THE MESSIAH OF PEACE

Biblical Performance Criticism Series

David Rhoads, Holly E. Hearon, and Kelly R. Iverson, Series Editors

The ancient societies of the Bible were overwhelmingly oral. People originally experienced the traditions now in the Bible as oral performances. Focusing on the ancient performance of biblical traditions enables us to shift academic work on the Bible from the mentality of a modern print culture to that of an oral/scribal culture. Conceived broadly, biblical performance criticism embraces many methods as means to reframe the biblical materials in the context of traditional oral cultures, construct scenarios of ancient performances, learn from contemporary performances of these materials, and reinterpret biblical writings accordingly. The result is a foundational paradigm shift that reconfigures traditional disciplines and employs fresh biblical methodologies such as theater studies, speech-act theory, and performance studies. The emerging research of many scholars in this field of study, the development of working groups in scholarly societies, and the appearance of conferences on orality and literacy make it timely to inaugurate this series. For further information on biblical performance criticism, go to www.biblicalperformancecriticism.org.

Books in the Series

Holly E. Hearon and Philip Ruge-Jones, editors
The Bible in Ancient and Modern Media

James A. Maxey
*From Orality to Orality:
A New Paradigm for Contextual Translation of the Bible*

Antoinette Clark Wire
The Case for Mark Composed in Performance

Robert D. Miller II, SFO
Oral Tradition in Ancient Israel

Pieter J. J. Botha
Orality and Literacy in Early Christianity

James A. Maxey and Ernst R. Wendland, editors
Translating Scripture for Sound and Performance

J. A. (Bobby) Loubser
Oral and Manuscript Culture in the Bible

Joanna Dewey
The Oral Ethos of the Early Church

Richard A. Horsley
Text and Tradition in Performance and Writing

Kelley R. Iverson, editor
*From Text to Performance:
Narrative and Performance Criticisms in Dialogue and Debate*

THE MESSIAH OF PEACE
A Performance-Criticism Commentary on
Mark's Passion-Resurrection Narrative

Thomas E. Boomershine

CASCADE *Books* • Eugene, Oregon

THE MESSIAH OF PEACE
A Performance-Criticism Commentary on Mark's Passion-Resurrection Narrative

Biblical Performance Criticism Series 12

Copyright © 2015 Thomas E. Boomershine. All rights reserved. Except for brief quotations in critical publications or reviews, no part of this book may be reproduced in any manner without prior written permission from the publisher. Write: Permissions, Wipf and Stock Publishers, 199 W. 8th Ave., Suite 3, Eugene, OR 97401.

Cascade Books
An Imprint of Wipf and Stock Publishers
199 W. 8th Ave., Suite 3
Eugene, OR 97401

www.wipfandstock.com

ISBN 13: 978-1-62564-545-6

Cataloguing-in-Publication data:

Boomershine, Thomas E.

    The messiah of peace : a performance-criticism commentary on Mark's passion-resurrection narrative / Thomas E. Boomershine.

    Biblical Performance Criticism Series 12

    xvi + 448 p. ; 23 cm. Includes bibliographical references and index.

    ISBN 13: 978-1-62564-545-6

    1. Bible—Mark—Criticism, interpretation, etc. 2. Bible—Gospels—Criticism, interpretation, etc. I. Bartholomew, Adam Gilbert. II. Title. III. Series.

BS2585.52 B5 2015

Manufactured in the U.S.A.   06/09/2015

To J. Louis Martyn and Walter Wink

CONTENTS

Preface | ix
Abbreviations | xv

    Introduction | 1
1 The Day before the Passover (14:1–11) | 36
2 The Passover Meal (14:12–25) | 72
3 The Night in Gethsemane (14:26–52) | 100
4 The Trials at the High Priest's House (14:53–72) | 155
5 The Handing Over to the Gentiles (15:1–20) | 202
6 The Crucifixion of Jesus (15:21–32) | 260
7 The Death and Burial of Jesus (15:33–47) | 294
8 The Resurrection (16:1–8) | 327
9 The Messiah of Peace | 359

APPENDIX 1
The Historical Context of Mark and His Audiences | 363

APPENDIX 2
A Sound Map of Mark's Passion-Resurrection Narrative | 368

APPENDIX 3
The Pronunciation of Koine Greek in the Roman Period | 387

APPENDIX 4
The Rhetorics of Biblical Storytelling | 391

APPENDIX 5
Markan Terminology | 406

APPENDIX 6
The Audiences of Mark | 410

APPENDIX 7
The Pronunciation of Jesus' Cry of Abandonment and the Bystanders' Mishearing (Mark 15:34–35) | 427
With Adam Gilbert Bartholomew

APPENDIX 8
The Mocking of Jesus and Samson and the LXX A Text of Judges | 430
With Adam Gilbert Bartholomew

Bibliography | 433
Index | 439

PREFACE

THIS PROJECT, COMPOSED OF THIS BOOK AND A SET OF VIDEO recordings, is a study of Mark's Passion and Resurrection Narrative (PRN) as a story that was told to audiences in the late first century by storytellers who believed that Jesus of Nazareth was the Messiah. The conclusion of recent Markan scholarship is that the historical context for the final composition of this story was the Roman-Judean war that began with the expulsion of the Roman occupation army in 66 CE and ended with the conquest of the final fortress of the Judean insurgency at Masada in 73 CE. The focus here is on the meaning and impact of the performances of Mark's story in the decades after the war.

An integral dimension of this essay is the video recordings of the story that can be seen at the website: **www.messiahofpeace.com**. My suggestion is that you go to the website and watch the recordings as you read the book. There will be symbols throughout the essay with the implicit direction to watch the video of the next story to be discussed. The presupposition here is that Mark's story was not a text read by readers. It was an interactive performance for audiences. If we want to understand Mark's story, we need to listen to the story and, in as far as possible, become part of the audience experience of the story. Of course, our problem is that those performances were nearly two thousand years ago. At some level we can only imagine those tellings of the story.

Recognizing our inherent limitations, however, there is a lot that can be discerned about the meaning and impact of this ancient story from listening to it closely. And what emerges from listening to Mark's story as a performance is very different than what emerges from reading it as a text. That difference—between the meaning of Mark's text read by readers and the meaning of Mark's story performed for audiences—has been my problem for forty-five years. I first recognized some of those differences when I learned this story in Greek and began telling it as part of my dissertation research in the summer of 1969. But I couldn't figure out a persuasive way to document that difference for my committee. In the end, after two years of negotiation, we agreed that I would submit my three hundred and some pages of detailed analysis of Mark's story as a story, with no conclusions about its meaning in its original context. In these intervening years, I have continued to study Mark's story as a story, and have told the whole gospel many times. In light of the many developments in biblical scholarship in the intervening years—e.g., the development of sound mapping by Margaret Lee and Bernard Brandon Scott, the extensive implementation of first narrative and now performance criticism, and the extensive performance of biblical compositions—there is now a context in which the analysis, the performance, and the conclusions can be presented.

This book is a recasting of that dissertation, with (as you will see) very distinctive conclusions about Mark's audiences and the meaning of Mark's story. Readers will make their own evaluation about whether the format of the present project works as documentation for the conclusions. But listening to the story is important. My suggestion is that most readers would best listen first to the English translation and then to the original Greek.

This book is not a comprehensive survey of Markan scholarship on the PRN. Nor is it a comprehensive comparison of the results of this study and the results of the research on Mark by other scholars. The value of this work will be a comprehensive and detailed study of Mark's passion-resurrection using a new methodology. But this research has evolved in continual dialogue with the community of biblical and, in particular, Markan scholarship. There are comparative discussions here of some of the major differences in the identification of Mark's audiences, rhetorics, and purpose but only with representative commentators such as Joel Marcus, whose commentary has been a steady source of insight as well as contrasting conclusions. The decision here was to limit the argument with others in order to focus on Mark and major issues in Markan interpretation such as the presence of what has been called anti-Jewish polemic and pro-Roman apologetic.

The positive results of this study are profoundly political, both in relation to this story in its original context, and in relation to the current period in history. The interpretation of the Jesus story is important now because of the paucity of imagination and energy for peace research in comparison to the research and development of resources for weapons and war. The separation between religion as a personal matter and corporate politics as an extension of the separation of church and state in the United States is an intellectual and political chasm with immense implications and potentially disastrous consequences. The community of biblical scholarship needs to address the issues of war and peace directly. We have groups studying war but none (to my knowledge) studying peace.

Preface

This book has distinctive features that are an integral part of a performance-criticism commentary. The introduction to each section and story of the commentary is the video of the performance of that part of the story at **www.messiahofpeace.com**. Attentive listeners will note that there are sometimes differences between the words in the performance and the translation in the text. This is both to be expected in different performances and is also a sign of the evolution of the translation as it has been continually revised including in the actual moments of each telling of the story. The long-term memory of the way I learned the story many years ago and the inspiration of the moment kicks in no matter how hard I try.

Another distinctive feature of this commentary is sound mapping. This terminology and the delineation of the cola and periods of ancient Greek are based on the pioneering work of Margaret Lee and Bernard Brandon Scott. The sound map in the appendix has thorough markings of the various features of the sound of the story. The sound map here integrates the analysis of cola and periods with the episodes, stories, and sections of the story identified in my dissertation chapter on the units of Mark's composition. In the commentary, only the verbal threads or sonic echoes are marked by bold print. The segment that follows the sound map in many of the stories is a discussion and frequent quotation of other ancient stories that have significant parallels with Mark's story, and that may have been in the background of the audiences' minds. The conclusion of the analysis of each story is a discussion of appropriate ways the story might be performed.

The terminology that will be used for the groups in Mark's context is also distinctive. I have followed John H. Elliott's recommendation that we adopt the terms used by Mark in order to more accurately characterize those groups in the first century. **Therefore, the terms *Jews*, *Judaism*, and *Jewish* will only be used when they are terms used by outsiders, such as the Romans.** We will use what we might call insider terms (*Judeans*, *Israelites*, and *Galileans*), as well as the names of the various sectarian groups. Furthermore, the term *Christian* will not be used in naming Mark's various audiences. The conclusion here is that these terms were only used widely in later contexts (post-second century CE) when the distinctive terms *Jewish* and *Christian* had become the preferred self-descriptions of these descendants of the religion of Israel.

While the commentary includes many highly technical elements such as textual variants in the extant Greek manuscripts, the pronunciation of Koine Greek and Aramaic, and the nuances of sound and meaning in Greek words, the goal has been to make this commentary accessible to a more general readership. For this reason, some basic facts and information have been included that will be well known to biblical scholars. Readers on both sides of the scholarly divide are encouraged to scan and skip elements that are not relevant to their interests. Nevertheless, readers are also encouraged to read every word.

Finally, the intention of the constant quotation of Greek in the commentary is to regularly inject the actual sounds of Mark's story into the analysis. It is one of the many complications that arise from paying close attention to the sound of an ancient story. The hope is that this will make it easier for those who have not studied Greek as well as for those who want to follow the story in Greek. An underlying conclusion of this study is that the distinctive sounds of the original Greek are a significant factor in the meaning and impact of Mark's story.

My debts to others are truly innumerable. My dissertation committee, in particular, J. Louis Martyn and Walter Wink, in the end made this book possible by their pioneering scholarship, and their assistance with a highly controversial dissertation. Since its founding in 1977, in the aftermath of the dissertation, the community of the Network of Biblical Storytellers has been an invaluable source of personal support and embodied demonstration of the viability of biblical storytelling and, in particular, the Gospel of Mark, which I first told as a whole at the first Festival of the Network in 1985. The members of the Society of Biblical Literature (SBL) Bible in Ancient and Modern Media (BAMM) research group, founded in 1983, have provided a research community that has built the foundations of performance criticism and the study of the Bible as performance literature. In particular, David Rhoads has been a colleague, friend, and trusted critic. His role as the editor of the Biblical Performance Criticism series in which this book appears is indicative of his generative role in enabling this book to be produced. It was he and Joanna Dewey, longtime friend and cochair of BAMM, who first suggested that I revise and publish the dissertation. My teaching colleagues at New York Theological Seminary and United Theological Seminary have supported my development of the distinctive pedagogy that is an essential dimension of teaching the Bible as performance literature. Finally, as a colleague in the doctoral program at Union, Adam Bartholomew was the first person to whom I told Mark's PRN in Greek. He has been a partner in this work during these years. His collaboration in the development of this book and in coauthoring some of the appendices has been a major contribution to its completion and its quality.

Among the many persons who have influenced my thought, Wayne Booth, Walter Ong, James Muilenburg, and Han Frei have been central figures in my intellectual development. I had the privilege of working with Wayne Booth as my professor and advisor during my undergraduate studies at Earlham College as he was completing his first major work, *The Rhetoric of Fiction*. James Muilenburg, as professor of my introduction to the Old Testament at Union Theological Seminary in 1962, was the first person I ever heard tell a biblical story. His later proposal in his presidential address to the Society of Biblical Literature advocating the development of rhetorical criticism provided the critical framework for my dissertation and subsequent research. I became acquainted with Walter Ong, SJ through his writings on communication and culture and later as a friend and scholarly colleague. His work has provided the foundation for the reconception and reevaluation of oral culture and the long and complex transition from oral to literate culture in the formation and interpretation of the Bible. Of these mentors of the mind, Hans Frei is the only one I never met personally. His book *The Eclipse of Biblical Narrative* was published the same year as my dissertation, and we were thinking many of the same thoughts in very different contexts. His analysis of the formation of the new paradigm of historical criticism during the Enlightenment is a great achievement that accurately describes the framework of current biblical interpretation and the division between the liberal and conservative churches. His description of "meaning as reference" establishes the need for a recovery of the meaning of biblical narrative as a story. It also lays the foundation for the recognition of the cultural relativity of the paradigms of biblical interpretation, and the need for a new paradigm for biblical interpretation in the emerging culture of the digital age.

While these persons have primarily been mentors I have known, I am poignantly aware of and want to acknowledge my indebtedness to my predecessors in the telling of Mark's story. I think of the storytellers in the history of Israel whose stories provided the foundation and sometimes the source of Mark's story. Then there are all those Judeans who passed on the stories of Jesus during the decades between Jesus and the composition of the gospel. And there are the myriads of storytellers and martyrs for whom Jesus as the non-violent Messiah of peace has been their inspiration.

I also want to acknowledge my indebtedness to the Jewish storytellers over the centuries who have preserved and passed on the storytelling traditions of Israel when most Christian intellectuals were doing philosophy and theology. They have been my precedent for the rediscovery of Mark as a Judean storyteller. All of us, Jews and Christians alike, are descendants of Israelite storytellers.

I am also indebted to the legions of African American storytelling preachers who have told the stories of the Bible during the centuries of slavery and Jim Crow. They have been signs of the power of storytelling. It was an anonymous preacher in a black Baptist church in Chicago whose hour-plus storytelling sermon in 1967 first convinced me that a long story like Mark could have been told at one time.

James Stock and his staff at Wipf and Stock Publishers have enabled the multiple versions of the book and, in particular, have encouraged the fully integrated digital version of the text and the videos. The editing of this manuscript with sound maps and new formats has been very complex. Jeremy Funk and Ian Creeger labored over this text with consummate care and intelligence. My deep gratitude is extended to K. C. Hanson, who served as editor and consultant for the book. In particular, the recasting of the terminology for the various groups in Mark's first-century context has benefitted from his decades of wrestling with this issue. In the end, the limitations and inadequacies of the manuscript are my responsibility. But those inadequacies have been signficantly reduced by the contributions of these colleagues.

At a personal level, my gratitude to the members of my family knows no bounds. Jean, Tom, and Michael and my parents, Garnet and Glenn, were my primary support group in the dissertation stages of this project. Amelia has been my partner in life and work in the later stages of reconceiving the project. The matrix that makes possible a lifelong work such as this is truly a work of grace.

ABBREVIATIONS

Ancient Sources

Ant.	*Antiquities* (Josephus)
Ann.	*Annales* (Tacitus)
KJV	King James Version
JW	*Jewish War* (Josephus)
Inst.	*Institutio Oratoria* (*The Orator's Education*)
LXX	Septuagint
m.	Mishnah
MT	Masoretic Text (Hebrew Bible)
NT	New Testament
Nero	*Nero* (Seutonius)
OT	Old Testament
Vit. Apol.	*The Life of Apollonius of Tyana* (Philostratus)

Contemporary Sources

AB	Anchor Bible
ABD	David Noel Freedman, ed., *The Anchor Bible Dictionary*, 6 vols., New York, 1992
ABRL	Anchor Bible Reference Library
AnBib	Analecta biblica
AYB	Anchor Yale Bible
BDAG	Walter Bauer, Frederick W. Danker, William F. Arndt, and F. Wilbur Gingrich, *Greek-English Lexicon of the New Testament and Other Early Christian Literature*. 3rd ed. Chicago: Univesity of Chicago Press, 2000
BDF	F. Blass, A. Debrunner, and R. W. Funk, *A Greek Grammar of the New Testament and Other Early Christian Literature*, Chicago: Univesity of Chicago Press, 1961
BTB	*Biblical Theology Bulletin*
ExpTim	*Expository Times*
GNT	Good News Translation
GRBS	*Greek, Roman, and Byzantine Studies*
HTKNT	Herders theologischer Kommentar zum Neuen Testament

ICC	International Critical Commentary
JBL	*Journal of Biblical Literature*
JSHJ	*Journal for the Study of the Historical Jesus*
JSNT	*Journal for the Study of the New Testament*
JTS	*Journal of Theological Studies*
KEK	Kritisch-exegetischer Kommentar über das Neue Testament
LCL	Loeb Classical Library
LSJ	H. G. Liddell, Robert Scott, and H. Stuart Jones, *A Greek-English Lexicon*, 9th ed. with revised supplement, Oxford: Clarendon, 1996
MHT	James H. Moulton et al., *A Grammar of New Testament Greek*, 4 vols., Edinburgh: T. & T. Clark, 1908
M-M	James H. Moulton and George Milligan. *The Vocabulary of the Greek Testament*, Grand Rapids: Eerdmans, 1930
NABRE	New American Bible Revised Edition
NASB	New American Standard Bible
NEB	New English Bible
NET	New English Translation
NETS	A New English Translation of the Septuagint, edited by Albert Pietersma and Benjamin G. Wright, Oxford: Oxford University Press, 2007
NIV	New International Version
NKJV	New King James Version
NJB	New Jerusalem Bible
NRSV	New Revised Standard Version
OTP	James H. Charlesworth, ed., *Old Testament Pseudepigrapha*, 2 vols., New York, 1983
REB	Revised English Bible
SJLA	Studies in Judaism in Late Antiquity
Str-B	Hermann L. Strack and Paul Billerbeck, *Kommentar zum Neuen Testament aus Talmud und Midrasch*, 6 vols., Munich: Beck, 1922–1961
TDNT	Gerhard Kittel and Gerhard Friedrich, eds., *Theological Dictionary of the New Testament*, translated by Geoffrey W. Bromiley, 10 vols., Grand Rapids: Eerdmans, 1964–1976
UBS	United Bible Societies Greek New Testament
ZTK	*Zeitschrift für Theologie und Kirche*

INTRODUCTION

MARK'S STORY OF JESUS' PASSION, DEATH, AND RESURRECTION has been one of the most important stories in human history. The reading and interpretation of this story has been the source of an experience of God's love and saving grace for millions of people. It has also been a source for Christian anti-Judaism that has been implicated in the deaths of millions of people. An investigation of the meaning and impact of this story in its original historical context may shed new light on this immense ambiguity in the experienced meaning of this story. A central dimension of that new light is the telling of the story of Jesus as the nonviolent Messiah of peace and reconciliation with Israel's Gentile enemies in the period after the Judean–Roman War. This new light will emerge from a new approach to the exploration of the meaning of Mark's story.

The purpose of this commentary is to listen closely to Mark's Passion-Resurrection Narrative (hereafter PRN) as a story that was performed for audiences in the period immediately following the conclusion of the Judean–Roman War (66–70 CE).[1] The detailed exegesis of biblical stories as *compositions of sound performed for audiences* is a new framework for biblical exegesis and interpretation. The need for a new methodology grows out of a new understanding of the communication culture within which the Gospel of Mark was composed.[2]

The Gospels have previously been explored in the context of a widely shared set of presuppositions about the communication culture of the ancient world. We as biblical interpreters have assumed that the ancient world was a literate culture in which the manuscripts of the Gospels were read by readers. We have imagined readers as individuals sitting alone with a

---

1. For a brief narration of the dynamics and some major events in the postwar period, see Appendix 1, "Mark's Postwar Context."

2. The other volumes of the Biblical Performance Criticism series are an appropriate context for this commentary. The reconception of the Bible as performance literature is an integral dimension of the emerging picture of the communication culture of antiquity.

manuscript and reading it, perhaps aloud, but generally in silence. In this picture, the experience of the original readers of the Gospels was a predominantly visual experience of examining the written marks on the manuscript pages in a manner that was basically the same as the way a scholar might read the Greek text of the Gospel of Mark today. We have assumed that the processes of detailed examination of the texts in silence would give us an experience of the biblical texts that is congruent with the way they were experienced in their original historical context—hence the ubiquitous reference in biblical commentaries and monographs to "the reader(s)."

Recent studies of the ancient media world reveal that this assumption that the Bible was an ancient library of texts read by readers is an anachronistic reading back into the ancient world of the practices of a later communication culture. First of all, most people in the ancient world couldn't read. This conclusion has emerged from studies of literacy in ancient Greece and Rome by classical scholars such as William Harris, Professor of History at Columbia University.[3] Harris concluded that while the rates of literacy varied widely in different regions and periods of ancient history, they were generally much lower than had previously been thought. His estimate is that the general rate of literacy in the ancient world never exceeded 15 percent among men in the cities and was markedly lower among women and in the countryside. Harris states:

> There was without doubt a vast diffusion of reading and writing ability in the Greek and Roman world, and the preconditions and the positive causes of this development can be traced. But there was no mass literacy, and even the level which I have called craftsman's literacy was achieved only in a certain limited milieu. The classical world, even at its most advanced, was so lacking in the characteristics which produce extensive literacy that we must suppose that the majority of people were always illiterate.[4]

Thus, the evidence indicates that literacy in the period of the composition and distribution of Mark's gospel was much lower than was previously assumed.

This dimension of ancient media culture correlates with the increasingly recognized fact that works like the Gospel of Mark were "published," that is offered to the public, by public oral performance for largely illiterate audiences rather than by the copying of texts to be read by individual

---

3. Harris, *Ancient Literacy*.
4. Ibid., 13.

readers. Whitney Shiner's study of the performance of Mark in the first century[5] sets the various dimensions of Markan performances in the context of the performance of written works in the culture of the Greco-Roman world.[6] Shiner cites a cynical account of the Isthmian Games in Corinth, from the same period as Mark, by Dio Chrysostom (40–120 CE), which provides a sense of the wider cultural context:

> That was the time when one could hear crowds of wretched sophists (rhetoric teachers) around Poseidon's temple shouting and reviling one another, and their disciples, as they were called, fighting with one another, many writers reading aloud their stupid works, and many poets reciting their poems, while others applauded them, many jugglers showing their tricks, many fortune tellers interpreting fortunes, lawyers innumerable perverting judgment, and peddlers not a few peddling whatever they happened to have.[7]

While it is unlikely that Mark or the storytellers who learned and performed his story would have been telling Jesus' story around Poseidon's temple during the Isthmian Games, they were part of the culture that Dio Chrysostom describes.

Another major factor driving ancient performance as the primary means of distribution of literary compositions, in addition to general illiteracy, was that books were expensive and not readily available. Early writing was done by chiseling inscriptions into stone monuments or tablets, a practice reflected in the story of Moses and the stone tablets of the Ten Commandments (Exod 24:12; 31:18; 32:15–16,19; 34:1). Thus, the meaning of the basic word for "writing" in Hebrew, *kethib*, is "to carve." As writing technology improved, a sharpened feather and later an iron *stylus* placed on the end of a feather, was dipped in ink and scraped on wood, pieces of clay called *ostraka*, wax tablets, papyrus, parchment, and finally vellum (animal skins). The writing on some form of "paper" made it possible to paste pieces of paper together and roll them into a scroll. Only in the first centuries of the Common Era (post–100 CE) was the *codex* developed in which pieces of parchment or vellum were folded in half and bound in the middle to form

---

5. Shiner, *Proclaiming the Gospel*.

6. Ibid., 11–36. There are many excellent introductory surveys to the communication culture of antiquity. The grandfather of these surveys was Moses Hadas, *Ancilla to Classical Reading*. See also the books in the Biblical Performance Criticism series, of which this book is a part, edited by David Rhoads, now being published by Cascade Books.

7. Dio Chrysostom, *Discourses* 8:9.

the pages of what we now call a book. Each copy had to be made by hand.[8] And while there was clearly a book business in the ancient world, manuscripts were primarily owned by communities, where they were performed, and by the wealthy.

The result of these discoveries about ancient communication culture is that when seen in the context of this culture, Mark was performance literature composed to be heard by audiences. When a text was read, the reader virtually always read aloud, even when reading in private and alone.[9] Mark was composed as sound with the assumption that those sounds would be reproduced when the story was performed for an audience, even if that audience was one, though generally it was many.

A feature of Markan performance is that the story was told from memory, sometimes with a manuscript in hand and often without a manuscript. The culture of the ancient world was a memorial culture in which memory was the center of learning and education. The measure of a person's knowledge was directly related to the number of speeches and stories that the person had mastered and recited. The memorization of written manuscripts was the primary task of education, and students memorized manuscripts every day.

The primary function of writing was to record sounds, and this function is reflected in the character of ancient manuscripts. Early biblical manuscripts such as the scrolls at Qumran have no word divisions, punctuation, capitalization, cola, periods, or paragraphs. They are a string of undifferentiated letters. Even if the performer had a manuscript in hand, the performer had to *virtually memorize* the language in order to be able to perform it smoothly.

The function of a written text of Mark's Gospel in the first century is comparable to the function of a musical score today. I have a small library of musical manuscripts for the piano and the organ. Their function is to record the sounds of a musical composition on paper so it can be played again. Whenever I use the manuscript, it serves as an aid to the playing of the composition, whether in private practice or in public performance. Sometimes I will study the score of a piece without playing the music, usually as part of the process of memorization. And while I often perform music with a manuscript, the performance of compositions, especially complex ones, from memory is sometimes the only way that it is possible to perform them.

---

8. For more detailed surveys of ancient writing technology, see Haas, *Writing Technology*.

9. B. W. Knox has identified some instances of silent reading in the ancient world: "Silent Reading in Antiquity," 421–35. But these are exceptions to the general rule, as Knox recognizes.

Performing music from memory also makes it possible to play more expressively and to relate more directly to audiences.

The analogy between music and reading is not a new idea. Quintilian wrote: "the art of letters and that of music were once united," and he goes on to cite examples from Aristophanes, Menander, and Cicero.[10] A function of manuscripts, then and now, is to enable *the sounds* of both music and words to be transmitted and reproduced.

In addition to the fact that ancient culture was a memorial culture and that education consisted in memorizing and reciting the works of significant authors, a further factor driving the memorization of manuscripts was the awkwardness of managing a scroll in a performance. It was fully possible to use a scroll, just as in choral performances today each member of the choir may have a musical score in hand. But for storytelling and rhetorical speeches, a manuscript eliminates the additional expressive ingredients of gestures and movement and makes the relationship to the audience more distant. In general, memorized performances of stories are better than performances with a manuscript. For all of these reasons, it is probable that many of the performances of Mark's story were done without a manuscript in hand. In that case, the manuscript served as an aid to the memorization of the sounds of the story prior to the performance.

The implication of the emerging picture of the communication culture of the ancient world is that the accurate exegesis of the meaning of these compositions in their original context requires a methodology congruent with the character of the manuscripts as a medium for the recording of sounds in performance. In contrast to informational genres, such as data storage and factual history, rhetorical genres require that the sounds of the composition be integral to the experience of the composition. Just as the experience of listening to music as it is performed is essential to the music's content, so the feelings accompanying the words of Mark's story are part of the content. Studying Mark in silence is like investigating the music of Bach and never listening to the music. An essential step in the study of Mark in its original historical media context, therefore, is to pay detailed attention to the sounds of Mark's story. If we want to understand Mark's composition as sound, we need to listen to his story.

This commentary has two component parts, the text and the videos of a performance of Mark's story in English and in the original Greek. The videos are available at **www.messiahofpeace.com**. I strongly suggest that you go to the site now and have it available to watch and hear as you read

---

10. Quintilian, *Inst.* 1.10.17–20.

the commentary. There is a brief oral introduction to the videos that would be a good place to begin.

Sound-Mapping Mark

The first component of the commentary on each story will be a "sound map" of Mark's story. Margaret Lee and Bernard Brandon Scott have provided us with a guidebook on the exploration of the sounds of first-century Koine Greek rhetorical compositions. They have proposed that we arrange the compositions of the New Testament in sound maps in order to make the units of sound in the compositions visible. In a sound map or "score" of an ancient composition, the goal is to create graphic signs of the sound of the story just as composers of music construct a score of their musical composition. The grammarians and rhetoricians of ancient Greek consistently describe the "colon" and the "period" as the basic units of sound in Greek oratory, drama, and poetry. The colon and the period were breath units, the colon being the words that can comfortably be said in one breath and the period as a combination of cola that build to a climax. A primary value of the delineation of these units of composition is that they represent the sound units in which the composers of Greek stories thought and spoke. Thus, the art of "colometry" seeks to identify the basic units of sound in ancient Greek and Latin compositions.[11] A detailed analysis and specific examples of the formal characteristics of the units of sound in Mark's composition is available in Appendix 2, "A Sound Map of Mark's Passion-Resurrection Narrative."

The function of the sound map is similar to the function of a place map: it provides clues about what to listen for and graphically represents the way the sound of the story is organized. The purpose of the structures of sound in Mark's story is to create emphatic climaxes that will be remembered. The composer of this story was a highly skilled storyteller who used sophisticated techniques for the structuring of sound to create meaning and memory. The invitation implicit in the sound map at the beginning of each story is to pay close attention to the sound of the story (videos at **www.messiahofpeace.com**), first in an approximation of the original sounds of Mark's story in English translation and then in Koine Greek.

However, it is necessary to recognize that we do not know exactly how the Koine Greek of Mark's story was pronounced in Mark's time. Erasmus developed the pronunciation system you will hear in these videos in the early sixteenth century. It has been and is now the most widely

---

11. See, for example, West, "Colometry."

used pronunciation system in the teaching of New Testament Greek. Even though actual speakers of Greek in Mark's time almost certainly did not pronounce Greek in exactly this way,[12] it is the pronunciation familiar to those schooled in academic Greek and will be more accessible for the majority of the readers of this commentary. And so, while we cannot reproduce an exact pronunciation of Mark's story, there are many dimensions of how these stories sounded that we can rediscover, such as tempo, volume, verbal threads, onomatopoeia, audience address and asides, dynamics of characterization, and climactic structure. And while we cannot determine the exact sounds of Koine Greek in the first century, the differences in the different pronunciation systems are relatively minor and have minimal effect on the overall impact of the sound of Mark's Greek.

The sound map of the cola and periods is the major step in the recovery of the sound of Mark's story. But there is more to the sound than the rhythm of its cola and periods. There is also the organization of the cola and periods into larger storytelling units marked by changes in time and place, repetitions and verbal threads, particular grammatical constructions, changes in the principal characters, and the basic subject matter. These markers also call for various lengths of pause, changes of pace, or climactic expression as the means of marking the end of a storytelling move before going on to the next. It is these ingredients that enable the storyteller to create suspense and closure. There is explicit evidence for the rhythmic sounding of the words in cola and periods in both manuscripts written in sense lines[13] and descriptions in rhetorical handbooks.[14] In regard to other ingredients of sound, Quintilian says explicitly that it is "natural that what is sublime should have a stately stride, that what is gentle should seem to be led along, that what is violent should seem to run and what is tender flow."[15] Since the manuscripts, unlike musical scores, give no directions about the appropriate volume, tempo, emotional tone, or rests to be employed, the exegete must deduce these ingredients from the clues within the content. Neither the rhythm of the performance described in the ancient rhetorical handbooks nor the clues in the text to the emotional tone have been attended to in commentaries, except on the rarest of occasions,[16] because the question of the sound of the story and the possible significance of the

---

12. For a fuller discussion of the original pronunciation of Koine Greek, see Appendix 3, "The Pronunciation of Koine Greek in the Roman Period."

13. Metzger, *Manuscripts*, 90, plate 19A.

14. See Lee and Scott, *Sound Mapping*, 104, quoting Dionysius of Halicarnassus.

15. Quintilian, *Inst.* 9.4.138–39; quoted in Lee and Scott, *Sound Mapping*, 120.

16. An example of an exception is found in Carson, *Gospel according to John*, 595, where he describes Pilate's question to Jesus, "What is truth?" as "curt and cynical."

sound for meaning has seldom been asked. Just as we cannot determine the pronunciation of Greek in Mark's time, we may not be able to determine the exact character of other ingredients of the story's sound. One thing, however, is certain: the generally dispassionate, evenly paced manner in which we have come to read the Bible in church[17] is a radical change from the way the compositions gathered in the Bible were originally performed. Just as we can approximate the pronunciation of Mark's Greek, we can at least get closer to the original character of the performance of his story.

A word of explanation about the sound maps of Mark that follow may be helpful. The sound maps that are included at the beginning of each story in the commentary are formulated to indicate the units of sound in the composition and the sonic links within the story. All sonic links within Mark's PRN and sometimes the links to earlier parts of the Gospel of Mark as a whole will be marked in bold. In addition to the sonic links in the Greek, the English words that translate the Greek words will also be marked in bold even though there may be no sonic linkage between the words in English. The units of sound will be marked by indentation. A new period always begins at the left margin. If it is a complex period with more than one colon, the additional cola are indented. A comma within a colon is further indented but will have no number on the left. The words of a period or colon that extend beyond one line will be right justified on the next line. The episodes will be indicated by a space and the stories and sections will be given titles. A more extensive discussion of the background of sound mapping in the Greek grammarians and a more comprehensive sound map will be found in Appendix 2.

Meaning in Texts Read by Silent Readers and in Stories Heard by Audiences

The most significant change resulting from experiencing Mark as performance literature instead of as a text read by readers is the character of meaning generated by the performance. In the communication culture of silent reading that has emerged since the invention of the printing press in which it has become possible for individuals to have their own copies of the Bible, texts of the Bible are analyzed as sources of what Hans Frei has termed "meaning as reference"—both "ostensive reference," namely historical

---

17. For example, Bonhoeffer, *Life Together*, 55–56. Bonhoeffer's reasoning is both logically and theologically incoherent. A hunch is that he heard some poor readings and was searching for some way of imposing order.

meaning, and "ideal reference," namely theological meaning.[18] This "meaning as reference" is associated with a process of achieving psychological distance in relation to the verbal content of the text. The psychological distance associated with silent reading largely eliminates the dynamics of interaction and sympathetic participation that were part of the original performance, thus freeing the reader from those ingredients of spoken language that have the power to draw one into participation in the story, and making it possible to stand outside the story in order to think critically about it and to evaluate the referential data. Such psychological distance for the purpose of critical reflection is an epistemological ideal of the culture of silent reading. Thus, a steady motif in the celebration of the distinctive learning that characterizes "higher" education is the celebration of "critical learning." Indeed "criticism" has become a characteristic word in the definition of valid study of the Bible, so that the major methodological achievements of modern study are labeled historical criticism, higher criticism, lower criticism, text criticism, form criticism, source criticism, redaction criticism, and more recently social-scientific criticism, reader-response criticism, rhetorical criticism, and narrative criticism. The term *criticism* names a fundamentally valued relationship with texts, achieved by means of psychological detachment and intellectual distance, which has been made most readily possible by means of the practice of silent reading. "Meaning as reference" assumes that the text refers both to history (political history, the history of the composition of the text) and to theology (doctrinal theology, political theology of the composers or the users). This type of referential meaning is the dominant form of the meaning of the text for a critical reader.

Mark's story has a very different character and meaning when told by a storyteller and heard by an audience than when it is read by a critical reader. The critical reading that dominates the use of the Bible today, at least among adults, is the fruit of the changes in communication culture that have taken place over the nearly two thousand years that separate us from Mark's original historical context.[19] Mark's audiences were predominantly oral-culture audiences even as they were shaped by the increasingly powerful literate culture. Most people in the late first century were illiterate and had, therefore, an oral-culture mindset.

A way of describing the difference in the way the Bible functions in these two different cultures is to compare different modern audiences of listeners. I have told Mark's story to a variety of audiences, young and old,

---

18. Frei, *Eclipse of Biblical Narrative*, 86–104.

19. Walter Ong has described the transformations of the word that have been associated with the major changes in communication technology and culture; see in particular Ong, *Presence of the Word*. See also Boomershine, "Biblical Megatrends."

black and white, conservative and liberal. But the biggest difference in audiences is where they fall on the scale of orality and literacy. Oral-culture audiences respond to the oral performance of Mark very differently from the way high-literate culture audiences respond. High-literate readers tend to be critical and distant audiences while oral-culture audiences tend to be more participatory and responsive.

First of all, an oral culture audience is usually a sympathetic audience that participates in the story. Such an audience does not maintain critical distance. An audience of high-literate readers is often an emotionally distant and unresponsive audience. You can see it in their faces and in their body language. An oral-culture audience smiles, even laughs frequently and easily at elements of the story and to the storyteller's various moves or appeals. A high-literate audience maintains a rigid posture and an expressionless face. If they are highly committed readers, they may even find a copy of Mark and militantly look at the text rather than at the storyteller in order to see if the story is being told "right."

There is the implication in a critical audience's lack of response that they are uncomfortable with and don't like the story or the storytelling and feel emotionally assaulted. There is the sense that they are resisting the appeals of the storyteller and the story and are examining the story and the storyteller. An oral audience, in contrast, identifies with the characters of the story. They recognize and even visibly and audibly affirm the congruence between the response of the characters and their own response. They appreciate the connection and what it makes clear for them. Their response may even be explicitly saying with a smile, "Oh you got me!" or moving their hand to their heart or their head or just holding up their hand or pointing at the storyteller. They will even clap at particular moments in the story and frequently at the end of the story.

A responsive audience is a delight for a storyteller. In that context, telling Mark's story is fun. A dimension of the fun is that the audience clearly experiences something of significance, sometimes even great significance, in their hearing and interacting with the story of Jesus. Often there is a dimension of surprise to their experience. They may even clap or cheer or cry. But perhaps the most important characteristic of a good audience is that they fully enter into the experience and response inherent in the story. They don't hold back, or if they do, it is because they are really wrestling with the implications of the story for themselves.

Another dimension of an experience of Mark in performance when compared with the experience of a critical reading of Mark is that in performance the meaning of the story is only minimally connected with ideas or facts. The story is far too visceral and emotional in its impact to allow time or psychological distance for reflection on ideas. That may come later. But in the moment of the performance, the meaning is more directly connected with the emotional impact of the events and characters involved. Nor is there a preoccupation in the audience with whether or not the story is historically true. It comes off as authentic and real and, therefore, as a description of, more or less, what actually happened. There is what Samuel Taylor Coleridge called a "willing suspension of disbelief." As a result, the telling of the healing of the leper or the stilling of the storm or Jesus' walking on the water or even the empty tomb is not experienced with a spirit of skepticism as impossible or historically improbable. Audiences willingly suspend disbelief in order to participate in a good story, and Mark's story has an inherent realism to it that invites this suspension of disbelief. Jesus comes off as a real person who encountered other real people in a believable time and space the audience can understand.

A listening audience of high-literate readers tends to be thinking about rather than participating in the story. Often they are thinking so hard that they can't feel anything, or their dominant feeling is discomfort with the storyteller's exhibition of feelings and efforts to awaken those feelings in the listeners. There are differences among individual readers along the spectrum of thinking and feeling, but the tendency of audiences of readers is to think. A dimension of that thinking is critical evaluation of the historical and theological claims that are implicit in the story.

This contrast between oral-culture audiences and literate-culture audiences is even more pronounced when high-literate readers read a story in silence. One of the reasons for the differences in meaning is that silent reading activates different sensory registers in the brain than listening to a story told. From a strictly perceptual perspective, a reader engaging the text with the eyes perceives a different set of stimuli than when listening to a story with the ears.[20] Silent readers actually experience a different story than listeners because the story is processed by different centers in the brain. And these differences between ancient oral-culture audiences and later reading audiences have become greater and more complex as time has passed.

We dare not overgeneralize about responses to narrative features. The difference is not absolute. Silent readers can and do imagine sounds to at least some extent. Some members of a high-literate audience and some readers of silent texts do identify with the characters of the story and participate in the experience of the story. Likewise some members of an oral-culture audience can sit back and critically evaluate a storyteller and

---

20. For a phenomenological study of sound, see Ihde, *Listening and Voice*, 3–16, 72–83.

the characters. But the contrasting tendencies are evident to anyone who attends the worship services of both an inner-city black Baptist or Hispanic Pentecostal church and a suburban white Presbyterian church.

Thus, the fundamental categories of meaning as history and theology in Enlightenment culture are not the categories of meaning implicit in Mark's story as heard by audiences who lived in the media culture of the first century. In the medium of performance, the meaning of the story did not consist, as it often does today, in the critical assessment of the Markan text as a source of referential information about the actual historical events it purports to record and of a highly nuanced set of theological ideas. The hearing of the story is an experience more analogous to watching a great film, and it differs markedly from reading it from a critical perspective in a book. Indeed, it is an experience of suspense and anticipation of events, of hope and disbelief, of closeness to or alienation from the characters rather than an experience of contemplation of a set of theological ideas or an evaluation of historical reports. Thus, the alternative to "meaning as reference" can be called "meaning as experience." And "meaning as experience" is dependent on the willingness of audiences to enter fully into the story and to identify with the characters of the story.

It is fully possible that by now some readers of this commentary may be thinking, *Yes, and that's just the problem with audiences. They are so easily taken in by emotion, by con men and storytellers! Give me critical readers!* And I would understand and even, to a degree, agree. But if our goal is to understand the meaning of Mark's story in its original context, then we have to take account of the fact that Mark's audiences were different from modern readers, and that Mark was very different from a modern theologian or historian. There were undoubtedly differences between the various members of the Markan audiences, and many audience members were critical of Mark and his hero. At the most basic level of a storytelling performance of Mark's two-hour-plus story, it is likely that some members of the audiences got fed up or bored and left in the middle of the story. And, as is reflected in the story at the end of the apocalyptic discourse (Mark 13:33, 35, 37) and in the Gethsemane story (14:34, 37–38, 40–41), it is likely that some folks in the audiences had become sleepy or had actually gone to sleep after nearly two hours of storytelling and needed to "wake up" or "stay awake." But those critical responses were of a different character from the critical distance of modern readers. Critical responses in ancient audiences happened because the listeners were angry, bored, or committed to the war against the Romans or to separation from Gentiles rather than to reconciliation and peace. With contemporary literate audiences, critical distance is associated with a refusal or inability to be emotionally engaged with the story because of intellectual loyalty to skepticism and critical detachment as a way of being.

How then are we to think about a "performance-criticism"[21] commentary? The proposal here is that we establish a dialectical relationship between engagement in the experience of the story and critical analysis.[22] The suggestion here is that you listen to the whole story in English and then Greek before reading the commentary and that you listen again to each story, both prior to and after reading the detailed commentary on that story. Performance criticism is an analysis of the sound and dynamics of Mark's story as it was performed for audiences, not of the text as a document read by readers. The proposal here is that the rhythm of first engagement with performance and then involvement in critical analysis will create a different relationship to this ancient composition and will reveal dimensions of its meaning both in its original historical context and in its contemporary context.

The Audiences of Mark

The data that emerges from the study of Mark's gospel as a composition performed for audiences indicates that Mark's audiences were composed primarily of Hellenistic Judeans[23] with a minority of Gentiles who lived in the

---

21. David Rhoads has been the driving force in the development of performance criticism. He named it, defined it, and has been its steady organizer and sponsor. A dimension of his leadership has been his service as editor of the Biblical Performance Criticism Series at Wipf and Stock of which this book is a part. For a fuller picture of his contributions, see the website at **www.biblicalperformancecriticism.org** and his articles and forthcoming book. Many have made contributions to the emergence of performance criticism as a new paradigm of biblical interpretation. Werner Kelber has made major contributions to the reconception of biblical interpretation in the light of twentieth-century research on the history of communications media by, among others, Father Walter Ong. While, as will become evident, I have significant disagreements with Kelber about the interpretation of Mark, I regard those disagreements as minor in comparison with my appreciation for the monumental work he has done in the comprehensive and detailed reinterpretation of the biblical scholarship of the past three centuries and the identification of new areas of research and development implicit in media study.

22. Walter Wink proposed this kind of rhythm in his manifesto against the "bankruptcy" of historical criticism in *The Bible in Human Transformation*, recently (2010) republished with an afterword by Marcus Borg. See, in particular, chapter 3, "Toward a New Paradigm for Biblical Study," 19–35.

23. This commentary will follow the recommendation of John H. Elliott that the most appropriate terminology for the community of Israelites in the immediate postwar period is "Judeans" rather than "Jews" and various terms for the followers of Jesus as the Christ rather than "Christians." This recasting of the terminology for the description of

last decades of the first century, approximately 70–100 CE, in the aftermath of the Judean–Roman War. These audiences were addressed as persons who did not believe that Jesus was the Messiah/Christ. While there may have been some followers of Jesus as Christ in the audiences, most were not members of communities of what Luke calls "the Way" (Acts 9:2; 19:9, 23; 24:22). Most Markan scholars now agree that Mark's story was composed in the context of the Judean–Roman War that reached its climax in 70 CE with the destruction of the Temple and the slaughter of tens of thousands of Judeans.[24] Josephus estimated that the total number of those killed during the war was more than a million, and another one hundred thousand were taken captive and either killed in Roman entertainments or sold into slavery. The focus of this scholarly consensus is the date of composition and the implicit historical context of the gospel. The data from a performance-criticism analysis of the gospel supports this consensus.

The conclusion that the gospel was performed for audiences of predominantly Hellenistic Judeans who were not followers of Christ, however, challenges the predominant view that Mark's audiences were composed of what have been called "Gentile Christians." The conclusion to which the performance evidence points is that the majority of the audiences were neither followers of Jesus nor Gentile, but predominantly Israelites who were not believers in Jesus as Messiah.

Let us first summarize the evidence that Mark was addressing audiences composed primarily of Judeans rather than Gentiles. A more extensive and detailed presentation of the data is available in Appendix 6, "The Audiences of Mark." There are many signs implicit in the story that Mark's audiences were made up primarily of Judeans. The most pervasive is the structure of address to the audience by the storyteller and the characters, primarily Jesus, whom the storyteller presents. The dynamics of audience address are different than the dynamics of address to readers. The major difference is that an audience is invited to identify themselves as the characters who are being addressed rather than as observers of a speech event reported in the document. In Mark's story, the audience is addressed by the storyteller and by the characters whom the storyteller embodies as various

---

the communities of the first century addresses the problem of the anachronistic use of the terms "Jews" and "Christians" that received their distinctive reference only in the second to fourth centuries with the formation of Rabbinic Judaism and the Christian Church. For an exposition of Elliott's recommendation and its adoption here, see Appendix 5, "Markan Terminology."

24. For the most comprehensive outline of the evidence for the setting of Mark in the aftermath of the Judean–Roman War, see Marcus, "Jewish War"; and Marcus, *Mark*, 1:33–35. Also see Appendix 1, "The Historical Context of Mark and His Audiences."

groups of Judeans: e.g., scribes, Pharisees, the crowd, the disciples, the twelve, and in Mark 13 as Peter, James, John, and Andrew. Only once does Mark the storyteller address the audience as non-Judeans, namely, in the explanation of Israelite cleanliness practices (Mark 7:3–4). In performance, this audience aside is a gesture of inclusion of non-Judeans, while as a document read by readers the narrative comment explaining "Jewish" customs has been perceived as the decisive indication of the identity of the majority of Mark's readers.[25]

Another important indication that the story is structured for predominantly Judean audiences is that the gospel is replete with explicit quotations and allusions from the Greek Septuagint translation of the Hebrew-Aramaic Scriptures. Mark clearly assumes that these quotations and allusions will be recognizable to the listeners. But, in contrast to John's gospel, for example, in which there are no Gentiles except perhaps for the Greeks[26] who appear briefly in 12:20 and for Pilate, and in which the audience is never addressed as Gentiles, Mark's gospel makes a conscious effort to explain some Judean customs and practices to his listeners and thereby includes Gentiles in the horizon of his audiences.[27] Thus, the evidence from the study of Mark as performance literature indicates that Mark addressed his story to audiences that were inclusive of some Gentiles along with the Judeans. But in order to participate fully in the story, it was necessary for the Gentiles to accept being addressed as persons who identified with the traditions of Israel.[28]

25. See, for example, Brown, *Introduction to the New Testament*, 163: "For the most part the recipients were not Jews since the author had to explain Jewish purification customs to them. Yet he could assume that they would know religious terms stemming from Judaism (Satan, Beelzebul, Gehenna, Rabbi, Hosanna, and Amen), so that they were probably Christians who had been converted by evangelizers familiar directly or indirectly with Jewish Christian tradition." In his discussion of the purity-laws controversy, Marcus states that the Markan community of predominantly 'Gentile Christians' may have included some 'Jewish Christians' who may have been inclined to observe "the tradition of the elders" (Marcus, *Mark*, 449, 452). Pesch also makes this allowance: "Ein erklärender (*gar*) Kommentar, der Hörern zugedacht ist, die mit pharisäischem, ja jüdischem Milieu nicht vertraut sind" (Pesch, *Markusevangelium*, 1:370).

26. See Carson, *Gospel according to John*, 436, for an acknowledgment that some have understood these to be Greek-speaking "Jews" and a sound argument that they are Gentile Godfearers, not necessarily from Greece but influenced by Greek culture. See also Brown, *Gospel according to John*, 1:314 and 466.

27. A further line of evidence for the identification of the range of Mark's audiences is the translation of Aramaic words into Greek (e.g., Mark 5:41; 15:22; 15:34). These translations are directed at anyone in the audience who did not understand Aramaic, which included most of the Israelites who lived in the Diaspora as well as Greek-speaking Gentiles.

28. For a detailed outline of the evidence regarding Mark's audiences and the patterns of audience address, see Appendix 6, "The Audiences of Mark." Also see

If the evidence points to audiences primarily made up of Israelites, it also points to the fact that the audiences were not already believers in Jesus as the Christ. The evidence from an analysis of audience address shows that Mark's rhetorical strategy was to bring his listeners to identification with the disciples and to belief in Jesus as the Messiah in the course of his story. When assessing the character of the intended audience, it is important to pay attention to the rhetorical strategy of the entire gospel. When the gospel is performed from beginning to end over the course of about two hours, the audience is addressed for the first hour of the story as characters who are on the periphery of relationship with Jesus—"those seated around him" (3:33–34), "the great crowd" (4:1), "those around him with the twelve" (4:10)—and only in the later part of the story, as "the disciples" (7:17; 9:31; 10:13–14, 23; 11:22; 12:43; 14:32), "the twelve" (10:33; 14:18, 22, 27), and finally, in the apocalyptic discourse, as the four, Peter, John, James, and Andrew (13:3). The implication of this structure of audience address is that the audiences were not initially addressed as followers of Jesus (that is, as members of churches). The story is structured to invite the listeners to move from identifying with those on the margins of relationship with Jesus to being part of the band of Jesus' disciples.

The PRN itself assumes that the audience will readily identify with the disciples, Peter, and the women who followed Jesus, *but only after imaginatively walking with Jesus for nearly two hours*. The structure of the story is, therefore, a sign that Mark's gospel was addressed to the Israelites of the Diaspora and their Gentile neighbors who were not members of communities who believed in and followed Jesus as Messiah in the context of the aftermath of the Judean–Roman War as an invitation to identify with the disciples of Jesus and their experience. Persons who identify themselves as followers of Jesus and as believers in his identity as the Messiah, whether Judean or Gentile, could certainly have their faith addressed and strengthened by the gospel, as is clear from the history of its later use by the church. But the rhetoric of the story indicates that the audiences are addressed as persons who do not initially identify themselves as disciples of Jesus but are only invited to this self-identification in response to the story of Jesus' ministry, passion, and resurrection. Thus, faith in Jesus as the Messiah is not assumed in the storyteller's address to the audience.

The PRN was the conclusion of a long story of some two hours in duration, composed and told first by Mark, an anonymous disciple who may have been a follower of Peter,[29] and thereafter by the storytellers who

---

Boomershine, "Audience Asides and the Audiences of Mark."

29. See Marcus, *Mark*, 1:17–24, for a review of the evidence for authorship.

learned and told his story. Mark's gospel was a proclamation that Jesus gave his life in order to establish a global kingdom of peace, and that his way of nonviolent peacemaking was vindicated by his resurrection. The stories preceding the PRN relate a series of events in which Jesus carried out his campaign against the powers of evil—first in Galilee by driving out demons, healing persons from various afflictions, and feeding of fellow Israelites; and then in the Gentile regions of Phoenicia and the Decapolis by carrying out a similar campaign of good deeds of exorcism, healing, teaching, and feeding among the "nations." After Peter's recognition of Jesus as the Messiah, Jesus prophesied that he himself would be handed over to the chief priests, scribes, and elders of Israel, and that they would condemn him to death and hand him over to the Gentiles, who would kill him, and that on the third day he would be raised. Following the prophecy of his own death and resurrection, Jesus outlined the cost of following him and set out for Jerusalem. When he entered Jerusalem, he carried out a nonviolent, prophetic protest in the Temple in defense of the Temple as a place of prayer for all nations, and in protest against what it had become in Mark's time: a den of insurgents, the final fortress of the warriors who carried out the war against the Romans. In Mark's story, Jesus' prophetic action set in motion the conspiracy among the Judean authorities that led to the fulfillment of Jesus' prophecy of his death.

The exploration of the sound structures of the PRN itself reveals that it is composed of eight sections.[30] After the plot to arrest Jesus and his last Passover, each subsequent section tells the story of the successive fulfillment of Jesus' third passion-resurrection prophecy, 10:33–34: arrest, trial, and condemnation by the Sanhedrin; the handing over and humiliation by the Gentiles; the crucifixion, death, and resurrection. Each of these sections of prophecy fulfillment ends surprisingly with a climactic description of the wrong responses of Jesus' supporters, with whom the audience has been invited to identify: first the disciples, then in succession Peter, the crowd, and the women who were present at his death and mourned him but who, when commissioned to go and tell the news of the resurrection, fled and told no one.

The central impact of this story is to announce Jesus as the Messiah of peace whose life, death, and resurrection are a sign of God's way of redemption of the human community—both Israel and "the nations"—from the powers of evil that oppress them. The climactic moments of the PRN involve the audiences in identification with the experience of sympathetic characters who respond in unambiguously wrong ways to Jesus' acceptance

---

30. See Appendix 2, "A Sound Map of Mark's Passion-Resurrection Narrative," for a description of the units of sound in the PRN and a sound map of the whole narrative.

of his nonviolent suffering and death as the will of God and as the way to victory over the powers of evil. From this position of involvement, the audience experiences the shame of the disciples' flight, the grief of Peter's denial, the shock of the crowd's rejection of Jesus and choice of Barabbas, and finally the fear associated with the commission to tell the story of the resurrection.[31]

A Note on the Possible Physical Appearance of Mark's Alexandrian Audiences

The largest Judean community in the Diaspora was located in Alexandria. Subsequent traditions revere Mark as the founder of the Coptic Church in Egypt, which had its origins in Alexandria.[32] Eusebius records the early sources of this tradition:

> Clement in the eighth book of his *Hypotyposes* gives this account, and with him agrees the bishop of Hierapolis named Papias. And Peter makes mention of Mark in his first epistle which they say that he wrote in Rome itself, as is indicated by him, when he calls the city, by a figure, Babylon, as he does in the following words: "The church that is at Babylon, elected together with you, saluteth you; and so doth Marcus my son" (1 Peter 5:13). *And they say that this Mark was the first that was sent to Egypt, and that he proclaimed the Gospel which he had written, and first established churches in Alexandria.* (italics added)[33]

Thus, an ancient tradition locates early proclamations of Mark's gospel in Alexandria. And it is probable that Mark's gospel was composed either during the later stages or in the immediate aftermath of the war in the late '60s or early '70s. We can, therefore, imagine performances of Mark's Gospel in the last three decades of the first century in Alexandria. This possible setting

---

31. See below in this introduction the section titled "The Rhetorics of Israelite Storytelling," and Appendix 4, "The Rhetorics of Biblical Storytelling" for an analysis of what I call the rhetoric of alienation and the rhetoric of involvement and implication in some of the major stories in Israel's storytelling tradition, including David and Goliath, Ahab and Jezebel, the Yahwist creation story (Genesis 2–3), the golden calf at Mount Sinai, and David and Bathsheba.

32. See Marcus, *Mark*, 1:30–37, for the evidence for Rome and Syria as the location of composition.

33. Eusebius, *Ecclesiastical History* 2.15.1–2; 2.16.1. The translations are from *The Nicene and Post-Nicene Fathers*, 2nd ser., vol. 1.

for some of the early proclamations of Mark was rumbling around in my mind when I made a delightful discovery.

In the last months of the final revision of this commentary, I was in New York City for the annual "Urban Angels" banquet of New York Theological Seminary. And on my last day I decided to visit the Metropolitan Museum of Art. When I entered the first gallery to the left of the ticket checkpoint, I was in the gallery of Egypt in the Roman period, precisely the time period we are exploring. And to my amazement, there were beautiful, magnificently preserved portraits of Alexandrians dated from the late first to the early second century. Those portraits are available on the website of the Metropolitan Museum (www.metmuseum.org/collection/the-collection-online/search?ft=Egypt+in+the+Roman+period, pages 1–5) and at **www.messiahofpeace.com**. This is how representative Alexandrians in the late first century looked! These portraits are a window into the performance world of Mark's gospel and the faces of the Judeans and Egyptians who may have been in Mark's audiences.

Two Recurring Motifs in the *Reading* of Mark

A frequent conclusion of Markan scholarship is that the audience for Mark's gospel were readers who were members of Gentile Christian congregations in various locales in the Roman Empire. Joel Marcus, for example, concludes that Mark's readers were members of a particular Gentile "Christian" congregation of which Mark was a member, in Rome or perhaps in Syria.[34] In each case scholars envision these communities as having had their origins in the religion of Israel but to varying degrees as having separated themselves and become self-consciously "Christian" communities.

Assuming an original audience of predominantly Gentile "Christian" communities, two mutually complementary motifs have been identified in the reception of Mark's narrative. The first is some degree of what has been called "anti-Judaism." This motif is seen as the source of the emphasis in Mark's story on the responsibility of the "Jews" for Jesus' death. In particular, the construction of the trial before the Sanhedrin and the crowd's choice of Barabbas and demand for Jesus' crucifixion to which Pilate reluctantly assented are seen as efforts by the author of this story to shift responsibility for Jesus' death from the Romans to the "Jews." When seen in this perspective, the purpose of this polemic against "Jews" was to reinforce "Christian" readers in their identity as "Christians."

---

34. Marcus, *Mark*, 1:33–37. Bauckham, *Gospel for All Christians* (note the title).

This "anti-Jewish" motif in Mark's story is then seen as the source for the further development of this theme in the subsequent stories of Matthew, Luke, and John. In those later stories, the degree of "Jewish" responsibility for Jesus' death was made even more emphatic. In Matthew, "the people as a whole" say, "His blood be on us and on our children" (Matt 27:25). In Luke, Pilate three times asserts Jesus' innocence and declares his intention to release Jesus, but in the end the voices of the people demanding Barabbas' release and Jesus' crucifixion "prevailed" (Luke 23:13–25). And in John, the ones demanding Jesus' crucifixion are repeatedly and explicitly named as "the Judeans." This motif in the Gospels was then the seed for what became Christian anti-Judaism. That religious polemic was further developed in the context of German scientific eugenics into the genocidal anti-Semitism that was a principal driving motive for the Holocaust and the deaths of millions of Jews. Thus, in this view Mark was the source for these later developments that extended and amplified the "anti-Judaism" inherent in Mark's story.

The second motif that has often been identified in the formation and reception of Mark's story was pro-Roman apologetic. This apologetic was, again according to this reading of Mark, the motive for the positive characterization of Pilate. In Mark's story of the Pilate trial, Pilate is characterized as a Roman governor who is sympathetic to Jesus and tries to release him. He only sentences Jesus to be crucified after the repeated demand by the crowd, "in order to satisfy the crowd." The underlying motive for this positive characterization is understood to be the defusing of any possibility that the Roman authorities would perceive the story of Jesus' death as anti-Roman and engage in further persecution of Christians. As E. P. Sanders has written,

> The stories of Pilate's reluctance and weakness of will are best explained as Christian propaganda; they are a kind of excuse for Pilate's action which reduces the conflict between the Christian movement and Roman authority.[35]

This motif is seen, therefore, as having even greater urgency in the aftermath of the Judean War, when the possibility of the association of Christians with Judaism could provoke further Roman retribution. And that urgency is reflected in the subsequent tendency in the later gospels to further intensify the portrayal of Pilate's efforts to get Jesus released: Matthew's stories of Pilate's wife's dream and washing his hands, and Pilate's repeated insistence in both Luke and John that he finds Jesus innocent of the charges and repeatedly tries to release him.

---

35. Sanders, *The Historical Figure of Jesus*, 274.

The combination of these two motifs has been characterized as the underlying reason for what is seen as Mark's literary intention of increasing the responsibility of Jews and decreasing the responsibility of Romans for Jesus' crucifixion and death. On this reading this two-fold tendency in Mark and in the Gospels that followed constitutes a principal meaning of Mark's story for its original readers. This reading has in turn been identified as the original and underlying source of Christian anti-Semitism. John Dominic Crossan has characterized this dual motif in the gospel accounts and has starkly stated its consequences:

> In its origins and first moments that Christian propaganda was fairly innocent. Those first Christians were relatively powerless Jews, and compared to them the Jewish authorities represented serious and threatening power. As long as Christians were the marginalized and disenfranchised ones, such passion fiction about Jewish responsibility and Roman innocence did nobody much harm. But, once the Roman Empire became Christian, that fiction turned lethal. In the light of later Christian anti-Judaism and eventually of genocidal anti-Semitism, it is no longer possible in retrospect to think of that passion fiction as relatively benign propaganda. However explicable its origins, defensible its invectives, and understandable its motives among Christians fighting for survival, its repetition has now become the longest lie, and for our own integrity we Christians must at last name it as such.

Crossan's conclusion about the relationship between Mark's PRN and Christian anti-Semitism is without question an accurate description of what happened in the reception and hearing of Mark's narrative in *subsequent* Christian history. The question here, however, is whether this was the purpose and meaning of Mark's narrative in its *original* historical context. Was it in fact anti-Jewish and pro-Roman? Is its original meaning accurately defined as Mark pointing the finger of condemnation at the Jews as primarily responsible for Jesus' death and the Romans as innocent?

The answer that emerges from this study will be a steady and consistent no. The evidence will indicate that this reading of the meaning and purpose of Mark's narrative is a distortion and perversion of its original meaning, purpose, and impact. When the gospel is heard in performance, its purpose comes through as passionately pro-Israelite. It was the story of a "peace party" in first-century Israelite religion. It was aimed at saving the people of Israel from the consequences of ongoing warfare against the Romans and the Gentiles by engaging them in a two-hour-long orally performed story that was rhetorically designed to draw Judean and Gentile listeners throughout the Roman Empire into sympathetic identification with characters who were to varying degrees attracted to and involved with Jesus, but who in the end turned away from a Messiah who advocated nonviolence against the Romans and the inclusion of Gentiles in God's saving purpose. When this story is read through the lens of what has been called "anti-Judaism" the impact of the story is reversed, transforming it from a story that invites audience involvement in the rejection of Jesus and nonviolence and the choice of Barabbas into a story that invites its readers to condemn "the Jews" for their violence against Jesus. Mark's passionate appeal to recognize *our* involvement in the death of the Messiah of peace has become "the Jews killed Jesus." This radical shift in meaning is the tragic result of forces that developed in later centuries when the vital nerve of sympathetic identification with the characters of Mark's story was severed by the combination of the change in the religious identity of the audiences of Mark and the emotionally detached reading of the story as a document. The proposal here is that the anti-Jewish/pro-Roman interpretation of Mark's PRN has been a misreading and a mishearing of the story's meaning and purpose that has been associated with the conclusion that Mark's original receivers were "Gentile Christian" readers.

The Rhetorics of Biblical Storytelling

The proposal that emerges from the analysis of Mark's story as performed for audiences is, therefore, that one major source of the anti-Jewish stream of interpretation of Mark's story is that the self-identity of the audiences changed from being predominantly Israelite/Judean to being Christian/non-Jewish. In combination with other factors, this change in the religious and cultural identity of the audiences and readers of Mark over the centuries also significantly altered their experience of the meaning of the story. A second, later and equally momentous factor has been the detachment from emotional engagement with the story that has accompanied the development of silent reading, namely, the reading of the meaning of biblical texts as a referential source for historical "facts" ("ostensive reference") and theological ideas ("ideal reference"), and criticism as a habitual practice for those silent readers.

The goal in this commentary is to listen for the original meaning and impact of this story for the audiences for whom the story was composed. This purpose requires us to experience the story in its original medium as a story and to repair the vital nerve of sympathetic engagement that has been severed by this combination of factors. A dimension of this reorientation that may be helpful for twenty-first-century interpreters of Mark is greater clarity about the rhetorical structures of storytelling in the traditions of Israel that preceded and shaped Mark's story.[36]

In order to clarify the precedents for Mark's rhetorical structures, the echoes of different storytelling rhetorics need to be distinguished. For the purposes of this discussion, they can be called *the rhetoric of alienation or condemnation* and *the rhetoric of involvement or implication*. We are all familiar with the rhetoric of alienation because of its perpetual presence in contemporary movies and politics. The rhetoric of involvement or implication is less familiar.

The Rhetoric of Alienation and Condemnation

The rhetoric of alienation and condemnation has a characteristic set of appeals and dynamics in respect to "aesthetic distance," a technical term in literary criticism meaning how *alienated from or close to* a character a listener or reader feels.[37] Aesthetic distance refers to the dynamics of relationship established between a receiver (generally a reader) and a character in a story. A highly sympathetic characterization will generate a dynamic of emotional intimacy and sympathy with a character—hence, a minimal degree of aesthetic distance. The characterization of a hostile, alienating character will result in a high degree of aesthetic distance.

The general plot structure associated with the rhetoric of alienation is the introduction of a conflict in which a character has a major role as an enemy. This bad-guy character never does anything good, right, or in any way sympathetic. The dynamics of aesthetic distance in relation to the character are only negative, and those dynamics are intensified in the course of the story. Elements that escalate negative aesthetic distance are negative images, the implementation of negative norms of judgment, recurring themes or motifs of wrongdoing, insight into hostile motives or attitudes, negative

---

36. Booth, *Rhetoric of Fiction*. The analysis of narrative rhetoric had its most significant development in the work of Wayne Booth. The great value of his book is the synthetic drawing together into a comprehensive framework of the various dimensions of interaction between a novelist and the readers of modern fiction. The various types of narrators and their points of view, the dynamics of characterization, the appeals to shared norms of judgment, and the structuring of plot are elements of rhetoric that are universal in storytelling. The problem for biblical interpretation is to recognize and account for the differences between ancient oral narratives, which were told to audiences, and modern novels, which were usually read in silence by readers—Charles Dickens, who read his stories for audiences, being an exception.

37. Ibid., 156.

asides or comments to the audience by the storyteller, plots to do evil, and evil actions by the character. Storytellers, novelists, and dramatists have a broad repertoire of gestures, tones, and attitudes for the intensification of the rhetoric of alienation. As the conflict in the plot escalates, the actions of the enemy become progressively more evil until the climax of the conflict in which the enemy is killed or destroyed. The appeal to the audience is to celebrate and rejoice at the death or marginalization of the character. This is the rhetoric of countless action movies and of political rhetoric such as the characterization of Sadaam Hussein in the buildup to the Iraq war and his eventual capture and execution.

There are many instances of this rhetorical structure in Israelite storytelling tradition. Examples of this rhetoric in Israel's storytelling traditions include Goliath, Pharaoh, Ahab and Jezebel, and Haman. Goliath is a classic example of this rhetoric of alienation. He is introduced as a giant warrior, and his challenge to send someone to fight with him fills the armies of Israel and the audience with fear. When David goes to meet him, Goliath curses him by his gods and mocks David: "Am I a dog, that you come to me with sticks?" (1 Sam 17:43). David taunts him in return in the name of the Lord of Hosts and then kills him with a sling, a stone, and Goliath's sword. For Israelites who originally heard this story, Goliath's cursing and mockery of David and Israel's God is highly alienating and creates high aesthetic distance. Every child who has heard this story over the centuries has cheered at Goliath's demise.

This set of negative rhetorical appeals is used in the storytelling traditions of Israel in the characterization of foreign enemies such as Haman and Jezebel and in the characterization of Israelites: e.g., Korah and his allies, who rebelled against Moses (Numbers 16), the Benjaminites in Gibeah who raped and killed the Levite's concubine (Judges 19–20), and Manasseh (2 Kgs 21:1–17). In each of these stories, the storyteller invites the audiences to join in the condemnation of these characters, a condemnation that the storyteller expresses by her tone of voice and body language. Silent reading of these texts, such as the story of the Levite's concubine, will create this visceral feeling of outrage at the behavior of the men of Gibeah and thus alienation from them even for modern readers. In the context of its original telling, the evil of the Benjaminites was poignantly experienced in the war between that tribe and the rest of Israel, in the deaths of tens of thousands of warriors, and in the destruction of the city of Gibeah. The dynamics of alienation and condemnation were made only more intense by means of the tone of voice and body language of the tellers of the story. In the Gospel of Mark, this rhetoric of alienation or condemnation is present in the characterization of the chief priests, scribes, and elders.

A *variation* of this rhetorical pattern is what can be called *the rhetoric of disappointment and alienation*. This is the more complex rhetorical pattern of characters who are initially presented as enemies, who become for a time sympathetic helpers but then revert to their status as enemies. At some point in the story these characters speak and behave in ways that raise the hope that they will change and do what is right and good. But that hope is disappointed and the characters are confirmed as evil and as an enemy.

The classic instance of this characterization in the storytelling traditions of Israel is Pharaoh. The pharaoh of the exodus is established as an enemy by his enslavement of the Israelites and his campaign to kill the male babies of the Israelites (Exodus 1). At several points in his interactions with Moses, Pharaoh relents and promises to let the people go; but then he changes his mind (the frogs—8:8-15; the flies—8:25-31; the hail—9:27-33; the firstborn—12:30-32). In each instance, especially when Pharaoh asks Moses to pray for him, the hope is raised that he may relent and let the people go. The climax of Pharaoh's reversions to his evil self is his pursuit of the Israelites with his army to the Red Sea. The audiences of Exodus are invited to rejoice with Miriam at the Egyptians (and by implication, Pharaoh) dead on the shore.

Another instance of this rhetorical structure is the characterization of Ahab. He is initially presented as evil ("did evil in the sight of the Lord more than all who were before him"—1 Kgs 16:30). In his dialogues with Elijah and in his hesitation to take Naboth's vineyard (1 Kgs 21:4), the hope is raised that he will do the right thing. Indeed, he repents of his evil plan to take the vineyard for a short time (21:27-29), but after a talk and conspiracy with his wife, Jezebel, she engineers the stoning of Naboth, and Ahab takes the vineyard. He later has a moderately sympathetic dialogue with the prophet Micaiah (22:13-28). But he rejects Micaiah's prophecy and returns to his way of not listening to the Lord and is killed at Ramoth-Gilead (22:29-40). Other instances of this rhetorical pattern are the characterizations of Nebuchadnezzar and Antiochus IV Epiphanes. This set of rhetorical appeals is used often in the characterizations of rulers and some of these men are the worst characters in the stories of Israel. This is the rhetorical structure of Mark's characterization of Pilate.

The Rhetoric of Involvement and Implication

The most complex rhetorical pattern of characterization can be called *the rhetoric of involvement or implication*, the noun *implication* carrying the verbal sense of being or becoming involved in or implicated in what is taking place. In contrast to the rhetoric of disappointment and alienation, this rhetorical strategy involves good characters who do something wrong, but with whom the storyteller appeals for sympathy in both their goodness and their failure.

The stories exhibiting this rhetorical strategy have a common structure in biblical literature. A covenant is made between God (or God's representative) and the central characters of the story—a covenant that often carries with it unambiguous norms in regard to what will constitute violation of the covenant. Various details create a high degree of sympathetic identification between the character and the audience. The characters are introduced in a positive manner. The actions and words of the character are in agreement with the ethical and cultural norms of the storyteller and the audience. There are intimate inside views of feelings and perceptions sympathetic in their emotional dynamics. This last narrative technique is one of the most readily identified marks of this rhetorical structure. There are often also recurring images, actions and even phrases that are used to draw the characterization and to reinforce the positive dynamics in the relationship between the audience and the character.

In the rhetoric of involvement or implication, this character who has been presented in a highly sympathetic manner then does something that is unambiguously wrong, but at the same time perfectly understandable for the listener. The character's action is a violation of the basic structure of the covenant between the character and the Lord. The consequences of this violation of the covenant are named and carried out in words and acts of judgment. Sometimes the character's grief and repentance from this violation of covenant are explicitly described, often as weeping, shame, or confession. Because the character's violation is something the listener can fully understand, the impact of this story structure for the audience is an experience of being involved and implicated in this action and its consequences. A frequent response of a listener to this rhetorical dynamic is a sharing of the feeling of guilt and grief, reflection on what led to this wrong-doing, and turning away from that action or thought. This audience response is particularly present when there is an immediate connection between the decisions of the character and existential issues facing the listeners. Thus, there is a direct correlation between the degree of sympathetic identification with the character and the degree to which the audience is itself involved in the character's action.

This narrative strategy is also characteristic of Israelite storytelling. The most graphic examples of this rhetorical structure occur in the central moments in the larger story of the covenant of the people with God: creation, the covenant with Yahweh and the golden calf at Sinai, David's violation of the covenant in his adultery with Bathsheba and murder of Uriah, the covenant renewal after the exile in Ezra's reading of the Torah at the Water Gate (Nehemiah 8), and the confession and baptism at Pentecost (Acts 2:23, 37, 41). The distinguishing feature of this rhetorical structure is a highly sympathetic characterization of a character with whom the audience is invited to identify, who then does something that is, according to the norms shared by the storyteller and the audience, wrong. And in each of the stories listed above, the story concludes with the recognition and confession of the violation of the covenant with God. A more detailed analysis of this rhetorical dynamic will help to clarify the impact of these stories. Only one example of this rhetorical structure will be analyzed here, but the other stories listed here are discussed in Appendix 4, "The Rhetorics of Israelite Storytelling."

The Man and the Woman in the Garden of Eden (Genesis 2–3)

The story of the man and the woman in the garden of Eden is a highly developed instance of this rhetorical structure. The earth-man is introduced by the story of the Lord mixing water and clay to form the man and then to give him life by breathing into him the breath of life. The Lord blesses the man by creating a garden into which the man is placed. The man's place in paradise is a strong invitation to the audience to identify with the man. The covenant between the Lord and the man is established by the pronouncement of the Lord in which the man is invited to eat from the fruit of all the trees in the garden except the fruit of the tree of the knowledge of good and evil, which is explicitly forbidden to him. The following episode in which God brings all of the creatures of the world to the man in his search for a companion is delightful and establishes a highly positive relationship with the Lord, the man and the woman. This sympathetic relationship with God has its climax in the image of the Lord bringing the woman to the man.

The formation of the woman is the culmination of the story of creation. The story implies that she is brought to the man naked. The man becomes an instant poet and proclaims her name in ecstasy. The sexual union of the man and the woman is explicitly implied in the description of their becoming one flesh. And the invitation to complete identification with the man and the woman culminates in the storyteller's aside to the listeners that they were naked and were not ashamed.

The serpent's temptation of the woman is an engagement of this superbly beautiful character with an enemy. An easily recognized hint to the audience of the woman's vulnerability to violation of the covenant with God is her exaggerated quotation of God's prohibition against eating from the tree of the knowledge of good and evil: "You shall not eat of the fruit of the tree that is in the middle of the garden, *nor shall you touch it*" (compare Gen 2:17 with 3:3). Every listener can remember and recognize that she has exaggerated God's command. The prelude to the eating of the fruit is an intensive threefold inside view of her seeing the fruit, anticipating its good taste, and recognizing that it is to be desired to make one wise—all qualities generally attractive to human beings. By taking the listener inside the woman's mind to see these attractive things and desire them with her, the narrator invites the listener into the most intimate sympathetic identification with her. When she eats the fruit and gives it to "her man with her" and he eats, the audience can identify fully with this action by the woman and the man.

The discovery of their violation of the covenant is immediate, both in their recognition that they are naked and in their ensuing conversation with the Lord. The pronouncement of the Lord's judgment against the serpent, the woman, and the man follows this violation of the covenant with its prophecies of the consequences with which every listener can identify (Gen 3:14–19). The story ends with the Lord clothing the man and the woman in an act of mercy and casting them out of the garden.

The distinctive characteristic of the storytelling dynamics of this story is the high degree of sympathetic identification established between the characters and the audience leading up to the violation of an unambiguous norm of judgment in their relationship with God. A virtual elimination of aesthetic distance is created by the utopian descriptions of the garden, the woman, and the man, which are universally attractive to men and women everywhere. By means of this identification the listeners become involved and implicated in the actions of the woman and the man. Sympathetic identification is, then, the central mark of the rhetoric of involvement and implication.

Tragically, the man's effort to blame the woman for his sin, meant as an ironic joke in the original telling, has been read without irony in major streams of the theological tradition, making women responsible for the fall. This is similar to the way the theological interpretation of the ironies in the PRN has led to the momentous conclusion that "the Jews killed Jesus." As is evident in the theological tradition associated with blaming the fall on the woman, the possibility is present that members of the audience and especially readers of the text will not identify with the character and will experience the story as alienation and condemnation rather than involvement and implication. But the story's rhetoric is structured to create audience involvement in the actions of the woman *and* the man.

Introduction

Meaning in Mark's Passion-Resurrection Narrative

Both the rhetoric of alienation and condemnation and the rhetoric of involvement and implication are present in Mark's PRN. The characterization of the chief priests is a flat characterization in which the dynamics of *alienation or condemnation* are established in the first episode of the PRN by their stealthy plotting and fear of Jesus' popularity (14:1–2) and are intensified until the climax of their mocking of Jesus on the cross (15:31–32). The climax of the rhetoric of alienation is the joining of the chief priests and scribes with the insurrectionists on Jesus' right and left in the taunting and mockery of Jesus.

The story of Pilate, in contrast, exhibits the *variation of the rhetoric of alienation* in which an enemy becomes a helper for a moment but then disappoints and reverts to his status as an enemy. This rhetorical structure has been interpreted as pro-Roman apologetic and a lessening of Roman responsibility for Jesus' death. This interpretation is a curious distortion of the impact of Pilate's characterization. The characterization has the same structure as that of Herod in the earlier story of the execution of John the Baptist. The fact that there are sympathetic dimensions to the characterization of Herod and that the possibility is raised that he will continue to protect John from his wife's rage in no way diminishes his responsibility for John's death. If anything, it heightens the scale of injustice and of alienation from Herod. The same is true of the characterization of Pilate. He has the power to execute Jesus or to release him. Because of political calculations like those of Herod, Pilate orders the crucifixion of a man he knows is innocent of any crime. The magnitude of his cynicism in regard to the tradition of Roman justice is stunning. The characterization of Pilate, like the characterizations of the chief priests and Herod, is structured by the rhetoric of condemnation.

The characterizations of the disciples, Peter, the women, and the crowd are complex and are structured by the *rhetoric of involvement and implication*. The audience is invited to sympathize and identify with these characters, *including the crowd*, in a variety of ways prior to a climactic action or response that is unambiguously wrong. The accurate identification of this rhetorical structure is an essential element in the appropriate interpretation of the stories. A central argument here is that the perception of Mark's story as "anti-Jewish" is related to the misperception of the rhetorical dynamics involved in the characterization of the crowd. The analysis of the characterization of the crowd in the commentary that follows is of particular importance. While the rhetorical strategy in Mark's presentation of the disciples, Peter, and the women is usually perceived as one of involvement or implication, the strategy in the presentation of the crowd at the Pilate trial has been widely understood to be that of alienation or condemnation.[38]

The problem with the rhetoric of involvement or implication is that the meaning and impact of the story is dependent on the audience's sympathetic identification with the characters. As is evident in the interpretation of the story of Adam and Eve as well as the gospel PRNs, in the absence of that vital connection with the characters, the same story that is structured to involve listeners in self-recognition and self-reflection can become a story that is experienced as alienating, causing listeners to criticize and condemn the character rather than to share the character's involvement in violation of the covenant with God.

One of the reasons why hearing the story rather than reading it in silence makes a difference is that the storyteller narrates the events and the words of the characters in a tone communicating more than factual information, and draws listeners into identification with characters who may be outwardly different. Full engagement in sympathetic identification with the characters of the story is fully possible also with silent reading if readers are attentive to and psychologically open to the clues to the storyteller's invitation. But if readers maintain a high degree of psychological distance in the reading of the story, its actual meaning can become virtually the opposite of the intended meaning, communicated inherently in the structure of the story. The source of that distance, therefore, may be a change either in the self-identity of the listener (from identifying oneself in the post-war first century as Hellenistic Judean to identifying oneself in the post-Nicea fourth century as a Christian) or in the psychological distance to the story (sympathetic hearing to critical silent reading) or both in combination. But, regardless of the cause of this shift, the story can undergo a radical transformation in its meaning. Thus, the story of the man and the woman in the garden can change, especially for male readers and theologians, from meaning "*we* violated God's covenant, and our effort to blame it on the woman is a joke" to "*the woman* violated God's covenant." Likewise in Mark's story, the meaning of the story, especially for later Christians who did not identify themselves as Jews, can shift from "*we* were involved in the death of the Messiah" to "the *Jews* killed Jesus."

---

38. A major school of Markan interpretation has, I think inaccurately, extended the identification of the rhetoric of alienation and condemnation to Mark's characterization of the disciples, Peter, and the women. Beginning with Theodore Weeden's seminal book, this reading of Mark's rhetoric had its most extensive development in Werner Kelber's identification of the rhetoric of alienation in relation to the representatives of the "oral Gospel" that Mark was displacing with his "written Gospel." See Weeden, *Mark—Traditions in Conflict*; and Kelber, *The Oral and the Written Gospel*.

This is then a brief orientation to the dynamics implicit in the now silenced text of Mark's story and the possible ways in which the story can be restored to sound and reexperienced. The problem for our exploration of Mark's PRN is that while Mark's original audiences were familiar with this kind of story and its appeals, most contemporary readers of Mark's story are at best only vaguely familiar with these earlier stories, and virtually none of those readers has ever heard them told in the grand and forceful style of public performances in Mark's world.[39]

Furthermore, experiencing the appropriate dynamics of the passion-and-resurrection story is dependent on having heard the whole gospel. The impact of the flight of the disciples, Peter's denial, and the women's silence, and also of the crowd's choice of Barabbas rather than Jesus is in all cases, including that of the crowd, dependent on the sympathetic relationship with the characters that is established in the earlier parts of the story. Thus, the traditional practice of reading individual stories out of context and in an emotionally detached manner works against the possibility of experiencing the original meaning of the story that is implicit in the rhetorical structure of the entire gospel. This tendency has only been increased by the practice of detached critical reading of biblical compositions in silence. This practice directly relates to the misperception of the central stories of Mark's PRN as structured according to the rhetoric of alienation rather than the rhetoric of involvement and implication. The conclusion that follows from this misperception is that Mark's purpose was anti-Jewish polemic rather than the creation of an experience of involvement in the events that led to the death of the Messiah of peace.

What then did Mark's story mean for his first-century audiences of Judeans and Gentiles in the aftermath of the greatest war in Israel's history? Jesus announced the coming of the kingdom of God with his actions and his words and set about defeating the powers of evil. His teaching was woven with his actions of exorcism, healing, and feeding—first for his fellow Galileans and then for Gentiles, on "the other side." His actions of healing on the Sabbath, touching and being touched by the unclean, eating with sinners and tax collectors, and doing good for the Gentile enemies of Israel are signs of Jesus' disagreement with the Pharisees' approach to Torah interpretation.

---

39. See Shiner, *Proclaiming the Gospel*, 89: the rhetorical handbooks identify three styles of speech: 1. plain, suited to teaching that addresses the intellect; 2. grand or forcible, aimed at the emotions; and 3. intermediate. In Shiner's view, Mark is "full of forceful emotion," and emotion serves "as a primary determinate of the meaning of the Gospel in its original setting." The plain style is clearly the style that Western Christian readers have come to practice when reading aloud in liturgical settings. It is the style favored by "critical readers," as we shall note below. Some "critical readers" find an oral performance that is full of emotion to be a hindrance to their critical reflection.

His disciples recognized his actions as signs that he was the Messiah. He spoke of both his coming martyrdom and the possible martyrdom of any who would follow him; and knowing what would happen, he set out to meet his destiny in Jerusalem.

When Jesus entered the city, he was welcomed as the coming king of Israel. He carried out a nonviolent demonstration in the Temple against the Temple's transformation from a place of prayer for all the nations (the Gentiles) into a fortress of war, a "den of insurgents." As the plot to kill him proceeds, his disciples are presented as highly sympathetic characters who promised to die with him rather than to run away and deny him. But as his prophecy of their flight and denial is fulfilled step by step, they step by step fail to keep their promises. The crowd, his most consistent supporter both in Galilee and in Jerusalem and therefore a character with whom the audience has in the earlier parts of the narrative been invited to identify, chooses an insurrectionist and demands that Jesus be crucified. This is shocking but also understandable to anyone who has been swept along in the emotions of a war and who is mystified or offended by Jesus' refusal to defend himself. The story's invitation is to experience *our* implication in the war against our enemies and our rejection of Jesus' way of nonviolence and peacemaking implicit in the choice of Barabbas. The resurrection of Jesus is a vindication by God of Jesus and his way and a commission to tell the story. The invitation of the women's silence is to sympathize with their silence and their fear of telling anyone because of the threat of martyrdom and at the same time to reject it as a violation of the divine commission to tell the story.

The Importance of Mark's Story

We began this introduction with the proposal that this is one of the most important stories in human history. As with all hyperbolic rhetoric, the purpose of such a proposal is to provoke reflection. The historical reason for such a statement is that this story and its interpretation has had significant impact for both good and evil in subsequent history. On the positive side of the ledger, Mark's PRN provided the model for the concluding story of the canonical Gospel tradition and was a source and an inspiration for the development of at least two if not all three of the other canonical gospels. The gospels in turn have been a source of redemptive experience of God in the lives of millions of people for the subsequent two millennia and have inspired many to sacrificial service for others.

In our time we cannot do anything about the fact that many modern audiences of the gospels do not self-identify as Jews or Judeans. But we can recover the original performance medium of the narrative along with its style of emotional engagement designed to draw not only Judeans but also Gentiles into identification with the Judeans whose story is told in the narrative. We can also recover the performance of the Gospel of Mark as a whole in order to experience its entire dynamic of development from beginning to end, which is the only just context in which to try to understand the details. That exegetical challenge will be a next step in the formation of the new paradigm of biblical study implicit in the development of performance criticism. Furthermore, we can get clear about the implication of the historical setting of the original performances of Mark in the aftermath of the revolt against Rome, namely, that rejection of Jesus was associated with the choice of the nation to go to war and with the fearful challenge of following a nonviolent Messiah. Mark's gospel announced that the kingdom of God and the deliverance of the human community from the powers of evil will happen by prayer and peaceful engagement with our enemies rather than by violence.

Justice is an issue in this discussion. There is an issue of justice for all of the Jewish martyrs who have suffered and died as a direct or indirect result of the proclamation of this story. The tragedy of the accusation, conviction, and retribution against the multitudes of Jews who have been found guilty of the death of the Messiah calls out for justice. A central argument of this study is that this result was in no sense what Mark intended. Later powers beyond Mark's control transformed the meaning of his story in ways that he would have found horrific. It is difficult to imagine anything more contrary to his purpose than what has happened in subsequent history.

There is also an issue of justice in relation to the gospel tradition and Mark. Mark has been accused and convicted in the forum of public opinion of a terrible, massive crime—specifically, perjury and inciting of genocide. The investigation of the evidence in regard to this multifaceted crime of such scale and ambiguity calls for attention. The evidence indicates that Mark is innocent of this indictment.

The most difficult challenge to understanding any person's efforts at communication is to hear what they are saying in context, which turns out to be a very complex process. Our biggest liability in making meaning out of what another person says is to respond only to isolated fragments of it and to assume that our context for understanding them is identical with theirs. In the interest of justice we should be as diligent in our efforts to understand Mark's context—his entire context, including his media context—as we are in our efforts to understand any other speaker or writer we encounter. This is the ideal towards which scholarship strives. Modern people seek to honor it in a therapeutic context. We often do not honor it in our present political and religious context.

We can listen for the central meaning of this story in its original context, namely, that Jesus' death and resurrection was a sign that Jesus was the Messiah of peace, whose life and death was a witness to the transformative power of the love of the other and a revelation of God's way of redemption for all people by nonviolent action against the powers of evil. The sympathetic hearing of this story is an invitation to reflect on the fact that we often choose, as a human community and as both Jewish and Christian descendants of Israel, the warrior and warfare as the way we will be delivered from the powers of evil and violence. We can also hear in it a proclamation that humanity can be saved from delight in violence and can learn Jesus' way of love, nonretaliation, nonviolent resistance, and forgiveness. These are some of the major dimensions of the apocalyptic framework of this story about the Messiah's engagement with the powers of evil, from which the human community is in steady need of deliverance. They are elements of the story that, in the aftermath of the greatest tragedy in the history of Israel, shocked Mark's original audiences of Judeans and Gentiles into reflection about their belief in the myth of redemptive violence and their implication in the crucifixion of Jesus, who rejected that myth.

The personal dimensions of this story are the challenges of nonviolent discipleship. Jesus' announcement of his impending death is followed by his declaration that this is the calling for all those who would follow him. The costly demands of this challenge are then experienced in: (1) the disciples' running away and Peter's denial; (2) the crowd's fully understandable choice (in the context of the war) of Barabbas rather than Jesus; and (3) the women's flight and silence in response to the commission that they tell the story and announce the resurrection of the one who walked this fearful path. Each of these climactic moments in the story is a vicarious experience of involvement in the understandable but unambiguously wrong response to the challenges implicit in following a Messiah of peace.

On the other side of the ledger, many people have heard this story as an accusation and condemnation of the Jews as Christ killers. Many pogroms against Jews during the Middle Ages were ignited by the reading of the PRN and specifically the Pilate trial on Good Friday. The PRN has been interpreted as an anti-Jewish story and was used as a foundation for the Nazi Holocaust. This story is also, therefore, implicated in the deaths of millions of Jews over the centuries and is appropriately hated by many. We need to look this potential meaning of the story in the face and ask the question, is anti-Jewish polemic an accurate perception of this story's original meaning and impact? The answer to this question is an unequivocal no. Is anti-Jewish polemic the inevitable consequence of reading and hearing the story in today's context? Again, the answer to this question is an unequivocal no. But this answer can perhaps only be articulated in combination with a call to reappropriate the narrative in the medium of its original grand and forceful performance. The exploration of the meaning of this story in its original historical context is, therefore, important in relation to both the positive and the negative dimensions of its reception and interpretation in subsequent centuries.

There is a profound congruence between the message of Mark's narrative and the medium of the gospel. Mark's advocacy of peace and reconciliation through the oral publication of the story of Jesus as the Messiah of peace was nonviolent in its method as well as its message. The empowerment of a network of oral storytellers by the composition of a narrative preserved in a written document was a nonviolent way of organizing against the myth of redemptive violence. Thus, the medium of Mark's story of the Messiah of peace is integrally related to his story's meaning. And the enigma of the women's silence was a typically Markan way of encouragement for all who were silent and didn't tell the story because of fear.

If this story can reveal and energize even some dimension of the way that will lead to global peace, it will be a very important story in human history. Any dimension of that possibility will have its source in the hearing of Mark's story in a different context than has happened in recent centuries. This commentary is an invitation to listen to Mark's PRN in a new way. The purpose of this introduction has been to outline the conclusions to which we have been led by the analysis of Mark's story as a story told to audiences in the decades after what is most appropriately called the Judean–Roman War. The validity of those conclusions will only emerge from a detailed engagement with the sounds of the story in their original historical context. That is the purpose of the detailed commentary that follows. The implication is that everyone who wants to understand Mark's PRN in its original context is invited to learn and tell the story to audiences rather than only to read Mark's document in silence. The hope is that this exegesis and the performance of Mark's story will be explored, evaluated, and developed by others and will lead to a more appropriate retelling and reinterpretation of Mark's story by the wider community.

1

THE DAY BEFORE THE PASSOVER (14:1–11)

THE THREE STORIES IN THIS FIRST SECTION OF THE STORY ARE linked together by the plot of the chief priests and scribes in which Judas becomes a key conspirator. This is a further instance of Mark's "sandwich" stories in which a related story is inserted into the middle of another story. Mark does this earlier when he surrounds the story of the woman who touched Jesus' garment by the story of Jairus' daughter (5:21–43), when the execution of John the Baptist is told in the context of the mission of the twelve (6:7–31), and when the debate about Jesus being possessed by Beelzebul is inserted into the story of Jesus' family looking for him because they thought he was out of his mind (3:20–35). In each instance, this interlacing of stories links the two stories together and encourages the listeners to explore that relationship. The story of the woman and Jairus' daughter are linked by the common motif of Jesus breaking the law—by disregarding the uncleanness of being touched by an unclean woman, and by taking a presumably dead girl by the hand. The linking of the highly successful mission of the twelve and John's execution implies that Jesus is grieved and troubled. The implication is that he wants to withdraw with the twelve after the disciples' successful mission makes it clear that he may share John's fate. And Jesus' denunciation of the scribes' charge that he is possessed by Beelzebul establishes the basis for his refusal to see his family when they come to get him. Thus, the weaving together of these two stories creates a connection between the plot of the priests and Judas, and the woman anointing Jesus with precious ointment in Bethany.

The Day before the Passover (14:1–11)

The Conspiracy of the Chief Priests and Scribes (14:1–2) ▶

Sound Map

1Ἠν δὲ τὸ πάσχα καὶ τὰ ἄζυμα μετὰ δύο ἡμέρας.
καὶ ἐζήτουν οἱ ἀρχιερεῖς καὶ οἱ γραμματεῖς πῶς αὐτὸν ἐν δόλῳ
                                      κρατήσαντες ἀποκτείνωσιν.
2ἔλεγον γάρ,
    Μὴ ἐν τῇ ἑορτῇ, μήποτε ἔσται θόρυβος τοῦ λαοῦ

Translation

1Now the feast of Passover and Unleavened Bread was the next day.
And the chief priests and the scribes were looking for a way
    to arrest him by a conspiracy and kill him.
2For they had been saying,
    "Not during the feast or there will be a riot of the people."

Notes on Details and Translation

14:1: the next day / μετὰ δύο ἡμέρας

This phrase has been the subject of controversy and misunderstanding. It is usually translated as "two days before" (NRSV) or "two days away" (NIV). When the Greek phrase, literally translated "after two days," is used, the first of the two days referred to is the current day and the second day is the next day. This holds for Jesus' prophecy that he will be killed and rise again "after three days" (μετὰ τρεῖς ἡμέρας—8:31; 9:31; 10:34). The day he is killed is day 1 (Friday), day 2 is Saturday, and day 3, the day on which he will rise, is Sunday. It is important to be clear about this detail. Mark is implying that the execution of the plot is urgent. The authorities want to arrest and kill Jesus before the Passover festivities begin *the next day*—when the crowds with whom Jesus has been popular are gathered, and there is potential for political explosion. Thus, the implication is that they have to arrest him *today*.

In the first century, the celebration of Passover had been integrated into the seven-day feast of Unleavened Bread. The Passover lambs were sacrificed on the first day of the feast of Unleavened Bread. This was an elaborate and time-consuming process in which thousands of lambs were slaughtered, each in an elaborate ritual that involved the laying on of hands, prayers, and the complete draining of the animal's blood. The Passover feast was prepared during this first day of the festival. The feast was then eaten during the evening of the second day of the festival of Unleavened Bread after sundown. (Days among Israelites ended at sundown rather than midnight as among Romans.)

Mark's story indicates that the day of the plot, anointing, and betrayal is Wednesday (Nisan 13). The correlations between the days (sundown to sundown) and Mark's story are as follows:

- Sunday (Nisan 10): the triumphal entry and first day in the Temple (11:1-11)
- Monday (Nisan 11): the cleansing of the Temple (11:12-19)
- Tuesday (Nisan 12): the conflicts with the Judean authorities and Jesus' conversation with the four disciples (11:20—13:37)
- Wednesday (Nisan 13): the plot, anointing in Bethany, and Judas' betrayal (14:1-11)
- Thursday (Nisan 14): the preparations for the Passover (14:12-16)
- Friday (Nisan 15): the Last Supper, the arrest, the trials, the crucifixion, the death, and the burial of Jesus (14:17—15:47)
- Saturday (Nisan 16) the Sabbath (Friday sundown through Saturday sundown)
- Sunday (Nisan 17) the women's purchase of the spices, the discovery of the empty tomb, the speech by the young man in white, the flight and silence (16:1-8)

by a conspiracy / δόλῳ

The NRSV translates the Greek word δόλος as "stealth," and the RSV renders it as "treachery." The authorities are looking for a way to arrest and kill Jesus on the day before the festival begins, with its large crowds and potential for rioting. The implication of their plot is that they are engaging in a conspiracy to commit murder, which is regarded as a capital crime now, though it was not legally a crime in antiquity, when only the deed itself constituted a crime. Mark is describing a state-sponsored crime in which the government itself is engaging in criminal behavior for the sake of preventing further defection from the government's policies in regard to the Temple, the law, and the Roman empire. Secrecy, treachery and stealth (NIV "sly way" is too cute) are dimensions of their strategy, but these words do not adequately convey the seriousness of their crime. An indication of this seriousness is that Jesus includes δόλος in his list of the acts that defile a man—equating it to a crime against God (7:22–23). The term *conspiracy* more adequately names the authorities' defection from the ways of the righteous.

Comments on the Meaning and Impact of the Story

14:1: The time

The PRN begins with an introductory comment by the storyteller to the audience, naming the time: "the feast . . . was the next day." The tone of this comment is ominous. Never before in Mark's story has time been the sole subject of the opening period of a story. The contextual information is that this is Wednesday, and the festival begins tomorrow.

The fulfillment of Jesus' prophecies

An implication is that the time has come for Jesus' prophecies of his suffering and death to be fulfilled. This implication is created by the verbal echoes linking the conspiracy of the chief priests and scribes with Jesus' earlier prophecies of his coming suffering and death. The italicized elements in the following quotations are the verbal connections:

> . . . it is necessary for the Son of Man to suffer many things, be rejected by **the chief priests and the scribes** and the elders and **be killed and on** the third **day** to rise. (8:31)

> The Son of Man will be handed over into the hands of men and **they** will **kill him;** and having been **killed, on the** third **day** he will be raised. (9:31)

> . . . and the Son of Man will be handed over to **the chief priests and scribes** and they will condemn him to death and hand him over to the Gentiles and they will . . . **kill him; and on the** third **day** he will be raised. (10:33)

> Now the feast of Passover and Unleavened Bread was **on the** next **day. And the chief priests and scribes** were seeking how they might arrest him by a conspiracy **and kill him.** (14:1)

The implication of this theme from the earlier prophecies at the beginning of the story is that the prophecies are about to be fulfilled. This implication is made more ominous by the notice that the chief priests and scribes have decided to use treachery or conspiracy in their determination to kill Jesus. Their earlier actions have been public events. Their conspiracy is the culmination of an implied series of secret meetings in which they have planned to arrest and destroy him.

The plot against Jesus

The earlier descriptions of the plot against him are the climactic endings of the stories of the healing of the man with a withered hand (3:6), the cleansing of the Temple (11:18), and the parable of the Wicked Tenants (12:12). The sonic themes linking these earlier stories with the notice of the plot in the PRN are printed in bold:

> And the Pharisees went out and immediately conspired with the Herodians, **how they could destroy him.** (3:6, NRSV)
>
> **And the chief priests and the scribes** heard it and **were seeking how they could destroy him.** (11:18)
>
> And they **were seeking how to arrest him** but they also feared the people. (12:12)
>
> **And the chief priests and scribes were seeking how they might arrest him** by a conspiracy and kill him. (14:1b)

Thus, the plot against Jesus has developed throughout Mark's story. The two new elements of the plot against Jesus (in 14:1) are the authorities' resorting to a conspiracy (δόλος) and their actively seeking to kill him "today." It is these two new elements that introduce that ominous tone. The authorities are feeling a sense of urgency and are resorting to more extreme measures.

2: The explanation of the authorities' urgency

The storyteller's explanation in the concluding period ("for") implies that he is answering an implicit question by the audience. Many of the cola and periods in Mark's story that begin with the conjunction γάρ have this function (e.g., 3:21; 5:8; 5:28; 6:18) of answering a question raised by the previous statement. Furthermore, this comment is one of only three instances (also 6:52 and 16:8) in which an audience aside occurs at the end of a major segment of the story. By introducing the period with "for" at the end of the description of the conspiracy to kill Jesus, Mark's implication is that the audience is asking, why? Why would the authorities, the respected leaders of Israel, resort to such extreme violations of the law? The storyteller's answer is that they were running out of time, and today is the last day they can safely arrest him: i.e., "Because they were saying to one another, 'Not during the feast, or there might be a riot by the people.'" Their fear of the people has already been established (11:18; 12:12) and is now a prohibitive factor to public arrest.

Just as in 6:52 and 16:8, this explanation raises more questions than it answers. The implication of this "scoop" on the internal conversations of the authorities is that the crowd's enthusiastic support of Jesus has been the only thing that prevented the authorities from arresting him earlier in the week. Does this then mean that they will give up their plot if they cannot arrest him in secret? And if the feast of Passover and Unleavened Bread begins tomorrow, does that mean that they have to arrest him today? And if they can't arrest him today, is there a chance that Jesus' prophecy of his arrest, suffering and death might not be fulfilled and that he could escape? The implied answer is that they must arrest him today. Tomorrow during the feast will be too politically risky.

This news is both ominous and hopeful. The authorities are now resorting to a criminal conspiracy in order to kill Jesus. But the conspiracy to murder Jesus must be carried out "today." This information is a glimmer of hope. If they can't arrest and kill him today, they will suspend the plot.

While this audience aside raises tantalizing possibilities, it also raises further profound questions. In the logic of the story, two contradictory elements come together in this episode. The first is the intensifying plot to kill Jesus. The assumption throughout the entire narrative is that this plot is profoundly wrong. All the actions to preserve some measure of secrecy that Jesus has taken to this point—telling his disciples to tell no one; forbidding the demons to speak because they know him; commanding various people such as the leper, Jairus and his wife, and the crowds to say nothing—have been positive actions because they have prevented the authorities' ongoing plot to destroy him from being accomplished. But now Jesus' enemies have decided to kill him immediately.

Jesus' positive steps to prevent the authorities' plot from coming to fruition are set in the context of Jesus' ongoing prophecies of his death. In addition to the three explicit prophecies, there are several earlier intimations of his death. When people ask why his disciples don't fast, Jesus says that they don't fast because the bridegroom is with them, but that they will fast when he is taken away from them (2:19–20); the implication is that he will be taken away from them. The execution of John the Baptist and Jesus' implicit grief in taking the disciples away to a lonely place implies that a similar death may be ahead for Jesus. The parable of the Wicked Tenants includes allusions to the death of John the Baptist ("some they killed") and Jesus (the murder of "the son"—12:1–12). In its context, this saying is a prophecy of Jesus' murder by the authorities. And finally, all of the notices of Jesus' efforts to keep his messianic identity secret themselves imply that there is a sinister plot that he is working against.

Modern movies have developed these kinds of intimations into a highly subtle art that utilizes particular harmonies and types of music, vague images that flashback or flash forward in the action, and tones or statements of subtle warnings in the voices of the main characters. I think in particular of the Bourne Conspiracy series. Mark's story uses many of the foreshadowing and flashback techniques available to ancient storytellers. And, even if we can't prove it since we have no audio or video recordings of storytellers from antiquity, what we do know about the style of ancient storytelling makes it virtually certain that the Markan storytellers used vocal tones and gestures that implied the coming tragedy. All of these elements are associated with Jesus' explicit and implicit prophecies of his suffering, death, and resurrection.

The fulfillment of prophecy in biblical tradition carries with it the implication that this is the will of God. And while many of the prophecies in the prophetic tradition are prophecies of disaster, the fulfillment of prophecy is always a sign of the fulfillment of the will of God. Often the prophecies of disaster are an appeal to change the patterns of behavior that are leading to disaster. Jonah is an explicit instance of this kind of prophecy. But in the Gospel of Mark, Jesus unambiguously presents these prophecies as the will of God. Thus, Peter's resistance to the first passion prophecy (8:32–33) is explicitly namely as satanic thinking in the way of human beings, not God. Likewise Jesus' prayer in Gethsemane that God would take the cup of suffering from him but that he wants God's will to be done is fulfilled in Jesus' decision to walk the way of the cross. Presumably God's will is good. This creates a wrenching paradox that is built into the passion-and-resurrection story from its beginning here. These events are, on the one hand, the workings of the powers of evil men, whose demented purpose is wrong. But these events are also the working out of the will of God and ultimate good. The rest of the passion-resurrection story is an invitation to enter deeply into the conflict that the storyteller at the very beginning called "the good news."

Thus, this episode recalls the passion prophecies and also brings to mind the entire story that has gone before. It raises the underlying question that runs throughout the second half of the story: if Jesus knows that he is going to be killed in Jerusalem, why does he continue to walk toward Jerusalem? Likewise the plot of the priests recalls the plot of Jesus' opponents that has been present throughout the entire story. The persistence of their plot in turn raises the question, why were Jesus' opponents so determined to destroy him? When heard against the background of the Judean–Roman War, these questions point to the messianic traditions of Israel and the radical discontinuity between Jesus' way and the way of the messiahs of Israel. The "anointed ones" of Israel, most graphically Saul and David, immediately gathered an army and attacked the enemies of Israel. Jesus recruits a band of disciples and attacks the powers of evil: sickness, demon possession, social ostracism of the "unclean," strict observance of Sabbath law, hunger, poverty, and injustice. Furthermore, he attacks these powers in the areas of the Gentiles as well as within Israel. And if the law is violated in the course of these actions, Jesus heals people and casts out demons without concern for either Sabbath law or cleanliness laws. And now he has attacked the business of the sacrificial cult in the Temple and has gathered the support of the crowds in the Temple for his prophetic critique of the transformation of the Court of the Gentiles from a place of prayer to a place of warfare.

This story requires Jesus' listeners—his disciples, and the audience of the story who are addressed as his disciples—to rethink their assumptions about the Messiah. Jesus' actions are different from the actions narrated in the Old Testament stories of the Messiahs of Israel. There are no traditions of Saul or David or any of the anointed kings of Israel healing people, casting out demons, or doing good for the enemies of Israel such as the Gerasene demoniac and the Syro-Phoenician woman. Messiahs do battle, not acts of mercy and lovingkindness. David did relent from killing Nabal at Abigail's request (1 Sam 25:2–42), and he had mercy on Shimei, who cursed him as he fled from Jerusalem (2 Sam 16:5–14; 19:18b–23). But these are the actions of a man of war who exercises discrimination and some restraint in those whom he kills.

Jesus stands in stark contrast to the messiahs of Israel because he does not make war against the enemies of his people and is wholly nonviolent. He does not even defend himself against attacks by persons and factions among fellow Israelites. Thus, Jesus now confronts his enemies within the community of Israel without any actions of violence in response to their planned violent attacks against him that he knows are imminent.

This is the underlying crux of the conflict between Jesus and the chief priests. Jesus' loyalty to the kingdom of God transcends his loyalty to the ethnic identity of Israelites and to the law that is the foundation of Israelite purity and separation from Gentiles. His concept of the kingdom of God is global rather than national. The implication of the story is that there is a conflict between the will of God and the will of the leaders of the nation of Israel.

However, while this conflict is always present in the background of the story, this episode is also an important indication about the storyteller's assumptions about the audiences' attitude toward Jesus and the authorities. The implication of the episode is that the audience does not want Jesus to be killed and is on his side against the authorities. But this conflict is not "anti-Jewish." It is conflict between different factions within the community of Israel.

The storyteller's concluding explanation is a note of possible hope. If Jesus can get through this day without being arrested, he may be able to escape the storm in the ominous clouds forming on the horizon. At every major turning point in this story, Mark the storyteller appeals to the hopes of the audience that Jesus may somehow be able to live and not die. All of this is implicit in this intimate episode of explanations and inside information in which Mark the storyteller raises tantalizing possibilities for the listeners about what may happen in the rest of the story. It also cements the relationship between the storyteller and the audience at the beginning of this climactic story.

The Performance of the Story

This episode was told as inside information to the audience. Both the imminence of the day and the explanation of the reason for the conspiracy are addressed to the audience by the storyteller. A gesture of putting your hand next to your mouth and speaking softly as if telling a secret may help to convey the spirit of this. This gesture and tone is also congruent with the priests' inside plotting. These periods are short and should, therefore, be told slowly.

The most important thing is to establish direct contact with the audience. It is said that the reason grandchildren and grandparents get along so well is that they have a common enemy. The same is true in storytelling, and the common enemy here is the chief priests and the scribes. Remember, however, this was a story told by Mark to predominantly Judean communities in the aftermath of the Judean–Roman War. He was probably one of the many Judeans in the late first century who were thoroughly alienated from the chief priests and scribes. Some of the chief priests and scribes made alliances with the various factions responsible for initiating the revolt and the war. As we will see throughout the story, the audience is always addressed as Israelites, who share Israelite norms, experience, and tradition. It is in no sense an anti-Jewish story. It is a story that was told by Judeans who believed that Jesus was the Messiah to other Judeans and to Gentiles in the aftermath of the greatest disaster in the history of Israel.

The Day before the Passover (14:1–11)

The Anointing at Bethany (14:3–9)

Sound Map

14:3Καὶ ὄντος αὐτοῦ **ἐν** Βηθανίᾳ **ἐν** τῇ οἰκίᾳ Σίμωνος τοῦ λεπροῦ
          κατακειμένου αὐτοῦ
ἦλθεν γυνὴ ἔχουσα ἀλάβαστρον μύρου νάρδου πιστικῆς
           πολυτελοῦς.
συντρίψασα τὴν ἀλάβαστρον κατέχεεν αὐτοῦ τῆς κεφαλῆς.

4ἦσαν δέ τινες ἀγανακτοῦντες πρὸς ἑαυτούς,
  Εἰς τί ἡ ἀπώλεια αὕτη τοῦ μύρου γέγονεν;
5ἠδύνατο γὰρ τοῦτο τὸ μύρον
  πραθῆναι ἐπάνω δηναρίων τριακοσίων
  καὶ δοθῆναι τοῖς πτωχοῖς.
καὶ ἐνεβριμῶντο αὐτῇ.

6ὁ δὲ Ἰησοῦς εἶπεν,
  Ἄφετε αὐτήν.
τί αὐτῇ κόπους παρέχετε.
καλὸν ἔργον ἠργάσατο ἐν ἐμοί.

7**πάντοτε** γὰρ τοὺς πτωχοὺς **ἔχετε** μεθ᾽ ἑαυτῶν,
  καὶ ὅταν θέλητε δύνασθε αὐτοῖς εὖ ποιῆσαι,
  ἐμὲ δὲ οὐ **πάντοτε ἔχετε**.
8ὃ ἔσχεν ἐποίησεν·
  προέλαβεν μυρίσαι τὸ σῶμά μου εἰς τὸν ἐνταφιασμόν.
9ἀμὴν δὲ λέγω ὑμῖν,
  ὅπου ἐὰν κηρυχθῇ τὸ εὐαγγέλιον εἰς ὅλον τὸν κόσμον,
  καὶ ὃ ἐποίησεν αὕτη λαληθήσεται εἰς μνημόσυνον αὐτῆς.

Translation

14:3But on that day Jesus was in Bethany in the home of Simon the leper,
  and when he was reclining for dinner
    a woman came in carrying an alabaster vase of very expensive
           ointment of pure nard.
Breaking the neck of the vase, she poured it over his head.

4Some of those present were angry among themselves,
  "Why was the ointment wasted like this?

5 It could have been sold for more than three hundred denarii and given to the poor."
And they rebuked her.

6 But Jesus said,
"Let her alone.
Why are you attacking her like this?
She has done a good thing for me.

7 **Look, you will always have** the poor with you
and whenever you want to you can do good for them,
but **you will** not **always** have me.
8 What **she could do**, she did:
she anointed my body beforehand for burial.
9 And truly I say to you,
wherever the gospel is proclaimed in the whole world
what she has done will be told in memory of her.

Audience Associations and Connections: Anointing Stories

There is a rich Israelite story tradition of anointing with oil as the central sign of the ordination of priests and kings. Mark's telling of this story evokes the audiences' memories of that tradition. The verbal thread that links these stories together is "to pour it on his head." Specifically, in the LXX, the verb that resonates with Mark's story is ἐπιχεῖν as in the story of the anointing of Saul: καὶ ἐπέχεεν ἐπὶ τὴν κεφαλὴν αὐτοῦ (LXX 1 Kgs 10:1). In Mark's story, the phrase is κατέχεεν αὐτοῦ τῆς κεφαλῆς, "poured it over his head" (14:3).

The first story in this tradition is the anointing of Aaron (Exod 29:7; Lev 8:12) in the service of his ordination by Moses as high priest (Exod 29:1–37; Lev 8:1–36). This sonic theme is also heard in the stories of the anointing of Saul (1 Sam 10:1) and Jehu (2 Kgs 9:6). The motif of anointing occurs most frequently in the stories of the anointing of the kings of Judah and Israel: David (1 Sam 16:13 David anointed by Samuel; 2 Sam 2:4 David anointed king over Judah; 5:17 David anointed king over Israel; 1 Kgs 1:39 Solomon anointed king; 2 Kgs 11:12 Joash anointed as king at age 7; 1 Kgs 23:30 Jehoahaz anointed king).

The tradition of the anointing of kings is fraught with secrecy, conflict, treachery, and murder. Samuel anoints David in secret with full awareness of the possible political consequences (1 Sam 16:1–5). Adonijah conspires to succeed David instead of Solomon (1 Kgs 1:5—2:25) and is supported by the priest Abiathar, though he never actually anoints him. Likewise the priest Zadok and the prophet Nathan are an active part of the coalition that succeeds in establishing the younger Solomon as king, and Zadok actually anoints Solomon (1 Kgs 1:39). Jehu is also anointed in secret by a young member of Elisha's company of prophets in an atmosphere of political conspiracy (2 Kings 9). Thus, this story evokes memories and associations with the tradition of political succession in Israel and all the conflicts that are associated with it.

The implication of the Markan storyteller's allusion to this tradition is that Jesus is anointed for his role as Messiah. But what Jesus' Messiahship means is unclear. His anointing takes place in the context of a conspiracy by his opponents in the political establishment of Israel, who may think he is a royal candidate. Whether Jesus aspires to be king remains ambiguous at this point in the story. His triumphal entry into the city, riding on a donkey, evokes the memory of Solomon riding on David's mule (1 Kgs 1:38) just prior to his being anointed by Zadok and established as king. And Jesus' controversies with the priests and other religious parties enlist the unambiguous support of the people in Jerusalem. James and John clearly expected that Jesus would become king (10:37), and Bartimaeus calls him "son of David" (10:47, 48) just prior to the triumphal entry. The possibility remains that Jesus is going to attempt to become king.

The Sounds of the Story

14:3

The beginning of the story in Greek is a series of smooth sounds. The first period has a high concentration of *ou* syllables: τοῦ λεπροῦ κατακειμένου αὐτοῦ and ἔχουσα ἀλάβαστρον μύρου νάρδου πιστικῆς πολυτελοῦς. The cola are fun to say because they are so liquid in sound. They are characterized by euphony and have almost no harsh or clashing sound. The one exception is the opening of the second period. The word συντρίψασα is one of relatively few instances of asyndeton (the absence of linking conjunctions, such as καὶ or δὲ) in the PRN. It has an onomatopoetic quality in which the sound of the word has the quality of the action of breaking the neck of the jar it describes.

4–5

The long periods and languorous sounds of the initial episode provide the maximum contrast to the short, harsh sound of the rebuke of the angry ones and Jesus' even stronger counterrebuke of them. The climax of the attack of the angry ones on the woman is a three-word period (καὶ ἐνεβριμῶντο αὐτῇ, "And they rebuked her") that punctuates their critique.

6–9

Jesus' initial response is even shorter and more pointed. The first three periods of two, four, and four words are verbal punches with plosive force. To use Muhammed Ali's memorable phrase, they "sting like a bee." The explanation of Jesus' rebuke has a tone of satire that is cutting in its rhetorical quality. The concluding period in praise of the woman is Jesus' strongest and most expansive praise in the entire gospel and is "over the top" in its impact.

Notes on Details and Translation

14:3: Simon, the leper / Σίμωνος τοῦ λεπροῦ

The appositive description of Jesus' host for the feast, Simon, as "the leper" is most naturally heard as a reference to someone who would be known by the audience. The only possible reference here is "the leper" earlier in the story (1:40–45) who begged that Jesus make him clean of his leprosy and then became the first one to tell about the great things Jesus was doing. The audience would have remembered this story if, as is probable, they had heard the whole story prior to the PRN. Assuming that was the case, the storyteller's implication is that Simon was now acting out of gratitude for his healing and welcomed Jesus and his disciples into his home in Bethany, where he had settled after his offering of proof of his cleansing to the priests in Jerusalem.

On that day / καὶ ὄντος

The opening phrase of the story is usually translated "while he was at Bethany" and makes no connection with the plot of the chief priests and scribes. But the Greek phrase Mark uses here—καὶ ὄντος αὐτοῦ **ἐν** Βηθανίᾳ—implies a connection. The other instance of this phrase in the PRN is the introduction to Peter's denial: Καὶ ὄντος τοῦ Πέτρου κάτω ἐν τῇ αὐλῇ is best translated "And meanwhile Peter was below in the courtyard." Peter's presence in the courtyard was established before the Sanhedrin trial: "Peter had followed him at a distance, right into the courtyard of the high priest, and he was sitting with the guards, warming himself by the light of the fire" (14:54). The introductory phrase establishes that Peter was there at the fire during the trial and sets the denial in the temporal context of Jesus' trial before the

The Day before the Passover (14:1–11)

Sanhedrin. Likewise the anointing of Jesus is set in the temporal context of the plotting of the authorities to arrest and kill Jesus on this last day before the feast. Possible translations are "meanwhile" or, to make the connection unmistakable, "on that day."

alabaster vase / ἀλάβαστρον

Alabaster vases or jars in antiquity were finely crafted vessels with a translucent beauty that was highly valued. Alabaster continues to be a precious stone that is used for sculpture and exotic vessels. Thus, beautiful alabaster vases, including an alabaster vase of ointment, have been discovered in the tombs of Egyptian pharaohs (see *Wikipedia* "alabaster"). The quality of alabaster is not adequately conveyed with the English word "jar" that is associated with canning and every day kitchenware. And Mark names the vessel only as "alabaster." A better translation than "jar" (NRSV) would be "alabaster vase."

ointment / μύρου

This word is often translated as "perfume" (NIV, NEB). In both the ancient and the modern world, only women use "perfume." Men in the ancient world, on the other hand, loved ointment as part of sensual massage and as a soothing source of moisture for dry skin in an arid climate. The prophets did not anoint the kings of Israel with perfume. And perfume does not have the same unguent qualities for massage as ointment. Also in English "**oint**ment" and "an**oint**" share the same basic sound. Thus, "ointment" is the best translation.

very expensive ointment of pure nard / νάρδου πιστικῆς πολυτελοῦς

These are the last words in Mark's luxurious description of the ointment: ἔχουσα ἀλάβαστρον μύρου νάρδου πιστικῆς πολυτελοῦς. The meaning of πιστικῆς is ambiguous, sufficiently ambiguous that the NRSV doesn't even translate it. The NRSV translation—"very costly ointment of nard"—only translates the other three words in the Greek phrase, as if πιστικῆς does not even occur in the Greek text. Three main possibilities have been suggested for its derivation. The first is that the word is derived from the adjective πιστικός, which means "faithful" in later writers. This is the derivation on which the translation "pure" is based in the RSV and NIV: "pure nard."[1] This

---

1. Cf. BDF, #113.2.

is unlikely because the only uses of the word in this way are from writers long after the first century. The second possibility, even more unlikely, is to derive it from the verb πίνω "to drink" with the meaning "liquid."[2] The third possibility is that the word is derived from a name. Three names have been identified:

(a) a Greek form of the Latin *spicatum*. This is a plant or herb, *myriophyllum spicatum*. It is currently also called Eurasian watermilfoil and is an invasive species in the northern lakes of the United States (see *Wikipedia*, "*spicatum*"). This plant is also called spike, from which the King James translators probably got the name "spikenard."

(b) the Greek form of the Aramaic word for the "pistachio tree." This derivation from Aramaic encounters the problem that the word in Mark is feminine while the Aramaic word is masculine. This would be easily explained if the word were used here as an adjective. But, if derived from Aramaic, it would be used as a noun and the change in gender is not easily explained. More important, pistachio nuts are not associated with precious ointment anywhere.

(c) a Greek form of the East Indian word *piçata*, the name of the plant Nardostachys Jatamansi. Of these three possibilities the most probable is the East Indian derivation because it is the name for a plant from which the highly valued "nard" was manufactured, as is reflected in its name. There was a lively spice trade with India in the first century, and "nard" from India was very expensive and wonderfully fragrant. The best translation, then, would be: "ointment of nard."

Mark ends this description with a word full of liquid vowels, πολυτελοῦς. Its denotative meaning in English, "very expensive, costly, precious," only communicates one dimension of its meaning. It is an utterly luxurious word that provides an appropriate climax to this verbally extravagant description. The King James translation retains the word order of the Greek and gives final emphasis to this word: "an alabaster box of ointment of spikenard very precious." The RSV adopts the word "costly" but preserves Mark's word order; thus, "an alabaster jar of ointment of pure nard, very costly." Unfortunately, the NRSV has not preserved Mark's emphasis. As we have seen, the NRSV doesn't even translate one of the words and moves the climactic word to a normal adjectival position in the phrase "an alabaster jar of very costly ointment of nard." The NIV also moves in this more literary direction: "an alabaster jar of very expensive perfume, made of pure nard." When evaluated as a translation of the sound of the Greek words, the NIV

2. See LSJ, 1408.

and NRSV are the least adequate. Mark's placement of this word at the end of the phrase gives climactic emphasis to the primary issue on which the ensuing conflict will focus, namely, the high cost of the ointment. And the sound of the Greek word communicates its connotative meaning beautifully. The King James "precious" sounds best but is somewhat antiquarian in relation to the Greek's basic meaning of costing lots of money. The best translation of the phrase for storytelling is, therefore, "an alabaster vase of very expensive ointment of pure nard."

breaking the neck of the alabaster vase / συντρίψασα τὴν ἀλάβαστρον

The literal meaning of the verb here is "to smash, crush," and the verb phrase is usually translated as "broke the jar." But it is impossible to pour ointment out of a smashed or broken jar, and it inevitably raises questions for an attentive listener. Alabaster vases for ointment often had a long neck. To gain access to the contents inside the jar, one would break the neck of the vase with a twist and pour the contents out of the newly formed spout. Therefore, this is best translated as "breaking the neck of the alabaster vase."

Comments on the Meaning and Impact of the Story

The gospel tradition of the anointing of Jesus

The anointing of Jesus has a richly developed history in the gospel storytelling tradition. Mark and Matthew recount this episode as a central event in the PRN. The woman who anoints Jesus is an anonymous woman who is apparently quite wealthy. Judging by the extravagance of her gift, she also had a deep affection for Jesus, but the reason for that affection is a mystery. A woman's affection is equally present in the versions of this story in Luke and John. In John's story (John 12:1–3), the woman is Mary, the sister of Lazarus. The anointing takes place during a dinner in Jesus' honor in the immediate aftermath of his raising of Lazarus from death, and in this context the motivation for her action is no mystery. John's story shares with Mark and Matthew the critique of the woman and Jesus' defense of the anointing as preparation for his burial. John names her critic as Judas Iscariot while Mark does not name him but only implies by Judas' immediate action of betrayal that he was one of those Jesus rebuked. However, John shares with Luke the detail that the woman anointed Jesus' feet rather than his head and wiped his feet with her hair (Luke 7:38; John 12:3). In Luke's story, the woman is a sinner, presumably a prostitute, who anoints Jesus' feet with ointment from an alabaster jar at a dinner held in Jesus' honor by Simon, a Pharisee. The dinner happens early in Jesus' Galilean ministry and is interpreted as a gesture of her gratitude for her sins being forgiven. No disciples are even present, and there is no connection with Jesus' burial. And, unlike in John's story, in Luke Jesus does not praise the woman as one whose story will be told as part of the ongoing proclamation of the gospel.

This story was a field day for the tellers of Jesus tales. It is a revealing instance of the diverse ways in which the stories of Jesus developed in the course of being retold over several decades after Jesus' death and resurrection. There is no decisive evidence about which version is earliest or whether there may have been an early story prior to all four of these extant stories. If this anointing story were evaluated in isolation, the most natural conclusion would be that Matthew and Luke were two independent early versions of an earlier oral tradition developed by Mark and John. Matthew's story is the briefest of the three, and Mark can naturally be heard as an elaboration and particularization of Matthew's version, but this goes against the dominant evidence that Matthew was a later recomposition of Mark and Q. Luke's version of the story is so distinctive that it appears to be an independent tradition. John's story has motifs in common with the stories in both the Matthew/Mark story (presented as a prelude to passion/burial, includes Judas' taking offense) and Luke (anointing of feet and wiping with hair), but John's story is also distinctive (takes place in the house of Lazarus; involves Mary, the sister of Lazarus; has a longer and more liquid description of the anointing and of its fragrance filling the house).

14:3: The ointment

The descriptions of the ointment are particularly interesting. Mark and John are virtually identical and have the most extensive descriptions of the ointment. John's description is λίτρον (a pound) μύρου νάρδου πιστικῆς πολυτελίμου, and thereby shares four of Mark's five words. John emphasizes the quantity of ointment, and twelve ounces (a Roman pound) was a lot of ointment. If John is later than Mark as is probable, he could have heard Mark's telling of this story either in performance or from reading a manuscript aloud and learning Mark's phrase. Luke's brief description—ἀλάβαστρον μύρου—shares two key words with Mark. Matthew's phrase—ἀλάβαστρον μύρου βαρυτίμου—uses a distinctive word in the final position that occurs in the literature of the period to describe precious, expensive ointments.[3] It is difficult to identify the transmission history of this phrase

---

3. See BAGD, 134.

precisely and what these four storytellers received and adapted one from the other. These things are certain: all of the tellers of Jesus' stories loved this story and developed it in distinctive ways. And they knew and recomposed each other's stories.

Linkage with the conspiracy

Mark's story of the anointing is linked to the story of the conspiracy with which the PRN begins. The conspiracy story ends with the implication that Jesus' opponents have decided that they must arrest him "today," before the beginning of the feast "the next day." In the Bethany story, the narrator's introduction sets Jesus' presence in Bethany in the context of the conspiracy that was going on at the same time in Jerusalem. Bethany has been established earlier (11:11, 12; and, by implication, 11:19, 20) as the resting place for Jesus and the twelve during their stay in Jerusalem. On the two previous days, Monday and Tuesday, Jesus has gone into Jerusalem. On each of those days, the chief priests and scribes had wanted to arrest him (11:18; 12:12) but did not because they were afraid of the crowd. The implication is, therefore, that on the day when Jesus' opponents had agreed to use treachery in order to arrest him before the feast, Jesus is spending the day in Bethany. The further implication of Jesus' presence on this last day before the Feast of Unleavened Bread and the Passover in Bethany rather than in the Temple as on the previous days is that the authorities' plot is broken and they will not be able to arrest and kill Jesus. This setting adds flame to the implied flicker of hope that Jesus may escape the plot of the authorities.

The setting probably implies that Jesus was having dinner with disciples and friends. The final word of the setting, κατακειμένου, means "to recline" and is usually used in descriptions of dinners (Mark 2:15; Luke 5:29; 7:37) at which men reclined on pillows and ate from common bowls on a table in the middle of the dining area. This meaning is more probable than that he was sleeping or resting.

The woman

The main subject of the story is an unknown woman who is characterized only by what she has and what she does. She has highly valuable ointment. The verbal extravagance of Mark's description of the ointment is unparalleled in his whole story. This storyteller, who spends words like a miser, lavishes words on the ointment. Its significance is carried by its description: exotic, extremely expensive, and luxurious. The sheer beauty of the sounds of the ointment establishes its quality. This also implies that the woman is rich. Only rich people could have access to such ointment and could afford to spend a workingman's income for a year in one single moment of extravagant affection.

Her anointing of Jesus is surprising. The women who anoint men in ancient culture were wives or prostitutes, as is reflected in Luke's version of the story (Luke 7:36–50). She has no authority or position that would make this an official action. That is, the reason for this act remains shrouded in mystery. She pours this precious ointment on his head. It must have been an act of affection, but the reason for her affection remains veiled in mystery.

Israelite associations with anointing

Nevertheless, Mark's words evoke the memory of the ancient Israelite tradition of pouring oil on the head as the symbolic act of inauguration of a king. The kings were then known as *messiahs*, "anointed ones." Thus, in the Septuagint translation of Hebrew into Greek, both Saul and David are named Christ (LXX Saul by David: 1 Kgs 24:7, 11; 26:9, 11, 16, 23; 2 Kgs 1:14, 16; of David: 2 Kgs 19:21; 22:51; 23:1). The woman's anointing of Jesus is the first time that Jesus has been anointed, and the title with which the gospel begins, (Ἀρχὴ τοῦ εὐαγγελίου Ἰησοῦ Χριστοῦ) "The beginning of the good news of Jesus, the anointed one," is actually confirmed. Whatever her motivation may be, she pours the oil over his head and anoints him.

4–5: The critics

Her action provokes an immediate conflict. The angry conversation between some of those present leads up to their severe rebuke of the woman. The indefinite pronoun "some" (τινες) raises the question of their identity. Nowhere else in the story have the objects of a reprimand by Jesus been so indefinite. In every other instance of serious conflict with Jesus, the other party is specified (see Mark 1:25; 2:6ff.; 8:32ff.; 9:25, 38ff.; 10:13ff.). And in the other instances where an indefinite pronoun is used in reference to people whose identity remains unclear, none of them is in conflict with Jesus (see 4:22; 8:3; 9:1, 38; 11:5; 14:47, 57). Only at the arrest and the crucifixion—14:47; 15:35, 36—is there a comparable indefiniteness for a significant character. The "one of those standing by" who struck the slave of the high priest is readily identified as one of the disciples. And those standing at the foot of the cross are Judean mockers of Jesus who could (mistakenly) link the sound of Jesus' Aramaic name for God with Elijah. In these instances, the context provides the clues to their identity. In Simon's home, they are characterized by their emotion of anger (the "angry ones"). The only clues to their more specific identity are derived from the context and the associations of their words.

The context is, first of all, geographic. Bethany is associated with Jesus and the twelve (11:11, 12, 19). The disciples are the most likely ones to be at Simon's house with Jesus. The key verb in their response, "to be angry" (ἀγανακτοῦντες), is associated with interactions within the band of Jesus and his disciples. Thus, Jesus is angry with the disciples when they forbid the mothers to bring their children to Jesus (10:14), and the disciples are angry at James and John for requesting positions of power in Jesus' new government (10:41). Mark's choice of an indefinite pronoun ("some of those present") may imply, however, that others were present at the meal in addition to the disciples. They could have been friends or associates in the Jerusalem area who were sympathetic to Jesus' movement. Whatever their particular identity, their criticism of the woman is associated with Jesus' command to the rich young man (10:21). The rich should sell what they have and give it to the poor. Their judgment has substance. At a denarius a day (Matt 20:2), the annual earnings of a laborer working six days a week would be 312 denarii. "More than 300 denarii" would be more than a workingman would earn in a year! This was really expensive ointment. Thus, the implication of the story is that some of Jesus' disciples and their friends were very angry at the woman for this extravagant action and rebuked her with the assumption that they were being good students of Jesus in doing so.

Their angry rebuke was a symptom of the great divide between the rich and the poor in ancient Israel and particularly in the period of the Judean–Roman War and its immediate aftermath. Most of the people in first-century Palestine were peasants like Jesus and his disciples. They were generally poor and lived off what they could make as farmers, tradesmen, and (in Galilee) fishermen. There was also a significant class of nobles, landed aristocracy who owned large tracts and lived in the cities in large, luxurious homes. Hatred of the upper class was widespread and was expressed during the Jerusalem siege in the killing of many of the aristocracy.[4] A dimension of the Judean–Roman War was class warfare between the poor and the rich. Mark's listeners, therefore, lived in a context in which a high degree of anger against the upper class was a dimension of the socioeconomic situation. In this context, the anger of some of those present at this anointing was thoroughly understandable to Mark's audiences.

---

4. See, e.g., Horsley, *Jesus and Empire*, 43–45; and Horsley and J. S. Hanson, *Bandits*, 72–73.

6–9: Jesus' response to the critics

The tone and impact of Jesus' speech is shaped by the relationship of his response here to his responses earlier in the story. Three stories earlier in the gospel have a similar structure to the Bethany story: the rebuke of Peter following Peter's messianic confession and Jesus' first passion prophecy (8:32–33), the controversy over the exorcist who was using Jesus' name but was not part of the twelve (9:38–41), and the controversy over mothers bringing children to Jesus (10:13–16). A structured citation of the stories with verbal threads in bold may help to clarify the relationship between these stories and the anointing story. I have modified the NRSV translation in order to indicate the verbal threads in the Greek.

The Messianic confession (8:32–33, NRSV):

> **Rebuke by Peter**
> And Peter took him aside and began **to rebuke** him (NRSV).
> **Rebuke by Jesus**
> But turning and seeing his disciples, **he rebuked Peter** and said, "Get behind me Satan.
> **For** you are setting your mind not on divine things but on human things."

The other exorcist (9:38–41, NRSV):

> **Rebuke by John**
> John said to him, "Teacher, we saw a man casting out demons in your name, and **we forbade him,** because he was not following us."
> **Rebuke by Jesus**
> But Jesus said, "**Do not forbid him.**
> **For** no one who does a deed of power in my name will be able soon after to speak evil of me.
> **For** he that is not against us is for us.
> **For truly I tell you**, whoever gives you a cup of water to drink because you bear the name of Christ will by no means lose the reward.

The children (10:13–16, NRSV)

> **Rebuke by the disciples**
> And people were bringing little children to him so that he might touch them;
> and **the disciples rebuked them.**

Rebuke by Jesus
But when Jesus saw this, **he was angry** and said to them,
> "Let the children come to me.

Do not forbid them.
For it is to such as these that the kingdom of God belongs.
And truly I tell you whoever does not receive the kingdom of God as a little child will never enter it."

Anointing at Bethany (14:3–9):

Rebuke by some
Some of those present **were angry** and were saying to one another,
> "Why was the ointment wasted like this?

It could have been sold for more than three hundred denarii
> and the money given to the poor."

And they **rebuked** her.

Rebuke by Jesus
But Jesus said,
> "**Let her alone.**

Why are you giving her trouble?
She has done a beautiful thing for me.

Look (γάρ), you will always have the poor with you,
> and whenever you want to, you can do good for them,
> but you will not always have me.

She has done what she could:
> she has anointed my body for burial before the time.

And truly I say to you,
> wherever the good news is proclaimed in the whole world,
> what she has done will be told in memory of her."

In each of these stories, the disciples take some decisive action involving either a rebuke or a prohibition. In each case, Jesus' initial response is a command in the imperative mood. The command is followed by an explanation that is introduced by the conjunction "for" or "because" (in Greek, γάρ). The conclusion of Jesus' response is a prophecy that is introduced by the formula "Truly I say to you." The apparent exception is the story of Peter's confession. There the prophecy with the formula "Truly I say to you" occurs at the end of the whole discourse: "Truly I say to you there are some standing here who will not taste death until they see that the kingdom of God has come with power" (Mark 9:1).

This structure—a command or instruction, an explanation, and an authoritative prophecy—is a characteristic form of Jesus' teaching to his disciples when he disagrees with an action they have taken. And as will become clear when we examine the details below, the anointing at Bethany is the most fully developed instance of this form. Each of the elements of this pattern of conflict between the disciples and Jesus is expanded and intensified. This expansion is, on the one hand, an inclusion of important details. But it is also an intensification of the form that creates a higher level of emotional intensity. The anointing at Bethany is the most fully developed and emotionally charged story in the gospel of a conflict between Jesus and his disciples.

The storyteller's introduction to Jesus' speech uses a formula—"But Jesus said" / ὁ δὲ Ἰησοῦς εἶπεν—that is always used prior to a surprising and unexpected response by Jesus (9:23, 39; 10:5, 18, 38, 39; 11:29; 12:17; 14:6, 62). Jesus is angry, even angrier than he was about the rebuke of the mothers bringing their children to him. Although in this instance the narrator does not describe Jesus' feeling, Jesus' own anger is expressed in three short, sharp verbal rebukes, a left-right-left combination with no pauses or connecting conjunctions.

The first verbal rebuke is a command: "Leave her" or "Let her alone." The second punch is a question: "Why are you giving her trouble?" That question is a direct parallel to the opening question of the angry ones: "Why was the ointment wasted like this?" I have heard this style of rebuke many times in arguments among angry children, young men, or adults on the streets of New York, particularly in the defense of women and children. This is an appropriate parallel because Jesus is defending the woman against an attack. Jesus' third punch is a statement that flatly contradicts their calling the anointing "a waste" (ἡ ἀπώλεια). He calls it "a good work/service" (καλὸν ἔργον).

Jesus' explanation of his reprimand is, as in the other instances of this pattern we have noted, introduced by γὰρ. It is translated here as "Look." In his explanation he takes up their critique that the ointment should have been sold and the money given to the poor. The angry ones essentially quoted what Jesus said to the rich young man. Jesus' explanation of his defense of the woman sets the anointing and giving to the poor in the context of this particular moment in time, namely, his imminent death. He also challenges them to do what they have demanded of the woman, namely, to give to the poor. This conditional colon—"whenever you want to, you can do good for them"—is distinctive to Mark's telling of the story. Both Matthew and John repeat the saying regarding the poor—"For the poor you will always have with you, but you will not always have me" (Matt 26:11; John 12:8)—with only a minor difference in word order. But they do not include this challenge to those who objected that the ointment should have been sold and given to the poor—a challenge to give to the poor themselves.

While there is no readily apparent reason why Matthew and John would have left out this saying, the tone of this saying may have been too satirical for their sense of Jesus' character. Jesus' challenge is an implicit accusation of hypocrisy. The only limitation on their ability to give to the poor at any time is their will. They are criticizing the woman for failing to do what they themselves are unwilling to do. It is a strongly satirical statement that mocks their critique of the woman. A paraphrase of Jesus' statement would be, "Whenever you want to, you can do good for the poor but the problem is you don't really want to. You would rather criticize others like this woman." The only saying of Jesus in his conversations with his disciples with a comparable degree of satire is, as we shall see, his comment to Peter when he finds him asleep: "Couldn't you even stay awake one hour?" But Jesus' comment there has a tone of grief and disappointment. In this story, the implication is that Jesus is criticizing his disciples with an unprecedented degree of anger. This tone may be the reason Matthew and John did not repeat the saying.

In the final colon of this three-colon period, Jesus sets giving to the poor in the context of his absence. The norm of judgment has been established earlier in the story in Jesus' explanation of why his disciples do not fast (2:19–20). To paraphrase that explanation, "My disciples do not fast because I am only here for a little while. After I am no longer here, they'll fast." There is no critique of fasting in that response, only a qualification of its appropriateness. The value of ethical practices is relative to the context in time.

Therefore, in this case, the goodness of giving to the poor is of relative value in the context of his impending death. To paraphrase again,

> The ointment was not sold and the money given to the poor
> because I am here for only a little while (you will not always have me).
> After I am no longer here (am buried),
> then you will give to the poor (whom you always have with you).

9: Jesus' praise of the woman

Jesus' response to the angry ones has a chiastic structure: the woman, the poor, and now again the woman. Jesus answers their original question—"Why was the ointment wasted like this?"—by interpreting what she did. The first colon is usually translated "She did what she could." If, as is possible, the infinitive "to do" is presumed here, the force of the colon is, "what she had the means to do she did."⁵ An implicit contrast is thereby drawn between the woman and the angry ones, who have the power to do good but do not do it. She did what she could. Jesus' answer to their question is, therefore, that she had the courage to act and the foresight to anoint Jesus' body for burial. In this sense, she acts as a prophet who foresaw the future. He thereby defends the woman by setting her action in the context of his impending death.

Jesus' concluding prophecy, introduced by the solemn formula "Truly I say to you," is the most extravagant praise Jesus ever gives anyone, even John the Baptist (9:13).⁶ It is his climactic contradiction to their denunciation of the woman.⁷ Jesus' prophecy is that her action will become an integral and perpetual part of the gospel storytelling tradition. In fact, the very telling of the story by Mark to his audiences is a fulfillment of the prophecy. Several of Jesus' prophecies in the apocalyptic discourse have been fulfilled in the experience of Mark's listeners if, as is probable, the story was told in the aftermath of the Judean–Roman War (stones thrown down, hearing of wars, people appearing before Gentile kings and Israelite courts, etc.). But this is the first of Jesus' prophecies introduced by the solemn formula "Truly I say to you" that is, in any explicit sense, fulfilled in the experience of Mark's audiences (see, for example, Mark 3:28; 9:1; 10:15; 11:23; 13:30). In the honor/shame culture of antiquity, one of the greatest honors anyone can receive is that the story of their heroic acts will be told in memory of them. The conclusion to Jesus' defense of the woman is a climactic reversal of their denunciation by his proclamation of honor. Jesus' praise is even more extravagant than her ointment.

We can infer from the "sandwich" structure of the insertion of the Bethany anointing into the story of the plot that the storyteller wanted to make a connection between the two elements of the story. In this case, the most probable connection is an explanation for the shocking action of Judas Iscariot in betraying Jesus. Luke's story (Luke 22:1–6) also makes a

---

5. Taylor rightly argues that the interpretation of the Greek phrase ὃ ἔσχεν (14:8) as meaning "what she could" depends on the listener supplying the infinitive "to do"; see Taylor, *Gospel according to St. Mark*, 532. This implied infinitive concludes the colon to which this statement is by contrast related, namely, the angry ones who have the means but do nothing for the poor. To paraphrase, "she did what she had the means to do but you have the means to do good for the poor and you do nothing."

6. For the significance of this phrase, see Malina, *New Testament World*, 41.

7. This is the only instance in Mark where a conjunction, in this case δὲ, is inserted into the formula ἀμὴν λέγω ὑμῖν. This conjunction is often but not always adversative. In this case, an implied contrast is its most likely force. The contrast cannot be to the preceding period, but it could be to the critics' denunciation. This would complete the pattern of antithetical response to each element of their response.

connection by going directly from the plot of the priests and scribes to Judas' betrayal. Luke's explanation is that Satan entered Judas' heart. Luke's story probably retells an earlier story of the passion in which the anointing was absent. In John, Judas is named as the one who criticized Mary for the anointing (John 12:4–6). In Mark, the motive for Judas' action is implied by the intense conflict between Jesus and the angry ones. (Mark does not name those who are angry. Matthew names them as "the disciples.") Judas was angry at Jesus' sharp rebuke when he and his friends criticized the rich woman for wasting the nard. Nevertheless, in this surprising way, a courageous rich woman anointed Jesus for his climactic conflict with the powers of evil and for his burial. His best supporter was an unknown woman who lavished an extravagant gift on him and thereby identified the supreme value of his life.

The Performance of the Story

Either moving to or pointing to another place in the storytelling space is a way of indicating the presence of Jesus in Bethany. This gesture can be made with a tone of joy and delight. The realization that Jesus is in Bethany on this critical day has the feeling of "Aha! Their plot is foiled." The description of Simon as "the leper" invites the listeners to remember and connect Simon with the earlier story of the healing of "the leper" (1:40–45). The description of Jesus reclining at dinner sets the scene for the entry of the woman. It is probably impossible to overdo the sheer pleasure of the description of the ointment. I think it is appropriate to also say the Greek words ἀλάβαστρον μύρου νάρδου πιστικῆς πολυτελοῦς either before or after the English. The impact of these words is as impossible to translate into another language as is the Italian of the operas of Verdi and Puccini. The gesture of breaking the neck of the vase and pouring the ointment is elegant and grand, fitting for the anointing of a king. The anger of some of those present is to be told without any note of judgment or criticism but with sympathy and full embodiment. Find the place of righteous anger at the extravagances of the rich in your experience and tell the story from that place. And don't hold back in pronouncing the *b* in "rebuke" with its full plosive force. There needs to be a high level of anger in their rebuke so that Jesus' words have something to which to respond.

Jesus' response is, first of all, protective and cuts off this attack. A gesture of stopping with your hand may be helpful. I don't think Jesus is angry as much as he is strong and forceful. There is a tone of strong criticism in his question about their giving her trouble, and of biting satire in his suggestion that they can give to the poor whenever they want to. His explanation of the significance of her action in relation to his burial is an appeal for recognition of what is happening; i.e., he is being prepared for imminent death. Jesus' solemn pronouncement of the honor she is to be given in the telling of her story is the stuff of award ceremonies and the granting of medals of honor. This is the biblical equivalent of the honor given to great warriors in the Homeric epics. This is an opportunity to express the height of personal glorification. It might be helpful to imagine yourself giving a medal or a trophy at some major event. And, of course, this is all spoken out of Jesus' love for his disciples, which has major components of frustration and exasperation at their blindness and stupidity.

I have found it difficult to express the intensity and complexity of Jesus' emotion in this speech. There is a powerful tradition of reciting Jesus' words with emotional distance and objectivity, which is hard to overcome. But I encourage you to explore Jesus' spirit—his gratitude to this anonymous woman for her gift, and his love for his disciples in this moment of their blindness to what was happening in their midst—and to search for a way to express what Jesus was thinking and feeling.

The telling of this story requires the storyteller to communicate a level of conflict between those who rebuked the woman and Jesus that is high enough to provide a sufficient motive for Judas Iscariot's betrayal of Jesus. The degree of alienation between Jesus and those who were angry must be strong enough to make sense of Judas' decision to join the conspiracy to kill Jesus.

The Betrayal of Jesus by Judas Iscariot (14:10–11) ⏵

This short story is the climax of the initial section of the PRN that describes the events of Wednesday, the day before the opening day of the Feast of Passover and Unleavened Bread.

Sound Map

10Καὶ Ἰούδας Ἰσκαριὼθ ὁ **εἷς τῶν δώδεκα**
    ἀπῆλθεν πρὸς τοὺς ἀρχιερεῖς ἵνα **αὐτὸν παραδοῖ** αὐτοῖς.
11οἱ δὲ ἀκούσαντες ἐχάρησαν
    καὶ ἐπηγγείλαντο αὐτῷ ἀργύριον δοῦναι.
καὶ ἐζήτει πῶς αὐτὸν εὐκαίρως **παραδοῖ.**

The Day before the Passover (14:1–11)

Translation

10 And Judas Iscariot, the **one of the twelve**,
   went to the chief priests **to hand him over** to them.
11 And when they heard it, they rejoiced
   and promised to pay him money.
And **he looked for** the best time **to hand him over**.

Notes on Details and Translation

14:10: Iscariot / Ἰσκαριώθ

The derivation of the epithet to Judas' name, *Iscariot*, is uncertain.[8] After more than a century of scholarly suggestions, we still don't know what it meant. A suggestion that emerges from listening to the story in the context of the post-70 period is that *Iscariot* sounds like *sicarius*, a Latin word meaning "dagger." The Greek term σικάριος appears in Acts 21:38 in the Roman tribune's reference to the four thousand "assassins" whom the Egyptian had led out into the desert.[9] The *scarius* was a curved dagger used by the Sicarii to carry out targeted assassinations of Judeans who supported and benefitted from the Roman administration. The Sicarii were one of the terrorist groups that joined the alliance of Judean revolutionary groups that initiated the Judean revolt and carried out the war against the Romans in 66–70 CE. They adopted the name of their preferred weapon as their group name. Their policy was the assassination of rich Judeans who collaborated with the Romans and participated in the highly stratified economic system. If Mark was composed and told in the early 70s in the immediate aftermath of the war, as is highly probable, the sound of the *Iskariot* name would have had highly charged associations. If the listeners made this connection with Judas' surname, an association between Judas Iscariot and the *sicarii* was a dimension of the implied background for Judas' motive in betraying Jesus.

---

8. See Brown, *Death of the Messiah*, 2:1413–16, for a detailed analysis of the possible derivations that have been proposed.

9. Brown's objections to this derivation are etymological and historical. The only explanation of why Mark reversed the first two letters from *si* to *is* is a derivation from a relatively obscure Aramaic form *'îsqaryā'ā*. The historical problem is that there is nothing in the tradition linking Judas with political revolution, and the evidence in Josephus for the Sicarii only describes them in the period during the war, decades after Jesus and Judas lived. See Brown, *Death of the Messiah*, 2:1415. If, however, Mark was performed in the period after the war, the audiences' associations with the sound of this epithet were in interpretive play.

10: the one of the twelve / ὁ εἷς τῶν δώδεκα

The article introduces a phrase that becomes a verbal thread in the subsequent story. None of the major translations translates the article that emphasizes Judas' distinctiveness. The phrase "one of the twelve" (without the article) is used later in the story by both Jesus in the Last Supper story (14:20) and by the storyteller in the arrest story to describe the betrayer (14:43). It is the verbal expression of the scandal and even horror at Judas' action. The scandal is grounded in the name for Jesus' disciples and closest friends, "the twelve" (3:13–19). This title and the individual names of the Twelve are listed shortly after the first notice that Jesus' enemies are seeking to destroy him. The article used here and translated as "the" is probably an "anaphoric" usage that refers back to the earlier naming of the twelve in the story.[10] In this instance, it refers back to the listing of the disciples, where the appositive following the name of Judas Iscariot is "who betrayed him": i.e., that previously mentioned one of the twelve.

hand over / παραδίδωμι

The main verb, δίδωμι, means "to give," and the preposition παρα can mean "to" or "over." It is used in this sense in 13:9–12 in Jesus' prophecy of the persecutions that will fall upon his followers: "they will hand you over to councils" (13:9), "when they hand you over" (13:11). This describes the action of police or soldiers giving a person into the authority of a court or other judicial body for trial and, potentially, sentencing for punishment. This same word also has the meaning of "betray" when the handing over is done by a trusted friend or family member. The term *traitor* is frequently used in English to describe such a person who has betrayed a cause by going over to the other side in a war. Traitors often are involved in betraying secrets to the enemy, which lead to the deaths of their compatriots. Both these meanings are appropriate in reference to Judas' action. He both hands Jesus over to the authorities and betrays Jesus' love and trust in a way that leads to Jesus' death.

Both senses of the verb are rendered in the various parts of the NRSV translation ("handed over"—10:33; "betrayed"—9:31; 14:10, 11, 18, 21, 41). The result is that in English the explicit verbal connection between the epithet for Judas and other statements describing Judas' action of "handing over" is lost. The translation of this period describing the action of Judas needs to preserve the verbal thread linking this episode to the earlier

---

10. BDF, #252.

passion prophecies. In the second passion prophecy, Jesus says, "The Son of Man is to be handed over into human hands . . ." (NRSV, 9:31), and in the third, most detailed prophecy, he says, "the Son of Man will be handed over to the chief priest and the scribes . . ." (NRSV, 10:33); in Greek, παραδίδοται εἰς χεῖρας ἀνθρώπων (9:31) and παραδοθήσεται τοῖς ἀρχιερεῦσιν καὶ τοῖς γραμματεῦσιν (10:33). Therefore, the phrase in the betrayal story is translated here as "went to the chief priests in order to hand over him to them" (ἀπῆλθεν πρὸς τοὺς ἀρχιερεῖς ἵνα αὐτὸν παραδοῖ αὐτοῖς, 14:10).

11: he was looking for the best way to hand him over / ἐζήτει πῶς αὐτὸν εὐκαίρως παραδοῖ

A literal translation of this colon is as follows: "he sought how him the best time he might hand over." This phrase repeats the description of the plot of the priests: "they sought how him . . . they might kill." While it is difficult to translate these two phrases in a way that preserves the verbal connection, it is clearly the composer's intention to link these two actions. The NRSV translates the plot of the chief priests and scribes as "were looking for a way to arrest Jesus by stealth and kill him" and the plot of Judas as "began to look for an opportunity to betray him," thereby losing the verbal echo. The translation here seeks to maintain the echo by translating the leaders' plot as "the chief priests and scribes were looking for a way to . . ." and Judas' plot as "he was looking for the best way to . . ."

Comments on the Meaning and Impact of the Story

14:3–11: Judas' motive and the Bethany anointing

The story of Judas' betrayal implies that he was one of those who were angry at the woman who anointed Jesus and was also, therefore, the object of Jesus' most stinging rebuke to his disciples in the entire story. The connections between the defection of Judas Iscariot and the anointing at Bethany in Mark's story are both explicit and implicit. The explicit connection is the word that Mark uses to describe Judas' action: "to leave, depart" (ἀπῆλθεν)—literally translated, "Judas Iscariot, the one of the twelve, departed to the chief priests . . ." A more accurate but wordier translation would be, "Judas Iscariot, the one of the twelve, left from there and went to the chief priests . . ." Thus, the verb that Mark uses explicitly describes Judas' action as departing from Bethany and going to Jerusalem to talk to the chief priests. This implies that he is among those who witnessed the action of the woman and became angry.

Judas' action of going to the chief priests in order to betray Jesus inevitably raises the question, why? First, the storyteller implies that Judas was one of those who were angry at the woman. The group's critique of her was a citation and a logical extension of Jesus' command to the rich young man to sell all his possessions and give them to the poor. The rich man then decided not to join the band of disciples. When Jesus defends the woman by his acceptance of the luxurious ointment, his acceptance and subsequent criticism of the group's anger constitutes a modification of his own political policy of unqualified support for the poor. Jesus' critique of the group, Judas included, is an implicit reason for Judas' act of betrayal.

The story might also have suggested to the audience a more personal reason for Judas' betrayal: he may have been angry at Jesus' extravagant honoring of the woman. Men can get very angry when other men elevate women over them. This was even more characteristic of men in the ancient world than now.

Furthermore, Jesus' acceptance of death in speaking about his burial rather than taking action against his enemies implies that he plans to pursue nonviolent rather than violent resistance. This might have suggested to the audience yet a third reason for Judas' betrayal.

The first and third explanations offered above might have suggested themselves to the audience all the more if they associated the name Iscariot with the Sicarii. The Sicarii were particularly angry at the wealthy for their extravagant lifestyle. In the anointing, Jesus both accepts this extravagant gift and even more extravagantly praises the woman for doing it, thereby allying himself with the rich and their offensive social practices. There was a long and well-established tradition of social banditry in Israel throughout the period of Roman domination. Richard Horsley has documented this from the time of Pompey's entry into Jerusalem in 64 BCE through the decades leading up to the war against Rome (66–70 CE).[11] The system of double taxation for the support of the Temple, and the Roman tribute tax for Judean peasant farmers, resulted in impoverishment and loss of land for a growing part of the population. These bandits (the Greek noun used to describe them was often λῃστής, a term used frequently in the Gospels; see especially Mark 11:17; 14:48; 15:17) attacked baggage trains and the wealthy landed aristocracy in order to support their impoverished families. This political critique of wealthy Judeans by the majority of the people was popular, and the majority of Judeans in Galilee and Judea supported and protected these bands of bandits. There was also a straight line of continuity between

---

11. See Horsley and J. S. Hanson, *Bandits*, 48–87; also the messianic uprisings in the aftermath of the death of Herod such as the revolts led by Simon and Athronges, ibid., 110–17. See also Rhoads, "Zealots," in *ABD* 6:1043–54.

the bands of bandits and the peasant armies of the Sicarii, the Zealots, John of Gischala and his followers, and Simon bar Giora and his followers. In the period of the telling of Mark's story, soon after the war, this was probably common knowledge in relation to the social origins of the war.

Judas' traitorous behavior was completely believable in the context of the actions of the Judean revolutionary groups during the war and especially during the Roman siege of the Temple. Josephus describes a series of traitorous actions by the various Judean revolutionary armies during the siege, including the murder of other Judeans who tried to escape through the walls; the battle between the revolutionary armies and the armies rallied by the chief priest, Ananus; and the betrayal of the people's best interest in the continuing resistance. As we have seen, the most immediate reference of the emphatic anaphoric article, "*the* one of the twelve," is to the one of the twelve who was most angry at the anointing.

The character of Judas Iscariot and the Judean–Roman War

Thus, when heard in the context of the immediate aftermath of the Judean War, the story leads to the hopes of first-century Judeans for a Messiah who would lead a war of independence against Rome and establish an independent Judean state. This motif will recur even more strongly in the search for the reasons why the crowd, Jesus' primary support and ally, suddenly ask for Barabbas instead of Jesus. The historical evidence about the extent of the independence movement in Jesus' time is ambiguous. The revolt of Judas the Galilean in 6 CE was a major outbreak of violent revolution during Jesus' youth. The seeds of the revolutionary movement were, therefore, present in Jesus' time. Those seeds were deeply grounded in the history of Israel and had found political expression in the refusal to accept Babylonian domination in the sixth century BCE and in the Maccabean revolt against Antiochus IV Epiphanes and Syrian domination in the second century BCE. There is, however, no evidence of an insurrection movement in the period of Jesus' life and in the immediate decades following (approximately 10–50 CE).

However, there is abundant evidence of insurrection in the years preceding Mark's gospel. The seeds sown in Israel's history of resistance to Hellenism and Roman domination led to the Judean War, which led in turn to the destruction of the Temple, the loss of the degree of Judean self-government enjoyed under the procurators, the loss of hundreds of thousands of lives, and the enslavement of an entire generation of young Judeans as is reflected in the Arch of Titus in the Forum in Rome.

The issue of warfare and the confidence in violence as the only way to defeat the entrenched institutions of the powers of evil, specifically the Romans, was a major issue, especially in the aftermath of the war. Both Pharisaic Judaism, under the leadership of the rabbis at the Academy in Jamnia, and Christian Judaism were wholly nonviolent movements that adopted different strategies for the continuation of the religion of Israel in the aftermath of the war. But neither the rabbis (until Akiba's endorsement of Simon bar Kokhba's revolt, 132–135) nor the followers of Jesus advocated violence as a political strategy. Nevertheless, in the context of Jesus' time and in Mark's time, Judas' motive is completely understandable. Mark is, however, unambiguous in his negative portrayal of Judas and his action. There is no sympathetic inside view of Judas' mind or motive that would lessen the audience's alienation from him as a character.

Judas as a character

The characterization of Judas in Mark, like that of the chief priests, is wholly negative. The contrast between Judas and the other disciples is implicit in the introductory phrase the "the one of the twelve." (See note above for the force of the definite article here that takes the listeners back to Mark's introduction of him in 3:19.) The negative characterization of Judas begins with the climactic phrase in the story of the call of the twelve in 3:13–19, where Judas is described in v. 19 with the epithet "who in fact handed him over." ("In fact" is the translation here of the Greek word καί, which after the relative pronoun gives the epithet greater independence [BDAG, καί, 2.f]). The reintroduction of Judas in 14:10 is only the second time he appears in Mark's entire story. When Judas now reenters the narrative, it is to take the first explicit step towards the fulfillment of Jesus' earlier prophecies that he would be "handed over," and to fulfill the dastardly deed predictively attributed to him when he was previously introduced. Mark uses here another form of the same verb that Jesus uses in the last two passion prophecies (παραδίδοται—9:31; παραδοθήσεται—10:33; παραδοῖ—14:10–11). Mark constructed this verbal linkage in order to make unmistakable for his listeners the connection between the prophecy and its tragically painful fulfillment by "the one of the twelve."

The judgment of betrayal is deeply grounded in the history of Israelite and Greco-Roman storytelling. The story of Brutus' involvement in the assassination of Julius Caesar has a similar resonance in the stories of antiquity. The difference is that Brutus did some good things before his action. In both instances, the probability is that Brutus and Judas acted out of a sense of higher loyalty to the nation. There are, however, no positive notes in Mark's characterization of Judas and no qualification of the implicit condemnation of Judas in the story. The characterization of the chief priests has the same structure. This story is a development of the negative dynamics of aesthetic distance in relation to the character of Judas. In the norms of the story, what he does is shocking in its degree of evil, particularly because he had been a trusted disciple and friend. Judas' action violates the sacred covenant between a rabbi and his students.

11: The chief priests' payment to Judas

The chief priests' promise to pay Judas money also makes an ironic connection with the rebuke of the woman. The verb "to give" was last used in the discussion of the angry ones: "this ointment could have been sold for more than two hundred denarii and the money *given* to the poor." The irony is that immediately after condemning the woman for not giving to the poor, Judas is now willing to accept money for betraying Jesus. In this context, Jesus' implicit accusation of hypocrisy on the part of those who rebuked her was accurate. As we saw earlier, the policy of taking money from the rich and giving it to the poor was associated with the Zealots. And in the aftermath of the war, many Judeans, like Josephus, saw the Zealots as the ones who had betrayed the people of Israel. This, in turn, was a part of Israelite tradition, reflected in the prophetic condemnation by Jeremiah and Ezekiel of those who advocated ongoing rebellion against Babylon prior to the first destruction of Jerusalem and the Temple in 587 BCE (e.g., Jer 23:9–40; 28:1–17 against Hananiah; Ezra 13:1–16).

The renewal of the priests' conspiracy

The most immediate meaning of Judas' betrayal in Mark's story is that the conspiracy of the chief priests and scribes is given new life. They had ruled out a continuation of the conspiracy if they could not arrest Jesus on Wednesday before the beginning of the feast of Passover and Unleavened Bread. Jesus was in Bethany on that day, and their plot was dead in the water. With Judas' offer, their plot is back in business. The storyteller's description of their rejoicing is a reference to this revival of their conspiracy to kill Jesus.

Judas makes possible the restoration of the priests' plot by becoming a coconspirator. In the initial plot, the chief priests and scribes "were looking for a way . . . to kill him" (14:1). Now Judas "was looking for a way to hand him over" (14:11). In this rounding repetition of the words that introduced the conspiracy of the chief priests and scribes, there are only two new words: εὐκαίρως, which is usually translated "the best time," and παραδοῖ, "to hand over," or as the treacherous act of a friend, "to betray." The storyteller makes the connection impossible for the listeners to miss. The priests' concern about the imminence of the feast is no longer a problem. Their new secret agent, Judas Iscariot, can look for the most opportune moment to hand Jesus over to them. That in turn means that the conspirators can put aside any concern about the possibility of the people rioting in response to a public arrest.

Judas Iscariot's treachery in handing Jesus over, therefore, fulfills Jesus' own prophecies that he would be handed over—in one instance, into the hands of men (9:31), and in the second, more detailed prophecy (10:33), to the chief priests and scribes. The two motifs of the plot, the plans of Jesus' enemies and the prophecies of Jesus, are again woven together through the traitorous action of Judas. The fact that Jesus stayed in Bethany on Wednesday, the last day before the festival, raised a glimmer of hope that Jesus might escape because of the priests' decision to suspend the plan to kill him during the festival. With Judas' betrayal and the fulfillment of the first major element of the prophecy, that glimmer of hope flickers away.

The Performance of the Story

The challenge of telling this story is to convey the painful paradox of Judas' action. Judas literally picks up and continues the authorities' project and becomes part of their conspiracy against Jesus. The connection between Judas' betrayal and the anointing in Bethany needs to be made explicit in word and tone. The pause between the two stories is short. A gesture or actual move from *here* to *there* can also help to make the connection for the audience between Bethany and the chief priests. The appositive phrase "the one of the twelve" is an opportunity to express your feelings as a storyteller about Judas, which can range from incredulity to condemnation. The description of Judas' betrayal invites the teller to indicate by some vocal tone that this is a fulfillment of Jesus' prophecy. The rejoicing of the priests and the promise to pay Judas invites a tone that indicates the irony of their joy and Judas' reward. And the concluding note of Judas' looking for the best time needs to be sounded in an ominous tone.

Finally, look for a way to express that this story is a destruction of the hope that Jesus might escape arrest. It will require experimentation in both word and gesture. A central feature of biblical storytelling is what can be called the hermeneutics of gesture. Much of the interpretation of the story is done with gestures, facial expressions, and movement. While we have some information about ancient gestures,[12] we have no direct information about the gestures associated with the telling of the Gospel of Mark. All of this is extremely subtle. That is the nature of storytelling.

---

12. See, e.g., Shiner, *Proclaiming the Gospel*, "Gesture and Movement," 127–42.

2

THE PASSOVER MEAL (14:12–25)

AFTER A PAUSE, THE STORY OF THE PASSOVER MEAL FOLLOWS the story of the plot. It is the story of Thursday during the day and that evening after sundown. The emotional contrast between the violence of the betrayal and the covenant intimacy of the supper heightens the impact of this story. That contrast is made explicit at the supper in Jesus' prophecy that one of the twelve will betray him.

In the context of the gospel as a whole, this story completes a major motif in the earlier story, the mystery of the bread (8:14–17). It is also the time of greatest intimacy between Jesus and his disciples. For the listeners, this story is the most intimate moment of being addressed by Jesus as one of his disciples. The implicit invitation to the listeners is that they fully accept that role and become one of Jesus' disciples.

This section that centers on the meal consists of three smaller stories: the Preparations for the Passover (14:12–16), the Prophecy of Betrayal (14:17–21), and the Last Supper itself (14:22–25).

The Preparations for the Passover (14:12–16)

Sound Map

14:12Καὶ τῇ πρώτῃ ἡμέρᾳ τῶν ἀζύμων, ὅτε τὸ πάσχα ἔθυον,
    λέγουσιν αὐτῷ **οἱ μαθηταὶ** αὐτοῦ,
    Ποῦ θέλεις ἀπελθόντες **ἑτοιμάσωμεν** ἵνα **φάγῃς τὸ πάσχα**;
13καὶ ἀποστέλλει δύο τῶν μαθητῶν αὐτοῦ καὶ λέγει αὐτοῖς,
    Ὑπάγετε **εἰς τὴν πόλιν**,
    καὶ ἀπαντήσει ὑμῖν ἄνθρωπος κεράμιον ὕδατος βαστάζων.
ἀκολουθήσατε αὐτῷ, 14καὶ **ὅπου** ἐὰν εἰσέλθῃ εἴπατε τῷ οἰκοδεσπότῃ ὅτι

The Passover Meal (14:12–25)

Ὁ διδάσκαλος λέγει,
Ποῦ ἐστιν τὸ κατάλυμά μου
ὅπου τὸ πάσχα μετὰ τῶν μαθητῶν μου **φάγω**;

15καὶ αὐτὸς ὑμῖν δείξει ἀνάγαιον μέγα ἐστρωμένον ἕτοιμον,
  καὶ ἐκεῖ **ἑτοιμάσατε** ἡμῖν.
16καὶ ἐξῆλθον **οἱ μαθηταὶ**
  καὶ ἦλθον **εἰς τὴν πόλιν**
  καὶ εὗρον καθὼς εἶπεν αὐτοῖς.
καὶ **ἡτοίμασαν τὸ πάσχα**.

Translation

14:12 On the first day of Unleavened Bread, when they would kill the
        Passover lamb,
  his disciples said to him, "**Where** do you want us to go from here
  and **make the preparations** in order **for you to eat the Passover**?"
13 And he sent two of his disciples, saying to them,
  "Go into the city and a man carrying a jar of water will meet you.
Follow him, 14 and wherever he enters, say to the owner of the house:
  'The Teacher says, **Where** is my guest room
  where I may eat **the Passover** with my disciples?'

15 He will show you a large room upstairs, furnished and ready,
  and **make preparations** for us there."
16 And **the disciples** set out
  and went **into the city**,
  and they found everything just as he had said to them.
And **they prepared the Passover**.

Notes on Details and Translation

The episodic structure of this story is ambiguous. A factor is the rhythm of the three-period episodes in the preceding and following stories, but this divides the speech between two episodes. The indications that this was composed in two episodes are the verbal threads that link the successive periods in each episode: "make preparations," "go/went into the city" and "Passover."

14:3: when the Passover lamb is killed. τὸ πάσχα ἔθυον.

The KJV translates this clause, "when they killed the passover." The word πάσχα is employed in Greek without qualification, but various contexts clearly suggest a variety of specific references. The word πάσχα refers fundamentally to the Passover festival, as in 14:1. In the present context, however, the reference is clearly to the Passover lamb or lambs. The same word occurs in the next period—"where do you want us to prepare for you to eat the Passover?"—where it refers to the entire meal, not just to the lamb. Recent translations almost always supply the word "lamb" (RSV, NRSV, NJB, NIV, NET, NABRev) or "lambs" (NEB, REB, TEV). The plural is more descriptive of what actually happened: thousands of Passover lambs were sacrificed in the Temple on Passover eve, just as tens of thousands of turkeys are slaughtered on the days before Thanksgiving. The unqualified character of the Greek word requires the listeners to sort through the possible connotations to the one suitable to the context. Since the verb "they used to" refers to a yearly practice, the most obvious one is "lambs." The Greek word, however, is singular and is anomalous in its context for that reason. Mark's choice of the singular may imply that he is inviting his listeners to make a connection with "the Passover lamb" that will be sacrificed, namely, Jesus. This is congruent with his highly allusive storytelling style. Translating the phrase in the singular preserves that possible allusion.

Where do you want us to go from here . . . in order to / ἀπελθόντες . . . ἵνα.

In the preparations story, this participle occurs in the disciples' question to Jesus: literally translated, "Where do you want *departing* that we prepare in order that you might eat the Passover?" (14:12). It is sonically linked with the description of Judas going to the chief priests at the beginning of the previous story: literally translated "And Judas Iscariot, the one of the twelve, *departed* to the chief priests in order to betray him" (14:10). This verbal thread that implicitly contrasts Judas' action with that of the disciples is syntactically difficult to translate and is not present in any of the major translations. The translation adopted here is "to go from here . . . in order to."

The Passover Meal (14:12–25)

Comments on the Meaning and Impact of the Story

14:12: the day

The storyteller first locates this story in time: "the first day of Unleavened Bread." This is the day spoken of in 14:1: "the feast of Passover and Unleavened Bread was the next day" (literally, "on the second day"). The plot section describes the events of Wednesday (14:1–11), and now it is Thursday (14:12). The further definition as the day "when the Passover lamb is sacrificed" also specifies the time as the day preceding the evening of the Passover meal.[1] The verbal connection between the beginning of the plot story and the description of the feast carries with it the ominous sense of the unfolding events of each day, now heightened by the knowledge that the plot against Jesus continues.

Mark's further clarification of the day as the day "when they would sacrifice the Passover" (τὸ πάσχα ἔθυον) contains an ambiguity that some members of Mark's audiences may have recognized. As noted above, the absolute term "the Passover" can mean the Passover festival, meal, or lamb, depending upon the context. The verb "they would sacrifice" makes it clear that it is "the lamb" that is referred to here. The lamb was the center of the Passover meal. After the lamb was sacrificed in the Temple, it was given back to the family who brought it to be eaten in the festival meal. However, in light of Jesus' impending death and the anomalous singular usage, the potential is there for the audience to find in it a new meaning: the time for the sacrifice of the Passover lamb, Jesus, is near at hand.

This suggestion is unmistakable in the Gospel of John, and John often makes explicit what is implied in Mark (e.g., naming Judas as the angry one in the anointing story—John 12:4–6). In John 19:14 the time that Pilate hands Jesus over to be crucified is specified as "the day of the Preparation for the Passover . . . about the sixth hour": that is, noon, the hour when Passover lambs began to be slaughtered.[2] Thus, according to John, Jesus ate his final meal with his disciples in the evening that began the day of Preparation. Here in Mark 14:12, in contrast, the disciples explicitly ask Jesus on the morning of the day of Preparation, "Where do you want us to go from here and make the preparations in order for you to eat the Passover?" Mark is not making the kind of explicit connection made in John. He never calls Jesus

---

1. In view of the fact that Israelite custom usually refers to the first day of Unleavened Bread as Nisan 14, the day which began with the Passover evening, it is unclear why Mark refers to the day of preparation, Nisan 13, as the first day of the feast. For the few extant references in Josephus and the rabbinic literature to the first day of Unleavened bread as Nisan 14, see Jeremias, *Eucharistic Words of Jesus*, 17.

2. Brown, *Gospel according to John*, 2:883.

the "Lamb of God" as John does. But when at the Passover meal Jesus offers a new interpretation for the bread and the wine as a covenantal sacrifice, the audience might remember the reference to the sacrifice of the Passover a short while earlier in the story and realize it has taken on a new meaning. At least one member of a Markan audience, namely the composer of the Gospel of John, may have heard that connection and made it more explicit in his telling of the story.

The disciples' question and Judas' betrayal

The disciples' question to Jesus—"Where do you want us to go from here to prepare in order for you to eat the Passover?"—is the antithesis of the opening to the previous episode: "Judas Iscariot, the one of the twelve, went from there in order to hand him over to the chief priests"(14:10). Judas departs from Bethany and goes to Jerusalem to hand him over, while the disciples ask about going into Jerusalem to prepare the Passover meal for him. The repetition of two forms of the same verb, "to depart, go from" (ἀπῆλθεν—14:10; ἀπελθόντες—14:12), at the beginning of these two contiguous stories, implies that both missions are launched from Bethany and, in combination with the repetition of the purpose clause, "in order" (ἵνα), draw attention to the different purposes for which the disciples and Judas leave Bethany to go into Jerusalem.

Prophecy fulfillment or good arrangements

A central question about the meaning of this story is whether this is a prophecy/fulfillment story, that shows Jesus' prophetic foreknowledge, or a story about Jesus' extensive prearrangements for the Passover meal.[3] The structural connections with the story of the preparations for the triumphal entry (11:1–6) indicate that the two stories have the same meaning. The elements of common story structure are as follows:

---

3. The discussion of this issue in the critical literature has primarily focused on whether this story, along with the story of the preparations for Jesus' triumphal entry (11:1–6), is legendary or historical. Those who see these stories as legendary (e.g., Bultmann, *History of the Synoptic Tradition*, 163–64, 283ff.; Wellhausen, *Marci*, 110ff.) regard the parallels between these stories and the Old Testament narratives of Moses and Samuel as evidence of legendary development. Those who regard the narratives as historical (e.g., Lagrange, *Evangile selon Saint Marc*, 371–75; Taylor, *Gospel according to St. Mark*, 535–39) see the narratives as implying prearrangements rather than divine foreknowledge on the part of Jesus.

The Passover Meal (14:12–25)

Jesus sends two of his disciples.
He commands them to go into the city or village.
He describes what will happen.
He tells them what to do and what to say.
They go and do what he said.
It all happens, "just as he had said."

In both stories, therefore, a series of detailed commands are given and immediately accomplished.

Two major stories in the Old Testament have this same structure and are evidence that this is a conscious story structure for Israelite storytellers. The first is the story from Exodus of Moses' preparations for the Passover (Exod 12:21–28). The larger story has two parts: first, a series of commands by the Lord to Moses and Aaron about the Passover (Exod 12:1–13) and the feast of Unleavened Bread (Exod 12:14–20), then Moses' instructions to the elders of Israel concerning preparations for the Passover (Exod 12:21–28). The extensive verbal parallels between the Septuagint (Greek) translation of the story from Exodus (in italics) and Mark's story of the Passover preparations indicate that Mark knew this story and is using the same formulas:

Exodus 12:21–28
Then Moses called all the elders of Israel and said to them,

After you have gone from here (ἀπελθόντες, Exod 12:21)

... **sacrifice the Passover** (lamb) (θύσατε τὸ πάσχα, 12:21)

... When **you enter** the land (ἐὰν δὲ εἰσέλθητε, 12:25)

... **you shall say** to them (καὶ ἐρεῖτε αὐτοῖς, 12:27)

... this **Passover** is a **sacrifice** (θυσία τὸ πάσχα, 12:27)

Mark 14:12–16
... when **they would sacrifice the Passover lamb** (ὅτε τὸ πάσχα ἔθυον, Mark 14:12)

his disciples said to him, "Where do you want us to **go from here** . . ." (ἀπελθόντες, 14:12)

"... and wherever he **enters** (ὅπου ἐὰν εἰσέλθῃ, 14:14)

say to the owner of the house (εἴπατε τῷ οἰκοδεσπότῃ, 14:14)

... where I may eat **the Passover**" (τὸ πάσχα, 14:14)

Thus, Jesus' instructions are patterned on Moses' instructions and use some of the same words (in bold). In fact, Mark's entire story has the structure of the story from Exodus:

Moses summons the elders' council of Israel (Exod 12:21).

Moses commands the elders what to do when they **go from where they are**: they are to **sacrifice the Passover (lamb)**, put its blood on the door and stay inside (Exod 12:21-22).

Moses describes what will happen during the night (Exod 12:23).

Moses tells them that when they **enter** the land they are to observe the rite and **say** to their children that the **Passover** is a **sacrifice** commemorating the Lord's protection (Exod 12:25-27a).

They **depart** and do what he said (Exod 12:27b-28).

That night the prophecy of Moses is fulfilled (Exod 12:29).

The implication of this structural connection between the acts of Moses and Jesus is that Jesus is a prophet like Moses, another Markan motif that is developed more extensively in the Gospel of John.[4]

In Mark, this implicit connection with Moses recalls Jesus' conversation with Moses on the mountain when Jesus is transfigured (9:4). To approach the story merely in terms of whether it is a prophecy/fulfillment story that shows Jesus' foreknowledge, or alternatively a story about his extensive prearrangements for the Passover, misses the deeper background of the story in the tradition of Moses and indeed in the tradition of Moses and the Passover, which is the setting of this new episode in Jesus' story.

The other Old Testament story with a similar structure reinforces the need to hear the Markan story in the context of Israel's traditions, this time a story about its first anointed king. This is the story of Samuel's instructions and prophecy to Saul that immediately follows the anointing of Saul and predicts the confirming signs of God's action in Samuel anointing him (1 Kgs 10:1-9 [LXX]; 1 Sam 10:1-9 [MT]). Once again it is best to read the whole story. The specific verbal parallels between Mark's story of the preparations for the Passover and the LXX translation of the story of Samuel and Saul are as follows:

> 1 Kgs 10:1-9 [LXX]:
>
> When you **go away** (ἀπέλθῃς) from me today you will meet two men (1 Kgs 10:2 [LXX])
>
> ... as you enter there **into the city**, you will meet

---

4. See for example, Martyn, *History and Theology*, ch. 6, "From the Expectation of the Prophet-Messiah Like Moses...," where Martyn traces the development of Jesus as a prophet like Moses through the Gospel of John.

(ἂν εἰσέλθητε ἐκεῖ εἰς τὴν πόλιν καὶ ἀπαντήσεις) a band of prophets (1 Kgs 10:5 [LXX])

Mark 14:12–16:
... his disciples said to him, "Where do you want us to **go from here**... (ἀπελθόντες Mark 14:12)

"Go **into the city** and a man **will meet** you (Ὑπάγετε εἰς τὴν πόλιν,

καὶ ἀπαντήσει Mark 14:13) carrying a jar of water ...

The probability that Mark's knowledge of this story about Samuel and Saul played a role in the way he told the story of the Passover preparation is indicated by the structural connections between the two stories. (1) The verb "to meet" (ἀπαντάω) is never used elsewhere by Mark and is only used one other time in the New Testament in Luke's story of the ten lepers (Luke 17:12). (2) Mark uses this verb to describe what will happen when the two disciples "go into the city." (3) Mark's story of Jesus and his disciples has the same structure as the Samuel-Saul story as a synopsis of the Samuel-Saul story shows:

1 Kgs 10:1–9 [LXX]:

Samuel describes what will happen when Saul goes away from him in an elaborately detailed prophecy (10:2–6)

Samuel commands Saul about what he is do (10:7–8)

Saul goes, does what Samuel commanded, and the signs all take place that day (10:9)

(4) Both stories follow an act of anointing: Saul is anointed by Samuel (1 Kgs 10:1 LXX), and Jesus is anointed by the woman (Mark 14:3). In Mark this connection may have also implied that this fulfillment of Jesus' prophecy was a confirmation of God's initiation of Jesus' anointing by the woman for his messianic mission. It is difficult, therefore, to imagine that Mark's use of a unique verb to tell the story of a similar event in a similar narrative that unfolds in the wake of an anointing is merely coincidence.

The implication of the fulfillment of Samuel's prophecy in the events that follow is that God authorized Samuel to anoint Saul as a "messiah" in Hebrew, a "christ" in Greek. Against that background story, the implication of the fulfillment of Jesus' prophecy of the events associated with the preparations is that Jesus is a prophet like Moses and Samuel, authorized by God to set in motion the events that are about to unfold.

To summarize, the structure of these four stories, one each about Moses, Samuel, and two about Jesus is virtually identical. All begin with an elaborate speech by the prophet composed of prophecies and commands. The speech is followed by a short summary that the ones addressed went out, the events foretold happened, and the things commanded were done.

In each case, this story structure points to the activity of God. Thus, Moses did not prearrange the slaying of the firstborn in Egypt nor did Samuel prearrange all of the various meetings and events following the anointing of Saul. The impact of these stories is to evoke the audience's recognition that these events could only have been initiated and arranged by God. The implication is that Jesus knew about the colt, the man carrying a jar of water, and the furnished upper room by his unique prophetic knowledge that also came from God.

The story thereby establishes Jesus' status as a true prophet, who stood in the tradition of Moses, Samuel, Elijah, and John the Baptist. The implication is that the meaning of Mark's story is deeper than a mere display of Jesus' prophetic powers. The connections with the stories of earlier prominent prophets in Israel's history gives depth to the story of Jesus for those who knew and recognized the connections with those earlier stories. The connection with the story of Moses implies that Jesus is a prophet like Moses preparing for a momentous new Passover. And the connection with the story of Samuel and Saul implies that God has anointed Jesus for his mission as the Messiah. This connection also implies that Mark assumed that a significant part of his audiences would recognize it and, therefore, knew the stories of Israel's tradition well.

Jesus as rabbi and his disciples

This story of the preparations for the Passover is a new development in the relationship between Jesus and his disciples. The disciples' question is appropriate to the relationship between a rabbi and his disciples in the first century.[5] The basic contract was that a rabbi's students would meet his physical needs for meals, cleaning, and errands in exchange for his teaching. This student-teacher relationship is established earlier in the story when the disciples get a boat for Jesus (4:36); distribute food at the feedings (6:37ff.; 8:6ff.); offer to build booths for Jesus, Moses, and Elijah (9:5); and get the donkey for him to ride into the city (11:1ff.). In earlier stories, the disciples have simply responded to Jesus' commands (e.g., 3:9; 11:1). But here, for the first time, the disciples take the initiative of asking how they might serve their master. It is a good and right sign of their willingness to serve Jesus and further heightens the contrast to Judas' action.

---

5. See, for example, Rengstorf, "διδάσκαλος," in *TDNT* 2:154.

Jesus' response confirms the loving relationship between himself and his disciples. For the only time in the gospel, he uses the name "Teacher" for himself and calls them "my disciples" (v. 14) The tone of this speech is a graphic contrast to the anger and even cynicism of his critique of those who rebuked the woman. This is the first time in Mark's story that Jesus has a meal alone with his disciples. Prior to this, their meals were shared with either tax collectors and sinners (2:15) or the crowd (6:35ff.; 8:1ff.), or have been interrupted by others (3:20ff.; 6:31ff.). Jesus expresses his love for his disciples in his instructions. He prepares for an uninterrupted, celebrative Passover feast with his closest friends.

16: the fulfillment of the prophecy

The climax of the story is the fulfillment of Jesus' prophecy: "and they found everything just as he had said to them." In the mouth of a storyteller, such an outcome is reported with an expression of amazement. Just as there is a sense of amazement at the fulfillment of Samuel's elaborate and detailed prophecy to Saul, so also here the fulfillment of Jesus' prophecy is amazing. In both of Mark's stories about Jesus involving preparations, first for the entry into Jerusalem and now for the Passover meal, there are explanations of the responses of those who cooperate with Jesus. The bystanders who let the disciples take the colt gladly allow their donkey to be used for the service of "the Lord," and it is implied that the owner of the house in Jerusalem was honored to have "the Teacher" use his upper room for the Passover. But while the implication that Jesus knew there was a donkey in the town is surprising, the implication that he knew there would be a man carrying a jar of water who would meet and lead the disciples to the house with a ready and available upstairs room is even more surprising. The impact of the story is wonder at the knowledge and authority of Jesus as a prophet and teacher, an authority that can only come from God. Finally, in relation to the overall question of meaning with which we began, this meaning is far more congruent with a story of Jesus as a prophet and "anointed one" than a story celebrating his ability to make good arrangements for his Passover meal with his disciples.

This nexus of story connections with the stories of the Septuagint translation of the Hebrew Scriptures is also an indication of the character of Mark's audiences and Mark's assumptions as a composer about their knowledge. Mark assumes that at least some of the members of his projected audiences would have recognized this nexus of relationships to the stories of Israel's tradition. While the connections are extensive, they require intimate familiarity with those stories in Greek. This is, therefore, a sign that the story was composed for audiences of Hellenistic, Greek-speaking Judeans who knew the Greek Scriptures well.

The Performance of the Story

This story begins with the quiet evocation of the first day of the festival, with all its crowds and excitement and the sacrifice of the Passover lamb. It then builds in a steady crescendo to the climax of the disciples' finding things just as Jesus had told them. Finally, it recedes to quiet again in the description of the disciples' preparations. The disciples' question is told with a tone of respect and affection. It can also convey the disciples' loyalty and warmth as faithful followers and friends of Jesus.

Jesus' response to the disciples' question needs more life than readers normally give it. The words are often spoken in a factual and somewhat pedantic tone that reflects the conclusion that Jesus is telling the disciples about the arrangements he has already made. But Mark probably spoke Jesus' words in the style of a prophet like Moses and Samuel with confidence and authority. I find it helpful to think of Samuel talking to Saul in the immediate aftermath of the anointing. It is important to communicate that Jesus is, on the one hand, a rabbi-teacher but he is also a prophet like Moses and Samuel. His instructions are given with a smile and joyful anticipation of the Passover meal. This is a happy story, in stark contrast to the story that precedes it. The tempo is measured but moves along with deliberate speed. Communicate that Jesus is pleased at the disciples' request.

The description of their journey into the city and discovery of everything just as he had said is a crescendo of amazement. It can be told slowly enjoying each phrase and building up to an expression of surprise and amazement with the words, "just as he had said!" The conclusion of the story is once again quiet and very slow, giving the audience time to see all the events of the actual preparations in their imagination.

The Prophecy of Betrayal (14:17–21)

The story of the Last Supper takes place on Thursday evening, the beginning of Nisan 15. Mark marks the time but very briefly, "When it was evening," that is, the hour or so before the setting of the sun (also 15:42). The place is not named, but the upstairs room is simply assumed in light of the previous story of the preparations.

The Passover Meal (14:12–25)

Sound Map

14:17Καὶ ὀψίας γενομένης ἔρχεται μετὰ **τῶν δώδεκα**.
18καὶ ἀνακειμένων αὐτῶν καὶ **ἐσθιόντων** ὁ Ἰησοῦς εἶπεν,
    Ἀμὴν λέγω ὑμῖν ὅτι
    εἷς ἐξ ὑμῶν **παραδώσει** με,
    ὁ ἐσθίων μετ' ἐμοῦ.
19ἤρξαντο λυπεῖσθαι καὶ λέγειν αὐτῷ **εἷς** κατὰ **εἷς**,
    Μήτι ἐγώ;

20ὁ δὲ εἶπεν αὐτοῖς,
    Εἷς τῶν δώδεκα,
    ὁ ἐμβαπτόμενος μετ' ἐμοῦ εἰς τὸ τρύβλιον.
21ὅτι ὁ μὲν υἱὸς τοῦ ἀνθρώπου ὑπάγει καθὼς γέγραπται περὶ αὐτοῦ,
    οὐαὶ δὲ τῷ ἀνθρώπῳ ἐκείνῳ δι' οὗ ὁ υἱὸς τοῦ ἀνθρώπου
                                        παραδίδοται.
καλὸν αὐτῷ εἰ οὐκ ἐγεννήθη ὁ ἄνθρωπος ἐκεῖνος.

Translation

14:17And when it was evening, he came with **the twelve**.
18And when they had reclined and **were eating**, Jesus said,
    one of you **will betray** me,
    one who is eating with me!"
19They began to be deeply grieved and to say to him, **one after another**,
    "Is it me?"
20He said to them, "**One of the twelve!**
    One who is dipping bread into the bowl with me!
21For the Son of Man goes as it is written of him,
    but woe to that man by whom the Son of Man **is betrayed**.
It would have been better for that man if he had not been born."

Notes on Details and Translation

14:18: When they had reclined / καὶ ἀνακειμένων αὐτῶν

The NRSV translation, "when they had taken their places," is an ingenious solution to a translation conundrum. The literal meaning of this phrase is "when they had reclined . . ." This will make no sense to modern readers who do not know the ancient custom. But it is also the historical probability, since most people in Palestine in this period lay down on pillows and propped their left side up on cushions with their heads and hands toward the short table in the middle where the food was laid out. Bowls held many of the various parts of the meals and were eaten by the family and guests dipping bread in the bowls. Other translations have translated this phrase anachronistically as "As they sat at supper . . ." (REB; also KJV) because of the later custom of sitting at tables as well as all the traditional pictures of Jesus and the twelve around a table. The literal meaning is adopted here in order to convey more accurately the Middle Eastern setting of the story.

19: they began to be deeply grieved . . ."Is it me?" / λυπεῖσθαι . . . Μήτι ἐγώ.

The NRSV translation, "they began to be distressed," is quite inadequate. The verb in Greek means to be in pain or grief, sometimes severe (BDAG). The translation "deeply grieved" is adopted here because it is more emotionally intense and precise. Jesus' accusation here is the most serious violation of relationship that is possible and "distressed" is too trivial. The translation "Surely, not I" (NRSV) is inappropriately formal for the exchange among intimate friends pictured here. The disciples' response in Greek consists of two words, Μήτι ἐγώ. The first word introduces a question that expects a negative answer, expressible in English either by "surely not," as the NRSV has translated it, or by tone of voice. The question of the appropriate tone of voice will be addressed below. The translation adopted here, "Is it me?" is grammatically incorrect but ubiquitous in common speech. It is also more emotionally expressive and, therefore, more appropriate for illiterate Judean men who were in no sense culturally sophisticated.

21: It would be better for that man if he had never been born / καλὸν αὐτῷ εἰ οὐκ ἐγεννήθη ὁ ἄνθρωπος ἐκεῖνος

Once again, the NRSV translation here, "It would have been better for that one not to have been born," is problematic. One of the purposes of the revision of the RSV was to change gender-specific language that excluded women. This is especially appropriate when the original Hebrew or Greek was generic. But here the Greek phrase is gender specific and unambiguously refers to a man. The phrase "that one," while gender inclusive, sounds curiously objective, as if it was not directed to Judas. In this case, the RSV translation, "It would have been better for that man," is preferable and more accurately conveys the dynamics of Jesus' words.

The Passover Meal (14:12–25)

Comments on the Meaning and Impact of the Story

The prophecy that is aleady fulfilled

The immediately striking dimension of Jesus' prophecy of betrayal is that the prophecy has already been, at least partially, fulfilled. That is, the audience already knows that Judas has defected to the chief priests and is seeking to hand Jesus over to them. This inside-scoop dimension of the story means that the audience can answer the disciples' question definitively about the identity of the betrayer. This connection to the preceding betrayal episode is made unmistakable by the storyteller's use of key words from that story: "the twelve" (δώδεκα), "to betray" (παραδίδωμι), and the phrase "one of the twelve" (εἷς τῶν δώδεκα). Everyone knows except the Eleven.

The emotional connotations of the supper are set by the earlier stories in the gospel. The association that the evening is the time of withdrawal and retreat for Jesus and the disciples has been established by the earlier stories of the boat trip following his teaching the crowd by the shore (4:35) and the trip out to Bethany after the triumphal entry (11:11). Their reclining together heightens the implication of intimate fellowship. Never before in the story have Jesus and his disciples been able to eat together alone.[6]

Jesus' first prophecy of the betrayal describes the betrayer in two phrases: "one of you, one who is eating with me." There is a note of incredulity as well as condemnation in this twofold repetition. It sounds as if Jesus can't believe it himself. Although the listener knows what Judas has already done, what is surprising here is that once again Jesus knows with such precision what is going to happen. The context of intimate fellowship around the Passover meal increases the sense of the enormity of this betrayal.

19: the grieving response of the disciples

The disciples' response after Jesus' first statement concretizes the horror of the betrayal. The verbal expression of the intensity of their grief at the possibility that one of them might be the betrayer is the emotion-laden construction of "to begin" with an infinitive: "they began to be deeply grieved ..." The intensity of their grief has also been established by the only earlier use of this word, "to grieve, become sad, distressed" (λυπέω), in the story of the rich prospective disciple who left in sadness rather than give away all his possessions. (10:22) The disciples' grief and the question it evokes

---

6. The only previous use of "to recline" (ἀνάκειμαι) is in the story of Herod's banquet (6:26) at which John is beheaded. In both instances, the verb refers to a leisurely meal eaten on a special occasion.

from them creates a uniquely double faceted impact for the audience. The listeners are given this inside view of the disciples' distress, but they also know that Judas is the one. The disciples' way of asking their question in Greek expresses the expectation of a negative answer. Not one of them can believe it is true that he is the one who will do this terrible thing. But each still asks the question. And it is a question, not a statement. Their grief and horror suggest also that none of them asks it purely rhetorically in a tone of confidence that he could not possibly be the one. Rather the tone is incredulity at the possibility. So the possibility that it is true, however incredible, hangs in the air.

18–21: the scandal and puzzle of Jesus' naming of the betrayer

Jesus' next words intensify the first description: "one of the twelve, one who is dipping into the bowl with me." These four descriptions form a crescendo of scandal:

> One of you will betray me,
> > one who is eating with me!
> One of the twelve!
> > One who is dipping into the bowl with me!

The degree of Judas' offense is built by sheer accumulation. The implicit norms in these repeated descriptions are, first, the violation of the covenant between a rabbi and his disciples and, second, the violation of the covenant of table fellowship. Jesus' response raises further questions for the listeners: why doesn't Jesus name him and confront him directly? And why doesn't he try to stop him? As will happen at the arrest and at the trial before the priests, Jesus appears to accept Judas' action and takes no action to prevent it. Instead Jesus focuses on the still secret betrayer.

The connotations of Jesus' prophecy of woe (that is, of impending disaster for the betrayer) are determined by Jesus' earlier woe pronouncements in the apocalyptic discourse. There Jesus predicts woe for those who are nursing "in those days" (13:17). It is an expression of distress and mourning because of what lies in the future. The connotations of the pronouncement of woe here are similar to those in the story in 1 Kings 13 (3 Kingdoms 13—LXX), where the old prophet of Bethel mourns the man of God who had prophesied against Jeroboam but who was tricked by the old prophet of Bethel into disobeying the LORD's command not to return to eat and drink, and because of his disobedience is killed by a lion. The old prophet declares, "Woe my brother," and instructs his sons to bury him with the man of God (3 Kgs 13:30–31—LXX). Just as the old prophet at Bethel mourns the man of God who had been deceived, so Jesus treats Judas as a man who has been deceived into breaking his covenant with him and who will suffer the terrible consequences. The meaning of Jesus' words is directly tied to the tone in which they are pronounced. The cry of woe is a mourning song pronounced in grief (see, for example, Jer 22:18 and Isa 1:4). Thus, Jesus' word of woe was spoken in a tone of sorrow, not condemnation. Thus, Jesus grieves for the man who is betraying him, even as he protects him from public disclosure.

Jesus contrasts the Son of Man (by implication, himself) and his betrayer: to paraphrase, this way of suffering and death has been written for the Son of Man, but it has not been written for the one of his chosen Twelve whose handing over is an act of betrayal. Jesus earlier used this concept of how it is written in another indirect passion prophecy in which he links the coming of Elijah as John the Baptist with his own death: "Elijah is indeed coming first to restore all things. How then is it written about the Son of Man, that he is to go through many sufferings and be treated with contempt? But I tell you that Elijah has come, and they did to him whatever they pleased, as it is written of him" (9:12–13). Here the concept of its being written is a synonym for the will of God. "It is written" means that it has been predestined by God.[7] But this way has not been written of Judas and is in no sense the purpose of God. It is *not* his destiny.

The audience can judge that Judas' action stands under divine judgment. But the final confirmation of Jesus' prophecy of woe for Judas remains to be fulfilled in the future. In view of the fact that Jesus' prophecy that Judas will betray him has already been fulfilled, the probability is high that this prophecy of Judas' judgment will also be fulfilled. But, unlike in Matthew, where Judas hangs himself, or in Acts, where he falls down in a field and his bowels gush out, in Mark the story ends without that fulfillment having taken place. The audience, however, has every reason to believe that Jesus' prophecy will be fulfilled. If anything, Jesus' response to Judas only deepens the puzzle of Jesus. The implication is that he even loves and grieves for the one who will betray him. Nevertheless, there is an implicit contrast drawn between the betrayer and the other disciples. There is no possibility of Jesus' reconciliation with his betrayer. It would be better for that man if he had

---

7. A scene in the movie *Lawrence of Arabia* catches the impact of Jesus' words here. As Lawrence and his army are crossing the hottest and most desolate part of the Arabian desert to attack the port of Aqabah, one of the men falls off his camel. They only discover this after they have made it to the oasis on the other side. Lawrence, against the objections of his Arab chief ally, goes back to get the man at the risk of his own life. When he brings him back in triumph, the Arab chief says in admiration, "It is written of you."

never been born. Jesus is portrayed as a prophet who foresees disaster for his betrayer.

20–21: the mystery of Judas' motive and Jesus' response

The question that looms over the entire story of the betrayal is Judas' motive: why would Judas do this? The only clues in the story point to the Bethany anointing and the political dynamics associated with the conflict between Jesus and some of his disciples over the woman's anointing him with very expensive ointment. For Mark's audiences, who heard this story either during or in the more or less immediate aftermath of the war, those clues resonate with the political conflicts that led to the war. In the background of the conflict between Jesus and Judas lies the issue of the Judean aristocracy's collaboration with the Romans and Jesus' command to the rich man to sell everything and give it to the poor (10:17–27).

Furthermore, when Jesus' response is heard against the background of the messianic traditions of Israel, his response to his betrayer is radically different from the responses of Saul and David to their betrayers. Saul's belief that David was betraying him may or may not have been misplaced, but he sought with all his might to kill him. When Absalom betrayed his father, David defended himself, and even though he tried to prevent Absalom's death, the war between their two armies led to Absalom's being killed. The stories of the anointed ones of Judah and Israel in 1 and 2 Kings are replete with stories of conspiracy, betrayal, and death. And whenever possible, the one being betrayed tries to escape and fights against his betrayer.[8] Judas Iscariot is then part of an ancient tradition in Israel and Judah of men who have conspired against and betrayed the anointed ones of Israel. Jesus' action is, however, unprecedented. He knows the conspiracy and his betrayer; but

---

8. For example, the graphic story of betrayal and flight from assassination in Jehu's ascent to the kingship in rebellion against the house of Ahab (2 Kgs 9:1–28). Jehu is anointed by one of the prophets at Elisha's command (2 Kgs 9:6). He then conspires against Joram, son of Ahab (2 Kgs 9:14). In a highly dramatic scene, Jehu drives his chariot to Jezreel where King Ahaziah of Judah had come to visit Joram, who was sick. After sending two horsemen to ask, "Is it peace?" both of whom did not return, Joram and Ahaziah drove out to meet Jehu. When Jehu denounced Joram, Joram shouted, "Treason, Ahaziah!" and both of them reined about and fled. Jehu shot Joram with an arrow between his shoulders and then pursued and ordered the assassination of Ahaziah. See also the death of Amaziah (2 Kgs 14:9), Zechariah son of Jeroboam who was assassinated by Shallum (2 Kgs 15:10), Pekahiah son of Menahem (2 Kgs 15:25), Pekah son of Remaliah (2 Kgs 15:30), and Amon (2 Kgs 20:23). In each of these stories, there is a conspiracy against the king and the king is killed. In most of these instances, the king is apparently caught unawares and has no opportunity to flee or to oppose the conspiracy.

he does not disclose his betrayer's identity and neither takes action against him nor does anything to protect himself from the conspiracy.

In the end, a dynamic of Jesus' words in this story is an expression of love for Judas. Jesus' response to Judas has some of the same spirit as David's response to Absalom's betrayal and death (see 2 Samuel 18). In response to Judas' hatred and desire to have Jesus killed, Jesus expresses both his shock at what Judas is doing as one of the twelve at this covenant meal and his grief at what this means for Judas. In contrast to Jesus' words at the anointing in Bethany, there is no anger in his words here—only incredulity and grief. Jesus responds to his awareness of this explicit action of hatred with love. This is not passive love that simply accepts whatever Judas does. Jesus names what Judas is doing publicly in the context of the community that he is attacking. But Jesus also makes no effort either to change Judas' mind or to take action to expose his identity or to prevent him from bringing his plot to completion. Nor does Jesus offer to negotiate or change his own course of action. Jesus' words are an expression of nonviolent determination.

The Performance of the Story

The challenge at the beginning of this story is to create a scene of camaraderie and celebration. A broad gesture indicating the group reclining and eating is the place to start. This warmth of fellowship provides the maximum contrast to Jesus' prophecy. The most important decision here is how to embody the character of Jesus. Jesus' character here is strong and courageous. It is necessary to practice Jesus' words in order to be able to capture the combination of grief and scandal. The gesture of Jesus here might be a finger pointing around the circle. And it is fully appropriate to include in that circle the members of the audience who are here addressed as the disciples. The storyteller's introduction of the disciples' response one by one can have the tone of shock and even a kind of horror at the possibility that each might be the one. The direct quotation of their response is the place to express their shock and grief at what Jesus is suggesting. A fist to the chest is an appropriate gesture. A slightly longer pause after their question lets the ambiguity of the question include the listeners.

The second set of terms naming the betrayer is a crescendo of intensity. It begins with the most ironic descriptor, "one of the twelve," and ends with the naming of the violation of the sacred covenant of table and Passover fellowship. The contrast between the Son of Man's choice of what God has willed for him and the woeful choice of the betrayer can be indicated by a nod of the head, yes, for the first and a shake of the head, no, for the second.

The final colon has the tone of a dirge that expresses Jesus' mourning of the fate that awaits the betrayer. There is no anger or bitterness in Jesus' words here, only grief and, yes, love.

The Last Supper (14:22–26) ▶

This story is the climax to the larger story of Jesus' last meal with his disciples. In the narrative of the Gospel of Mark, this is also the first meal of Jesus with his disciples because all of the earlier meals were either interrupted or incomplete (2:15; 3:20; 6:31). In the three Synoptic Gospels, Jesus' last meal with his disciples is the Passover feast. This story was then heard by Mark's listeners against the background of their memories of Passover—both the original stories and their own Passover celebrations. The sonic echoes (in bold) also link this story with the earlier feeding stories (6:30-44; 8:1-9).

Sound Map

14:22Καὶ ἐσθιόντων αὐτῶν λαβὼν ἄρτον εὐλογήσας ἔκλασεν καὶ ἔδωκεν
αὐτοῖς καὶ εἶπεν,
    Λάβετε.
τοῦτό ἐστιν τὸ σῶμά μου.

23καὶ λαβὼν ποτήριον εὐχαριστήσας ἔδωκεν αὐτοῖς,
    καὶ ἔπιον ἐξ αὐτοῦ **πάντες**.
    24καὶ εἶπεν αὐτοῖς,
    Τοῦτό ἐστιν τὸ αἷμά μου τῆς διαθήκης
    τὸ ἐκχυννόμενον ὑπὲρ πολλῶν.
25ἀμὴν λέγω ὑμῖν ὅτι οὐκέτι οὐ μὴ **πίω** ἐκ τοῦ γενήματος τῆς ἀμπέλου
ἕως τῆς ἡμέρας ἐκείνης ὅταν αὐτὸ **πίνω** καινὸν ἐν τῇ βασιλείᾳ τοῦ
θεοῦ.

Translation

14;22And **while they were eating, he took bread,
blessed it, broke it, and gave it to them**, and said,
    "Take it.
This is my body."

23Then he took a cup, and after giving thanks he gave it to them
and they all drank from it.

24And he said to them,
"**This is my blood** of the covenant,
which is poured out for many.
25Truly I tell you, never again will **I drink** of the fruit of the vine
until that day when **I drink it** new in the kingdom of God."

Comments on the Meaning and Impact of the Story

The central motif in this story is Jesus' reinterpretation of the meaning of the unleavened bread and the wine of the Passover meal. The storyteller first links this story with the prophecy of betrayal: "while they were eating." The implication is that Jesus' prophecy did not end the meal but was an announcement in the midst of their dinner together and that Judas Iscariot was still present in the circle.

14:22: the meaning of the bread throughout the gospel

Jesus' actions of taking the bread, blessing it, breaking it, and giving it to them repeat and recall the words and ritual gestures in the two earlier stories of the feeding of the crowds of Judeans and Gentiles (6:41; 8:6–7). The verbal connections are so extensive that the sonic linkage cannot be missed. In the first feeding story, Jesus "took the five loaves . . . blessed and broke the loaves and gave them to the disciples to set before them" (καὶ λαβὼν τοὺς πέντε ἄρτους . . . εὐλόγησεν καὶ κατέκλασεν τοὺς ἄρτους καὶ ἐδίδου τοῖς μαθηταῖς παρατιθῶσιν αὐτοῖς—6:41). In the story of the feeding of the four thousand, Jesus "took the seven loaves and having given thanks he broke and gave [them] to his disciples to set before and they set them before the crowd" (καὶ λαβὼν τοὺς σέπτε ἄρτους εὐχαριστήσας κατέκλασεν καὶ ἐδίδου τοῖς μαθηταῖς ἵνα παρατιθῶσιν καὶ παρέθηκαν τῷ ὄχλῳ—8:6). The key words of this ritual action are present in all three stories. The only significant difference is that Mark uses a synonym of "to bless" (εὐλόγησεν) in the second feeding, "to give thanks" (εὐχαριστήσας), from which we get the term *Eucharist*. In the Passover meal story, these two verbs are also used: "to bless" over the bread, and "to give thanks" over the cup. In addition to using the verbal threads, the probability is that the storyteller also used the same ritual gestures in each of the three stories. The sonic linkage of these three stories in the Gospel of Mark and in Israel's Scriptures is one of the most extensive leitmotifs of Mark's PRN.

For everyone who has heard these earlier stories, this story recalls the unanswered questions left hanging after each of the earlier feeding stories.

After the feeding of the five thousand, Jesus sends the disciples ahead in the boat and then comes to them walking on the water. After Jesus gets in the boat, Mark tells his listeners that the disciples were totally astounded. He then explains why: "because they did not understand about the loaves, but their hearts were hardened" (6:51–52). This is typical of Mark's storytelling: he gives an explanation that raises more questions than it answers (e.g., 16:8). The questions are inevitable: what didn't the disciples understand about the loaves? And why were they like Pharoah, who hardened his heart against the Lord and Moses? So the question is left hanging and unanswered: what did the disciples not understand about the loaves?

This question is made even more pressing by the dialogue between Jesus and his disciples in the boat after the second feeding. In that story, Jesus feeds the four thousand and immediately gets into a boat with the disciples and goes to Dalmanutha. The Pharisees meet him there and ask for a sign. Jesus refuses to give them a sign and is so angry and frustrated (which the storyteller communicated by his tone and gestures) that he gets back into the boat to go back to the other side. The disciples forgot to bring any bread to eat on the way across the sea, and Jesus, in response to their anxiety, asks them a series of questions about the feedings. In the telling of the story, these questions were addressed to the audience as the disciples:

> "Why are you talking about having no bread? Do you still not perceive or understand? Are your hearts hardened? You have eyes, don't you see? You have ears, don't you hear? And don't you remember? When I broke the five loaves for the five thousand, how many baskets full of broken pieces did you collect?" They said to him, "Twelve." "And the seven for the four thousand, how many baskets full of broken pieces did you collect?" And they said to him, "Seven." Then he said to them, "Don't you understand?" (8:17–21, NRSV)

In the story itself there is no answer to these questions. As a result the audience can't answer Jesus' questions with any certainty. They can guess, but there are no answers. The effect of this long speech is, on the one hand, funny. But while the audience is invited to laugh at the disciples and at Jesus' rabbinic frustration, they also have to laugh at themselves because they can't answer the questions either. Maybe they can guess at the significance of the twelve and seven baskets. But even now we aren't sure what it meant. I tend to think that "the twelve" was probably associated with the twelve tribes of Israel. But the best anyone can come up with for "the seven" is the seven hills of Rome, which is a possible inference for Hellenistic Judeans and Gentiles in the Roman Empire but is still pretty obscure.

However, while Mark's directions for the trip from Tyre through Sidon to the other side of the Sea of Galilee are a "long way round" (7:31), he clearly indicates that the trip ended in "region of the Decapolis," the ten Gentile cities on the east side of the Sea of Galilee and the Jordan. This is an unambiguous indication that Mark locates the feeding of the four thousand in the same general area as the story of the Gerasene demoniac, the Gentile regions on the other side of the Sea of Galilee.

Thus, even if the significance of the baskets was as ambiguous to Mark's audiences as it is to us, which is itself uncertain, he is describing two feedings to five thousand Judeans and four thousand Gentiles on the two sides of the Sea of Galilee. However, even if Mark's audiences understood the two feedings as given to Israelites and Gentiles, the answer to the central question—what do the loaves mean?—remains a mystery. And the two episodes following the feedings (6:51–52 and 8:17–21) raise the question to a high level of intensity.

Jesus' statement at the Passover meal repeats the liturgical formula from the earlier feeding stories and answers the question about the significance of the bread: "Take. This is my body." The loaves were Jesus' body.[9] Thus, it is implied that these feedings were sacred meals in which Jesus gave himself to the crowds of Judeans and Gentiles and now to the disciples. The immediate connotations of the phrase "my body" (τὸ σῶμά μου) are determined by Jesus' use of these words in his rebuke of those who attacked the woman: "She has anointed my body (τὸ σῶμά μου) beforehand for burial" (14:8). "My body" is then associated with Jesus' death. Furthermore, the immediate context of Jesus' words is the prophecy of betrayal. The implication is that Jesus, knowing who will hand him over to be killed, gives himself to both the faithful disciples and his betrayer. Just as the words to his betrayer are spoken in a spirit of grief and love, here this action of self-giving is a supreme sign of love.

24: the meaning of the cup

Next Jesus takes "the cup," that is, in the context of the Passover meal and of Jesus' later reference to "the fruit of the vine," a cup of wine. Mark introduces this cup of wine by repeating with one variation ("gave thanks" in place of "blessed") the ritual words with which he introduced the bread: "taking,

---

9. For the most extensive examination of the motif of the mystery concerning the loaves, see Quesnell, *Mind of Mark*. Quesnell's study is a thorough and comprehensive redaction-critical study that explores the meaning of the enigmatic ending to the story of Jesus walking on the water: "they didn't understand about the loaves but their hearts were hardened" (6:52). His exploration also leads to eucharistic meaning.

"giving thanks," "gave it to them." However, while these words of introduction to the bread make an implicit connection with the bread in the earlier feeding stories, there has been no earlier mention of a cup of wine and its significance. There is, however, an implicit connection to the prophecy of Judas' betrayal that immediately precedes this story. The storyteller reports that Jesus took the cup, gave thanks, gave it to them "and they all drank from it" (v. 23). If they "all" drank from the cup, that meant Judas drank from the cup as did the rest of the disciples. Furthermore, the storyteller makes the word "all" (πάντες), the last word in the phrase. It could be translated: "And they drank from it—all of them." It is probable that Mark placed the word "all" in this emphatic position in order to imply that Judas also drank from the cup of the new covenant.

Jesus' interpretation of the cup has verbal connections to an earlier story in the tradition, the covenant sacrifice of the oxen at Sinai (Exod 24:8), and those verbal threads are extensive. In the Exodus story, the Israelites arrived at Mount Sinai, and Moses went up to meet the Lord on the mountain. The Lord then spoke the Ten Commandments to the people and the Covenant Code to Moses (Exod 20:22—23:33). In response to the Lord, Moses wrote down all the words and built an altar and sacrificed oxen. He took the book of the covenant and read it in the hearing of the people, and then "Moses took the blood and dashed it on the people and said, 'See the blood of the covenant that the LORD has made with you in accordance with all these words'" (Exod 24:8). Mark's story echoes the sounds of the Greek translation of this covenantal story (LXX):

> Moses **took the blood . . . and said,** "Behold, **the blood of the covenant**
>
> λαβὼν δὲ Μωυσῆς τὸ αἷμα . . . καὶ εἶπεν Ἰδοὺ τὸ αἷμα τῆς διαθήκας—Exodus 24:8
>
> And Jesus **took** the cup and having given thanks, he gave it to them and they drank from it—all of them. **And he said** to them, "This is my **blood of the covenant . . .**"
>
> καὶ λαβὼν ποτήριον εὐχαριστήσας ἔδωκεν αὐτοῖς, καὶ ἔπιον ἐξ αὐτοῦ πάντες **καὶ εἶπεν** αὐτοῖς, Τοῦτό ἐστιν τὸ **αἷμά** μου **τῆς διαθήκης**—14:23-24

Mark makes the connection unmistakable for everyone who has heard the Moses story in Greek. The wine is identified with Jesus' blood and with the blood of the oxen that sealed the Mosaic covenant between the Lord and the people of Israel. By analogy, Jesus is the covenant sacrifice as were the oxen in the Exodus story, and drinking the cup is like receiving the sprinkling of the blood at Sinai.

Jesus' reinterpretation of the blood of the covenant at Sinai has two major elements: "this is *my* blood of the covenant" and "poured out for many." The phrase "*my* blood" both connects this cup with the blood of the covenant at Sinai and distinguishes it as Jesus' blood rather than the blood of the oxen. In a similar manner, the phrase "poured out for many" makes an implicit contrast with the Sinai covenant. The Greek word πολλῶν is the genitive plural of πολλοί. The phrase "hoi polloi" has come down into English as a phrase that means the common folk.

Mark builds meaning by repeating the sounds of words. So what would listeners who had heard the whole gospel have remembered in connection with the phrase, "poured out for **many**"? The following list is indicative:

- Galileans in Capernaum: "he cured **many** who were sick with various diseases" (1:34)
- tax collectors and sinners: "**many** tax collectors and sinners were also sitting with Jesus and his disciples—for there were many who followed him" (2:15)
- a great multitude from Judea, Idumea, beyond the Jordan, and around Tyre and Sidon: "for he had healed **many**" (3:10)
- the demons in the Gerasene demoniac: "My name is Legion, for we are **many**" (5:9)
- the five thousand Judeans in Galilee: "Now **many** saw them going and recognized them, and they hurried there on foot from all the towns" (6:33ff)
- the four thousand Gentiles in the Decapolis: "In those days when there was again a great crowd [a crowd of **many**]" (8:1ff)

The most immediate associations of the term are then a broadly representative community that includes Judeans, Gentiles, tax collectors and sinners, the sick, and persons possessed by evil spirits.

In his study *The Eucharistic Words of Jesus*,[10] Joachim Jeremias observes that this phrase is an echo of the "Suffering Servant Song" in Isaiah 52:13—54:12. He argues that in Isaiah's Servant Song the "many" of 52:12-13, who are astonished at the Servant when they finally see and understand, include not only the nations and the kings (52:15) but a much broader group that includes the speaker as well as "all" (53:4-6). This implies that these are the same ones who—according to 53:5-6, 11-12—are forgiven

---

10. Jeremias, *Eucharistic Words of Jesus*, 227-31.

their sins, transgressions, and iniquities. Therefore, the phrase "for many" is not exclusive (many, but not all) but rather, in the Semitic manner of speech, inclusive (the totality, consisting of many).[11] In this sense, therefore, Mark's phrase τὸ ἐκχυννόμενον ὑπὲρ πολλῶν is to be rendered "which is poured out for the peoples of the world."

If the meaning of "the many" in this interpretation of the cup was significantly shaped by its connection with and contrast to the Exodus story, the implied comparison is that the covenant at Sinai was for Israelites while this covenant is extended to Israelites and Gentiles, clean and unclean. In the context of the Judean–Roman War and its aftermath, this implies that the covenant established by "my blood of the covenant" includes the enemies of Israel such as "Legion" as well as the people of Israel.

25: the vow of abstinence

The climax of the Passover meal is Jesus' vow of abstinence from wine until the coming of the kingdom of God. Like the word concerning the bread and the prophecy of being handed over, it contains phrases that were heard earlier in Mark's narrative, namely "that day" and "kingdom of God." Both these terms describe an eschatological future in Mark and are spoken by Jesus in his role as a prophet.[12] In the plot and Passover meal sections that begin the PRN, Jesus is presented as a prophet. In his prophetic role, Jesus introduces two of his prophecies with the solemn words, "Amen, I tell you," namely, the prophecy of the worldwide telling of the woman's extravagant act of anointing him, and the prophecy that one of the twelve will betray him. The prophecy concerning the preparations for the Passover meal is not introduced with this formula, but in all three of these stories his prophecies are fulfilled either immediately (the disciples find it as he said; Judas has already set his betrayal in motion) or in the experience of the listeners (who are hearing the story of the woman's extravagance from Mark's mouth).

In this new prophecy, with the solemn formula "Amen, I tell you," Jesus swears that he will abstain from the fruit of the vine until he drinks it new in the kingdom of God. It is Jesus' first prophecy concerning himself in the PRN, and it is the first prophecy concerning himself (e.g., the passion prophecies) that is introduced with this solemn formula. This prophecy is

---

11. Ibid., 229: Jeremias goes on to say, "The Johannine tradition interprets it in this way, for in its equivalent to the bread-word . . . it paraphrases 'for many' as 'for the life of the world' (John 6:51c)."

12. Thus, various forms of the phrase "that day" (ἡμέρας ἐκείνα) occur in Mark 2:20; 13:17, 19, 24, 32; "kingdom of God" (βασιλεία τοῦ θεοῦ) in 1:15; 4:26, 30; 9:1, 47; 10:14, 15, 24, 25.

The Passover Meal (14:12–25)

the climax of the supper story. But whereas earlier prophecies are validated by evidence either within the story itself or within the audiences' experience of the story, evidence for this prophecy is neither given in the story nor presumed in the audiences' experience to validate or confirm the prophecy. This prophecy rather points to the eschatological future of the kingdom of God.

Jesus' commitment to his vow to abstain from wine until the eschatological future of the kingdom of God is pointed to again later in the narrative when, at the cost of suffering greater pain, Jesus refuses the wine mixed with myrrh before he is fastened to the cross (15:23).[13] What does it mean? Why is it the climax of Jesus' last meal with his disciples? Why is Jesus steadfast in keeping this vow to the end? Just as the bread and the wine allude to earlier Israelite traditions, does Jesus' commitment to abstinence from wine also allude to something in the traditions of Israel?

Joachim Jeremias has presented a comprehensive survey of the various possible backgrounds for this vow.[14] The most persuasive background he identifies is that Jesus' vow is connected with the warrior traditions of Israel. Vows of abstinence are associated with the warriors who took vows of abstinence from women or food while they were "in the tents" or engaged in battle. The story of Uriah's faithfully keeping his vow of abstinence when David desperately wanted him to break his vow and sleep with Bathsheba is an example of such a vow (2 Sam 11:6–13) being kept at the cost of a righteous man's life. Another instance occurs when Saul lays an oath on his troops prior to a battle: "Cursed be anyone who eats food before it is evening and I have been avenged on my enemies." But Jonathan does not hear the vow and dips the staff of his spear in a honeycomb and eats a little honey. This breaking of the vow and its implicit curse become a major issue that almost leads to Jonathan's death (1 Sam 14:24–46). Vows of abstinence were not taken lightly in ancient Israel.

Thus, Jesus takes a demanding vow like those taken by his messianic predecessors. And, precisely because of its lack of connection to the earlier stories in Mark, it is a memorable vow whose importance is only made clear later in the story. Jesus keeps this vow at great cost both prior to his crucifixion and in his death by refusing the bystander who mockingly tries to give

---

13. Jesus also refuses the drink of *oksos* just before he dies (15:36). This may be an allusion to Ps 69:21 (69:22 LXX) where the offer of *oksos* is an abusive action. Jeremias, *Eucharistic Words of Jesus*, 212n5, calls attention to Jesus' steadfast keeping of this vow: "When Jesus refused the wine mingled with myrrh which was offered to him as a narcotic the reason could have been that he was bound by his declaration of intent to abstain."

14. Ibid., 207–18.

him sour wine. Jesus' abstinence from wine during the ordeal of his crucifixion and death is, therefore, a sign of his personal strength and courage, recalling the warriors of Israel. But the fulfillment of his vow of abstinence in the celebrative drinking of wine in the kingdom of God remains in the eschatological future.

The Performance of the Story

This story can be told quietly in a manner that creates the ritual of the meal. The most important implicit dimension of this story is the tone of love and commitment in Jesus' words to the disciples. The storyteller assumes that many in the audience had associations with sacred meals. For many in Mark's audiences, those memories were Passover feasts, but for everyone who has heard the whole gospel, those memories are the earlier feeding stories. The introduction of the story needs to evoke those memories. The storyteller can indicate the circle of those reclining around the table with a gesture that includes the audience. The introduction of the bread and the wine is told with the same gestures that were used in the two earlier feeding stories: taking, blessing, breaking, and giving. The command, "take it," while an imperative, is best spoken in the tone of passionate desire that what is offered should be received as a gift of love and self-sacrifice. The implicit allusion to Moses' sacrifice of the oxen at Sinai means that there is a stress on the word "*my* blood of the covenant" in the words of the interpretation of the meaning of the cup. The extension of the covenant in "my blood" to "many" can be embodied by a gesture of inclusion of everyone in the audience and beyond.

The background of the vow of abstinence invites us to give voice to the vow in the tone and spirit of the ancient tradition of taking vows prior to battle. It is quite likely that in the original performances of this story there was a gesture of victory that accompanied the phrase "drink it new in the kingdom of God." It is possible that this gesture was a raised hand, or two hands raised in victory. This gesture is connected with the martial dimensions of the messianic tradition and is the final moment before Jesus goes into nonviolent battle against the powers of this evil age.

The storyteller's gesture ends the story on a strong note. Jesus cannot appropriately be presented in this story as a stoic who went to his death passively in a spirit of resignation to his fate. The story invites us to present Jesus as one who goes into this conflict, this spiritual battle, as a strong man vowing to abstain from wine until the battle of the kingdom of God has been won and he can drink the new wine of victory.

This is the only section of the PRN that ends with Jesus' words and actions. The responses of various characters provide the endings for the rest of the sections. But this section ends with Jesus' vow that he makes in anticipation of triumphant victory. The end of the story needs to be told in that triumphant spirit. It is the spirit of the heroic stories of the ancient Near East reformed in the context of the recognition that everyone, friend and enemy, Israelite and Gentile, needs to be delivered from the powers of evil by the power of God embodied in Jesus and enacted in this feast of covenantal love.

3

THE NIGHT IN GETHSEMANE (14:26–52)

THIS SECTION, LIKE THE SECTIONS OF THE PLOT (PLOT/ANOINTing/betrayal) and the Passover meal (preparations / betrayal prophecy / bread and wine) has three stories: the twofold prophecy of the disciples' flight and Peter's denial (26–31), Gethsemane (32–42), and the arrest (43–52). The initial story of Jesus' prophecy of the disciples' flight and of Peter's denial sets the agenda for both this section of the story and the one to follow in 14:53–72, each of which ends with the fulfillment of Jesus' prophecy in this story. This section ends with the flight of the disciples and the naked young man (50–52); the next section ends with Peter's denials (66–72). The story is constructed to enable the listeners to recognize the structure of prophecy/fulfillment.

This section is also another instance of the "sandwich" structure present in the earlier section (14:1–12) where the story of the anointing was bracketed by the stories of the plot against Jesus. In the present section, the stories of Gethsemane and the arrest are bracketed by the motif of the disciples' flight (14:27, 50–52). The next section (14:53–72) has a similar structure that interlocks the two stories of the Sanhedrin trial and of Peter's denial.

The most important element in the narrative structure of these sections is the motif of Peter's denial that brackets both this section and the next. In the first of the three parts of the present section (14:26–31), Jesus' prophecy of the flight of all the disciples quickly develops into the passionate argument between Jesus and Peter concerning whether Peter will flee as well. This argument sets the stage for the story's development through both this section and the next, concluding with the denial by Peter.

This sort of structuring is also a mnemonic device that makes the stories easy to learn and remember for retelling. The frequency of this structure in Mark is one of the signs that the composer of this story sought to facilitate others' learning and telling it.

As in the earlier "sandwich" sections of the gospel as a whole (see also 3:20–35; 5:21–43; 6:7–30), its presence also raises the question of its impact. In both these sections Mark makes the responses of Jesus' disciples the climactic elements of the story. We shall see that the entire PRN also ends with the response of Jesus' followers, namely, the flight and silence of the women. What is Mark's purpose in making these responses (rather than the events of Jesus' passion that fulfill his earlier passion prophecies) the climax of these two sections as well as of the resurrection section that concludes the entire narrative?

The Prophecy of Running Away and Denial (14:26–31)●

As has been noted above, this first story in the section introduces the central elements of the plot for this and the following section of the PRN, which interweaves the story of Peter's denials with the Sanhedrin trial. The resolutions of the motifs introduced here in 14:26–31 are reported in the stories of the disciples' running away (14:50–52) and Peter's denial (14:66–72). The accurate discerning of the impact of this story is a key to the entire story of Jesus' passion.

Sound Map

14:26Καὶ ὑμνήσαντες ἐξῆλθον εἰς τὸ Ὄρος τῶν Ἐλαιῶν.
27Καὶ λέγει αὐτοῖς ὁ Ἰησοῦς ὅτι
    Πάντες σκανδαλισθήσεσθε, ὅτι γέγραπται,
    Πατάξω τὸν ποιμένα, καὶ τὰ πρόβατα διασκορπισθήσονται.
28ἀλλὰ μετὰ τὸ ἐγερθῆναί με **προάξω ὑμᾶς εἰς τὴν Γαλιλαίαν.**
29ὁ δὲ Πέτρος ἔφη αὐτῷ,
    Εἰ καὶ **πάντες σκανδαλισθήσονται,** ἀλλ' οὐκ ἐγώ.

30καὶ λέγει αὐτῷ ὁ Ἰησοῦς,
    Ἀμὴν λέγω σοι ὅτι
    σὺ σήμερον ταύτῃ τῇ νυκτὶ
    πρὶν ἢ δὶς ἀλέκτορα φωνῆσαι
    τρίς με ἀπαρνήσῃ.
31ὁ δὲ ἐκπερισσῶς ἐλάλει,
    Ἐὰν δέῃ με συναποθανεῖν σοι,
    οὐ μή σε **ἀπαρνήσομαι.**
ὡσαύτως δὲ καὶ πάντες ἔλεγον.

Translation

14:26 When they had sung the hymn, they went out to the Mount of Olives.
27 And Jesus says to them,
> "**You will all be offended and run away**;
> for it is written, 'I will strike the shepherd,
> and the sheep will be scattered.'
> 28 But after I have been raised, **I will go before you to Galilee**."

29 But Peter said to him, "Even if **they all are offended and run** away, not me!"

30 Jesus says to him, "Truly I tell you,
> you, this day, this very night,
> **before the cock crows twice,**
> **you will deny me three times!**"

31 But he said vehemently, "Even if I must die with you, **I will never deny you**."
And all of them said the same thing.

Notes on Details and Translation

14:27: "be offended and run away" / σκανδαλίσθήσεσθε

The Greek verb that introduces this story and is translated in the NRSV as "become deserters" literally means "to be offended, scandalized." It is one of the most difficult words to translate in the Gospel of Mark because no single word in English accurately conveys the meaning of the Greek. The noun related to this verb, σκάνδαλον, means "a stone of stumbling." It refers to the stones on which wearers of sandals stub their toe. The response to this experience is universal, namely, to be really ticked at the stone. "To be scandalized" at a stone of stumbling is to be radically offended. Paul uses this word with precisely this sense in 1 Cor 1:23: "We preach Christ crucified, a stumbling block (σκάνδαλον) to Judeans . . ." The association of this word with flight or desertion comes from the quotation here of Zech 13:7, which follows Jesus' prophecy: "the sheep will be scattered" (i.e., will run away). This prophecy is then that the disciples will be radically offended or angry at Jesus' arrest. But in the story of the arrest their offense is in response to Jesus' speech in which he accepts arrest as the fulfillment of Scripture (14:48–49). Thus, the disciples are offended at the fulfillment of Jesus' prophecy and his acceptance of arrest, not at those who are arresting him such as Judas.

The NRSV translation creates a verbal thread in English that is not present in Mark's Greek. In contrast to the frequent pattern of translating the same Greek word with different English words in order to avoid redundancy, here the NRSV uses the term "become deserters" (v. 27) and "deserted" (v. 50) to translate two different Greek verbs and to create a verbal thread in English that does not exist in the original Greek. In this prophecy story, the Greek verb σκανδαλίζω is translated in both occurrences (14:27, 29) as "become deserters." Then in the arrest story the Greek verb φεύγω, which means "to flee, run away," is also translated as "all of them deserted him."

While the translation "become deserters" verbally links Jesus' prophecy (14:27) and the fulfillment of Jesus' prophecy in the disciples' flight (14:50), and also renders the military connotations of flight during battle accurately, that translation doesn't connect at all with the internal response of being offended at Jesus' action which is the primary meaning of Jesus' word here. Furthermore, desertion usually refers to leaving a military unit secretly before the battle rather than during the battle. Earlier in Mark, the verb σκανδαλίζω has been used three times to describe (1) the seeds that take root in rocky ground and then die as a result of persecution (4:17); (2) the response of the people of Nazareth to Jesus (6:3); (3) the cause of doom for anyone who either leads "one of these little ones who believe in me" to be "scandalized" or are "scandalized" themselves by their hand, foot, or eye (literally, "if your hand causes you to be offended. . ."—9:42–47). The seeds that die are "scandalized" by the persecution they encounter; the Nazarenes are "scandalized" at Jesus' words in the synagogue; and the disciples are "scandalized" by the other exorcist who is casting out demons in Jesus' name but is not part of their group. The general meaning of the word in Mark is to be led into sin, to be repelled or take offense at Jesus by refusing to believe or by becoming apostate; in every context it is extremely negative. The translation here, " to be offended and run away," is then the best of several inadequate options, because it includes both the flight prophecied in the quotation from Zechariah ("will be scattered") and the cause specified in the verb σκανδαλισθήσονται. It is better than "become deserters" both because it is truer to the story and because its function is to describe the disciples' response in a manner that also connects with and describes the possible offense Mark's story will generate in the audience as they hear the story. But the description of the disciples' ultimate action of flight needs to be included along with the reason for the flight; hence the two words rather than one. There is no single adequate English word for the Greek word σκανδαλίζω here.

28: after I have been raised / μετὰ τὸ εγερθῆναι με

This phrase establishes an important verbal thread that links two parts of the larger story: Jesus' prophecy here that he will go before the disciples to Galilee after the resurrection, and the fulfillment of the prophecy in the announcement by the young man in the tomb (16:7).

30: Truly I say to you, you today, this night, before the cock crows twice, three times you will deny me / Ἀμὴν λέγω σοι ὅτι σὺ σήμερον ταύτῃ τῇ νυκτὶ πρὶν ἢ δὶς ἀλέκτορα φωνῆσαι τρίς με ἀπαρνήσῃ

The NRSV translates this prophecy as "Truly I tell you, this day, this very night, before the cock crows twice, you will deny me three times." This is an improvement over the RSV, which collapses two different time designations, "today" and "this night," into a single "this very night." But even the NRSV fails to translate the emphatic *you* with which Jesus begins his response to Peter. The NRSV accurately captures the fact that the Greek text has three words or phrases for naming the time of Peter's denial. Each successive one narrows down the interval between the present and the time that Peter will do whatever Jesus is about to say he is going to do. "Today" indicates that the denial will happen in the next twenty-four hours. "This night" foretells that the denial will happen in the next twelve hours. And "Before the cock crows" puts the denial at the hour just before dawn (BDAG, ἀλεκτοροφωνία) in five or six hours. In the telling of the story, the movement from a longer to a shorter time frame makes the denial more and more imminent. This makes a difference. Jesus begins by pointing the finger at Peter with an emphatic *you*, verbally jabbing the one who has just said he was going to be different from all the others. "Today" means without delay. There will barely be time between Peter's bragging and whatever action of Peter Jesus foresees. Then another more imminent time: "this night." This brings whatever Jesus has in mind a little closer. Finally, with the third time designation, Jesus predicts that Peter's denial will be soon. Whatever Peter is going to do, it will be almost immediate: "before the cock crows twice."

But we still don't know what Jesus is going to say Peter will do! What is it that Peter is going to do before the cock crows twice? This clause also needs to be better translated than is customary. All the translations we have consulted say in effect, "you will deny me three times." But this minimizes the suspense of Jesus' prophecy. The Greek word order is, "three times me you will deny." This leaves the verb that names Peter's action till the very end. The best we can do and still have good English is "three times you will deny me!" At least this word order delays the verb as long as possible.

The Night in Gethsemane (14:26–52)

Comments on the Meaning and Impact of the Story

The most striking dimension of this story is that this is the first time in the entire gospel story in which Jesus does not have the last and authoritative word. Never before has a direct negative response to a statement or prophecy of Jesus been reported. Earlier in the story, the authorities respond negatively among themselves (2:6; 3:6; 11:18) but never openly to Jesus. Peter rebukes Jesus after the first passion prophecy (8:32), but the storyteller only summarizes his words. Furthermore, no one other than Jesus has ever had the last word in a discussion with him. In the conflict stories, Jesus always has the last word (e.g., in the healing of the paralytic [2:6–11], in the healing of the man with a withered hand [3:2–5], in the Beelzebul controversy [3:22–30], in the conflict about the purity laws with the Pharisees [6:5–13], in the divorce controversy [10:2–9], in the authorities' attack on Jesus' authority in the Temple [11:27–33], and in the Sadducees' question about the resurrection [12:18–27]). Likewise in his discussions with the disciples, Jesus' concluding statements are always decisive (e.g., in the first passion prophecy and the rebuke of Peter [8:31–33], in the controversy about who is the greatest [9:33–37], about the other exorcist [9:38–41], with the children [10:13–16], about James and John's request to sit at the right and left [10:35–45), and at the anointing in Bethany [14:3–9]).

But in this story, Peter makes a qualification of Jesus' first prophecy that they will *all* be offended and run away ("not me!") and vehemently contradicts Jesus' prophecy that he will deny him three times ("Even if I must die with you, I will never deny you!"). Furthermore, the conclusion of the story is that all of the disciples agree with Peter. This story structure—statement by Jesus, counterstatement, statement by Jesus, contradiction—is unprecedented. Thus, this story presents an unresolved argument in which the statements of Peter receive the greatest emphasis. It raises the question, who will be right—Jesus or Peter?

The context of this prophetic argument is established by the connotations of the end of the Passover meal. This all takes place "after they had sung the hymn," probably the second part of the Hallel,[1] as the concluding act of the Passover meal. That meal has been the time of closest fellowship between Jesus and his disciples in the story. Also this new setting, the Mount of Olives, has been a familiar place in the earlier story as the setting for Jesus' instructions about the entry into Jerusalem (11:1ff.) and his long apocalyptic discourse (13:3ff.). In this context, the prophecy that the disciples will be offended at him and run away is a total surprise. The earlier prophecy of

---

1. Cf. Lagrange, *Evangile selon Saint Marc*, 382; Lohmeyer, *Evangelium des Markus*, 311.

Judas' betrayal was only a confirmation of what the audience had been told earlier. And this new prophecy concerns not "one of the twelve" but "all of you." Jesus' word, σκανδαλίζω, refers to emotionally charged repulsion or offense (see note above). The reason for their offense is not named. There is no precedent for such a prophecy. These men have been Jesus' faithful disciples; and while they have been puzzled, in awe, frightened, and troubled at him, they have stuck with him through everything.

It is important to recognize that the first words of Jesus, "All of you will be offended," and the implicit gesture of inclusion are signs that the storyteller addressed Jesus' words to the audience as in the apocalyptic discourse (Mark 13) and in the story of the Passover meal. That is, in the original performances of Mark, these words were not addressed to the disciples as a group on an imaginary stage but to the audience. And to be offended and walk away is a quite plausible description of an audience response. However, the prophecy is also surprising as a description of a possible audience response if the audience has been listening to the story for nearly two hours.

Jesus then explains this surprising prophecy. His explanation is a quotation, with minor alterations,[2] of Zechariah's prophecy that the scattering of the sheep will follow the smiting of the shepherd (Zech 13:7b). The specific reference in Zechariah is unclear to us, but Jesus remembers Zechariah's words as a prophecy about his own suffering and his disciples' response. In paraphrase, Jesus' words to his disciples might have sounded something like this: "The reason why I predict that all of you will be offended and run away is that Zechariah has prophesied that the striking of the shepherd will result in the scattering of the sheep."

One of Mark's minor alterations in his quotation of Zechariah is to change the word order so that the verb, "will be scattered" is the final and climactic word:

> LXX Zech 13:7b—Smite the shepherd and **scattered will be** the sheep.

---

2. I find persuasive Stendahl's argument that the LXX rather than the Hebrew is the basis for this quotation; see Stendahl, *School of St. Matthew*, 81ff. Stendahl includes a full listing of the various texts of Zech 13:7b. The only minor modification in Mark's quotation of the LXX translation of Zechariah is the use of the first person, "I will strike" (πατάξω) rather than the second-person plural imperative in LXX B, "strike" (πατάξετε) or the second-person-singular imperative in LXX A, again "strike" (πατάξον). The probability is that Mark is quoting LXX A because he uses the same verb for "scattered," διασκορπισθήσονται, rather than ἐκσπάσατε as in LXX B. The importance of this detail is that it indicates that Mark was quoting the Septuagint translation in Greek that was the Scriptures for audiences of Judeans in the Greek world of the Hellenistic cities. Another Markan connection with LXX A occurs in the story of the mocking: see Appendix 8.

Mark 14:27b—I will smite the shepherd and the sheep **will be scattered**.

This minor change creates an emphatic connection between the two verbs that conclude the two parts of Jesus' prophecy: "All of you **will be scandalized (offended and run away)** . . . the sheep **will be scattered**." Thus, the quotation of Zechariah's prophecy establishes this direct connection between being scandalized and running away.[3]

A promise of a postresurrection return to Galilee concludes the prophecy. The conjunction ἀλλὰ, often translated as "but," is usually used by Mark to signal major reversals. Here the reversal is from the disciples' "scattering" to the reunion in Galilee. In the gospel story as a whole, Galilee is most strongly associated with Jesus' early ministry where the disciples were called and the first decisive events took place (e.g., 1:14, 16, 28, 39; 3:7). The initial section of the Gospel of Mark, including the teaching discourse (4:1–34), is set in Galilee. But after this initial series of Galilean stories, the only additional reference to Galilee is the setting for the second passion prophecy and the conversation about who is the greatest—the latter taking place in Capernaum (9:30, 33). Thus, the dominant associations of Galilee in the story are with the early ministry. Galilee is where they started out together and where Jesus was enthusiastically accepted. In light of the opposition they have experienced in Jerusalem, Jesus' leading them back to Galilee will be going home. The implication of the prophecy of a return to Galilee is a promise that they will be reconciled after the disciples have run away.

Peter responds to the prophecy that they *all* will be "scandalized and run away" with a qualification: "Not me!" This episode has the same structure as the prophecy of betrayal (14:18–19): (1) a setting of Jesus and the disciples ("came with the twelve,"/ "when they had sung a hymn"); (2) a prophecy of Jesus ("one of you will betray me,"/ "all of you will be offended and run away"); (3) a response by the disciples ("Is it me?"/"Not me!").

In the betrayal prophecy, the disciples' response assumes that Jesus' prophecy is true and the only question is which one of them is the betrayer. Thus, Peter earlier granted the probability that the prophecy of betrayal

---

3. The question of the function of this quotation has been discussed extensively; e.g., see Lindars, *New Testament Apologetic*, 127–32; also Suhl, *Die Funktion der alttestamentlichen Zitate*, 62–65. For an early suggestion that the prophecy of denial was part of an anti-Petrine polemic, see Klein, "Verleugnung des Petrus," 285–328. Eta Linnemann's article, "Verleugnung," 1–32, is an extensive critical examination of Klein's hypothesis. Lindars argues that the quotation's purpose here is not polemical but apologetic and provides an explanation for the flight of the disciples. This interpretation is based on the presupposition that Mark's audience already knew that the disciples had run away and needed some help in dealing with their shock at that report.

would turn out to be true, and implicitly he was among those who seriously asked the question, "Is it me?" albeit unable to believe that it was![4] But in response to this new prophecy, while assuming the probability of the prophecy ("even if they all are offended and run away"[5]), he makes one exception—himself! In contrast to joining the disciples in their response to the betrayal prophecy, therefore, Peter offers a counterprophecy: "Even if they all are offended and run away, not me!"[6]

The credibility of Peter's response here builds on the dynamics of distance that have been created between the character of Peter and the audience. If Peter has been presented as a sympathetic character, the storyteller presented his words straight and the audience took his counterprophecy seriously and identified with him in his conflict with Jesus. If, on the other hand, Peter has been presented as a fool and a coward, the storyteller told his counterprophecy with a note of irony and cynicism and elicited a response of dismissal.[7]

A brief survey of the dynamics of distance in the characterization of Peter throughout Mark's gospel will enable us to answer this question. In the opening section of the gospel, Simon is a major character and is the first disciple to be named. The storyteller implies that Simon is important by calling Andrew "the brother of Simon." He is, with Andrew, the first to be called to follow Jesus, and his immediate acceptance of Jesus' call puts him in the same league as Elisha, who immediately answers Elijah's summons to follow him (1 Kgs 19:19–20). The story of his mother-in-law's sickness implies that Simon is married, and that he has welcomed his mother-in-law into his house, a not insignificant virtue. It also implies that he is leaving a family to follow Jesus. And the next morning, Simon is the leader among Jesus' disciples when they seek and find him praying (1:36ff.). From the beginning, Simon is the most fully developed character in the story other

---

4. The disciples' response to Jesus' betrayal prophecy begins with the word μήτι, which is used to introduce a rhetorical question that anticipates a negative answer. See μήτι in BDAG.

5. Cf. BDF, #371.

6. The conjunction ἀλλά at the beginning of the apodosis of a conditional sentence means, "yet, certainly, at least"; cf. BDAG, 38, #4. To paraphrase Peter's response, "Even if, as a I grant you, they all may run away, at least I will not."

7. A major theme in recent interpretation of Mark has been the reading of Peter's characterization as anti-Petrine polemic. The basic idea is that the negative dimensions of Peter's character were intended to alienate Mark's readers from Peter and the *theios aner* theology that he represents. In *The Oral and the Written Gospel*, Werner Kelber has expanded this polemic to include Peter as a representative of the oral gospel tradition that Mark is countering by his written gospel. The discussion here will focus on the characterization of Peter as it was experienced in performance.

than Jesus, and everything he does is good. The dynamics of distance are all positive.

In the story of the calling of the twelve (3:13ff), Simon is at the head of the list and is the only individual given what is often termed a surname, Peter (Πέτρος) which means "Rock." James and John are given a joint surname, Boanerges, "sons of thunder." By implication, the latter are the second tier of importance after Simon, while Andrew is only named after James and John. The connotations of the surname Peter, "Rock," are stability and strength.[8] However, the conventional term for this second name, *surname*, does not accurately convey the connotations of the giving of the name. A better term is *nickname*. There is a warmth of friendship associated with the nicknames that friends give each other. So for the purposes of this commentary, we will call the name Peter Jesus' nickname for Simon rather than Simon's surname.

The most important moment in the characterization of Simon Peter is the messianic confession (8:29ff.). The storyteller's use of the title χριστός in the opening sentence of the gospel (1:1), the structure of the story leading up to Peter's confession, and Jesus' response to that confession all imply that Peter has accurately perceived who Jesus is. Mark presents Peter's response to Jesus' question as a decisive right answer. It is the major turning point in the story and names a conclusion that the storyteller has been reinforcing since the beginning. As a result, Peter's rebuke of Jesus following the passion prophecy (8:31–32) is believable and sympathetic. There is no precedent for this sudden reversal of expectations in relation to the entire tradition of the messiahs of Israel. In fact, the dynamics of the story imply that Simon Peter is expressing what the audience is feeling, and that he is a spokesman for the listeners as well as the other disciples.

Jesus' rebuke of Peter as "Satan" is, then, the most emotionally charged conflict between Jesus and one of the disciples prior to this prophecy of scandalization and denial. That is, the story creates a high degree of sympathetic identification with Simon Peter, and the rebuke is experienced by listeners who have identified with Simon Peter as a rebuke of them. The discipleship discourse that follows this confrontation is addressed to the audience as Jesus' disciples, and this only heightens the dynamic of identification with Peter.

In the transfiguration narrative that follows Peter's confession, the sympathetic aspects of Peter's character are heightened further. Peter's response to the transfiguration and the appearance of Moses and Elijah is preeminently sympathetic. His words to Jesus offering to build three booths make for one of the most humorous moments in the whole story. Mark's

---

8. Cf. Cullmann, "Πετρος," in *TDNT*, 6:100ff.

explanation that Peter was afraid implies that his response was a bumbling, stammering kind of Everyman response. Furthermore, the storyteller's explanation to the audience of Peter's inner thoughts and feelings ("He didn't know what to say because he was afraid") is the first inside view of one of the disciples. The dynamics of distance here create a higher degree of sympathy and identification with Peter than with any character in the story other than Jesus.

Peter is once again the spokesman for the disciples in the discussion with Jesus following the rich young man's departure (10:23ff.). His statement that they have left everything to follow Jesus is true, and the listeners know the specific things that Peter has left: his mother-in-law and by implication his wife and his home in Capernaum (1:29-30). In the aftermath of the cleansing of the Temple, Peter remembers Jesus' curse of the now-withered fig tree in another inside view of Peter's mind. And Mark's listeners can confirm the accuracy of Peter's memory as he remembers Jesus' curse because they just heard the story. And finally, Peter is part of the inner group of four to whom Jesus addresses the apocalyptic discourse (13:3-37).

In summary, Peter is the most fully developed character in the entire story, other than Jesus. He is a sympathetic character throughout the story. His responses are always human and believable, and even when Jesus rebukes him, the audience can fully identify with him. There are two sympathetic inside views of his inner thoughts and emotions, and no other disciple is described with such intimacy. Peter's words are reported in direct discourse in four different stories (the Messianic confession [8:29], the transfiguration [9:5], the left-everything discourse [10:28], and the discussion about the fig tree [11:21]) and once in indirect discourse (the rebuke [8:32]). John is the only other single disciple whose words are quoted, in the story of the other exorcist (9:38). The other disciple speeches are either by a group (the prayer in the morning [1:36-37], the question about Elijah [9:11], and the question about the signs of the end [13:3]) or by James and John as a pair (the request to sit on Jesus' right and left [10:35-40]). By implication, Peter is involved in all these communal speeches except the request of James and John.

Thus, the two most extensive characterizations in Mark's story are Jesus and Peter. A comparison of the distance dynamics in both characterizations reveals that the characterization of Peter is more consistently sympathetic than the characterization of Jesus. The reason for that is relatively simple. Jesus is frequently alien because of his utterly puzzling actions and words such as calming the storm, walking on water, feeding five thousand and four thousand people, and his prophecies of death and resurrection. These are often the times when he is more like God than like human beings. Peter, on the other hand, is consistently human and, therefore, more consistently sympathetic. Even when he is wrong in Jesus' opinion, his response is fully understandable and reflects the natural response of the audience.

29: the credibility of Peter's counter-prophecy

As a result of the relationship that has been established between the character of Peter and the audience, therefore, Peter's words have credibility. In the context of what is known from the earlier parts of the story, Peter's prophecy is at least as credible as Jesus'. Why should Peter be offended now and run away? Furthermore, in the story of the supper, Peter was one of the disciples who asked, "Is it me?" in response to Jesus' prophecy that one of them will betray him. And every listener knows that he was right to introduce it with a Greek word that expresses disbelief that it could be. Therefore, both the previous dynamics of his characterization and the immediate context reinforce the believability of Peter's prophecy that he will not be offended and run away, even if the rest of the disciples do.

30: the prophecy of denial

Jesus' response is even more surprising. The prophecy of Peter's denial is the last of Jesus' "Amen" sayings. Jesus has reserved this solemn formula of introduction—"Truly I say to you . . ."—for his most solemn and important pronouncements such as the promise that the woman's anointing him will be told forever, the prophecy of betrayal, and his climactic vow of abstinence. This is the most specific of all the "Amen" sayings. And it is the only saying that begins with an emphatic personal pronoun: literally translated, "Truly I say to you, *you*, today, this night, before twice the cock crows . . ." The threefold description of the time becomes more specific and imminent: "today" (in the next twenty-four hours), "this night" (in the next six to eight hours), "before the cock crows twice" (before dawn).[9] The exact number of

---

9. The precise time reference of the phrase, "before the cock crows twice," is ambiguous. Mayo's hypothesis that it refers to the bugle call for the change of the guard (the gallicinium) is one possible explanation; see Mayo, "*Gallicinium*," 367ff. The changing of the Roman guard for the fourth watch was at 3:00 AM (first watch: 6–9 PM, second watch 9–12 PM, third watch 12–3 AM, fourth watch 3–6 AM). The clues in the story, however, indicate that Mark was thinking of the hour before dawn. The introduction to the Pilate trial places the meeting of the Sanhedrin to plan their strategy and their delivery of Jesus to Pilate as being "early" (πρωΐ) and "immediately," that is, right after Peter's denial and the Sanhedrin trial (15:1). The unqualified uses of "early" (πρωΐ) specify a time at or shortly after dawn (the trip back into Jerusalem [11:20] and the unknown hour of the lord's coming [13:35]). Pilate opened up for business at 6:00 AM. The trial is placed early in the morning, no later than 7:00 AM since the crucifixion happens at

denials is part of the prediction. And the final word of the prophecy, "deny," is the most surprising. This word has been used only once earlier in the story in Jesus' pronouncement about discipleship, following the rebuke of Peter (8:33–34): "If anyone would come after me, let them deny themselves and take up their cross and follow me." In that context, the meaning is "to deny, repudiate" yourself, and the consequence is to take up your own cross. In this prophecy, the total reversal of that command is predicted. Jesus predicts that Peter, instead of repudiating himself, will repudiate him and will not take up his cross and die with him.

31: Peter's second counterprophecy

Peter's response is a vehement and direct contradiction of the prophecy. The word describing Peter's manner, which is also a direction to future storytellers about how Peter's words are to be told, is an intensified adverbial form (ἐκπερισσῶς) that means something like "wildly, out of all proportion." Peter's response is an ultimate pledge of allegiance. The conditional clause in Peter's statement describes a general or universal situation: "Even if it is necessary for me to die with you . . ." Thus, he pledges that he will renounce himself totally. His vow that he will never deny Jesus is equally emphatic. The negative particles that Peter uses here (οὐ μή) have been used earlier only by Jesus, and five of those instances are in solemn "Amen" sayings (9:1, 41; 10:5; 13:30; 14:25; also in 13:2, 19—both prophecies of disaster). Thus, prior to this vow of Peter, Mark uses this form of emphatic negation only in Jesus' most solemn prophecies. Peter rejects Jesus' prophecy as emphatically as Jesus offers it.

The concluding summary reports that the disciples all agreed with Peter. Since the prophecy of denial concerned only Peter, their response also refers back to the prophecy of scandalization. The conclusion of the story is, therefore, a pledge of allegiance to the death by the disciples. This pledge is an expression of their unanimous rejection of Jesus' predictions about what they will do. The storyteller suggests nothing that would discredit their statements. And because of the unexpected character of Jesus' prophecies and the previous evidence throughout the earlier story of the disciples' and specifically Peter's loyalty, the prophecies of Peter are as credible as those of Jesus.

9:00 AM ("third hour"). Mark uses the particle "immediately" (εὐθὺς) to describe direct temporal contiguity (e.g., 14:43, 45). "Immediately" then indicates that Mark thinks of Peter's denial and the second crowing of the cock as occurring at a time near dawn, just before the Sanhedrin's strategy meeting. Therefore, Mark probably understood Jesus' prophecy as predicting a time near dawn and the cockcrow as referring to the crowing of roosters rather than the Roman trumpet signaling the changing of the guard.

This story is a battle of prophecies, not unlike the battles between Jeremiah and the false prophets (e.g., the battle between Jeremiah and Hananiah in Jeremiah 28). Every statement is a prediction about what is going to happen in the future. And Mark gives the last word to Peter's counterprophecies. The story presents Peter's prophetic pledges of loyalty positively. Peter's resistance to Jesus' prophecies creates a polarization because of the level of emotion that is present. Peter's vehemence is an appropriate response to the radicality of Jesus' prophecy. Thus, the context that is established for the two sections of the story that follow—the arrest and the Sanhedrin trial—is a sympathetic characterization of the disciples and particularly of Peter in their resistance to Jesus' prophecies that they will forsake and repudiate him.

The Performance of the Story

This story is to be told as a crescendo of volume and emotion. The first sentence, describing the hymn and the journey to the Mount of Olives, is quiet and addressed to the audience. Jesus' initial prophecy announcing what they *all* will do invites a sweeping gesture that first points to the imaginary place where the disciples stood, but then includes the audience. The prophecy of scandalization needs to be inclusive and to describe the possible responses of both the disciples and the audience. The words and the gesture include the audience in the prophecy and are given as a prediction of the audience response and of the disciples' response. The telling of Peter's response may include a move by the storyteller into Peter's space so that his words are addressed to the place where Jesus was standing. Neither Peter's response nor Jesus' response to him is addressed to the audience. Rather, the storyteller occupies Peter's physical space as Peter and addresses an imagined Jesus, and likewise Jesus' physical space as Jesus addresses an imagined Peter. The tone and volume of Peter's prophecy is louder than Jesus' words. Jesus' prediction of Peter's denial can be either louder and more forceful in turn, or deliberately quieter. Peter's response needs to be loud in volume, vehement in tone, and told with gestures of allegiance, probably with a fist shaken and then struck over the heart. The summary of the disciples' agreement is a bit softer than Peter's vow but equally intense. The storyteller addresses it to the audience without any note of irony or of implicit prediction of the disciples' failure to keep their vows of allegiance to the death. It is an indirect statement spoken in the same tone as Peter's pledge.

Prayer in Gethsemane (14:32–42)

The story of Jesus' struggle at Gethsemane is primarily composed of speeches by Jesus to his three closest disciples and to his Father. In fact, this story is the last in which Jesus is the main initiator of the action of the story. Hereafter he responds to the actions of others against him. The episode of Jesus' prayer is the most intimate and sympathetic moment in the entire characterization of Jesus. But it is surrounded by the story of Jesus' plea to his disciples to stay awake and his three discoveries of them sleeping. Mark's intention to make this a story of supreme intimacy with Jesus before the stories of his trials and execution is evident in his frequent use of the historical present tense.

Sound Map

14:32Καὶ ἔρχονται εἰς χωρίον οὗ τὸ ὄνομα Γεθσημανί,
    καὶ λέγει τοῖς μαθηταῖς αὐτοῦ,
    Καθίσατε **ὧδε** ἕως **προσεύξωμαι**.
33καὶ παραλαμβάνει τὸν Πέτρον καὶ τὸν Ἰάκωβον καὶ τὸν Ἰωάννην
                                    μετ' αὐτοῦ,
    καὶ ἤρξατο ἐκθαμβεῖσθαι καὶ ἀδημονεῖν.
34 **καὶ λέγει αὐτοῖς**,
    Περίλυπός ἐστιν ἡ ψυχή μου ἕως θανάτου.
μείνατε **ὧδε** καὶ **γρηγορεῖτε**.

35καὶ προελθὼν μικρὸν ἔπιπτεν ἐπὶ τῆς γῆς,
    καὶ **προσηύχετο** ἵνα εἰ **δυνατόν** ἐστιν **παρέλθῃ ἀπ' αὐτοῦ ἡ ὥρα**.
36καὶ ἔλεγεν,
    Αββα ὁ πατήρ, πάντα **δυνατά** σοι.
παρένεγκε τὸ ποτήριον τοῦτο **ἀπ' ἐμοῦ**.
ἀλλ' οὐ τί ἐγὼ θέλω
    ἀλλὰ τί σύ.

37καὶ ἔρχεται καὶ εὑρίσκει αὐτοὺς καθεύδοντας,
    καὶ λέγει τῷ Πέτρῳ,
    Σίμων, **καθεύδεις**;
οὐκ ἴσχυσας μίαν ὥραν **γρηγορῆσαι**;
38**γρηγορεῖτε** καὶ **προσεύχεσθε**, ἵνα μὴ ἔλθητε εἰς πειρασμόν.
τὸ μὲν πνεῦμα πρόθυμον
    ἡ δὲ σὰρξ ἀσθενής.

39καὶ **πάλιν ἀπελθὼν προσηύξατο** τὸν αὐτὸν λόγον εἰπών.

40καὶ πάλιν ἐλθὼν εὗρεν αὐτοὺς καθεύδοντας.
ἦσαν γὰρ αὐτῶν οἱ ὀφθαλμοὶ καταβαρυνόμενοι,
   καὶ οὐκ ᾔδεισαν τί ἀποκριθῶσιν αὐτῷ.

41καὶ ἔρχεται τὸ τρίτον καὶ λέγει αὐτοῖς,
   Καθεύδετε τὸ λοιπὸν καὶ ἀναπαύεσθε;
ἀπέχει.

ἦλθεν ἡ ὥρα.
ἰδοὺ παραδίδοται ὁ υἱὸς τοῦ ἀνθρώπου εἰς τὰς
   χεῖρας τῶν ἁμαρτωλῶν.

42ἐγείρεσθε ἄγωμεν.
ἰδοὺ ὁ **παραδιδούς** με ἤγγικεν.

Translation

32They come to a place called Gethsemane
   and he says to his disciples, "Sit **here** while I pray."
33And he takes with him Peter and James and John,
   and he began to be deeply distressed and troubled
     34**and he says to them**, "My soul is very sad, even to death.
Remain **here** and **stay awake**."

35And going a little farther, he threw himself on the ground
   and **he prayed** that, **if it were possible, the hour might pass from him.**
36And he said, "Abba, Father, **all things are possible** for you.
Take this cup **from me**.
But not what I want but what you want."

37And **he comes** and **finds them sleeping, and he says** to Peter,
   "Simon, **sleeping?**
Couldn't you **stay awake** one hour?
38**Stay awake and pray** that you may not come into the time of trial.
The spirit is willing but the flesh is weak."

39**And again he went away and prayed**, saying the same words.
40**And again he came and found them sleeping**.
Because their eyes were weighed down.
   And they didn't know what to say to him.

41 **And he comes** a third time **and says to them,**
"Still **sleeping** and taking your rest.
It is received.

The hour has come.
Look, **the Son of Man is betrayed into the hands of sinners.**

42 Get up, let's go.
Look, my betrayer is at hand."

Notes on Details and Translation

14:32–41: ερχονται/λέγει/παραλαμβάνει/ἔρχεται/εὑρίσκει

This story has the greatest concentration of the historical present tense in the PRN. The historical present is a present tense verb that describes events that have happened in the past. This is a distinctive feature of Mark's storytelling style. Its effect is to make the story more immediate and to create the sense of these events happening now. None of the usages of the historical present are translated with present tense verbs in the NRSV. While the use of present-tense verbs when mixed with past-tense verbs is a little strange, it is a more accurate representation of Mark's intention to make the story vividly present. Such a mixture is also common in the stories we tell to each other every day of the events of the day or things about which we have heard from others.

34: my soul is very sad / περίλυπός ἐστιν ἡ ψυχή μου

The NRSV has translated this phrase as "I am deeply grieved" rather than giving the RSV rendering, "My soul is . . ." The issue for performance is that the phrase "my soul" more accurately conveys the sense of the Greek in which Jesus is talking about his deepest self. The translation "I" does not communicate that distinctive depth of emotion. The more literal rendering, "my soul," is better.

36: All things are possible for you / πάντα δυνατά σοι

Jesus' address to God is a literal restatement of his response to the father of the demon-possessed boy (9:23) and to the disciples in the discussion following the encounter with the rich young man (10:27). In the story of the boy, Jesus' response to the father is, "All things are possible for him who believes" (πάντα δυνατὰ τῷ πιστύοντι—9:23). And his response to the disciples' question about who can be saved is, "for all things are possible for God" (πάντα γὰρ δυνατὰ παρὰ τῷ θεῷ—10:27). The best way to preserve the verbal thread is to preserve the word order and the phrase in each case. Therefore, the best translation here is, "All things are possible for you" rather than the NRSV "To you all things are possible." This verbal thread linking Jesus' prayer with his earlier word of encouragement to the father implies that Jesus is here remembering his own counsel.

41: it is received / ἀπέχει

This word is one of the most enigmatic words in Mark's gospel. In the most well-attested reading (Sinaiticus, A B C K L W X and many miniscules) the colon is only this unmodified and puzzling word. The enigma is reflected in the diverse textual tradition. One tradition of texts in the Western textual family (DWθφ13 565 1071 et al.) has a longer sentence: ἀπέχει τὸ τέλος. This tradition takes the verb as intransitive, with the resulting meaning: "far-off is the end." This variant's external attestation is, however, quite weak, and the additional words τὸ τέλος appear to have been added to clarify the enigmatic verb (against Taylor, *Mark*, 556–57, who accepts this reading). The most frequent basis for recent translations has been Jerome's Latin Vulgate translation, *sufficit*, with the meaning "it is enough" or simply "Enough!" (NRSV). This translation is, however, only supported by comparatively late evidence.[10]

The single verb is the most well-attested reading, but it is also the most difficult reading. The primary meaning of the active verb elsewhere in the New Testament and related literature is the commercial sense: "to receive in full."[11] Since the verb is, in this reading, impersonal,[12] the problem is the inference of the subject. When the story is heard, the immediate context is the disciples' sleeping: "it" = "sleeping and taking your rest." In this case the commercial meaning would be the ironic statement of what Jesus has received from the disciples: it, namely your sleeping, is received in full. This would take Jesus' word here as a final comment on the disciples' "gift" to him of sleeping in response to his plea that they watch with him. This theme is an echo of Jesus' first response to Peter:

> "Simon, sleeping? Couldn't you even stay awake one hour?"
> Σίμων, καθεύδεις; οὐκ ἴσχυσας μίαν ὥραν γρηγορῆσαι; (14:37)

10. See BDAG, #1.
11. Ibid.
12. BDF, #129.

"Still sleeping and taking your rest?"
Καθεύδετε τὸ λοιπὸν καὶ ἀναπαύεσθε; (14:41)

If this was the meaning heard by Mark's audiences, it was Jesus' final ironic comment on the disciples' sleeping in the same tone as his initial comment to Peter. The translation here—"It is received"—preserves the shortness of the single word better than the longer but clearer translation: "Your gift is received in full."

Comments on the Meaning and Impact of the Story

14:32: Gethsemane

The place is simply called Gethsemane, "an olive press"; it is, by implication, a specific place on the Mount of Olives. Once again, as in the stories of the anointing at Bethany, the Passover preparations, and the Last Supper, here Jesus begins with a command that indicates his authority as the teacher of his disciples: "Sit here while I pray." But in this case, his command establishes the distinctive theme of this story, his need for the support of the disciples while he prays.[13] Jesus has prayed twice earlier in the story—after the first day in Capernaum (1:35) and in the hills after feeding the five thousand (6:46)—but always alone. This time he specifically asks them to stay during the entire time of his prayer. He wants them to be with him.

33: taking with him Peter, James, and John / καὶ παραλαμβάνει τὸν Πέτρον καὶ τὸν Ἰάκωβον καὶ τὸν Ἰωάννην μετ' αὐτοῦ

The second dimension of the setting, "taking with him Peter, James, and John," draws together several verbal echoes from the earlier stories. The specific words of these verbal connections in English are as follows:

> But he . . . **takes along** the father and the mother of the child and those **with him** (5:40)
> And after six days Jesus **takes along Peter, James and John** (9:2)
> **And taking along** the twelve **he began to** say to them (10:32)
> **And taking along with him Peter and James and John he began to** be deeply troubled (14:33)

---

13. The temporal conjunction ἕως, usually translated "while," here denotes either the end of a period of time ("until I have finished praying") or a period contemporaneous with his praying ("as long as I am praying"); cf. BDAG, 1, a, b and 2, b. The force of the word here is more related to contemporaneous period, "as long as."

The Night in Gethsemane (14:26–52)

Apart from these four cola, with their extended resonance with the sound of 14:33, the key word in this verbal thread, "to take along" (παραλαμβάνω), occurs in only two other places in the gospel narrative: the disciples taking Jesus along (παραλαμβάνουσιν) in the boat (4:36); the traditions of the Pharisees, "which they take along (παρέλαβον) to observe" (7:4). This setting draws together the major associations of two motifs in the earlier stories. The first is the one exhibited above, of Jesus' taking along his close companions for significant events, and his uniquely close relationship to Peter, James, and John at such times.

Jesus' distress

The depth of Jesus' emotional state is evoked by the phrase "he began to . . ." (ἤρξατο and an infinitive), which connects "he began to be deeply distressed" here with the third passion prophecy, with its attendant intense emotion: "he began to tell them what was to happen to him" (ἤρξατο αὐτοῖς λέγειν τὰ μέλλοντα αὐτῷ συμβαίνειν—10:32) and "he began to be deeply distressed and troubled" (ἤρξατο ἐκθαμβεῖσθαι καὶ ἀδημονεῖν—14:33). The impact of this verbal thread is to set fulfillment of the passion prophecies in the context of Jesus' close companionship with these three disciples.

35–36: the inside view of Jesus' prayer

Having set the scene first with all the disciples and then with the inner circle, the storyteller now describes what happened. He begins with the first inside view of Jesus' feelings in the PRN. For the first time in the gospel, with the possible exception of Jesus' grief at their hardness of heart in response to the man with the withered hand (3:5), this inside view gives the listeners an experience of Jesus in deep distress.[14] The earlier inside views of Jesus' feelings are as follows:

- the leper—"And feeling compassion . . ." (1:42)
- the man with the withered hand—"And looking on them with anger and being grieved at their hardness of heart . . ." (3:5)

---

14. The Greek verb here, ἐκθαμβεῖσθαι, "to be distressed, troubled," is an emotionally intense word as is indicated by the intensive particle ἐκ, which also occurs in the adverb describing Peter's intense emotion in response to Jesus' prophecy that he will deny him: ἐκπερισσῶς. This verb has been used earlier in the gospel only once, where it describes the crowd's reaction to seeing Jesus just after the transfiguration (9:5). Its other subsequent use in Mark names the women's response to seeing the young man in the tomb (16:5, 6).

- the rejection at Nazareth—"And he was amazed at their unbelief" (6:6)
- the first feeding—"he felt compassion for them . . ." (6:34)
- the second feeding—"I have compassion for the crowd . . ." (8:2)
- the children—"But seeing this, Jesus was angry and said to them . . ." (10:14)
- the rich young man—"But Jesus, looking at him, loved him . . ." (10:21)

As you can see, the most frequent insight into Jesus' feelings is that he felt compassion (σπλαγνίζω). In each prior instance, the feelings are in response to someone else. These earlier insights into Jesus' feelings are the background for the present notice of his internal emotions. Both words—"distressed" (ἐκθαμβέω) and "troubled" (ἀδημονέω)—describe deep anguish. Never before in the story has Jesus been so troubled.

Jesus names his distress by paraphrasing a refrain from the Psalms: ἵνα τί περίλυπος εἶ, ψυχή; "Why are you grieved, Soul?" (LXX 41:6, 12; 42:5; RSV[MT] "Why are you cast down, O my soul?" 42:5, 11; 43:5). Jesus' words are, "My soul is deeply grieved, even to death" (περίλυπός ἐστιν ἡ ψυχή μου ἕως θανάτου). The reflexive question in the Psalms assumes that there is no basis for such distress, and an imperative follows: "Hope in God; for I will praise him. My salvation is my God" (LXX). But Jesus takes up the wording of the psalm not as a question but as a statement. The implication of Jesus' statement is that there is every reason for him to be depressed. Furthermore, the degree of this depression is total: "even to death" (ἕως θανάτου). That phrase also comes to his mind from the tradition. It is used more than once to describe situations of the most extreme distress (Jonah 4:9; Sir 34:12; 51:6). In the gospel, Jesus' statement is an unprecedented expression of anguish.

34: command and plea to the disciples

Jesus follows his sharing of his grief with Peter, James, and John with a new command. It is parallel to his earlier instruction to all the disciples: "Sit here" (14:32), "Stay here" (14:35) but is much more emotionally intense. To his instruction to stay close to him he adds, "Stay awake!" That command echoes Jesus' repeated exhortation in his earlier talk with Peter, James, John, and also Andrew on the Mount of Olives.[15] "Stay awake" (γρηγορεῖτε) was the last word of his speech then (13:34, 35, 37). There he was warning them

15. The major sonic connections between the apocalyptic discourse and the Gethsemane story are (1) "to pray"—13:18, 33 and 14:32; (2) the inner group, Peter James and John—13:3 and 14:33; (3) "to watch, stay awake"—13:34, 35, 37 and 14:34.

to be vigilant and on watch. The primary meaning here is more literally to stay awake, but it also has the earlier meaning of being on watch.[16] This connection to the apocalyptic discourse also implies that this night is a time of eschatological conflict between the forces of good and evil.

Thus, the first unresolved conflict between Jesus and the disciples in the conversation on the way out to the Mount of Olives is followed by a major shift in the audience's relationship to Jesus. Jesus' distress is described both by the storyteller and by Jesus himself. This is the most sympathetic moment in the characterization of Jesus to this point in the story. It is also a moment of deep companionship between Jesus and his disciples.

35–36: the prayer

Jesus' prayer is his third prayer in the overall story, the previous prayers being in a deserted place after the first day in Capernaum (1:35) and on the mountain after the feeding of the five thousand (6:46). This is the first time that the details of how he prayed and what he said are told. The fact that he threw himself on the ground is a sign of extreme spiritual distress; similarly, when the newborn baby of "Uriah's wife" and David is sick, David "fasted and went in and lay all night on the ground." (2 Sam 12:16).

Jesus' prayer has two parts: a statement reported in indirect discourse and a statement reported in direct discourse. A factor in the emotional impact of the prayer is the cumulative force of the parallelism between the two parts of the prayer:

> if it were **possible**   the hour might pass **from** him
> all things are **possible** to you   take this cup **from** me
>   But not what I want but what you want.

The prayer as reported in indirect discourse is a request for deliverance from "the hour" that is qualified by a simple condition, "if it is possible" (εἰ δυνατόν ἐστιν). The direct quotation of Jesus' words is parallel to the storyteller's indirect quotation, and substitutes "this cup" for "the hour," and "all things are possible" for "if it is possible."

The phrase "the hour" recalls Jesus' descriptions of the climactic hour of eschatological conflict in the apocalyptic discourse: "Say whatever is given to you in that hour" (13:11), and "But about that day or hour no one knows"

---

16. The only other uses of the verb "to stay awake, watch" (γρηγορέω) in Mark's composition occur in the apocalyptic discourse. The frequency of the verb's usage in that recent speech means that the audience could easily make the connection between these two episodes in the story.

(13:32). The use of the phrase "This cup" as a synonym for "the hour" recalls his offering of "the cup" as his blood at the Passover meal (14:24).

Jesus' prayer repeats his own earlier statements. The most memorable is Jesus' dialogue with the father of the demon-posssessed boy:

> The father: If it is possible, (ἀλλ' εἴ τι δύνῃ) have pity on us and help us.
> Jesus: If it is possible? (Τὸ εἰ δύνῃ) All things are possible (πάντα δυνατά) for him who believes. (9:22–23)

In Jesus' prayer, the sequence is, "if it were possible," in the storyteller's indirect quote, followed by the direct quotation of Jesus' words: "All things are possible!" This is an echo of the father's plea and Jesus' response. Here in Gethsamane it sounds as though Jesus is remembering his words to the father. Confident that all things are possible, Jesus pleads that he not have to drink this cup of his blood poured out for "the many." Jesus' affirmation—"all things are possible to you"—also recalls his assurance to the disciples about the possibility of salvation because all things are possible with God (10:27).

The logic of the prayer is unmistakable. Since the condition of possibility has been met, the implication at this moment is that both requests will be answered and that Jesus will not have to die. The hope is again raised for a moment that Jesus may be able to escape this imminent suffering. All the allusions to his earlier teaching (and, in particular, his word to the father of the boy that is immediately confirmed in the exorcism of the demon) mean that it is really possible for him not to suffer and die. But in the final words of his prayer, he expresses his readiness to accept the fact that this possibility may not become the reality. The two cola of the period are in antithetical parallelism ("not what I . . . but what you"), with an ellipsis of the implied verb (θέλεις) in the second half: literally translated, "But not what I want, but what you." It is a total reversal of Jesus' twice-reiterated prayer that he be freed from the path of suffering he himself prophesied. Nevertheless, it does raise the question that is not fully answered, even for Jesus: what does God want?

The effect of the prayer is to draw the listeners into a relationship of deepest sympathy with Jesus' request that his suffering and death might be avoided. The movement from indirect to direct discourse makes the second part of the prayer more immediate. As a result, the human and, therefore, sympathetic dimensions of Jesus' characterization are highest at this moment when he repeats his own teaching in his prayer and asks for the removal of the cup. Because of the highly sympathetic character of Jesus' passionate plea for deliverance, Jesus' expression of willingness to submit to the possibility that God wills him to drink the cup is painful. The implication of the prayer is that the events to follow are the will of God and are *not* the will of Jesus. Even though he has foretold all this to his disciples, in the end he has not chosen this course but has chosen only to subject his will to the will of his Father.

37–41: the disciples' sleeping

The discovery of the disciples' sleeping is in the historic present tense: "And he comes and finds them sleeping, and he says to Peter . . ." The use of the historic present makes the sense of Jesus' discovery more immediate. This also continues the inside view of the telling of the story from Jesus' perspective in the previous episode. This description of the action from Jesus' point of view is repeated in each of the episodes in which Jesus discovers the disciples' sleeping. Jesus' point of view becomes, therefore, the dominant perspective for the entire Gethsemane story. This combination of factors makes this story the most down-to-earth, fully human episode in the whole gospel. This in turn is a rhetorical appeal for the closest level of sympathetic distance in relation to Jesus.

The storyteller's use of Peter, the nickname Jesus gave Simon (3:16), recalls the camaraderie associated with a nickname. The selecting out of Peter from the others for special attention also brings to mind the prophetic dispute between Jesus and Peter on the way to the Mount of Olives—the conflict between Peter's vow to be the exception to Jesus' prophecy of the disciples' offense and flight, and Jesus' prophecy that Peter would, not just once but three times, deny him. Jesus' prophecy about Peter forms the background for Jesus' disappointment and grief at finding Peter asleep. This is the only time in Mark's entire story that Jesus addresses Peter by name. When this disciple is first introduced into the gospel, the storyteller calls him Simon. But ever since 3:16 when Mark told the listeners that Jesus gave Simon the nickname Peter, the storyteller himself calls him Peter. But here, the only time Jesus addresses him by name, Jesus calls him Simon, his formal, old name (1:16, 29, 30, 36; 3:16). The contrast between the warmth of the nickname and the formality of the given name is made starkly present by Jesus' use of the formal name immediately following the storyteller's use of the nickname.[17]

---

17. The Gospel of John develops this dynamic of the contrast between the two names of Simon Peter in the postresurrection story of the breakfast at the sea and Jesus' threefold cross-examination of Peter; each instance of examination is introduced by the formal name, "Simon, son of John" after the storyteller's introduction to the story, "Jesus said to Simon Peter. . ."(21.15).

Jesus' two questions of Simon Peter are rhetorical questions that require an affirmative answer.[18] Both questions address Jesus' plea that the three disciples stay awake. But the second, "Couldn't you even stay awake one hour?" is a reference to Peter's pledge to die with Jesus. It is also a more distant reference to his repeated command to the four disciples (Peter, James, John, and Andrew), at the end of his long talk with them about the coming of the kingdom of God, to stay awake (13:35–36). Whether the storyteller presented Jesus' tone here as mocking or sad is ambiguous. The level of conflict in the prophetic argument and Peter's vehement promise that immediately precedes this episode would tip the balance toward mockery. But, if it is implied that Jesus knows what is going to happen. as the prophecies imply, Mark may have presented Jesus' words in a tone of resignation and grief. However, the fact that Jesus' next words are a command to wake up, pray and resist the weakness of the flesh suggests strong words about staying the course rather than resignation.

Jesus' new instruction after his mockery of Simon's failure to stay awake is now directed at all three disciples; the Greek verbal endings change from singular to plural. His command is verbally connected to the first part of his own prayer (literally translated):

> he prayed **in order that**, if it is possible, there might pass from him the hour (προσηύχετο ἵνα εἰ δυνατόν ἐστιν παρέλθῃ ἀπ' αὐτοῦ ἡ ὥρα—14:35)

> pray **in order that** you might not come into the time of trial (προσεύχεσθε ἵνα μὴ ἔλθητε εἰς πειρασμόν—14:38)

Both prayers are purpose (ἵνα) clauses in Greek, "in order to," "so that." Just as Jesus prayed that the hour might pass him by, so also he tells Peter to pray that he may not have his own time of trial and testing. Jesus is essentially telling Peter to pray the same prayer he is praying for himself. The implication is that Jesus knows what is coming for Peter as well as for himself. The earlier uses of the verb "to test, tempt" (πειράζω) all occur in situations of conflict for Jesus (when he is tested by Satan—1:13; when the Pharisees test him after the feeding of the four thousand and on the issue of divorce—8:11 and 10:2; when the Pharisees and Herodians test him about paying taxes to Caesar—12:15).

---

18. The grammatical dimension of these rhetorical questions is that when the negative particle οὐ is used in an interrogative sentence, an affirmative answer is expected; cf. BDF, #427. Thus, Jesus' question, "Could you not stay awake one hour?" expects an affirmative answer.

Since Jesus' words are spoken in the context of his own agonizing watch and anticipation of what lies ahead, they express his anger and grief at the failure of his closest friends to share his time of trial. The fact that they go to sleep and thereby directly disregard Jesus' impassioned plea contrasts with their immediate obedience to his commands throughout the earlier story, most recently in the preparations for the Passover. The implicit shared expectation of the storyteller and the audience is that the disciples would watch with Jesus, especially in this time of his deepest distress. Their sleeping is both a surprise and a disappointment. Jesus' response is totally justified and appropriate.

There is an additional dimension of the impact of Jesus' plea to stay awake. The grammatical move from the singular to the plural (καθεύδεις; οὐκ ἴσχυσας, singular; γρηγορεῖτε καὶ προσεύχεσθε, plural) may be a verbal sign of a move from addressing the imagined Peter to addressing the audience. A major challenge for the audiences of long stories is to stay awake. If Mark has been telling the story for an hour and a half or so prior to the start of the PRN, one dimension of the impact of Jesus' emphatic exhortations to "stay awake"—first just prior to the beginning of the passion story (in the apocalyptic discourse) and now in the Gethsemane story just before the climactic events of Jesus' suffering and death—is to appeal for the audience to stay awake for the rest of the story. Jesus' appeal to the disciples has, therefore, an immediate experiential meaning for the audience. It is an implicit appeal to each member of the audience to be a faithful disciple and to stay awake with him in his time of testing.

This existential dimension of Jesus' exhortation to stay awake for the audience is made even more explicit by the concluding reason he gives for their prayer: "the spirit is willing, but the flesh is weak." In his article on the verb "to tempt, test" (πεῖρα), H. Seesemann observes that in most instances watchfulness is advised because of the imminence of the last events (e.g., "Stay awake, for you do not know when the time will come"—13:33; also 13:35). The reason Jesus gives here for staying awake is the weakness and susceptibility of the flesh,[19] in contrast to the spirit of determination with which Peter and all the disciples vowed to die with Jesus rather than be offended and run away or deny him. This advice is an existential description of the problem that faces Peter, James, and John and the listeners, namely, the power of the needs of the body—in this case, for sleep.

The next sequence of Jesus' prayer and the disciples' sleeping is reported in a single episode by summary repetitions: "And again he went away and prayed, saying the same words. And again he came and found them

---

19. Seesemann, "πεῖρα," in *TDNT*, 6:31ff.

sleeping" (14:39-40). There will be yet a third such sequence in the episode that follows. The impact of threefold repetitions in biblical storytelling is to build intensity (cf. Jesus' threefold question to Peter—John 21:15-17). This second repetition intensifies the dynamics of the earlier episodes.

40b: the inside view of the disciples

The summary of Jesus' prayer and of his finding the disciples sleeping is followed by an aside to the audience. The assumption of every audience aside by the storyteller explaining something that has just happened is that the audience is surprised or puzzled. In this case, the surprise is that the disciples were sleeping again. Every sleepy listener can understand the storyteller's explanation and sympathize with the disciples: "their eyes were weighed down." A force beyond the control of the disciples' spirit has put them to sleep, namely, the wine of the Passover feast.

A second aside describes their internal response to being discovered asleep for the second time. The storyteller names this internal response with words that echo his aside explaining Peter's bumbling question about building booths for Jesus and Moses and Elijah in the transfiguration story:

Because he didn't know what to say (οὐ γὰρ ᾔδει τί ἀποκριθῇ—9:6)

And they didn't know what to say to him (καὶ οὐκ ᾔδεισαν τί ἀποκριθῶσιν αὐτῷ—14:40)

In the transfiguration story, the storyteller's inside view of Peter's befuddlement gives the reason for the embarrassment and inferiority communicated in the storyteller's report of Peter's dumb statement to Jesus: "Rabbi, it is really good for us to be here; do you want us to make three booths, one for you, one for Moses, and one for Elijah?" (9:5). In the transfiguration story, Peter's words may even be funny. Here in Gethsemane, the disciples' not knowing what to say reflects their implicit embarrassment and sense of futility. The storyteller shows Jesus and the three looking at each other—all of them speechless. But the tone of the storyteller's explanation conveys the shame the disciples were feeling.

The storyteller's twofold inside view of the three disciples is the longest inside view of the disciples since the transfiguration. In this context, it makes complete alienation from the disciples impossible, not because what they have done is right, but because the narrator describes their sense of futility and implicitly reports their shame. A dimension of the audience's sympathy for the disciples may have been that they too were struggling with staying awake while listening to this long story. If so, their sleepiness is associated with the disciples' futility and shame. As one who steadily struggles with falling asleep during speeches and sermons and dinners after good food and wine, I too have experienced a minor version of the shame of both the disciples and Mark's audiences at inappropriate sleep.

41–42: the last words between Jesus and his disciples

Jesus' last words to the disciples in the entire gospel begin with a climactic, third repetition of his discovery of them sleeping. The episode is introduced by verbs in the historical present: "And he comes the third time and says to them . . ." Attention is drawn to this use of the historical present here by the contrast with the past-tense verbs in the previous episode. The impact of this grammatical form is to make Jesus' third discovery more immediately present for the listeners. Jesus' words—"Still sleeping and taking your rest,"[20]—are a more intense reiteration of his earlier question to Peter, "Simon, sleeping?" It is an expression of Jesus' disappointment at their ongoing response to his recurring plea for them to stay awake and watch with him.

Jesus' final comment on their response is the enigmatic one word, ἀπέχει, which can be translated here, "It (your sleeping) is received" (see note above). It is Jesus' last ironic expression of his disappointment at the disciples' sleeping. This single word in Greek is the climax of the motif of the disciples' sleeping. This threefold repetition builds a crescendo of sympathy for Jesus. The Gethsemane story as a whole creates the highest degree of sympathetic identification with Jesus to this point in the story. The disciples' failure to stay awake is also told in an intimate manner. While their failure to stay awake is clearly wrong, the storyteller describes their sleeping in a manner that every listener can fully understand. This is rhetoric of implication.

Jesus' statements at the end of the Gethsemane story primarily describe what is happening. The statement "the hour has come" refers back to the storyteller's description of Jesus' prayer: "he prayed that, if it were possible, the hour might pass from him" (14:33). In the context of Jesus' prayer, the implication of the hour's coming is that God's will is being done, and that God's will is not Jesus' will.

Both of Jesus' statements regarding the betrayal are introduced by the particle ἰδού, literally translated as "behold," and translated here as "Look."

---

20. The NRSV translates this as an interrogative sentence—"Still sleeping and taking your rest?"—like Jesus' question to Peter: "Simon, sleeping?" There is, however, no indication in the Greek of an interrogative sense here, as the punctuation of the Nestle/Aland and UBS texts rightly signal. It is a simple declarative statement that describes Jesus' ongoing discovery of his friends sleeping.

The first description of the betrayal is a virtually literal repetition of the second passion prophecy:

The Son of man will be **handed over into the hands** of men
ὁ υἱὸς τοῦ ἀνθρώπου παραδίδοται εἰς τὰς χεῖρας ἀνθρώπων—9:31

Look, **handed over is the Son of man into the hands** of sinners
ἰδοὺ παραδίδοται ὁ υἱὸς τοῦ ἀνθρώπου εἰς τὰς χεῖρας τῶν ἁμαρτωλῶν—14:41

Between these two statements only the word order, the implied tense of the verb, and the final word differ. The verb in both instances is the identical present-tense form, by which the future sense is implied in the prophecy. The ἰδοὺ and the repetition of the prophecy call the listeners' attention to the imminent fulfillment of Jesus' prophecies. Mark is saying, in effect, pay attention; the fulfillment of Jesus' prophecies is about to happen. Furthermore, the announcement of Judas' arrival refers back to Jesus' more specific prophecy that one of the twelve will hand him over (14:18ff.). Jesus' words, therefore, set the stage for the arrest by calling attention to the fulfillment of his prophecies that is at hand.

The immediate prelude to the arrest is Jesus' announcement to the three disciples of what is about to happen. The Gethsemane story has drawn the listener closer to Jesus than at any previous point in the gospel. His agony, his prayer to God, the failure of his closest friends, the inside views of his feelings and thoughts—all combine to make Jesus supremely sympathetic here. His speech is the climax. Without a hint of self-pity or anger, he announces what is about to happen and goes forward to meet it. The major effect of the entire Gethsemane story, therefore, is the heightening of the intensity of the sympathetic and profoundly human aspects of Jesus' characterization. The insight into the disciples' shame maintains some of their credibility. But the primary perspective here is the perspective of Jesus. With the exception of the inside view of the disciples' eyes being weighed down and their not knowing what to say to him, everything is described from Jesus' point of view. Neither his requests to God nor those to his friends are met. There is one exception that is indicated by the fulfillment of his prophecy. His prayer that his Father's will, not his, be done is being fulfilled.

The Performance of the Story

The overall tone of this story is somber and quiet, and the tempo is slow. Each of the episodes is highly emotional. As always in biblical stories (cf.

Jesus' examination of Peter in John 21), the threefold repetition is an indication of increasing emotional intensity. However, in this story there is actually a five-step crescendo: the plea to watch in the time of distress, the prayer, and the threefold discovery of the disciples' sleeping. Only the second discovery of the disciples' sleeping has no words of Jesus, but the crescendo continues to build there as well. The story is composed as a series of episodes, each of which has a crescendo within itself, but each episode is also another step up in intensity. This story is the most extended crescendo of intensity in the whole gospel.

The first episode (Jesus' two requests to the disciples [14:32–34]) begins with the quiet of Gethsemane and Jesus' command to "Sit here." This episode has a tone of friendship and camaraderie in a time of deep anguish. Jesus' second request to the three is more passionate than the first. A gesture of audience inclusion is probably called for, with Jesus' requests both to the group and to the three. The gesture of inclusion with Peter, James, and John establishes the motif of Jesus' addresses to the audience as the three disciples.

In both this first episode and in the prayer, the same thoughts and feelings of Jesus are presented first in indirect discourse (vv. 33b, 35b) and then as direct discourse (vv. 34a, 36). The indirect discourse is the storyteller's description of Jesus' thoughts and feelings. These indirect descriptions have the tone and emotional tenor of the words but are stated from a more objective, detached position, as descriptions of what Jesus is experiencing. The words in direct discourse are then a presentation of Jesus' words in which the storyteller embodies Jesus. This combination creates a crescendo of both volume and emotion.

I have found it difficult to dramatize Jesus' prayer (35a) of falling on the ground. It is possible to kneel, and it is possible that Mark the storyteller knelt. The other possibility is to point to Jesus' position on the ground for the indirect description of his prayer and to stand with hands folded for the actual prayer, "Abba, Father . . ."

The prayer (vv. 35b–36) is highly intense, with first the storyteller's inside view of Jesus' distress and then with Jesus' own words. Again it is a crescendo of emotion that reaches its climax in his plea that "this cup" be taken away. The words of Jesus here are an expression of the deepest anguish. The ancient storyteller would have told this in a highly passionate manner. The indications we have from ancient performance are that their manner was often what we would call bombastic.[21] Jesus was presented as a strong man who faced his hour of pain with great strength and courage.

---

21. Cf. Shiner, *Proclaiming the Gospel*, 88–89.

After a pause, the final words of acceptance of God's will are quieter but, if anything, more intense. It is possible for the modern storyteller to overdo this, but the temptation is to say Jesus' words in a dispassionate manner because of the tradition of Jesus' divinity. It may be helpful to remember your own experiences of distress and depression as a point of connection with Jesus' prayer. This is the most human moment in the characterization of Jesus, when Jesus as a man prays to God for deliverance from the suffering that is ahead.

The first discovery of the disciples' sleeping (37–38) can be told in several different ways, and it is best to try them all in order to discern what has the deepest resonance and authenticity.[22] Jesus' discovery and his first word to Peter, "Sleeping?" may be spoken as an expression of sadness, surprise, anger, cynicism, or disappointment, or you may find some combination. The precedents to this story are Jesus' words of frustration about the disciples' inability to understand the significance of the loaves (8:14–21), and the series of conflicts with the disciples (passion prophecy [8:31–33], who is the greatest [9:33ff], children [10:13–16], anointing [14:3ff]), and the prophecy conflict on the way to Gethsemane [14:27ff]). This story is the climax of all those interactions. Jesus' instruction to Peter to stay awake and pray is both a command and a plea. For teachers and parents, it may be helpful to connect with your own experiences of frustration and disappointment with your students or children.

The second discovery of the disciples' sleeping (14:40) is a series of descriptions of the internal feelings and responses of Jesus and the disciples. The challenge here is to render the full range of emotions in the way that you report their experience. Most important is to make fully sympathetic the disciples' inability to stay awake and their finding no words to explain it. There is no intimation of judgment of their failure here but only an explanation, with which every listener can identify, of their inability to resist sleeping.

The third time that Jesus comes back (14:41) needs to be marked with climactic emphasis as the culmination of the first and second return. Once again, the tone of Jesus' words is complex. Resignation, disappointment, grief, cynicism, abandonment—all are present here. If you decide to follow the traditional translation, "Enough!" the tone is having come to the end of patience; if you use the translation, "It is received," the tone is grief

---

22. See Swanson, *Provoking the Gospel of Mark*, for a process of exploration of how the various episodes of the story can be played by student actors who are invited to perform the story as a drama. While I doubt that this was the manner in which Mark's Gospel was originally told, it has been very effective as a pedagogical approach. The testing of (shall we say) what plays is often revealing about authentic meaning.

The Night in Gethsemane (14:26–52)

and disappointment. There is a marked change in tempo and attitude with the hour, the anticipation of betrayal, and the arrival of the betrayer. Jesus' instructions to the disciples are to be spoken as the orders of a commander to his troops before battle.

Once again the only way to find an appropriate tone for this entire story is to try out these possibilities. However, in all these instances, my suggestion would be that you search for a way of telling this story that has the deepest connection with the performances of the first century and with your audiences, whoever they may be. This means there is wide latitude for different performances, as I am certain that Mark was aware that people would tell his story in different ways. But ancient people also revered their sacred stories and sought to preserve the exact ways the stories were told.[23] This may appear to be a contradiction, but it is better understood as a dialectical tension between two poles. Then and now the commitment to pay attention to the original character of the gospel is the best protection against the distortion and misinterpretation of the story that has plagued its history. In this story, it is a distortion to drain Jesus of the grief and distress that both the storyteller and he explicitly name (14:33–34) and to make Jesus' passion dispassionate. Of course, the unavoidable problem is that the identity of the audiences has changed so radically in different periods of history. That is why a nuanced and deeply informed storytelling sensibility can make it possible for the story to be retold in different ways for the ever-new audiences of the contemporary context in a manner faithful to and consistent with the tradition initiated by the original performances of the story in the first century.

A significant resource for discovering an authentic way of telling this story is the composition of place that was discovered by Ignatius of Loyola, the founder of the Jesuits, in the cave at Manresa in Spain.[24] In this story, you would imagine yourself in the garden of Gethsemane and would compose the place in all its sensory specificity: the sights, sounds, tastes, touches, and smells of that night in the garden overlooking Jerusalem. The story invites the storyteller to express, both Jesus' distress as he prays, and the disciples' shame at their sleeping. The prayer of this story is an opportunity to contemplate what may be involved for you in following God's purpose

---

23. The four major manuscripts of the gospel storytelling tradition are a clear indication that the stories of Jesus in the first century were still in a fluid state and were retold in different ways. The four best versions of that extensive storytelling tradition have come down to us.

24. See http://www.ewtn.com/library/MARY/IGNAITU2.HTM for an excellent narrative of the life of Ignatius and the context of his transformative experience in the eleven months of prayer and contemplation in a cave at Manresa.

for your life. It is also an opportunity to explore your own willingness to stay awake with Jesus. The practice of lighting candles and praying with Jesus for a significant part of the night on the Thursday night of Holy Week is a long-established tradition of entering into the experience of this night. The prayer may help make it possible to tell the story with a greater sense of having been present in Gethsemane.

The Arrest in Gethsemane (14:43–52)

The arrest is the third and climactic story of the night on the Mount of Olives, which is the third major section of the PRN. The PRN has been building to this climax since Jesus' prophecy of the disciples' offense and running away, which followed immediately after the story of the last Passover meal. The arrest of Jesus is the successful culmination of the conspiracy of the chief priests, scribes, and elders. It is also the beginning of the detailed fulfillment of the passion prophecies, most explicitly the third passion prophecy. The third prophecy is the only one in which Jesus sees himself as being "handed over" to the chief priests and the scribes, and the only one that details the events leading to his death: condemned to death, delivered to the Gentiles, mocked, spat upon, and scourged (10:33–34). However, the climax of the story of Jesus' arrest and the flight of the disciples is the fulfillment of Jesus' prophecy that the disciples will be offended and will run away. This story is, therefore, composed of an intensive web of connections with earlier stories in the gospel.

Sound Map

14:43Καὶ **εὐθὺς** ἔτι αὐτοῦ λαλοῦντος παραγίνεται Ἰούδας **εἷς τῶν δώδεκα**
 καὶ μετ' αὐτοῦ ὄχλος **μετὰ μαχαιρῶν καὶ ξύλων**
  παρὰ τῶν ἀρχιερέων
  καὶ τῶν γραμματέων
  καὶ τῶν πρεσβυτέρων.
44δεδώκει δὲ ὁ **παραδιδοὺς** αὐτὸν σύσσημον αὐτοῖς λέγων,
 Ὃν ἂν **φιλήσω αὐτός** ἐστιν.
κρατήσατε αὐτὸν καὶ ἀπάγετε ἀσφαλῶς.

45καὶ ἐλθὼν **εὐθὺς** προσελθὼν αὐτῷ λέγει, Ῥαββί,
 καὶ **κατεφίλησεν αὐτόν**.
46οἱ δὲ ἐπέβαλον τὰς χεῖρας αὐτῷ
 καὶ **ἐκράτησαν αὐτόν**.
47εἷς δέ [τις] τῶν παρεστηκότων σπασάμενος τὴν **μάχαιραν**

The Night in Gethsemane (14:26–52)

ἔπαισεν τὸν δοῦλον τοῦ ἀρχιερέως καὶ ἀφεῖλεν αὐτοῦ τὸ ὠτάριον.

48καὶ ἀποκριθεὶς ὁ Ἰησοῦς εἶπεν αὐτοῖς,
    Ὡς ἐπὶ λῃστὴν ἐξήλθατε **μετὰ μαχαιρῶν καὶ ξύλων** συλλαβεῖν με;
49καθ' ἡμέραν ἤμην πρὸς ὑμᾶς ἐν τῷ ἱερῷ διδάσκων καὶ οὐκ **ἐκρατήσατέ** με.
ἀλλ' ἵνα πληρωθῶσιν αἱ γραφαί.

50καὶ ἀφέντες αὐτὸν **ἔφυγον** πάντες.
51καὶ νεανίσκος τις συνηκολούθει αὐτῷ περιβεβλημένος **σινδόνα** ἐπὶ **γυμνοῦ**,
    καὶ κρατοῦσιν αὐτόν.
52ὁ δὲ καταλιπὼν τὴν **σινδόνα γυμνὸς ἔφυγεν.**

Translation

43And **immediately**, while he was still speaking,
    that **Judas, one of the twelve**, arrives
    and with him a crowd **with swords and clubs**
    from the chief priests, the scribes, and the elders.
44Now **the betrayer** had given them a sign, saying,
    "**The one I kiss** is the man.
Arrest him and lead him away under guard."

45And he came and immediately went up to him and says, "Rabbi,"
    and **he kissed him.**
46And they laid hands on him **and arrested him.**
47But one of those who stood by drew **his sword**
    and struck the slave of the high priest and cut off his ear.

48And Jesus answered and said to them,
    "Have you come out **with swords and clubs**
    as if I were an insurrectionist to capture me?
49Day after day I was with you in the Temple teaching,
    and you did not **arrest** me.
But let the Scriptures be fulfilled."

50And forsaking him **they** all **fled.**
51And a certain young man was following him,
    clothed in **a linen cloth** over his **nakedness**
    and they arrest him.
52But leaving the **linen cloth, he fled naked.**

Notes on Details and Translation

14:43: that Judas, one of the twelve / Ἰούδας εἷς τῶν δώδεκα

A fascinating detail of the textual tradition is that Mark may have also included a masculine article before Judas' name. The two most important Markan manuscripts, codex Vaticanus and codex Alexandrinus, have the article ὁ prior to the name Judas, to read: ὁ Ἰούδας εἷς τῶν δώδεκα. Because of the article's redundancy, it is more likely that later scribes would have left out the article than that they would have added it. If this article was in the original performances, its oral impact would have been as an anaphoric article that refers back to the earlier descriptions. The translation here accepts the article and renders its force: "that Judas, one of the twelve."

48: an insurrectionist / λῃστὴς

Different translations translate this word variously as "robber," "thief," "brigand," "bandit," "outlaw." Jesus uses this word here in his question to the crowd about the swords and clubs they have brought to capture him, a nonviolent rabbi. This term is also used later in the PRN for those who were crucified with Jesus (15:27). The only prior occurrence of this term in Mark is in Jesus' quotation of Jer 7:11 in his speech at the Temple cleansing: "Is it not written, 'My house shall be called a house of prayer for all the nations'? But you have made it a den of robbers" (Mark 11:17—NRSV). Since in the LXX text of Jeremiah the word λῃστῶν is a translation of the Hebrew word *pharzim*, the meaning of the Greek word in the Septuagint is certainly "robbers."[25]

The question is what this term would have meant to Mark and his audiences, who lived in the immediate aftermath of the Judean–Roman War. Josephus uses this term extensively to refer to the various groups that composed the revolutionary army. Josephus' usage establishes that this term was used to describe the coalition that provoked and carried out the revolt in the same general period when Mark was writing and telling his gospel. Translations like "robber," "thief," and "bandit" accurately describe these revolutionary groups insofar as they stole from rich Judeans who supported the Roman government in order to fund their revolution. But for modern audiences, this term only means that they were criminals, not warriors for an independent Judean state. In our context in the early twenty-first century, many would call them assassins, terrorists, rebels, or insurrectionists. Since the war was such an important event in Mark's context, the probability

---

25. BDB, 829.

The Night in Gethsemane (14:26–52) 135

is both that he used the term to refer to the coalition and that his audiences heard the word as a reference to them. As the commentary will make clear, that meaning is fully congruent with the meaning and impact of Mark's story in its post-70 context. The term will, therefore, will be translated here as "insurrectionist."

50: forsaking him / ἀφέντες αὐτὸν

This participial phrase, "to leave, forsake him," is the introduction to the disciples' flight. The NRSV translates this with the same word, "to desert," that the translators used in the prophecy (14:27, 29) for a different Greek word: σκανδαλίζω. Since the guiding purpose of this translation is to render the verbal threads of the Greek into English, a correlative principle will be to avoid the creation of verbal threads in English that are not present in Greek. Therefore, even though "deserted" is a fully appropriate rendering, the word "forsake" is adopted here in order to make it clear in English that the word here at the arrest is a different word in Greek from the one Mark used in the earlier prophecy to describe this response by the disciples. "Forsake" is also synonymous with "to be offended and run away," the translation of σκανδαλίζω in 14:27, 29. It also implies that the disciples leave him because they find offensive the way he accepts arrest as a fulfillment of the Scriptures.

50–52: fled / φεύγω

This word is used twice to describe the flight of first the disciples and then the naked young man. The Greek word can be variously translated "to flee" or "to run away." The NRSV chooses to vary the translation: "All of them deserted him and *fled*" (14:50), and "he left the linen cloth and *ran away* naked" (14:52). It is important to preserve the verbal thread present in the Greek text. So it is translated "flee" both times. The repetition of the sound in narrating the action of the young man underscores and intensifies the response of all the disciples. The general response is now made vivid in a brief account about one of them. The young man's response dramatizes in a vivid and unforgettable way that they were so put off by Jesus' choice not to fight that one of them even fled in a condition that was deeply shameful. The repetition of the verb has a sonic impact that accompanies the visual impact of the description. The first sounding of the verb is like the first beat of a drum. The second sounding of it is like striking the drum again, but with more force. That second strike expresses the climactic function of the episode as a vivid portrayal of the flight of one man in a state of the most graphic shame.

44, 46, 51. seize / κρατέω

The thematic word that runs through this story of the arrest is the verb, "to seize, arrest" (κρατέω). It is a complex verbal thread that ties this story together, sounded in the first, second, and fourth episodes of the story (14:44, 46, 51). The NRSV translates the first two occurrences as "arrested." But for the third occurrence, in the episode of the young man, the NRSV translators change the translation to "caught hold of." The preservation of the verbal thread is important, and the third instance is translated here in the historical present tense, which contributes to the vividness of the episode.

The NRSV's change of translation for the third occurrence of the verb coordinates with the way it sets off the episode of the young man as a separate paragraph, reflecting the decision of the editors of the UBS Greek text. This paragraphing is a long-standing editorial tradition. The separate paragraph (and in the UBS Greek text a separate heading, "The Young Man Who Fled") is an indication that the editors have concluded that the story of the young man is a separate story that was added to an earlier pre-Markan passion narrative. But while the story of the young man only occurs in Mark, he clearly told this story as the climax to the arrest, not as a little appendage after the arrest story. This then is the second verbal thread that ties the episode of the young man to the episodes that precede it. The first is the word "fled" at the climax of the story. The second is the attempt to "arrest" the young man along with Jesus that provokes his flight. In the formatting of the text here, the story of the flight of the disciples and the young man is set off as a new episode, but it is the climactic episode in a series of four, not a disconnected new paragraph. The editorial arrangement of the Greek and English text should reflect the intentions of the final composer rather than conclusions about the history of the tradition.

Comments on the Meaning and Impact of the Story

14:43: connections to earlier stories

The first episode in this story establishes the setting for Jesus to be handed over to the powers of this age, as he has been predicting since the first passion prophecy to Peter and the disciples (8:31). The initial words, "And immediately while he was still speaking . . . ," connect this story to the events in Gethsemane and, specifically, to Jesus' speech to the disciples. Mark used

The Night in Gethsemane (14:26–52) 137

a similar clause earlier in 5:35 to connect the ongoing story of the raising of Jairus' daughter to the end of the story of the woman who touched his garment: "While he was still speaking, they came from the synagogue elder's house" ("Ἔτι αὐτοῦ λαλοῦντος ἔρχονται ἀπὸ τοῦ ἀρχισυναγώγου . . ."). Here the connection is between the stories of Gethsemane and the arrest. These initial words are also signs that there is a sudden increase in tempo here, in music an *accelerando*.

Characterization of Judas

The description of Judas picks up the verbal thread that was sounded in the stories of Judas' betraying Jesus to the chief priests and the prophecy of betrayal:

> Judas Iscariot, the one of the twelve (Ἰούδας Ἰσκαριὼθ ὁ εἷς τῶν δώδεκα—14:10)
>
> One of you will betray me (εἷς ἐξ ὑμῶν παραδώσει με—14:18)
>
> One of the twelve (Εἷς τῶν δώδεκα—14:20)
>
> that Judas, one of the twelve (ὁ Ἰούδας εἷς τῶν δώδεκα—14:43)

The introductory article and repetition of the appositive, "that Judas, one of the twelve," makes the fulfillment of Jesus' prophecy at the supper even more unmistakable. The emotional force and tone of this repetition of Judas' name and identity as a disciple expresses the offense and horror associated with the prospect of betrayal by one of those closest to Jesus. While the tone of Jesus' voice in the betrayal prophecy may have been grief, the dominant tone of the narrator here is offense. The historic present tense announces Judas' arrival in the most immediate manner: "that Judas, one of the twelve, arrives . . ."

The crowd from the chief priests, scribes, and elders

When the crowd is introduced, it is identified as being "with" Judas, armed with swords and clubs, and from the chief priests, scribes, and elders. This description distinguishes this crowd from "the crowd" that has been Jesus' primary source of support and survival against the plot of the chief priests and scribes in the earlier stories of Jesus' contests in the Temple (i.e., 11:18, 32; 12:12, 38; also "the people" in 14:2). The word order is literally "and with him a crowd . . ." This is then Judas' crowd. They are identified as Jesus' enemy because they have come from the chief priests, the scribes, and the elders. This threefold group of the Jerusalem authorities has been named earlier only in the first passion prophecy (8:31) and in the story of their questioning Jesus' authority to cleanse the Temple (11:27). In the PRN, the group seeking to arrest and kill Jesus has been the chief priests and the scribes (14:1). The addition of "the elders" and "the crowd" to the conspiracy to destroy Jesus implies that the group has now widened. This crowd is armed with swords and clubs, the first reference to weapons since the execution of John the Baptist (6:27, where a weapon of execution is implied).

Once again the two motifs of the plot merge. The conspiracy of the authorities is being successfully implemented. Judas has given them a way to arrest Jesus in the middle of the night without any danger of a riot by the people. And the prophecies of Jesus that one of the twelve would betray him (14:18, 20) and that he would be betrayed into the hands of men (9:31) are being fulfilled.

44: Judas' plan

The storyteller's aside to the audience, "Now the betrayer had given them a sign," gives the listeners a flashback with the inside information of the plan on which the conspirators had agreed.[26] It also heightens the alienating characterization of this group and its leader. Mark's description of Judas as "the one who betrayed him" (ὁ παραδιδοὺς αὐτὸν) picks up still another verbal thread associated with him (3:19; 14:42) earlier in the story. Judas' choice of a sign of affection as his way of marking the group's prey is a cynical symbol of his betrayal of his relationship with Jesus. The basic meaning of the word Judas uses here (φιλήσω) is "to like, love" and would be literally translated as "The one I will love is the man." It is traditionally translated "kiss," because that is the meaning implied by Judas' act of greeting Jesus (14:45). It is quite possible that Mark's listeners would have caught this additional level of irony.

Judas' command to the crowd to arrest Jesus links this story with the leitmotif of the authorities' evolving conspiracy to arrest and kill Jesus:

> **And the chief priests and the scribes** heard it and **were seeking how** they could destroy **him**; for they feared him, because **the** whole **crowd** was spellbound by his teaching.

---

26. The verb here δεδώκει, translated as "given," is an unusual Attic form of the pluperfect active tense from which the augment has been dropped (cf. MHT, 2:190). Since this tense in Greek describes the continuance of a completed action in the past, its usage here (14:44) reinforces that this is a narrative comment that interrupts the action in Gethsemane and flashes back to a description of the earlier plans of the enemy.

Καὶ ἤκουσαν οἱ **ἀρχιερεῖς** καὶ οἱ **γραμματεῖς** καὶ **ἐζήτουν πῶς αὐτὸν ἀπολέσωσιν. ἐφοβοῦντο** γὰρ αὐτόν, πᾶς γὰρ ὁ **ὄχλος** ἐξεπλήσσετο ἐπὶ τῇ διδαχῇ αὐτοῦ. (11:18)

And they **were seeking how to arrest him** but **they also feared the crowd**, because they knew that he had told the parable to them.

Καὶ **ἐζήτουν αὐτὸν κρατῆσαι**, καὶ **ἐφοβήθησαν τὸν ὄχλον** ἔγνωσαν γὰρ ὅτι πρὸς αὐτοὺς τὴν παραβολὴν εἶπεν. (12:12)

The chief priests and the scribes were seeking how to arrest him by a conspiracy and kill him.

καὶ **ἐζήτουν οἱ ἀρχιερεῖς καὶ οἱ γραμματεῖς πῶς αὐτὸν** ἐν δόλῳ **κρατήσαντες** ἀποκτείνωσιν (14:1)

Arrest him and lead him away under guard.

κρατήσατε αὐτὸν καὶ ἀπάγετε ἀσφαλῶς. (14:44)

The final word of his instruction, ἀσφαλῶς, translated here with the NRSV as "under guard," is an adverb that literally means "securely." Judas wants to make sure Jesus doesn't get away. Mark, by his words and probably by his tone and attitude in reporting Judas' words, makes it unmistakably clear that Judas acted out of a high degree of hostility and enmity toward his rabbi. Judas' instructions to the crowd have the same tone as a military commander might in giving orders to his troops.

46: the seizing of Jesus

Mark describes the actual arrest as the carrying out of the plan Judas had laid out for the crowd. Several elements of the description heighten the antagonistic and alienating crescendo of sound that builds up to Judas' climactic kiss. The repetition of Mark's favorite particle, "immediately" (εὐθύς), picks up the sequence of action interrupted by his flashback to Judas' plan, and once again establishes the rapid tempo. Judas' approach to Jesus is described in stages that are the storytelling equivalent of a scene in an action movie: καὶ ἐλθὼν εὐθὺς προσελθὼν αὐτῷ (literally translated, "and coming immediately going up to him." [14:45]). The participles that surround εὐθύς are patently redundant. (Matthew and Luke both have only one verb here.) But the effect is to convey the violence of Judas' action in carrying out his plan. Mark also uses the historical present (λέγει) to introduce Judas' calling

Jesus "Rabbi." Peter uses this title in the stories of the transfiguration (9:5) and the wilted fig tree (11:21) as a term of respect and affection. Judas' calling Jesus by this title heightens the intensity of his despicable action. The climax of Judas' action is the kiss. The verb κατεφιλέω means the act of kissing in either greeting or farewell and is virtually always used in an affectionate context. Thus, Judas couples a sign of affection with a title of respect in order to identify Jesus for arrest and execution. It is his climactic action of treachery and betrayal. If Mark's postwar audiences connected him with the Sicarii, Judas' action here is consistent with the treachery of the Sicarii, who would approach someone in apparent friendship and then stab them when they got close. Judas acts as one of the Sicarii.

The actual arrest, "they laid hands on him" (οἱ δὲ ἐπέβαλον τὰς χεῖρας αὐτῷ), fulfills another earlier prophecy. Jesus has twice foretold that he will be delivered into the hands, first, of men (9:31), and most recently, of sinners (14:41). The reiteration of this verbal thread, *hands* (χεῖρας), makes the fulfillment of the prophecy unmistakable. Jesus' earlier characterization of the arresting ones as sinners also emphasizes the moral status of their action. The evil plot of Jesus' enemies begins to bear fruit at this point in the story. And the implicit appeal to the audience is to respond with a corresponding level of antagonism. In the classic plot structure of escalating conflict between the forces of good and evil, this is the time for a shootout and the destruction of the evil ones.

47: struck the slave of the high priest

This coming to fruition of the conspiracy against Jesus establishes the context for the striking of the slave of the high priest. The precise identity of the striker is left ambiguous. The grammatical construction implies a contrast between "a certain one" and the rest of the group, in this case, of those standing by (εἷς δέ τις τῶν παρεστηκότων). The only groups standing by are the crowd and the disciples. The storyteller implies, therefore, that the fighter is one of the disciples. With the exception of "sword" elsewhere in this story to describe the crowd (14:43, 48), the words of this period are new words in the gospel. This total absence of verbal threads connecting it with earlier elements in the story is striking, because the previous episodes of the story have been full of connections with the preceding stories. This attack is, therefore, in the plot and in its language, a complete surprise.

The underlying question here is how Mark told this story: What was the tone and attitude of the storyteller? Did he describe this attack as a good thing with a raised fist and an implicit call to fight, or simply as an objective fact, or even perhaps with a tone of critique? Clues are built into the story. First, this is a long sentence. Sentence length is an indication of tempo: long sentences are usually spoken more rapidly, short sentences more slowly. The description of the attack is the climax of this episode of the story, and either maintains or even increases the tempo and intensity of the immediately preceding statements that are introduced by εὐθὺς, "immediately." In recent earlier stories, the long periods at the end of those stories have been climactic, authoritative statements by Jesus: the praise of the woman at the end of the anointing at Bethany (14:9) and the vow of abstinence at the end of the Passover meal (14:25). The precedents for this long period, which forms the climax of the arrest episode, indicate that it was probably told in a rapid tempo and with high emotion.

The probability is then that this attack was told positively as a response of righteous anger against Judas and his gang. Finally, someone fights back in Jesus' defense. In the context of the antagonism of Judas and the authorities against Jesus, Mark's description of this attack invites a response of joy and hope that others will join in the fight and set Jesus free. The identification with and respect for Jesus has reached its highest point in this three-story section of the narrative that is titled here the Night in Gethsemane (14:26–52). Given the level of hostility that has been generated by the story against Jesus' enemies, the implicit invitation in the story (and therefore in the manner of its performance) was for everyone in Mark's audience to cheer at these words, at least inwardly, but quite possibly in actuality. The story invites a response of complete sympathy with the attack and a hope for more. This would then be what Whitney Shiner calls "an applause line."[27]

48: Jesus' answer

Jesus' response to the crowd with Judas is introduced as the next step in the escalation of the conflict. He responds in words rather than action. The introduction to his words is a formula, literally translated, "and answering Jesus said to them" (καὶ ἀποκριθεὶς ὁ Ἰησοῦς εἶπεν αὐτοῖς—14:48). This formula is rarely given literally in modern translations (NRSV "Then Jesus said to them"; KJV, "And Jesus answered and said to them"). Mark often uses this formula to introduce responses to a situation of tension but with no adversarial implication (e.g., Peter's response at the transfiguration—9:5; Jesus' response to the disciples' shock—10:24; Jesus' response to the fig tree—11:14; also 12:35). Furthermore, the conjunction at the beginning of

---

27. For an illuminating discussion of applause lines in Mark, see Shiner, *Proclaiming the Gospel*, 153–70.

Jesus' response is the connecting καὶ rather than the frequently adversative conjunctions δὲ or ἀλλὰ (as in Luke 22:51). That is, no adversative introduction to the striking of the high priest's servant is implied. In other words, Mark did not say, "*But* Jesus answering said to them . . ." The introduction implies instead that Jesus' words will be in continuity with the striking of the slave of the high priest. If anything, Jesus' actual words are a reversal of the expectation raised by the introductory καὶ.

The early parts of Jesus' speech refer back to the first episode of the arrest (14:32 "with swords and clubs") and to the earlier conflicts in the Temple. The listening audience can easily recognize the sonic connections of this story with the Temple stories:

> "And as he was walking in the Temple, they . . . came to him
> καὶ ἐν τῷ ἱερῷ περιπατοῦντος αὐτοῦ ἔρχονται πρὸς αὐτὸν (11:27)

> And answering, Jesus said teaching in the Temple
> Καὶ ἀποκριθεὶς ὁ Ἰησοῦς ἔλεγεν διδάσκων ἐν τῷ ἱερῷ (12:35)

> Day after day I was with you in the Temple teaching
> καθ' ἡμέραν ἤμην πρὸς ὑμᾶς ἐν τῷ ἱερῷ διδάσκων (14:49)

Furthermore, the only previous use of the term "bandit, insurrectionist, Zealot" (λῃστής) is in Jesus' speech during the cleansing of the Temple (11:17). As has been explained in the note above, this word is best translated "insurrectionist," "revolutionary," or "insurgent" rather than "bandit," "robber," or "thief," in order to convey its dominant meaning for Mark's audiences in the aftermath of the Judean–Roman War. The verbal context of the speech, therefore, is Jesus' earlier conflicts with the religious authorities.

The major conflict with the Temple authorities was Jesus' cleansing of the Temple. Mark's telling of the story connects that event with the Judean–Roman War by the climax of Jesus' prophetic protest. Jesus' speech in the Temple is as follows:

> "Is it not written, 'My house shall be called a house of prayer for all the nations?'" But you have made it a den of robbers."
> (NRSV)

> Οὐ γέγραπται ὅτι ʽΟ οἶκός μου οἶκος προσευχῆς κληθήσεται πᾶσιν τοῖς ἔθνεσιν. ὑμεῖς δὲ πεποιήκατε αὐτὸν σπήλαιον λῃστῶν. (11:17)

Jesus' speech echoes statements by both Isaiah (56:7—LXX) and Jeremiah (7:11—LXX):

The Night in Gethsemane (14:26–52) 143

"Is it not written, 'My house will be called a house of prayer among all the nations?' But you have made it a den of robbers (insurrectionists)"—NRSV with one modification in parentheses.

Οὐ γέγραπται ὅτι ʽΟ οἶκός μου οἶκος προσευχῆς κληθήσεται πᾶσιν τοῖς ἔθνεσιν; ὑμεῖς δὲ πεποιήκατε αὐτὸν σπήλαιον λῃστῶν. (11:17)

The Septuagint translation of Isaiah is,

ὁ γὰρ οἶκός μου οἶκος προσευχῆς κληθήσεται πᾶσιν τοῖς ἔθνεσιν.

For my house will be called a house of prayer among all the nations. (Isa 56:7)

The Septuagint translation of Jeremiah is,

μὴ σπήλαιον λῃστῶν ὁ οἶκός μου οὗ ἐπικέκληται τὸ ὄνομά μου ἐπ'αὐτῷ ἐκεῖ, ἐνώπιον ὑμῶν;

mimicking the wording and order of the Greek text and literally translated as, "Is it not a den of thieves, my house where my name is called upon by him there, before you?" (Jer 7:11)

As you can see, the first period of Jesus' statement is an exact quotation of Isaiah. Jesus also echoes Jeremiah. The first three and the last two words of Jesus' quotation are an exact quotation of five of the first six words as well as of key phrases in the Septuagint translation of Jeremiah's prophecy. In the next period of Jeremiah's speech, he prophesies in the name of the Lord: "I will do to the house that is called by my name, in which you trust, and to the place that I gave to you and to your ancestors, just what I did to Shiloh" (Jer 7:14, NRSV). Shiloh, eighteen miles north of Jerusalem, had been the central place of worship in the time of Samuel (around 1050 BCE; see e.g., 1 Sam 4–6) and was destroyed (probably in the mid-eleventh century in the aftermath of the Philistine victory described in 1 Sam 4:10).[28] Jeremiah was arrested in the immediate aftermath of his prophecy of the Temple's destruction (sometime in the period 610–600 BCE) and initially condemned to death by the priests and false prophets (Jer 26:8, 11). As a result, this quotation of Jeremiah and Isaiah in Jesus' speech resonates with events centuries before. Jeremiah was arrested and condemned as deserving the sentence of death because he prophesied against the city and the Temple. And the Babylonians destroyed both the city and the Temple. By his allusion to Jeremiah, Jesus' also prophesies the Temple's destruction. And, most significant, his use of Jeremiah's phrase "a den of robbers/rebels" (σπήλαιον

---

28. See Halpern, "Shiloh," in *ABD*, 5:1214.

λῃστῶν, Mark 11:17) would have been heard by Mark's listeners as an exact description of what happened in the Temple in the summer of 70 CE. In the last stages of the war, the armies of the insurrection were besieged in the Temple for months, and the Temple, with the support of some of the priestly establishment, became a fortress of λῃστάς (in Mark's time "insurrectionists" or "insurgents"). And once again in 70 CE, as in the time of Jeremiah, the prophecy from a prophet of Israel was fulfilled, and the Temple was destroyed.

Jesus' allusion to their coming to arrest him as an insurrectionist or insurgent is ironic. The first two statements of Jesus' speech are in antithetical parallelism. Both end with the personal pronoun "me" preceded by a verb:

> Have you come out as if I were an insurrectionist with swords and clubs to capture me? Day after day I was with you teaching in the Temple, and you did not arrest me.
>
> Ὡς ἐπὶ λῃστὴν ἐξήλθατε μετὰ μαχαιρῶν καὶ ξύλων συλλαβεῖν με; καθ' ἡμέραν ἤμην πρὸς ὑμᾶς ἐν τῷ ἱερῷ διδάσκων καὶ οὐκ ἐκρατήσατέ με. (14:48–49)

The contrast between "insurrectionist" (λῃστὴν) and "in the Temple teaching" heightens the antithesis and the irony. Thus, Jesus' speech highlights the contradiction in the crowd's actions. The rhetorical question concerning their coming to seize him as an insurrectionist requires an affirmative answer. Mark the storyteller may have even smiled and laughed a little at the absurdity of this situation. Jesus' second statement points out that their failure to arrest him earlier in the Temple is a sign that he has committed no crime. The implication is that he has done nothing wrong and that this arrest is totally unjust.

There is a profound irony in the actions of Judas and the crowd that will be a theme in the accusations against Jesus. Jesus has been totally nonviolent throughout his life. In contrast to the expectations of a Messiah, he is never violent. Nor does he ever advocate violence. The closest he comes to violence is the cleansing of the Temple. But that is a prophetic protest, in which no one gets hurt. The irony of the crowd's action is that they come to arrest him as an insurrectionist, an advocate of violence. And the accusations against him will be that he has advocated the destruction of the Temple, and that he has claimed to be the King of the Judeans and therefore the legitimate ruler who is justified in using all necessary means to take power. The crowd, therefore, accuses him of being precisely what he has opposed and has never been.[29]

A major factor in the impact of this speech is its relationship to the striking of the high priest's slave in the preceding episode. In contrast to the other three gospels, the Gospel of Mark does not show Jesus criticizing the attacker or responding to the injury of the high priest's servant. Instead Mark's Jesus, like the fighter, responds directly to the action of the crowd. In addition, the narrator's introduction, "And Jesus answered and said to them" (see comment above), implies continuity between that act and Jesus' speech. Jesus' words are a description of an injustice, a criminal arrest of one who did nothing more than teach in the Temple. The hope is raised that Jesus will call the disciples to resist the arrest and set him free. The natural conclusion to this description of injustice and armed conflict would be a summons to violent resistance such as: "Fight! Set me free!"

The impact of this speech in its original context was related to the manner in which the storyteller presented it. Was there a tone of defiance and injustice in the way that the storyteller spoke Jesus' words, or did he tell Jesus' speech as an ironic description of the absurdity of the crowd's coming to arrest him as an insurgent and in anticipation of a battle? A major factor in this assessment is the structural parallel between the rhetorical dynamics of this speech and the prayer in Gethsemane. In both cases, the possibility that Jesus' suffering may be avoided is implied and then ended by a reversal at the end of the speech, in which Jesus resigns himself to whatever may be the will of God.

49b: acceptance of arrest as the fulfillment of the Scriptures

A sign of the logic and tone of the arrest speech is the relationship between Jesus' conclusion, "This is happening in order that the Scriptures may be fulfilled," and his prior statements. Jesus' statement means that this arrest is

---

29. A recent documentary film about the life and death in Brazil of Sister Dorothy Stang, a seventy-three-year-old American nun from Dayton, is another instance of this kind of irony. Sister Dorothy was killed by ranchers in the northern state of Para who are cutting down the rainforest for the logs and to create more grazing land for cattle. Sister Dorothy was an advocate for and organizer of sustainable use of the land by establishing peasant farms in the rainforest where each tenant is given a 250 acre plot, 20 percent of which is cleared for farming and 80 percent of which is maintained as rainforest. During the trial of those who were indicted for her murder, the defense accused her of being an organizer of violence and importing weapons. In the context of her life and teaching (the last thing she said to the two men who killed her was, "Blessed are the poor for theirs is the kingdom of heaven"), this charge is ironic. When her friends heard this at the trial, their jaws dropped in shock and they smiled at the irony of this charge.

happening in order to fulfill the will of God. And in both the Gethsemane prayer and the arrest speech, the concluding statements of acceptance of God's will begin with the strongly adversative conjunction "But" (ἀλλά) and are elliptical. In the following citation, the elements of the sentences that are inferred are bracketed:

> Abba, Father, all things are possible to you.
> Take this cup from me.
> *But* [do] not [do] what I want, but [do] what you [want]. (14:36)
>
> Have you come out as against an insurgent with swords and clubs to capture me?
>
> Day after day I was with you in the Temple teaching and you did not arrest me.
>
> *But* [this is happening] in order that the Scriptures might be fulfilled. (14:48b–49)

In each instance, the conclusion of Jesus' speech unexpectedly breaks the line of reasoning established in the rest of the speech. The strongly adversative conjunction ἀλλά is a clear sign of the logical discontinuity.

Furthermore, the listeners are required to supply the major verbs that heighten the climactic impact of the conclusion. In 14:49 Jesus' sentence is an elliptical construction with a concluding purpose clause.[30] The final colon has an adversative relationship to the first part of the speech. And the audience is invited to identify the statement that would have been the logical conclusion to Jesus' train of thought. In fact, the implication of the story's structure is that the storyteller expects the audience to identify that statement in order to make Jesus' final statement a decisive reversal of expectations and hopes.

If in addition Jesus' words were spoken ironically, the logic of the speech was undercut from the beginning. If Mark smiled and shook his head at the irony of the crowd's actions, any possibility that Jesus might call for violent resistance is ruled out from the beginning of his speech by his implicit attitude of acceptance of the irony rather than defiance. Thus, Jesus' response is a classic instance of nonviolent resistance to evil. Jesus is neither violent nor passive.

His final statement in the speech is the only use in Mark of the formula "in order that the Scriptures might be fulfilled." But Jesus has also made other statements that connect what is happening to him with the Scriptures. He quotes Zechariah in his prophetic talk with the disciples on the way

---

30. BDF, #448.7: "Elliptically ἀλλ' ἵνα 'on the contrary (but) this happened (or a similar verb), in order that." See also #480.5 on the omission of the implied verb.

to Gethsemane (14:27). But his reference to the "Scriptures" also refers to the Scriptures as a whole as in his conflict with the Sadducees: "you know neither the Scriptures nor the power of God" (12:24). This is the sense of his statement to Judas and the disciples when he tells them that he is walking the way that has been "written" for him (14:21). In effect, as when he yields to the will of God in the conclusion of his prayer in Gethsemane (14:36b) that leads to his acceptance of his imminent arrest in his final words to the disciples in the garden (14:41–42), in his final statement here, Jesus identifies what is happening as the fulfillment of the will of God. It is the will of God that Jesus accept being handed over to sinners. The evidence of the completion of God's purpose is the fulfillment of prophecy as spoken both by the prophets of the Old Testament and by Jesus himself.

Thus, the meaning of the speech is tied to its structure and context. Its context is the arrest and the violent action by one of those standing by, presumably one of the disciples. Its structure establishes a line of reasoning that is climactically reversed. But Jesus' initial statements are in direct continuity with that action. On the one hand, the logic of the speech elicits a sympathetic reaction to Jesus' descriptions of the actions of those who have illegally and unjustly arrested him, and raises the hope that Jesus may resist arrest and call for his disciples to fight. That is, the striking of the high priest's slave raises the hope of violent resistance. On the other hand, the probability that Mark spoke Jesus' words with a tone of irony means that Jesus is, from the beginning of his speech, accepting arrest and eliminating a violent way out of the apparently inexorable course of events.

The disappointment created by Jesus' rejection of violent resistance is set in the context of the fulfillment of Scripture as quoted by him at the beginning of their journey to Gethsemane: "You will all be offended and run away (σκανδαλίζω), for it is written, "I will strike the shepherd and the sheep will be scattered" (14:27). In the end, the impact of Jesus' speech is to establish his resolute determination to fulfill the will of God and to see this conflict through to the end in a spirit of love and nonviolence while recognizing the irony of the actions of all those around him, both of his opponents and of his supporters.

50: the disciples' flight

Among the questions raised by Jesus' prophecy that the disciples will be offended and run away is, why? In the telling of the story, the prophecy is addressed to and includes the audience as well as the disciples. Therefore, the question is, why will we all be offended and run away? This speech provides the answer: Jesus' nonviolent resistance to the unjust arrest of a prophet like Isaiah and Jeremiah is the answer to the question. And they ran away because they didn't want to be arrested and killed. Mark assumes that we all will be offended because Jesus doesn't fight. This expectation is not surprising. As John J. Collins has shown, the basic tradition of the Messiah in Israel is the warrior king:

> The concept of the Davidic messiah as the warrior king who would destroy the enemies of Israel and institute an era of unending peace constitutes the common core of Jewish messianism around the turn of the era . . . There was a dominant notion of a Davidic messiah, as the king who would restore the kingdom of Israel, which was part of the common Judaism around the turn of the era.[31]

And the messianic traditions of Israel are consistent with the heroic stories of the wider human community. Warrior traditions and confidence in the myth of redemptive violence continue to be the dominant hope of the human community for deliverance from the powers of evil.[32]

The concluding prophecy, originally of Zechariah but taken up by Jesus in this new context, is immediately fulfilled. The disciples *all* flee. The final, climactic word in Mark's Greek text is "all": ἔφυγον πάντες, literally translated, "they fled—all!" "All" is the key word of connection to Jesus' prophecy that "all" of them would be offended and run away. The introductory participial phrase, "And leaving him" (καὶ ἀφέντες αὐτὸν), heightens the irony of the disciples' flight, because it is used earlier to describe the response of the chief priests, the scribes, and the elders at the end of Jesus' parable of the Wicked Tenants: "So they left him and went away" (καὶ ἀφέντες αὐτὸν ἀπῆλθον, 12:12).

Now it is Jesus' friends who, like his opponents, are offended and leave him. Flight is always associated earlier in the gospel with fear—in the flight of the Gerasenes after the pig stampede (5:14) and in Jesus' recommendation of flight when the desolating sacrilege is seen (13:14). The disciples' response to Jesus' speech is to be offended and to escape. They do not follow their leader, who is faithful to the way of nonviolent resistance.

51–52: the flight of the young man

The young man is apparently not one of the twelve. Mark's description of him focuses on the scant clothing in which he was following Jesus. While

---

31. Collins, *Scepter and the Star*, 68.
32. See Wink, *Engaging the Powers*, 13–31.

the clothing detail is unusual, the major significance of this notice in the story is to establish the context for the young man's naked flight. His scant clothing also implies that it was a warm night. The crowd's seizing him is in the historical present tense, which heightens the shock and immediacy of his arrest. His arrest is initially sympathetic because he is being seized like Jesus. The climax of the night on the Mount of Olives is, therefore, an even greater surprise.

The young man's naked flight is the climactic symbol of the flight of the disciples. In almost every instance nakedness is associated with shame and humiliation in the traditions of Israel. There are three major uses of the word "naked" (γυμνὸς) in the Greek Old Testament: (1) as a description of the poor (Job 24:7, 10; 31:19; Eccl 5:14; Ezra 18:16); (2) in reference to birth (Job 1:21; Eccl 5:14); and (3) most frequently, as a sign of shame or guilt (Gen 3:7, 10, 11; 2 Chr 28:15; Job 26:6; Hos 2:3; Amos 2:16; 4:3; Mic 1:8; Ezek 16:7, 22, 39; 23:29; 2 Macc 11:12). This association of nakedness with shame is most graphically present in descriptions of defeat in battle:

> . . . those who handle the bow shall not stand, / and those who are swift of foot shall not save themselves, / nor shall those who ride horses save their lives; // and those who are stout of heart among the mighty / shall flee away naked in that day, says the LORD. (Amos 2:15–16 [NRSV], referring to the day of judgment on Judah)

> . . . so shall the king of Assyria lead away the Egyptians as captives and the Ethiopians as exiles, both the young and the old, naked and barefoot, with buttocks uncovered, to the shame of Egypt. (Isa 20:4, NRSV)

> They hurled themselves like lions against the enemy, and laid low eleven thousand of them and sixteen hundred cavalry, and forced all the rest to flee. Most of them got away naked and wounded, and Lysias himself escaped by disgraceful flight." (2 Macc 11:11–12 [NRSV], describing the defeat of Lysias by Judas Maccabeus and his followers).

Mark's description of the young man's naked flight is in continuity with this tradition. In the context of the Hellenistic world of the first century, the shame of nakedness reflects an Israelite cultural value shared by Mark and his audiences that stands over against the Greek and Roman celebration of nakedness, particularly in public statuary. In an Israelite context, therefore, the vignette of the naked flight of the young man brings the flight of the disciples to a disgraceful climax.

And yet, the young man's flight, while shameful, is also sympathetic. While in direct conflict with the norm of loyalty embraced by the disciples themselves in the story of Jesus' prophecy, it is also completely understandable as a human response to being arrested and executed. This is another of the many instances in Mark's narrative of characters doing something that is both wrong and understandable.

26–52: the audience's invited reflections on the arrest section

In the pause that follows this climactic ending, the audience is given time to reflect back over the whole section of the story of what happened on the Mount of Olives, beginning with Jesus' prophecy. Just as Jesus had foreseen, the disciples were offended and ran away. All of their promises of loyalty and of dying with him were forgotten. But the impact on the audience of the story of the disciples' flight is determined by the sympathetic relationship with them established in that earlier story. The naked flight of the young follower, while dramatizing the shame of the disciples' flight, is also sympathetic. It is told as the humiliation of a friend and as a sharing of his shame rather than as the joyful downfall of an enemy. It is impossible for the listeners to stand back and condemn the disciples and the young follower as traitors like Judas. The impact of the story is to invite the listeners to a sympathetic sharing of the disciples' shame. In the silence, Mark the storyteller gives the listeners a moment to reflect on that shared experience.

And where does this reflection lead? It leads first to reflecting on the reasons why Jesus' acceptance of arrest is so offensive, and why the disciples all ran away. As we have seen and heard, the context of this reflection is the traditions of warfare and of soldiers in battle. Jesus' acceptance of arrest does not fulfill the expectations of a leader in battle. From a military point of view, the disciples' flight is understandable. Their commander does not fight. In the end, he does not support or praise the one who does fight. And he does not call on them to fight.

Second, the story invites the listeners to reflect on Judas' betrayal. While his motivation remains shrouded in mystery, the clues all point to the response of one who was deeply committed to the use of violence and to the revolt against Rome. His action of betrayal is extraordinarily treacherous and violent. It is reminiscent of the assassination of Abner by Joab, who took him aside to speak privately in apparent confidence and trust and then stabbed him in the stomach (2 Sam 3:27). Later, Joab does the same thing to Amasa. He approaches Amasa in apparent friendship, saying, "Is it well with you, my brother?" Then taking Amasa by the beard to kiss him with his

The Night in Gethsemane (14:26–52)

right hand, he stabs him with the sword in his left hand in the belly "so that his entrails poured out on the ground and he died" (2 Sam 20:8–10, NRSV). Joab is the precursor of Judas.

However, the primary allusions of Judas' action for Mark's audiences are to the treacheries and betrayals that were a dimension of the Judean–Roman War. Treachery and assassination of the leaders of various factions of the Judean resistance, and particularly of those who favored reconciliation with Rome, was a frequent event both prior to and during the war. The characteristic act of the Sicarii, with whom Judas' surname, Iscariot,[33] may have been associated for Mark's listeners, was to approach a Judean supporter of the Roman-imposed government in apparent friendship in the marketplace and to kill him with the curved dagger, the *sicarius*. The Sicarii were the most fanatical group among the nationalists who carried out the revolt and war against Rome. That is, the implication of the story is that Judas was disappointed by Jesus' failure to act in the tradition of the messiahs of Israel and to lead a revolt against Rome. And he was willing to betray and kill his teacher because of his commitment to the cause of Israel's independence from Roman rule. For Mark's audiences in the decade of the 70s after the war, this was both a natural inference and a familiar scenario. Judas effectively assassinates Jesus.

But Jesus does not take, nor has he ever taken, the role of a military leader. The story of the prophecy and the ensuing argument that introduced the night on the Mount of Olives established the shared expectation that the disciples would stand with Jesus and not run away. That is, even though Jesus knows they will fail, his implicit expectation is that they would be arrested with him. Therefore, all of the disciples must be judged as having failed, according to the operative norms of the story. And even though Jesus did not call them to fight, he did have the right to expect them to observe the operative norms of the traditions of Israel and of the broader heroic traditions of the ancient world, in which loyalty to the leader was expected regardless of the circumstances. But they forsook their leader and ran away in the midst of a battle. From this perspective, they acted as cowards and deserters and are guilty in the modern world of a military crime punishable by court-martial and possible execution. This judgment is set in the context of a high degree of sympathetic identification with the disciples, in part because Jesus' expectations are new and difficult norms for the disciples and for Mark's audience.

---

33. See the note on his name in the commentary above, on 14:10. [X-REF]

The rhetoric of implication in the arrest section

This story is, therefore, structured by the rhetoric of involvement and implication. It combines a high degree of sympathetic identification with characters who do something in clear violation of a sacred covenant. Every listener can identify with the disciples. Jesus' acceptance of arrest as the fulfillment of Scripture is profoundly troubling. Every listener can understand the reason why the disciples ran away. Their leader refused to fight and instead accepted arrest as the will of God. Yet, as is established by the argument between Jesus and Peter with which this section begins, running away from Jesus rather than standing with him is unambiguously wrong. Thus, the story of the young man's flight puts climactic emphasis on the disciples' shame in running away in the face of the immediate prospect of being arrested with Jesus. However understandable, the disciples' flight conflicts with the courage required for covenant loyalty to their teacher. Thus, the final perspective from which the night on the Mount of Olives is to be seen is watching a young follower of Jesus run away naked.

The Performance of the Story

The telling of this story requires the teller to communicate a wide range of emotional dynamics and to make a series of complex decisions about how the story is to be told. Regardless of the decisions that you make about the way you tell this story, the most important invitation is that you live into the story deeply in all of its ambiguity so that you can tell it as an eyewitness, who has experienced what happened on that night in Gethsemane.

The tempo of this story is much faster than the tempo of the Gethsemane story. This story has an action-movie tempo. The description of Judas and the crowd is told as the description of an armed mob. As you will notice in the translation, it is possible that there was an article before Judas' name, in which case it would be Judas would be described as "that Judas, one of the twelve." This is a possible time to point at Judas and his gang as they arrive. The storyteller's description of their plan and Judas' instructions to the crowd entail inside information given to the audience. That is, the storyteller interrupts the description of this cascade of actions to give the audience essential information so that they understand what is happening. There is no sympathy in the storyteller's voice for Judas and his gang. They are Jesus' enemies and are determined to get him killed.

The description of Judas' identification of Jesus with a kiss is to be told with a tone of disbelief and scandal. It is a moment of implicit assassination of a teacher who loved and trusted his assassin, even as the teacher knew

The Night in Gethsemane (14:26–52)

what the assassin was going to do and protected his secrecy. The actual laying of hands on Jesus and arresting him is both a factual fulfillment of what had been predicted and an unbelievable development. But the striking of the high priest's slave needs to be told as good news and as a note of hope. It is the climax of the crescendo that began at the beginning, "While he was still speaking..."

The most difficult decision in this story is how to present Jesus' speech. Ideally, at the beginning of the speech, your telling will communicate both resistance and even defiance, combined with dispassionate recognition and possibly even a shrug of amusement at the irony of the crowd's action. The overall impact of Jesus' first two statements needs to make clear Jesus' accusation of the crowd for the injustice of their action. The end of the speech, where Jesus accepts the arrest as the fulfillment of the Scriptures, is a recognition of the inevitability of his death and a statement of his determination to fulfill his destiny; this is similar to his earlier statement at the Last Supper that the Son of Man goes as it is written of him. The challenge here is to present these words as statements of spiritual strength with no note of weakness, resignation, or self-pity.

The telling of the flight of the disciples and the naked flight of the young follower needs to convey the shame of their action. The disciples' flight is also the fulfillment of Jesus' earlier prophecy and may have a note that recalls the prophecy. The story of the young man is the climax of the whole story. His being seized can be told as an occasion of fear even bordering on terror. But his running away naked requires some tone of shame. A gesture of shaking the head may help to communicate this.

The connections with your own experience may help you to find an authentic way of telling this story. You might explore your memories of experiences of being betrayed or let down in public by someone you loved and trusted. Experiences of injustice provide another possible line of connection. Recalling your own experiences either of running away from conflict or of lashing out at an adversary in anger may help you find points of emotional connection with the dynamics of this story. The stories of the assassinations of the advocates of peace and nonviolence in our time have many of the dynamics of this ancient story. The stories of the deaths of Mahatma Gandhi, Itzak Rabin, Martin Luther King Jr., and now Sister Dorothy Stang are deeply linked with the story of Jesus. Pondering those stories may also provide points of connection with the dynamics of Jesus' story here. There are also many martyr stories from the post-Reformation period in Europe of the arrest and execution of both Roman Catholics and Protestants, which have connections with this story.

I would recommend an Ignatian meditation of composition of place with this story of Jesus' arrest. Imagine yourself in the garden with Jesus. What are the sounds, the sights, the smells, the tastes of the Passover meal and the wine, and the touches of sitting on the ground leaning against an olive tree? One dimension of the prayer associated with this place is a prayer of willingness to accept whatever suffering and shame may be a necessary part of the fulfillment of your purpose and destiny. This can also be a meditation on your own willingness to stand with Jesus and be counted rather than to run away from him out of fear or disappointment. One of the ironies of nonviolence is that it is often harder to maintain courage as a participant in nonviolent intervention than it is in situations of battle or violent confrontation. The energy to inflict others with injury or death is sometimes easier to identify than the energy to absorb suffering while maintaining a course of resistance. Another possible dimension of this meditation is to learn from Jesus' spirit how to engage the injustice of opponents with precise description but spoken in a spirit of detachment rather than rage. The potential gift of this meditation and of learning to tell this story with personal integrity is greater clarity about your own spirituality in relation to Jesus.

4

THE TRIALS AT THE HIGH PRIEST'S HOUSE (14:53–72)

THE CENTER OF THE STORY OF JESUS' TRIAL BEFORE THE Sanhedrin is his public confession that he is the Messiah. This is the climax of the motif of the Messianic secret in Mark. The Sanhedrin's immediate condemnation confirms that Jesus' desire to keep his identity a secret was both wise and necessary.[1] However, the story of Jesus' trial is set in the context of the story of Peter's denial that is "the sandwich" for the trial and Jesus' confession. As in the arrest section, the climax of the trial section is the response of Jesus' most voluble disciple to Jesus' confession and condemnation. It is, in effect, Peter's trial. His denial is also a fulfillment of the prophecy of Jesus that initiates the larger story of the night on the Mount of Olives, 14:26–31).

---

1. One of the clearest indications of the blindness created by the media assumptions of historical criticism is the history of "the Messianic secret" in Markan scholarship. Wrede's monumental study of this theme in Mark does not raise the possibility that this was a motif in the plot of Mark and the potential threat to Jesus of the public announcement of his identity. When Mark is told as a story, the Messianic secret creates a puzzling mystery that helps to sustain an audience's interest throughout a long story until its resolution in the trial before the Sanhedrin. The assumption that the motive for this element of the story was not to create narrative suspense but a theological doctrine that Mark was seeking to communicate through the story is a dimension of what Frei calls "the eclipse of biblical narrative."

Jesus' Trial before the Sanhedrin (14:53–65)

Sound Map

14:53 Καὶ ἀπήγαγον τὸν Ἰησοῦν πρὸς τὸν **ἀρχιερέα**,
　　καὶ συνέρχονται πάντες **οἱ ἀρχιερεῖς**
　　　　καὶ οἱ πρεσβύτεροι
　　　　καὶ οἱ γραμματεῖς.
54 **Καὶ** ὁ Πέτρος ἀπὸ μακρόθεν ἠκολούθησεν αὐτῷ ἕως ἔσω **εἰς τὴν αὐλὴν**
　　　　　　　　　　　　　　　　　　　　　　　　τοῦ **ἀρχιερέως**,
　　καὶ ἦν **συγκαθήμενος** μετὰ τῶν ὑπηρετῶν
　　καὶ **θερμαινόμενος** πρὸς τὸ φῶς.

55 Οἱ δὲ **ἀρχιερεῖς** καὶ ὅλον τὸ συνέδριον ἐζήτουν κατὰ τοῦ Ἰησοῦ μαρτυρίαν
　　εἰς τὸ θανατῶσαι αὐτόν, καὶ οὐχ ηὕρισκον.
56 Πολλοὶ γὰρ **ἐψευδομαρτύρουν κατ' αὐτοῦ**,
　　καὶ **ἴσαι αἱ μαρτυρίαι** οὐκ ἦσαν.

57 Καί τινες **ἀναστάντες ἐψευδομαρτύρουν κατ' αὐτοῦ λέγοντες ὅτι**
　　58 Ἡμεῖς ἠκούσαμεν αὐτοῦ **λέγοντος ὅτι**
　　Ἐγὼ καταλύσω τὸν ναὸν τοῦτον τὸν **χειροποίητον**
　　καὶ διὰ τριῶν ἡμερῶν ἄλλον **ἀχειροποίητον** οἰκοδομήσω.
59 Καὶ οὐδὲ οὕτως **ἴση** ἦν ἡ **μαρτυρία** αὐτῶν.

60 Καὶ **ἀναστὰς** ὁ **ἀρχιερεὺς** εἰς μέσον **ἐπηρώτησεν** τὸν Ἰησοῦν λέγων,
　　Οὐκ ἀποκρίνῃ οὐδέν;
　　　　τί* οὗτοί σου **καταμαρτυροῦσιν**;
61 ὁ δὲ ἐσιώπα καὶ **οὐκ ἀπεκρίνατο οὐδέν**.

Πάλιν ὁ **ἀρχιερεὺς ἐπηρώτα** αὐτὸν καὶ λέγει αὐτῷ,
　　Σὺ εἶ ὁ Χριστὸς ὁ υἱὸς τοῦ εὐλογητοῦ;
62 ὁ δὲ Ἰησοῦς εἶπεν,
　　Ἐγώ εἰμι, καὶ ὄψεσθε τὸν υἱὸν τοῦ ἀνθρώπου
　　　　ἐκ δεξιῶν καθήμενον τῆς δυνάμεως
　　　　καὶ ἐρχόμενον μετὰ τῶν νεφελῶν τοῦ οὐρανοῦ.

63 ὁ δὲ **ἀρχιερεὺς** διαρρήξας τοὺς χιτῶνας αὐτοῦ λέγει,
　　Τί ἔτι χρείαν ἔχομεν μαρτύρων;
64 ἠκούσατε τῆς βλασφημίας.
Τί ὑμῖν φαίνεται;

οἱ δὲ πάντες κατέκριναν αὐτὸν ἔνοχον εἶναι θανάτου.
65 Καὶ ἤρξαντό τινες ἐμπτύειν **αὐτῷ**

καὶ περικαλύπτειν **αὐτοῦ** τὸ πρόσωπον
καὶ κολαφίζειν **αὐτὸν**
καὶ λέγειν **αὐτῷ**, Προφήτευσον.
Καὶ οἱ ὑπηρέται ῥαπίσμασιν **αὐτὸν** ἔλαβον.

Translation

53They led Jesus away to **the high priest**
 and all **the chief priests and the elders and the scribes** gathered together.
54And Peter followed at a distance, right into the courtyard of the high priest,
 and he was sitting with the guards,
 warming himself by the light of the fire.

55Now **the chief priests** and the whole council were looking for testimony against Jesus
 to put him to death; but they found none.
56Because many **bore false witness against him**
 and **their testimony** did not agree.

57Some **stood up and bore false witness against him, saying**:
 58"We heard this man **say**,
 'I will destroy this temple **made with hands**
 and in three days I will build up another, **not made with hands**.'"
59But even on this their **testimony** did not **agree**.

60And **the high priest stood up** in their midst and **questioned** Jesus,
 "**Have you no answer to the charges they are bringing** against you?"
61But he was silent and gave no answer.

Again **the high priest questioned** him and says to him,
 "Are you the Messiah, the Son of the Blessed?"
62But Jesus said,
 "I am, and you will see the Son of Man
 seated at the right hand of Power
 and coming with the clouds of heaven."

63And **the high priest** rent his clothes and says,
 "Why do we still need witnesses?
64You have heard his blasphemy.
How does it appear to you?"

And they all condemned him as deserving death.
65 And some began to spit on him,
> to blindfold him,
> and to strike him,
> and to say to him, "Prophesy!"
And the guards took him away beating him.

Ancient Associations and Connections

Mark's audience would have brought to this story a set of social memories connected with the trials of prophets and righteous ones in the courts of Israel as well as stories of earlier acts of courage in enemy camps.

The stories of David's exploits when Saul was trying to kill him were part of the social memory that forms the background for Peter's following Jesus into the courtyard of the high priest. The story of David sneaking into Saul's encampment and taking his spear and water jar has similar associations:

> Then David set out and came to the place where Saul had encamped; and David saw the place where Saul lay, with Abner son of Ner, the commander of his army. Saul was lying within the encampment, while the army was encamped around him. Then David said to Ahimelech the Hittite, and to Joab's brother Abishai son of Zeruiah, "Who will go down with me into the camp to Saul?" Abishai said, "I will go down with you."
>
> So David and Abishai went to the army by night; there Saul lay sleeping within the encampment, with his spear stuck in the ground at his head; and Abner and the army lay around him. Abishai said to David, "God has given your enemy into your hand today; now therefore let me pin him to the ground with one stroke of the spear; I will not strike him twice." But David said to Abishai, "Do not destroy him; for who can raise his hand against the LORD's anointed, and be guiltless?" David said, "As the LORD lives, the LORD will strike him down; or his day will come to die; or he will go down into battle and perish. The LORD forbid that I should raise my hand against the LORD's anointed; but now take the spear that is at his head, and the water jar, and let us go." So David took the spear that was at Saul's head and the water jar, and they went away. No one saw it, or knew it, nor did anyone awake; for they were all asleep, because a deep sleep from the LORD had fallen upon them. (1 Sam 26:5–13, NRSV)

Most of this story was undoubtedly told in a whisper in order to convey the threat of their presence in Saul's encampment. It may be a precedent for the manner in which the notice of Peter with the guards as well as the first part of the story of Peter's denial was told.

There are two major stories of the trials of prophets that were probably part of the social memory of many in Mark's audiences. The first is the trial of Jeremiah. The trial is a response to the prophecies of Jeremiah in the Temple by the priests and false prophets. Jeremiah is then arrested and tried by the officials and all the people. The priests and the prophets serve as prosecutors in the trial. Excerpts from the story are printed here but I would encourage you to read Jeremiah 26–39 as background for the trial of Jesus:

> At the beginning of the reign of King Jehoiakim son of Josiah of Judah, this word came from the Lord: Thus says the Lord: Stand in the court of the Lord's house, and speak to all the cities of Judah that come to worship in the house of the Lord; speak to them all the words that I command you; do not hold back a word. It may be that they will listen, all of them, and will turn from their evil way, that I may change my mind about the disaster that I intend to bring on them because of their evil doings. You shall say to them: Thus says the Lord: If you will not listen to me, to walk in my law that I have set before you, and to heed the words of my servants the prophets whom I send to you urgently—though you have not heeded—then I will make this house like Shiloh, and I will make this city a curse for all the nations of the earth.
>
> The priests and the prophets and all the people heard Jeremiah speaking these words in the house of the Lord. And when Jeremiah had finished speaking all that the Lord had commanded him to speak to all the people, the priests and the prophets and all the people laid hold of him, saying, "You shall die! Why have you prophesied in the name of the Lord, saying, 'This house shall be like Shiloh, and this city shall be desolate, without inhabitant'?" And all the people gathered around Jeremiah in the house of the Lord.
>
> When the officials of Judah heard these things, they came up from the king's house to the house of the Lord and took their seat in the entry of the New Gate of the house of the Lord. Then the priests and the prophets said to the officials and to all the people, "This man deserves the sentence of death because he has prophesied against this city, as you have heard with your own ears." (Jer 26:1–11, NRSV)

The second story is the trial of Isaiah, apparently *in absentia*, as it was told in the *Martyrdom and Ascension of Isaiah*. The book as a whole is a composite work, with some sections composed in the period of Antiochus IV Epiphanes, and others as late as the late first century or early second century CE. The earlier sections of the book shared the historical context of the stories of the martyrdoms of Eleazar and the seven boys and their mother in 2 Maccabees 6–7, and were part of the prophet martyr traditions of Israel. The story of Isaiah's trial is as follows:

> And Belkira accused Isaiah and the prophets who (were) with him, saying, "Isaiah and the prophets who (are) with him prophesy against Jerusalem and against the cities of Judah that they will be laid waste, and also (against) Benjamin that it will go into captivity, and also against you, O lord king, that you will go (bound) with hooks and chains of iron. But they prophesy lies against Israel and Judah. And Isaiah himself has said, 'I see more than Moses the prophet.' Moses said, 'There is no man who can see the Lord and live.' But Isaiah has said, "I have seen the Lord, and behold I am alive.' Know, therefore, O king, that they (are) false prophets. And he has called Jerusalem Sodom, and the princes of Judah and Jerusalem he has declared (to be) the people of Gomorrah." And he brought many accusations against Isaiah and the prophets before Manasseh. But Beliar dwelt in the heart of Manasseh and in the heart of the princes of Judah and Benjamin, and of the eunuchs, and of the king's counselors. And the words of Belkira pleased him very much, and he sent and seized Isaiah. (*The Martyrdom and Ascension of Isaiah* 3:6–12 *OTP*, 159–60)

The stories of the trials and deaths of the prophets were a familiar motif in the storytelling traditions of Israel prior to Mark. And while Mark has no echoes of exact words from these stories, there are many similar dynamics and motifs that reflect the conflicts between the prophets and the priests as well as the battles that took place around and within the Temple. Those common motifs include the lists of opponents ("the priests and the prophets and all the people"), the charge of prophesying against the Temple, the verdict of death, and the charge of claiming to have a unique relationship with God.

The end of the book of Susanna, a popular Israelite novel dated sometime in the second century BCE, is an earlier instance of several similar motifs to those in Mark's story, including the bearing of false witness. Susanna was a very popular story and occurs in two different forms. Both are integral to the Greek translation of the book of Daniel. One version is Theodotian's

The Trials at the High Priest's House (14:53–72) 161

Greek translation; the other is the Septuagint translation. The NRSV translation summarized and quoted below is a translation of Theodotion's Greek text of Daniel.

Susanna was a very beautiful woman who was married to Joakim, a righteous and very rich man with a beautiful garden. I will quote the introduction of the two elders:

> That year two elders from the people were appointed as judges. Concerning them the Lord had said: "wickedness came forth from Babylon, from elders who were judges, who were supposed to govern the people." These men were frequently at Joakim's house, and all who had a case to be tried came to them there. (Sus 1:5–6)

These two lusted after Susanna and hid in the garden one hot day when Susanna was bathing alone. They gave her a choice that she would lie with them or they would testify that they had seen her with a young man. She refused and cried out. When people came, the elders carried out their threat and accused her of adultery. At the trial they both bore false witness against her. After she was condemned to death and was being led away to execution, the young Daniel, inspired by the Holy Spirit, shouted to the people to come back and reexamine the witnesses. When he questioned them separately, he asked them what tree Susanna and the young man were under. The first said a mastic tree and the second an evergreen oak. He exposed that their testimony did not agree, and that they bore false witness:

> Then the whole assembly raised a great shout and blessed God, who saves those who hope in him. And they took action against the two elders, because out of their own mouths Daniel had convicted them of bearing false witness; they did to them as they had wickedly planned to do to their neighbor. Acting in accordance with the law of Moses, they put them to death. Thus innocent blood was spared that day. (Sus 1:60–62, NRSV)

Notes on Translation and Details

14:53: all / πάντες

The word "all" occurs at the beginning ("all of the chief priests," v. 53) and at the end of the story ("they all condemned him," v. 64b) It indicates the scale and the style of this story. It is a big story with big gestures that include all the audience in the trial. It also provides the contrast with "many" who lie in their testimony (v. 56) and with "some" who abuse Jesus after the verdict (v. 65).

54: the light of the fire / τὸ φῶς

This last word of the introductory episode that describes where Peter was sitting with the guards is usually translated "fire," as in the NRSV and NIV. The word that Mark uses, however, is not the usual word for "fire," τὸ πῦρ. The word Mark uses, τὸ φῶς, usually means "light" and is used only rarely and metaphorically to mean "fire." This word heightens the imminent threat Peter is under as he sits with the guards, because he can be recognized in "the light." The translation here, "the light of the fire," preserves that allusive richness. It is also a clue about the tone of the word, namely, ominous and threatening.

56–58: bore false witness / ψευδομαρτυρέω

This word is a reference to the ninth of the ten commandments, "You shall not bear false witness against your neighbor" (Exod 20:16). This commandment deals with the possibility of perjury by witnesses in trials. The NRSV translates this word as "gave false testimony" and thereby eliminates the explicit echo of the commandment. The translation here preserves the sonic connection and the explicit implication that those who testified against Jesus were guilty of a capital crime in Israelite law, as is reflected in the trial story in Susanna (Sus 1:60–62).

60–61: have no answer / gave no answer / οὐκ ἀποκρίνῃ οὐδέν / οὐκ ἀπεκρίνατο οὐδέν

This repeated phrase is a double negative in Greek—literally, "Do you not answer nothing?" in the question of the high priest, and, "did not answer nothing" in Jesus' silent response. It cannot be translated literally into English because a double negative constitutes a positive in English.[2] But it is possible to translate the phrase with the same English words and thereby make the connection more explicit: hence, "have no answer" and "gave no

---

2. A related story from contemporary classrooms tells well: A linguistics professor was lecturing about double negatives and said, "In English, a double negative constitutes a positive. And in Russian, a double negative is an emphatic negative. But in no language does a double positive constitute a negative." And a student in the back of the room said, "Yeah, right."

answer." This phrase is also repeated in the Pilate trial and will be translated with the same words there.

60–61: he says / λέγει

Mark uses the historical present tense to introduce two elements in this story: the high priest's second question to Jesus—"Are you the Messiah?"—and the high priest's response to Jesus' affirmation/confession: "Why do we need more witnesses?" Both uses are clearly intended to make these climactic questions immediate and present in the audience's experience. Once again, while a minor element, the use of the present rather than the past tense in English translation has a similar impact as the original Greek did.

63: rent his clothes / διαρρήξας τοὺς χιτῶνας αὐτοῦ

This phrase is usually translated "tore his clothes/garments" and is thereby given a sonic connection with the Temple curtain being torn in two (15:38) and the heavens being torn open (1:10). This translation creates a sonic connection where Mark does not. In this story, Mark uses the phrase διαρρήξας τοὺς χιτῶνας αὐτοῦ. In both the baptism and the tearing of the Temple curtain, Mark uses a form of the verb σχίζω, "to split, divide, tear apart," from which we have the English word "schism." The tearing of the heavens and the Temple curtain are acts of God. My hunch is that Mark wanted to make no connection between the high priest's condemnation of Jesus and the acts of God. Therefore, this Greek verb should be translated with a different word in English. Hence the translation here is "rent his clothes."

64: how does it appear to you? / τί ὑμῖν φαίνεται;

This question that the high priest asks the gathered court literally means something like, how to you does it appear? The NRSV translates this as "What is your decision?" which is a good dynamic-equivalent translation. The problem is that it reduces the directness of the storyteller's question to the listeners about their own perception and response to Jesus' messianic confession and to the trial. This is the time in the gospel when the listeners are virtually required by the storyteller to decide whether or not they believe that Jesus is the Messiah. The translation, "how does it appear to you?," is a more direct and inclusive question about what the audience has seen and heard in the gospel story.

65: to spit, hit, slap / ἐμπτύειν, κολαφίζειν, ῥαπίσμασιν

These Greek words, which mean "to spit," "to hit," and "to strike or slap," describe the physical abuse directed at Jesus by some of those present at the trial. They are onomatopoetic sounds that convey the content of the story by the very sound of the words themselves. Rough transliterations are *emptuein* (which has some of the same character as the English "spittoon"), *kolaphizein* (which has some of the sound in English of a "coiled fist"), and *hrapismasin* (which has a similar sound to the English "raps" or "rapist"). The sound of the words invites the teller of this tale to articulate the consonants of the English words with dramatic force and to punctuate the sounds with similarly violent gestures. This is performative language that *does* what it describes.

Comments on the Meaning and Impact of the Story

14:53: the success of the conspiracy

Mark's story of Jesus' trial before the Sanhedrin begins with the successful completion of the conspiracy to arrest him with the help of Judas Iscariot. Judas' command to the arresting crowd in the previous story was, "Seize him and **lead him away**" (κρατήσατε αὐτὸν καὶ **ἀπάγετε**—14:44). The repetition of the key word in Judas' command makes the completion of both his command and the conspiracy explicit: "And they **led Jesus away** to the high priest" (**ἀπήγαγον** τὸν Ἰησοῦν πρὸς τὸν ἀρχιερέα—14:53). Furthermore, the repetition of the names of the coalition of authorities ("the chief priests, the elders and the scribes") who sent the crowd and now gather together reinforces the connection between the illegal arrest and this illegal trial in the middle of Passover night. The trial is thereby set in the context of the arrest and its atmosphere of extreme hostility.

54: Peter's kept vow and danger

The description of Peter's following Jesus is a note of good news. Peter kept his vow! Peter's prophecy or vow is fulfilled: "Even if they all are offended and run away, not me!" (14:29). The key word here, "to follow," echoes the earlier use of this verb to describe Peter's obedience to Jesus' initial calling of him and his brother (1:16 ff), the discipleship discourse after Peter's Messianic confession (8:34 ff), and Peter's affirmation of what the disciples have done: "Look, we have left everything and followed you" (10:29). Peter's following Jesus now was a climactic fulfillment of his discipleship and, heard in the context of stories such as David's going down into Saul's camp, an act of courage. It may have even been an applause line in Mark's story. But even if there was no applause, it was told in a tone of affirmation, perhaps with a clenched fist that signified, yes! Of course, this fulfillment also raises the question that follows from Jesus' response to Peter's promise that he will not be offended and run away: will Peter deny him or die with him?

The possibility that Peter may be identified and arrested is immediately implied in the description of the gathering in the courtyard of the high priest. Peter follows right into the middle of the enemy camp and sits with the guards in "the light." They have already tried to arrest the young man who was following Jesus in the garden. That vignette, related only three periods earlier, highlight's Peter's courage here. The implication of the setting is that if Peter is identified, he will be arrested and share Jesus' fate.

55–61: the structure of the trial story

The story of the trial itself is a unique combination of a kind of storytelling dialectic: reports of the developments in the trial followed by asides by the storyteller to the audience explaining what is actually going on. The reports re-create the heated and raucous atmosphere of the trial; the "inside" asides to the audience are quiet and intimate. Each new development in the trial is framed as a violation of Israelite legal practice: (1) a capital trial at night for which the whole Sanhedrin gathers, (2) seeking testimony to put the defendant to death and finding none, (3) the witnesses' bearing "false witness."[3] Mark assumes that his audience knows enough about Israelite legal tradition and earlier trials in Israel's history, such as the trials of Jeremiah, Isaiah, and Susanna, that they can ratify his description of the trial as a multifaceted travesty of justice. His initial report describes the trial in terms of the authorities' dilemma: they were seeking testimony to put Jesus to death, but they couldn't find any. This report echoes the plot with which the story began: "And the chief priests and the scribes were seeking how they might arrest him by a conspiracy and kill him" (καὶ ἐζήτουν οἱ ἀρχιερεῖς καὶ οἱ γραμματεῖς πῶς αὐτὸν ἐν δόλῳ κρατήσαντες ἀποκτείνωσιν—14:1b) This report, spoken in a loud voice, perhaps tinged with derision, reemphasizes the travesty of justice that is happening to Jesus and Mark's implicit charge of an illegal trial.

3. A focus of scholarly discussion has been the effort to determine the degree to which the trial as reported by Mark violated the laws regarding trial practice in first-century Judean law: see the summary in Brown, *Death of the Messiah*, 1:350–72. The focus here will be on identifying the appeals to the audiences and the implicit assumptions about what the audiences knew.

Mark's explanation of the reasons for their dilemma is related in an aside to the audience that provides inside information, perhaps softly, about what was really happening in the trial. This aside assumes that the projected audiences know enough about judicial practice to affirm the storyteller's implicit accusation that the trial was irregular and unjust. The two functionally interrelated reasons for the surprising inability of the Sanhedrin to find testimony to put Jesus to death are (1) many witnesses bore false witness, and (2) their testimony did not agree. According to Israelite law, a capital conviction required the valid and concurrent testimony of two witnesses (Num 35:30; Deut 17:6; 19:15). Furthermore, as the story of Daniel's intervention in the trial of Susanna demonstrates, the way to determine the truth of a number of witnesses was to see whether their testimony agreed. The story of Susanna's trial also makes it clear that those bearing false witness were guilty of a capital crime punishable by death, according to the law of Moses (see the account of Susanna above; also Deut 19:16–21).[4] Thus, Mark makes it clear from the very beginning of the trial both that the Sanhedrin had no case against Jesus and that those who testified against him were guilty of the capital crime of bearing false witness. And Mark assumes that his audiences know enough about the law to agree with him.

56–59: the false witnesses who did not agree

Mark then cites the testimony of "some." This testimony was probably reported at full volume with vehemence and finger-pointing to dramatize the charge of Jesus' treason against the Temple and the nation. The testimony of the witnesses echoes some phrases in earlier statements by Jesus that the audience has heard. The false witnesses' testimony is, "We heard this man say, 'I will destroy this Temple made with hands and in three days I will build another not made with hands'" ('Εγὼ **καταλύσω** τὸν ναὸν τοῦτον τὸν χειροποίητον καὶ ***διὰ τριῶν ἡμερῶν*** ἄλλον ἀχειροποίητον οἰκοδομήσω—14:58). Two earlier statements of Jesus in the gospel have sonic connections (noted in bold and italics) with this accusation. The first is Jesus' statement as he is leaving the Temple in response to one of his disciples, who was overwhelmed at the size of the stones and of the Temple buildings:

> Do you see these great buildings? Not one stone will be left here upon another that will not be **destroyed**." (οὐ μὴ ἀφεθῇ ὧδε λίθος ἐπὶ λίθον ὃς οὐ μὴ **καταλυθῇ**—13:2)

---

4. For further information about the commandment against false witness, see Moore, *Judaism*, 2:148n6.

The second accusation is a clear echo of the passion prophecies:

> And **after three days** he will rise. (καὶ μέτα τρεῖς ἡμέρας ἀναστήσεται—9:31; 10:34)

That is, the audience can confirm on the basis of their own hearing that Jesus said something like these phrases. But what Jesus actually said has been completely distorted by these witnesses. The implication of these accusations and their similarity to Jesus' earlier sayings is that these witnesses are liars committing what we would call perjury. They have taken fragments of Jesus' statements and twisted them into a prophecy against the Temple. The audience is invited to be the jury and to recognize that this is indeed a case of "bearing false witness" as in Daniel's interrogation of the lying elders in the story of Susanna. The witnesses are distorting Jesus' words. In effect, Mark as the teller of this story is appealing as a defense attorney to the audience as the jury.

Mark's concluding aside to his audience (14:59) reiterates that even the false witness of these lying criminals seeking to put an innocent man to death did not agree. Since only one example of their false testimony is cited, it was impossible for Mark's listeners to confirm his judgment that their testimony did not agree. But, in view of conflict between what some witnesses testified and what the audience knows Jesus actually said, there is every reason to believe Mark. Thus, the episode both explains and confirms that the Sanhedrin were unable to find incriminating evidence against Jesus.

And if the Sanhedrin can find no evidence against him, they will have to release him. To whatever degree the story of Susanna may be in the background of Mark's audiences' minds, that memory would have increased the intensity of the hope that, like Susanna, Jesus can escape condemnation and death. And regardless of the background, the storyteller's comments carry this implication. Mark evokes the hope that justice will prevail and that Jesus will be released.

60: the first interrogation by the high priest

The high priest's interrogation of Jesus is reported from an objective perspective without any further asides to the audience. However, the storyteller's point of view about this trial has been firmly established in the previous episodes. The repetition of the introductory participle that introduces the false witnesses—"standing up"/ ἀναστὰς—sets the high priest's interrogation in that discredited context. The high priest's question implies that Jesus has made no response to these false witnesses, and that the high priest assumes or at least pretends that their charges are valid. However, the listeners know that they have no evidence against Jesus. The implication of the high priest's dramatic action of standing up in the midst of the gathering is that he also recognizes that the effort to find witnesses who can give valid testimony against Jesus has failed, and that he has to try a different strategy. The high priest, therefore, turns to direct interrogation of Jesus in order to provoke him. His only hope now is to get Jesus to incriminate himself.

61: Jesus' silence and ancient law

Jesus' refusal to answer the high priest's question implies that Jesus also recognizes that they have no evidence against him and is intentionally silent. Silence was a legitimate form of defense in ancient law. Apollonius calls it "the fourth excellence in a court of law" and points to Socrates as a model (*Vit. Apol.* 8.2). Josephus reports that Jesus, son of Ananias, appeared four years before the war began (66 CE) and cried out dirges against the city and sanctuary. When he was brought to trial before the Roman governor Albinus and even when flogged brutally, he continued only to repeat his cries, "Woe to Jerusalem." In response to the governor's questions about who he was, where he came from, and why he was crying out, he answered nothing and was acquitted.[5] Furthermore, the form of the verb "to answer" that Mark uses here (ἀπεκρίνατο) is the unusual middle voice in the aorist tense that was used as a technical term in ancient legal practice for responses, in this case, for no response.[6]

The probability is that the storyteller reported Jesus' silence with an attitude of joy and delight. Jesus needs only to say nothing more and they will have to release him. Jesus' silence recalls the motif of the messianic secret and his frequent puzzling commands to the disciples, the demons, and those who were healed that they say nothing to anyone (1:34, 44; 3:12; 5:43; 7:36; 8:26, 30; 9:9). Jesus' own silence at this critical time conforms to these earlier commands to others and raises the hope even higher for the failure of the trial. The sonic connection between the high priest's question and Jesus' response—"**Do you answer nothing** . . . But he was silent and **answered nothing**" (Οὐκ ἀποκρίνῃ οὐδέν; . . . ὁ δὲ ἐσιώπα καὶ **οὐκ ἀπεκρίνατο οὐδέν**–14:60-61)—heightens the impact of Jesus' silence and implies that he is silent out of defiant refusal to answer these false charges.

---

5. Josephus, *JW* 300–305. For a comprehensive interpretation of Jesus' actions at the trials and the crucifixion as disengagement and obstruction, see Campbell, "Engagement, Disengagement, and Obstruction," 283–300.

6. M-M, 64.

The Trials at the High Priest's House (14:53–72) 169

53–60: the rhythm of public report/private audience aside

A central feature of this story is the alternation between loud and soft in the telling. This "loud-soft" pattern recurs four times in this story and is correlated with the content. The public elements were spoken publicly as an orator would speak in a public forum while the private, inside elements were spoken softly to the audience as privileged communication between the storyteller and the audience. The pattern is easily identified:

53	**And they led Jesus away to the house of the high priest, and all the chief priests and the elders and the scribes gathered together.**	LOUD
54	And Peter followed him at a distance right into the courtyard of the high priest and he was sitting with the guards warming himself by the light of the fire.	soft
55	**Now the chief priests and the whole council sought testimony against Jesus in order to put him to death, but they found none**	LOUD
56	Because many bore false witness against him and their testimony did not agree.	soft
57	**And some stood up and bore false witness against him, saying,**	LOUD
58	**"We heard him say, 'I will destroy this Temple made with hands and in three days build another not made with hands.'"**	
59	And even so, their testimony did not agree.	soft
	And the high priest stood up in the middle and questioned Jesus, saying, "Have you no answer to what these men are testifying against you?"	LOUD
60	But he was silent and answered nothing	soft

The introduction to the high priest's second question is a virtual repetition of the introduction to his first question:

And **the high priest** standing up in the middle **questioned** Jesus, saying … καὶ ἀναστὰς ὁ **ἀρχιερεὺς** εἰς μέσον **ἐπηρώτησεν** τὸν Ἰησοῦν λέγων … (14:60)

Again **the chief priest questioned** him and says to him … πάλιν ὁ **ἀρχιερεὺς ἐπηρώτα** αὐτὸν καὶ λέγει αὐτῷ (14:61b)

The repetition of the introduction and the storyteller's tone establishes the possibility that the other elements of the previous episode will be repeated:

the high priest will ask another question and Jesus will be silent. The logic of the story is that if Jesus is silent, he will be found not guilty and released.

Mark, however, makes two changes when he repeats this introduction. First, he reports the high priest's question in the imperfect tense instead of the aorist. The force of the imperfect here is "the idea of incomplete action in the past."[7] The first question is unanswered and awaits fulfillment in a further action. In this context, it implies that the high priest has not given up and is even more insistently trying again to get Jesus to respond and, hopefully, incriminate himself. Second, the storyteller introduces the high priest's actual question with "he says" in the historic present tense. This has the effect of making the high priest's question more immediate.

The high priest's second question, in contrast to the first, however, is not based on false testimony. In fact, his question recalls the central statements of Jesus' identity throughout the entire gospel story. There are four earlier statements with sonic connections to the high priest's question, "Are you the Christ, the Son of the Blessed One?" (Σὺ εἶ ὁ Χριστὸς ὁ υἱὸς τοῦ εὐλογητοῦ):

> The high priest's question repeats Peter's confession word for word—"You are the Christ" (Σὺ εἶ ὁ Χριστός—8:29)—though with the intonation of a question instead of a declaration.

> "Son of God" or its equivalent, "my Son," is heard from God at both the baptism and transfiguration, and from the demons:

> The voice from heaven speaks at the baptism: "You are my beloved Son." (Σῦ εἶ ὁ υἱός μου ὁ ἀγαπητός—1:11)

> The voice from the cloud speaks at the transfiguration: "This is my beloved Son." (οὗτός ἐστιν ὁ υἱός μου ὁ ἀγαρπητός—9:7)

> The demons speak: "You are the Son of God." (Σῦ εἶ ὁ υἱός τοῦ θεοῦ—3:11)

Thus, the sonic echoes of the high priest's climactic question have been in the air from the beginning of the story, in variations of "Son of God" spoken by God at the critical events of the baptism and transfiguration, as well as by the demons; and in the confession of Peter (8:29), which the high priest repeats exactly but in the tone of a question when he brings the two titles together. In other words, the high priest's question is a theme and variation of one of the most important leitmotifs in the entire gospel story. God, the demons, and Simon Peter are authoritative eyewitnesses who have given a common answer to the question of Jesus' identity.

---

7. MHT, 3:64.

Thus, there is a reversal in this second question of the high priest. His first question refers to the testimonies of false witnesses, but the second question resonates with the testimonies of reliable witnesses throughout the gospel. Mark probably reflects this reversal of content in the way that he reports the high priest's questions. The patterns of storytelling throughout the gospel indicate that the second question of the high priest is quiet and slow. Many of the places of climactic emphasis in the story build up to a quiet, slow, and emotionally intense climax, such as the ending of the whole gospel. The contrast of the quiet tone of the high priest's second question to the loud/soft pattern in the earlier story heightens the impact of the question (see the chart above).

While the high priest now confronts Jesus with titles that Jesus has implicitly acknowledged throughout the gospel, in every previous instance where a character in the story has recognized who he is, Jesus has silenced them.[8] This general command to silence about something Mark's audience suspects is true on the testimony of both Mark and the voice from heaven raises the question for Mark's audience, why does Jesus command silence about his identity? In the scholarly literature, this has been called the Messianic secret. Both within and at the end of the first series of healing/conflict stories, the unclean spirits fall down before Jesus and shout, "You are the Son of God!" (1:24–25, 34; 3:12). Jesus' response is to sternly order or rebuke them "lest they make him known." The inevitable question for the listeners is, why would Jesus rebuke the spirits? The only clue to this puzzle is the storyteller's report, following the healing of the man with a withered hand, that the Pharisees and the Herodians were plotting to destroy him (3:6).

Later in the gospel, Jesus' immediate response to Peter's statement that he is the Messiah is again to command the disciples to say nothing about him. And again the question for the audience is, why command silence? The first passion prophecy follows and the answer to the question is implicit in the prophecy of his betrayal and death. But the prophecy does not directly answer the question raised by Jesus' command to silence. Mark's audience has to make that connection.

Coming down from the mountain where Peter, James, and John witnessed Jesus' transfiguration and heard the same voice from heaven that

---

8. This general rule excludes the voice from heaven in the baptism story where the voice speaks to Jesus alone: "You are my beloved son." This testimony to Jesus as Son of God is overheard by Mark's audience, but there is no indication that any of the characters in the story who witnessed Jesus' baptism heard it. Contrast Matt 3:17, where "This is my beloved Son" is clearly a testimony to the people who witness Jesus' baptism. Contrast also Mark 9:7, commented on below.

Jesus heard at his baptism, saying to them, "This is my beloved Son," (9:7), Jesus again commands silence, until after his resurrection. Once again this implies that Jesus accepts the title. So why does he command silence? His naming of his resurrection as the time after which the disciples can tell others about Jesus' messiahship echoes the way he has just responded to Peter, where he implicitly accepted Peter's declaration that he was the Messiah, yet spoke only of the suffering, death, and resurrection of the Son of Man. Again this suggests but does not clearly state a possible answer.

The question raised by Jesus' commands to silence about his identity is raised with somewhat less intensity by the other commands to silence, each of which is a response to works of healing or to the prophecy of death and resurrection (1:44; 5:43; 7:36; 8:30). This curious and often climactic feature of this series of stories running through the first half of Mark's narrative keeps provoking the question, why does Jesus command people to silence? Why does Jesus keep telling people to say nothing about the mighty works he has done? Despite the clear testimonies to Jesus as Son of God and Messiah by reliable witnesses—especially God—in the hearing of and for the benefit of Mark's listeners, Jesus' failure to explicitly embrace those testimonies, combined with his commands to be silent about them, raise the question for the listeners: who does Jesus think he is? His own opinion about his identity remains a mystery.

Thus, Jesus' commands to silence and his own silence are the background for the high priest's question. Will Jesus maintain the silence he enjoins on others? Will he continue to equivocate about the titles that reliable witnesses have given him, especially now that he is on trial for his life? It is typical of mystery stories to raise such questions and give no decisive answer until the end of the story. The solving of the mystery only comes at the end. And a motif such as this is most dramatically experienced when the whole story is heard at one time.

Thus, in the moment of silent suspense between the high priest's question and Jesus' answer, the audience is invited to remember Jesus' earlier responses to messianic discussions and his puzzling silence in relation to his own identity. The expectation of Jesus' probable response and the hope that is being raised by the dynamics of the trial converge in an implicit, hopeful expectation: Jesus will remain silent and say nothing.

Jesus' response is, therefore, a reversal of the audience's expectations and a disappointment of the hopes raised by the earlier course of the trial. Instead of remaining silent in response to the high priest's question about his identity, and in contravention of his command to others throughout the narrative, he speaks. The introduction to Jesus' statement, "But Jesus said . . ." ὁ δὲ Ἰησοῦς εἶπεν, is a clue to what is coming, because the storyteller has

The Trials at the High Priest's House (14:53–72)

used this formula as an introduction for unexpected, surprising answers of Jesus throughout the story (9:23, 39; 10:5, 18, 38, 39; 11:29; 12:17; 14:6). Jesus' statement is the exact opposite of silence and provides the high priest with just the self-incriminating evidence the council has been seeking. Jesus confesses his identity openly and directly.

The probability is that the high priest's question and Jesus' answer were spoken as a reversal of the earlier pattern of loud/soft shown in the charts above to "soft/loud" here. If so, the high priest's question was voiced quietly while Jesus' answer was a crescendo of apocalyptic vision in the tradition of both Daniel and the prophet Isaiah. Jesus' confession echoes both canonical Isaiah (the vision of the throne room in Isaiah 6) and the *Martyrdom and Ascension of Isaiah* (see above). In that case, the words "I am" would have been soft, and the vision of the Son of Man would have been a crescendo of prophetic affirmation.

62: the sonic echoes in Jesus' confession

Jesus' confession echoes several statements earlier in the gospel story. The most resonant echoes are those from earlier stories in Mark that have the same words as Jesus' statement here. The confession "I am" (Ἐγώ εἰμι) echoes Jesus' self-identification to the disciples when he comes to them walking on the water:

> Take heart; *I am*. Don't be afraid.
> Θαρσεῖτε, ἐγώ εἰμι. Μὴ φοβεῖσθε. (6:50)

Thus, the first of these echoes, "I am," recalls the disciples' numinous experience of the apparition-like appearance of Jesus moving across the waters of the windblown sea in the early hours of the morning. This self-identification to his terrified disciples resonates with God's self-identification at the burning bush (Exod 3:14)[9] and with the frequent motif in the Psalms of God's command over the sea—especially in Ps 77:19, where God is said to make his way through the paths of the sea. Furthermore, Jesus' assurance, "Don't be afraid!" is associated with theophanies in which God or God's angel appears to humans (e.g., Gen 15:1; 26:24; Dan 10:12, 19; Mark 16:6; Luke 1:13, 30). Thus, the sonic resonance of Jesus' first words in response to the high priest recalls the theophany experience of the disciples on the sea, in which Jesus' walking on the sea and his words—"I am. Don't be afraid"—imply that he is God.

---

9. See Brown, *Gospel according to John*, appendix 6, 1:533–38 for the use of ἐγώ εἰμι in an absolute sense as the name of God.

Jesus' prophecy that those hearing him "will see[10] the Son of Man seated on the right hand of Power and coming 'with the clouds of heaven'" also echoes his prophecy to the disciples in the apocalyptic discourse:

> Then they **will see 'the Son of Man coming in clouds' with** great **power** and glory.
> Καὶ τότε **ὄψονται τὸν υἱὸν τοῦ ἀνθρώπου ἐρχόμενον ἐν νεφέλαις μετὰ δυνάμεως** πολλῆς καὶ δόξης. (13:26, NRSV)

It also repeats key words from Jesus' teaching about the Messiah as David's son in the Temple:

> The Lord said to my Lord, / "**Sit at my right hand** . . ."
> Εἶπεν κύριος τῷ κυρίῳ μου, **Κάθου ἐκ δεξιῶν μου** . . . (12:36, NRSV)

The words in bold, "sit at my right hand," are repeated in Jesus' answer to the high priest:

> **I am, and you will see the Son of Man seated on the right hand** of power and coming 'with the clouds of heaven.'
> **Ἐγώ εἰμι, καὶ ὄψεσθε τὸν υἱὸν τοῦ ἀνθρώπου ἐκ δεξιῶν καθήμενον τῆς δυνάμεως** (14:62, NRSV)

These leitmotifs in Mark resonate with earlier themes in the traditions of Israel. The first is an echo of Psalm 110:

> The LORD said to my lord, / '**Sit at my right hand** . . .'
> Εἶπεν ὁ κύριος τῷ κυρίῳ μου **Κάθου ἐκ δεξιῶν μου** (Ps 110:1, NRSV)

This psalm goes on to describe God's subjugation of the enemies of the king whom God is addressing.

The major tradition echoed in the rest of Jesus' prophecy concerning the Son of Man is Daniel's vision:

> I beheld in a night vision and behold with **the clouds of heaven** there was one **coming** like a **Son of Man** . . .
> ἐθεώρουν ἐν ὁράματι τῆς νυκτὸς καὶ ἰδοὺ **μετὰ τῶν νεφελῶν τοῦ οὐρανοῦ** ὡς **υἱὸς ἀνθρώπου ἐρχόμενος** . . . (Dan 7:13, NRSV)

The vision of the Son of Man in Daniel is an introduction to the "Ancient One's" appointment of this "one like a human being" as the king of a universal and everlasting kingdom in which all peoples, nations, and languages will serve him. In Daniel (from the second century BCE) this is announced

---

10. The personal ending of the Greek verb translated "you will see" is plural.

The Trials at the High Priest's House (14:53–72) 175

as the climax of the vision of the four great beasts, which represent the empires of the Babylonians, the Medes, the Persians, and the Greeks—empires that had dominated Israel since the exile, which began in 598 BCE.

But Jesus' prophecy of the coming of the Son of Man on the clouds of heaven for all to see is announced following his claiming the titles Messiah and Son of the Blessed with his climactic "I am." This prophecy to the Sanhedrin goes beyond the echoes of Daniel and even beyond his own vision of that future coming of the Son of Man (13:24–27) that he shares with his disciples immediately before his passion. It is the climax of his many statements about himself as the Son of Man. Several of these statements have been noted above, but I will quote all of them here and would suggest that you read them aloud in order to experience a little more of Mark's composition of this leitmotif throughout his story:

> But so that you may know that the Son of Man has authority on earth to forgive sins . . . (The healing of the paralytic, 2:10, NRSV)
>
> The sabbath was made for humankind, and not humankind for the sabbath; so the Son of Man is lord even of the sabbath. (Plucking grain on the sabbath, 2:28, NRSV)
>
> And he began to teach them that the Son of Man must suffer many things, and be rejected by the elders and the chief priests and the scribes, and be killed, and after three days rise again. (First passion prophecy, 8:31, NRSV)
>
> Those who are ashamed of me and of my words in this adulterous and sinful generation, of them the Son of Man will be ashamed when he comes in the glory of his Father with the holy angels. (Messianic confession and discipleship discourse, 8:38, NRSV)
>
> . . . he ordered them to tell no one about what they had seen [at the transfiguration], until after the Son of Man had risen from the dead (Transfiguration, 9:9, NRSV)
>
> How then is it written about the Son of Man, that he is to go through many sufferings and be treated with contempt? (Transfiguration, 9:12, NRSV)
>
> The Son of Man is to be betrayed into human hands, and they will kill him, and three days after being killed, he will rise again. (Second passion prophecy, 9:31, NRSV)
>
> . . . and the Son of Man will be handed over to the chief priests and the scribes, and they will condemn him to death; then they

will hand him over to the Gentiles; they will mock him, and spit upon him, and flog him, and kill him; and after three days he will rise again. (Third passion prophecy, 10:33, NRSV)

For the Son of Man came not to be served but to serve, and to give his life a ransom for many. (James and John seeking honor, 10:45, NRSV)

And then they will see the Son of Man coming in clouds with great power and glory. (Apocalyptic discourse, 13:26, NRSV)

For the Son of Man goes as it is written of him, but woe to that one by whom the Son of Man is betrayed! (Betrayal prophecy, 14:21, NRSV)

And he came the third time, and said to them, "Are you still sleeping and taking your rest? Enough! The hour has come; the Son of Man is betrayed into the hands of sinners." (14:41)

Jesus utters all but one of these sayings (9:9) in direct discourse. There are two basic themes in these statements: the authority and power of the Son of Man; and the prophecies of his passion, resurrection, and coming on the clouds. Thus, in his own self-descriptions and in the statements and prophecies about himself as Son of Man, Jesus describes his distinctive role in the deliverance of the world from captivity to the powers of evil. In effect, Jesus outlines a way of positive and decisive engagement with the powers of this evil age by actions in the service of others, including his willingness to suffer and die rather than to bring about the suffering and death of others.

In his response to the chief priest's direct question about his identity, by means of the designation "Son of Man" as he himself has spoken of it throughout the gospel story, Jesus both agrees with the high priest's description of his identity as the Messiah and Son of God and redefines its meaning. The implication of his third-person statement about the Son of Man is that he will be the triumphant Son of Man of Dan 7:13 and the triumphant messianic figure of Psalm 110, whose enemies are the spiritual powers of evil.

The chief priest's question and Jesus' answer thus draw together the central statements regarding Jesus' identity throughout the story. Furthermore, Jesus directly answers the lingering questions in the story about his own self-conception. He affirms that he is the Messiah, the Son of God, but he redefines these titles and the strategies of redemption and deliverance implicit within them in the categories of the Son of Man. His prophecy about the coming of the Son of Man also implies that all of his earlier Son of Man statements were also reinterpretations of the role and mission of the

Messiah. Throughout the story, therefore, Jesus has been acting as Messiah and teaching his disciples about the meaning of that title and role.

63: the high priest's condemnation

By breaking his silence about his identity implicit in the titles named by the high priest, however, Jesus assures his condemnation. The high priest's response is immediate. The tearing of his garments was a ritual gesture of grief because of the necessity of pronouncing a sentence of death.[11] The high priest's question to the council regarding witnesses refers back to earlier testimony of the witnesses and the council's original search for testimony in order to put Jesus to death. His charge of blasphemy recalls the initial charge of the scribes at the healing of the paralytic in response to Jesus' pronouncement "Your sins are forgiven" (2:5, 7). The reason for the charge there was Jesus' implicit assumption of divine authority in forgiving the man's sins. Here the charge is based on Jesus' messianic confession and his description of himself as a divine figure seated at the right hand of God. Regardless of the particular legal issues involved in the charge of blasphemy,[12] the primary implication of the high priest's charge is that he regards Jesus' confession as blasphemy against God.

64: the question addressed to the audience

The high priest's climactic question—"How does it appear to you?"—asks each listener to make their own decision about Jesus' testimony. In the telling of the story, this question is addressed directly to the members of the audience: how does it appear to you? Because of its centrality in the impact of this story for its original audiences, the storytelling dynamic of the high priest's question needs precise identification. Prior to the high priest's question, the storyteller directly addresses the audience several times and gives them inside information about what is happening in the trial. Indeed, he alternates between oratorical description of the public trial and private asides to the audience that explain what is really happening in the trial. Even

---

11. The later (second-century) Mishnaic requirement (*Sanhedrin* 7:5) that the judges at a blasphemy trial must tear their clothes on hearing the blasphemy may reflect earlier legal practices. While there are many earlier stories of persons tearing their garments in grief (e.g., Jacob in Gen 37:34; David in 2 Sam 1:11–12; Joshua in Josh 7:6; Elisha in 2 Kgs 2:12) that may have been known by Mark's audience, no direct parallels to a presiding judge tearing his garments have been identified.

12. For a comprehensive summary of the various legal and historical issues related to the trial of Jesus, see Brown, *Gospel according to John*, 2:791–802.

the storyteller's description of Jesus' silence was probably told expectantly rather than objectively, thereby implying that Jesus recognizes the fact that the prosecution can find no valid testimony against him, and that he is intentionally silent in order to provide no self-incriminating evidence.[13] In the aftermath of Jesus' confession of his identity as the Messiah, the storyteller takes the role of the high priest and addresses the audience as the Sanhedrin: "What need do we have for further witnesses? You have heard his blasphemy. How does it appear to you?" The members of the audience, addressed as members of the Sanhedrin, are asked to make a decision based on what they have heard. Is Jesus' confession of his identity as the Messiah true or false? Is his statement blasphemy, or is it a statement of the truth?

The high priest's loud and highly dramatic speech is, therefore, an appeal to a twofold jury: (1) in the story, Jesus is on trial, and the Sanhedrin is the jury. (2) In the telling of the story, the storyteller asks the question as the high priest and the audience is the jury. On this second level of the storyteller's appeal to the audience for a judgment, what are the major lines of evidence that Mark has presented in his story?

1. A series of witnesses—the storyteller (who implicitly presents himself at the beginning of the gospel as a witness), God at both the baptism and the transfiguration (1:9–11), the demons (1:34 and 4:12), and Peter (8:29)—have implicitly testified that Jesus is either the Messiah or the Son of God. Their testimony is recalled by the high priest's question.

2. The audience can confirm on the basis of evidence they have heard that the testimony of the witnesses called by the authorities (14:55–59) is a distortion of Jesus' words and is false.

3. Jesus himself has now testified that he is the Messiah and in his testimony has indirectly referred to all of his earlier statements regarding the Son of Man. Jesus' confession, therefore, is based on a frequently

---

13. A recent movie, *A Few Good Men*, has a trial scene with some similar dynamics. A colonel of the United States Marines is called as a witness in the court-martial of two young marines who followed orders of a code red and beat an underperforming recruit, who died of his injuries. The only chance that the young defense attorney for these marines has of proving their innocence of a charge of murder and preventing their execution is to provoke the colonel into admitting that he issued the code red. In the film the audience knows from several lines of evidence that the colonel issued the order. When finally asked directly, the colonel defiantly answers that he ordered the code red. In the movie trial, the colonel is the bad guy, and his admission is effectively a confession of murder. In Mark's story, Jesus is the good guy. But in both trials, the main character provides the evidence for his conviction by his answer to a direct question. In both trials, the audience is implicitly asked to serve as the jury. In the movie, the audience is asked to find the colonel guilty. In Mark, the audience is asked to find Jesus innocent of the charge of blasphemy.

repeated theme that runs through the entire gospel. Furthermore, several of Jesus' prophecies have recently been fulfilled: the preparations for the triumphal entry into Jerusalem, the withering of the fig tree, the prophecies of war and trials (which have been fulfilled in the audience's recent experience), the preparations for the Passover, the prophecies of betrayal by one of the twelve, and the disciples running away. The audience has conclusive evidence that Jesus is a true prophet.

4. The high priest's rejection of Jesus' claim is set in the context of the authorities' plot to destroy him. Given the audience's knowledge of the motive of the high priest and the entire Sanhedrin, the validity of the high priest's charge of blasphemy is compromised and can be judged by the audience jury as false. Furthermore, the Sanhedrin's condemnation of Jesus is clearly politically motivated.

5. On multiple grounds, the trial is a travesty of Israelite justice.

Therefore, on the basis of the evidence presented in the story, the audience, addressed as the council, is invited to answer the high priest's question—"How does it appear to you?"—with the decision that Jesus' confession is the truth rather than blasphemy.

64–65: the Council's verdict and abuse

The council's condemnation of Jesus as guilty and deserving of death is the fulfillment of the second part of Jesus' final passion prophecy, as is made unmistakably clear by the repetition with minor variations of the same words:

> the Son of Man will be handed over to the chief priests and the scribes and **they will condemn him to death** . . .
> ὁ υἱὸς τοῦ ἀνθρώπου παραδοθήσεται τοῖς ἀρχιερεῦσιν καὶ τοῖς γραμματεῦσιν καὶ **κατακρινοῦσιν αὐτὸν θανάτῳ** (10:33, NRSV)
>
> **they** all **condemned him** as deserving **death**
> οἱ δὲ πάντες **κατέκριναν αὐτὸν** ἔνοχον εἶναι **θανάτου** (14:64b, NRSV)

The notice that they spit on him also fulfills another element in Jesus' prophecy. But the bitterness of the irony is increased by the fact that Jesus' prophecy foretells the abuse that the Son of Man will suffer at the hands of the Gentiles: "and they will hand him over to the Gentiles and they will mock him and spit on him" (10:33b–34). The storyteller appeals to specifically Israelite norms of judgment here. The norm is that handing Jesus over to the Gentiles is handing him over to the enemies of Israel, and that the systems of Gentile justice will subject him to even greater mockery and abuse. But even Jesus did not foresee that the chief priests and scribes would be so spiteful.

Their mocking command that he prophesy, apparently about who is going to slap him next, is also doubly ironic because their action fulfills Jesus' earlier prophecy and because Jesus predicted that it would be the Gentiles who would mock him, not other Israelites. Their implicit assumption and what they are seeking to demonstrate by this mocking game is that he is a false prophet. Their mockery derives from a specific Israelite tradition: "the prophet who presumes to speak a word in my name which I have not commanded him to speak, or who speaks in the name of other gods—that same prophet shall die" (Deut 18:20). Therefore, from the point of view of the storyteller, the responses of the Sanhedrin are wrong in virtually every possible way.

The climax of the trial is the short notice that the guards (οἱ ὑπηρέται), the group with whom Peter was sitting (14:54), hit or beat Jesus as they led him away. The potential of similar treatment for Peter is thereby implied. The Sanhedrin's despicable actions toward Jesus heighten the audience's alienation from them. The characterization of the Sanhedrin has the characteristic pattern of the rhetoric of condemnation.

The council's condemnation of Jesus is also an implicit explanation for Jesus' earlier efforts to keep his messianic identity secret. As soon as he confesses openly who he is, he is condemned to death. Indeed, Mark implies that Jesus could have escaped condemnation and death by keeping the secret. His confession alone gives them a basis for condemning him to death.

53–65: the Israelite motive and appeal in the story of the trial

When heard against the background of other trials of prophets and righteous Israelites, this story is an appeal for Judeans and Gentiles who identify with the traditions of Israel to recognize Jesus' courage and loyalty to God and to the mission he has received from God. It is also a major indictment of the religious leaders of Israel. The question underlying this story, similar to the question about Judas that underlies the betrayal story, is, why did the leaders of Israel want to kill Jesus? The clues to this mystery lead back through the story to the conflicts in the Temple's court of the Gentiles, the controversies over the appropriate observance of the law and the forgiveness of sins, and Jesus' implicit claims to a unique relationship with God. The implication about the Jerusalem authorities' immediate motive for wanting to kill Jesus is his prophetic protest in the Temple. Jesus' prophetic sign and demonstration in the Temple is presented by Mark as a protest against the replacement of a universal place of prayer in the court of the Gentiles with a place for the business of the sacrificial system. The implication of Jesus' prophetic demonstration and speech is that the priests were perverting the purpose of the court of the Gentiles as a place of prayer for Gentile as well as Judean visitors to Jerusalem and the Temple. The business of changing money and selling sacrificial animals in the outer courtyard made it impossible to pray there. Jesus' quotation of Jeremiah may also have been heard by Mark's postwar audiences as a prophetic protest against the alliances of some of the chief priests with the leaders of the rebellion and against making the Temple a den of warriors/insurrectionists (λῄστης) and the center of the final battle with the Romans.

The major connections in the larger plot of the gospel, however, are with the issues of the law and of Jesus' authority to reinterpret the law as in the dispute over the forgiveness of the paralytic's sins, the healing of the man with a withered hand on the Sabbath, the healing of an unclean woman, the suspension of the cleanliness and dietary laws, and the healing and feeding of Gentiles. Implicit in many of these conflicts is the issue of the appropriate relationship of Judeans with Gentiles. That is, the reasons for the Sanhedrin's opposition to Jesus in the story are distinctively Judean issues, all of which are grounded in the understanding of the law and its role in Judean life. And the audience is asked to make judgments about these competing understandings of the law. In the trial, the conflicts between Jesus and the religious authorities come down to the issue of Jesus' identity and whether or not he is the Messiah, the Son of God, and, therefore, an authoritative interpreter of the law.

The dynamics of this climactic story do not support the frequent picture of Mark's audience as Gentile Christians. The issues in the trial are not internal church issues around a Divine Man or a suffering Son of Man Christology. And most important, the dynamic structure of the story is not anti-Jewish. The appeals of the storyteller are based on distinctively Israelite legal norms. Thus, blasphemy is a unique feature of Israelite religious law. The central appeal of the story is to find Jesus' messianic confession to be the truth rather than blasphemy. Furthermore, the central indictment of the Sanhedrin implicit in the story centers on the perversion of Israelite law in the conduct of the trial, an indictment based on the assumption that the audience knows the basic rules of Israelite legal practice. That knowledge was more widespread among Judeans than Gentiles.

The underlying dynamic of the plot is the raising of the hope that Jesus may be able to escape condemnation because of the false and contradictory testimony of the witnesses. That hope is broken by Jesus' own courageous testimony. When asked directly about his identity, Jesus answers with unequivocal clarity. Jesus asserts his identity as Messiah and Son of God under the greatest stress and at the cost of being condemned to death. The impact of the story is to magnify the respect and honor for Jesus as a prophet and as Messiah as well as to further increase the audience's emotional distance and alienation from the chief priests, the scribes, and the elders.

The Performance of the Story

The performance of the story of Jesus' trial before the Sanhedrin requires painting the big picture of a major political and religious trial, and intimately filling in details for the audience of what is actually happening. It may be helpful to establish two different places a step or two apart in the performance space, to associate each place with telling different kinds of events, and to physically move back and forth from objectively describing the trial (in one place) to delivering inside information directly to the audience (in another place). To communicate the telling of inside information as distinct from objective description of the ostensive event, you may choose to raise a hand to one side of your face or to lean forward.

The trip to the house of the high priest sets the scene for the whole trial story. The gathering of the Sanhedrin can be told as a busy assembling of the court. A key word in this sentence is "all," and this word needs to convey that this was a big gathering. In effect, this opening draws the picture of the setting of the trial. The fact that "all" of the chief priests, scribes, and elders gathered in the middle of the night is both surprising and threatening. Introducing this surprising threat with big gestures is central to describing this scene.

Peter's following Jesus sounds a note of gladness and fulfillment. Peter does it! The description of his place around the fire needs to be told with a tone that suggests threat as well as secrecy. A whisper and a sidewise glance may help to convey the character of this setting for both stories to follow.

The description of the council's quest for evidence is best told as an indictment, and their failure to find any is to be told with a note of hope. It is important to convey that this judicial procedure is highly irregular. But also their inability to find the evidence is told happily and implies that they may be unable to convict Jesus. The "inside" explanation about the reason for their inability to convict him is told as an aside or direct comment to the audience. You may want to move closer to your audience at this point and let your tone be soft and confidential. The atmosphere here is like a spy thriller.

The Trials at the High Priest's House (14:53–72)

The witnesses' testimony is an opportunity to embody and personify the false witnesses. There is probably a finger pointed at Jesus' place and a tone of vociferous accusation. It will be hard to overdo the degree of rage expressed by the false witnesses. It is up to the audience to compare the statements of the witnesses with the earlier statements of Jesus and to find the charge invalid. But once again the loudness of the accusation is undercut by the quiet of the storyteller's inside info to the audience.

The high priest's question is even more accusatory and has more bluster then the testimony of the witnesses. But the embodiment of the high priest invites walking around a little and asking his question with a tone of accusation and a certain disdain. The description of Jesus' silence is once again spoken quietly, but it is also extremely hopeful and fraught with the possibility of release. The shortness of the colon also provides the space to say this slowly so that the audience can clearly figure out the implications of Jesus' silence.

The high priest's second question is quiet and is in marked contrast to all that has gone before. Whether it is spoken as an implicit accusation or as a real question will be for you to decide. Both are possible. My own inclination is to tell this as a real question since it is the central question of the whole story. The storyteller as the high priest needs to address this question to the place where Jesus is imagined to be standing rather than to the audience. Jesus' answer is a crescendo of volume and intensity. My sense is that his initial positive answer is a direct and simple statement of fact with no note of either protest or urgency of assertion. The announcement of the Son of Man's coming is a prophetic pronouncement spoken with the full authority of a prophet. It is strong and highly assertive, and it builds to a crescendo of affirmation.

The high priest's response is introduced with a gesture of tearing the inner garments of his robe. It is not out of the question that you might actually tear something, although that would require some attention to costume that may not be possible. The high priest's words are spoken directly to the audience. If possible, look directly at every member of the audience so that the audience is explicitly addressed as the Sanhedrin. The question, "How does it appear to you?" is a climax of the story.

The sentence of death is performative discourse in which the word does what it describes. There is no concern about overdoing this sentence. It is high drama. This entire concluding episode is told in a tone of condemnation and mockery that returns to the earlier description of the trial scene in its grandeur. It is possible to tell this with an underlying tone of grief and disbelief at the injustice of the trial and this judgment.

This story does not invite the teller to underplay the telling of this story. It may be possible for some tellers to convey the full impact of this trial by understating what is happening. But I doubt it. You will find the most appropriate way for you to tell this story if you imagine yourself in that place and describe what is happening there so that your audience is also present at the event and experiences it fully.

The contrast between the nonviolence and strength of Jesus with the violence and desperate determination of the council is at the heart of the dynamic of this story. It embodies the universal conflict between the advocates of nonviolence, peace, and reconciliation with enemies and the rage of those who find such policies threatening and frightening.

Peter's Trial and Denial (14:66–72)

Sound Map

14:66Καὶ ὄντος τοῦ Πέτρου κάτω **ἐν τῇ αὐλῇ** ἔρχεται μία τῶν **παιδισκῶν**
        τοῦ ἀρχιερέως.
67καὶ **ἰδοῦσα τὸν Πέτρον** θερμαινόμενον ἐμβλέψασα αὐτῷ λέγει,
    Καὶ σὺ μετὰ τοῦ Ναζαρηνοῦ ἦσθα τοῦ Ἰησοῦ.
68ὁ **δὲ ἠρνήσατο λέγων,**
    Οὔτε οἶδα οὔτε ἐπίσταμαι σὺ τί λέγεις.

καὶ ἐξῆλθεν ἔξω εἰς τὸ προαύλιον.
69καὶ ἡ **παιδίσκη ἰδοῦσα αὐτὸν** ἤρξατο πάλιν λέγειν τοῖς παρεστῶσιν ὅτι
    Οὗτος **ἐξ αὐτῶν ἐστιν.**
70ὁ **δὲ πάλιν ἠρνεῖτο.**

καὶ μετὰ μικρὸν πάλιν οἱ παρεστῶτες ἔλεγον τῷ Πέτρῳ,
    Ἀληθῶς **ἐξ αὐτῶν εἶ.**
καὶ γὰρ Γαλιλαῖος εἶ.
71ὁ **δὲ ἤρξατο ἀναθεματίζειν καὶ ὀμνύναι** ὅτι
    Οὐκ οἶδα τὸν ἄνθρωπον τοῦτον ὃν λέγετε.

72**καὶ εὐθὺς ἐκ δευτέρου ἀλέκτωρ ἐφώνησεν.**
καὶ ἀνεμνήσθη ὁ Πέτρος τὸ ῥῆμα ὡς εἶπεν αὐτῷ ὁ Ἰησοῦς ὅτι
    Πρὶν **ἀλέκτορα φωνῆσαι δὶς** τρίς με ἀπαρνήσῃ.
καὶ ἐπιβαλὼν ἔκλαιεν.

The Trials at the High Priest's House (14:53–72)

Translation

66Meanwhile Peter was down below **in the courtyard**,
    and one of the **servant girls** of the high priest came by
    67and **when she saw Peter warming himself**, she looked
                                          at him and says,
    "And you were with that Nazarene, Jesus."
68But **he denied it** saying,
    "**I don't know** or understand what you are talking about."

And he went out into the forecourt and the cock crowed.
69And **the servant girl saw him** and began again to say to the
                                                        bystanders,
    "This man **is one of them**."
70And again **he denied it**.

Then after a little while the bystanders again said to Peter,
    "Surely **you are one of them**, because you are a Galilean."
71But he began to curse himself and to swear an oath,
    "**I do not know** this man you are talking about."

72**And immediately the cock crowed** for a second time.
And Peter remembered that Jesus had said to him,
    "Before **the cock crows twice, three times you will deny me**."
And beating on himself, he wept.

Ancient Associations and Connections

One of the earliest novels in antiquity is Chariton's *Callirhoe*. Most scholars date this story to the second half of the first century. If this dating is correct, it was written in the same period as the Gospels. The following summary will include two quotations with thematic connections to the Gospel.

    Callirhoe and Chaereas are young and beautiful children of noble families in Syracuse. They fall in love and are joyfully married. But in a jealous rage, induced by a plot of jealous suitors, Chaereas kicks the now newly pregnant Callirhoe in the abdomen and she apparently dies. She is buried in a tomb and wakes up in the tomb only to be captured by pirates, who rob the grave and take her away and sell her as a slave. Meanwhile, after discovering she is still alive, Chaereas and his loyal friend Polymarchus sail off to rescue her. But their warship is captured by other pirates, and they are sold as slaves. After being arrested for the crimes of other slaves, they are sentenced to be crucified:

> Without even seeing them or listening to their defense he [the governor Mithridates] immediately ordered the sixteen cellmates to be crucified. They were duly brought out, chained together at foot and neck, each carrying his own cross. The executioners added this grim public spectacle to the requisite penalty as a deterrent to others so minded. Now Chaereas said nothing as he was led off with the others, but on taking up his cross Polycharmus exclaimed, "It is your fault, Callirhoe, that we are in this mess. You are responsible for all our troubles!"[14]

Polycharmus' lament is overheard, and a servant tells the governor, Mithridates, who interrogates Polycharmus on threat of torture about the identity of this woman. Polycharmus is reluctant:

> Sir, it is a long story, and it will no longer do me any good. I will not bother you with chatter at the wrong time. Besides, I am afraid that if I dally my friend will pass on ahead of me, and I want to die with him.[15]

Everyone is moved, and Mithridates asks him, now with sympathy, to tell him the whole story. Polycharmus concludes his story: "I beg you, sir, tell the executioner not to separate even our crosses." His story moves Mithridates, in part because he had met Challirhoe and been overwhelmed with love for her, and he rushes to save Chaereas before he dies. Chaereas is just mounting his cross when they find him, take him down from the cross, and treat him as a royal guest with a great banquet.

This episode in Chariton's story shares many common motifs with Mark: friendship and loyalty, crucifixion, dying with a friend, acknowledging the past in a situation of trial. Whether or not Mark's audiences knew this specific story, the existence of this story, dated to the same historical period as Mark, is a sign that these highly specific themes were in the air at the time of the composition of the gospel.

In this story, the hero's friend wants to die with him, and his testimony saves the hero from the cross. The hero is taken down from the cross, his status is verified, and he is treated to a great dinner. Of course, this is a romantic fictional story in which everything eventually turns out happily, and no one except the bad guys die. But it also makes clear what the audiences of the late first century hoped for: the hero will escape death, and his closest

---

14. Chariton, *Callirhoe* 4.2.
15. Ibid., 4.3.

friend will be faithful to the death. Those hopes are a significant dimension of the cultural setting and audience expectations that shaped the impact of Mark's story.

Among the many stories in the Israelite storytelling tradition with the basic elements of the rhetoric of involvement and implication, two stories from the storytelling traditions of Israel particularly help to clarify the background of Peter's denial. The stories of the man and the woman in the garden of Eden and of Nathan telling the parable of the poor shepherd and his lamb to David are examples of the highly distinctive ways Israelite storytellers engaged their audiences in the realization of sinfulness.[16] I will summarize the context and quote the most directly analogous sections of these stories. In contrast to other Israelite stories that were immediate background for Mark's stories, these stories reflect the storytelling traditions on which Mark was drawing in his shaping of the story of Jesus.

The second story of creation in Genesis 2-3 begins with the creation of the man and the garden of Eden in which the Lord God places him. The creation-of-the-garden episode ends with the Lord God commanding the man not to eat of the tree of the knowledge of good and evil, and predicting what will happen if he does:

> And the LORD God commanded the man, "You may freely eat of every tree of the garden; but of the tree of the knowledge of good and evil you shall not eat, for in the day that you eat of it you shall die." (Gen 2:15-17, NRSV)

After the culmination of creation in the creation of the woman, the serpent tempts her to eat from the tree that was forbidden by God. The description of her decision to eat the fruit is a long inside view of her perceptions of the fruit and of the inner movements of her mind. Her eating the fruit and giving it to the man is immediately followed by the inside view of their realization of their nakedness and their implicit shame:

> So when the woman saw that the tree was good for food, that it was a delight to the eyes, and that the tree was to be desired to make wise, she took of its fruit and ate; and she also gave it to her man, and he ate. Then the eyes of both were opened, and they knew that they were naked; and they sewed fig leaves together and made loincloths for themselves. (Gen 3:6-7)

The story ends with the humorous efforts of the man and the woman to blame their transgression on others; the man blames the woman, and the

---

16. For a more extensive discussion of the Yahwist creation story, see the introduction above (27-28) and Appendix 4 (396-97).

woman the serpent. But the Lord will have none of it and severely punishes them.

This story appeals to its audiences to identify with highly sympathetic characters who explicitly violate the commandment of God. Their realization of what they have done is described in an inside view that creates audience intimacy with the man and the woman as they realize what they have done.

Nathan's parable follows the story of David's adultery with Bathsheba, her pregnancy, and the death of Uriah. Nathan tells David the parable of the poor man whose one beloved lamb is taken by a rich man and prepared for his guest to eat. David's anger is kindled against the man, and David says,

> "As the Lord lives, the man who has done this deserves to die; he shall restore the lamb fourfold, because he did this thing, and because he had no pity." Nathan said to David, "You are the man!" (2 Sam 12:5–7, NRSV)

Nathan then pronounces what will happen in David's house:

> And David said to Nathan, "I have sinned against the Lord." Nathan said to David, "Now the Lord has put away your sin; you shall not die. Nevertheless, because by this deed you have utterly scorned the Lord, the child that is born to you shall die." (2 Sam 12:13–14, NRSV)

David fasts and weeps for seven days, lying on the ground all night. As the teller does in the story of the man and the woman in the garden, so in this story the teller also appeals to audiences to identify with a highly sympathetic character who violates God's commandments and realizes with shame and grief what he has done. As outlined in the introduction and the appendix, these are instances of the rhetoric of implication and involvement.

While it is unlikely that the story of Peter's denial would have evoked immediate memories of the stories of the man and woman in the garden and of David and Nathan, these are stories the audience would have heard. They would have been familiar with the pattern of sympathetic characters violating an important norm of behavior and feeling ashamed of what they had done. The listeners were thereby prepared to recognize the meaning and impact of Peter's story.

The Trials at the High Priest's House (14:53–72)

Notes on Details and Translation

14:66–67

The servant girl's identification of Peter is a long period in Greek that communicates the stages in her realization of who he is. The NRSV splits it into two sentences and breaks up the drama and growing intrigue of her recognition of Peter. It is punctuated here as one English sentence that builds to the climax of her fingering him.

67: looked at / ἐμβλέψασα

The NRSV translates this verb as "stared" to describe the servant girl's recognition of Peter. A better translation is "looked at," in order to dramatize the second stage of her visual examination of Peter.

she says / λέγει

Mark once again uses the historical present to introduce her accusation. It is translated in the present tense here to convey the heightened sense of presence that Mark intends.

that Nazarene, Jesus / τοῦ Ναζαρηνοῦ ἦσθα τοῦ Ἰησοῦ

The word order in the Greek emphasizes Jesus' identity as a Nazarene and an outsider to Jerusalem. The NRSV inexplicably changes the word order to "Jesus, the man from Nazareth" and eliminates this subtle note of identification of Jesus and Peter as aliens. Mark clearly intends to create this dynamic since every other instance of "Nazarene" in the story follows Jesus' name (1:24; 10:47; 16:6). The servant girl's naming Jesus first as a Nazarene implies her sense of Jesus' and Peter's foreignness to the big city. It is also better to translate her accusation as "And you were with that Nazarene, Jesus" rather than the more formal and less direct "You also were with the Nazarene, Jesus."

68: the cock crowed

Many of the ancient Greek manuscripts of Mark have the phrase "and the cock crowed" following the description of Peter's going out into the forecourt. The two best manuscripts, Codex Vaticanus and Codex Sinaiticus along with a few other manuscripts (LWΨ 892) and several manuscripts of the Syriac and Coptic versions, do not have this phrase. It has been a disputed variant, and earlier modern versions of the Greek text, such as the Nestle-Aland (1963), have followed Vaticanus and Sinaiticus and excluded it from the text, whereas the more recent UBS Greek texts have included it in brackets.

The attestation in the two best manuscripts, both Vaticanus and Sinaiticus, is striking. And an explanation of the addition is that later editors wanted a more literal fulfillment of Jesus' prophecy and added the phrase for this reason. Its absence from the other gospels can also be explained as their learning the original version of Mark's story prior to the later addition. The external attestation, therefore, supports the omission.

The internal evidence is complex. If included in the story, this is an aside to the audience that is consistent with Mark's storytelling style. He often calls attention to small details in an indirect manner and leaves it up to the audience to make the appropriate inference. These are also the kinds of details that later storytellers left out. And in this case, Matthew, Luke, and John all do not have this notice of the first cockcrow. Since later performance traditions deemphasized Mark's attention to detail, it can be argued (and my first conclusion has been) that it is more difficult to explain why later scribes would have added this note than why they would have left it out. The exclusion of this notice from Vaticanus and Sinaiticus can be explained as a harmonization of Mark with the other three gospels.

However, the effect of the notice of the cockcrow is to insert an audience aside that detracts from the threat and identification with Peter that is the primary rhetorical structure of the story. It also deemphasizes the climactic description of the denials at the end of the first two episodes. The introduction of each of the three denials is a crescendo of threat. This notice minimizes that effect. On balance, therefore, the combination of external and internal evidence indicates the probability that this notice of the first cockcrow was a later editorial addition.

72: immediately / εὐθὺς

"Immediately" is the signature word in Mark's storytelling that he uses frequently as a verbal thread to increase the immediacy of the events he is describing. Its use as the introduction to the cock's crow calls climactic attention to this fulfillment of Jesus' prophecy. The NRSV modification of the phrase, "At that moment," is a classic instance of translation for the eye rather than the ear.

The Trials at the High Priest's House (14:53–72)   191

and beating on himself, he wept / καὶ ἐπιβαλὼν ἔκλαιεν

This phrase, translated in the NRSV as "broke down and wept," is difficult, and both Matthew and Luke have different treatments of the moment (Matt 26:75: "And he went out and wept bitterly" [καῖ ἐξελθὼν ἔξω ἔκλαυσεν πικρῶς]); Luke simply omits it.[17] Mark's participle, ἐπιβαλὼν, is often taken to mean "set about, begin," and is often translated as if there were an infinitive following it, "began to weep."[18] But ἔκλαιεν is an imperfect indicative, not an infinitive. A wide variety of options have been offered for the translation of this word (a good summary is given in BDAG, 367-68). BDAG distinguishes two basic meanings among texts in which the verb is intransitive active, as it is here. The first group consists of Mark 4:37 and 14:72. In 4:37 the meaning is clear from the context of the storm: "and the waves *beat into* the boat" (NRSV). This meaning is attested by nonbiblical texts. BDAG treats the meaning of this verb in 14:72 in a special paragraph, stating that the meaning is "in doubt," and listing the various proposals. BDAG concludes "Prob. Mk intends the reader to understand a wild gesture connected with lamentation." With Peter as the subject and taken reflexively,[19] the verb seems to have the same basic meaning as in 4:37: "and beating himself, he wept." The verb indicates the gesture that the storyteller used in telling the end of this episode.

Comments on the Meaning and Impact of the Story

14:66: linkage to the Sanhedrin trial

This story is connected with the story of Jesus' trial by the phrase Καὶ ὄντος, translated here as "meanwhile," that is, at the very same time. Its only previous use is in the introduction to the anointing of Jesus (14:3), where it makes the temporal link of simultaneity between the authorities' making plans to arrest Jesus on Wednesday and his being in Bethany "on that day,"

---

17 For an extensive discussion of the alternative renderings of this puzzling phrase, see Taylor's excellent summary (Taylor, *Gospel according to St. Mark*, 376). Plummer's comment is indicative of the difficulty of this phrase: "we must be content to share the ignorance of all the ages as to what Mk means by ἐπιβαλὼν" (Plummer, *Gospel according to St. Mark*, 342).

18. Cf. BDF, #308.

19. Marcus rightly notes that one would expect a reflexive pronoun (such as ἑαυτον) if the verb had a reflexive meaning: "beating himself." The pronoun is not, however, grammatically required to make the verb reflexive, and Mark regularly requires the listeners to infer words. The composer's stylistic goal here is to make the period as short as possible.

the translation here of this phrase in 14:3. The opening colon of the story establishes the temporal link between the Sanhedrin trial and Peter's denial: "Meanwhile Peter was down below (κάτω) in the courtyard." This also establishes the storyteller's visual perspective as being "up above," where Jesus is being tried and looking down at Peter. It probably indicates the gesture that was used, pointing down at Peter. This initial description is the storytelling equivalent of the classic wide shot in movies that precedes a close-up. The simultaneity of these two events also establishes an atmosphere of threat to Peter.

Another dimension of this linkage to Jesus' trial is the contrast between the two trials. Jesus is on trial for his life and confesses his identity as the Messiah. Peter is also on trial for his life, but he denies his identity as Jesus' disciple.

Several words from the initial episode of the trial story (14:54) are repeated in this first period of the story (that were unhelpfully given two verse numbers, 66 and 67) and make the connection to Peter's following Jesus into the courtyard: "Peter/in the courtyard/of the high priest/warming himself" (Πέτρου /ἐν τῇ αὐλῇ /τοῦ ἀρχιερέως /θερμαινόμενον—14:66–7). The threatening atmosphere of the earlier setting in the courtyard of the high priest is intensified by the death sentence and the overt hostility of the Sanhedrin and the guards toward Jesus after his confession.

The storyteller's appeal to sympathize and identify with Peter, established throughout the larger narrative and reinforced in his argument with Jesus, is heightened by his following Jesus (14:54). The hope is raised that he will follow through with his vow and die with Jesus. As can be seen from the episode of Polycharmus and Chaereas, being crucified with a good friend was a popular motif in the stories of the late first century. The story of the arrest has intensified the hostile and alienating characterization of everyone associated with the high priest. As a result, the servant girl is immediately connected with the high priest, and her identification of Peter implies that she was part of the armed mob that arrested Jesus.

67: the impact of the changes in point of view

The shifts in the storyteller's point of view are a distinctive dimension of this initial episode in the story of Peter's denial. The story begins with the storyteller's looking down (κάτω) at Peter in the courtyard, presumably from an upper level of the high priest's house. The servant girl is introduced from this same perspective: "a servant girl of the high priest came." But the recognition of Peter is told from her point of view. The storyteller describes

The Trials at the High Priest's House (14:53–72) 193

what she saw. In Greek, two participles make her gradual recognition of Peter explicit. Translated literally, the colon is, "and seeing Peter warming himself, looking at him she says. . ." (ἰδοῦσα τὸν Πέτρον θερμαινόμενον ἐμβλέψασα αὐτῷ λέγει—14:67). The impact of this description is similar to the impact of the two participles and historical-present verb that describe Judas' approach to Jesus in the arrest story, literally translated, "And coming immediately, going up to him he says . . ." (καὶ ἐλθὼν **εὐθὺς** προσελθὼν αὐτῷ λέγει—14:47). Film directors got the idea of a gradual close-up on a character from this kind of dramatic storytelling. This is Mark's way of making these moments of the culmination of threat and fear experientially present for the audience. The Markan composer doesn't waste words, and this colon is a crescendo of danger.

the maid's indictment of Peter

The servant girl's charge is that Peter is associated with a condemned criminal: a literal translation reads, "And you with the Nazarene were, that Jesus."[20] (Καὶ σὺ μετὰ τοῦ Ναζαρηνοῦ ἦσθα τοῦ Ἰησοῦ—14:67). Mark has twice earlier used the preposition "with" (μετά) to indicate close association with Jesus: in the prophecy of betrayal—"one who is eating **with** me" (ὁ ἐσθίων **μετ'** ἐμοῦ), and "one who is dipping **with** me" (ὁ ἐμβαπτόμενος **μετ'** ἐμοῦ)—and second in the Gethsemane story—"and taking Peter and James and John **with** him" (καὶ παραλαμβάνει τὸν Πέτρον καὶ τὸν Ἰάκωβον καὶ τὸν Ἰωάννην **μετ'** αὐτοῦ). The connotations of this phrase have been established by these earlier uses.

The servant girl's emphatic description of Jesus as "that Nazarene" communicates her hostility and her sense of his alien status in Judea. The major impact of her accusation is the audience realization of the threat Peter faces by "warming himself," a description that recalls the earlier notice that "he was sitting with the guards, warming himself by the light of the fire" (14:54). Peter has been recognized in the light of the fire.

68: Peter's first denial

The storyteller's introduction to Peter's response, "But he denied it" (ὁ δὲ ἠρνήσατο), is a shift in point of view back to that of the storyteller as observer. The storyteller makes it crystal clear to the audience that Peter's

---

20. George Lucas, the creator of the film *Star Wars*, may have gotten the idea for the distinctive speech patterns of Yoda, Luke Skywalker's mentor in the ways of the Jedi, from literal translations of ancient Greek like this.

words of evasion are a fulfillment of Jesus' prophecy on the Mount of Olives: "three times you will deny me" (τρίς με ἀπαρνήσῃ—14:30). Peter's reply to the servant girl is like that of a witness who tries to make light of an accusation by throwing the burden of proof on the accuser: "I don't know or even understand what you are talking about." The listeners can count: one.

69: the escalation of the threat of identification

There are similar shifts in the storyteller's point of view in the second episode. Peter's going out into the forecourt is again described from an observer's viewpoint above the action. The storyteller's point of view then shifts to the servant girl's perspective, as she once again sees and recognizes Peter. This time, however, she accuses Peter of being "one of them" to others standing in the courtyard. The identity of the bystanders can only be inferred from the context. The possibilities are the guards, other members of the arresting crowd that brought Jesus to the high priest's house who hung around to see what would happen, and random folk. Whoever they were, the servant girl's accusation moves the threat level up several degrees. The storyteller's introduction to the servant girl's statement, "she began again to say" (ἤρξατο πάλιν λέγειν), uses the grammatical formula "to begin" plus an infinitive. This formula has been used by the composer of the story almost exclusively as an introduction for emotionally intense statements (1:45; 2:23 [a shocking action]; 5:17, 20; 6:2; 8:11, 31, 32; 10:28, 32, 41, 47; 11:15; 12:1; 13:5; 14:19, 33, 65). Exceptions are 4:1; 6:7, 34, 55. This formula indicates that Mark introduced the servant's statement in a tone of voice with a higher level of emotional intensity. And her first word, οὗτος, is used by Mark for definite and emphatic identifications, as it was in Jesus' identification of those sitting around him as members of his family (3:35), as it was in God's identification of Jesus as his son at the transfiguration (9:7), as it was in the parable when the wicked tenants identify the owner's son (12:7), and as it was by the centurion at the cross: "Truly this (οὕτως) man was the Son of God" (15:39). Thus, there are several elements in this episode that combine to build the emotional intensity of the servant girl's accusation.

70: the second denial

The report of Peter's second denial is a very short and thereby slow and climactic summary, "And again he denied it" (ὁ δὲ πάλιν ἠρνεῖτο). This is another instance in the PRN of a storytelling pattern present throughout Mark's gospel. Mark uses short sentences to create climactic impact (e.g.,

6:6, 52; 8:9, 21; 10:22; 11:14; 12:12, 17b, 34b; 14:11b, 31b, 50; 16:8). To this point in the PRN this is the shortest sentence outside the speeches of Jesus and the high priest. The shortness of the sentence is a sign that Mark gives it major emphasis rather than merely repeating the first denial. This is a storytelling crescendo of emotional intensity and volume. That's two.

70b–71: the third charge and denial

The third charge in the indictment of Peter is made by the bystanders and is a confirmation of the servant girl's accusation. In this instance, they not only repeat her basic charge, "one of them," but they also offer corroborating evidence: "for you are a Galilean."

Peter's third denial has a level of vehemence that at least equals and probably exceeds his earlier vehement vow to die with Jesus rather than deny him. One sign of this is that Mark uses once again the grammatical formula "to begin" (ἤρξατο), plus an infinitive—a formula that he reserves for introductions of intense moments in the story as in the introduction to the servant girl's second accusation of Peter. Also the introduction to Peter's speech has two infinitives, as does the description of Jesus' agony in Gethsemane: "he began to be distressed and troubled . . ." (ἤρξατο ἐκθαμβεῖσθαι καὶ ἀδημονεῖν—14:33). Furthermore, as in the Gethsemane story, so here the verbs are intense in their emotional associations. The first, "to invoke a curse" (ἀναθεματίζειν), means that violation of the oath he is swearing would result in his being cursed. In effect, he curses himself. One did not invoke curses against oneself lightly in the ancient world. The second, "to swear" (ὀμνύναι), is used earlier in the story to describe Herod's solemn oath that bound him to execute John (6:23) rather than to break his oath to Herodias' daughter.

The storyteller's indirect report of Peter's invoking a curse on himself and swearing invites each listener to imagine what he actually said: for example, "May God damn me to hell; I swear . . ." The only comparison from earlier in this story to this oath's vehemence is Peter's own vow of allegiance to Jesus, even to death (14:31). Peter's oath in denial of Jesus is an even more thundering climax of volume and intensity. Peter repeats the first two words of the first denial, "I do not know" (Οὐκ οἶδα); and then, instead of merely disclaiming knowledge and understanding of the accusation as in his first denial (v. 68), he now explicitly denies any acquaintance with Jesus.

Thus, the three denial episodes have a climactic structure. This structure indicates that each was told with increasing volume and intensity. The accusations become more and more threatening, and Peter's denials become increasingly intense until he vehemently denies any relationship with Jesus. The structure of the story enables the audience to count Peter's denials. That's three.

72: the cock crow and Peter's remembering Jesus' prophecy

The immediate crowing of the cock for the second time fulfills Jesus' prophecy. Literally translated, the words are:

> "before the second cock crow sounds" (πρὶν ἢ δὶς ἀλέκτορα φωνῆσαι—14:31)

> "for the second time the cock crowed" (ἐκ δευτέρου ἀλέκτωρ ἐφώνησεν—14:72)

The virtual word-for-word repetition of Jesus' prophecy makes the fulfillment unmistakable.

There is a sudden shift in the storyteller's point of view in the report of Peter's remembering what Jesus had said. For the first time Mark goes inside Peter's mind and reports the words of Jesus he remembers. Earlier in the story Peter saw that the fig tree had withered, and he remembered that Jesus had cursed it the previous morning (11:21). But he does not remember Jesus' specific words. Here Peter remembers Jesus' words. His memory is an abbreviated and slightly modified version of Jesus' prophecy. In this way, the story has a high degree of verisimilitude with the way memory actually works. However, Peter's memory formulates Jesus' words in a highly dramatic manner, focusing narrowly on the precise time of his denial, and juxtaposing δὶς and τρίς to effect a striking contrast, a contrast that unfortunately cannot be adequately translated (i.e., "twice/thrice" is the closest English equivalent, but it sounds antiquated; and "two times/three times" is wooden and wordy).

The actual words are once again translated literally in the word order of the Greek:

> Jesus' prophecy: Truly I say to you, you, today, this night, **before twice the cock crow sounds, three times me you will deny.**

> Ἀμὴν λέγω σοι ὅτι σὺ σήμερον ταύτῃ τῇ νυκτὶ πρὶν ἢ δὶς ἀλέκτορα φωνῆσαι τρίς με ἀπαρνήσῃ—14:30

> Peter's memory of Jesus' prophecy: **Before the cock crow sounds twice, thrice me you will deny.**

> Πρὶν ἀλέκτορα φωνῆσαι δὶς τρίς με ἀπαρνήσῃ—14:72

The impact of this inside view is to create a high degree of sympathetic distance in relation to Peter. Rather than standing off at a disassociating distance and reporting Peter's realization as a condemnation, the storyteller describes this moment in the tone of Peter's horror and grief as he realizes what he has done.

Of course, the judgment that Peter has failed to keep his promise and has instead done exactly what Jesus predicted is also made explicit. Every listener can remember the story of the battle of prophecies that took place earlier that night, and the hope that was raised by Peter's earlier following of Jesus right into the courtyard of the high priest. At this climactic moment, that hope is disappointed. But in the context of the growing threat to Peter's life in the servant girl's recognition and identification of him and the crowd's even more specific recognition, Mark's audience can also understand and sympathize with Peter's denials. The poignancy and power of this moment in the story is the result of the combination of the clarity of the norms of judgment and the high degree of sympathetic distance.

The dynamics of this story are extremely complex. The story has many of the same dynamics as the story of the man and the woman in the garden of Eden after they eat the fruit, and the story of David's realization of his adultery at the end of Nathan's parable of the poor shepherd and his lamb. These stories are structured by the rhetoric of implication, in which listeners are invited to be involved in intimate experience of wrongdoing and to experience with the characters the painful realization of what they have done.

72: Peter's grief

Peter's response to the realization of what he has done is grief. As has been described above, a focus on the ancient performance of this story suggests that the enigmatic Greek word ἐπιβαλὼν (translated in the NRSV and NIV as "broke down") is a description of the gesture of beating on the chest that dramatized Peter's grief: "And beating himself, he wept" (καὶ ἐπιβαλὼν ἔκλαιεν—14:72).

The sound of this word in Greek is onomatopoetic and carries with it the actual sound of beating it describes. Furthermore, while several speeches have one or two-word periods (e.g., 14:41–42), this narrative period of three words, like the climax to the rebuke of the woman who anointed Jesus (καὶ ἐνεβριμῶντο αὐτῇ—14:5b), is spoken slowly and is surrounded by silence. This episode brings together an intensive inside view of Peter's emotions, unambiguous norms of judgment, and a short, climactic three-word period.

A major factor in the impact of this story is the sudden change in the perspective in this last episode. Throughout the three denial episodes, Mark tells the story from the relatively detached viewpoint of an observer, or from the viewpoint of Jesus' opponents, primarily the servant girl. There are no descriptions of the action of the story from Peter's point of view. As a result, the audience can literally count off the denials at the end of each episode. Peter's failure to keep his vow is described from an observer's point of view.

But in the final episode, after the prophecy of all three denials has been fulfilled, the storyteller describes Peter's realization of what he has done from inside Peter's own mind, as Peter remembers Jesus' prophecy. This shift in perspective changes the dynamics of the story and makes Peter an even more sympathetic character. As a result, the final sentence, "And beating upon himself, he wept," is an intimate report of Peter's shame and sorrow. This change in perspective requires the audience to see the denials from Peter's viewpoint, as he realizes what he has done. The sympathetic relationship to Peter, established early in the gospel and deepened by the prophecy argument on the way to Gethsemane and by his following Jesus to the high priest's house, reaches its highest level in this moment of grief.

66–72: the impact of the denial as a climax of the plot

This episode is also the climax of the plot introduced in the story of the prophecy battle between Jesus and Peter on the way to Gethsemane. The question established in that story was whether Jesus or Peter is right about the future. Will the disciples all run away? Will Peter not run away even if the others do? Will Peter die with Jesus or deny him? Those questions have now all been answered. This element of the plot is woven into the larger plot of the story established by Jesus' passion prophecies and the plot of the authorities to destroy him. Will Jesus' prophecies of suffering and death be fulfilled? Will the authorities' plot to destroy him succeed? The first two parts of Jesus' passion prophecies have now been fulfilled in the arrest and the trial: he has been betrayed into the hands of evil men and condemned to death.

What then does the interweaving of these elements of the plot reveal about Mark's purpose? A similar plot structure is present in both the preceding section of the story, The Arrest on the Mount of Olives (14:26–52), and the section we are presently discussing, The Trial before the Sanhedrin and Peter's Denial (14:53–72). The arrest of Jesus on the Mount of Olives and the fulfillment of his prophecy spoken there are imbedded in the story of the disciples' response to the arrest. This structure gives climactic emphasis to the disciples' flight. The trial of Jesus before the Sanhedrin is imbedded in the story of Peter's following and denying Jesus, and the climax of the story is Peter's realization of the fulfillment of Jesus' prophecy of his denials. Thus, in both sections of the story, Mark gives climactic emphasis to the wrong but fully understandable responses of Jesus' disciples. Because of the sympathetic characterization of the disciples and especially Peter, the story invites the audience to reflect on these responses to Jesus' failure to fight, his nonviolent acceptance of arrest as the fulfillment of the Scriptures, and his confession that he is the Messiah. Those responses are in turn set in specific contexts in the story. Being offended and running away is the disciples' response to Jesus' acceptance of arrest, and denying Jesus is Peter's response to Jesus' messianic confession and condemnation to death. It is these responses that receive climactic emphasis in the story.

The purpose implicit in this plot structure is to involve the audience in sympathetic identification with the disciples and Peter as they respond in ways that are profoundly wrong. The effect of this rhetoric of involvement and implication is to invite the audience to reflect on their own responses to Jesus' actions. Will they be offended and run away? Will they when tested by persecution deny any association with Jesus or belief in him? In each instance, the audience has experienced these responses in specific ways. The response of offense and running away is associated with the shame of the young man running away naked. And the response of denial is associated with Peter's grief. In response to Jesus' willingness to suffer, the disciples and Peter have acted as cowards who have been unwilling and afraid to suffer with him for the sake of the kingdom of God.

However, when heard against the background of both the heroic stories of both the Greco-Roman world and the messianic stories of ancient Israel, the disciples' response is fully understandable. One might fight to the death for one who is also fighting against the enemies of the nation. But following a messianic hero who asks you to suffer and die with him in nonviolent battle with the powers for the sake of the transnational kingdom of God is more difficult. This is the decision that the story is structured to provoke in the hearts and minds of the listeners. It is a classic example of the rhetoric of implication.

The Performance of the Story

The telling of this story begins in the imagined place of the trial that has been identified in the story space. From there the opening gesture locates Peter down below in the courtyard so that you are looking down at him from up above. Peter's name here is spoken with warmth rather than with neutral objectivity, and his presence is related with eager anticipation. After all, he is living up to his promise! He, of all the disciples, had not run away, at least not for good. If he was with the others when they ran, he had second thoughts. He had regained his earlier courage. And here he is still, ready to die with Jesus as he is being condemned.

The servant girl's discovery can be dramatized by walking over into the campfire space and first glancing and then moving closer to and looking intently at the imagined Peter. The introduction of the servant girl and her discovery has a note of growing threat that connects with the earlier description of Peter warming himself *by the light of the fire*. The tone of her statement, even in her very few words, moves from initial tentative recognition ("Hey, you were") to a crescendo of confident accusation ("with that Nazarene Jesus!"). She is not asking a question but is addressing Peter directly. Giving her words a different intonation and even a different accent helps to increase the threat. Her voice is similar to the voice of Herodias' daughter asking the king for the head of John the Baptist on a platter. Her voice also needs to imply that she was an eyewitness there in the garden.

The introduction and naming of Peter's first denial is addressed to the audience. But in the half breath between the two cola, the focus of address shifts to the imagined servant girl. Peter's words can be spoken in several ways: as a kind of country-bumpkin "aw, shucks"; as a laughing dismissal of this silly girl's misidentification; or an expression of incredulous disbelief. Whatever you find is best, it is light rather than heavy. This episode is also relatively quiet.

Peter's move to the forecourt can also be dramatized with a few steps to another spot in the storytelling space, preferably closer to the audience. Once again the storyteller's tone communicates Peter's trying to get away from the servant girl. The servant girl's second accusation to those standing around can be addressed to the audience or to the imagined bystanders in the onstage courtyard. The phrase "began to say to the bystanders" is an opportunity to build a crescendo of intensity that reaches its climax in her accusation. This second identification is a much stronger accusation, with a strong gesture of pointing at him accompanying the words "*this* man." The storyteller's report of Peter's denial is slow and even more intense. Given that this denial is summarized in indirect discourse rather than quoted in Peter's words, it is best spoken with the tone of an observer. It is addressed to the audience so that they can count the denials. This episode is louder.

The bystanders' charge is more intensely accusatory, especially in the citation of Peter's Galilean identity. As I've outlined above, Peter's third denial is a climax of volume and emotional intensity. Peter's invoking a curse on himself has the tone of "God damn me!" spoken in rage. It is probably not possible to overdo the vehemence of this denial. The gesture of taking an oath with the hand or fist over the heart is fully appropriate here.

The description of the cock crow has the tone of the tolling of a bell and is immediately quiet. Peter's remembering is told from inside Peter's mind as he recites Jesus' words to himself with a tone of grief and horror at realizing what he has done. Whether or not the proposed translation of the Greek word ἐπιβαλὼν is accepted, a gesture of striking the chest hard is an appropriate expression of Peter's grief. This final sentence in the story is slow and intimate, with each word surrounded by silence. The tone is not objective or detached but is an expression of Peter's intense grief.

5

THE HANDING OVER TO THE GENTILES (15:1–20)◉

The two stories of this section fulfill a climactic part of the third passion/resurrection prophecy: "and they will hand him over to the Gentiles, and they will mock him and spit on him and flog him" (10:33–34). In the story of the Pilate trial, Jesus is handed over to the Gentiles and flogged; in the story of the mocking by the Roman soldiers, he is mocked and spit on. The framing of the section as Judean/Gentile, the introduction of Barabbas, and the crowd's choice to release an "insurrectionist" rather than Jesus deepens the connections between the stories of the PRN and the audiences' recent experience of the Judean–Roman War.

The Trial before Pilate (15:1–15)◉

Sound Map

15:1Καὶ εὐθὺς πρωῒ συμβούλιον ἑτοιμάσαντες **οἱ ἀρχιερεῖς**
 μετὰ τῶν πρεσβυτέρων
 καὶ γραμματέων
 καὶ ὅλον τὸ συνέδριον
 δήσαντες τὸν Ἰησοῦν ἀπήνεγκαν καὶ **παρέδωκαν Πιλάτῳ.**
2καὶ ἐπηρώτησεν αὐτὸν ὁ **Πιλᾶτος,**
 Σὺ εἶ ὁ βασιλεὺς τῶν Ἰουδαίων;
ὁ δὲ ἀποκριθεὶς αὐτῷ λέγει,
 Σὺ λέγεις.

3καὶ **κατηγόρουν** αὐτοῦ **οἱ ἀρχιερεῖς** πολλά.
4ὁ δὲ **Πιλᾶτος** πάλιν ἐπηρώτα αὐτὸν λέγων,

Οὐκ ἀποκρίνῃ οὐδέν;
    ἴδε πόσα σου **κατηγοροῦσιν**.
5 ὁ δὲ Ἰησοῦς **οὐκέτι οὐδὲν ἀπεκρίθη**,
    ὥστε θαυμάζειν τὸν Πιλᾶτον.

6 Κατὰ δὲ ἑορτὴν **ἀπέλυεν αὐτοῖς** ἕνα δέσμιον ὃν παρῃτοῦντο.
7 ἦν δὲ ὁ λεγόμενος **Βαραββᾶς** μετὰ τῶν **στασιαστῶν** δεδεμένος
                    οἵτινες ἐν τῇ **στάσει** φόνον πεποιήκεισαν.
8 καὶ ἀναβὰς ὁ **ὄχλος** ἤρξατο αἰτεῖσθαι καθὼς ἐποίει **αὐτοῖς**.

9 ὁ **δὲ Πιλᾶτος ἀπεκρίθη** αὐτοῖς λέγων,
    Θέλετε ἀπολύσω ὑμῖν **τὸν βασιλέα τῶν Ἰουδαίων**;
10 ἐγίνωσκεν γὰρ ὅτι διὰ φθόνον **παραδεδώκεισαν** αὐτὸν οἱ **ἀρχιερεῖς**.
11 οἱ **δὲ ἀρχιερεῖς** ἀνέσεισαν **τὸν ὄχλον**
    ἵνα μᾶλλον τὸν **Βαραββᾶν ἀπολύσῃ** αὐτοῖς.

12 ὁ **δὲ Πιλᾶτος πάλιν** ἀποκριθεὶς **ἔλεγεν αὐτοῖς**,
    Τί οὖν [**θέλετε**] ποιήσω [ὃν λέγετε] **τὸν βασιλέα τῶν Ἰουδαίων**
13 οἱ **δὲ πάλιν ἔκραξαν**,
    Σταύρωσον αὐτόν.

14 ὁ **δὲ Πιλᾶτος ἔλεγεν αὐτοῖς**,
    Τί γὰρ ἐποίησεν κακόν;
οἱ δὲ περισσῶς **ἔκραξαν**,
    Σταύρωσον αὐτόν.
15 ὁ **δὲ Πιλᾶτος** βουλόμενος τῷ **ὄχλῳ** τὸ ἱκανὸν ποιῆσαι
    ἀπέλυσεν αὐτοῖς τὸν Βαραββᾶν,
    καὶ **παρέδωκεν τὸν Ἰησοῦν** φραγελλώσας ἵνα σταυρωθῇ.

Translation

1 **And immediately**, early in the morning, **the chief priests**,
    having prepared a plan **with the elders and scribes and the whole council**,
    bound **Jesus**, led him away and **handed him over to Pilate**.
2 And **Pilate questioned him**,
    "Are you the King of the Judeans?"
But **answering** him **he says**,
    "You say so."

3 And the chief priests accused him of many things.
4 So **Pilate questioned him** again,

"Have you no answer?
You can see how many charges they **bring against** you."
5 But **Jesus gave no answer** so that **Pilate wondered**.

6 Now at the festival **he used to release for them** any one prisoner for whom they asked.
7 And there was a man called **Barabbas** in prison
with **the insurrectionists** who had committed murder **during the insurrection**.
8 And **the crowd** came up and began to demand that Pilate do for them according to his custom.

9 **And Pilate answered** them and said,
"Do you want me **to release** for you **the King of the Judeans**?"
10 Because he knew that it was out of jealousy
that **the chief priests had handed him over**.
11 But **the chief priests** incited **the crowd**
to ask instead for **Barabbas to be released to them**.

12 **And Pilate again** answered and said to them,
"What then shall I do with the man you call '**King of the Judeans**'?"
13 **And again they shouted**,
"Crucify him!"

14 Pilate said to them,
"Why, what crime has he committed?"
But **they shouted** vehemently,
"Crucify him!"
15 **And so Pilate**, wanting to satisfy **the crowd, released for them**
Barabbas
and having flogged Jesus, **he handed him over to be crucified**.

Ancient Associations and Connections

The audiences brought their memories of the trials of prophets and other Israelites in Israelite and Gentile courts to the hearing of this story. The most immediate associations with the story of the trial before Pilate were the trial stories that the audiences had just heard: the trial before the Sanhedrin (14:53–65) and the trial of John the Baptist *in absentia* (6:14–29). Since we have just discussed the story of the Sanhedrin trial, only the story of John the Baptist's trial before Herod will be discussed here. This is a sound map of the story of the Herod trial:

The Handing Over to the Gentiles (15:1–20)

King Herod heard of it, for Jesus' name had become known.
Some were saying, "John the baptizer has been raised from the dead;
    and for this reason these powers are at work in him."
But others said, "It is Elijah";
    and others said, "It is a prophet, like one of the prophets of old."

But when Herod heard of it, he said, "John, whom I beheaded, has been
                                      raised."
For Herod himself had sent men who arrested John, bound him,
    and put him in prison on account of Herodias, his brother Philip's
                                      wife,
    because Herod had married her.
For John had been telling Herod, "It is not lawful for you to
                              have your brother's wife."

And Herodias had a grudge against him, and wanted to kill him.
But she could not, for Herod feared John,
     knowing that he was a righteous and holy man,
     and he protected him.
When he heard him, he was greatly perplexed;
    and yet he liked to listen to him.

But an opportunity came when Herod on his birthday gave a banquet
    for his courtiers and officers and the leaders of Galilee.
When his daughter Herodias came in and danced,
    she pleased Herod and his guests.

And the king said to the girl,
    "Ask me for whatever you wish, and I will give it."
And he solemnly swore to her,
    "Whatever you ask me, I will give you, even half of my kingdom."

She went out and said to her mother, "What should I ask for?"
She replied, "The head of John the baptizer."

Immediately she rushed back to the king and requested,
    "I want you to give me at once the head of John the Baptist on a
                                      platter."
The king was deeply grieved;
    yet out of regard for his oaths and for the guests,
      he did not want to refuse her.

Immediately the king sent a soldier of the guard with orders to bring
                                      John's head.

> He went and beheaded him in the prison,
> > brought his head on a platter,
> > and gave it to the girl,
> > and the girl gave it to her mother.
> When his disciples heard about it, they came and took his body
> > and laid it in a tomb. (6:14–29, NRSV)

A dimension of the multifaceted connections between these two trials is that the characterizations of Herod and Pilate have the same dynamic structure. In effect, Herod's conduct of the informal trial and execution of John serves as a precedent for Pilate's actions in the trial of Jesus. The dynamics of distance in relation to Herod are initially rather positive. He may have arrested John for his denunciation of Herod's marriage, but he respected John and liked to listen to him. And he protected John against Herodias' hatred of him. But when he faced the political consequences of revoking his vow in front of all his guests, Herod executed an innocent man in gross violation of the rule of law. Mark's appeal to the audience is to condemn Herod for his illegal and immoral action.

The precedent established by this story for the audience is multifaceted. For kings and governors, political expediency is more important than are the laws of justice. This is true whether those rulers are Idumean/Judean or Roman. Likewise rulers are often weak and unscrupulous in defending innocent prophets against the evil plots of persons and groups whose power and reputations may be damaged by public prophetic critiques. It is, therefore, not surprising that Pilate acts like Herod. That similarity also carries with it an appeal to condemn Pilate, who recognizes Jesus' innocence, for his illegal and immoral action in crucifying Jesus.

When we turn to the larger context of the traditions of Israel, there are three major stories about trials of Israelites in Gentile courts. All of these were probably composed during or shortly after the period of the reign of Antiochus IV Epiphanes (165–74 BCE): the trial of Shadrach, Meshach, and Abednego before Nebuchadnezzar (Daniel 3), the trial of Daniel before Darius (Daniel 6), and the trials of Eleazar and the family of seven boys and their mother before Antiochus IV Epiphanes (2 Macc 6:18—7:42). These stories were very popular and were widely told in the approximately two hundred years prior to Mark's story. These stories are the immediate precedents in the traditions of Israel for the performances of Mark's story of the Pilate trial.

Because of the length of these stories, they will not be printed here. These stories are different from each other in many ways. The story of Shadrach, Meshach, and Abednego is highly stylized and has many characteristics of heroic legends, while the story of the Maccabean martyrs has a more historical character. Another difference is that the story of Shadrach, Meshach, and Abednego is like a fairy tale in which the good guys are delivered from the fiery furnace and Nebuchadnezzar praises the God of Israel and promotes them. The conversion of the violent and vengeful king establishes a hopeful precedent. Even Gentile kings who demand the worship of idols can be changed. In contrast, in the story from 2 Maccabees, Eleazar and the seven boys with their mother are brutally executed, and Antiochus is totally unrepentant.

Even with this major difference, the characterizations of King Nebuchadnezzar and Antiochus IV Epiphanes are strikingly similar. Both militantly demand that Israelites[1] cease from observing their religion, and both put on trial and execute those Israelites who refuse. In the story of Nebuchadnezzar, the demand is that Israelites worship the idol that the king has set up, while in the story from Maccabees, Antiochus IV Epiphanes demands that Israelites eat pork and thereby publicly break the laws of their religion. Both kings are arrogant and highly alienating characters. Both kings are filled with rage at the defiance of their subjects and at the subjects' willingness to die rather than to violate the laws of their religion. Thus, Nebuchadnezzar is "so filled with rage that his face was distorted" (Dan 3:19, NRSV) while a recurring phrase to describe Antiochus is that he "fell into a rage" (7:5, 39, NRSV).

The characterization of Antiochus IV Epiphanes is probably the most consistently evil and alienating character in all of ancient Israelite literature. He is worse than Pharaoh. His public torture and execution of an entire family of seven boys and their mother is without precedent. He truly lives in infamy along with Adolf Hitler among the most evil rulers of history. There are no positive dynamics in all the stories about him in the literature of Israel.

The story of the trial and attempted execution of Daniel by Darius, the king of Persia, in Daniel 6 is different. Darius is a highly positive character who is caught between his loyalty and respect for Daniel and the presidents and satraps who conspire against Daniel because Darius has put him above them in the governmental hierarchy. After he is tricked by the conspirators into signing a decree that anyone who prays to anyone, divine or human, other than the king will be thrown into a den of lions, Daniel is found guilty of continuing to pray to God. But Darius is "determined to save Daniel and until the sun went down he made every effort to rescue him" (6:14, NRSV).

---

1. The usage of the term "the Judeans" in Dan 3:8, 12 corresponds to the pattern of usage John H. Elliott has identified (see Appendix 5). The term is used by outsiders in a context of denunciation and accusation.

But the conspirators demand that he execute the decree, since "no interdict or ordinance that the king establishes can be changed" (6:15, NRSV).

The king then orders that Daniel be thrown into the den of lions but also expresses to Daniel his hope that God will deliver him. The king fasts all night and rushes to the den in the morning, calling out to Daniel. When he discovers that Daniel has been delivered, he throws the conspirators with their wives and children into the den of lions and issues a decree that all in his kingdom "tremble and fear before the God of Daniel." Darius is, therefore, a model of a Gentile ruler who is sympathetic to Israelite prophets and seeks to rescue them in the context of conspiracies manipulating the law against them. His characterization establishes the narrative precedent of a Gentile ruler sympathetic to Israelites.

It has already been noted above in the commentary on Jesus' trial before the Sanhedrin that the story of the trial of Isaiah in the *Martyrdom and Ascension of Isaiah* is another story in the background of Mark's story of Jesus' trials. It shares with the Pilate trial the motif of a conspiracy against the prophet by other Israelites. In Isaiah's case the conspiracy is led by a false prophet, Belkira.

These stories from Israel's earlier traditions establish a set of expectations and possibilities that provide the context for hearing Mark's story of the Pilate trial. But whether Mark's audiences knew them in detail or not, the earlier stories reflect the range of possibilities that were part of people's experience in the period. However, the probability is that the great majority of Judeans knew these stories, and that they provided the background for their hearing of Jesus' trial before Pilate.

The Sounds of the Story

The sounds of the Pilate trial are filled with an unusually dense series of sonic echoes of earlier stories in Mark, particularly the trial before the Sanhedrin but also the third passion prophecy and the earlier stories of the plot against Jesus. While a discussion of the sounds of the story may be somewhat dense in itself, this story is so important that a separate analysis of the sounds is needed.

The first period of the story (15:1) is a complex period of two cola, which builds to the climax of Jesus' delivery to Pilate. The first colon has the most comprehensive list of the Judean groups involved in the conspiracy to kill Jesus. The second colon of this period introduces the new subject of Pilate. The period as a whole echoes the entire motif of the conspiracy, but its most immediate connection is with the third passion prophecy, specifically

The Handing Over to the Gentiles (15:1-20)

the prophecy that the chief priests and the scribes will hand Jesus over to the Gentiles (10:33). That prophecy is fulfilled in their handing Jesus over to Pilate.

This density of connection with the earlier stories also intensifies the contrast with the new elements of the story. Besides introducing Pilate as a character, the second period also introduces the new motif of Jesus' being called the King of the Judeans, a title that has never been used before. The third period, Jesus' response to the charge, is the shortest period in the first episode, and Jesus' two-word response to Pilate is the shortest colon in this episode. The shortness and distinctiveness of Jesus' words, "You say" (Σὺ λέγεις), heighten the contrast to his earlier response to the chief priest, "I am" (Ἐγώ εἰμι). This climactic short colon is characteristic of Mark's storytelling.

The second episode of the trial (15:3–5) has three periods and continues the echoing of earlier stories. In the first period of this episode, the chief priests' accusation (κατηγόρουν) brings to completion an initiative by a group in a Galilean synagogue, apparently composed of Pharisees and Herodians, who were watching to see whether he would heal the man with a withered hand on the Sabbath "so that they might accuse him" (ἵνα κατηγορήσωσιν αὐτοῦ—3:2). The accusation by the chief priests is the first simple period in the story and thereby receives emphasis.

The second period in this episode is Pilate's second interrogation of Jesus. It is the most complex. The second colon of this period is an exact quotation of the high priest's first question to Jesus ("Have you no answer?" Οὐκ ἀποκρίνῃ οὐδέν;—14:60). The third colon of the period refers to the chief priests' accusations. The description of Jesus' silent response to Pilate uses other forms of the same words used to describe Jesus' silence in response to the high priest (14:61a). These sonic echoes call immediate attention to the difference between Pilate's response of wonder and the high priest's response of condemnation. The placement of Pilate's name at the end of the final period of the interrogation creates a rounding with the ending of the first period (15:1) and a heightening of the surprise of Pilate's response.

The simple period (15:6) describing the custom of the release of one prisoner introduces the key word for the rest of the story, ἀπολύω, "to release" (15:6, 9, 11, 15). It makes explicit the possibility that Jesus might be released. The single complex colon making up the second period describes Barabbas. It has two key words, στασιαστῶν and στάσει, best translated as "insurrectionists" and "insurrection." These two words are emphasized by the alliteration between them. These words also have a quality of onomatopoeia, containing in Greek the hissing sound of assassination, daggers and swords cutting through the air. The climax of this episode is the simple third period that describes the coming up of the crowd. This is an unusual and surprising introduction of a new character in the middle rather than at the beginning of a story. Because of its earlier associations with the conflict between Jesus and the chief priests (see below), the sound of the crowd's coming up (ὁ ὄχλος) is a note of hope and new possibilities.

The next three episodes share a common structure. Each consists of a question to the crowd by Pilate and a response by the crowd to Pilate. Repetitions in biblical storytelling are always a sign of a crescendo of intensity and often of volume. In this instance, it is a crescendo of both volume and intensity.

The first exchange between Pilate and the crowd is introduced by a complex period with a surprising conclusion. Pilate's unexpected offer to release Jesus combines the key word "to release" with a repetition of the charge of treason against the state: "King of the Judeans" (15:2). Repetitions imply a change of tone. It is probable that the storyteller presented Pilate's recital of this title here with at least a moderate tone of respect, in contrast to his earlier initial disdain, based on the assumption that the crowd regarded Jesus as their king. It is also the case that Pilate's words now are much louder and are addressed by the storyteller as Pilate to the audience as the crowd.

The storyteller's explanation of Pilate's internal motive (15:10) is a simple period that is softer in volume and is addressed to the audience with the insider tone of privileged insight into this Gentile's surprisingly accurate perceptions. The dynamic of the third period of this episode, the priests' inciting of the crowd and the request for Barabbas, is complex both in its periodic structure and its implications. This report in indirect discourse requires the audience to infer the inciting words and actions of the priests to the crowd, and the crowd's demand for the release of Barabbas. The storyteller's tone also conveys his shock at this unprecedented reversal in the crowd's political loyalty. My hunch is that the need to express the storyteller's surprise and shock is the reason the crowd's request for Barabbas is reported in indirect rather than direct discourse as in the subsequent episodes.

The second exchange between Pilate and the crowd is composed of two complex periods, each having two cola. A factor in the impact of the episode is the contrast between the relatively long colon of Pilate's question about what to do with "the King of the Judeans" (12:12) and the short cola (12:13b, 14d) of the crowd's demand for crucifixion. The shorter cola are slower, louder, and climactic.

The climax of the trial is the third exchange between Pilate and the crowd. It is two complex periods. The colon of Pilate's question is shorter and more emphatic than his first questions. As can be seen in the sound map, the first two periods of the episode have cola of five, four, four, and

The Handing Over to the Gentiles (15:1–20)

two words. This is Mark's way of creating maximum impact in sound, as will be evident in the final story of the gospel (16:8). It is also often a feature of climaxes in musical compositions. Thus, the climax of the dialogue between Pilate and the crowd is short, slow, and loud. Major emphasis falls on the word περισσῶς ("vehemently"), which introduces the defiant tone of the crowd's final response.

The period describing Pilate's decision is quieter. The two cola of this complex period reflect the structure of the possible outcomes of the trial: Barabbas or Jesus. The participial phrase describing Pilate's motive, namely, to do "what is sufficient" (τὸ ἱκανὸν) for the crowd, sets the release of Barabbas and the flogging and crucifixion of Jesus in the context of the crowd's demands. The descriptions of the "release" of Barabbas and the "handing over" of Jesus repeat the key words from earlier in the story ("release," 15:6, 9, 11; "hand over," 15:1, 10). These sonic connections are the basis of the irony of Barabbas' being released rather than Jesus, and the fulfillment of Jesus' prophecy of his being handed over to the Gentiles to be flogged and killed (10:34). There is also a rounding of the story in the repetition of Jesus' being "handed over" at the beginning of the story to Pilate (15:1) and now at the end to the soldiers for crucifixion. Finally, the sound of the participle, φραγελλώσας, has an onomatopoetic connection to the flogging it denotes.

Notes on Details and Translation

15:1: prepared a plan / συμβούλιον ἑτοιμάσαντες

These two words that describe the actions of the Sanhedrin prior to handing Jesus over to Pilate are an exegetical conundrum. In the NRSV, they are translated as "held a consultation": "As soon as it was morning, the chief priests held a consultation with the elders and scribes and the whole council" (15:1). The conclusion about Mark's picture is then that the chief priests organized an early morning meeting of the entire Sanhedrin immediately prior to handing Jesus over to Pilate.

The meaning of the noun συμβούλιον is ambiguous and can refer either to a "meeting, council session" or to the result reached at a meeting, "a plan, purpose" (cf. BDAG). The textual tradition of Markan manuscripts reflects a grappling with this ambiguity. In both instances of this word in Mark, the verbal form that follows it differs widely in different manuscripts. The textual variants and their attestations are as follows:

3:6 ἐποίησαν ℵ C Θ 892c	15:1 ποιήσαντες A B K N W Γ Ψ al

ἐποίουν A K P Γ al	ἐποίησαν D Θ 565 2542s it; Or
ἐποιοῦντο W	ἑτοιμάσαντες ℵ C L 892 pc
ποιοῦντες D a	
ἐδίδουν B L 28 al	

As can be seen, in both 3:6 and 15:1 most of the manuscripts have some form of the verb ποιέω, "to do, make." The only other readings (at the bottom of both lists) are ἐδίδουν ("to give") in 3:6 and ἑτοιμάσαντες ("having prepared") in 15:1. The most probable explanation of this variation is that most of the textual copyists found the reading "to give" in 3:6 and "having prepared" in 15:1 difficult and substituted some form of ποιέω. On textual grounds, therefore, these two more difficult readings are best. For this reason, the editors of the twenty-fifth edition of the Nestle-Aland text accepted these two readings (ἐδίδουν, ἑτοιμάσαντες) as the most probable original forms but changed their minds about 15:1 in the most recent editions. Thus, the current editions have adopted Codex Vaticanus as the best text for both 3:6 and 15.1, ποιήσαντες, which has led in turn to the NRSV translation, "the chief priests *held a consultation* with the elders and scribes and the whole council." In contrast, both verbs in the twenty-fifth Nestle-Aland text refer to συμβούλιον as "the plan" that emerged from the meeting rather than to the meeting itself, i.e. "having made/prepared a plan." This is the more probable original reading.

These phrases are part of the motif that runs through Mark's story of the authorities' plot to destroy Jesus. The chief priests' conspiracy and plotting against Jesus has been a major motif in the story, especially since Jesus' arrival in Jerusalem. In both uses of the term, therefore, it is most likely that Mark is describing this conspiracy. In fact, the NRSV translates ἐδίδουν συμβούλιον with this sense: "The Pharisees went out and immediately conspired with the Herodians against him" (3:6). Given that the attestations in Vaticanus for 3:6 and Sinaiticus for 15:1 are the most difficult and were most likely to be amended, the reading in the twenty-fifth edition is better. In that case, the plan is the focus of the phrase, and it is is translated here as "having prepared a plan." Mark draws a picture of a group of prosecutors preparing their case before the trial.

If this reading was original, the chronology of events in Mark's original story was *not* that the Sanhedrin had a *second meeting* prior to Pilate's opening for business at 6:00 a.m. It is rather that sometime between the end of the trial and the delivery of Jesus to Pilate, probably immediately after the trial, the entire council developed a *plan* for how they were going to present the case for Jesus' guilt of a capital crime to Pilate. They then adjourned,

The Handing Over to the Gentiles (15:1–20)

and shortly before 6:00 a.m. the chief priests bound Jesus and took him to Pilate's Jerusalem headquarters to stand trial. Whether or not this account is a historical description of what actually took place, it is a more believable scenario than two meetings of the whole council. And it is in continuity with the actions of the authorities throughout the story.

2b: But he answered and said / ὁ δὲ ἀποκριθεὶς . . . λέγει

Mark uses this formula to introduce Jesus' response to Pilate's question, "Are you the King of the Judeans?" literally translated, "But answering . . . he says." This introduction formula is used consistently, with some grammatical variation in the verbs, throughout the gospel to introduce unexpected, surprising responses (6:37; 7:28; 9:19; 10:3, 24; 15:2, and here in 15:12). It always has an adversative force, "But he answered . . ." That translation is adopted here rather than the NRSV, "He answered . . . ," which omits the adversative "But."[2]

5: gave no answer / οὐκέτι οὐδὲν ἀπεκρίθη

The colon describing Jesus' silence—"he gave no answer" οὐκέτι οὐδὲν ἀπεκρίθη—is an almost exact repetition of Jesus' response to the first question of the high priest in the Sanhedrin trial. The only difference is the change from the middle to the passive voice, with no difference in meaning, and that is impossible to show in English. It is, therefore, translated here with the same words, "gave no answer," in order to make the verbal connection between the two interrogations explicit.

7: bound with the insurrectionists who had committed murder during the insurrection / μετὰ τῶν στασιαστῶν δεδεμένος οἵτινες ἐν τῇ στάσει φόνον πεποιήκεισαν

Clarity about the associations of this phrase is critically important in understanding the impact of the portrayal of Barabbas for Mark's audiences.

---

2. The NIV translation here is a particularly egregious example of the stylistic practice of reversing the Greek order of naming the speaker followed by the quotation: e.g., "'Are you the King of the Judeans?' asked Pilate. 'You have said so,' Jesus replied" (15:2–3, NIV). This translation practice is an example of translating for silent readers rather than for oral performance, since it eliminates the oral practice of introducing the one who is speaking first, so that the audience knows the speaker prior to the actual words. When the NIV translation is performed, the audience is required to wonder who is speaking until after the quotation, even if the storyteller changes tone for each character.

It is probable that Mark composed his gospel either in the last stages of the Judean–Roman War (69–70 CE) or, more likely, in its more or less immediate aftermath (71–73 CE). The general consensus among scholars is that Josephus wrote his book *The Jewish War* between 75 and 78 CE, only a couple years later than Mark. A detailed comparison of the words in the Barabbas-Jesus episodes of Mark with the stories of Josephus reveals that Josephus uses the same family of words to describe the war and the insurgents as are used in the four Gospels to describe Barabbas and the two men who were crucified with Jesus. That is, Mark and Josephus, who composed their works in the same decade after the war, use the same words with similar connotations. The word στασιαστής is the most frequent term that Josephus uses for the insurrection forces (68 times). It is one of four terms he uses as virtual synonyms for the Judean armies: στασιαστής (68 times), Ζηλωτής (55 times), λῃστής (33 times), and τύραννος (37 times). This description in Mark of those with whom Barabbas is imprisoned is the *only* use of the term στασιαστής in the New Testament.

Josephus uses the term φόνον, "murder," most frequently to describe the crimes of the various revolutionary forces against other Judeans, sometimes opponents and often other ordinary citizens of the city (*JW* 4.139, 145, 184, 348, 437, 544, 560). For example, John of Gischala allowed his men to do whatever they desired, "the murder (φόνον) of men and the violation of women were their sport" (*JW* 4.560). Josephus also uses the term στάσιν, usually translated as "sedition" in the Loeb translation of *The Jewish War*, to describe riots and insurrections, sometimes in response to Roman actions but also in internal battles between Judean factions. And in book 5, Josephus uses the term to describe the entire revolt: "I therefore proceed to relate the after history of the rebellion (στάσις)" (*JW* 5.20). Thus, there is a remarkable congruence between the key terms that Mark uses in this description with the words that Josephus uses to describe the revolution and the insurgent armies in his history of the Judean–Roman War.

This evidence from Josephus indicates that Mark's description of Barabbas evoked associations with the leaders of the insurrection for his audiences, who lived in its immediate aftermath. The NRSV translation, "rebels," is accurate, but the word does not carry the associations for contemporary audiences that are implicit in Mark's historical context. "Terrorists" may carry more of those associations for audiences now. But "insurrectionists" is another form of the word "insurrection" and has the same sound, just as στάσει and στασιαστῶν are two forms with the same lexical root that are sonically connected in Greek.

8: began to demand / ἤρξατο αἰτεῖσθαι

The phrase Mark uses for the crowd's petition—ἤρξατο αἰτεῖσθαι—is another instance of Mark's attention to the details of the story's sound. As we have noted above, the Markan composer uses the formula ἤρξατο + an infinitive in contexts of intense emotion, often conflict or anger (e.g., "Peter began to invoke a curse on himself"). The NRSV and many other translations (NASB, NET, NIV, NKJV, NJB, REB, NABRE) translate this with some form of the English verb "ask." That verb is much too polite for this context, and a more intense word is called for in this context. Liddell and Scott include "demand" among the possible meanings of αἰτέω, and it has more accurate connotations here.[3]

10: he knew / ἐγίνωσκεν

This is an inside view of Pilate's reason for his surprising offer to release Jesus. The primary meaning of the verb is "to know," and it conveys Pilate's inner state better than the NRSV/RSV translation, "he realized."

11 so that instead Barabbas might be released for them / ἵνα μᾶλλον τὸν Βαραββᾶν ἀπολύσῃ αὐτοῖς

This translation is close to the NRSV ("to have him release Barabbas for them instead"). In contrast to the REB ("to ask instead for the release of Barabbas") and NJB ("to demand that he should release Barabbas for them instead"), there is no verb, like "ask" or "demand," making the crowd the explicit agents of the chief priests' desire. The translation offered here, like that of the NRSV, is more literal. But our translation maintains the Greek word order, so that the adverb "instead" comes first. If storytellers do not rush these words, but pause momentarily between "instead" and "Barabbas," they set up the audience to prepare for the unexpected one Mark is about to name.

14: evil, wrong / κακόν

Pilate uses this term in his final question to the crowd that the NRSV translates as, "Why, what evil has he done?" This translation poses the issue of Jesus' guilt in theological categories of good and evil rather than legal

---

3. The NJB uses this stronger word to describe the tone of the chief priests' inciting of the crowd to oppose the release of Jesus: "to demand that he should release Barabbas for them instead."

categories of crime and legal offense. The NIV translates Pilate's question in legal categories: "Why? What crime has he committed?" The NIV legal translation is insufficiently apocalyptic for Mark. While the NRSV translation is somewhat incongruous for a trial, this broader category may be precisely what Mark had in mind. The adjective in the neuter case is used elsewhere in the New Testament and early Christian literature as a substantive meaning "evil" in virtually every instance. As we will see in the discussion of the performance of the story to follow, Pilate's questions are addressed directly to the audience, as were the questions of the high priest at the end of the Sanhedrin trial. Pilate's question here can be understood as a broader question to the audience about what Jesus has done that is so bad as to justify crucifixion, rather than as a way of seeking to create verisimilitude in relation to the actual historical trial some forty or more years before the telling of the story.

However, the decisive consideration here is that the question in Greek ends with this word "evil," so that the matter of evil is the dominant issue left hanging in the air. Since evil is the more accurate category here, it is adopted as the preferred translation. It carries both the legal sense of right and wrong as well as the apocalyptic sense of the battle between the spiritual forces of good and evil. While "wrong" may serve just as well as "evil" in English as the final word of the sentence—thus, "What has he done wrong?"—Mark's meaning is more accurately translated as "What has he done that is evil?"

11: incited / ἀνέσεισαν

This verb only occurs here in Mark and in Luke's Pilate trial story (Luke 23:5) in the New Testament. The verb is usually (NRSV, NIV, RSV) translated as "stirred up." Thus, Luke's usage of this word in the council's second indictment of Jesus to Pilate is translated: "He *stirs up* the people by teaching throughout all Judea, from Galilee where he began even to this place" (NRSV). Luke uses this term in the priests' criminal indictment against Jesus. Mark also uses this term here as an implicit criminal indictment but against the chief priests. In both New Testament instances of the word, therefore, it is used as an indictment. In common English, "inciting" a crowd to riot is a crime, but "stirring up" a crowd is only normal politics. "Incited," therefore, carries more of Mark's meaning here. The Sanhedrin continues to act in a criminal manner.

14b: vehemently / περισσῶς

This adverb is the base form of the word ἐκπερισσῶς, the word Mark uses to describe Peter's response to Jesus' prophecy of his denial (14:31). In both instances it means "excessively": "all the more" (NRSV), "all the louder" (NIV). However, in order to preserve the verbal connection between Peter's response and the response of the crowd, the same word must be used. For this reason, it is translated here as "vehemently" as in 14:31.

Comments on the Meaning and Impact of the Story

15:1 The time of the Pilate trial

The description of the time, "immediately early" (εὐθὺς πρωΐ), connects the trial before Pilate with the previous section, the trial before the Sanhedrin and Peter's denial. Mark's use of his characteristic adverb, "immediately," implies that the handing over of Jesus to Pilate took place right after Peter's denial. The aorist participle[4] places the time of the Sanhedrin's formulation of a plan for the upcoming trial at a particular time just before the handing over of Jesus to Pilate. Since Peter's denial is described as happening in the immediate aftermath of Jesus' trial, the implication is that the council's development of a plan happened right after or during Peter's denial, "immediately" before the handing over of Jesus to Pilate. Since Pilate opened for business at 6:00 a.m., "early" here means between 5 and 6 a.m.

the chief priests with the elders, scribes and the whole council / οἱ ἀρχιερεῖς μετὰ τῶν πρεσβυτέρων καὶ γραμματέων καὶ ὅλον τὸ συνέδριον

The list of the various religious authorities who are involved in the development of the strategy for the trial and in handing Jesus over to Pilate is Mark's most comprehensive list that draws together all the groups seeking his death mentioned at the beginning of the Sanhedrin trial:

14:53 and all the chief priest and elders and scribes

14:55 And the chief priests and the whole council

15:1 the chief priests with the elders, scribes and the whole council

This list carries with it an unprecedented implication in the tradition of Israel. Never before has the entire community of the religious leaders of Israel

---

4. Both alternative textual readings—ποιήσαντες and ἑτοιμάσαντες—are aorist; see detailed note on 15:1, above, pp. 211-12.

joined together to deliver a prophet of Israel to the Gentiles. In the context of the stories of the Maccabean martyrs and the martyrdom of Isaiah, it is almost unthinkable that the community of Israel's leaders would hand over a fellow Israelite for such humiliation and suffering at the hands of the Gentiles. In the case of Eleazar and the mother and her seven sons, they were arrested by Antiochus' soldiers; and in the case of Isaiah, he was accused by a faction of false prophets led by the prophet, Belkira, and was arrested by Manasseh. But even in the case of Isaiah, he was delivered into the hands of Israelite, not Gentile, authorities. Matthew calls attention to the horror of giving over innocent blood in Judas' recognition of what he has done and his suicide (Matt 27:4).

Pilate, the Gentiles / Πιλᾶτος, τὰ ἔθνη

The identification of Pilate as a representative of "the Gentiles" is implicit in the verbal thread that connects this handing over with Jesus' third passion prophecy:

> And the Son of Man will be handed over to the chief priests and the scribes, and they will condemn him to death; **then they will hand him over to the Gentiles** (παραδοθήσεται αὐτὸν τοῖς ἔθνεσιν); they will mock him and spit upon him, and flog him, and kill him. (10:33–34, NRSV)

> the chief priests with the elders, scribes and the whole council, having bound Jesus, led him out and *handed him over to Pilate.* (παρέδωκαν Πιλάτῳ 15:1)

In effect, Mark repeats the phrase from Jesus' third passion prophecy (with a different form of the verb παραδίδωμι),[5] replacing "the Gentiles" with "Pilate." Notice also how in both uses of this phrase, the action of handing over follows an action involving the Israelite religious leaders, so that "Pilate" is introduced as the representative of "the Gentiles." In the prophecy, there is a clear contrast between the actions of the Israelite authorities, who will condemn him to death, and the Gentiles, who will mock him, spit on him, flog him and kill him. Thus, in Jesus' most detailed prophecy of his suffering, death, and resurrection (10:33–34), the actions of the Gentiles (15:16–19) are foreseen as much more violent than those of the Israelite religious authorities.

---

5. The Greek verbs that form the verbal connection between Jesus' prophecy and the Pilate trial are future- and aorist-tense forms of the same verb, "to hand on, over" (παραδίδωμι).

The prior instances of the term, "the Gentiles," carry the connotations of "the others" in all of its uses in Mark's story (10:33, 42; 11:17; 13:8, 10), including in Jesus' quotation of Jeremiah in the Temple (11:17). Mark consistently uses this term in the sense of *them* rather than *us*. And with the exception of the Jeremiah quotation, this name has a connotation of being ethically wrong. For example, in Jesus' discussion with the disciples after the request of James and John for positions of power, Jesus contrasts his way of service with the way of the Gentiles, whose "rulers lord it over them and their great ones are tyrants over them" (10:42). In the Gospel of Mark, the Gentiles are clearly *other than* Jesus and his Israelite disciples. Furthermore, the composer of the story also assumes that his audiences will share these norms.

In the hearing of the story, the repetition of the words of the passion prophecies signals that the fulfillment of the prophecies is about to happen. The fulfillment of Jesus' prophecy that he will be handed over to the Gentiles in this opening of the Pilate trial is explicit and unmistakable for Mark's listening audiences. Mark's use of the term "Gentiles" is characteristic of Israelite literature[6] and is a decisive sign that Mark assumed that his audiences would share this negative norm of judgment. This is further evidence that Mark composed his gospel for audiences that were predominantly Judean, and that he initially characterizes Pilate as a Gentile enemy.

This allusion to "the Gentiles" generated by the sonic repetition of key words from the prophecy (10:33–34) in the introduction to the trial before Pilate establishes the audience's expectations of Pilate. The most immediate memory of a trial before the Gentiles in the tradition of Israel is the trial of Eleazar and the seven boys before Antiochus IV Epiphanes. The horror of that story and the violence of the torture and death of those innocent Israelites are associated with the memories of "the Gentiles." The first expectation of what is to follow is implicit in the fulfillment of Jesus' prophecy, namely, the tortures that Jesus explicitly predicted that he would suffer at the hands of the Gentiles (mocking, spitting, flogging, killing). The further expectation is that Pilate will act in the same manner as Antiochus IV Epiphanes. Although the tale of Darius and Daniel may exist in the mythical memory, the Syrian mass murderer established the dominant expectations for how Gentile rulers will treat Israelites. Pilate is, therefore, implicitly an enemy from the moment of his entrance into the story.

---

6. Bertram and Schmidt, "ἔθνη," in *TDNT*, 2:364–69.

2: Are you the King of the Judeans? / Σὺ εἶ ὁ βασιλεὺς τῶν Ἰουδαίων;

Pilate's opening question to Jesus, "Are you the King of the Judeans?" implies that the chief priests reported this as the indictment against Jesus. This implied indictment is associated with "the plan" that the whole body identified in the aftermath of the trial. The storyteller's implied logic is that the Sanhedrin agreed that an indictment of Jesus on blasphemy charges would have been dismissed by Pilate as insignificant for Roman law and would lead to Jesus' release. The indictment on the charge that Jesus claimed to be King of the Judeans, on the other hand, would be a capital crime of seeking to overthrow the Roman government, a crime for which the Roman punishment was crucifixion.

2–5: Pilate's interrogation / the high priest's interrogation

The impact of Pilate's interrogation of Jesus is shaped by its extensive and complex parallelism to the interrogation by the high priest. These structural and sonic connections are as follows (marked in bold):

> And . . . the high priest **asked** Jesus, "**Have you no answer** to what these men testify **against you?**" **But** he was silent and **did not answer. Again** the high priest **asked him** and said to him, "**Are you** the Christ, the Son of the Blessed One?" Jesus said, "I am . . .

> καὶ ἀναστὰς ὁ ἀρχιερεὺς εἰς μέσον **ἐπηρώτησεν** τὸν Ἰησοῦν λέγων, **Οὐκ ἀποκρίνῃ οὐδέν;** τί* οὗτοί σου **καταμαρτυροῦσιν;** ὁ δὲ ἐσιώπα καὶ **οὐκ ἀπεκρίνατο οὐδέν. πάλιν** ὁ ἀρχιερεὺς **ἐπηρώτα αὐτὸν** καὶ λέγει αὐτῷ, **Σὺ εἶ** ὁ Χριστὸς ὁ υἱὸς τοῦ εὐλογητοῦ; ὁ δὲ Ἰησοῦς εἶπεν, Ἐγώ εἰμι . . . (14:60–62)

> And Pilate **asked** him, "**Are you** the King of the Judeans?" But he answered him, "You say so." . . . And Pilate **asked him again,** "**Have you no answer?** See how many charges they bring **against you.**" **But Jesus answered nothing** . . .

> καὶ **ἐπηρώτησεν** αὐτὸν ὁ Πιλᾶτος, **Σὺ εἶ** ὁ βασιλεὺς τῶν Ἰουδαίων; ὁ δὲ ἀποκριθεὶς αὐτῷ λέγει, Σὺ λέγεις . . . ὁ δὲ Πιλᾶτος **πάλιν ἐπηρώτα αὐτὸν** λέγων, **Οὐκ ἀποκρίνῃ οὐδέν;** ἴδε πόσα σου κατηγοροῦσιν. ὁ δὲ Ἰησοῦς οὐκέτι **οὐδὲν ἀπεκρίθη.** (15:2–5)

The structure of the high priest's interrogation is, first question ("Have you no answer?"), followed by Jesus' silence; second question ("Are you the Messiah. . ."), followed by Jesus' confession/response. That structure is reversed in the Pilate trial: first question ("Are you the King of the Judeans?"), followed by Jesus' nonconfession response; second question ("no answer?"), followed by Jesus' silence. The impact of this structural reversal is to heighten the contrast between Jesus' responses to the high priest and to Pilate and the responses of the high priest and Pilate to Jesus' silence. This sequence of reversals of expectations reaches its climax in the contrast between the final responses of the high priest and Pilate to their interrogations of Jesus. The high priest condemns him as guilty of a capital crime while Pilate reconsiders the entire situation and ponders what is going on here.

2: You say / Σὺ λέγεις

The beginning of Pilate's question uses the same formula as does the last question of the high priest, "Are you . . .?" But, in contrast to the titles used by the high priest ("the Messiah" and "Son of . . .") that have been used frequently earlier in the story, no one before Pilate has used the title King of the Judeans in Mark's story.[7] Jesus' response to Pilate contrasts starkly to his response to the high priest's question. As noted above in the comment on this verse in the Notes on Details and Translation, the formula that Mark uses here, ὁ δὲ ἀποκριθεὶς . . . λέγει, always introduces unexpected and surprising responses. Jesus' response, Σὺ λέγεις, literally means "You are saying" or "You say." But regardless of its literal meaning, Jesus' response is ambiguous and equivocal, especially when heard in contrast to his unequivocal "I am/ Ἐγώ εἰμι" in response to the high priest. That is, Jesus' response to Pilate is the perfect response to a question to which an answer of either yes or no would be potentially incriminating. Jesus throws the question back into Pilate's lap. It is interesting that these exact words are present in all four canonical stories of the Pilate trial (John adds "that I am a king"). This response of Jesus in its exact form was a memorable response in the storytelling tradition of this trial.

Jesus' response to Pilate's question had a double meaning for Mark's listeners. One meaning is created by the contrast between his response to Pilate and his response to the high priest. As a result of the comparison to the earlier trial, the audience knows something that Pilate does not know, that is, Jesus' unambiguous response to the question, "Are you the Christ,

---

7. The only earlier use of the term οἱ Ἰουδαῖοι is in Mark's explanation of Judean customs to the Gentiles in his audiences (7:3).

the Son of the Blessed?" Because of the contrast to his earlier response, the listeners can recognize that Jesus does not accept this title King of Judeans. That is, the meaning of Jesus' saying *for the audience* is, therefore, "I am not." But *for Pilate*, the answer is ambiguous and therefore nonincriminating.

There is a further, crucial dimension to the meaning of Jesus' response. Jesus' response makes it clear that he rejects a traditional political definition of his identity and role. As he implied in his earlier teaching in the Temple (12:35–37), Jesus does not claim to be a son of David and a legitimate heir to David's throne. That is, Jesus' statements to the crowd in the Temple imply that he rejects the Davidic definition of the role of an "anointed one." His rhetorical question, "Why do the scribes say that the Messiah is the Son of David?" (12:35, NRSV) and subsequent citation of David's song (Ps 110:1), imply that he does not accept the equation of the role of the Messiah with the reestablishment of David's kingdom. Even though Jesus responded positively to Bartimaeus when he called him, "Son of David" (10:48ff.), his teaching to the crowd in the Temple is a rejection of the Davidic Messiah tradition. It is also a rejection of the people's acclamation during Jesus' entry into Jerusalem: "Blessed is the coming kingdom of our father David!" (11:10). That acclamation implies that the people hoped that he would reestablish the kingdom of David as an independent state. Therefore, in contrast to the implied hopes and expectations of the people, Jesus' response to Pilate means, *to the audience*, that he is not the King of the Judeans, and that he will not lead a military revolution against the Romans.

These are the only words that Jesus speaks in his defense before Pilate. We have seen earlier that Jesus' silence would have been perceived in Mark's context as a legitimate defense. The impact of Jesus' response is to raise again the possibility that his defense will be successful and that he will be released. This is also another dimension of the contrast to his response to the high priest. In that trial, Jesus' response to the high priest's direct question, "Are you the Messiah, the Son of the Blessed One?" reversed the hope that he might escape condemnation raised by the lying and contradictory witnesses and Jesus' silence. Jesus' response to the high priest's question was a direct and unambiguous, "I am." However, while perhaps courageous, it was, as testimony in his own defense, a disaster. But his response to Pilate's question is equivocal and, once again, legally shrewd as was his silence at the trial before the Sanhedrin. A light of hope glimmers once again.

It is also important to be clear here about the implication of Jesus' statement for his own self-definition. This has been a major issue throughout the story implicit in the various titles that Jesus himself has used and that others have used for him, as well as in the motif of the messianic secret. In these two responses—once to the high priest and once to Pilate—Jesus defines his own identity. In effect he says, I am the Messiah; and, I am not the King of the Judeans. To state this more explicitly, Jesus communicates, I am the fulfillment of the hopes of Israel for an anointed one who will save the nation; but also I am not the Son of David, an anointed king who will set the people of Israel free from Roman domination by military action. This self-definition of Jesus is clearest to the Markan audiences who have heard all the stories that have preceded these trials. But it is also implied that this self-definition can be recognized by the crowd in Jerusalem, who are highly sensitive to the nuances of political self-designation in relation to their hopes for future leaders.

4–5: the second interrogation

The second round of interrogation before Pilate has the same structure as the first round in the trial before the high priest: an action by the chief priests ("accused him of many things"), a question by Pilate ("Have you no answer?"), and a response by Jesus.

> Then the high priest stood up before them and **asked** Jesus, **"Have you no answer?** What is it that they testify against you?" *But* he was silent and **made no answer."** (14:60–61)
>
> καὶ ἀναστὰς ὁ ἀρχιερεὺς εἰς μέσον **ἐπηρώτησεν** τὸν Ἰησοῦν λέγων, **Οὐκ ἀποκρίνῃ οὐδέν**; τί* οὗτοί σου καταμαρτυροῦσιν; ὁ δὲ ἐσιώπα καὶ **οὐκ ἀπεκρίνατο οὐδέν**. (14:60–61)
>
> Pilate **asked him** again, **"Have you no answer?** See how many charges they bring against you." *But* Jesus **answered nothing**, so that Pilate wondered. (15:4–5).
>
> ὁ δὲ **Πιλᾶτος** πάλιν **ἐπηρώτα** αὐτὸν λέγων, **Οὐκ ἀποκρίνῃ οὐδέν**; ἴδε πόσα σου κατηγοροῦσιν. ὁ δὲ Ἰησοῦς **οὐκέτι οὐδὲν ἀπεκρίθη**, ὥστε θαυμάζειν τὸν Πιλᾶτον. (15:45)

This structural reversal from Jesus' sequence in the Sanhedrin trial (first silence, then an answer) to Jesus' sequence in the Pilate trial (an answer followed by silence) in and of itself creates a sense of surprise. And the surprise is heightened by the specific elements of the episode.

The chief priests move to the center as the spokesmen for the whole council. While their accusations are not quoted, the listeners can supply the accusations from the earlier trial before the Sanhedrin. Pilate's question to Jesus assumes that Jesus is silent in response to the chief priests' accusations. The parallel between Pilate's question and the high priest's interrogation probably signals the tone that the storyteller gave to Pilate's question: it too is hostile and accusatory. But the second half of Pilate's statement is a warning and an attempt to alert Jesus to what his accusers are saying: "See how many charges they bring against you." This is Pilate's first departure from the script established by the high priest's interrogation.

so that Pilate wondered / ὥστε θαυμάζειν τὸν Πιλᾶτον

Jesus' silence in response to Pilate's second question is a surprise: why doesn't he deny their charges that are undoubtedly false just as were the charges of the false witnesses at the trial before the Sanhedrin? But, in contrast to the first trial, the surprise is explicitly identified here in the description of Pilate's internal response: "so that Pilate wondered." The grammatical construction that Mark uses here, "so that" with an infinitive (ὥστε θαυμάζειν), is consistently used throughout Mark's story to describe an extreme response (1:27; 2:2, 12; 3:10, 20; 9:26)[8] or a crisis (1:45; 4:1, 37).[9] And the two previous uses of the verb θαυμάζω ("to wonder, marvel, be astonished, be surprised") occur in situations of great surprise: i.e., the townspeople's discovery of the healed demoniac (5:20) and Jesus' response to the unbelief of his home synagogue (6:6). Both the verb and the construction are reserved for a particular storytelling function and indicate the heightened manner in which these phrases were spoken. In this case, Pilate's wonder is both an expression of his surprise at Jesus' response, and an expression of the storyteller's surprise at Pilate's sympathetic response to Jesus. Jesus' silence and Pilate's wonder are reversals of the audience's expectations, based on earlier trials of Israelites before Gentiles (specifically based on the trial of the Maccabean martyrs).

The structural dimension of this surprise is the complex parallelism between the two trial stories. While there are many parallel elements, the

---

8. These extreme or exaggerated responses introduced by "so that" (ὥστε) and an infinitive are the introduction to the crowd's amazed response to Jesus' casting out the demonic spirit from the man in the synagogue (1:27); the extreme enthusiasm of the people in Capernaum who packed into the house to hear Jesus (2:2); the crowd's response of amazement to the healing of the paralytic (2:12); the crowd's pressing in on Jesus and by implication nearly crushing him in response to his healings (3:10); the crowd's enthusiasm that prevents Jesus and his disciples from eating (3:20); the crowd's extreme response to the stillness of the boy from whom the violent demon was driven out: "He's dead!" (9:26). This pattern constitutes a virtual storytelling instruction that these responses are to be told in an exaggerated tone. Mark's implicit instruction is, make these a big deal.

9. The crises introduced by "so that" (ὥστε) and an infinitive are the leper's proclamation of what Jesus had done for him so that Jesus can't go into the cities (1:45); the crowd's pressing in on Jesus forces him to get into a boat (4:1); the storm's waves fill up the boat and the disciples awaken Jesus in fear (4:37).

two interrogations end in different ways. The trial before the Sanhedrin ends with a confession and a condemnation. The condemnation is a fulfillment of Jesus' prophecy and has, therefore, a precedent. But the interrogation before the Gentiles has ended with Pilate's wondering, a result that has no precedent and could not have been anticipated. Instead of the hope for Jesus' release being broken by his being handed over to the Gentiles, Pilate's response reawakens that hopeful possibility. The implication of Pilate's "wondering" is that the chief priests' plan isn't working while Jesus' strategy of silence and refusal to incriminate himself is.

Furthermore, Pilate's response is congruent with the story's specifically Israelite norms of judgment. This is another dimension of the antithetical parallelism between the two trial stories. In the trial before the Sanhedrin, the response of the high priest and the council to Jesus' messianic confession conflicts with the norm of judgment inherent in the story. The entire story, from the opening sentence, is based on the storyteller's claim that Jesus is the Messiah, and that claim has been reinforced in some manner in virtually every succeeding story. The conclusion of the high priest and the council that Jesus' messianic confession is blasphemy conflicts with this norm of the story. Pilate's wonder at Jesus' silence and his terse, non-incriminating response to the charge of claiming to be the King of the Judeans is fully congruent with the story's norms. The result is to make Pilate, the Gentile enemy, somewhat more sympathetic. Once again, when all seemed lost, a hint of a possible means of Jesus' escape appears. Yet ambiguity remains: what precisely did Pilate wonder about? Clearly he is surprised at Jesus' silence, but is there more?

6: he used to release one prisoner / ἀπέλυεν αὐτοῖς ἕνα δέσμιον

The storyteller now steps forward and gives the audience further background information that heightens the possibility that Jesus might be released. While there is little historical evidence from existing ancient sources that Pilate had a custom of releasing one prisoner at the people's request at Passover, the Markan audiences had no reason to doubt this statement. The key word in this sentence for the plot of the story is ἀπολύω, "to release."

7: Barabbas / Βαραββᾶς

Mark's second background comment to the audience introduces Barabbas in terms that resonated deeply for audiences in the period after the Judean–Roman War. Mark describes Barabbas as, literally translated, "bound with the insurrectionists who during the insurrection murder had committed" (μετὰ τῶν στασιαστῶν δεδεμένος οἵτινες ἐν τῇ στάσει φόνον πεποιήκεισαν—15:7). In the comments on details above, we pointed out that among the four terms that Josephus uses for the Judean revolutionary forces, namely, στασιαστής ("insurgents"), Ζηλωτής ("Zealots"), λῃστής ("bandits," or better "insurrectionists"), and τύραννος ("tyrants"), the word στασιαστής is the most frequent term. Josephus also uses the term φόνον, "murder," frequently to describe the crimes of the insurgents against other Judeans. Josephus uses the term στάσιν to describe riots and insurrections, sometimes in response to Roman actions but also in internal battles between Judean factions. And in book 5 of the *Jewish War* he uses this term to describe the entire revolt (see note above). Thus, in addressing his audiences in the post-70 period, Mark uses the same terms to describe Barabbas and his associates that Josephus uses to describe the groups that led the war against the Romans.

Mark's use of terms that Josephus employs for the various insurgent groups is not idiosyncratic in the four canonical stories of the Pilate trial. The descriptions of Barabbas in the other gospels are also congruent with Josephus' usage. Matthew describes Barabbas as δέσμιον ἐπίσημον, usually translated as "a notorious prisoner" (Matt 27:16). Josephus usually uses the term ἐπίσημον to describe "distinguished," "eminent," or "honorable" citizens, often victims of the insurgent forces because they in some way opposed their policies. But in his initial description of John of Gischala, the most violent of the leaders of the insurrection, Josephus uses the word in the same sense as Matthew: "the most unscrupulous and crafty of all who have ever gained notoriety" (ἐπίσημον) (JW 2.585). Luke's description of Barabbas is, "This was a man who had been put in prison for an insurrection that had taken place in the city and for murder" (ὅστις ἦν διὰ στάσιν τινὰ γενομένην ἐν τῇ πόλει καὶ φόνον βληθεὶς ἐν τῇ φυλακῇ—Luke 23:19, NRSV). Once again, Josephus frequently uses the terms στάσιν and φόνον to describe the actions of the various factions of the insurrection. Finally, John simply names Barabbas as a λῃστής. This term, usually translated "brigand, robber," is also one of Josephus' major terms for the insurgents (33 instances).

Thus, while each of the four evangelists uses different terms to describe Barabbas, they are all terms that Josephus uses to describe the insurgent groups and their characteristic actions during the war. The four canonical Gospels were all composed in the decades from 70 to 100 CE, in the immediate aftermath of the war. In this historical context, Mark's use of these terms for Barabbas evoked associations with the Judean–Roman War for Mark's audiences. "The insurrection" was a term fraught with horrific memories for every Judean who lived in the shadow of that disastrous war.

Just as the ancient sources that have come down to us feature no evidence for a custom of a Passover release, so also they contain no evidence of an insurrection in Jerusalem in the decade from 30 to 40 CE. The possibility exists, as many have argued, that this episode of the Pilate trial was a later development of the Pilate trial tradition. But regardless of this episode's historicity, which we are finally unable to determine with certainty in part because of the paucity of ancient sources, the meaning of this episode for Mark's audiences remains clear.

8: and coming up the crowd / καὶ ἀναβὰς ὁ ὄχλος

With the arrival of the crowd, the storyteller resumes the account of the events of the trial. The arrival of the crowd is presented as a moment of climactic importance at the end of the episode. And the tone of the crowd's demand that Pilate observe the custom is intense. In the context of the description of the custom, the implication is that the crowd needs only to ask for Jesus and Pilate will release him. Everything in the characterization of the crowd prior to this episode creates the expectation that they will ask for Jesus to be released. Since the issue of the dynamics of the characterization of the crowd is of major importance for the meaning of the trial, a detailed examination of the characterization is needed.

Mark's Characterization of the Crowd

The questions concerning the historical reference of the crowd have confused the identification of the impact of this characterization. Many scholars, such as Raymond E. Brown and John Dominic Crossan, have made distinctions between this crowd and the crowds at the cleansing of the Temple, the triumphal entry into Jerusalem, and Jesus' ministry in Galilee. The argument has been that these were different crowds, and that there is no connection between the crowd at the Pilate trial and earlier crowds even in Jerusalem.[10]

While this is undoubtedly the historical reality, it is essential to distinguish between, on the one hand, the historical meaning of the story as a source of ostensive referential knowledge about the empirical facts of ancient events for audiences of twenty-first-century historians and, on the other, the meaning of the story as it was heard by ancient audiences. In the hearing of the story, the crowd is a character just as Jesus, the scribes, and

---

10. Brown, *Death of the Messiah*, 2:801: "Markan readers would have no reason to identify this crowd that has come up with any that has gone before."

the disciples are characters in the story. And "the crowd" is always the same character, whether in Galilee or Jerusalem. If Mark wants to distinguish between different crowds so that the audience does not confuse them, he names them in a way that will make that distinction. Thus, at the arrest, Mark explicitly names a particular crowd "armed with swords and clubs from the chief priests, the scribes, and the elders" (14:43, NRSV). The composer distinguishes *this* crowd as an opponent of Jesus from "the crowd" that has been Jesus' primary support against his opponents. Mark does not give the crowd at the Pilate trial a distinctive name such as "the Jerusalem crowd" or "the crowd from the chief priests, the scribes, and the elders."

A brief survey of the characterization of the crowd will help to specify the impact of the crowd's sudden appearance in the Pilate trial. The crowd is named first as a character in the story of the paralytic (2:4). The crowd has so packed the house that those bringing the paralytic are unable to get in. The conflict with the scribes is focused on the issue of Jesus' right to forgive sins. Their charge of blasphemy introduces the norm of judgment that will be the basis for the condemnation of Jesus at the trial before the Sanhedrin, namely, blasphemy. The healing of the paralytic is a confirmation of Jesus' authority to forgive sins, and the crowd implicitly recognizes and celebrates his power. Thus, the amazement of "all" refers to the crowd (2:12), and their exclamation, "We have never seen anything like this," is a delightful moment of unbridled enthusiasm. And their positive response to Jesus is demonstrated in following him to the sea, where he teaches them (2:13). The crowd is introduced as a positive and sympathetic character.

The next appearance of the crowd occurs in 3:9, once again after a conflict between Jesus and the Herodians and Pharisees over the healing of the man with a withered hand on the Sabbath (3:1–6). This story ends with the intensification of the conflict with other religious parties over Jesus' authority to heal on the Sabbath, and the plot of the Pharisees with the Herodians to destroy him. Here in 3:9 the crowd appears as Jesus' enthusiastic supporter after the conflict. In both instances (2:4; 3:9) the crowd expresses extreme enthusiasm for Jesus in the immediate context of his conflicts with other Judean religious groups that oppose him, and forms a kind of alliance with him in the aftermath of these conflicts.

These two stories introduce the basic features of the characterization of the crowd: their attraction to Jesus' teaching and actions, and their loyalty to him in the context of his conflicts with other religious groups. The dynamics of distance in relation to the crowd are wholly positive, and the Markan storyteller appeals to the audience to identify with the crowd. In the performance of the gospel, the responses of the crowd are opportunities for the storyteller to express extreme enthusiasm, joy, and laughter.

The next appearance of the crowd is one of the major moments of audience inclusion in the entire story. The story of Jesus and his family follows the Beelzebul controversy, in which the scribes who had come down to Galilee from Jerusalem accuse Jesus of being possessed by the devil (3:22–30) and are condemned as guilty of an unforgivable sin for blasphemy against the Holy Spirit. In the subsequent story, Jesus' mother and brothers call to him as the crowd is sitting around Jesus. In the telling of the story, the storyteller's gesture to indicate a gathering around Jesus is a gesture that includes the audience. Jesus' concluding statement, "Here are my mother and my brothers," is addressed to the audience as the crowd, as "those seated around him in a circle" (τοὺς περὶ αὐτὸν κύκλῳ καθημένους—3:34). This may be a description of the setting in which Mark and his audience are arranged. But, whatever the storytelling configuration of the Markan storyteller and the listeners, it is the most intimate moment of audience address and inclusion to that point in the story. In effect, the audience is invited to identify with the crowd as members of Jesus' family.

The next story tells of Jesus' teaching the crowd by the sea (4:1). The crowd's enthusiasm forces Jesus to get into a boat. This is a potential moment of laughter in the story. This moment heightens the sympathetic identification of the audience with the crowd as a character. In the telling of the parable of the sower, the storyteller "becomes" Jesus and addresses the audience as the crowd gathered by the sea. The rest of Jesus' teaching in this section of the story (4:10–32) is addressed to the audience as an "in" group of "those around him along with the twelve" (οἵ περὶ αὐτὸν σὺν τοῖς δώδεκα). In the telling of the story, the move from addressing the large crowd along the shore to speaking to the smaller group is indicated by a reduction in the storyteller's volume and the storyteller's gesture of inclusion of the audience. The effect of this is to invite the listeners to identify with this closer relationship with Jesus as those who are "with the twelve," and who are beneficiaries of his "secret" teaching about the kingdom of God (4:11).

This movement in the story from addressing the audience as the enthusiastic crowd to addressing them as those around him with Jesus' disciples is an implicit invitation to move from identifying with the crowd to identifying as disciples of Jesus. This happens several times in Mark's story: with the crowd by the sea and then the appointment of the twelve (3:7–12 and 3:13–19), with the teaching of the crowd by the sea and then the address to "those who were around him with the twelve" (4:1–9 and 4:10–32), with the summary of the cleanliness-laws discourse to "the crowd" (7:14–16) and then the explanation of the parable to "his disciples" (7:17–23), with the feeding of the great crowd of four thousand (8:1–10) and then the discourse with the disciples about having no bread (8:14–21). The storyteller's appeal to each member of the audience signals a move for the audience from identification with the crowd that listens to Jesus to identification with the more intimate group of Jesus' disciples. This appeal is embodied in the performance of the story with a more intimate tone and with gestures signaling audience inclusion.

In the stories of the woman who touched Jesus' garment and of Jairus' daughter, the first negative notes are sounded in the characterization of the crowd. When Jesus comes back from the Gerasenes, the crowd is characterized once again as a group of enthusiastic followers who first pin Jesus to the sea (5:21) and then follow him as he goes to Jairus' house. But Jesus then forbids anyone but the three disciples to go with him. Similarly, after the death of John the Baptist, "many" crowd around Jesus and then chase him around the sea so that when he arrives at the lonely place for his retreat with the disciples, a great crowd (πολὺν ὄχλον) is there on whom he has compassion so that he both teaches and feeds them. In these instances the crowd's enthusiasm is inconvenient, but Jesus responds to them with sympathy and compassion. The characterization of the crowd invites the storyteller to present them like a group of children who are sometimes overly enthusiastic.

A central moment in the characterization of the crowd is the discipleship discourse following Peter's identification of Jesus as the Messiah (8:34ff). In the aftermath of Jesus' rebuke of Peter, the storyteller addresses the audience as "the crowd with his disciples" (τὸν ὄχλον σὺν τοῖς μαθηταῖς). This merging of "the crowd" with "his disciples" is the first time that the storyteller as Jesus has addressed the audience as a fully unified group composed of "the crowd" and "his disciples." This moment of development in the characterization of the crowd is followed by the first inside view of the crowd's emotional response. When the crowd sees Jesus as he comes down from the mountain after the transfiguration, they are "astonished" (9:15). The Greek word here is ἐξεθαμβήθησαν, for which a more literal translation would be "amazed out of their minds." The storytelling function of this word in Mark's story is made clear by the other use of this identical word as the description of the women's response to seeing the young man in the tomb (16:5). Mark uses this word to describe the experience of a theophany. This scene evokes the memory of the people of Israel seeing Moses coming down from the mountain (Exod 34:30). Here the crowd responds to Jesus in a manner directly connected with the response of the people of Israel to seeing Moses. And the audience is invited to identify with the crowd as Israelites in their awe and astonishment at seeing Jesus.

The crowd appears in the story twice more prior to the climactic episodes in Jerusalem, as the group whom Jesus teaches before the teaching-about-divorce story (10:1), and as the group leaving Jericho with Jesus on

The Handing Over to the Gentiles (15:1–20)

the way up to Jerusalem: "as he was leaving Jericho with his disciples and a large crowd" (10:46). Thus, before the Jerusalem ministry, the crowd is characterized by its attraction to Jesus (2:4; 3:20; 4:1; 5:21,24; 6:34). The emotional relationship between Jesus and the crowd is one of growing closeness. The relationship moves from the crowd in the Capernaum house where the paralytic is healed to the intimacy of Jesus' family to Jesus' talk about discipleship after Peter's confession. And, most important, a sympathetic relationship is established between Jesus and the crowd in the aftermath of his conflicts with the leaders of the other Judean religious parties (2:13; 3:9, 32; 7:14). "The crowd" is never associated with Jesus' opponents.

This alliance between Jesus and the crowd against the leaders of the religious establishment is the main motif in the characterization of the crowd during Jesus' Jerusalem ministry. Following the cleansing of the Temple, the storyteller explains that the chief priests and the scribes were afraid of him because of the crowd's positive response to his prophetic teaching and action (11:18). The storyteller's comment to the audience about the crowd is highly sympathetic: "they were afraid of him because the whole crowd was spellbound by his teaching" (ἐφοβοῦντο γὰρ αὐτὸν, πᾶς γὰρ ὁ ὄχλος ἐξεπλήσσετο ἐπὶ τῇ διδαχῇ αὐτοῦ—11:18, NRSV).

The next two descriptions of the crowd are comments by the storyteller to the audience that explain the authorities' decision not to arrest Jesus because of their fear of "the crowd." The first explains why the chief priests, the scribes, and the elders chose not to respond to Jesus' demand that they tell him whether John's baptism was from men or from God: "they were afraid of the crowd because all regarded John as a true prophet" (11:32, NRSV). After the parable of the Wicked Tenants, the storyteller's comment implies that the crowd is Jesus' protection: "they wanted to arrest him, but they feared the crowd. So they left him and went away" (12:12). The final notice about the crowd in the stories of Jesus' Jerusalem ministry is the crowd's response to Jesus' attack on the scribes' ruling that the Messiah must be the Son of David (12:35–37, NRSV): "the large crowd was listening to him with delight."

Thus, throughout Jesus' Jerusalem ministry the crowd is his primary ally and protector against the various opponents who want to discredit and arrest him. The crowd's strongly sympathetic characterization throughout the gospel reaches its highest point in this alliance. It is Jesus and the crowd against the other Judean political/religious parties and their leaders. With the possible exception of the inconvenience that the crowd's enthusiasm sometimes causes Jesus, there are no negative elements in the entire characterization. The dynamics of aesthetic distance are more consistently positive in the characterization of the crowd than for any other character in the story, even of the disciples, who frequently do not understand Jesus. The effect of the characterization is to create a high degree of sympathetic identification with the crowd.

As a result of this characterization of the crowd, the expectation built into the story when the crowd "comes up" (ἀναβὰς) to Pilate is that the crowd will oppose the chief priests and demand the release of Jesus. It is unclear whether "coming up" means that the crowd arrived at the trial after Pilate's initial interrogation of Jesus, or whether they were already present and pressed forward after the interrogation, but the implication leans toward their pressing forward.

The grammatical construction of this period (15:8) marks the crowd's coming up as a climactic moment in the story. Circumstantial participles after καί and δέ usually occur in the first period of episodes of the story (e.g., 14:17–18: the Last Supper and prophecy of betrayal; 14:39–40: the second prayer and return of Jesus in Gethsemane; 14:66–67: the setting and the servant girl's seeing Peter). But Mark consistently uses this construction in a concluding position for climactic moments (e.g., 14:52: the young man's flight; 14:72: Peter's realization and grief; 15:37: Jesus' death; 16:4: the discovery of the stone rolled back). Thus, Mark signals by his grammar that this moment is of major importance.

The crowd is Jesus' last hope. All the hopes for Jesus' release that the story has created and disappointed now focus on the crowd. The crowd is at this moment in the telling of the story a supremely sympathetic character with whom the audience is invited to identify completely. The only barrier that might prevent Jesus' release is if the crowd is unable to get Pilate to observe the custom. The "coming up" of the crowd raises the hopes for Jesus' release and the saving of his life to the highest level.

9: Do you want for me to release to you the King of the Judeans?
/Θέλετε ἀπολύσω ὑμῖν τὸν βασιλέα τῶν Ἰουδαίων;

Since the crowd's demand is only reported in indirect discourse, the audience can only infer the actual words of the demand. Pilate's response to their demand is a complete reversal of expectations. The similarities between the characterizations of Antiochus IV Epiphanes and Herod with that of Pilate have created the expectation that he, like his predecessors, will reject any effort to get Jesus released. The introduction used by the storyteller, ἀπεκρίθη αὐτοῖς λέγων, had been used earlier to introduce surprises, as in the response of the Syro-Phoenician woman to Jesus' implicitly labeling her a dog (7:28; see above detailed note on 15:2b). Pilate's statement implies

The Handing Over to the Gentiles (15:1–20)   233

that he has perceived what the crowd will ask, and instead of resisting it, he surprisingly suggests it. His question is a rhetorical question that expects a positive answer. He picks up the title King of the Judeans, presumably used by the priests in the earlier interrogation (cf. 15:1–2) and essentially offers to release Jesus.

10: For he knew / ἐγίνωσκεν γὰρ

The storyteller recognizes the audience's surprise at Pilate's question and explains the reason for Pilate's response. The storyteller's aside is a wholly believable description of Pilate's internal motive for his offer to release Jesus. His perception of the chief priests' motive corresponds with the negative portrayal of the chief priests throughout the story.[11] Their fear of the crowd because of its alliance with Jesus could quite naturally have a strong element of jealousy and envy. That is, the storyteller's explanation of Pilate's perception of the chief priests' corruption corresponds with their earlier actions that the audience knows—particularly the priests' conspiracy with the scribes to kill Jesus and their payoff of Judas Iscariot.

11: the chief priests incited the crowd to have him instead release Barabbas for them / οἱ δὲ ἀρχιερεῖς ἀνέσεισαν τὸν ὄχλον ἵνα μᾶλλον τὸν Βαραββᾶν ἀπολύσῃ αὐτοῖς

This response of the crowd is a total reversal of everything that the story has led the audience to expect. The crowd has been Jesus' ally against the chief priests and has effectively protected him from arrest. The people's support

---

11. The storyteller's explanation of the authorities' motive here is a further instance of giving the audience insight into the authorities' internal responses, as in the audience aside following the parable of the vineyard: "for they knew that he had told the parable to them" (ἔγνωσαν γὰρ ὅτι πρὸς αὐτοὺς τὴν παραβολὴν εἶπεν—12:12). In both instances, the explanation of the surprising response from the authorities creates a moment of "inside information" between the storyteller and the audience against the authorities. This is also an instance when the subtle dynamics of interaction between the storyteller and the audience are eliminated in contemporary literary translations. A literal translation of the Greek here is, "And they sought to arrest him and they feared the crowd. For they knew that to them he had told the parable. And leaving him, they went away" (12:12). The NRSV translation of these sentences changes the word order and eliminates the storyteller's explanatory comment to the audience: "When they realized that he had told this parable against them, they wanted to arrest him but they feared the crowd. So they left him and went away." Here the translators fail to understand the storytelling dynamic of audience asides that explain a puzzling or surprising action in the previous sentence. Translators create a more literary translation that eliminates the original oral dynamic of the story and the relationship between the storyteller and the audience.

for Jesus and the resulting prospect of a riot if the chief priests arrested him openly is the motive for the authorities' conspiracy at the beginning of the PRN (14:1–2). The crowd has enthusiastically followed Jesus joyfully throughout his Galilean ministry and has both welcomed him into Jerusalem and supported him in his conflicts there. The shock of this reversal of expectations is in part the result of the absence of any preparation. The earlier failures of Jesus' followers—Judas' betrayal, the flight of the disciples, and Peter's denial—were all foreseen by Jesus. While Pilate's surprising offer to release Jesus is explained by the storyteller, this much greater surprise is left to the audience to explain. Why would the crowd choose Barabbas instead of Jesus?

For Mark's audiences in the post-70 period after the Roman–Judean War, the answer is easily provided from their immediate context. Barabbas is connected with the insurrection and with murder. The people chose a political revolutionary leader like those who led the nation of Israel into the insurrection against the Romans. Jesus has not fulfilled the military expectations of the messiahs of Israel. He has not restored the kingdom of David as the crowd proclaimed at his entry into Jerusalem. The crowd's choice here corresponds with Israel's choice throughout its ancient history. Thus, the religious and political leaders of Israel rejected Jeremiah's recommendation of accommodation with the Babylonians in the period leading up to the destruction of the Temple in 587 BCE.

The answer to the question implicit in the crowd's response is immediately apparent to the audiences of Mark's story in the aftermath of the Judean–Roman War. The nation chose Barabbas and the way of war rather than Jesus and the way of peace and reconciliation with the Gentiles, which he carried out in his ministry. The entire story of Jesus' ministry reverses the messianic expectations built into the stories of Saul, David, and the other anointed ones of Israel's history. Thus, the subsequent events known to Mark's audiences make sense of the chief priests' success in inciting the crowd to demand Barabbas instead of Jesus. The crowd expected and chose a military leader. And Mark's audiences know the horrendous consequences of that choice in their immediate experience.

Furthermore, these clues to the surprising response of the crowd to Pilate's offer are built into the language of the story. As has been established earlier, the words Mark uses to describe Barabbas are the same words Josephus uses to describe the revolt and its leaders. Thus, it was easy for Mark's audience to infer the reason for the crowd's demand for Barabbas. Mark provides the dots and the audiences can draw the lines of connection from their own most vivid experience.

The Handing Over to the Gentiles (15:1–20)

The impact of this reversal in the story is shaped by the relationship that has been established between the audience and the crowd. While the chief priests have consistently been portrayed as enemies of Jesus, the crowd has been Jesus' most consistent support, often in opposition to the chief priests. Prior to this story, the crowd's actions have always been positive and delightful. A high degree of identification with the crowd has been created in the course of the story. In effect, the crowd is *us*, the people with whom the audience can fully identify. In the context of this sympathetic identification with the crowd, the crowd's demand for Barabbas creates audience involvement and implication in the crowd's action. Just as the flight of the disciples and Peter's denial are told in a manner that creates engagement and implication in their failure, so also the crowd's demand for Barabbas' release is reported in a manner that creates a high degree of sympathetic involvement in the crowd's action. This is not the action of an enemy that the audience can condemn and from which it can emotionally distance itself. It is the action of the character with whom the audience has most deeply identified. The crowd is *us*, the audience listening to the Markan storyteller.

This storytelling dynamic is the rhetoric of implication. It happens whenever a highly sympathetic character with whom the audience has identified does something that is, in the norms of the story, wrong. As I outline in the introduction and in Appendix 4, "The Rhetorics of Biblical Storytelling," this story structure is present throughout the Scriptures—for example, in the stories of the man and the woman in the garden, of the people of Israel at Mount Sinai, of Samson and Delilah, of David and Bathsheba, of Jonah, and of Ezra and Nehmiah, to name only a few. The impact of this rhetoric is to require the audience to reflect on the reason for this wrong action from a perspective of identification rather than condemnation. The inferred reason for this wrong action in the story is a present experience or issue that the audience faces in its present time: i.e., the worship of fertility-cult gods and goddesses (Genesis 2–3; Exodus 32), the taking of foreign women as lovers (the Samson story in Judges), the lust that leads to adultery and murder (2 Samuel 11–13), and persistence in the implacable hatred of enemies (Jonah). In Mark's story, the issue in the present time of the audience is the insurrection against the Romans and belief in the myth of God's redemptive violence. The impact of the story is, then, the recognition of *our* implication in the choice of insurrection and war.

12:" What then shall I do with the one you call King of the Judeans?" / Τί οὖν [θέλετε] ποιήσω [ὃν λέγετε] τὸν βασιλέα τῶν Ἰουδαίων;

Pilate's question is a response to a statement by the crowd that is not reported but only inferred. The crowd presumably said something like, "Give us Barabbas!" Both Pilate's question, "What shall I do with the one you call "King of the Judeans?" and the crowd's response, "Crucify him," are introduced by the adverb "again" (πάλιν). While this term would initially appear to be more appropriate prior to the second demand for the crucifixion (15:14b), it refers here to the crowd's indirectly reported demand to release Barabbas (15: 11), not to an earlier demand for crucifixion. The word "again" implies that the crowd's initial demand for Barabbas' release was, like this one, a "shout" (ἔκραξαν), loud and insistent rather than civil and relatively quiet. Marcus notes that the introduction to the crowd's response is the verb κράζειν, which Mark frequently uses to refer to the shouts of demons (3:11; 5:5,7; 9:26).[12] This verbal connection implies that the crowd has been possessed by the spirit of evil in its demand for crucifixion of Jesus.

13–14: Crucify him! / Σταύρωσον αὐτόν

The crowd's demand that Jesus be crucified is another major reversal of expectations. There has been no preparation earlier in the story for the radicality of this demand. In the discipleship discourse (8:34), Jesus earlier named taking up the cross as a dimension of following him. But there it was a metaphor for self-sacrifice and nonviolent resistance. In his prophecies Jesus predicted that he would be killed but never that he would be crucified. Furthermore, this demand by the crowd has no prompting by the chief priests. The crowd comes up with this idea itself.

This response by the crowd further intensifies the implicit question of the crowd's motive for this sudden transformation from adulation and affection to hatred. Why would the crowd demand Jesus' crucifixion? Once again, a major dimension of the answer is implicit in the present experience of the audience in the postwar context. As Josephus describes at several points in his history of the war, the advocates of the war killed their

---

12 Marcus, *Mark*, 2:1030–31, 1037. The most recent use of this verb was to introduce the cry of "many" (not "the crowd") at the triumphal entry which does not seem demonic: "And those who went before and those who followed shouted, 'Hosanna! Blessed is he who comes in the name of the Lord! Blessed is the kingdom of our father David that is coming!'" (11:9). This may be an indication of nothing more than the composer using a word with different connotations in different contexts.

fellow countrymen who advocated reconciliation or who tried to leave the besieged Temple.

The dynamics of audience address in the Pilate trial are a further development of the dynamics of the trial before the Sanhedrin. In the Sanhedrin trial, the high priest's question "You have heard his blasphemy! How does it appear to you?" is addressed to the audience as the Sanhedrin. The answer to the high priest's question, based on the norms of story, is that Jesus is not guilty of blasphemy and is the Messiah. The Sanhedrin's condemnation is the opposite of the answer invited by the story. The distance dynamics of characterization of the Sanhedrin are highly alienating. The impact of the Sanhedrin's condemnation of Jesus as being worthy of death is to create further audience alienation from the Sanhedrin. Their judgment is clearly wrong. The entire story has led to the conclusion that Jesus' Messianic confession is the truth, not blasphemy.

9, 12, 14: Pilate's questions to the audience as the crowd

In the Pilate trial, Pilate asks three questions of the crowd. In the telling of the story, these questions are addressed by the storyteller as Pilate to the audience as the crowd. The third question (15:14) is the climax of Pilate's interrogation of the crowd and, therefore, of the audience. And, in contrast to the highly alienating characterization of the Sanhedrin, the characterization of the crowd has been highly sympathetic and invites the audience to identify with the crowd. As a result, Pilate's questions (like the high priest's question "How does it appear to you?") are addressed by the storyteller as Pilate to the audience. For the audience, Pilate's questions are addressed to *us*, not *them*.

14: "What has he done that is evil?" / Τί γὰρ ἐποίησεν κακόν;

Pilate's final question to the crowd focuses on Jesus' offense: what evil has he done that is worthy of crucifixion? The only prior use of the key word, κακόν, occurs in the cleanliness discourse as an adjective: "From inside, out of the hearts of people come **evil thoughts** (NRSV—"intentions")" (ἔσωθεν γὰρ ἐκ τῆς καρδίας τῶν ἀνθρώπων οἱ διαλογισμοὶ οἱ **κακοὶ** ἐκπορεύονται—7:22). It is the overall category for the list of acts contrary to the law that follows. The connotation of the word in the Pilate trial concerns the evil, sin, or crime that Jesus has done. Pilate's questions are left unanswered by the crowd. As a result, the effect of the question is similar to the high priest's concluding question, "How does it appear to you?" Pilate's question demands an answer from the audience. And once again the answer based on the norms of the story is that Jesus has committed no sin, crime, or evil. It is the direct opposite of the crowd's response: "Crucify him." The finality of the crowd's second demand is emphasized by the adverb "vehemently" (περισσῶς).

For the audience, an implied dimension of the episode is the question: why would the crowd suddenly turn against Jesus? There are two levels to the question. It is, on the one hand, a historical question to be asked by Mark's audience some forty years after the trial: why would the crowd have done this forty years ago? It is also a question about the present time of Mark's audiences: what answer to this question is implicit in our experience now? The answer to which the story points is implicit in the choice of Barabbas. Jesus' crime was the failure to fulfill the crowd's hopes and expectations of a Davidic Messiah who would liberate Israel from Roman domination. For Mark's postwar audiences, the insurrection against the Romans is the answer to Pilate's question. Jesus' crime was his failure to provide military leadership.

There is also a theological dimension to the question. If, as the story implies, Jesus is God's chosen Messiah and the Son of God, Pilate's question is also a question about *our* response to God. What has God done wrong? Why have we rejected God? Why this vehement expression of hostility and hatred toward God? The answer to this question resonates through Israel's history and the tradition of the prophets. It leads back to Israel's repentance during the exile, to Israel's defiance of the Babylonians and the destruction of the first temple, to the tragedy of Israel's history of warfare from the time of the establishment of the kingdom with the reign of Saul until the destruction of the northern kingdom and then the southern kingdom. Jesus, and by implication God, has inaugurated another way of establishing the kingdom of God, which is indicated by Jesus' actions, teaching, and now by his suffering and imminent death. The major contrast between Jesus as Messiah and the earlier anointed ones of Israel is that Jesus is not violent. His crime is then that he is not a warrior, a general, or a revolutionary. The implication of the story is that the crowd has rejected God's intervention in human history and the way to liberation from the powers of evil that Jesus has inaugurated. The crowd has chosen instead (μᾶλλον) the way of Barabbas. For Mark's audience, the implication is that *we* made that decision and are now suffering the consequences of that decision, just as the people at the Watergate (Nehemiah 8–9) recognized that in the exile they were suffering the consequences of their violation of the covenant.

The Handing Over to the Gentiles (15:1–20)

15: wanting to satisfy the crowd / βουλόμενος τῷ ὄχλῳ τὸ ἱκανὸν ποιῆσαι

Pilate's response to the crowd's vehement demand that Jesus be crucified is to release Barabbas and hand Jesus over to be crucified. The motivation for Pilate's twofold decision is made perfectly clear by an inside view of his intent. The Greek phrase describing Pilate's motive, βουλόμενος τῷ ὄχλῳ τὸ ἱκανὸν ποιῆσαι, literally means "wanting for the crowd the sufficient to do" and is usually translated as "wishing to satisfy the crowd." BDAG suggests the phrase "to do someone a favor."[13] This description of Pilate's motive recalls the storyteller's inside view of Herod's motive for the execution of John: "the king was deeply grieved but out of regard for his oaths and for the guests, he did not want to refuse her" (see 6:26, NRSV). The logic of the story is, therefore, that the crowd has the same role in the execution of Jesus as Herodias and her dancing daughter had in the execution of John. However, while "the crowd" may be the decisive factor in Pilate's decision, his decision is unambiguously wrong. Pilate, knowing that Jesus is innocent of any crime, acts in a manner that is as corrupt and unjust as Herod's beheading of John. His motive is political expediency rather than justice.

The supreme irony of the story is that the crowd is the decisive factor in Jesus' crucifixion. Pilate's release of Barabbas meets their demand that he observe the custom of releasing a prisoner at Passover. His condemnation of Jesus meets the crowd's demand for Jesus' crucifixion. Pilate's condemnation of Jesus uses the key word of the trial's introduction, "to hand over" (παραδίδωμι), and thereby fulfills the prophecy of Jesus again. The flogging (φραγελλώσας) is synonymous to the third verb in Jesus' prophecy of the Gentiles' maltreatment of the Son of Man, μαστίζω, "to beat, flog" (10:34). Pilate is the subject of this participle. While the implication may be that Roman soldiers flogged Jesus at Pilate's command, the plain meaning is that Pilate himself, as the representative of the Gentiles, flogged Jesus with the leather straps tipped with jagged metal. The hope that Pilate would do what is just is broken, and he is confirmed as an enemy. The prophecy is fulfilled, and the last hope for Jesus' release is gone.

The Rhetoric of Involvement and Implication in the Pilate Trial

In light of the history of this story's interpretation, the question is, what was the dynamic meaning of this story for its original audiences? The conclusion of many scholars is that Mark's intention in this story was to shift

13. BDAG, 472.

the responsibility for Jesus' crucifixion onto "the Jews" and to exculpate the Romans. In this reading, Mark's intention is to condemn "the Jews" and to communicate that they are responsible for Jesus' death. A related conclusion has been that Mark was a document read by an audience of Gentile Christian readers rather than an oral story structured for performance to predominantly Judean audiences. The argument here is that this conclusion is only possible if one does not listen to the story and experience its dynamics. The story is structured by the rhetoric of implication rather than by the rhetoric of condemnation.

The dynamics of distance in the characterization of Pilate and the crowd are the keys to this story's meaning and impact. Prior to this story, the crowd is presented as a highly sympathetic character, particularly in its alliance with and protection of Jesus in Jerusalem (11:18, 32; 12:12, 38). In the context of Jesus' possible release, the crowd is the supreme hope. The storyteller's appeal is for the audience to join with and support the crowd in its anticipated action. As a result of this dynamic of distance, it is impossible for the audience to stand off and condemn the crowd in the same way that the audience is invited to condemn the chief priests, the scribes, and the elders. The authorities are unquestionably guilty of sin and criminal activity. And the structure of the characterization of the chief priest, scribes, and elders is the rhetoric of alienation and condemnation.

But the necessity of the same judgment on those with whom the audience has been closely identified has a completely different impact. This story is structured to lead the audience into the recognition that *we*, that is, the audience in identification with the crowd, are implicated in Jesus' death. The same story dynamic is present here as in the stories of the disciples' flight, Peter's denial, and (as we will see) the women's flight and silence. In both the earlier stories, the structure leads the audience into sympathetic identification with characters who respond to Jesus' arrest and trial in ways that are profoundly wrong according to the norms of the story. But in the Pilate trial, the recognition of the crowd's wrong does not come through a symbol of shame (such as the young man's naked flight) or through an inside view (of Peter's grief). In this story the crowd's involvement is made clear through an inside view of Pilate's motive for Jesus' crucifixion, namely, his desire to satisfy the crowd. The crowd, with whom the audience has been identified, is implicated in the complex of the causes of Jesus' death. It is not *them* but rather *us* who have demanded the crucifixion of the Messiah. As the highly sympathetic characterization of the crowd prior to the Pilate trial indicates, the rhetorical structure of the characterization of the crowd is the rhetoric of involvement and implication.

Pilate's characterization is also central to the story's impact. At the beginning of the trial, Pilate is presented as a Gentile whose questions have an even more hostile tone and intent than the high priest's. Pilate is characterized as a Gentile enemy directly analogous to Antiochus IV Epiphanes. But, in the middle of the trial, his sympathetic recognition of Jesus' innocence, his offer to release "the King of the Judeans," and his perception of the chief priests' hostile motive is a major reversal of expectations. Pilate's surprise at Jesus' silence corresponds to the effect of the story. His last question to the crowd—"What has he done that is evil?"—implies that he has found Jesus innocent, a further accurate perception. But he then condemns Jesus for a crassly political motive in the same manner that Herod condemned John the Baptist. This final reversal of expectations reestablishes Pilate as an inimical character. This is not a sympathetic characterization that removes Pilate and by implication the Romans from responsibility for Jesus' death. In the end Pilate acts in a manner that is typical of the Gentile oppressors of Israel. And, as we will see, the final characterization of Pilate in the story of Jesus' burial further reinforces his characterization as a cynical Roman tyrant.

The irony of the story from a Judean perspective in the aftermath of the war is that the people were involved in bringing about Jesus' execution. The cause of Jesus' death is an unholy alliance between the crowd, the Israelite religious authorities, and the Romans.[14] However, as Jesus' final passion prophecy indicates, the death of the Son of Man at the hands of the Gentiles is to be expected. What is unexpected and is not foreseen in the prophecy is that Jesus' primary ally throughout his ministry, the crowd, becomes a major agent in his crucifixion by the Gentiles. Thus, Jesus' prophecy is fulfilled but in a way that no one predicted.

These stories have an impact similar to the impact of dominant stories in the tradition of Israel's storytellers from the garden of Eden and the exodus through the stories of David and the destruction of the Temple and Jerusalem. As is evident in the story of Pentecost (Acts 2), the experience

---

14. The widely held conclusion that it is historically probable that the Judean religious authorities in alliance with the Romans shared responsibility for Jesus' death may be accurate. But the conclusion that often accompanies that assessment is that Mark's motive in implicating "the crowd" along with the religious authorities was to shift the responsibility from the Romans to the Jews as part of an anti-Jewish polemic. There is no evidence in the rhetorical dynamics of Mark's story to support this correlative conclusion about Mark's purpose. The purpose inherent in the structure of Mark's story is to involve the members of his audiences in the dynamics that led to Jesus' death rather than to involve them in condemning "the crowd." In fact, this widely accepted, anti-Judaic reading of Mark is exactly the opposite of the performance dynamics of Mark's story in its original context.

of implication in the sins of the people against the Messiah invites Israelite audiences to reflect on what led to these actions, and to turn away from these actions in repentance. In this story of the Pilate trial, the experience of implication invites audiences to reflect on the choice of Barabbas and the condemnation of Jesus. At its heart the story invites its listeners to turn away from the faith that violence and war will save us from the powers of evil.

If this was a primary meaning of the Pilate trial, the crowd's choice between the way of Barabbas and the way of Jesus is wholly understandable in a contemporary as well as an ancient context. The crowd is acting on the common belief, then and now, that the only way to overcome the powers of evil as embodied in our ever-changing enemies is through violence and warfare. Audiences in the twenty-first century are bombarded with endlessly inventive variations of this myth of redemptive violence in movies and television. That myth is the foundation of the movie business and the delight of audiences around the world. In this sense, few Christians actually believe that Jesus is the Messiah. At some foundational level, most Christians agree with the great majority of the human community, who believes in the myth of redemptive violence. According to this myth, a realistic view of the world means violence is the only way to control and overcome the powers of evil. It is not only the audiences of Mark who are implicated in the death of Jesus. Everyone who in a multitude of ways chooses and delights in the myth of redemptive violence in its many forms is implicated in Jesus' death and is invited by the story to reflect on this faith.

The Performance of the Story

The introductory description of the authorities' meeting and handing over of Jesus has several elements. The tone of the meeting or plan has a sinister character. The list of the authorities is the most inclusive list yet, and the climactic phrase "the whole Sanhedrin" invites a gesture of outspread arms. It conveys that everybody was at this meeting. The tone of Pilate's name needs to be the identification of an enemy, a representative of the Gentiles, who is going to kill Jesus. The whole first sentence builds to the climax of the last two words: "handed him over to Pilate." It is important to tell this in a way that indicates that this is a fulfillment of Jesus' prophecy, and that the fulfillment of the prophecy is imminent.

Pilate's opening question to Jesus invites a characterization of him in the imperial manner of the Roman power structure: cynical, hostile, accusatory. *Gruff* is a word that comes to mind. Some have proposed that the emphasis of Pilate's question should fall on "you" as a satire directed at Jesus.

The Handing Over to the Gentiles (15:1–20)

But this is highly improbable because he is repeating the implied accusation of the Judean authorities. The charge is that Jesus has claimed to be the King of the Judeans, a capital crime of treason against the Roman state. The emphasis of the question needs to fall on the charge that is ultimately inscribed on the tablet fixed to the cross over Jesus' head.

The tone of Jesus' response is more complex. It is strong rather than weak. It is ambiguous and can be taken as both yes and no. A paraphrase is something like, "That is your idea" and by implication means, "*You* say so, but not me." Jesus' words are to be said in a strong voice with the head up looking straight ahead with dignity. The gesture of hands bound probably in front of the body is also important as a reminder that Jesus was bound. There is no tone of resignation or admission of guilt. Furthermore, everyone who has heard Mark's story knows that Jesus has never claimed to be the King of the Judeans. In contrast to the statements by the storyteller (1:1), Simon Peter (8:29), and Jesus himself (14:62) that he is the Messiah, neither Jesus nor any sympathetic character in the story has ever claimed that Jesus is King of the Judeans. The implication of the story is that the Sanhedrin manufactured this title during their planning meeting.

The summary of the chief priests' accusations conveys their implacable hostility. And Pilate's second question is also hostile and gruff (15:4). It may be that the report of Jesus' silence was told in a manner that anticipated the audience's surprise at Jesus' response. If so, it gives greater credibility to Pilate's surprise. The first hint that Pilate may be sympathetic to Jesus is the inside view of his "wonder" in response to Jesus' silence. The description of his surprise needs to be a sympathetic description of his internal response. It needs to sound a note of hope.

Mark's descriptions of the custom of prisoner release and of Barabbas are comments addressed to the audience as background information (15:6–7). They are an interruption in the description of the trial. This is a moment of intimacy between the storyteller and the audience. Stepping forward, leaning in, and directly including the audience in this inside information may heighten this closeness. A quieter and more intimate tone and a gesture of the hand beside the mouth may also be helpful. Mark's tone in the description of Barabbas is unclear. Given the recent experience of Mark's audiences, it is possible that Barabbas and his murderous associates are described in a tone of critique and even condemnation. In the context of the recent disaster perpetrated by people like him, it certainly is not told with a clenched fist in a tone of celebration and admiration. But since the description of Barabbas is so important in the audience's experience of the rest of the trial, it is more likely that the tone is more like a relatively objective news report, which leaves the audience free to make their own judgment about the choice that will follow. The other possibility is that Mark here expresses his hostility toward his opponents in the sectarian conflict in a manner similar to Josephus' description of the leaders of the insurrection.

The coming up of the crowd and the report of their demand to Pilate is structured to be told with a tone of hope and joy. This is the fulfillment of Jesus' long and positive relationship with the crowd. And the crowd's intervention carries with it the expectation that they will ask for Jesus to be released.

The report of Pilate's offer to release "the King of the Judeans" is a reversal of expectations and is, therefore, to be told with a tone of surprise. The sense of this is that no one would have ever predicted that Pilate would make such a proposal. This tone of surprise can only be conveyed in the introduction to Pilate's question, and that may be the reason why the introduction is relatively long (ὁ δὲ Πιλᾶτος ἀπεκρίθη αὐτοῖς λέγων—15:9). The style of Pilate's question continues the same basic tone and voice of the interrogation. It may be a kind of grudging offer to meet the demand for Jesus' release that he anticipates. The storyteller's explanation of Pilate's offer is another inside comment told directly to the audience in response to their surprise at Pilate's offer. It answers the audience's question: why would Pilate offer to release Jesus?

The chief priests' successful inciting of the crowd to demand Barabbas is the most radical reversal of expectations in the entire story. In view of the consistent pattern of the expression of the storyteller's attitude towards the crowd present throughout the gospel, it is probable that Mark expressed his shock at the crowd's defection. His attitude may even have been a kind of horror at what *we* have done. The impact of the report is to raise the question, why? Why would the crowd suddenly join with the chief priests? Why would they demand Barabbas instead of Jesus?" The implicit assumption of the story is that the audience is able to supply the answer immediately to this question. Prior to this, as in the surprise of Pilate's offer to release Jesus, the storyteller explains the reasons to the audience. But there is no implication here that the crowd's response is a mystery. Furthermore, it is important that this not be told as a condemnation. That would be antithetical to the rhetoric of the story. The dynamic of the story at this point is not condemnation but involvement. The telling needs to express both the storyteller's attitude toward this development and the development itself.

Pilate's question about what he is to do with Jesus (15:12) is addressed to the audience as the crowd. The tone of his question may include a note of exasperation and annoyance in response to the crowd's rejection of his offer. The tone of the storyteller's introduction of the crowd's demand to crucify Jesus is ambiguous. The possibilities are that it is given in the vehement tone of the demand itself, in a tone of disbelief and horror, in a tone

The Handing Over to the Gentiles (15:1–20) 245

of condemnation, or in the objective and dispassionate tone of a neutral observer. In view of the complexity of the story, it is unlikely that the tone of the introduction was vehement. The tone of a neutral observer is possible. But the dominant pattern in the story is that the storyteller expresses his own attitude toward the events about which he is reporting. If so, the tone of this introduction is disbelief, horror, and grief. This same issue is present in the performance of the stories of Judas' betrayal, the disciples' flight, and Peter's denial. The probabilities in all these instances are that the storyteller expressed his own attitude about these actions by Jesus' disciples. This is even more probable in reporting this action by the crowd, Jesus' major support in his conflict with the authorities. Thus, it is likely that Mark introduced the crowd's demand for crucifixion with a tone of horror, grief, and disbelief. It is unlikely that he could report this objectively with a tone of emotional detachment.

Recognizing the importance of the storyteller's attitude in this story raises the question of how the crowd's actual words, "Crucify him," are to be told (15:13). I have always assumed that the storyteller told these words with the hostile attitude of the crowd. In effect, the storyteller would then introduce the crowd's response with an attitude of disbelief and grief and then dramatize the crowd's words and fully express their hostility. But in a recent meeting during which I told this story, another scholar reported that she experienced my performance as the most anti-Jewish telling she had ever heard. This response has convinced me that it is necessary, with contemporary audiences prone to hear polemic, to also express an attitude of grief and disbelief in reporting the crowd's actual words, as well as in the introductions.

The volume of the story steadily increases from the report of the custom of prisoner release. Pilate's concluding question to the crowd (15:14a), addressed by the storyteller as Pilate to the audience as the crowd, is the climax of Pilate's speeches. It is exceeded in volume only by the crowd's second, vehement demand for Jesus' crucifixion (15:14b), matched by the storyteller's even more intense grief at reporting it. The climax of Pilate's speech (15:14) is the word "wrong" or "evil." Just as this question hangs over the story of the trial as a whole, it may be good to allow the question to hang in the air for a moment before reporting the crowd's response. The crowd's second demand for crucifixion is louder and constitutes the climax of the crescendo of this exchange between Pilate and the crowd and of the storyteller's grief in relating it.

The last complex period that describes Pilate's decision is quieter. It is important to convey the climactic irony of Pilate's motive, "wanting to satisfy the crowd," and your attitude as the storyteller of disbelief and irony at this development. The report of the dual release is the final dashing of the hope that Jesus might be released. It is also the supreme irony for Mark and his listeners in light of the implicit consequences of the way of Barabbas in the recent history of Israel. The concluding colon is the bitter fulfillment of Jesus' prophecy of his treatment by the Gentiles. There is absolutely no note of sympathy or compassion in the description of Pilate's cowardly and cynical action. The final implication of the performance of the Pilate trial is that the flogging and handing over of Jesus for crucifixion is a travesty of justice.

The Mocking by the Roman Soldiers (15:16–20)

This story is the climax of the section that fulfills in detail the prophecy of abuse by the Gentiles. The acoustic signal that this is the climax of the section is the rounding of the ending of the Pilate trial, "and he handed him over in order to be crucified" (ἵνα σταυρωθῇ) and the ending of the mocking by the soldiers, "and they led him out in order to crucify him" (ἵνα σταυρώσωσιν αὐτόν).

Sound Map

16 **Οἱ δὲ στρατιῶται** ἀπήγαγον αὐτὸν ἔσω τῆς αὐλῆς, ὅ ἐστιν πραιτώριον,
    καὶ συγκαλοῦσιν ὅλην τὴν σπεῖραν.
17 καὶ **ἐνδιδύσκουσιν αὐτὸν πορφύραν**
    καὶ περιτιθέασιν αὐτῷ πλέξαντες ἀκάνθινον στέφανον.
18 καὶ ἤρξαντο ἀσπάζεσθαι αὐτόν,
    Χαῖρε, **βασιλεῦ τῶν Ἰουδαίων**
19 καὶ ἔτυπτον αὐτοῦ τὴν κεφαλὴν καλάμῳ
    καὶ **ἐνέπτυον** αὐτῷ,
    καὶ τιθέντες τὰ γόνατα προσεκύνουν αὐτῷ.

20 καὶ ὅτε **ἐνέπαιξαν** αὐτῷ, **ἐξέδυσαν** αὐτὸν τὴν πορφύραν
    καὶ **ἐνέδυσαν** αὐτὸν τὰ ἱμάτια* αὐτοῦ.
καὶ ἐξάγουσιν αὐτὸν ἵνα σταυρώσωσιν αὐτόν.

Translation

16 **The soldiers** led him away into the courtyard of the palace, that is
                                                                the praetorium,
    and called together the whole cohort.
17 And **they clothed him in a purple cloak**

and put on his head a crown woven of thorns.
18And they began to salute him, "**Hail, King of the Judeans!**"
19and they struck his head with a cane
and **they spit** on him
and kneeling they paid homage to him.

20And when **they had mocked** him, **they unclothed him of the purple cloak**
and **reclothed him in his own clothes.**
And they led him out **to crucify him.**

Ancient Associations and Connections

This story evoked the Markan audiences' memories of earlier stories of ritual humiliation of Israelites by their Gentile enemies. The oldest of these stories was the story of Samson. The central verb of this story tradition, ἐμπαίζω, "to ridicule, make fun of, mock," is used twice in one textual family of the LXX translation of the Samson story (Judg 16:25, 27). In fact, the LXX A text has virtually the same exact phrase as Mark's summary: καὶ ἐνέπαιξαν αὐτῷ (Judg 16:25) and καὶ ὅτε ἐνέπαιξαν αὐτῷ (Mark 15:20). The NRSV translation is based on the Hebrew text and renders this phrase as "he performed for them." But the Greek in Codex Alexandrinus[15] means "they mocked, made fun of him." This may well be an instance in which the LXX translators made an ambiguous Hebrew phrase clearer. Furthermore, this may be a sign that the Markan composer had heard the A text of the Septuagint and was sounding that note in his new composition.

The Greek of the verses of Codex Alexandrinus where the verb occurs is,

Καὶ ἐκάλεσαν τὸν Σαμψὼν ἐξ οἴκου φυλακῆς, καὶ **ἐνέπαιζον αὐτῷ**
... τρισχίλιοι ἄνδρες καὶ γυναῖκες ἐμβλέποντες ἐμπαιζόμενον τὸν Σαμψὼν. (Judg 16:25, 27)

A fairly literal translation of the verses in which the verb occurs in Codex Alexandrinus is,

---

15 The textual history of the LXX text of Judges is particularly complex. The editors of the Ralfs edition have included two texts of Judges in their text. Judges is the only book with this format. The texts are Codex Alexandrinus and the text of Theodotian, printed on the top and bottom half of each page respectively. They have printed them in this format because both may preserve elements of the original text. In this story, the probability is that Mark knew and is alluding to the textual tradition of the Greek translation of Judges recorded in Codex Alexandrinus.

> And they called Samson out of the prison and **they mocked him** . . . and on the roof there were some three thousand men and women who watched Samson being mocked.

The NRSV translation of the Hebrew text of the larger story in which this verbal thread occurs is as follows:

> Now the lords of the Philistines gathered to offer a great sacrifice to their god Dagon, and to rejoice; for they said, "Our god has given Samson our enemy into our hand." 24When the people saw him, they praised their god; for they said, "Our god has given our enemy into our hand, the ravager of our country, who has killed many of us." 25And when their hearts were merry, they said, "Call Samson, and let him entertain us." So they called Samson out of the prison, **and he performed for them**. They made him stand between the pillars; 26and Samson said to the attendant who held him by the hand, "Let me feel the pillars on which the house rests, so that I may lean against them." 27Now the house was full of men and women; all the lords of the Philistines were there, and on the roof there were about three thousand men and women, **who looked on while Samson performed**. (Judg 16:23–27, NRSV)

As evidenced by his biblical quotations and allusions throughout the gospel, it is highly probable that Mark knew some version of the Septuagint very well, and the indication here is that he knew the Greek translation recorded in Codex Alexandrinus. Because of the complexity and uncertainty of the Septuagint textual tradition, however, the most that can be said is that the composer of Mark may have known this form of the Samson story and that his allusion to the story included this verbal thread. But, regardless of the presence or absence of the specific word for mocking, the Samson story is part of the background for Mark's audience.

The other story of Gentile ritual mocking of Israelites is the story of the Maccabean martyrs (2 Maccabees 7). I will only include here the story of the torture and death of the oldest three boys, which has the most explicit verbal connections with Mark's story (NRSV):

> It happened also that seven brothers and their mother were arrested and were being compelled by the king, under torture with whips and thongs, to partake of unlawful swine's flesh. 2One of them, acting as their spokesman, said, 'What do you intend to ask and learn from us? For we are ready to die rather than transgress the laws of our ancestors.'

> 3The king fell into a rage, and gave orders to have pans and cauldrons heated. 4These were heated immediately, and he commanded that the tongue of their spokesman be cut out and that they scalp him and cut off his hands and feet, while the rest of the brothers and the mother looked on. 5When he was utterly helpless, the king ordered them to take him to the fire, still breathing, and to fry him in a pan. The smoke from the pan spread widely, but the brothers and their mother encouraged one another to die nobly, saying, 6'The Lord God is watching over us and in truth has compassion on us, as Moses declared in his song that bore witness against the people to their faces, when he said, "And he will have compassion on his servants."'
>
> 7After the first brother had died in this way, they brought forward the second for their sport. They tore off the skin of his head with the hair, and asked him, 'Will you eat rather than have your body punished limb by limb?' 8He replied in the language of his ancestors and said to them, 'No.' Therefore he in turn underwent tortures as the first brother had done. 9And when he was at his last breath, he said, 'You accursed wretch, you dismiss us from this present life, but the King of the universe will raise us up to an everlasting renewal of life, because we have died for his laws.'
>
> 10After him, the third was the victim of their sport. When it was demanded, he quickly put out his tongue and courageously stretched forth his hands, 11and said nobly, 'I got these from Heaven, and because of his laws I disdain them, and from him I hope to get them back again.' 12As a result the king himself and those with him were astonished at the young man's spirit, for he regarded his sufferings as nothing.

The torture and death of the second and third boys is introduced by the same family of words for mocking, for which the root verb is ἐμπαίζω, which occur in Mark. The torture of the second boy is introduced with these words:

> After the first brother had died in this way, they brought forward the second for their sport [ἐμπαιγμὸν, "for mockery"] and they tore off the skin of his head with the body of his hair . . .
>
> Μεταλλάξαντος δὲ τοῦ πρώτου τὸν τρόπον τοῦτον τον δεύτερερον ἤγον ἐπὶ τὸν **ἐμπαιγμὸν** καὶ τὸ τῆς κεφαλῆς δέρμα σὺν ταῖς τὸ σῶμα κατὰ μέλος. (2 Macc 7:7)

And the third boy's execution begins:

After him, the third was the victim of their sport (ἐνεπαίζετο, "was mocked").

Μετὰ δὲ τοῦτον ὁ τρίτος **ἐνεπαίζετο** ... (2 Macc 7:10)

I would highly recommend a reading aloud of 2 Macc 6:18—7:42 as the immediate background for this story and indeed for the rest of Mark's story. The characterization of Antiochus IV Epiphanes, and the effort of apparently Greek friends of Eleazar to find a way for him to pretend to eat the forbidden meat and not be executed, as well as the pathos of the mother's address to her last little boy are important elements of the story.

These stories of the torture and execution of Israelites by Gentiles were probably known by Mark's audiences and were the immediate background against which Jesus' story was heard.

The Sounds of the Story

Once again the sounds of the story need extensive description. The periods of this story are all complex (two or more cola), with the exception of the final simple period: "and they led him out to crucify him." This ending of a story with a simple, short period is a frequent pattern of Markan endings.[16] This concluding period sounds the theme of this part of the story that is established at the end of the preceding story (15:15): "in order to crucify him" (ἵνα σταυρώσωσιν αὐτόν). As Lee and Scott have observed, the most striking

---

16. The role of particular cola in Mark's composition is sometimes ambiguous. Lee and Scott, *Sound Mapping*, make a strong argument that the unit of the soldiers' mocking begins with the colon καὶ παρέδωκεν τὸν Ἰησοῦν φραγελλώσας ἵνα σταυρωθῇ ("and having flogged him he handed Jesus over to be crucified," 15:15b). This cola is the first instance of the new sound pattern (καὶ + verb + αὐτόν) in 15:12b–24 after a frequently repeated pattern of ὁ (οἱ) δὲ in 15:11–15a). However, the sound patterns of the story are coordinated with the content. A new story unit is often introduced by the name and description of the principal character of that story (see the introduction of the woman in the story of the anointing at Bethany [14:3] and the story of Peter's denial [14:66]). New stories are also introduced by the naming of a new place or a new time (see 14:1, 3, 12, 17 and many other verses, which clearly begin a new story). In this case, Pilate is the subject of the periods beginning in 15:1, and he is still the subject in 15:15. In 15:16 a new main character (the soldiers) and a new place (the praetorium) are introduced. The soldiers are the subject of the story through the crucifixion of the "insurrectionists" with Jesus (15:27), although a new character, Simon of Cyrene, is introduced in 15:21, initiating a new episode in the story of what the soldiers did. Furthermore, the parallel ἵνα clauses—ἵνα σταυρωθῇ (15:15) and ἵνα σταυρώσωσιν αὐτόν (15:20)—are most naturally heard as the climactic endings of their respective stories and as a rounding of the section. The markers for the subunits of the crucifixion story are ambiguous. But the probability is that the flogging and handing over of Jesus was the climax of the Pilate trial, and that a significant pause came prior to the introduction of the soldiers.

The Handing Over to the Gentiles (15:1–20) 251

element of the sound of this story is the drumbeat of the story. Each of the cola in the story (with the exception of the calling together of the whole cohort at the beginning) has a structure of καὶ ("and") + a verb + αὐτὸν/αὐτῷ ("him," in some grammatical form appropriate to the particular Greek verb).[17] This establishes a beat in the sound of the story like the rhythm of a whipping or a hammer driving nails. That beat is repeated ten times in this story and you have to hear it to appreciate its impact. Combined with the last colon of the Pilate trial and the four instances in the story of the preparations for the crucifixion (15:21–25), which follows this story of the mocking, this beat occurs fifteen times in this section of Mark's story, most of them in immediate and uninterrupted sequence.

The sound of the story reinforces the violence of its content. The story begins and ends with Jesus' being first "clothed" in purple (15:17) and then "declothed" of the purple (ἐνδιδύσκουσιν αὐτὸν πορφύραν/ἐξέδυσαν αὐτὸν τὴν πορφύραν—15:20), thereby rounding the story. The final position of maximum impact is given to the major theme and the major sound of this section of the story, "in order to crucify him" (ἵνα σταυρώσωσιν αὐτόν). Beginning with the Pilate trial, this verb is repeated in various forms seven times (15:13, 14b, 15, 20, 24, 25, 27). Linked with the description of Simon of Cyrene carrying Jesus' cross (ἵνα ἄρῃ τὸν σταυρὸν αὐτοῦ), with the mocking taunt to come down from "the cross" by the passersby (15:30) and the authorities (15:32), and with the derision by the rebels "crucified with him" (15:32), the sounds of crucifixion ring like a tolling bell throughout these sections of the story.

The cola in the middle of this story of the mocking by the soldiers are also highly onomatopoetic. In English as well as in Greek, they have the harsh sounds of the beating and spitting they describe: καὶ ἔτυπτον αὐτοῦ τὴν κεφαλὴν καλάμῳ καὶ ἐνέπτυον αὐτῷ "And they **struck** (ἔτυπτον) his head with a cane and they **spit** (ἐνέπτυον) on him . . ." (15:19). The shortness of the "spitting" colon is a sign that it was to be enunciated emphatically. The soldiers' mocking repetition of the initial accusation by the chief priests and Pilate that he claimed to be "King of the Judeans" implies that the soldiers laughed at this Judean "king." In the fourth period, the story's theme of mocking introduces the period with the plosive force of the verb, ἐνέπαιξαν, and is followed by the pairing of the verbs for "unclothed, undressed, stripped" and "reclothed, re-dressed" (ἐξέδυσαν/ἐνέδυσαν) in the successive cola.

---

17. Lee and Scott, *Sound Mapping*, 200.

This story also sounds the fulfillment of another element of Jesus' earlier prophecies of his passion and resurrection by repeating key words (here, in bold) from the last of those prophecies (10:33–34). Jesus' prophecy was,

καὶ **παραδώσουσιν αὐτὸν** τοῖς ἔθνεσιν
καὶ **ἐμπαίξουσιν αὐτῷ**
καὶ **ἐμπτύσουσιν αὐτῷ**
καὶ μαστιγώσουσιν αὐτὸν
καὶ ἀποκτενοῦσιν

and **they will hand him over** to the Gentiles
and **they will mock him**
and **spit on him**
and flog him
and kill him (NRSV)

The "handing him over to the Gentiles" was fulfilled at the beginning of the Pilate trial in the handing over to Pilate (15:1). The next stage in the fulfillment of the prophecy was heard in the last colon of the Pilate trial: "and he handed over Jesus, having flogged him, in order to be crucified" (καὶ παρέδωκεν τὸν Ἰησοῦν φραγελλώσας ἵνα σταυρωθῇ—15:15). The completion of the "handing over to the Gentiles" is Jesus' being handed over from the Gentile governor to the Gentile soldiers.

The story of what the Gentile soldiers do to Jesus does not always repeat the exact words of the prophecy. In the prophecy Jesus used the word μαστιγώσουσιν for "flogging." At the conclusion of the Pilate trial in 15:15, Pilate hands Jesus over to be crucified "having flogged Jesus," and the Greek word is φραγελλώσας. In the story about the soldiers, the flogging is named as part of the torture (15:19), and this time Mark names it even differently: "they struck his head with a cane" (καὶ ἔτυπτον αὐτοῦ τὴν κεφαλὴν καλάμῳ). Other words do make sonic connections with the prophecy. The word for "spit" in the prophecy is εμπτωσουσιν (10:34). In the story of the soldiers' mocking, it is the same word with only a grammatical difference: ἐνέπτυον (15:19). Thus, the same word is used in both the prophecy and the soldiers' torture. Also the word for the soldiers' mocking is an aorist (past) form of the future form used in Jesus' prophecy: εμπαιξουσιν (10:34) / ἐνέπαιξαν (15:20). Through both sonic connections and alternative ways of naming the same actions, therefore, Mark makes the fulfillment of Jesus' prophecy unmistakable for the audience and easy to remember for those who would tell his story.

The Handing Over to the Gentiles (15:1–20)

Notes on Details and Translation

17, 20: they clothed him / unclothed him / reclothed him / καὶ ἐνδιδύσκουσιν αὐτὸν /ἐξέδυσαν αὐτὸν/ἐνέδυσαν αὐτὸν

The major verbal thread in this story is the clothing and unclothing of Jesus in purple and then clothing him again in his own clothes. In the NRSV this is translated as "clothed him in a purple cloak" / "stripped him of the purple cloak" / "put his own clothes on him." The clear intent of the composer of the story is to weave a motif focused on the ritual of clothing. He accomplishes this through words that produce a sonic repetition that the translation eliminates. Translating this as "clothed, unclothed, and reclothed" preserves the verbal thread that was structured into the story and calls attention to this central dimension of the mocking of Jesus.

17, 20: the purple / πορφύραν

This term, which is usually translated as "a purple cloak," is simply the noun for "purple." Whether Mark was referring to a robe or a cloak, and whether it was purple or red is uncertain. Purple was a royal color and emperors and royal officials did apparently have purple cloaks, but they were very expensive to make. This is also the name for the cloak worn by Roman soldiers[18] that were a mass-produced red. While it is unlikely that the Roman garrison in Jerusalem would have had a purple cloak, it would have been easy for one of the soldiers to take off his own cloak and put it on Jesus. This is probably what Mark pictured. Since cloaks only covered the back and were tied at the neck, the irony of this garment is magnified if the implication of the final description of the mockery—"they reclothed him in his own clothes"—is that they had stripped him before putting the cloak on him since a cloak would not have covered the front of the body.

19: with a stick / καλάμῳ

The word for the instrument with which the soldiers struck Jesus in the head is an ambiguous word. Its first meaning is "a reed." But this makes no sense in the context of a Roman mockery. Soldiers would look silly making mockery with a reed. It is also unlikely that it is an allusion to Isa 42:3: "a bruised reed he will not break," where the reference is to what the Servant of the Lord will not do. Furthermore, the same word is used to describe the implement that the bystander used to extend the sponge of sour wine

---

18. BDAG, 855.

to Jesus. A reed is too flexible to support a sponge being lifted up several feet. It is more probable that Mark is using the word in the sense of a cane or stick, which is the meaning of this Greek word in Artemidorus' work, *Oneirocritica* 2.48: "It is bad luck to be beaten (in a dream) . . . by a cane (καλάμῳ) because of the noise that it makes."[19] Therefore, the translation "cane, stick" is adopted here.[20]

Comments on the Meaning and Impact of the Story

The frame of the story is established by two sets of verbal connections with what has gone before. The first set is the sonic repetition at the beginning of the Pilate trial (15:1) and at the end of that trial (15:15) of the word "handed over" (παρέδωκεν), which takes up Jesus' prophecy that he would be "handed over" (παραδώσουσιν) to the Gentiles (10:33). In 15:1 the entire Judean religious leadership hands Jesus over to Pilate; in 15:15 Pilate hands Jesus over to the soldiers, setting the stage for the mocking and torture that follow in 15:16-20. The second set is the sonic links between the setting of the mockery by the soldiers and the setting of the earlier trial before the Judean religious establishment. These connections are as follows:

> They **led** Jesus away to the high priest . . . And Peter followed him at a distance, right **into the courtyard** of the high priest.
>
> **Καὶ ἀπήγαγον** τὸν Ἰησοῦν πρὸς τὸν ἀρχιερέα. . . . καὶ ὁ Πέτρος ἀπὸ μακρόθεν ἠκολούθησεν αὐτῷ ἕως **ἔσω** εἰς **τὴν αὐλὴν** τοῦ ἀρχιερέως. (14:53-54)
>
> The soldiers **led** him away **into the courtyard** of the palace, that is the praetorium
>
> Οἱ δὲ στρατιῶται **ἀπήγαγον** αὐτὸν **ἔσω τῆς αὐλῆς** (15:16)

These repetitions set the story of the mocking by the soldiers unmistakably in the camp of the enemy. This association of "the soldiers" (οἱ στρατιῶται) as the Roman enemies of Israel is reinforced by the connotations of this term in both the Septuagint and the Gospels. With one exception, this term in the Septuagint refers to the soldiers of the Gentiles: Antiochus Epiphanes (2 Macc 5:12; 4 Macc 17:23), Nicanor (2 Macc 14:39), and Ptolemy Philopatur (3 Macc 3:12). The exception is its use to describe Israelite warriors in one passage, in 4 Macc 3:7, 12. In the Gospels the noun "soldier" always refers to Roman soldiers (Matt 8:9; 27:27; 28:12; Mark 15:16; Luke

---

19. BDAG, 502, meaning 2.
20. Marcus, *Mark*, 2:1040.

7:8; 23:36; John 19:2, 23, 24, 32, 34). And in Mark as well as John, there are no earlier stories of "good" Roman soldiers as there are in the Gospels of Matthew and Luke, which share a story about a centurion with soldiers under him (Matt 8:5–13; Luke 7:1–10). Thus, the setting of this story resonates with both earlier expectations established by Jesus' prophecy concerning the treatment of the Son of Man by the Gentiles and the atmosphere of the earlier trials. This setting is an explicit sign that the norms of judgment throughout Mark's story are Israelite norms. The anticipation established by this setting is that this will be a racially charged ritual of humiliation.

The setting of this mock ritual is the courtyard of the palace.[21] The naming of the praetorium may be an indication that this courtyard was outside rather than inside the palace. A cohort was a tenth of a legion, which meant approximately six hundred men.[22] The courtyard that Mark imagined was, therefore, a large courtyard that could function as a kind of amphitheater for a kind of entertainment.

The bitter irony of the soldiers' mockery of Jesus is created by the juxtaposition of images of royalty with actions of explicit humiliation. The purple cloak, the salute, the title King of the Judeans, and the kneeling are all signs of royalty. The explicit actions of mockery are the crown of thorns, spitting on him, and striking his head with a stick or cane. The most graphic action of humiliation is only implied at the end of the story when it is noted that the soldiers put his own clothes back on him, which in turn implies that they had stripped him naked before putting on the purple cloak. This is the climax of the crescendo of humiliation of an Israelite man by Gentiles and is clearly structured to appeal to the audience's Israelite sensibilities. And, as has been noted above (see *Ancient Associations and Connections*), the story has the same structure of sympathetic appeals as the mockery of Samson and the Maccabean boys.

This is the most explicit instance of the term, "the Judeans," as a name used by those outside the community of Israel. With the possible exception of Pilate's first question to Jesus, his use of the title, King of the Judeans is not derisive or mocking. It is implied that the chief priests introduced the title as the central accusation of Jesus' imperial ambitions and revolutionary intent. Pilate then uses the term in his dialogue with the crowd as their name for Jesus: i.e., "the one you call 'King of the Judeans.'" But no Judeans had ever used that term, and the crowd rejects Jesus and, by implication, this name. Even the chief priests and scribes in their mockery later in the story use the term "the King of Israel." In the mocking by the Roman soldiers, the

---

21. Marcus, *Mark*, 2:1039.
22. Brown, *Death of the Messiah*, 1:248.

title "King of the Judeans" is spoken in contempt and derision. This is the connotation of the name "the Judeans" at the climax of Mark's story. In this instance, it is a term used in derision by Gentile outsiders.

Violent contrasts are built into the story by the associations of the words of the story denoting violence with earlier actions of honor and affection. Jesus' garments have been the source of healing power for the woman with a flow of blood (5:27–30) and the sick folks in Gennesaret (6:56), and a sign of Jesus' identity as the Son of God (9:3). Here garments are used to mock and shame Jesus. The previous use of the verb "to salute" (ἀσπάζομαι) was when the crowd ran up to "greet" (NRSV) Jesus after the transfiguration (9:15). Here saluting is an act of derision. Jesus' head has received a supreme gesture of affection and honor in the woman's anointing him with precious ointment (14:3). Now his head is beaten with a cane. The Gerasene demoniac's first response to Jesus (5:6) was to do obeisance before him (προσεκύνησεν, NRSV "bowed down before") in fear. Here the soldiers do obeisance in mock homage. These previous associations heighten the irony of the soldiers' mockery. Spiteful and degrading treatment of loved and honored persons is the epitome of violence.

An integral dimension of the impact of the story is that the mockery also explicitly fulfills two more parts of Jesus' passion prophecy:

> They will hand him over to the Gentiles; and **they will mock him and spit on him** and flog him . . .
>
> Καὶ παραδώσουσιν αὐτὸν τοῖς ἔθνεσιν **καὶ ἐμπαίξουσιν αὐτῷ καὶ ἐμπτύσουσιν αὐτῷ** καὶ μαστιγώσουσιν . . . (10:33–34)
>
> 19and they struck his head with a cane and **they spit on him**
> and kneeling they paid homage to him.
> 20And when **they had mocked him**
>
> 19καὶ ἔτυπτον αὐτοῦ τὴν κεφαλὴν καλάμῳ καὶ **ἐνέπτυον αὐτῷ**,
> καὶ τιθέντες τὰ γόνατα προσεκύνουν αὐτῷ.
> 20καὶ ὅτε **ἐνέπαιξαν αὐτῷ** . . . (15:19–20);

The actions of fulfillment of Jesus' prophecy form a chiasm with the prophecy: the appearance of the words *mock, spit,* and *flog* (in that order) in the prophecy and the appearance of the same words in reverse order (*flog, spit, mock*) in the trial and mocking stories. This creates a rhythm of memory for both the storyteller and the audience. All the abuse at the hands of the Gentiles that Jesus prophesied happens.

The fulfillment of this prophecy marks the end of the hope raised in the earlier episodes that Jesus may be able to escape death. The custom of

The Handing Over to the Gentiles (15:1–20)

release and the previous support of the crowd were the last hope. This leaves hovering in the air the issue that is implicit throughout the story but made graphically present in the context of Jesus' prayer in Gethsemane: how can this be the will of God?

The rounding of the sounds of the story at the beginning and the end creates the implication of the highest degree of humiliation to this point in the story:

> And they **clothed him in a purple cloak**
>
> καὶ **ἐνδιδύσκουσιν αὐτὸν πορφύραν** (15:17)
>
> ... they **unclothed him of the purple cloak** and **reclothed him** in his own clothes
>
> **ἐξέδυσαν αὐτὸν τὴν πορφύραν** καὶ **ἐνέδυσαν αὐτὸν** τὰ* ἱμάτια* αὐτοῦ (15:21)

The implication of the statement that they put his own clothes back on him is that they had stripped him naked before they had put the purple cloak on him. It is difficult to imagine a more humiliating position for a Judean man of the first century. The evidence that the normal Roman practice was to crucify men naked suggests that Mark's audiences would have inferred this.[23] The naked flight of the young man at the arrest (14:51–52) has already established nakedness as a symbol of humiliation. The young man's naked escape was, however, under the cover of darkness and was witnessed only fleetingly by a relatively small crowd. Jesus' exposure here was before hundreds of Roman soldiers in the full light of day. The division of his clothes by the soldiers after the crucifixion also implies that he was crucified naked.

This story increases the emotional distance from the Gentiles generally and the Roman soldiers specifically—a distance introduced in Jesus' final passion prophecy and at the beginning and end of the Pilate trial. Pilate and his agents, the soldiers, are characterized as evil men who stand in the tradition established by Antiochus IV Epiphanes. The climax of the story reemphasizes the impending conclusion for which this mocking is only a preparation: they will crucify Jesus (15:20d). This alienation from the soldiers and Pilate is accompanied by an ever-increasing sympathy for Jesus.

---

23. An explicit ancient source for the Roman practice of crucifixion naked is in *Oneirokritika* (book 2, chapter 53) by Artemidorus Daldianus. See http://reference-works.brillonline.com/entries/religion-past-and-present/artemidorus-daldianus-SIM_01119?s.num=10/; also https://archive.org/stream/oneirocritica01arte#page/234/mode/2up/. Artemidorus was a second-century professional diviner who wrote about the interpretation of dreams. For the most recent English translation, see Harris-McCoy, *Artemidorus' Oneirocritica*.

He suffers racial humiliation as a Judean, as a prophet of Israel, and as a wholly innocent man. Because we have become accustomed to the motifs of this story, analogies are needed to describe the impact of this story for its original audiences. Stories with a similar impact in more recent times are stories and pictures of the castration and whipping of African slaves, and stories of African Americans being tarred, feathered, and hanged by the Ku Klux Klan in the American South. Accounts of Jews being stripped naked by Nazi soldiers prior to being lined up and shot in front of mass graves also carry a contemporary impact similar to the impact of the mocking story for Mark's audience. The dynamics of this story are explicitly racial and are structured to appeal for sympathy for Jesus as a Judean who is suffering this mockery at the hands of Gentiles. Furthermore, the unmistakable claim of the story is that Jesus is suffering this humiliation as the Messiah.

The Performance of the Story

The challenge in telling this story is to weave together the dramatizing of the soldiers' actions with the expression of your own attitude as the storyteller about what is happening., The drumbeat of the story's rhythm is the background of the story. It can be the underlying rhythm for a crescendo of expression of your attitude and feelings as the storyteller about what is happening. The climax is the concluding comment by the storyteller—"When they had finished mocking him . . ."—that introduces the conclusion of the soldiers' play. The stories of the mocking of Samson and the seven boys are the storytelling tradition that this story continues and develops. This comment by the storyteller can also mark a transition from the representation of the soldiers' playful mockery to the description of their action from the perspective of the storyteller. (A similar dynamic is probably present in the two reports of the crucifixion. See the commentary on 15:24-25.) This concluding comment and summary of the end of the mock enthronement ceremony is the time for the storyteller to express fully her or his own attitudes toward the soldiers' actions.

The setting of this story needs to be drawn by expansive gestures. The praetorium was a big courtyard, large enough for six hundred soldiers, so this is a big story. The gestures then need to indicate the size of the courtyard and the cohort. The preparations for the mockery of clothing Jesus in the purple cloak and the thorn crown can be told with the gestures and satirical ceremony of the soldiers' putting the cloak and the crown on Jesus with expansive gestures of honor and pompous ceremony.

The Handing Over to the Gentiles (15:1–20)

The main part of the story requires a dramatizing of the soldiers' actions: the exaggerated mockery of their saluting him as King of the Judeans, the striking of his head, the spitting, and the mocking obeisance. The violence of their actions and their racial mockery are communicated by the harsh pronunciation of the words. The tone is shaped by the attitudes of the soldiers. This is play for them and an opportunity for some fun prior to an unpleasant but necessary duty. They are making fun of a Judean whom they have heard claimed to be the King of the Judeans and, therefore, their superior. They are putting him in his place.

The attitude of Mark, the Judean teller of this story, toward the Roman soldiers was not dispassionate or objective. The possible attitudes about the soldiers' actions that may appropriately be expressed include disgust, anger, disdain, incredulity, and horror. The concluding description of their stripping him, putting his clothes back on him, and leading him out to crucify him is where the storyteller can tell the story with whatever attitude expresses the teller's feelings about this event. Our contemporary tendency to exercise restraint in the expression of feelings is not supported by the evidence of highly dramatic styles of rhetorical expression in the ancient world. The composer of this story is restrained in his description of the details of these events. But that is not an indication that the ancient storyteller was restrained in the expression of emotion. For most contemporary audiences, our tendency will be to minimize the emotion rather than to fully express it. Mark's expansive and detailed dramatization of the soldiers' mockery makes the event present, and that is the goal of the storyteller now (15:20).

6

THE CRUCIFIXION OF JESUS (15:21–32)

THIS SECTION IS COMPOSED OF THREE SHORT STORIES. THESE short stories are comparable to the opening section of the plot in which two one-episode stories, the plot of the priests and Judas' betrayal, are the introduction and conclusion to the central longer story of the anointing. Here the stories of the preparations and the mocking of Jesus by Judeans introduce and conclude the crucifixion. A sign of this sectional structuring is the rounding at the ending of the section that repeats key words from the ending of the previous story. In the Pilate trial section, both the trial and the mocking by the soldiers end with a form of the phrase "in order to crucify." In the Crucifixion section, both the crucifixion story and the mocking story end with the motif of "those crucified with him."

The preparations are the gruesome details of the carrying of the cross, the carrying of Jesus to the Place of a Skull, and the offer of wine. The crucifixion story includes three notices of crucifixion with a sound like the repeated hammering of the nails, alternating with the reports of casting lots for his clothing, the inscription, and the crucifixion of two others with him. The climax of the section is the story of the three groups of Judeans who verbally abuse and mock him: Jerusalemites passing by, a group of chief priests and scribes, and the two insurgents who were crucified with him.

The Preparations (15:21–23)

Sound Map

21Καὶ ἀγγαρεύουσιν παράγοντά τινα Σίμωνα Κυρηναῖον ἐρχόμενον ἀπ' ἀγροῦ,

τὸν πατέρα Ἀλεξάνδρου καὶ Ῥούφου,

The Crucifixion of Jesus (15:21–32)

ἵνα ἄρῃ τὸν σταυρὸν αὐτοῦ.
22καὶ φέρουσιν αὐτὸν ἐπὶ τὸν Γολγοθᾶν τόπον,
ὅ ἐστιν μεθερμηνευόμενον Κρανίου Τόπος.
23καὶ ἐδίδουν αὐτῷ ἐσμυρνισμένον οἶνον,
ὃς δὲ οὐκ ἔλαβεν.

Translation

21And they compel a passerby who was coming in from the country,
                                           Simon of Cyrene,
the father of Alexander and Rufus,
to carry his cross.
22And they carry him to the Golgotha place,
which means skull place.
23And they tried to give him wine mingled with myrrh,
but he did not take it.

Ancient Associations and Connections

The story of the martyrdom of Eleazar in 2 Maccabees 6 is a direct precedent for the story of Jesus' crucifixion because of the common motif of the martyr's suffering in order to maintain sacred vows of abstinence. In the Eleazar story, the vow of abstinence is from eating pork. In the Jesus story, the vow of abstinence is from drinking wine.

The Martyrdom of Eleazar: 2 Maccabees 6:18–31 (NRSV)

The following is the story of the martyrdom of Eleazar during the persecution of faithful Israelites by Antiochus IV Epiphanes:

> Eleazar, one of the scribes in high position, a man now advanced in age and of noble presence, was being forced to open his mouth to eat swine's flesh. But he, welcoming death with honour rather than life with pollution, went up to the rack of his own accord, spitting out the flesh, as all ought to go who have the courage to refuse things that it is not right to taste, even for the natural love of life.
>
> Those who were in charge of that unlawful sacrifice took the man aside because of their long acquaintance with him, and privately urged him to bring meat of his own providing, proper for him to use, and to pretend that he was eating the flesh of

the sacrificial meal that had been commanded by the king, so that by doing this he might be saved from death, and be treated kindly on account of his old friendship with them. But making a high resolve, worthy of his years and the dignity of his old age and the grey hairs that he had reached with distinction and his excellent life even from childhood, and moreover according to the holy God-given law, he declared himself quickly, telling them to send him to Hades.

'Such pretense is not worthy of our time of life,' he said, 'for many of the young might suppose that Eleazar in his ninetieth year had gone over to an alien religion, and through my pretense, for the sake of living a brief moment longer, they would be led astray because of me, while I defile and disgrace my old age. Even if for the present I would avoid the punishment of mortals, yet whether I live or die I will not escape the hands of the Almighty. Therefore, by bravely giving up my life now, I will show myself worthy of my old age and leave to the young a noble example of how to die a good death willingly and nobly for the revered and holy laws.'

When he had said this, he went at once to the rack. Those who a little before had acted towards him with goodwill now changed to ill will, because the words he had uttered were in their opinion sheer madness. When he was about to die under the blows, he groaned aloud and said: 'It is clear to the Lord in his holy knowledge that, though I might have been saved from death, I am enduring terrible sufferings in my body under this beating, but in my soul I am glad to suffer these things because I fear him.'

So in this way he died, leaving in his death an example of nobility and a memorial of courage, not only to the young but to the great body of his nation. (2 Macc 6:18–31, NRSV)

The Sounds of the Story

The story of the preparations for the crucifixion was told slowly. While all three periods of this story are complex, after the first colon that introduces Simon of Cyrene, the following cola in Greek have a similar length of four to seven words. These short cola are the sign of the slow tempo, because the recital of four to seven words with one breath is slower than longer cola that have to be told more rapidly. A visible sign of the tempo is the number of accents in each colon of the story. After the initial colon introducing Simon of Cyrene (8 accents), the subsequent cola in the story have a strikingly similar and gradually decreasing number of accents (5, 7, 4, 5, and 3) with the shortest and, therefore, the slowest colon being the refusal of the wine. This is an example of the storytelling technique of building to a climax by a gradual slowing of the tempo for which the most striking example is, as we will see and hear, the end of the gospel (16:8).

Even though it is not possible to translate the story into English with such verbal economy, the story in English has sufficient economy to make a slow tempo possible. There is also more continuity in the length of the cola in the preparations story than in any other story in the PRN. This means that the same basic tempo is maintained throughout the story. The final colon in the story, of Jesus' refusing the wine, is the shortest, with only four words. The words are also all exceptionally short in Greek, the first three having only one syllable. This creates an emphasis for each word. It can be mimicked in English by means a deliberate pacing of the one-syllable words of the translation. The emphatic report of Jesus' refusal of the wine gives the listeners time to remember his vow of abstinence that is the climactic ending of the Passover meal with the disciples, and to reflect on his strength and courage.

Another dimension of the sound of the story is the concentration of verbs in the historical present. The first two of the three major verbs in this story are in the present tense (15:21 and 22) and have the same introduction, καὶ, and the same ending, -ουσιν. This creates a sense of immediacy and continues the drumbeat of the soldiers' actions that begins with taking Jesus into the praetorium and calling together the cohort (15:16).

The parallelism of the name of Golgotha, transliterated into Greek from the Hebrew, and the Greek translation of the name associates this place with death. These two phrases in Greek, translated literally into English, are "the Golgotha place" (τὸν Γολγοθᾶν τόπον) and "Skull Place" (Κρανίου Τόπος). Because of the parallel phrases, the word that receives the greatest emphasis is "skull" (Κρανίου), with its associations with death.[1]

---

1. The central memorial at the Choeung Ek Genocidal Center, commonly called the "killing fields," outside Phnom Penh, Cambodia, is a Buddhist stupa with the skulls of those killed by the Khmer Rouge forces during the Cambodian civil war (1975–79). Because of American involvement in the events that led to the war, going to Choeng Ek for me as an American was an experience of implication. Online: en.wikipedia.org/wiki/Choeung_Ek.

Notes on Details and Translation

15:21: Alexander and Rufus / Ἀλεξάνδρος καὶ Ῥοῦφος

Alexander (Ἀλεξάνδρος) is a Greek name that was a favorite among Judeans as well as Gentiles.² Rufus (Ῥοῦφος) is a Latin name found frequently in its Greek spelling, as it is in Mark.³ The inference has been frequently drawn that this naming of Simon's sons means that the Christian community for whom Mark wrote his gospel knew these two men.⁴ This implication has sometimes been connected with the conclusion that Mark's gospel was written for the church in Rome. This is a possible inference but not a necessary or even probable one. Men and women in ancient literature are often identified by their children without any implication that those children would be known to the audiences of the stories. Elsewhere in Mark, the first named woman of the witnesses of Jesus' death is named in Mark 15:40 as "Mary, of James the younger and Joses' mother" (καὶ Μαρία ἡ Ἰακώβου τοῦ μικροῦ καὶ Ἰωσῆτος μήτηρ); later in 15:47 as "Mary the mother of Joses" (Μαρία ἡ Ἰωσῆτος) and in 16:1 as "Mary the mother of James" (Μαρία ἡ [τοῦ] Ἰακώβου). There is no implication in this description that the listeners would have known James and Joses or, for that matter, Mary. Similarly, men are frequently introduced by the naming of their father. Thus in Mark "Levi, the son of Alphaeus" (2:14), "James, the son of Alphaeus" (3:18), "James and John, the sons of Zebedee" (10:35), and "the son of Timaeus, Bartimaeus" (10:46) are named by their fathers without any implication of audience knowledge of the fathers or the sons. This is simply the convention of naming persons by reference to their parents or their children.

---

2. BDAG, 42. Bauckham, *Jesus*, 85–86 gives statistics for the 99 most popular male names among Israelites between 330 BCE and 200 CE. They show that the name Alexander was nineteenth in the order of popularity.

3. BDAG, 907.

4. Several commentators argue that the naming of Simon's sons was an allusion to persons known to the readers of Mark (Collins, *Mark*, 736; Marcus, *Mark*, 1:27–28; Bauckham, *Jesus*, 52). This is a dimension of the tradition of Mark's gospel being written for a Roman Christian congregation. The fact that Rufus was a Latin name is another clue that has reinforced this possibility (see also Marcus, *Mark*, 2:1040–41). For an analysis of the difference between this naming as a narrative comment to readers and as a storyteller aside to audiences, see Boomershine, "Audience Asides."

The Crucifixion of Jesus (15:21–32)

22: they carry him / φέρουσιν αὐτὸν

Mark frequently uses this verb to mean bringing or leading a person from one place to another (1:32; 2:3; 7:32; 8:22; 9:17, 19–20). However, its basic meaning is "to carry, bear," and it is used in this sense in the stories of the healings in Capernaum (1:32) and of the paralytic (2:3). While the tradition that Simon carried Jesus' cross only after Jesus was no longer able to bear it has become solidly lodged in communal memory, the only statement in Mark, Matthew, and Luke is that Simon carried the cross; there is no reference to Jesus' becoming exhausted after a time of cross-bearing. The implication in these three gospels is that Jesus was so weakened by the flogging that he could not carry it at all. The further implication of the verb, φέρουσιν, is that he could not even walk so that he had to be carried. Since we have to choose one English word for this ambiguous verb in Greek, "to carry" is more striking and probably more historically descriptive. This implication of the severity of the flogging is reinforced by the shortness of the time between Jesus' being fastened to the cross and his death; dying by crucifixion often took days.

the Golgotha place, which means Skull Place / τὸν Γολγοθᾶν τόπον/ Κρανίου Τόπος

This translation is shorter and gives greater emphasis to the parallelism and to the central word, "skull."

23: tried to give / ἐδίδουν

This verb is a relatively rare instance of the conative imperfect that is used to describe an incomplete action.[5] It is interesting that this construction is also used at the beginning of the torture of Eleazar:

> Eleazar, one of the scribes in high position, a man now advanced in age and of noble presence, was being forced to open his mouth to eat swine's flesh (ἀναχανὼν ἠναγκάζετο φαγεῖν ὕειον κρέας). But he, welcoming death with honor rather than life with pollution, went up to the rack of his own accord, spitting out the flesh, as all ought to go who have the courage to refuse things that it is not right to taste, even for the natural love of life. (2 Macc 6:18–20, NRSV)

---

5. MHT, 3:65, translate this verse as "tried to give."

The context makes it clear that the act of force on the part of Eleazar's persecutors was not successful. Turner, therefore, translates it "the attempt was made to force him to eat."[6] In the case of Eleazar, persecutors tried to give him pork, and here the soldiers "*tried* to give Jesus wine mingled with myrrh, *but he did not take it.*"

Comments on the Meaning and Impact of the Story

15:21: the description of Simon of Cyrene

The description of Simon of Cyrene, who was compelled to carry Jesus' cross, is highly sympathetic. Cyrene was a region of modern Libya. Simon was, therefore, African in his origins. The probability is that Mark's audience would have understood Simon to be a pilgrim, as was the Ethiopian eunuch (Acts 8:26–40), who traveled from North Africa to Jerusalem to worship, and in Simon's case to participate in the celebration of Passover. This was a frequent pattern for Diaspora Judeans from all over the world. His coming in from the country was probably a reference to his lodging outside the city, just as Jesus and his disciples stayed in Bethany and traveled in and out of the city (11:11, 12, 20, 27; 14:3).

The naming of Simon's sons is a common way of introducing a new person in a story. We argued above in the detailed note on these names that it is highly unlikely that Mark was alluding to persons who were known to his audiences. Since Mark's gospel was composed for performance, it would have been told in many places to many different audiences. (See the introduction to this volume for the evidence of this view of Mark's audiences.) An allusion to people known to the audience is only possible if the gospel was written for one small community.

The naming of Alexander and Rufus creates a sense of intimacy with Simon and the impression that Mark, the composer of this story, knew of Simon and his sons and possibly knew them personally. In carrying Jesus' cross, Simon is also doing something that is connected with Jesus' earlier command to his disciples: "Let him take up (ἀράτω)[7] his cross" (8:34). Thus Mark the storyteller creates highly sympathetic vibes in relation to Simon. The implication of the soldiers' conscripting Simon to carry Jesus' cross is

---

6. MHT, 3:65.

7. This is the same verb used of Simon in 15:22. The nuance of this verb according to BDAG (28) is "to lift up and move from one place to another."

that Jesus was unable to carry it himself because he had been severely weakened by the flogging.

22: the implication that the soldiers carried Jesus to Golgotha

As has been noted above, the verb describing the journey to Golgotha can mean both "to bring" and "to carry." There is nothing in the story that clarifies whether the soldiers carried or led Jesus to the "Skull Place." As a result, both meanings are possible for the audience. The ambiguity allows the audience to imagine that Jesus was so weakened by the flogging that, not only could he not carry his cross but also he had to be carried himself.

The translation of the Hebrew place-name *Golgotha* is the only translation into Greek of something other than the words of Jesus. The translation is made for the benefit of Diaspora Judeans and Gentiles who did not know Hebrew, which included most Judeans, since most lived not in Palestine but in the Diaspora, especially after the war. The importance of the translation is that the term, "Skull Place," is an image of death.

23: the impact of the soldiers "trying" to give Jesus wine

The soldiers' offering of wine mingled with myrrh carried with it the implication that it was offered as a sedative. Furthermore, the grammatical construction carries the implication that the soldiers tried to force Jesus to drink some wine. Thirst as well as pain was one of the tortures of crucifixion so that some drink after the journey to the place of execution and prior to a tormenting thirst was welcome. Myrrh was believed to have an additional sedative effect, and drinks such as this were offered to the condemned. Thus *Sanhedrin* 43a in the Babylonian Talmud mandates:

> when one is led out to execution, he is given a goblet of wine containing a grain of frankincense, in order to addle his wits, for it is written, 'Give strong drink to one who is perishing, and wine to those in bitter distress' [Prov 31:6].[8]

Jesus' refusal of the wine is connected in the story with his vow of abstinence from wine at the Passover meal with the disciples: "Truly I tell you, never again will I drink of the fruit of the vine until that day when I drink it new in the kingdom of God" (14:25). The maintenance of vows at the cost of pain and death is a motif in the martyrdoms of Eleazar and the seven boys and their mother in 2 Maccabees (see above). It is also a motif in the

---

8. Cited by Marcus, *Mark*, 2:1049.

excruciating story of Jepthah and his daughter (Judg 11:29-40) and also in the story of Samson, who failed to maintain his vow (Judg 16:15-31). As the narrative comment at the end of the story of Eleazar's martyrdom makes clear, this kind of faithfulness was revered in Israel's traditions:

> So in this way he died, leaving in his death an example of nobility and a memorial of courage, not only to the young but to the great body of his nation. (2 Macc 6:31, NRSV)

Thus, Mark told the story of Jesus' maintenance of his vow as a similar example of nobility and courage in the face of a martyr's death. And, even though there is no implication that the Roman soldiers knew of his vow, Jesus' courage was, like that of the Maccabean martyrs, demonstrated in his rejection of an insistent invitation by Gentiles to break his vow of abstinence.

The Greek verb ἐδίδουν, used for the soldiers' attempt to *give* Jesus wine (see detailed note above on the tense of this verb) and the verb for Jesus' refusal to *take* the wine also repeats a sonic theme from the last supper story of giving and taking bread and wine:

> And . . . **taking** bread . . . he **gave** it to them and said, "**Take** it . . ." And **taking** a cup . . . he **gave** it to them and all of them drank from it.
>
> Καὶ . . . **λαβὼν** ἄρτον . . . **ἔδωκεν** αὐτοῖς καὶ εἶπεν, **Λάβετε**, . . . καὶ **λαβὼν** ποτήριον . . . **ἔδωκεν** αὐτοῖς, καὶ ἔπιον ἐξ αὐτοῦ **πάντες**. (14:22-23)
>
> And they **tried to give** him wine mingled with myrrh but he did not **take** it. (15:23)
>
> καὶ **ἐδίδουν** αὐτῷ ἐσμυρνισμένον οἶνον, ὃς δὲ οὐκ **ἔλαβεν**.

Jesus' refusal of the wine offered and perhaps pushed on him by Roman soldiers who are about to crucify him is also the reversal of the ritual gift of the Last Supper. At the supper, Jesus took the cup of wine and offered it to his disciples and they all drank from it. At the crucifixion, the Roman soldiers try to give Jesus wine and he does not take it.

The Performance of the Story

The tone is a lament. The tempo of the story is slow and deliberate. The funeral marches of Beethoven and Chopin are examples of this tempo.

The entire story, with the exception of the aside to the audience about Simon's sons, is told from the storyteller's perspective as an observer reporting these events. The most important dynamic in the telling of the story is the sense of immediacy, which is created through the use of the historical present in the principal verbs of the first two periods. It is important as the storyteller to create the sense that this is the account of an eyewitness who is describing an event that is taking place now before the audience's eyes. It is the ancient equivalent of an "on-the-spot" television report.

The main gestures of the story are pointing to the places and events that are taking place in the story. Identifying those imaginary places in the setting of the story's performance and pointing to the same places consistently is an important dimension of the telling of the story. The most important dramatic gesture in the story is the shaking of one's head at Jesus' refusal of the wine. It is an opportunity to both dramatize Jesus' response and to show respect for Jesus' courage.

The goal for the performance of this story is to make the event present in the experience of the audience and to create maximum sympathy for Jesus in his suffering and humiliation.

The Crucifixion of Jesus (15:24–27)

Sound Map

24καὶ σταυροῦσιν αὐτὸν
    καὶ διαμερίζονται **τὰ ἱμάτια αὐτοῦ**,
    βάλλοντες κλῆρον ἐπ' αὐτὰ τίς τί ἄρῃ.
25ἦν δὲ ὥρα τρίτη
    καὶ **ἐσταύρωσαν αὐτόν**.
26καὶ ἦν ἡ ἐπιγραφὴ τῆς αἰτίας αὐτοῦ ἐπιγεγραμμένη,
    Ὁ βασιλεὺς τῶν Ἰουδαίων.
27Καὶ **σὺν αὐτῷ σταυροῦσιν** δύο λῃστάς,
    ἕνα ἐκ δεξιῶν καὶ **ἕνα ἐξ** εὐωνύμων αὐτοῦ.

Translation

24**And they crucify him**
    and divide **his garments**
    casting dice on them to see who takes what.
25It was **the third hour**
    and they crucified him.

26 And the inscription of the charge against him read,
   "**The King of the Judeans.**"
27 And **with him they crucify** two insurrectionists,
   one on his right and **one on** his left.

Ancient Associations and Connections

This story has some sonic connections with and evokes memories of the traditions of Israelite martyrs and righteous sufferers, including the Maccabean martyrs (2 Maccabees 6–7), the *Martyrdom of Isaiah*, and Psalm 22 (21 LXX). There are also thematic connections with the tradition of the taunt in both the Scriptures and Homer.

Psalm 21 LXX (MT 22)

The two episodes of the story of Jesus' crucifixion, together with the story of his death that follows, contain three verbal threads, more or less extensive, with the LXX translation of Psalm 22 (in the MT, the basis of most English translations, Psalm 21 in the LXX). The composer of this story assumes that his listeners were familiar with this psalm and would hear the echoes of the psalm in the story. The quotations below are the first of the three sonic echoes of LXX Psalm 21 in the crucifixion story. The first quotation is the LXX text followed by the NETS translation. The LXX chapter and verse numbers with the MT numbers are in parenthesis:

> Psalm 21:19 LXX (MT 22:18)
> διεμερίσαντο τὰ ἱμάτιά μου ἑαυτοῖς
> καὶ ἐπὶ τὸν ἱματισμόν μου ἔβαλον κλῆρον.
>
> they **divided** my **clothes** among themselves,
> and for my clothing they **cast lots**.
>
> Mark 15:24
> καὶ διαμερίζονται τὰ ἱμάτια αὐτοῦ,
> βάλλοντες κλῆρον ἐπ' αὐτὰ τίς τί ἄρῃ.
>
> and they **divide** his **garments**
> **casting dice** on them to see who takes what.

The three sonic connections to this psalm constitute the most extensive echo in Mark's Gospel with the Greek Scriptures of Hellenistic Israelites.

The Crucifixion of Jesus (15:21–32)

The Sounds of the Story

This story and the next two stories—the crucifixion, the death, and the burial—are marked by indications of the time. The evening that begins this day, Friday, was named in the introduction to the Last Supper: "and when it was evening" (καὶ ὀψίας γενομένης—14:17), and the morning was identified in the introduction to the Pilate trial, "And immediately, early in the morning," (Καὶ εὐθὺς πρωῒ—15:1). The "third hour" named in the first episode of this story (15:25) is the third hour of the morning: nine o'clock. The "sixth" and the "ninth" hours that begin the story of the death (15:33–34) are then noon and three o'clock in the afternoon. The naming of "evening," ὀψίας, once again, at the beginning of the story of the burial, marks the period prior to sunset at the end of Friday.[9]

The first two episodes of the crucifixion story begin and end with complex periods, each of which has the central verbal thread: "and they crucify" (σταυροῦσιν—15:24, 27). The episode of the mocking has complex periods describing the mockery—first by those who pass by, and then by the chief priests and scribes. The episode ends with a simple period that echoes the end of the crucifixion episodes, naming again those who were crucified with Jesus but now adding them to the list of those who derided him: σὺν αὐτῷ σταυροῦσιν (15:27) / οἱ συνεσταυρωμένοι σὺν αὐτῷ (15:32b). This is a good example of the effect of Greek periods that build to a climax of intensity. The periods that describe the mockery of Jesus by fellow Israelites (15:29–31a) create a gradual increase in volume and tempo that reaches its peak in the priests' mocking invitation for "the Messiah, the King of Israel" to come down from the cross. The final period describing the derision by those crucified with Jesus is a climax of irony. This unit has the sound structure of a phrase in music that begins quietly in the episode relating the crucifixion, builds to a climax of volume in the mockery episode, and then ends more quietly in the final period but with a peak of ironic intensity. This shape of the story's sound contributes to the climactic irony of Jesus' being mocked by Romans who divide his clothes, by fellow Israelites who distort his prophecies, and even by the insurgents with whom he is crucified.

The word "crucify" occurs at both the beginning and the end of the first episode of the story (15:24–25), creating a rounding of the episode. This rounding is probably a sign that there was a major pause after the naming of the hour and the second crucifixion notice (15:25), a time of silence during which the audience can meditate on what has just happened. There is

---

9. See Brown, *Death of the Messiah*, 2:1211–12: "Jewish law would have the crucified taken down and buried before sunset, which would mark the beginning of another day. By narrative flow, then, the setting is somewhere between 3 P.M. and sunset."

also a change in tense from the historical present (σταυροῦσιν) to the aorist (ἐσταύρωσαν), which indicates a shift in the storyteller's relationship to the audience. The formula "now it was" (ἦν δὲ—15:25) is used consistently by Mark as an introduction to a comment addressed directly to the audience. In storytelling, this is a change of tone from the reporting of an event by an observer to a more intimate, inside tone for the conveying of background, translation, or additional information. This change of tone is a sign that the storyteller here shifted to a sharing of feelings about what is happening in the story. As a result, the crucifixion is reported from two different perspectives, with two different tones: from the perspective of an eyewitness describing what is taking place in the present (15:24), and from the perspective of a storyteller some years later, looking back on the event in the past (15:25). It is quite possible that the storyteller expressed feelings of grief in these words and perhaps even showed those feelings with tears.

The initial naming of the third hour had the sound of a tolling bell. It is a fateful sound that repeats the theme Jesus established in his final words to the three disciples in Gethsemane: "the hour has come" (ἦλθεν ἡ ὥρα—14:42). In this instance, the storyteller picks up Jesus' theme and develops it as a central motif in the story of Jesus' death. It is introduced by what Lee and Scott call "the sound signature" of this unit, "now it was" (ἦν δὲ), that contrasts to the long series of periods beginning with καὶ + a verb + αὐτὸν, which began with the conclusion of the Pilate trial and ended with the first notice of the crucifixion (15.15b-24).[10] In all these periods but one, in which Simon of Cyrene is the object, the soldiers are the subject, and Jesus is the object of their actions.

A central dimension of the sound of this story is the verbal threads that link this story with earlier motifs in the larger story by repeating earlier words in this new context. The repeated word "crucify" in the first episode of this story (σταυρόζω) echoes the crowd's cries demanding crucifixion (15:13-14), the climax of the mocking by the soldiers (15:20) and the report about Simon carrying Jesus' cross (15:21). The second period is linked with Jesus' words about the hour (14:35, 41). The charge written on the sign repeats the implied accusation of the chief priests that is the subject of Pilate's first interrogation of Jesus, "the King of the Judeans" (ὁ βασιλεὺς τῶν Ἰουδαίων). The naming of those crucified with him as λῃστής ("insurgents, bandits, robbers, insurrectionists") recalls Jesus' accusation of the arresting crowd, "As against an insurrectionist (λῃστὴν) have you come out with swords and clubs to arrest me" (14:48), and his accusation of the Temple

---

10. Lee and Scott, *Sound Mapping*, 202.

authorities that they have turned the Temple into "a den of insurgents" (σπήλαιον λῃστῶν 11:17).

Notes on Details and Translation

15:24: crucify/divide / σταυροῦσιν/διαμερίζονται

Both these verbs are in the present tense, the second in the present middle, which connotes "divide *among themselves*."[11] Mark uses the present tense to create a sense of immediacy, and translation in the present tense in English, while a little strange, approximates the impact of Mark's usage here.

who takes what / τίς τί ἄρῃ

This phrase is translated in the NRSV as "what each should take." This is a good translation but does not render the impact of the short double interrogative pronouns that both start with *t*. An alternative translation that preserves more of the sharpness of the Greek is, "who takes what."

27: they crucify. σταυροῦσιν.

As in the report of Jesus' crucifixion (15:24), the report of the crucifixion of the two others who are crucified with Jesus is in the historical present tense. Mark uses the historical present selectively for the elements of the story that are most graphic and deserving of being made present in the experience of the audience.

two insurrectionists / δύο λῃστάς

The translation of this Greek word is difficult. The normal translation is "robbers" or "bandits" (RSV, NRSV; "rebels," NIV). The problem with these translations is that they imply these are petty thieves with no political association. It is unlikely that the Romans would have crucified Judean men for thievery since they tended to reserve crucifixion for crimes against the state. The term "bandits" or "brigands" can carry the implication of thievery for the sake of a cause, but only if the rest of the story makes that clear. In this instance, Mark gives no particulars, so the term can only be translated on the basis of its implications. What are then the threads of implication here?

---

11. BDAG, 233.

As we have seen, Mark alludes at many points to the war against the Romans. The war was an intensely present memory for listeners in the period immediately after the war. This term is one of the major terms that Josephus uses to describe those who led the insurrection against the Romans in 66–70 CE. The translation must, therefore, indicate that their crime was different from petty thievery. The implication of the story is that they were involved along with Barabbas in "the insurrection." But, as in many other places in the story (including in the place where Mark alludes to Jesus' mother but mentions only her other children, 15:40), Mark leaves it to his audience to make the inference. However, in a translation for twenty-first-century audiences the implication that these two were involved in revolutionary activities needs to be made explicit. The possible terms are "insurgents," "insurrectionists," "revolutionaries" or "rebels." "Insurrectionist" is the most accurate term for the Judean fighters associated with "the insurrection" (15:7). Other appropriate terms are "insurgents" or "revolutionaries" because they were attempting to overthrow an external power and establish an independent government. Any of these translations carries more accurate connotations than "brigands" or "bandits." "Insurrectionist" is chosen here to make an explicit connection with those held in prison with Barabbas who committed murder during "the insurrection."

Comments on the Meaning and Impact of the Story

15:24–27: the litany of crucifixion

The Roman soldiers are the subject of all the verbs from the beginning of the story of the mocking by the soldiers (15:16–20) through the crucifixion of Jesus and the dividing of his clothes (15:24). The beginning of this story is the climax and shortest colon in that sequence: καὶ σταυροῦσιν αὐτὸν, "And they crucify him." This colon introduces a series of three cola that repeat this horror to which the entire PRN has been building:

And they crucify him (v. 24a)

they crucified him (v. 25b)

And with him they crucify two insurrectionists (v. 27a)

Each of these three cola is either preceded or followed by a second colon or two adding detail to the picture.

And they crucify him and divide his garments

    casting dice on them to see who takes what. (v. 24b)

The Crucifixion of Jesus (15:21–32)

It was the third hour and they crucified him (v. 25a)

And the inscription of the charge against him read, "The King of the Judeans." (v. 26)

one on his right and one on his left. (v. 27b)

The first two of these supplementary cola, coming between reports of the crucifixion, create a brief interval before repeating the soldiers' action. The result is that the verbs "they crucify . . . they crucified . . . they crucify" have the sound of hammer blows.

The first and third instances of the verb "crucify" are in the historical present tense, which increases the sense of immediacy in the hearing of the story. This phrase also continues the verbal thread begun in the crowd's demand for crucifixion. This leitmotif, the historical present tense, the repetition of the verb "crucify," and the solemn tempo of the narration are the subtle stylistic elements that contribute to the impact of this story event. Mark's story is highly restrained and stands in contrast to contemporary movies and novels, in which the crucifixion story is retold with all the gory details. The film *The Passion of the Christ* stands as the most grotesque instance of this tradition of rejecting the evangelists' way of telling the story. Mark's story calls upon a dense (unspoken) background of Israelite martyr stories and relies on the audience to fill in the details in their own imaginations. Since crucifixion was well known in the ancient world, this would have been easy for the listeners to do.

24: the impact of the Roman soldiers' division of Jesus' clothes

The dividing of Jesus' clothes refers, first of all, back to the mocking of Jesus by the Roman soldiers and to the implication that he was stripped naked in front of the cohort for that mocking (15:20). The dividing of Jesus' clothes continues the drumbeat of the fifteen preceding cola, beginning in 15:16, with καὶ + a verb (parataxis) that have the soldiers as the subject. The verb reporting the dividing of Jesus' clothing is once again in the historical present tense, the tense that has been alternating with past-tense verbs, both aorist and imperfect, through this entire series of cola narrating the soldiers' actions.

The order of the first period in this new, climactic episode, is crucifixion followed by the division of Jesus' clothes. It invites the audience to fill in what is implied. The implication of the division of the garments at the beginning of the story is that Jesus was stripped naked before being crucified (cf. 15:20, "reclothed him in his own clothes"). This is a poignant appeal for sympathy with Jesus as a Judean subjected to humiliation by the Gentile soldiers.

The description of the dividing of Jesus' clothes is also an allusion to Psalm 21 (LXX), the quintessential psalm of righteous suffering in the tradition of Israel. The echo of the psalm is unmistakable for anyone in the audience who knew the psalm:

> Psalm 22:18 (21:19, LXX):
>
> **they divided my clothes among themselves,**
> and for my clothing **they cast lots**. (NETS)
>
> καὶ **διεμερίσοντο τὰ ἱμάτιά μου** ἑαυτοῖς,
> καὶ ἐπὶ τὸν ἱματισμόν μου **ἔβαλον κλῆρον**.
>
> Mark 15:24:
>
> and **they divide his garments**
> **casting dice** on them to see who takes what.
>
> καὶ **διαμερίζονται τὰ ἱμάτια αὐτοῦ**,
> **βάλλοντες κλῆρον** ἐπ' αὐτὰ τίς τί ἄρῃ.

The series of allusions to the psalm throughout the story of Jesus' death (see "Associations and Connections," above) is a sign that the storyteller assumes the audience will recognize this connection. This in turn is another sign that the storyteller assumes the audiences of the story are Judeans since the narrator could only count on intimate familiarity with the Psalms among Judeans. The implication of these connections to Psalm 22 (21, LXX) is that Jesus is like the righteous sufferer of the psalm. The allusion thus reinforces the characterization of Jesus as the righteous sufferer and the characterization of those who are dividing his clothes among themselves as his enemies. These characterizations in turn intensify the sympathetic distance of the audience in relation to Jesus, and the audience's alienation from the soldiers. As Jesus had predicted (10:34), he is being killed by the Gentiles.

This allusion introduces the most extensive and explicit allusion to the Scriptures in Mark's PRN. The connections with Psalm 22 (21, LXX) are an indirect commentary that the Scriptures are being fulfilled in Jesus' death. The gospel's frequent allusions to and quotations of the Scriptures in turn imply that these events told in Mark's gospel are the will of God. The implication of the allusion is that even this event of supreme humiliation and suffering is encompassed by the will and purpose of God. This allusion to Psalm 22 (21, LXX) also reinforces the motif of God's activity in the plot explicitly established earlier in the PRN by the fulfillment of Jesus' passion prophecies and by his prayer in Gethsemane. And while there have been clues to God's purposes in the events of Jesus' suffering, what precisely God has in mind remains shrouded in mystery for the audience and, as will become even more graphically apparent, for Jesus himself.

25: the tone of the time of the crucifixion

The report of the time of the crucifixion is, as was noted above, an aside to the audience, given with a more personal tone. The impact of the three reports of Jesus' crucifixion is similar to my memory of Walter Cronkite's report on the afternoon of John F. Kennedy's assassination. Cronkite first said, in a grave tone but in his newscaster voice, "President Kennedy was shot and killed today in Dallas, Texas." Then, after a long pause, he repeated with a tone of deep personal sorrow, "The President is dead." There were also several points during the newscasts of that day when Cronkite reported the time when Kennedy was shot and the time of his death, but I don't remember his specific words. Cronkite's expression of sorrow in his second pronouncement of Kennedy's death corresponds to the tone of Mark's second pronouncement of Jesus' crucifixion. The motif of "the hour" had been established earlier in the story (in Jesus' prayer that the hour might pass from him [14:35]), and in Jesus' words to his disciples in Gethsemane: "The hour has come" (14:41c). There is a sense in which Jesus' prayer in Gethsemane functions as a prophecy that is fulfilled in this moment of the crucifixion. The impact of this report is to mark the exact time of an event of great importance.

26: the aside to the audience naming the charge

The report of the inscription of the charge against Jesus is another aside by the storyteller that provides background information for the audience. The title King of the Judeans has been used only in the Pilate trial and in the mocking by the soldiers. As has been seen above, this title is by implication only introduced by the chief priests and is never used by either the storyteller or Jesus. The Markan storyteller calls Jesus Messiah, and Jesus accepts that title from Peter. Otherwise from Jesus' own lips we hear him calling himself Son of Man, and indeed clarifying Peter's naming him Messiah by himself speaking of the Son of Man. This sonic pattern plus the contrast between Jesus' responses to the questions of the high priest and Pilate implies that Jesus never claimed to be King of the Judeans. That is, the implication of the storyteller is that Jesus is innocent of the charge for which he is being crucified. There is no sign earlier in the story that Jesus intended to overthrow the Roman government and to establish himself as king. There was probably a tone of irony in the storyteller's voice as he repeated the inscription of the charge for which Jesus was being crucified.

27: the "insurrectionists" crucified with Jesus

The irony of this false charge is only deepened by the identity of those with whom Jesus is crucified. It is profoundly ironic that Jesus is being executed with two insurrectionists, who are implicitly associated with the movement that would lead to the war and its disastrous consequences. Jesus had established at the arrest that the crowd from the chief priests, the scribes, and the elders was wrong in coming out to arrest him as an insurrectionist (λῃστής, 14:48). He was a nonviolent teacher, who never advocated violence of any kind. Another dimension of the irony of Jesus' being crucified with revolutionaries is that James and John had asked to sit in positions of power and authority "on his right and on his left" on the way up to Jerusalem (10:37). In response Jesus asked them if they were able to drink the cup that he would drink and to be baptized with the baptism with which he would be baptized. This was an allusion to his martyrdom. But those who are dying with Jesus are not his disciples but "insurrectionists" who had committed murder. The implicit theme of the entire story of the gospel has been that Jesus is a radically different Messiah than the earlier warrior-king tradition with which "the anointed one" was associated in the stories of the kings of Judah and Israel, especially Saul and David. For him to be crucified with men who were part of a violent revolutionary movement is supremely ironic.

The Performance of the Story

The story of Jesus' execution has been prepared by the actions of the soldiers in the immediately preceding story as well as by the entire PRN. The challenge in telling this story is to maintain a balance between objectivity and emotional expression. The crescendo of lament steadily grows with Simon carrying Jesus' cross, with the carrying of Jesus to Golgotha, and with the offer and refusal of wine. The lament continues with the word "crucify" and the pain that word implies. The lament is further developed by the report of the dividing of Jesus' garments by the Roman soldiers, the first of the three connections between the events and Psalm 22 (21, LXX). The second description of the crucifixion, introduced by the tolling of the hour, is an opportunity for you as the storyteller to express your own grief at Jesus' crucifixion. It is a slow sentence that allows plenty of time for the full expression of the emotional intensity of this moment. The irony of the false charge against Jesus and his crucifixion with two "insurgents" can only be conveyed by the tone of the storyteller.

The Mocking by Judeans (15:29–32)

Sound Map

29Καὶ οἱ παραπορευόμενοι ἐβλασφήμουν αὐτὸν
  κινοῦντες τὰς κεφαλὰς αὐτῶν καὶ λέγοντες,
  Οὐὰ ὁ **καταλύων τὸν ναὸν καὶ οἰκοδομῶν ἐν τρισὶν ἡμέραις**,
30**σῶσον σεαυτὸν καταβὰς ἀπὸ τοῦ σταυροῦ**.
31ὁμοίως καὶ **οἱ ἀρχιερεῖς** ἐμπαίζοντες πρὸς ἀλλήλους
                                       μετὰ **τῶν γραμματέων** ἔλεγον,
  Ἄλλους **ἔσωσεν, ἑαυτὸν** οὐ δύναται **σῶσαι**.
32ὁ **Χριστὸς ὁ βασιλεὺς** Ἰσραὴλ **καταβάτω** νῦν **ἀπὸ τοῦ σταυροῦ**,
  ἵνα ἴδωμεν καὶ πιστεύσωμεν.
καὶ οἱ **συνεσταυρωμένοι σὺν αὐτῷ** ὠνείδιζον αὐτόν.

29And those who passed by blasphemed him,
  wagging their heads and saying,
  "**Aha, you who would destroy the Temple and build it in
                                                    three days,**
30**save yourself and come down from the cross.**"
31Likewise **the chief priests** mocked him to one another with
                                       the scribes and said,
  "**He saved** others, but he cannot **save himself**;
32let **the Messiah, the King** of Israel, **come down** now **from the cross**
  so that we may see and believe."
And **those who were crucified with him** reviled him.

Ancient Associations and Connections

The sonic connections and evocations of memory of this story are the traditions of *Martyrdom and Ascension of Isaiah* and Psalm 22 (LXX 21). There are also thematic connections with the tradition of the taunt in the story of David and Goliath (1 Sam 17:41–47) and Homer's story of the climactic battle between Hector and Achilles.

Psalm 22 (21, LXX)

The two episodes of the story of Jesus' crucifixion, together with the story of his death that follows, contain three verbal threads, more or less extensive, with the LXX translation of Psalm 21 (Psalm 22 in the MT, the basis of most English translations). Mark's Judean listeners were probably familiar with this psalm in Greek and heard these echoes in Mark's story. The quotations below are the verses in the psalm that are echoed in the mocking of Jesus by other Judeans. The first quotation is the LXX text followed by the NETS (New English Translation of the Septuagint) translation.

Psalm 22:7–8 (21:8–9, LXX)

πάντες οἱ θεωροῦντές με ἐξεμυκτήρισάν με,
ἐλάλησαν ἐν χείλεσιν, **ἐκίνησαν κεφαλήν**
Ἤλπισεν ἐπὶ κύριον, ῥυσάσθω αὐτόν·
σωσάτω αὐτόν, ὅτι θέλει αὐτόν.

All who saw me mocked at me;
they talked with the lips; **they moved the head**:
"He hoped in the Lord; let him rescue him;
let him **save** him, because he wanted him." (NETS)

Mark 15:29–30:

Καὶ οἱ παραπορευόμενοι ἐβλασφήμουν αὐτὸν
κινοῦντες τὰς κεφαλὰς αὐτῶν καὶ λέγοντες,
Οὐὰ ὁ καταλύων τὸν ναὸν καὶ οἰκοδομῶν ἐν τρισὶν ἡμέραις,
σῶσον σεαυτὸν καταβὰς ἀπὸ τοῦ σταυροῦ.

And those who passed by blasphemed him,
wagging their heads and saying,
"Aha, you who would destroy the Temple and build it in three days,
save yourself and come down from the cross."

This verbal echo of Psalm 21 (LXX) is the second in the series of three. Once again, the composer assumes that the listeners know the psalm with sufficient familiarity to recognize the allusion and its implicit fulfillment of the prophecy inherent in the psalm.

The Crucifixion of Jesus (15:21–32)

Martyrdom and Ascension of Isaiah

There is also an important thematic connection between the mocking of Jesus by fellow Israelites and the mocking of the prophet Isaiah by other Israelites in the *Martyrdom and Ascension of Isaiah*. The story of Isaiah's martyrdom and ascension is a composite work of an early Israelite story with later Christian additions. The oldest element (1:1—3:12 and 5:1–16) was probably composed in Hebrew in the period of the persecution by Antiochus IV Epiphanes and the Maccabean revolt in the second century BCE (167–164 BCE).[12] In light of the fact that it is a relatively obscure work, with the only extant texts of the entire work in Ethiopian, it is uncertain whether Mark's audiences would have known this in the late first century (70–100 CE). However, in view of the early date of the Hebrew sections of the *Martyrdom and Ascension of Isaiah*, it is quite possible that Hellenistic Judeans would have known this story in the period of the composition and early performances of Mark. It is notable for its distinctive motif of the mocking and martyrdom of a prophet by other Israelites. The translation of the section of the story that is relevant to Mark's crucifixion narrative runs as follows:

> And while Isaiah was being sawed in half, his accuser, Belkira, stood by, and all of the false prophets stood by, laughing and (maliciously) joyful because of Isaiah. And Belkira, through Mekembekus, stood before Isaiah, laughing and deriding. And Belkira said to Isaiah, "Say, 'I have lied in everything I have spoken; the ways of Manasseh are good and right, and also the ways of Belkira and those who are with him are good.'" And he said this to him when he began to be sawed in half.
>
> And Isaiah was in a vision of the Lord, but his eyes were open, and he saw them. And Belkira spoke thus to Isaiah, "Say what I say to you, and I will turn their heart and make Manasseh, and the princes of Judah, and the people, and all Jerusalem worship you." And Isaiah answered and said, "If it is within my power to say, 'Condemned and cursed be you, and all your hosts, and all your house!' For there is nothing further that you can take except the skin of my body." And they seized Isaiah the son of Amoz and sawed him in half with a wood saw.

12. See Knibb, in Charlesworth, *OTP*, 1:143–50. The only complete extant text is an Ethiopic translation of a probable Greek original. Major sections of the *Martyrdom and Ascension* were later Christian additions to the earlier Hebrew story. The additions are generally called the *Testament of Hezekiah* (3:13—4:22) and the *Vision of Isaiah* (chs. 6–11). The section quoted here is from the early element of the narrative from the Maccabean period.

> And Manasseh, and Belkira, and the false prophets, and the princes, and the people, and all stood by looking on. And to the prophets who (were) with him he said before he was sawed in half, "Go to the district of Tyre and Sidon, because for me alone the Lord has mixed the cup." And while Isaiah was being sawed in half, he did not cry out, or weep, but his mouth spoke with the Holy Spirit until he was sawed in two (*Martyrdom and Ascension of Isaiah* 5:2–14).[13]

The importance of the story of Isaiah's martyrdom for the understanding of Mark is that it makes clear the Israelite provenance of the crucifixion story. Both are stories told by Israelites to other Israelites in relation to conflicts within the Judean community. It is a clear indication that stories of the mockery and execution of a prophet by Judean opponents were present in Jesus' and Mark's period. Furthermore, the dynamics of this story are similar to the dynamics of Mark's story. The most striking similarity is that the prophet is mocked by his Israelite opponents—the false prophet, the religious and political authorities, and the people—while he is being executed. There is also the common motif of "the cup" of suffering. The composer of Mark emphasizes the mocking of the prophet more explicitly by the development and variety in the taunts of the opponents. There are also differences: Jesus does not denounce or curse his accusers, does not see a vision of God, and does not speak to his friends while he is being executed. But the story of Isaiah's martyrdom makes it clear that Mark's story is an integral part of a distinctive Israelite storytelling tradition.

David and Goliath (1 Sam 17:41–7)

The other major connection of this story with the stories of both Israelite and Greco-Roman tradition is the tradition of the taunt. This is present in the classic story of David and Goliath and is a major feature of Homer's epic, *The Iliad*. The story of the taunting prelude to the battle between Goliath and David is as follows:

> 41 The Philistine came on and drew near to David, with his shield-bearer in front of him. 42 When the Philistine looked and saw David, he disdained him, for he was only a youth, ruddy and handsome in appearance. 43 The Philistine said to David, 'Am I a dog, that you come to me with sticks?' And the Philistine cursed David by his gods. 44 The Philistine said to David, 'Come

---

13. The translation of the reconstructed version of this early work cited here is by Knibb in Charlesworth, *OTP*, vol. 1.

The Crucifixion of Jesus (15:21–32)

to me, and I will give your flesh to the birds of the air and to the wild animals of the field.'

45But David said to the Philistine, 'You come to me with sword and spear and javelin; but I come to you in the name of the Lord of hosts, the God of the armies of Israel, whom you have defied. 46This very day the Lord will deliver you into my hand, and I will strike you down and cut off your head; and I will give the dead bodies of the Philistine army this very day to the birds of the air and to the wild animals of the earth, so that all the earth may know that there is a God in Israel, 47and that all this assembly may know that the Lord does not save by sword and spear; for the battle is the Lord's and he will give you into our hand.' (1 Sam 17:41–47, NRSV)

Hector and Achilles (*The Iliad* 22)

The battle of taunts between Hector and Achilles that precedes the actual battle and the slaying of Hector runs as follows:

"I will no longer fly you, son of Peleus," said he, "as I have been doing hitherto. Three times have I fled round the mighty city of Priam, without daring to withstand you, but now, let me either slay or be slain, for I am in the mind to face you. Let us, then, give pledges to one another by our gods, who are the fittest witnesses and guardians of all covenants; let it be agreed between us that if Jove vouchsafes me the longer stay and I take your life, I am not to treat your dead body in any unseemly fashion, but when I have stripped you of your armour, I am to give up your body to the Achaeans. And do you likewise."

Achilles glared at him and answered, "Fool, prate not to me about covenants. There can be no covenants between men and lions, wolves and lambs can never be of one mind, but hate each other out and out all through. Therefore there can be no understanding between you and me, nor may there be any covenants between us, till one or other shall fall and glut grim Mars with his life's blood. Put forth all your strength; you have need now to prove yourself indeed a bold soldier and man of war. You have no more chance, and Pallas Minerva will forthwith vanquish you by my spear: you shall now pay me in full for the grief you have caused me on account of my comrades whom you have killed in battle."

He poised his spear as he spoke and hurled it. Hector saw it coming and avoided it; he watched it and crouched down so that it flew over his head and stuck in the ground beyond; Minerva then snatched it up and gave it back to Achilles without Hector's seeing her; Hector thereon said to the son of Peleus, "You have missed your aim, Achilles, peer of the gods, and Jove has not yet revealed to you the hour of my doom, though you made sure that he had done so. You were a false-tongued liar when you deemed that I should forget my valour and quail before you. You shall not drive your spear into the back of a runaway—drive it, should heaven so grant you power, drive it into me as I make straight towards you; and now for your own part avoid my spear if you can—would that you might receive the whole of it into your body; if you were once dead the Trojans would find the war an easier matter, for it is you who have harmed them most."[14]

These classic stories of taunting prior to battle make clear the centrality of taunting in stories of battle and death in the ancient world. Taunting was a ritual of intimidation and humiliation. Success in winning the war of words brings success in the actual battle. This storytelling tradition is the context within which the centrality of taunting in the story of Jesus' crucifixion and death makes sense. The most striking contrast of Mark's story with these is that Jesus says nothing in return to the taunting by his Roman and Israelite adversaries. Jesus doesn't play the game of ritual combat.

The Sounds of the Story

The blasphemous taunt of the people passing by, "You who would tear down the Temple and build it again in three days," is a paraphrase of the accusation of the false witnesses at the trial before the Sanhedrin: "I will destroy this Temple made with hands and in three days build up another not made with hands" (14:57). Mark's use of the verb ἐβλασφήμουν, "they blasphemed," to describe the taunt of those who passed by redirects the high priest's charge of blasphemy against Jesus to Jesus' opponents. A similar reversal of the charge of blasphemy occurred early in the gospel with the scribes' accusing Jesus of blasphemy at the healing of the paralytic (2:7). This accusation is followed by Jesus' pronouncement of the scribes' accusation that he was possessed by Beelzebul as blasphemy against the Holy Spirit (3:29).

The chief priests' mocking Jesus to one another along with the scribes recalls the deep irony of Jesus' prophecy that he would be mocked by the Gentiles (10:34). The Roman soldiers fulfill that prophecy (15:20). But Jesus

---

14. Homer, *Iliad* 22.

never prophesied that fellow Israelites would mock him. The naming of the chief priests mocking him "with the scribes" echoes the frequent identification of the alliance of Jesus' opponents earlier in the story (8:31; 10:33; 11:18, 27; 14:1, 43, 53; 15:1). The challenge of the passersby that Jesus save himself, developed in the chief priests' taunt that he "saved others," is an ironic repetition of a frequent theme in Jesus' ministry of healing and teaching. Jesus' saving acts are a virtual litany in the gospel story. They are characterized with this verb "to save" by others such as Jairus and the woman who touched Jesus' garment (5:23, 28), by Jesus about the saving faith of others (the woman, 5:34; Bartimaeus, 10:52), by the storyteller about Jesus' healing ministry (6:56), and in Jesus' teaching about discipleship (8:35). These are sonic connections that enable the listening audience to link the Roman crucifixion of Jesus and his mockery by fellow Israelites with earlier elements in the story.[15]

An overall tone of story is the combination of irony and grief. The taunting from the passersby and the religious authorities is framed by the story of those who are crucified with Jesus. The simple periods that tell the story of the insurgents crucified with him provide the launch and the landing for the more complex periods of the mockery. Furthermore, these periods of the story of those crucified with him are given the position of emphasis at the end of each sound unit in this story.

Comments on the Meaning and Impact of the Story

15:29: the blasphemous mockery of those passing by

The climax of the crucifixion is the taunting and mockery of Jesus as he is hanging on the cross—first by those Jerusalemites passing by, then the chief priests and scribes, and finally by those with whom he is crucified. The poignant irony of this mockery is that all those who mock Jesus now are Israelites. Jesus had predicted mockery by the Gentiles (10:33–34) but never by his fellow Israelites.

Mark immediately introduces his own judgment about their action: "Those who passed by *blasphemed*" (15:20). Blasphemy was the charge on which the Sanhedrin condemned Jesus (14:64). Blasphemy was and is the act of slander and defamation of God. It was a capital crime in Israelite law, as is reflected in the Sanhedrin's judgment against Jesus. It is the strongest condemnation of those who mocked Jesus that was available to Mark. The

---

15. Lee and Scott, *Sound Mapping*, have identified the onomatopoetic character of the words here. For a further exposition of the densely woven verbal threads outlined by Lee and Scott, see Boomershine, "Mark, the Storyteller," 27, 59, et al.

verb "to mock" (ἐμπαίζω), which Mark uses to describe the words of the chief priests and the scribes, has highly negative associations in Israelite tradition. It is, for example, the basis for condemnation of the men of Gibeah who "made sport of, mocked" the Levite's concubine (Judg 19:26) and of the Philistines who "mocked" Samson (Judges 16). Mark implicitly accuses those who passed by and the chief priests and scribes of a crime against God and asks his audiences to join him in that judgment. It must be noted here that this norm of judgment is another sign that this story is being told by a Judean to predominantly Judean audiences.

The phrase that describes the blasphemy of those who passed by is "shaking/wagging their heads" (κινοῦντες τὰς κεφαλὰς αὐτῶν). This is the second allusion to the LXX translation of Psalm 21 (Ps 22 in Hebrew and English translations). In earlier uses, this action is a sign of extreme distress (e.g., of Daniel in Dan 4:19 [LXX]) or derision (e.g., Sir 12:18; 13:7; Job 16:4). In Ps 22:7–8 (21:8–9, LXX) this gesture occurs immediately prior to the only quotation of the words of the psalmist's enemies:

> All who saw me mocked at me;
> they talked with the lips; **they moved the head**:
> "He hoped in the Lord; let him rescue him;
> let him **save** him, because he wanted him." (NETS)

This allusion to the psalm has the same basic function as the earlier allusion to the division of the garments (15:24), but this time the enemies are not Gentiles but Israelites. In the psalm, the identity of the psalmist's enemies is left ambiguous, but the implication is that they are neighbors and fellow Israelites who are beginning to divide the property in anticipation of the psalmist's death. The passersby in Mark's story are introduced as the enemies of the righteous sufferer and as Israelites who are acting like the Roman soldiers (15:20; cf. 10:33–34).

The implicit accusation from the passersby (that Jesus prophesied against the Temple) is a paraphrase of the key words of the accusation from the false witnesses at Jesus' Sanhedrin trial (14:58):

> We heard this man say, "I will destroy this Temple made with hands and in three days I will build up another not made with hands."
>
> Ἡμεῖς ἠκούσαμεν αὐτοῦ λέγοντος ὅτι Ἐγὼ καταλύσω τὸν ναὸν τοῦτον τὸν χειροποίητον καὶ διὰ τριῶν ἡμερῶν ἄλλον ἀχειροποίητον οἰκοδομήσω.

The words of those who "blaspheme" Jesus here (15:29) are:

Aha, you who would destroy the Temple and build it in three days
Οὐὰ ὁ καταλύων τὸν ναὸν καὶ οἰκοδομῶν ἐν τρισὶν ἡμέραις

This allusion to the Sanhedrin trial is ironic in the same way that the written sign on the cross is, which names Jesus King of the Judeans. The earlier stories of Jesus' words about the Temple have made it clear that the charge against Jesus by the witnesses before the Sanhedrin is false and is a distortion of Jesus' words. This mocking repetition of the false witnesses' charge is doubly ironic because Jesus is mocked for words that he never said. The implication of the story is that the charges against Jesus at both trials were false testimony fabricated to create the appearance of capital offense.

The challenge to Jesus, "Save yourself" (σῶσον σεαυτὸν), has sonic connections with Jesus' earlier teaching: "Whoever wants to save his life (τὴν ψυχὴν αὐτοῦ σῶσαι) will lose it but whoever loses his life for my sake and the gospel will save it" (8:35). In this case, the indirect allusion to Jesus' earlier words confirms Jesus' courage and willingness to live out his own teaching. It is another kind of irony since the intention of the passersby is to denigrate and mock Jesus. But, for the attentive listener, their words are an affirmation of Jesus' fulfillment of his nonviolent witness. Jesus is a martyr for the kingdom of God who has rejected the option of saving himself and is losing his life for the sake of the gospel.

the possibility of Jesus' coming down from the cross

Furthermore, in light of Jesus' earlier miracles, the possibility that Jesus could come down from the cross is by no means out of the question. This possibility is also a motif in other stories of crucifixion in the first century. The most graphic occurs in an episode of Chariton's romance novel, *Callirhoe,* which was summarized above in the "Ancient Connections and Associations" section of the commentary on the story of Peter's denial.[16] In addition to sharing with Mark the common motif of two men being crucified together, it also shares the motif of coming down from the cross.[17] In that story, Chaereas and Polycharmus, the companion and best friend of Chaereas, have been imprisoned with a group of pirates who made an escape from jail by killing their guards. When the pirates (along with Polycharmus and Chaereas) are

---

16. X-REF

17. This motif has also been identified by Marcus, *Mark,* 2:1044. He cites a report in Josephus' *Life* (420–421) that Josephus intervened with the Roman general Titus to save three friends who were being crucified. Titus gave the order, and the three were taken down from their crosses and received treatment.

quickly recaptured, they are sentenced to be crucified. After speaking the name of Callirhoe in reproach, Polycharmus is taken away to Mithridates, the king, to whom he tells their story. Mithridates recognizes that this is the same Chaereas who is husband to Callirhoe, with whom he is madly in love:

> Mithridates sent them all to save Chaereas before he died. They found the others already hanging on their crosses, and he was just mounting his. From far off they each shouted appeals: "Spare him!" "Come down!" "Do not hurt him!" "Let him go!" So the executioner stopped his work, and Chaereas descended from the cross, regretfully, for he had been glad to be leaving his miserable life and unhappy love. (4.3.6)

As we have seen and heard earlier, Mark raises in every new episode of the story the possibility that Jesus might escape death. The story of Chaereas makes it clear that the possibility of coming down from the cross was in the air in Mark's time and was not an impossible joke. However, the taunters are probably presented as assuming that it is impossible.

31: the taunting by the chief priests and scribes

The chief priests pick up and develop the mocking cries of those passing by. The thematic verb of this section of the story, "to mock" (ἐμπαίζω) introduces their words. In the traditions of Israel as translated in the Septuagint, this verb is usually associated with taunting and mockery across racial or ethnic boundaries. Even a selective list of instances of mockery across ethnic lines is extensive: e.g., the wife of Pharaoh about Joseph (Gen 39:14), Yahweh about the Egyptians (Exod 10:2), Baalam to his donkey (Num 22:29), Samson by the Philistines (Judg 16:25, 27 [LXX A]), Yahweh to the Egyptians (1 Sam 6:6), Saul and his fear of being made sport by the Philistines (1 Sam 31:4 and 1 Chr 10:4), Jeremiah about the idols of the nations (Jer 10:15), the nations to Israel (Ezek 22:5), the Syrians with the third brother of the Maccabean martyrs (2 Macc 7:10), the Gentiles against the Israelites in Judas Maccabeus' speech to his troops before the battle with Nicanor (2 Macc 8:17). Mockery of Israelites by other Israelites is rare but not unprecedented in Israelite tradition, as the mockery of Isaiah by the false prophet, Belchira, shows (*Martyrdom and Ascension of Isaiah*, 5:2–3). But it is highly unusual, and in most instances it is scandalous as in the case of the Levite's concubine where the LXX uses the word ἐμπαίζω, "mocked, made sport of," for the treatment of the Levite's concubine by the men of Gibeah in Judg 19:25; 20:5. (The Hebrew of these verses is translated variously "raped," "abused," "forced.") This word is used also to describe Israel's response to the Lord's

The Crucifixion of Jesus (15:21–32) 289

messengers in 2 Chr 36:16. Thus, the mockery of Israelites by other Israelites is associated with scandal in the literature of Israel. It virtually never happens, because mockery is only directed against one's ethnic enemies. This tradition is reflected in Jesus' prophecies. Jesus had prophesied that the Son of Man would be mocked by the Gentiles (10:33–34), but he never foretold that he would be mocked by other Israelites. In doing this, therefore, the chief priests and the scribes act like Gentiles in the eyes of Israelite tradition.

The first part of the chief priests' mockery (15:31) is an in-group conversation with the scribes. They first state their recognition that Jesus had saved others, an admission that evokes the audience's memory of all those Jesus had saved: the leper, the paralytic, the man with a withered hand, the Gerasene demoniac, the woman who touched his garment, Jairus' daughter, the Syro-Phoenician woman's daughter, the deaf and mute man, the blind man of Bethsaida, the boy possessed by a demon and his father, and Bartimaeus. Their mocking of Jesus' inability to save himself is ironic because Jesus has clearly decided at several earlier points in the story, including in Gethsemane, not to save himself but to be obedient to God's will. He is doing what he taught his followers to do: lose their life for the sake of the gospel (8:35).

Just as the passersby alluded to the charge against Jesus in the Sanhedrin trial, so the priests' second statement opens with the titles for which Jesus was condemned in the two trials: "the Christ" (14:61) and "the King of the Judeans" (15:2,26). Their change of the second title to the "King of Israel" is, if anything, a more emotionally resonant name for a leader of the nation.[18] Their use of this title in mockery is a sign that they believe both titles are a joke. It is also likely that the storyteller presented their mockery with taunting laughter.

Finally, the chief priests and scribes repeat and develop the challenge of those passing by the cross for Jesus to come down from the cross. Their new idea is to name a purpose for his descent from the cross, namely, "in order that we might see and believe" (ἵνα ἴδωμεν καὶ πιστεύσωμεν—15:32). Ironically, the priests' taunt repeats some of the key words from Jesus' earlier quotation of Isa 6:9–10 in his explanation of his purpose in speaking in parables:

> in order that seeing they might not perceive and that hearing
> they might hear and not understand, lest they might turn again

---

18. The contrast between "the King of the Judeans" and "the King of Israel" also reflects the difference between outsider and insider language to which John H. Elliott refers: see Appendix 4, "Markan Terminology."

and be forgiven. (ἵνα βλέποντες βλέπωσιν καὶ μὴ ἴδωσιν . . . μήποτε ἐπιστρέψωσιν—4:12)

The implication of this allusion is that the priests are unaware that their use of these terms fulfills Jesus' earlier prophecy of the response to his teaching.

the implicit explanation of the Judean leaders' disbelief

A dimension of the Isaiah prophecy in Mark is to provide an internal explanation for the incomprehension and disbelief of many, including the leaders of the nation (i.e., the chief priests, the scribes, and the elders). The recognition of this connection to Jesus' earlier explanation of his parabolic teaching to the disciples is dependent on the audience's memory of that earlier story, but the composer of Mark clearly assumes this capability in the audience. In this instance, the implication of this connection with Jesus' quotation of Isaiah is that the chief priests and scribes do not understand the character and significance of Jesus' life and death. The reversal of logic built into the story means that this ironic mockery of Jesus as "the Messiah, the King of Israel" is another confirmation of the truth of his identity as Messiah.

32b: the derision by those crucified with him

The final period of the crucifixion story completes the motif of the men crucified with Jesus. The audience's context for hearing the story of Jesus' compatriots in crucifixion was the earlier Israelite martyr stories. A motif in the story of the Maccabean martyrs in 2 Maccabees 7 is that the mother, prior to her own death that concludes the story, provided encouragement and support for her sons as they were being tortured and killed:

> The mother was especially admirable and worthy of honorable memory. Although she saw her seven sons perish within a single day, she bore it with good courage because of her hope in the Lord. She encouraged each of them in the language of their ancestors. Filled with a noble spirit, she reinforced her woman's reasoning with a man's courage, and said to them, "I do not know how you came into being in my womb. It was not I who gave you life and breath, nor I who set in order the elements within each of you. Therefore, the Creator of the world, who shaped the beginning of humankind and devised the origin of all things, will in his mercy give life and breath back to you again, since you now forget yourself for the sake of his laws." (2 Macc 7:20–23, NRSV)

The motif of support for a dying prophet-martyr by other prophets is also found in the story of the martyrdom of Isaiah:

> And Manasseh, and Belkira, and the false prophets, and the princes, and the people, and all stood by looking on. **And to the prophets who (were) with him** he said before he was sawed in half . . . (*Martyrdom and Ascension of Isaiah* 5:12–13).[19]

The implication of the description of those who were looking on is that the prophets were also present both before and during Isaiah's being sawed in half. These elements of consolation for those who are dying in the martyr-story tradition also provided some solace to those hearing these horrible stories that those who died received some support during their executions. The derision from the men crucified with Jesus is even more poignant in its contrast to these earlier martyr stories. Every potential source of consolation is denied Jesus. The comparison to the earlier Israelite martyr stories implies that Jesus suffers more than any of the previous martyrs of Israel.

The Greek word that Mark uses to describe the derision by those crucified with Jesus, ὠνείδιζον, has a range of meanings: "to reproach, heap insults upon, revile."[20] It is the opposite of comfort and consolation. The derision is reported indirectly, without any quotation of their words. We cannot know what the Markan audiences may have inferred about what they said. But the implication of the context is that these men had nothing in common with Jesus. That is, the fact that the revolutionaries reviled and insulted Jesus is a clear indication that they did not regard him as one of them in any sense. The derision of Jesus by the insurrectionists means that Jesus was radically different from "the zealous." A specific dimension of the contrast is that Jesus was nonviolent and did not sponsor or encourage violence in any form, including warfare. His consistent teaching and pattern of action is that the kingdom of God will be established by means other than violence against the enemies of the kingdom. The witnesses to the coming kingdom of God may suffer violence, but they will triumph by faithful endurance. The mocking of Jesus by these men associated with the insurrection emphasizes this contrast. Those who pass by, the chief priests and scribes, and the insurrectionists alike share a common incomprehension of the kingdom of God and the means by which it will be established.

---

19. The translation of the reconstructed version of this early work cited here is by Knibb in Charlesworth, *OTP*, vol. 1.

20. BDAG, 570.

The Performance of the Story

The storyteller's introduction to the mockery episode is a prosecutor's charge of blasphemy against those passing by. A gesture of accusation, pointing the finger at them, is fully appropriate. The implication of this charge is that the passersby are guilty of a capital crime. The tone is similar to the tone of the high priest in his condemnation of Jesus. The words of the passersby are to be told as a dramatic presentation of their tone and attitude. The first word, in Greek, οὐά, and in English, "Hey you," is a full-voiced taunt.[21] Since these mockers quote the false witnesses at the Sanhedrin trial, their tone here is the same as their earlier compatriots. But the volume of their taunts is considerably louder outside along the road than the earlier testimony in a courtroom.

The critical question here is your attitude as the storyteller toward what you are reporting. Does the storyteller simply embody the attitude of the passersby and the authorities, or does the storyteller express an attitude toward what is being told? And if the storyteller's attitude is to be expressed, what is it—anger and hostility or scandal and grief? In light of the associations in earlier Israelite stories of scandal and grief with this kind of mockery, the most appropriate attitude here is scandal and grief rather than anger and hostility. This can be most directly expressed in the introductions to the words of the passersby and the authorities, but it is also possible to use gestures of grief even as you are displaying characters' emotions of hostility and mockery. That is, the challenge in performing this story is to convey both the attitude of those who mocked Jesus and your own attitude toward what they were doing and saying.

The mockery by the chief priests builds the crescendo of laughter and disdain. The first part of their taunt is addressed to the scribes standing with them, while the second part, beginning with "Let the Christ..." is addressed to Jesus on the cross. This change in the point of address can be dramatically represented by addressing the first part to the imagined scribes beside you and the second to the imagined Jesus on the cross, either in front or to one side of you. It is important to keep the imaginary location of the cross in the

---

21. K. C. Hanson has argued that οὐά should be translated "Shame on" as the reciprocal of μάκαριος ("How honorable"). In this translation, the onlookers at the crucifixion are publicly shaming Jesus for his comments about the Temple: "Shame on you who would destroy the Temple and build it up again in three days..." See Hanson, "How Honorable." This article only came to my attention after the videos of the translation had been recorded and, therefore, after a change in the translation could be made in the document. Hanson's translation makes the mocking of the passersby more congruent with the honor/shame culture of the first-century Mediterranean and is recommended for future tellings of Mark's story.

The Crucifixion of Jesus (15:21–32)

same place, probably best to one side of the storytelling space. The mockery of Jesus' titles and the humorous possibility that the mockers might believe are the climax of the authorities' speech. This is the high point of the crescendo in volume, and it is appropriately interlaced with mocking laughter.

The derision of those crucified with Jesus is reported in indirect discourse. While this period is quieter than the chief priests' taunt, it is, if anything, even more ironic. There may also be a note of the storyteller's grief here at the absence of any consolation or camaraderie for Jesus as he dies. But the climactic tone here is the derision of the revolutionaries.

The energy of this section of the story is to intensify the audience's sympathy for Jesus. Jesus' silent suffering on the cross in response to this litany of mockery by his Roman enemies and his fellow Israelites is the most compelling dimension of the story. It is a sign of Jesus' courage and commitment to the way of the kingdom of God.

7

THE DEATH AND BURIAL OF JESUS (15:33–47)

THE STORIES OF THE DEATH AND BURIAL OF JESUS COMPLETE the fulfillment of the prophecies of his suffering and death. The ending of this section with the story of Jesus' burial is the only positive ending of a section since the last Passover. The mocking response of the bystanders to Jesus' cry of dereliction continues the motif of the taunting and the breaking of the last hope of Jesus' deliverance from death. However, the responses to Jesus' death are all positive, and they constitute the last episode of the story of Jesus' death. The death and burial stories have the highest concentration of complex periods in the PRN. The responses of God, the centurion, the women, and Joseph of Arimithea are climactic gestures of honor and mourning expressed in the long and slow periods of these stories.

The Death of Jesus (Mark 15:33–41)

Sound Map

15:33Καὶ γενομένης **ὥρας ἕκτης** σκότος ἐγένετο ἐφ' ὅλην τὴν γῆν
                                                          ἕως ὥρας ἐνάτης.
34καὶ τῇ **ἐνάτῃ ὥρᾳ** ἐβόησεν ὁ Ἰησοῦς φωνῇ μεγάλῃ,
    Ελωι ελωι λεμα σαβαχθανι;
    ὅ ἐστιν μεθερμηνευόμενον Ὁ θεός μου ὁ θεός μου, εἰς τί ἐγκατέλιπές
                                                                                                                                                                    με;

35καί τινες τῶν παρεστηκότων ἀκούσαντες ἔλεγον,
    Ἴδε Ἠλίαν φωνεῖ.
36δραμὼν δέ τις [καὶ] γεμίσας σπόγγον ὄξους περιθεὶς καλάμῳ

The Death and Burial of Jesus (15:33–47)

ἐπότιζεν αὐτόν, λέγων,
Ἄφετε ἴδωμεν εἰ ἔρχεται **Ἠλίας** καθελεῖν αὐτόν.
37ὁ δὲ **Ἰησοῦς** ἀφεὶς **φωνὴν μεγάλην ἐξέπνευσεν**.

38Καὶ τὸ καταπέτασμα τοῦ ναοῦ ἐσχίσθη εἰς δύο ἀπ' ἄνωθεν ἕως κάτω.
39Ἰδὼν δὲ ὁ κεντυρίων ὁ παρεστηκὼς ἐξ ἐναντίας αὐτοῦ
    ὅτι οὕτως **ἐξέπνευσεν** εἶπεν,
    Ἀληθῶς οὗτος ὁ ἄνθρωπος **υἱὸς θεοῦ** ἦν.
40ἦσαν δὲ **καὶ** γυναῖκες ἀπὸ μακρόθεν θεωροῦσαι,
    ἐν αἷς **καὶ** Μαρία ἡ Μαγδαληνὴ
    καὶ Μαρία ἡ Ἰακώβου τοῦ μικροῦ καὶ Ἰωσῆτος μήτηρ
    καὶ Σαλώμη,
41αἳ ὅτε ἦν ἐν τῇ Γαλιλαίᾳ ἠκολούθουν αὐτῷ
        καὶ διηκόνουν αὐτῷ,
καὶ ἄλλαι πολλαὶ αἱ συναναβᾶσαι αὐτῷ εἰς Ἱεροσόλυμα.

Translation

33And **at the sixth hour**, darkness came over the whole land
        until the ninth hour.
34**And at the ninth hour Jesus** cried out **with a loud voice**,
    "Eloi, Eloi, lema sabachthani?"
That means, "My God, my God, why have you forsaken me?"

35And when some of the bystanders heard it, they said,
    "Listen, he is calling **Elijah**."
36And someone ran and filled a sponge with sour wine, put it on a stick,
        and held it up for him to **drink**, saying,
    "Wait, let us see whether **Elijah** will come to take him down."
37**But Jesus** gave **a loud cry and breathed his last**.

38And the curtain of the Temple was torn in two, from top to bottom.
39And when the centurion, who stood facing him, saw how he **breathed
        his last**, he said,
    "Truly this man was **Son of God**!"
40There were also women watching from a distance
    and among them were Mary Magdalene,
    and Mary the mother of James, the younger, and Joses,
    and Salome,
    41who followed him when he was in Galilee and served him
    and many other women who had come up with him to Jerusalem.

Ancient Associations and Connections

Several motifs in this story resonate with the story of the martyrdom of Eleazar in 2 Macc 6:18-31: the offering of meat/drink from which the martyr has vowed to abstain, the bystanders who become malicious, the groaning words before death. See the commentary above on Mark 15:21-23, "The Preparations" for the crucifixion, where this story is quoted in full.

The Sounds of the Story

The tonal atmosphere and rhythm of the story of Jesus' death is established by Jesus' cry of lament and grief. The story begins in the deep quiet of the descent of darkness over the land. That quiet is pierced by Jesus' loud cries and the mocking misinterpretation of his cry by the bystanders. This is a difference of volume and of tempo. Jesus' cry of abandonment and the responses to his death have the tempo of a funeral march. The response of the bystander who runs to get some sour wine is fast and loud. This contrast establishes the irony of his misperception of Jesus' words.

Once again, as in the first and last episodes of the crucifixion story (15:24-25; 29-32), this climactic section of Mark's story is composed of a combination of simple and complex periods. The naming of the hour and the deep darkness is a simple period that sets the context for the complex period of Jesus' cry of abandonment. Jesus' remembering of the beginning of Psalm 22 (LXX 21) is a complex period with the explicit direction of the volume of Jesus' cry. The translation for the Greek-speaking audience is heard here as a third period that establishes the episodic rhythm of the story and allows time for the storyteller to move from dramatizing Jesus' cry to addressing the audience with the translation in her own voice. Jesus' cry is explicitly described as "with a loud voice" (φωνῇ μεγάλῃ). The loud quotation of the Aramaic words of the psalm give it a sound of authenticity as the storyteller repeats what are presented as the actual sounds that Jesus cried.[1] The translation of Jesus' words into the sounds of Greek that were familiar to the audience has a different tonal quality ('Ο θεός μου), since the translation is an interruption in the flow of the story and a direct address to the audience. Mark provides the translation for his listeners, which in turn indicates that some, probably most, of his prospective listeners did not know Aramaic.

The two periods of the bystanders' mocking misinterpretation of Jesus' prayer are both complex periods that end with references to Elijah. The

---

1. See Brown, *Death of the Messiah*, 2:1051-56 for a full account of the textual and language issues involved in assessing Jesus' cry.

The Death and Burial of Jesus (15:33–47)

sonic connection between the Aramaic word for God in Jesus' cry and the name of the prophet is not present in an English translation of the prophet's name, but it is present in an English or Greek transliteration of his name in Hebrew or Aramaic. If we employ standard English phonetics in the transliteration of the Aramaic word "my God" we get *Ĕlōē*. Likewise, if we use standard English phonetics to transliterate the name of Elijah as it sounds in Greek,[2] the transliteration is *Ālēyă*. Both words, then, share the consonant *l* and the long vowel *ē*. The sound of the two words is sufficiently similar that a bystander's misperception is understandable.

The composer of this story clearly assumes that the audience will be able to understand this misperception and to get the joke. Whether this is an intentional joke or simply poor hearing by the bystander is not addressed. But the bystander treats it as a joke and holds up the wine to Jesus in order to heighten the hilarity of the possibility of Elijah's fiery-chariot deliverance. The similarity in the sound of the name of God, Ελωι, and the sound of the name of Elijah in Aramaic (transliterated into Greek letters) is the linchpin of his humor and needs to be rendered in English.[3]

The period describing Jesus' death is short and climactic. The "loud voice" echoes the words in the introduction to Jesus' cry. The end of the period has the quality of onomatopoeia with the volume of the loud cry followed by the word ἐξέπνευσεν, which sounds like Jesus' last breath.[4]

The final three periods in this story describe the responses to Jesus' death by God, the centurion, and the women who came up to Jerusalem with Jesus. God's response is a simple and relatively short period. The centurion's response is a complex period with three cola, and the women's response of implied grief is the longest and most complex period in the entire PRN.

The most striking sound in the first period recounting the responses to Jesus' death is the verb phrase ἐσχίσθη εἰς δύο: "torn in two." The sound of this verb has been associated with an act of God by its only earlier use, in description of the tearing open of the heavens at Jesus' baptism: "the heavens were torn open" (σχιζομένους τοὺς οὐρανοὺς—1:10). In the baptism, the tearing open of the heavens is associated with God's joy and blessing on his beloved Son. Here the tearing of the curtain is associated with God's grief and the ritual tearing of garments that is heard in the onomatopoeia of these words.

---

2. Mark's Greek version of the name is the same as that used in the LXX, which is close to a Greek transliteration of one version of the Hebrew name.

3. See Appendix 7 for more discussion of the problem of enabling English-speaking listeners to make the connection between Eloi and the name of the prophet.

4. Lee and Scott, *Sound Mapping*, 210–11.

The centurion's response also resonates with the baptism story. The baptism ends with the voice from heaven saying, "You are my Beloved Son" (Σὺ εἶ ὁ υἱός μου ὁ ἀγαπητός—1:11). The centurion's response to what he sees is, "Truly this man was son of God" (Ἀληθῶς οὗτος ὁ ἄνθρωπος υἱὸς θεοῦ ἦν—15:39). The introduction to his response—literally translated, "that thus he breathed out"—repeats Jesus' "breathing out" (ἐξέπνευσεν) and sonically connects the centurion's response with Jesus' death.

The story of Jesus' death ends with the description of the company of women who had come up to Jerusalem with him and were watching his death from a distance. This is surprising because there has been no earlier notice of the presence of women with Jesus and his disciples in Galilee or during their trip up to Jerusalem that began at the latest with their journey to Judea (10:1). While all these women are shrouded in mystery in Mark's story, their presence on Golgotha is the first notice since the arrest that any of Jesus' companions from Galilee were with him during his trials and execution.

The women's grief is implied in this longest and most complex period of the PRN. It has the tone and slow rhythm of a dirge. It is an appropriate climax to Mark's description of the responses of the witnesses of Jesus' death. The litany of the names of the three women gives each of them a separate colon in which the audience has time to imagine their faces and their times with Jesus in Galilee.

Notes on Details and Translation

15:33 the "sixth/ninth hour" or "noon/three o'clock"

The translation of the time notices in the story raises once again the question of how to translate the verbal connections in the story. The RSV has a literal translation, in contrast to the later NRSV. The RSV translates the time notices as "the sixth hour," and "the ninth hour," just as in 15:25 it reads "the third hour." The NRSV has changed these to "nine o'clock," "noon" and "three o'clock." The reason for the change in the NRSV is not esoteric: it clarifies the actual reference by means of contemporary expressions so that there is no misunderstanding by contemporary audiences.

Attention to the sounds of the story introduces a new factor in the translation. In as far as possible, it is important for performance to render the sonic connections that constitute the sound fabric of the various parts of the story. In this case, "the hour" is a verbal motif that was established in the Gethsemane story: Jesus' first prayer is that **"the hour** might pass him by." He expresses Peter's failure to stay awake as, "Couldn't you even stay awake for **one hour**?" And the climax of the story has this verbal motif as one of Jesus' final words to his disciples: "**The hour** has come." Mark makes the connection between these references to "the hour" in Jesus' words in Gethsemane and these references to "the hour" of his crucifixion and death by the repetition of the same word. The translation into the terms of "o'clock" here eliminates those connections. Furthermore, "the hour" has the connotations of the tolling of a bell. The RSV translation may require a word of explanation to a modern audience, but its steady sounding of "the hour" renders more of the original impact of this leitmotif.

39: Son of God / υἱὸς θεοῦ

The meaning of the centurion's response to Jesus' death is ambiguous. The first layer of ambiguity is his tone: is his tone sincere or satirical and mocking? The second ambiguity is the meaning of his words in the context of the whole story. We will address the grammatical issues first.

The centurion's statement is, Ἀληθῶς οὗτος ὁ ἄνθρωπος υἱὸς θεοῦ ἦν; a literal translation is, "Truly this man Son of God was." Various forms of this title are a leitmotif throughout the gospel.[5] Assuming that the instance of this title in 1:1 is a later addition, the first occurence of this leitmotif is at Jesus' baptism, when the voice from heaven says, "You are my Beloved Son" (1:11). In 3:11 the unclean spirits whom Jesus silences in the summary of his early ministry also use this name but with the article: "You are the Son of God" (σὺ εἶ ὁ υἱὸς τοῦ θεοῦ—3:11). In 5:7 the Gerasene demoniac calls Jesus "the Son of the Most High God." At the transfiguration, God says to the three disciples, "This is my Son whom I love" (9:7). And finally the chief priest asks him, "Are you the Messiah, the Son of the Blessed?" (14:61). In each of these four instances, the definite article is employed with the word "Son" and is definite in meaning even though the phrase is varied and only once couples "son" with "of God."

Many scholars have seen the absence of the article in the centurion's statement as meaning that this is not a full and definite christological confession of Jesus as "*the* Son of God" but rather a more generic recognition of Jesus as "*a* son of God." While this is possible, the phrase is actually

---

5. The term "Son of God" occurs in Mark 1:1 in many early and good manuscripts of Mark. However, as can now seen with a click, the addition in Sinaiticus of the abbreviation of υἱὸς θεοῦ, υυ θυ, is a later superscript scribal addition to the text. Since Sinaiticus is our oldest complete manuscript of Mark, it is decisive evidence that this phrase was added to the text, and that the best manuscript tradition of the original text did not have it. The text can be seen online at http://codexsinaiticus.org/en/manuscript.aspx?book=34&lid=en&side=r&zoomSlider=0/.

ambiguous and can be heard as either definite or generic. Colwell has found that a definite predicate noun usually lacks the article when it comes before the verb, as it does in 15:39,[6] and the scribal addition in 1:1 shows that the phrase can be definite without the article. Harner's[7] careful and nuanced study of Mark's use of arthrous and anarthrous nouns in a predicate both before and after the verb shows that Mark was capable of designating definite and indefinite predicates clearly. If he had wanted to say "a son of God," he could have placed the verb before the anarthrous noun. If he had wanted to say "the Son of God," he could have placed the verb before an arthrous noun. In several instances, the anarthrous noun is clearly indefinite (6:49; 11:17, 32; 14:70). In 2:28 and 3:35 the anarthrous nouns turn toward being definite but with more of a qualitative function than identification of a specific person. So the grammar turns out to be quite ambiguous.

As Marcus observes, since Mark had the capacity to be unambiguous, he may have wished the centurion's statement to be ambiguous.[8] He may have expected the listeners to hear the centurion in the context of the Hellenistic and Roman practice of deifying a great past leader,[9] and at the same time to expect the listeners to see him joining many others in the narrative who were saying more than they knew.[10] The grammatical evidence indicates, therefore, that the ambiguity of the centurion's title for Jesus was intentional.

The tone of the centurion's statement must be determined, therefore, on other grounds. There are three considerations. First, the centurion's words occur in an episode of highly sympathetic responses to Jesus' death by God and the women. A mocking tone on the part of the centurion would be out of keeping with the tone of the other two responses.

Second, the centurion is described as standing facing Jesus (ὁ παρεστηκὼς ἐξ ἐναντίας αὐτοῦ). This recalls the "bystanders" at the cross (15:35) who are described with the related word (τινες τῶν παρεστηκότων), whose tone was mocking. Collins perceptively discerns here an implied difference between the bystanders and the centurion, such as Mark makes between Jesus and Peter in their two "trials," and between Jesus and Barabbas in the Pilate trial.[11] These implicit comparisons draw the audiences' attention to the contrasting responses and roles of different characters in these

---

6. Colwell, "Definite Rule," 20.
7. Harner, "Qualitative," 75–87.
8. Marcus, *Mark*, 2:1058. See also Collins, *Mark*, 769.
9. Harner, "Qualitative," 79.
10. Marcus, *Mark*, 2:1058.
11. Collins, *Mark*, 710, 721, and 766.

central episodes of the story. Thus, the contrast between the bystanders' mocking joke and the centurion's sincere confession is a further instance of this pattern in Mark's storytelling.

The third consideration is that the centurion's statement is a reversal of the audience's expectations established in 15:20 when the Roman soldiers mocked Jesus. The centurion's response is in surprising contrast to both the earlier mocking by the soldiers and the joking tone of the bystanders who hear Jesus' cry to God. Embedded with the sympathetic responses of God and the women, the centurion's response is a rhetorical reversal of expectations of these elements in the story's plot. These three factors indicate that the Markan storytellers' tone in reporting the centurion's use of the term "Son of God" was probably sincere and straightforward. It was an expression of honor in the voice of a Roman centurion experienced in the ways of death.

40–41: the women and Jesus' mother

Only one of the three women has been named earlier in the story. In the story of Jesus' teaching in the Nazareth synagogue, the people say,

> Isn't this the carpenter, the son of Mary, and the brother of James and Joses . . . ? οὐχ οὗτός ἐστιν ὁ τέκτων, ὁ υἱὸς τῆς Μαρίας καὶ ἀδελφὸς Ἰακώβου καὶ Ἰωσῆτος. (6:3, NRSV)

In this story she is named as

> Μαρία ἡ Ἰακώβου τοῦ μικροῦ καὶ Ἰωσῆτος μήτηρ, literally translated, Mary, of James the younger and Joses mother. (15:40)

The implication of the verbal thread of these names is that James and Joses are Jesus' younger brothers, and that this Mary is, therefore, Jesus' mother! This is typical of Mark's allusive manner. But this is a connection that is only caught by someone who has listened to (or attentively read) the whole story. Thus, in these closing periods of the story of Jesus' death, Mark alludes to the presence and grieving responses of Jesus' heavenly Father and his earthly mother.

This allusion to Jesus' mother also picks up the story of Jesus' family. Prior to the Nazareth story, alluded to here by the names James the younger (brother) and Joses, Jesus' family is introduced as the frame or "sandwich" for the Beelzebul controversy (3:20–35). In the same manner that the story of Jairus' daughter is the sandwich for the story of the woman who touched Jesus' garment (5:21–43), so the story of Jesus' family introduces and concludes the story of Jesus' conflict with the scribes who came down to Galilee from Jerusalem and accused him of being possessed by the devil:[12]

3:20–21:

Then he went into a house.
And the crowd gathered again, so that they could not even eat bread.

And when his family heard this, they went out to seize him.
Because they were saying,
    "He's out of his mind."

3:31–35:

And his mother and his brothers came,
    and standing outside, they sent for him, calling him.
And a crowd was sitting around him and they say to him,
    "Your mother and your brothers and your sisters are outside
                                     looking for you."

And he answered and says to them,
    "Who are my mother and my brothers?"
And looking around at those who were sitting in a circle around him,
                                         he says,
    "Here are my mother and my brothers.
Whoever does the will of God is my brother and sister and mother."

This story is the most negative characterization of Jesus' family in the entire gospel tradition. The scribes' accusation that he is possessed by Beelzebul is only another step from his family's conclusion that he is out of his mind. Thus, his family is described as being allied with the scribes from Jerusalem whose accusation Jesus takes very seriously and names as blasphemy and an eternal sin. Furthermore, this entire controversy, including Jesus' redefinition of his family, takes place in the house he has entered with his disciples. The implication of the story is that he never goes out to meet his mother and brothers, who are waiting outside the house to talk to him. In the telling of the concluding story in this section, the audience is addressed as the crowd sitting around him in a circle. This may in turn reflect at least one of the settings in which Mark told his story—with people sitting around the storyteller.

Thus, the story implies that Jesus never went out to talk with his biological family, and that he regarded his followers as his brother and sister and

---

12. This is my translation and sound map.

The Death and Burial of Jesus (15:33-47)

mother rather than his family.[13] In the context of familial loyalty in Judean culture, this is a major family rupture. When heard as a whole, Mark's story of Jesus' family has three major episodes, this conflict story; the Nazareth synagogue story, in which his hometown folk essentially reject him (6:1-6); and this story of the responses to Jesus' death.

In this context, it is interesting that Mark's initial description of Jesus' family in 3:21 is highly allusive, as is this description of Jesus' mother and brothers in the story of his death. The Greek phrase translated as "Jesus' family" is οἱ παρ' αὐτοῦ, literally "those from him." Joel Marcus (1:270) sets this in the context of the history of Greek literature:

> In classical Greek this term denotes envoys and ambassadors, but in the LXX and other Hellenistic literature it means either adherents and followers (e.g., 1 Macc 11:73; 12:27; 2 Macc 11:20) or parents and other relatives (e.g. Prov 31:21; Sus 33; Josephus *Ant.* 1.193; cf. Taylor, *Gospel according to St. Mark,* 236).

Marcus rightly concludes that the familial interpretation is necessary in Mark because of the distinction from the disciples in the preceding story (3:13-19) and the more precise description after the Beelzebul story of these folks as Jesus' mother and brothers (3:31). Thus, throughout the story, Mark's habit of sandwiching stories strengthens the case for identifying the people in 3:20-21, both the disciples and the family, to be the same as those in 3:31-35.

In the story of Jesus' death, Mark again describes Jesus' family in an indirect manner. By echoing the earlier association of Jesus' mother Mary with the names of these same brothers, Mark asks the listeners to remember that she initially thought he was crazy. The implication of identifying her and the brothers in the story of Jesus' death is that she changed her mind and traveled with him in Galilee and up to Jerusalem.

Mark frequently requires the audience to make connections such as this. To name only a few instances earlier in the PRN, Mark invites the listeners to figure out that Judas is one of those who rebuke the woman (14:4ff.), that the one who struck the slave of the high priest is one of the disciples (14:47), and that those who misunderstood Jesus' prayer on the cross were Judeans (15:35). And in these instances, there are no sonic connections, as there are with Mary, the mother of Jesus' brothers. Other instances of more explicit allusions are the references to Judas as "*the* one of the twelve" (14:10), which is sonically linked with his initial naming (3:19);

---

13. A number of scholars infer that this story reflects the experience of family conflict and alienation in the early Christian community. For an excellent summary, see Marcus, *Mark,* 1:271, 280.

and to Simon as "*the* leper" (14:3), which linked to the first major healing story (1:40–45). Mark constantly alludes to earlier parts of the story by these sonic connections. This indirect, allusive reference to Jesus' mother answers the question of why Mark did not simply say "Jesus' mother," as John does in his later retelling that often makes explicit what Mark implies.

The storytelling function of this indirect manner is to require and reward the audience when they pay attention and remember. Each new allusion is a discovery. In this case, the audience's recognition that Mark is referring to Jesus' mother heightens the impact of the story. The allusion has an effect similar to seeing an important someone from a distance and, vaguely at first and then definitely, recognizing her or him. This indirect reference to Jesus' mother is, therefore, consistent with Mark's storytelling style throughout the crucifixion story and the gospel. Many of the most emotionally intense facts—Jesus' nakedness in the praetorium and on the cross, his courageous keeping of his vow of abstinence from wine, Barabbas' representative connection with the war—are implied rather than explicitly named. Mark thereby constantly invites his audience to be actively engaged in the story.

Mark's naming of James as "James the Young" may also be intriguing for the audience. "Young" or "younger" in relation to what? All the major translations translate this name without supplying the implied word "brother." The audience is invited to fill it in when they catch the allusion to the earlier identification of him as Jesus' brother in 6:3.

Mark identifies Mary in the two subsequent stories of the burial and resurrection in the same allusive manner—the first employing the name of one brother, and the next employing the name of the other brother. In these sonic echoes Mark omits the word "mother." We as listeners have to fill in the ellipsis: Μαρία ἡ Ἰωσῆτος, literally, "Mary, the one of Joses" (15:47) and Μαρία ἡ τοῦ Ἰακώβου, "Mary, the one of James" (16:1). This is a frequent Markan practice in naming a person in relation to someone else. In 1:19 Mark names James as Ἰάκωβον τὸν τοῦ Ζεβεδαίου, "James the 'son' of Zebedee." The listener must fill in the specific relationship. In all these instances, the translators supply the implied missing word: in 1:19 the word "son," and in 15:47 and 16:1 the word "mother." This is appropriate since Mark uses the word "mother" at the end of the first description of this woman in 15:40, and the listeners can easily supply it in these later instances. But the continuing identification of her by means of her other sons continues the sonic echo of the words of the folks in the Nazareth synagogue in response to Jesus' teaching there—"Isn't this the carpenter, the son of Mary and the brother of James and Joses and Judas and Simon and aren't his sisters here with us?" (6:3)—and of the earlier story of Jesus' family (3:21), which by

The Death and Burial of Jesus (15:33–47)

implication includes his mother and his brothers, who came to take him home because they thought he was crazy.

Comments on the Meaning and Impact of the Story

15:34: the context and impact of Jesus' cry.

The tonal atmosphere and rhythm of the story of Jesus' death is established by Jesus' cry of lament and grief. The story begins in the deep quiet of the descent of darkness over the land. That quiet is pierced by Jesus' loud cries and the mocking misinterpretation of his cry by the bystanders at the crucifixion. This is a difference of volume and of tempo. Jesus' cry of abandonment and the responses to his death have the tempo of a funeral march. The response of the bystander who runs to get some sour wine is fast and loud. This contrast establishes the irony of his misperception of Jesus' words.

The setting for Jesus' cry is the three hours of darkness from the sixth hour, 12 noon, until the ninth hour, 3 p.m. The naming of the hours sounds like the tolling of a bell. The darkness is a symbol of the powers of evil, the antithesis of light. John names this antithesis in his hymn of joy at the beginning of his story of Jesus: "The light shines in the darkness and the darkness did not overcome it" (John 1:5, NRSV). For these three hours, the darkness has overcome the light and controls the whole land. Jesus cries out at the end of these hours of darkness, at the ninth hour. The naming of the hours—crucified at the third hour, darkness at the sixth to the ninth hour, cry at the ninth hour—enables the listeners to count the hours Jesus has been on the cross.

Jesus' prayer is a quotation of Psalm 22:1 (21:2, LXX), the theme of the song of a righteous sufferer. It is also the climax of the allusions to the psalm that began with the division of his garments (15:34) and continued in the mockers' shaking their heads and challenging him to save himself (15:29-30). (See commentary above on 15:24-32, "Ancient Associations and Connections.") These are the first words of Jesus since his two-word response to Pilate's hostile interrogation: "Are you the King of the Judeans?" and Jesus' response: "You say so" (Σὺ λέγεις—15:2). The impact of Jesus' recitation of the opening words of the psalm is to express to God his feeling that God had abandoned him. The implication is that Jesus remembered this traditional song at this moment of agony and humiliation.[14]

The story of Jesus' death consists of two parts: Jesus' cry of abandonment (vv. 33–34) and the mockery by those who heard him (vv. 35–36). The climax of the first part is the storyteller's translation of the prayer from Aramaic into Greek for the audience. The impact of the original Aramaic is to increase the reality of the description by repeating the actual words Jesus cried. The translation is a form of storytelling commentary in which the storyteller interrupts the story to give the audience information about Jesus' cry of anguish. Thus, the Aramaic quotation reports Jesus' cry in the context of its original historical occurrence around 30 CE. The Greek translation, in which the storyteller expresses her or his own anguish, sets the cry in the context of the storyteller's relationship with the audience in the present moment of the story at any subsequent time. Both Jesus' sense of abandonment and the storyteller's anguish are thereby made present. The effect of the episode is to establish identification with Jesus as a righteous man praying to God during the most intense suffering. And, as a result of the connection between the quotation of Jesus' words in Aramaic and the storyteller's translation of this most memorable line of the psalm, along with the preceding allusions in 15:24 and 34, the entire crucifixion section is set in the context of Israel's tradition of righteous suffering.

35: the bystanders' mocking of Jesus' prayer.

The two periods of the bystanders' mishearing of Jesus' prayer are both complex periods that end with references to Elijah. The bystanders' mishearing of Jesus' cry to God, "Eloi," as a call to Elijah is particularly confusing in the English translations because of insufficient attention to the details of English pronunciation (see Appendix 7).

The composer of this story assumes that the audience will be able to understand this misperception. Whether this is an intentional joke or simply poor hearing by the bystanders is not addressed. But the implication is unambiguous that these bystanders are fellow Israelites who, unlike the Roman soldiers, could pick up the subtleties of the sounds of Aramaic, even if mistaken.

---

14. In order to deal with the scandal of the implication of Jesus' desolation and sense of abandonment, some have suggested that Jesus' quotation of the first line of the psalm implies his remembering the whole psalm that ends on a positive note of faith and fulfillment. There is no evidence of such an allusion and, as we have seen and heard, Mark is very good at making allusions. I doubt, therefore, that many people in Mark's audiences made the connection with the later, more positive parts of Psalm 21 (22).

The report of the bystanders' mishearing or laughing distortion of what Jesus said only increases the audience's sympathy for Jesus. In popular Israelite belief in the first century, Elijah was the one to rescue the godly in their time of need.[15] He was a rough equivalent to the Lone Ranger in twentieth-century American folklore. The ancient fairy tale went something like this: at the last minute, when all other options are gone, call on Elijah and Elijah will come down in his fiery chariot and whisk you away. Furthermore, as we noted above in the story of the near crucifixion of Chaereas,[16] the possibility of coming down from a cross at the last moment was a motif in first-century storytelling. However, Mark's audience knows that Jesus was praying to God, not Elijah. And he is asking why God had forsaken him, not for Elijah or God to come and save him. This is another instance in which the audience is assumed to know things that are unknown to the characters in the story as in Jesus' prophecy of treachery by "one of the twelve," unknown to the eleven but known by the audience to be Judas Iscariot.

36: the final try to give Jesus wine.

The storyteller's introduction to the bystander's offering of sour wine is ambiguous—both positive and negative—in its connotations. There are several initial implications that the offering of wine will be an action of kindness and compassion:

1. The conjunction δὲ in 15:36 sometimes has an adversative force that communicates a disjuncture between this person who runs to fill the sponge with "sour wine," ὄξους, and those mockers who misinterpret Jesus' prayer. This combined with the pronoun τις, "a certain one," implies that this one might be different from "some of the bystanders." A paraphrase would be: "Some of the bystanders, when they heard this, laughed and said, 'Hey, listen to that! He's calling Elijah.' But another one of them, running over and filling a sponge full of sour wine..."

2. The verb "to give to drink" (ποτίζω) is used positively by Jesus earlier in the story: "Whoever gives you a cup of water to drink because you bear the name of Christ will by no means lose the reward" (9:41, NRSV). The soldiers' attempt to offer wine to Jesus prior to his crucifixion (15:23) is the one element of the preparations that has no implication of mockery. The connotations of "sour wine" (ὄξος) are not necessarily negative since it was a popular beverage for the lower classes.[17]

---

15. Cf. Str-B, 1042.
16. See Chariton, *Callirhoe*, 4.6.
17. BDAG, 715.

3. Circumstantial participles in an introduction are usually used in a positive context. The only prior instance of this construction in the PRN is in the introduction to the anointing of Jesus with the ointment (14:3), where it concretizes the surprise of the woman's action: συντρίψασα τὴν ἀλάβαστον, "breaking the neck of the alabaster." In this colon about the sour wine, there are three circumstantial participles that create a crescendo leading up to his statement: δραμών, "running," γεμίσας, "filling," περιθείς, "putting." This construction usually leads up to something good.

There are also some negative associations implicit in the description of the wine giver. First, the introduction includes an allusion to Psalm 69:20 (68:22, LXX): "I looked for pity, but there was none; and for comforters, but I found none. They gave me poison for food, and for my thirst they gave me vinegar to drink." Mark's narration in Greek repeats two key words from the psalm:

> and for my thirst they gave me **sour wine to drink**
>
> καὶ εἰς τὴν δίψαν μου ἐπότισάν με ὄξους (Ps 68:22, LXX)
>
> And someone running and filling a sponge with **sour wine** and putting it on a stick, held it up for him **to drink**
>
> δραμὼν δέ τις [καὶ] γεμίσας σπόγγον ὄξους περιθεὶς καλάμῳ ἐπότιζεν αὐτόν. (15:36)

This psalm is a first-person lament describing in great detail the hostility shown to a righteous sufferer by personal enemies in the community of Israel. The allusion to the psalm created by the wording of the narrative sets the action and the statement of this bystander in the context of the denial of comfort to a righteous sufferer and suggests that both the action and the words are meant as a taunt. The composer of Mark's story assumed that the listeners would recognize the psalm and catch the allusion.[18]

The second negative association with the wine giver is that the word "reed, cane, staff" (καλάμῳ) is associated with the soldiers' hostile mockery of Jesus (15:19): "and they struck his head with a cane (καλάμῳ)." The memory of this earlier use of a κάλαμος reinforces the negative association of the allusion to the psalm. Furthermore, the soldiers tried to give Jesus wine before they crucified him.

The statement of the bystander, "Wait, let's see if Elijah will come and take him down," builds on a motif in the earlier taunts by those who mock

---

18. Lindars, *New Testament Apologetic*, 100 assumes this negative meaning: "The fact that the offer of vinegar is meant in a hostile sense is shown by its close connection with the taunt about Elijah."

The Death and Burial of Jesus (15:33–47)

Jesus (i.e., the repeated challenge of the passers-by and chief priests that he come down from the cross [15:30, 32]). It also builds on the mishearing of the other bystanders who say that Jesus is calling Elijah (15:35), a statement that Mark told as a mocking taunt. Thus, the storyteller may have reported the preparations of the wine giver hopefully. If so, the taunting tone of the wine giver's words is a reversal of the expectations generated by the introduction. Indeed, the wine giver's first word is associated with the taunting of the chief priests and scribes. Thus, the opening hortatory subjective construction, "Wait, let's see . . ." (Ἄφετε ἴδωμεν), is addressed to the others at the foot of the cross and takes the same tone as the statement of the chief priests addressed to the scribes with them: "Let the Messiah, the king of Israel, come down" (15:32, NRSV). This climactic taunt, just before the description of Jesus' death, may have been accompanied by taunting laughter in the original telling of this story.

But what sense did it make for a bystander to give Jesus wine in order to see whether Elijah was coming? The implication of Jesus' cry of dereliction is that he was near death. Since thirst was one of the causes of death by crucifixion, a little wine might keep him alive a little longer. And the bystander's first word, "Wait," implies that he is trying to slow down the death process a little. After all, if Jesus dies right away, there will be no time for Elijah to come and take him down. Thus, in this story of raised and dashed hopes this bystander offers the final hope that Jesus will get a last-minute reprieve or at least will experience some compassion. But the conclusion here is that Mark told the wine giver's words as the witnesses' last joke on the dying Jesus.

Thus, any possibility that this last action by the bystanders might be a note of compassion is immediately dashed. Jesus dies. The formula with which Jesus' death is introduced, "But Jesus" (ὁ δὲ Ἰησοῦς), is always adversative and is used to introduce responses that are in contrast to what was previously expected or initiated (see e.g., 14:6, 20, 62; 15:2b). In this case, the possibility that Jesus would drink the wine because he was thirsty (as in John's version of the story, John 19:28–30) and possibly hang on a bit longer is broken. Instead, the phrase "But Jesus" (ὁ δὲ Ἰησοῦς) introduces the fulfillment of Jesus' vow of abstinence.

37: Jesus' final cry and death

Jesus' loud cry is a sonic connection with the introduction to his prayer from Psalm 21 (LXX):

15:34 Jesus cried out with a loud cry (ἐβόησεν ὁ Ἰησοῦς φωνῇ μεγάλῃ)

15:37 But Jesus giving a loud cry (ὁ δὲ Ἰησοῦς ἀφεὶς φωνὴν μεγάλην)

This repetition of the words introducing Jesus' cry of agony reinforces the connotations and the volume of Jesus' prayer and the intense sympathy it invited. Thus, the climactic words, "giving a loud cry," were spoken loudly. The implication is that Jesus' response to this final act of spite against him is to refuse the wine, to cry out, and die. Jesus remained faithful to his vow of abstinence from "the fruit of the vine" (14:25) to the end and demonstrated thereby his strength and courage. The last word of the simple, short period naming Jesus' death, ἐξέπνευσεν ("breathed out his last"), has the quality of onomatopoeia with the volume of the loud cry followed by this word, which sounds like a last breath.[19]

38: the implied meanings of the tearing of the Temple curtain

The final three periods in this section of Mark's story describe the responses to Jesus' death—first by God, then by the centurion, and finally by the women who came up to Jerusalem with Jesus. God's response is a simple and relatively short period. The precise significance of this first response, the tearing of the Temple curtain, is shrouded in ambiguity. The tearing of garments was a gesture of grief in ancient Israel, and that is its primary association here. The gesture of tearing the garments is also the climax of the Sanhedrin trial, and some have suggested that the tearing of the Temple curtain is thereby associated with judgment as well as grief. However, if Mark wanted to make the connection to the high priest's act of judgment, he would have used the same word in both places. Instead, as the climax of the trial, Mark says that the high priest "rent his garments" (διαρρήξας τοὺς χιτῶνας αὐτοῦ—14:63), and the phrase here is "torn in two from top to bottom" (ἐσχίσθη εἰς δύο ἀπ' ἄνωθεν ἕως κάτω—15:38). Others have suggested that the tearing of the curtain symbolizes the elimination of the barrier between people and God; but there is no implication of this theological motif in the tearing of the curtain in Mark's story. Therefore, the verbal thread with the baptism is the most important clue to Mark's meaning:

> . . . he saw the heavens **torn open** and the Spirit like a dove descending on him

---

19. Lee and Scott, *Sound Mapping*, 210–11.

... εἶδεν **σχιζομένους** τοὺς οὐρανοὺς καὶ τὸ πνεῦμα ὡς περιστερὰν καταβαῖνον εἰς αὐτόν (1:10, NRSV)

And the curtain of the temple **was torn** in two, from top to bottom.

Καὶ τὸ καταπέτασμα τοῦ ναοῦ **ἐσχίσθη** εἰς δύο ἀπ' ἄνωθεν ἕως κάτω. (15:38, NRSV)

The implication of the tearing of the Temple curtain is that God responds sympathetically and grieved at Jesus' death. God had not forsaken Jesus but was present throughout Jesus' ordeal as a Father watching his beloved Son die.

The rending of the Temple curtain is also another instance of indirect communication of inside information to the audience that is not known to the characters of the story, in this instance, Jesus. The implication of Jesus' singing the song of the righteous sufferer—"My God, my God, why have you forsaken me?"—is that he felt that God had abandoned him and left him alone. Indeed, Jesus dies with those words on his lips. The tearing of the curtain is God's immediate response. As a result, the audience knows what Jesus did not know. God had not abandoned him but was present with him in his suffering and death.

The sympathetic character of God's action is heightened by its contrast to the response of the bystanders following Jesus' cry of dereliction (15:35–36). In fact, since the time of Jesus' condemnation by Pilate, everyone, with the exception of Simon of Cyrene, has been against him: the soldiers, the passersby, the authorities, those crucified with him, and, in this story of Jesus' death, those standing at the foot of the cross. The audience's sympathy for Jesus has grown since the time of the soldiers' mocking, and it finds its first expression in God's tearing of the Temple curtain. Most important, God's point of view is decisively shown. God is for and with Jesus.

39: the centurion's response of recognition and honor

The response of the centurion is the second response to Jesus' death. The connotations of the initial introduction to the centurion's statement are negative. As the Roman officer in charge of the execution, he is directly responsible for Jesus' death. The centurion is Jesus' executioner. Furthermore, he is standing at the foot of the cross, as were the taunters in the previous episode with all the negative associations with them. Finally, the phrase usually translated "opposite, facing him," ἐξ ἐναντίας αὐτοῦ, uses an adjective that means "against, contrary to" (as in the description of the wind "against" the disciples in the boat [6:48]), and is always used in contexts of hostility or opposition elsewhere in the New Testament (e.g., Matt 14:24; Acts 27:4; 28:17; 1 Thess 2:15; Titus 2:8). Thus, the initial connotations of the description of the centurion reinforce the expectation that his response will be hostile. After all, the soldiers under his command mocked Jesus, crucified him, and took his clothes.

The conclusion of the narrator's introduction describes what the centurion saw: "that in this way he breathed his last" (ὅτι οὕτως ἐξέπνευσεν). This is an inside view that has the same storytelling effect as the inside view of Pilate's "wonder" at Jesus' silence. In both instances, the inside view reverses the alienating dynamics of distance in the previous characterization.

This description of the centurion's perceptions refers back to the way in which Jesus died: prayed in a loud voice, refused the wine, gave a loud cry, and breathed out. The implication of the storyteller's description of Jesus' death is that he refused the wine again just as he had done before he was fastened to the cross. And the listeners know that Jesus was keeping the vow of abstinence from wine he had taken at his last meal. In addition to its connection with the vows of abstinence from eating unclean foods in the stories of the Maccabean martyrs, Jesus' vow of abstinence was also associated with the vows of soldiers during war, such as Uriah's vow of abstinence (2 Sam 11:6–13). For a soldier such as the centurion, who often saw men die, Mark's implication is that the centurion recognized the courage and strength evident in Jesus' cries and in his persistent refusal of the consolation of wine.

This sympathetic reference to how Jesus died as the conclusion of the introduction to the centurion's speech rules out the possibility that the centurion's statement was told as a final taunt, ironic in tone: "Truly, **this** man was Son of God?!"[20] Furthermore, the immediate context of the centurion's response is the sympathetic responses to Jesus' death by God and the women. And it is a climax to the motif of the Gentiles that is introduced in the first half of the gospel (5:1–20; 7:24—8:26) and developed further in the prophetic demonstration in the Temple (11:15–19). Mark's report of the centurion's response is another instance of the conversion of Gentile executioners in the tradition of the martyrs of Israel as in Daniel and 3 Maccabees (Dan 3:28; 6:24; 3 Macc 6:20–29).

The centurion's words, therefore, reverse the expectations established for the audience by the PRN as a whole and by the first phrase of the introduction to his words. The adverb "truly" has been used earlier only by the bystanders who recognized Peter as a Galilean (14:70), and carries the connotation of certain identification. The centurion's response echoes

---

20. For an excellent explication of this possibility, see Fowler, *Let the Reader Understand*, 202–9.

The Death and Burial of Jesus (15:33–47)

God's words at the baptism and transfiguration. The baptism ends with the voice from heaven saying, "You are my Beloved Son" (Σὺ εἶ ὁ υἱός μου ὁ ἀγαπητός—1:11). And the voice from the cloud at the transfiguration says, "This is my Son whom I love" (οὗτός ἐστιν ὁ υἱός μου ὁ ἀγαπητός—9:7 [NIV]). The centurion's response to what he sees is, "Truly this man was son of God." (Ἀληθῶς οὗτος ὁ ἄνθρωπος υἱὸς θεοῦ ἦν—15:39 [NIV]).

This statement by a Roman centurion in the aftermath of the Judean–Roman War had far-reaching resonance for predominantly Judean audiences. In effect, this statement implies Jesus' victory over Roman claims of divine identity and authority for the emperors. The Roman Senate had established the tradition of the apotheosis or deification of the emperors of Rome by its designation of Julius Caesar as *Divus Iulius* in 42 BCE. Octavian, Caesar's nephew, began calling himself *Divi filius,* "son of God" as a way of promoting his status, during the Second Triumvirate, the rule of Rome by the three Caesarians: Marc Antony, Marcus Aemilius Lepidus, and Octavian. Octavian, later named Augustus, even displayed this title on his coins.[21] Vespasian, who was emperor from 69 to 79 CE, during the probable period of the composition and initial performances of Mark's gospel, used the imperial cult as a means to establish his authority. Both he and his son, Titus, were declared divine after their deaths, and Domitian, Vespasian's youngest son, who was Emperor from 81 to 96 CE, demanded that he be addressed as *dominus et deus,* master and god.

Thus, the Roman imperial religion was a major presence in the Greco-Roman world of the late first century. It is possible that members of Mark's audiences heard the centurion's statement in different ways. Some of Mark's listeners may have heard the centurion's words to mean that he recognized Jesus as a son of God alongside the emperors past and present rather than as the one and only Son of God in the monotheistic tradition of Israel's religion. But many would have heard this as meaning that the centurion saw Jesus as "**the** Son of God." Mark's intent in using this phrase is reflected in the words of the voice from heaven at Jesus' baptism, "You are my beloved Son" (1:11), which forms with the centurion's statement a "rounding" frame for the whole gospel. But, regardless of its specific meaning, the centurion's statement was a major reversal of expectations and a highly charged political and religious sign of the power of Jesus' death. His statement is a sign that Jesus by his death has won the victory of the religion of Israel over the ideology and religion of Roman imperial power.[22] That implication of Mark's story

---

21. See *Wikipedia*: "Julius Caesar," "Second Triumvirate," "Gaius Octavian," "Augustus."

22 Brown (*Death of the Messiah*, 2:1149) rejects the proposal that this would have been heard "over against the Roman solider's allegiance to the emperor: 'This man, not

took another three centuries to finally be recognized and established by the abolition of the imperial cult during the reign of Theodosius I (387–395 CE) and the establishment of Christianity as the official religion of the Roman Empire. The officer of the army of the Gentiles has seen the truth.

40–41: the women witnesses who mourned Jesus' death

The story of Jesus' death ends with the description of the company of women who had come up to Jerusalem with him and were watching his death from a distance. This is surprising because there has been no earlier notice of the presence of women with Jesus and his disciples in Galilee or during their trip up to Jerusalem that began at the latest with their journey to Judea (10:1). While all of these women are shrouded in mystery in Mark's story, their presence on Golgotha is the first notice since the arrest and flight of the disciples and Peter's denial that any of Jesus' companions from Galilee were with him during his trials and execution. The description of the women is a direct address to the audience by the storyteller.

This concluding long, slow period has the rhythm of a dirge or lament and implies that the women were grieving. It is an appropriate climax to Mark's description of the responses of the witnesses of Jesus' death.[23] The litany of the names of the three women gives each of them a separate colon in which the audience has time to imagine their faces and their times with Jesus in Galilee.

The name of only one of the three women has been heard earlier in the story: "Mary, the mother of James the younger and Joses" (Μαρία ἡ

Caesar, is the Son of God.'" (thus Bligh, "Note," 53). This is an instance in which the implications of what Mark's postwar audiences would have heard are subject to debate. The possibility that Mark's audiences were predominantly Judean who did not believe in Jesus as Messiah rather than Gentiles who were members of believing communities and, therefore, were more prone to hear anti-imperial implications may be a new component in the debate.

23. The dominance of source criticism and the preoccupation with looking for the disjunctures in Mark's story are reflected in the editorial arrangement of this story in recent English translations (RSV, NRSV, NIV, GNT, NEB). In all these translations, the story of the women is separated from the tearing of the Temple curtain and the centurion's declaration as a distinct paragraph. In the NEB it is even separated by a full space and given a heading indicating it as the beginning of a new story. This is a reflection of a source-critical conclusion that this was a Markan editorial inclusion of a separate pre-Markan source that is essentially unrelated to what comes before and after this notice. A performance-criticism analysis reveals that this is the climax of the responses to Jesus' death and is a fully integral conclusion of the story of Jesus' death. This editing of the story is an inappropriate use of source criticism that profoundly changes the impact of the ending.

The Death and Burial of Jesus (15:33–47)

Ἰακώβου τοῦ μικροῦ καὶ Ἰωσῆτος μήτηρ—15:40). We discussed the significance of the way this Mary is named in the Notes on Details and Translation above. The implication of these names is that James is the younger (literally little) brother of Jesus, and that this Mary is Jesus' mother! This implication depends on Mark's listeners' remembering the story of Jesus' teaching in the Nazareth synagogue, where the people say, "Isn't this the carpenter, the son of Mary, and the brother of James and Joses and Judas and Simon?" (ὁ υἱὸς τῆς Μαρίας καὶ ἀδελφὸς Ἰακώβου καὶ Ἰωσῆτος καὶ Ἰούδα καὶ Σίμωνος—6:3).

This conclusion seems initially improbable. Why would Mark refer to Jesus' mother in such an indirect manner? Why not simply say "Jesus' mother?" The answer is that this is Mark's characteristic manner of storytelling. He frequently forces his audience to makes connections such as those. In making the connection with the Nazareth story, the listeners may also remember the other story involving Mary, where she and his brothers are standing outside sending for him (3:31–35 which explicitly names "his mother"; also the introduction to this section in which "his family" came to get him: 3:21). In a manner characteristic of Mark's style, that story brackets the story of the Jerusalem scribes' accusation that Jesus accomplishes his healings in league with Beelzebul, the prince of demons (3:22–30). Prior to this, therefore, there is only one time Jesus' mother was actively present in the story, and in that earlier appearance she shared her family's view that Jesus was crazy and came to take him home.

In contrast, here after Jesus' death, the description of the women, including his mother Mary, is wholly positive in its connotations. The verb "to follow" (ἀκολουθέω), is always a good action (see e.g., 14:54). Galilee is the place of Jesus' early triumphs and the verb "to serve" is used to describe the angels in the wilderness (1:13), Peter's mother-in-law (1:31) after her healing, and the Son of man (10:45). The storyteller's report that women followed Jesus and served him in Galilee is, first of all, a surprise because no women among the band of the disciples have ever been mentioned earlier in the story. Nevertheless, this report evokes the memories of the Galilean ministry and the journey to Jerusalem. If the presence of his mother is implied, this description also implies that she changed her mind about her son.

And how do women respond to seeing the death of a man whom they have followed and, by implication, loved? They mourn. Once again, Mark only implies the grieving of the women. The implication is typical of Israelite martyr stories. The climactic reference to the mother is a major motif in the story of the seven sons killed by Antiochus IV Epiphanes (2 Macc 7:20–29). This direct address to the audience is, therefore, an indirect description of Jesus' mourners: his mother, two women to whom he was close, and many other women who had come up to Jerusalem with him. At the end, the entire story of Jesus' crucifixion and death is seen from their perspective.

It is also worthy of note that in these closing periods of the story of Jesus' death, Mark alludes to the presence of and the grieving responses of Jesus' heavenly father and of his earthly mother. These allusions frame the declaration of Jesus as "Son of God" by the Roman officer in charge of Jesus' crucifixion.

The Performance of the Story

The setting of the deep darkness over the land can be dramatized by a gesture of descending night and a tone of the darkest night. The tolling of the hours can be done with a deep chime or bell. The presentation of Jesus' cry invites the storyteller to embody his cry and to present him crucified before the audience. Whether or not to spread the arms in the position of a crucified one is a judgment call. My sense is that Mark probably did use that gesture and invites us to follow his implicit direction. The storyteller explicitly names the volume of Jesus' cry so there can be no mistake about his directions to make it loud. The translation of Jesus' cry from Aramaic into Greek and later into English, however, is a direct address to the audience and is spoken in a softer and more intimate tone. This is also an opportunity for you as the storyteller to express your feeling about what you are reporting. This episode is the supreme appeal for sympathetic identification with Jesus as a man suffering desolation and abandonment.

The tone of the bystanders' misidentification of Jesus' cry as directed to Elijah rather than God is probably a joke accompanied by laughter. The introduction to one bystander's wine offering can be told sympathetically in order to increase the bitterness of his mockery. The shift from a sympathetic introduction to the mocking tone of his taunt is hard to do. It helps to make the pause between the introductory colon and the mocker's words a little longer. Jesus' refusal of the wine can be presented with a turning away from the sponge or slight shaking of the head as the gesture that accompanies Jesus' name and the loud cry. It is fully appropriate to breathe out a last breath and have a moment of silence before going on to the responses.

The tearing of the Temple curtain invites the gesture of tearing the garments in grief. A Roman military salute of the fist to the heart is the gesture for the centurion's declaration of divine honor. The centurion's voice is a tough, commanding voice. The gesture for the long and slow description of the women's mourning can be a steady beating of the chest. The pronouncement of their names has the tone of the recital of the names of the relatives of the deceased at a funeral. The storytelling dynamic is to invite the listeners to identify with the women as they witness Jesus' death.

The Burial of Jesus (15:42–47)

Sound Map

42Καὶ ἤδη ὀψίας γενομένης, ἐπεὶ ἦν παρασκευή, ὅ ἐστιν προσάββατον,
43ἐλθὼν Ἰωσὴφ ὁ ἀπὸ Ἀριμαθαίας εὐσχήμων βουλευτής,
ὃς καὶ αὐτὸς ἦν προσδεχόμενος τὴν βασιλείαν τοῦ θεοῦ,
τολμήσας εἰσῆλθεν πρὸς τὸν Πιλᾶτον
καὶ ᾐτήσατο τὸ σῶμα τοῦ Ἰησοῦ.
44ὁ δὲ **Πιλᾶτος ἐθαύμασεν εἰ** ἤδη **τέθνηκεν,**
καὶ προσκαλεσάμενος **τὸν κεντυρίωνα** ἐπηρώτησεν αὐτὸν
εἰ πάλαι **ἀπέθανεν,**
45καὶ γνοὺς ἀπὸ τοῦ **κεντυρίωνος** ἐδωρήσατο τὸ πτῶμα τῷ Ἰωσήφ.

46καὶ ἀγοράσας **σινδόνα** καθελὼν αὐτὸν ἐνείλησεν τῇ **σινδόνι**
καὶ **ἔθηκεν αὐτὸν** ἐν μνημείῳ ὃ ἦν λελατομημένον ἐκ πέτρας,
καὶ προσεκύλισεν **λίθον ἐπὶ τὴν θύραν τοῦ μνημείου.**
47ἡ δὲ **Μαρία ἡ Μαγδαληνὴ καὶ Μαρία ἡ Ἰωσῆτος** ἐθεώρουν **ποῦ τέθειται.**

Translation

42When evening had come, since it was the day of Preparation, that is,
the day before the sabbath,
43Joseph of Arimathea, a respected member of the council,
who was also waiting for the kingdom of God,
took courage and went to Pilate and asked for the body of Jesus.
44And **Pilate wondered if** he was already **dead**;
and summoning **the centurion**, he asked him **if he had** already
died,
45and having confirmed it from **the centurion**, he granted the
corpse to Joseph.

46And he bought **a linen cloth**, and taking him down,
he wrapped him **in the linen cloth**,
and **laid him** in a tomb that had been hewn out of the rock
and rolled **a stone against the door of the tomb**.
47**And Mary Magdalene and Mary the mother of Joses** saw where
the body was laid.

Notes on Details and Translation

15:42–46: the translation custom of dividing Mark's periods into multiple sentences

There are several elements of the translation of this story in the prevalent English translations that need to be modified for performance. Mark's periods in this story need to be preserved in translation rather than divided into separate sentences. The NIV separates the descriptions of Joseph of Arimathea going to Pilate and the burial of Jesus into two discrete sentences, and the NRSV has two sentences for the burial. Mark's purpose in creating these long periods, with three or four cola each, is to create the atmosphere of a funeral. They are long and slow in order to communicate the passage of considerable time and the solemnity of the burial. Dividing them into several sentences eliminates the somber rhythm of Mark's cadences.

43: took courage / τολμήσας

The description of Joseph of Arimathea's going to Pilate is an act of courage because of the risk that he might be painted with the same brush as Jesus. Mark uses this term earlier as a description of the absence of internal courage in the conclusion of Jesus' dialogue with the good scribe: "After that no one dared (ἐτόλμα, had the courage) to ask him any question" (12:34, NRSV). The risk in both instances is public shame. That he went "boldly" (NRSV, NIV) carries the implication that he was aggressive but does not convey the risk involved. The RSV translation, "took courage," conveys the primary meaning of this word and more accurately conveys the dynamic of Joseph's interior decision and the external risk.

45: body, corpse / σῶμα, πτῶμα

Mark creates a contrast between Joseph's request for Jesus' body and Pilate's granting it. The word Mark uses for Joseph's request is σῶμα while the word for Pilate's assent is πτῶμα. The word σῶμα is Jesus' word for his body at the anointing at Bethany (14:8) and at the Last Supper (14:22). It has positive connotations. On the other hand, πτῶμα means "corpse," and its only prior use is in the description of the disciples of John the Baptist recovering the decapitated corpse of their leader (6:29). In this instance, all the major English translations create a verbal connection by translating both words as "body" rather than preserving the distinction Mark makes. As we will see,

The Death and Burial of Jesus (15:33–47)

that change is an important dimension of this final characterization of Pilate as a cynical enemy.

44–45: already / ἤδη

According to the UBS fourth edition of the Greek New Testament, Mark changes adverbs in narrating, first, Pilate's internal wondering whether Jesus was already dead (15:44), and, second, his external question to the centurion concerning the time of Jesus' death (15:45). According to the preferred reading of the UBS text, Pilate wondered if Jesus was ἤδη, "already" dead, and, therefore, asks the centurion (v. 45) whether he had been dead πάλαι, "for some time" (NRSV). But there are two variants in the textual tradition of Mark for the adverb in 15:45. The reading πάλαι is well attested (Sinaiticus, Alexandrinus, and a long list of uncial and miniscule manuscripts), but so also is ἤδη (Vaticanus, Bezae, and two other uncial and one miniscule manuscripts). The editors of the UBS fourth edition have chosen πάλαι, probably because the textual evidence is slightly stronger, and they have given it a *B* rating in their ranking of certainty. But πάλαι is awkward here because its primary meaning is "long ago, formerly," and the efforts to translate it are wordy and misleading. The NRSV translates it "for some time," and the GNT has, "a long time." In the story Jesus could not have been dead for more than three hours and probably less, so it was not long. In this case, my conclusion is that it is more likely that Mark was creating a sonic echo here, and that the adverb he used was ἤδη, the alternative variant to πάλαι. In other words, he uses ἤδη twice, just as he does in the feeding of the five thousand (6:35). For this reason I would argue that ἤδη is the preferred reading here. The proposed translation is, "And Pilate wondered if he was *already* dead; and summoning the centurion, he asked him if he had *already* died."

Comments on the Meaning and Impact of the Story

42: the time of the burial

The story of Jesus' burial begins with a new notice of the time, "evening." What time is implied for the burial? Jesus died shortly after 3 p.m., so it was between roughly 3:15 and sunset.[24] The picture in the story is that Joseph of

---

24. It is helpful to repeat here (see commentary on "Crucifixion and Mocking") Brown's clarification of the meaning of ὀψίας: "Jewish law would have the crucified taken down and buried before sunset, which would mark the beginning of another day. By narrative flow, then, the setting is somewhere between 3 P.M. and sunset. In itself

Arimathea went to Pilate early enough in the evening that there was time for Pilate to send for the centurion and have a short meeting, for Joseph to buy a shroud and take Jesus down from the cross and lay him in the tomb before the Sabbath began at sundown. Given that sundown in late March or early April was sometime between 7 and 7:30 p.m., these things could have been done in two hours or so since the distances were around a quarter mile. Thus, "evening" here refers to sometime around 5 p.m. The implication of Mark's story is that the time of the day made the burial urgent.

This explanation is another indication of Mark's projected audiences. The day is named twice, "the day of preparation, that is, the day before the Sabbath." The appositive explanation implies that some in the audiences would not know what the term, "day of Preparation," (παρασκευή) meant. This comment addresses the ignorance of Judean practices by Gentiles in potential audiences, just as the earlier explanation of Israelite purity laws had been made for Gentiles in the audience (7:3-4). However, Mark also assumes that he does not need to explain that the imminence of the Sabbath means that Jesus needs to be buried before sundown. This may imply that Mark assumes that his audiences would know Israelite law, which required hanged bodies to be buried before sundown: "When someone is convicted of a crime punishable by death and is executed, and you hang him on a tree, his corpse must not remain all night upon the tree; you shall bury him that same day, for anyone hung on a tree is under God's curse" (Deut 21:22-23). It may also be that everyone in Mark's projected audiences would have known that bodies needed to be buried lest they become carrion for birds.

Given general audience knowledge of Judean observance of the Sabbath, the body had to be buried before sundown on Friday, or it could not be taken off the cross until Saturday after sundown because the transport of the body would constitute work. Vultures and other birds such as crows that fed on carrion ate dead bodies on crosses. As Juvenal says in his *Satires* (14.77-78), "The vulture hurries from dead cattle and dogs and crosses to bring some of the carrion to her offspring."[25] The composer of the gospel assumes that the gory details of crucifixion were common knowledge. Thus, while Mark assumes that some in the potential audiences of his story

opsia does not convey precise information about relationship to the opening of the next day" (*Death of the Messiah*, 2:1211-12). In a footnote Brown cites two passages where qualifying phrases fix the time, placing "evening" after the setting of the sun (1:32) and after the time of the meal, which would have been eaten only after sunset (14:17). However, in the Last Supper story, there is an implied distinction between the time of the journey into the city and the meal. The implication is that they walked the two miles to Jerusalem from Bethany in the evening before sunset and celebrated the Passover after sunset.

25. Juvenal, *Juvenal and Persius*, 271.

would not know technical terms for Sabbath, he also assumes that everyone, Judeans and Gentiles, will know about Judean Sabbath observance and the fate of crucified corpses.

43–46: the dynamics of distance in the characterization of Joseph of Arimathea

The characterization of Joseph of Arimathea is, in the end, positive. But the dynamics of the characterization are similar to the characterization dynamics of the centurion. Mark's first description of Joseph as "a respected member of the council" has negative connotations. In the earlier description of the trial before the Sanhedrin, Jesus was condemned as worthy of death by "all" (14:64). If Joseph is a "respected" member of the Sanhedrin, the implication is that he had joined in this verdict. However, Mark's report that he was looking for the kingdom of God implies that he shared the eschatological hope of Jesus. This further implies that he may not have joined in the condemnation of Jesus. There is no implication here that Joseph was a secret disciple, as John later developed the story (John 19:38). But this notice is a surprise and a reversal of expectations for a member of the Sanhedrin establishment. This also may be the reason Mark uses, for the only time in his story, the term βουλευτής, "council" rather than συνέδριον, "Sanhedrin" (14:55; 15:1), since the latter has highly negative connotations. Furthermore, Joseph's willingness to risk opposition and perhaps recrimination is implied in the inside view of his courage (τολμήσας) in going to Pilate and asking for the body of Jesus. While his status in the ruling establishment gives him some protection, he is the first friend of Jesus' movement who acts with courage in the whole story. The overall dynamic is a movement from the first term in the description of Joseph, which initially suggests that he is an adversary of Jesus, to both a sympathetic description ("who was also waiting for the kingdom of God"—15:43) and a supremely kind act that entails some significant risk to himself.

As has been noted above, Joseph's request is for the body (σῶμα) of Jesus, the same word used earlier by Jesus (14:8,22). This request is a reversal of the pattern of actions against Jesus, which has been prevalant since his arrest. Because of the prevalence of crucifixion in the cities of the Roman Empire, Mark's audiences probably knew that without Joseph's intervention, Jesus' naked body could have been left to be picked apart on the cross by scavenger birds or, if taken down by soldiers, simply thrown into a common grave in the Jerusalem dump near Golgotha. Joseph's response to Jesus' death is in direct continuity with the sympathetic witnesses to Jesus' death: God, the centurion, the women, and now Joseph (15:38–40).

44: Pilate's "wondering"

Pilate's response to Joseph is an inside view of Pilate's internal thoughts rather than a summary, in indirect discourse, of what Pilate said to Joseph. Just as Pilate "wondered" at Jesus' silence in response to Pilate's own second interrogation (15:5), so also here Pilate "wonders" if Jesus is already dead. The verb "to die" here is in the perfect tense (τέθνηκεν), which conveys the sense of a past event that continues in a present state or condition.[26] Thus, Mark reports what Pilate was wondering (in my own paraphrase): "I wonder if he is already dead. It's pretty quick." Because of what has already been reported, the listeners know that Jesus is dead. The inside view of Pilate's thoughts is, therefore, alienating rather than positive. Pilate's response to Joseph's request is set in an adversarial context. In contrast to Mithridates' saving Chaeraes from death, (see comment above on 15:30), Pilate wants to make sure that Jesus is really dead before granting Joseph's request. Joseph is the protagonist, and Pilate has once again returned to his role as the Roman antagonist. This is not a pro-Roman characterization.

44–45: Pilate and the centurion

The summoning of the centurion recalls the centurion's testimony after Jesus' death. The associations with the centurion are relatively positive but associations with Pilate are not. Pilate's question is reported in indirect discourse and continues the hostile tone of his internal wondering. The use of the aorist tense here (ἀπέθανεν) frames his question as looking back to the punctiliar moment of death: "if he had already died." Pilate is presented, therefore, as resisting Joseph's request until the centurion's confirmation of Jesus' death. The implication is that Pilate wanted to make sure that Jesus was dead. Pilate's attitude here reflects Roman attitudes toward the victims of Roman sport. In the Circus Maximus (first constructed in the sixth century BCE) and later in the Coliseum (begun in 70 CE and completed in 80 CE during the same period as the composition and early performance of Mark's gospel), gladiators fought to the death and conquered peoples were thrown to wild beasts. At the end of each event, soldiers checked out the victims to make certain that each was dead. If not, the victim would be

---

26. Cf. BDF, #341; see also MHT, 3:82–85.

dispatched with a quick thrust of the sword. Pilate also wants to be sure that Jesus is truly dead, and only then does he grant Jesus' "corpse" to Joseph.

The granting of Joseph's request is once again reported in indirect discourse. The implication is that Pilate used the word "corpse" (πτῶμα), with its starkly different connotations instead of Joseph's word, "body." Joseph asks for Jesus' "body" and Pilate gives him Jesus' "corpse."

15:1–15:45: the dynamics of distance in the characterization of Pilate

This episode is the end of the characterization of Pilate in Mark's story. The storyteller establishes a complex distance relationship between his audiences and Pilate. Pilate is introduced as the representative of the Gentiles and an enemy of Jesus and the Israelites by the connection between Jesus' final passion prophecy and the introduction to the Pilate trial. Thus, Jesus' final passion prophecy is: "and they (*the chief priests and scribes*) *will hand him over to the Gentiles* and they will mock him, and spit upon him and flog him and kill him" (10:33–34). And the introduction to the Pilate trial is, "*the chief priests*, elders, *scribes* and the whole Sanhedrin bound Jesus, led him away, and *handed him over to Pilate*" (15:1). Mark substitutes "Pilate" for "the Gentiles." Pilate's initial questions (15:2, 4) to Jesus parallel the questions of the chief priest (14:60, 61) at the Sanhedrin trial and carry, therefore, the antagonistic associations of that earlier interrogation. The initial dynamics of emotional distance for the audience in relation to Pilate are, therefore, strongly alienating.

In contrast, Pilate's wondering, his offer to release Jesus, and his questions to the crowd are a highly positive reversal of expectations that create a sympathetic lessening of aesthetic distance in relation to Pilate as a character. But the inside view of his crassly political motive for the unjust condemnation of Jesus to flogging and crucifixion, "wanting to satisfy the crowd," and the detailed fulfillment of Jesus' prophecy of his treatment by the Gentiles reestablishes and even heightens the initial alienation from Pilate.

This complex relationship to Pilate is then the context for this distinctive story of Mark.[27] Pilate's desire to make sure that Jesus is dead confirms

---

27. This story of Joseph's going to Pilate and asking for Jesus' body, like the story of the young man who fled naked at Jesus' arrest (14:51–52), is not present in the other three gospels. Brown has the most comprehensive survey of the proposed explanations for this difference in the gospel accounts (*Death of the Messiah*, 2:1219-22). The most prevalent suggestion is that the other evangelists did not know Mark's story, but that a post-Markan redactor, unknown therefore to Matthew, Luke, and John, added this

his alien status as a Gentile enemy like Antiochus IV Epiphanes and the armies of Rome. Thus, Pilate is characterized as an enemy who becomes sympathetic for a short time but who then becomes even more alien in his unjust and cynical actions. The characterization of Pilate is in no way pro-Roman apologetic.

46: the meaning of Joseph's burial

The description of the burial is a detailed factual account of Joseph's honorable burial of Jesus. This is a supremely kind act by Joseph. Jesus is given an honorable burial in a tomb rather than being thrown in a dump as often happened with the crucified. There are two sonic connections with the earlier story that shape its associations here. First, a "linen cloth" (σινδόνα) is the same word as the garment of the young man who left his linen garment and ran away naked (14:52). Its use here is thereby associated with the covering of Jesus' nakedness and shame. Second, the cynic who offered Jesus sour wine used the verb "to take down" (15:36) in reference to Elijah. Here the same word is used to describe Joseph's taking Jesus down from the cross. Joseph, not Elijah, takes Jesus down.

47: the two women at the burial

The conclusion of the burial is a description of two women from the group of mourners named at the climax of the story of Jesus' death. The two women are the first two named at the death site: Mary Magdalene and Mary, the mother of James the younger and Joses. The reference to Mary does not include the word "mother" but is an abbreviation (Μαρία ἡ 'Ιωσῆτος)[28] and a reference back to the earlier, more elaborate description, where she is

---

in order to create a second confirmation of Jesus' death for the apologetic purpose of establishing that his resurrection was not a mere resuscitation from a coma. Brown rejects this highly speculative proposal and concludes that an imperfect but better solution is that the later evangelists thought that even raising the question of the truth of Jesus' death by Pilate was unnecessary and could backfire. Therefore they omitted it. (ibid., 1222) My proposal is, in contrast also to Brown, that the dynamic of Mark's characterization of Pilate suggests that the later evangelists did not want to emphasize this negative characterization of Pilate and his final hostile attitude to Jesus and just left it out.

28. See BDF, #162 and 266(3) for the common practice of using the article, followed by a name in the genitive to designate a person who is in some way related to the named person. The context has to imply the relationship. In 15:47 the listeners know from the earlier mention of Mary that she is the mother of Joses. There the noun "mother" is explicit; here it is implied by the context.

called "Mary the mother of James the young and Joses" (Μαρία ἡ Ἰακώβου τοῦ μικροῦ καὶ Ἰωσῆτος μήτηρ—15:40). This again brings to the attentive listeners' memory the reference in 6:3 that Joses was a brother of Jesus, again implying that Mary is the mother of Jesus as well. The same verb, "to see, watch" (θεωρέω), that was used to describe the women watching Jesus die (15:40) is also used here. This time it is used as an inside view of what they saw: "where he was laid." In this characteristic indirect manner, Mark here invites the listeners to see Jesus' body in the tomb through the eyes of the two women who grieved his death and burial, one of whom was his mother. This reestablishment of the perspective of Jesus' mourners is the climax of the entire section. This notice reinforces the characterization of the women as highly sympathetic characters and reiterates the storyteller's invitation to identify with the women as the climax of the story of Jesus' death. Indeed, in the silence that concludes the story, the audience is invited to remember the entire preceding story of Jesus and his ministry in Galilee from the women's point of view.

The Performance of the Story

The first half of this story is told in the tone of the adversarial relationship between Judeans and Pilate that is assumed in the first introduction of Pilate at the opening of the trial. He is introduced there as the fulfillment of Jesus' prophecy that the Judean authorities would hand him over to the Gentiles, who would mistreat and kill him. Pilate has fulfilled that prophecy and continues that characterization of the Gentiles to the end.

The story begins in the slow tempo of a funeral march. This continues the pulse of the final period of the death story about the women mourners. The description of the time has three components: "evening," day of preparation, day before the Sabbath. It is the most complex description of the setting for a new event in the whole PRN. The explanation of the day of preparation as "the day before the Sabbath" is a gesture of help to audiences that include people who will not know this. It can be heightened by a gesture of inclusion, not unlike the welcome at a viewing.

The description of Joseph has the tone of the appearance of a surprising and unexpected friend. While there is no implied negative or critical tone in the naming of Joseph as a well-respected member of the council, he is identified as part of the group that condemned Jesus, creating initial possible apprehension in the listeners about what he might be up to. The notice that he was looking for the kingdom of God relieves any possible apprehension by establishing him as a positive character. So this needs to be told in a warm and friendly tone. The naming of his courage and request to Pilate is an opportunity to embody Joseph's resolute and dignified character.

The telling of Pilate's interrogation requires the storyteller to make a decision about whether to tell this indirect discourse of Pilate in the tone and attitude of the storyteller or as an indirect expression of Pilate's tone and attitude. The choice of indirect discourse may be an indication that Mark told this as an expression of his own attitude. If he had wanted to express Pilate's tone, he would have used direct discourse and simply quoted him: "Is he already dead?" Therefore, in the storyteller's own voice, the tone can range from incredulous to critical. Identify your own attitude about Roman delight in violence and death and to the indifferent hostility to the hundreds of thousands of Judeans the Romans killed. The granting of the corpse suggests that a dismissive gesture of throwing it away will help to communicate Pilate's Roman disdain for crucified provincials.

The story of Joseph's burial of Jesus is totally sympathetic in tone and expresses the grief of the Markan storytellers. The identification of the tomb carved out of the rock can have a tone of honor. It is a funeral march in tone and tempo. The naming of Mary Magdalene and Mary the mother of Joses is affectionate in tone and is an indirect expression of their grief as they watched Jesus' burial. A gesture to the place where he was laid can enable the audience to see the place in their imagination. There is lots of time for the telling of this story and for the silence at its ending.

8

THE RESURRECTION (16:1–8)

THE CLIMACTIC SECTION OF THE PRN HAS ONLY ONE STORY and is the shortest section in the larger narrative. While there are some markers that sound like divisions between stories, the overall unity and climactic structure of the episodes are signs that it was composed and told as one story without major pauses between three short stories. The shortness of the section is congruent with the gradual shortening of the periods until the last two-word period. The composer of this story often builds climactic impact by shortening the periods. And in this final section he builds the climax of the gospel story by shortening the resurrection story.

This section flows seamlessly from the preceding section in which the women witnesses are the subject of the rounding periods at the end of the death and burial stories, as are the concluding periods in, for example, the stories of the Pilate trial and the mockery by the soldiers. The women now go into action. The audience's identification with the women in the climactic endings of the death and burial stories is the dynamic linkage to this final section of the gospel in which Jesus' concluding prophecy of resurrection is fulfilled. The response to that fulfillment in the young man's announcement, however, remains an open question for every listener beginning with the women. To paraphrase William Shakespeare, to tell or not to tell, that is the question.

Sound Map

1Καὶ διαγενομένου τοῦ σαββάτου **Μαρία ἡ Μαγδαληνὴ**
        καὶ **Μαρία ἡ [τοῦ] Ἰακώβου**
        καὶ **Σαλώμη**
ἠγόρασαν ἀρώματα ἵνα ἐλθοῦσαι ἀλείψωσιν αὐτόν.

2καὶ λίαν πρωῒ τῇ μιᾷ τῶν σαββάτων ἔρχονται **ἐπὶ τὸ μνημεῖον**
ἀνατείλαντος τοῦ ἡλίου.

3καὶ ἔλεγον πρὸς ἑαυτάς,
  Τίς **ἀποκυλίσει** ἡμῖν **τὸν λίθον** ἐκ τῆς θύρας **τοῦ μνημείου**;
4καὶ ἀναβλέψασαι θεωροῦσιν ὅτι **ἀποκεκύλισται ὁ λίθος**.
ἦν γὰρ μέγας σφόδρα.

5καὶ **εἰσελθοῦσαι εἰς τὸ μνημεῖον** εἶδον νεανίσκον
  καθήμενον ἐν τοῖς δεξιοῖς
  περιβεβλημένον στολὴν λευκήν,
  καὶ **ἐξεθαμβήθησαν**.
6ὁ δὲ λέγει αὐταῖς,
  Μὴ **ἐκθαμβεῖσθε**.

Ἰησοῦν ζητεῖτε τὸν Ναζαρηνὸν τὸν ἐσταυρωμένον.
ἠγέρθη.

οὐκ ἔστιν ὧδε.
ἴδε ὁ τόπος ὅπου ἔθηκαν αὐτόν.

7ἀλλὰ ὑπάγετε εἴπατε τοῖς μαθηταῖς αὐτοῦ καὶ τῷ Πέτρῳ ὅτι
  Προάγει ὑμᾶς εἰς τὴν Γαλιλαίαν.
ἐκεῖ αὐτὸν ὄψεσθε, **καθὼς εἶπεν ὑμῖν**.

8καὶ **ἐξελθοῦσαι** ἔφυγον ἀπὸ τοῦ μνημείου.
εἶχεν γὰρ αὐτὰς τρόμος καὶ ἔκστασις.

καὶ οὐδενὶ οὐδὲν εἶπαν.
ἐφοβοῦντο γάρ.

Translation

1When the sabbath was past, **Mary Magdalene, Mary the mother of James, and Salome**
  bought spices, so that they might go and anoint him.
2And very early on the first day of the week, they went out **to the tomb**
  as the sun was rising.

3And they were saying to one another,
  'Who will **roll away the stone** for us from the door **of the tomb**?'
4And looking up, they saw that **the stone had already been rolled back**!

The Resurrection (16:1–8)

Now it was a really big stone!

5 And **going into the tomb**, they saw a young man,
   sitting at the right hand
   clothed in a white robe,
   and **they were astonished.**
6 But he said to them, '**Do not be astonished.**

You are looking for Jesus of Nazareth, **who was crucified.**
He has been raised.

He is not here.
Look at the place **where they laid him.**

7 But go, tell his disciples and Peter,
   '**He is going ahead of you to Galilee.**
There you will see him, **just as he said to you.**'

8 And **they went out and fled from the tomb.**
For trembling and amazement had seized them.

And they said nothing to anyone.
For they were afraid.

Ancient Associations and Connections

The most important connections with the resurrection story are the political and religious reasons for the women's silence and fear with which the story ends. What reasons for the women's silence and fear would have occurred to Mark's audiences as they pondered their response to the implicit commission to tell the story?

In addition to the memories of the Judean–Roman War, the story of the great fire in Rome in 64 CE and Nero's persecution and killing of Christians was probably widely known in the late first century. There are two extant accounts of the great fire by Suetonius (69/72–130 CE) in *The Lives of the Twelve Caesars* and Tacitus (56–117 CE) in *The Annals,* both written in the early second century. Tacitus remembered the fire from his childhood, and Suetonius had ample sources for his history of the Caesars (Julius Caesar through Domitian) from eyewitnesses and official documents. Suetonius describes only the fire while Tacitus includes the subsequent persecution of Christians. Both recount the fire as an intentional act of Nero. Tacitus' description of Nero's placing the blame for the fire on "the Christians" and instituting a widespread persecution of the sect is the earliest historical information about Roman imperial persecution of the Judean sect that became Christianity, which continued intermittently until the reign of Constantine (306–337 CE). For Mark's listeners as early as 71–75 CE, this would have been a primary connection with the fear of the women. This radical persecution had happened only a decade or so prior to Mark's gospel and it is likely that this would have been a present memory for audiences of Mark.

Suetonius' account is as follows:[1]

> XXXVIII. He (Nero) spared, moreover, neither the people of Rome, nor the capital of his country. Somebody in conversation saying—
>
> *Emou thanontos gaia michthaeto pyri*
>
> When I am dead let fire devour the world—
>
> "Nay," said he, "let it be while I am living" [emou xontos]. And he acted accordingly: for, pretending to be disgusted with the old buildings, and the narrow and winding streets, he set the city on fire so openly, that many of consular rank caught his own household servants on their property with tow, and (368) torches in their hands, but durst not meddle with them. There being near his Golden House some granaries, the site of which he exceedingly coveted, they were battered as if with machines of war, and set on fire, the walls being built of stone. During six days and seven nights this terrible devastation continued, the people being obliged to fly to the tombs and monuments for lodging and shelter. Meanwhile, a vast number of stately buildings, the houses of generals celebrated in former times, and even then still decorated with the spoils of war, were laid in ashes; as well as the temples of the gods, which had been vowed and dedicated by the kings of Rome, and afterwards in the Punic and Gallic wars: in short, everything that was remarkable and worthy to be seen which time had spared [614]. This fire he beheld from a tower in the house of Mecaenas, and "being greatly delighted," as he said, "with the beautiful effects of the conflagration," he sang a poem on the ruin of Troy, in the tragic dress he used on the stage. To turn this calamity to his own advantage by plunder and rapine, he promised to remove the bodies of those who had perished in the fire, and clear the rubbish at his own

---

1. Suetonius, *Nero*, 38.118–22.

expense; suffering no one to meddle with the remains of their property. But he not only received, but exacted contributions on account of the loss, until he had exhausted the means both of the provinces and private persons.

Tacitus' documentation of the persecution of Christians at the time of the great fire of 64 CE in Rome is generally accepted as historically reliable and authentic.[2] Tacitus clearly regards Nero with hostility and disdain.

Mark's original audiences would not have known this particular account since it was composed some decades later. But the events described by Tacitus, in which it is implied that both men and women were killed, were known widely and would have been a present memory for Mark's listeners:

> But all human efforts, all the lavish gifts of the emperor, and the propitiations of the gods, did not banish the sinister belief that the conflagration was the result of an order. Consequently, to get rid of the report, Nero fastened the guilt and inflicted the most exquisite tortures on a class hated for their abominations, called Christians by the populace. Christus, from whom the name had its origin, suffered the extreme penalty during the reign of Tiberius at the hands of one of our procurators, Pontius Pilatus, and a most mischievous superstition, thus checked for the moment, again broke out not only in Judaea, the first source of the evil, but even in Rome, where all things hideous and shameful from every part of the world find their centre and become popular. Accordingly, an arrest was first made of all who pleaded guilty; then, upon their information, an immense multitude was convicted, not so much of the crime of firing the city, as of hatred against mankind. Mockery of every sort was added to their deaths. Covered with the skins of beasts, they were torn by dogs and perished, or were nailed to crosses, or were doomed to the flames and burnt, to serve as a nightly illumination, when daylight had expired.
>
> Nero offered his gardens for the spectacle, and was exhibiting a show in the circus, while he mingled with the people in the dress of a charioteer or stood aloft on a car. Hence, even for criminals who deserved extreme and exemplary punishment, there arose a feeling of compassion; for it was not, as it seemed, for the public good, but to glut one man's cruelty, that they were being destroyed.

---

2. Tacitus, *Ann.*, 15.44.

Thus, it is probable that the imperial persecution of Christians was widely known in the last decades of the first century and would have been known by Mark's audiences.

Notes on Details and Translation

16:1: Mary, the (mother) of James / καὶ Μαρία ἡ [τοῦ] Ἰακώβου

Once again Mark follows the practice common in Greek of employing the article in concord with the name to which it refers followed by a name in the genitive to designate a person who is in some way related to the named person. This elliptical way of speaking relies on the context to make clear the precise relationship. In 15:40 the noun "mother" made the relationship explicit.[3] This name, "Mary, of James," makes a sonic connection with "Mary, the mother of James and Joses," named as one of Jesus' mourners at the end of the death story (15:40). This same Mary was named then again at the end of the burial (15:47) as "Mary, of Joses." The deliberate artistry of Mark's storytelling style is evident in the way he varies his naming of her by naming both sons the first time, and then first one and then the other the two succeeding times. In each of these instances, Mark invites his listeners to remember the naming of Jesus' family by the synagogue community in Nazareth in Mark 6:3, where it was said explicitly that James and Joses were the brothers of Jesus. Even in the details of grammatical construction like this, Mark engages the audiences in filling in the gaps of the story. In this case, the implication of this ellipsis and sonic echo is that this woman is Jesus' mother.

2: And very early . . . when the sun had risen / καὶ λίαν πρωΐ . . . ἀνατείλαντος τοῦ ἡλίου

Mark introduces these notices of the time at the beginning and the end of the description of the women's going out to the tomb. This is the only time in Mark's entire story in which a description of the time is used at both the beginning and the end of a period: "*Very early on the first day of the week*, they went out to the tomb, *when the sun had risen*." The first colon evokes the visual image of the darkness just before dawn. The word πρωΐ names the early part of the daylight period, and the word λίαν pushes this time of early light to its beginnings. In the world of Mark's story, darkness descended just prior to Jesus' cry of abandonment (15:33). That time of darkness in

---

3. See BDF, #162 and #266(3).

the world of the story is continued in the first period, which describes the women going to buy the spices "when the Sabbath was passed," that is, in the postsundown darkness of the day after the Sabbath. Mark creates an image of the women getting up and setting out for the tomb, just as the darkness is beginning to give way to dawn.

Having invited his listeners to picture the women setting out in the predawn darkness, Mark ends the period with a notice that the sun had risen! This two-step progression is typical of Mark's style.[4] The effect for the audience is a storytelling moment of the emergence of the new day from the darkness to the rising of the sun. It is the first hint of the possibility that the prophecy of the resurrection has been fulfilled. Thus, Mark ends the period with the first intimation of the new light of the resurrection. It is the storytelling objective correlative of an Easter-morning sunrise service.

None of the major translations except the King James Version render this moment of the emerging light. Instead they pull "when the sun had risen" back into the setting of the scene to make it complete before narrating the action of the women. The NRSV, for example, translates 16:2 as follows: "And very early on the first day of the week, when the sun had risen, they went to the tomb." The NAB does the same: "Very early when the sun had risen, on the first day of the week, they came to the tomb." In this reordering of Mark's cola, there is no element of surprise in the emergence of the light during the women's journey to the tomb, and no gradual transition from the darkness of the night when they bought the spices to "very early" when they got up and set out for the tomb to the new light of "the risen sun." In the translation of this story, modern translators of this brief story have changed the order of Mark's cola because they have apparently not listened to the story and the rhetorical impact of Mark's ordering of the cola.

4b: Now it was really big! / ἦν γὰρ μέγας σφόδρα

This is a second instance of modern translators' changing the order of Mark's cola, and along with it the rhetorical effect of the way Mark told his story. In the Greek text of Mark's story, this period is the climax of the episode of the women going out to the tomb: "And looking up, they saw that the stone had already been rolled back. Now it was a really big stone!" It is unusual syntax. But, when told, this audience aside is a climactic moment of inside communication between the storyteller and the audience. It is an explanation to the audience of the question raised by the content and the over-the-top tone of the report of the women's discovery of the stone rolled

---

4. Collins, *Mark*, 795.

back. The audience's implicit question is, why were they so amazed that the stone had been rolled back? And the storyteller then answers, Because it was really big. This is another hint that something more than normal cemetery maintenance was involved in this big stone's being rolled back.

Not appreciating this function of the storyteller's response to the puzzled audience, most translators have absorbed this audience aside into the previous period. This is a particularly graphic instance of the difference between a literary and an oral translation that merits an extended discussion. Hence, the NRSV reads: "When they looked up, they saw that the stone, which was very large, had already been rolled back" (16:4, NRSV). The NIV, by breaking the periods of this story into paragraphs, does the same thing as the NRSV, but takes the further step of changing the function of these two merged periods—from reporting a surprising contrast to what the women expected to find when they arrived at the tomb to introducing their act of entering into the tomb:

> Very early on the first day of the week, just after sunrise, they were on their way to the tomb and they asked each other, "Who will roll the stone away from the entrance of the tomb?"
> But when they looked up, they saw that the stone, which was very large, had been rolled away. As they entered the tomb, they saw ... (16:3–5a, NIV)

In a text, paragraphing tells a reader where to place a pause. In this case the placement of the "big stone" appositive at the beginning of a new paragraph instead of at the end of the previous paragraph transforms its rhetorical impact from a climactic mystery to introductory, relatively unimportant, information.

The Good News Translation (GNT) punctuates the audience aside as a separate sentence but moves it from its climactic position to a position prior to the women's discovery of the stone having been rolled back:

> On the way they said to one another, "Who will roll away the stone for us from the entrance to the tomb?" (It was a very large stone.) Then they looked up and saw that the stone had already been rolled back.

And, as you can see, it also places the explanation in parentheses, implying that it is an authorial comment to a reader.

The King James Version and the New American Bible render Mark's story structure more accurately and punctuate the audience aside about the stone as a concluding phrase. Hence, the NAB translates 16:3–4 as, "When they looked up, they saw that the stone had been rolled back; it was very large." But only the King James Version translates γὰρ, Mark's primary cue that what follows is a storyteller aside to the audience: "And when they looked, they saw that the stone was rolled away: for it was very great." Both of these translations punctuate the two clauses with a half-stop (semicolon in the NAB and a colon in the KJV), thus reducing its impact as a separate climactic, short period.

Mark's intent as a composer becomes clear when the story is told and heard. Mark often uses audience asides, usually introduced as here by the conjunction γὰρ, as the climax of episodes. These asides to the audience are a moment of intimacy and shared delight, often accompanied by a smile or a twinkle in the eyes. They are always an opportunity to explain something that was puzzling in the material immediately prior to the comment (though sometimes, as in 6:51–52 and 16:8, the explanation raises more questions than it answers).

Consider, for example, the concluding cola in the story of the healing of Jairus' daughter: "And immediately she got up and started walking around the room. Because she was twelve years old." The aside to the audience answers the audience's question, how can she be walking if she is a little girl? That question is raised because Jairus' description of his "little girl" implies the possibility that she is very little, too young to walk.

To return to the empty-tomb story, the audience aside about the size of the stone is a response to the audience's puzzlement about the degree of the women's extreme surprise, implicit in the storyteller's tone, at the discovery of the stone rolled back. The description of the "really big stone" is a moment of storytelling delight and mystery. Its storytelling function is a combination of describing this "really big stone" and further anticipation of the surprises that are just inside the tomb. It is one of the best laugh lines in the whole gospel. The decision of the NRSV and NIV to convert this climactic period in Mark's composition into a minor phrase in the previous English sentence is a syntactical mistake that eliminates the impact of Mark's storytelling composition. In order to render Mark's meaning in these concluding audience asides, the translation needs to have a full stop between the puzzling statement and the explanation to the audience. In that moment, the storyteller can change from describing what happened to addressing the audience directly and providing the explanation to the puzzle. The rhetorical function of the conjunction γὰρ is to provide a verbal cue to the audience of this move from description to explanation, narration of action to commentary on the action. When evaluated in relation to the function of punctuation as markers of sound and breath, a semicolon or colon is not a big enough breath. The moment requires a full stop. As we will see, this aside is a prelude to the climactic asides to the audience at the ending of the resurrection story.

5: a young man seated at the right hand clothed in a white robe / νεανίσκον καθήμενον ἐν τοῖς δεξιοῖς περιβεβλημένον στολὴν λευκήν

The most widely used translations make clear once again what happens when translators reverse the order in which Mark narrates the elements of his story. This short description of the young man evokes in the listeners' memories of two earlier events in Mark's story. The first is Jesus' confession to the high priest during his trial:

> "I am, and you will see the Son of Man **seated at the right hand of Power.**" (14:52, NRSV)
>
> ὄψεσθε τὸν υἱὸν τοῦ ἀνθρώπου **ἐκ δεξιῶν καθήμενον** τῆς δυνάμεως (14:62)
>
> young man **seated at the right hand**,
>
> νεανίσκον **καθήμενον ἐν τοῖς δεξιοῖς** (16:5)

The second is the description of the young man in Gethsemane who, when grabbed by his σινδόνα, his linen cloth, left it behind and fled naked:

> And a certain young man was following him, clothed in a linen cloth over his nakedness.
>
> Καὶ **νεανίσκος** τις συνηκολούθει αὐτῷ **περιβεβλημένος** σινδόνα ἐπὶ γυμνοῦ (14:51)
>
> ... clothed in a white robe
>
> **νεανίσκον** ... **περιβεβλημένον** στολὴν λευκήν (16:5)

The "seated at the right hand" clause evokes the memory of Jesus' vision of the Son of Man at "the right hand" in a position where he shares the power of God seated at the right side of the heavenly throne. Therefore, the young man we meet through the eyes of the women upon entering the tomb is first of all implicitly a messenger from the heavenly realm. After implying the young man's origin at God's right hand, Mark goes on to describe him in a way that evokes the memory of the young man whose naked flight was the climax of the story of the flight of the disciples (ἔφυγον, 14:50; ἔφυγεν, 14:52) from Jesus' captors in Gethsemane. In contrast to the earlier young man, who was scantily dressed in a linen cloth that just covered his nakedness, this young man is dressed in a white robe, a στολὴν, whose color may remind the listeners of divine messengers and of the whiteness of Jesus' garments at the time of his transfiguration (9:3). Coming after the description that associates the young man with Jesus' description of the position of the Son of Man next to God, his being dressed in a white robe, as Jesus was at his transfiguration, reinforces the association of this young man with the realm of God.

Both the NRSV and the NIV inexplicably reverse the order of the descriptions of the young man: "a young man, dressed in a white robe, sitting on the right side . . ." (NRSV; in the NIV, same wording but without the commas). This new order leads the listeners to remember the young man in Gethsemane before evoking the association with the Son of Man's place at the right hand of Power, an association that, when heard in Mark's order, connects the white robe with the transcendent realm glimpsed also at the transfiguration. Out of the context of association with Jesus seated at the right hand of Power, there is a chance that the listeners will first associate the young man in the tomb with the young man who fled in the garden. As the first association, there are a number of other directions the listeners' imaginations can go other than association with Jesus' position of exaltation. And indeed interpreters have made associations between the white robe and the baptismal garment.[5] This possibility has been exacerbated by a change in translation of the phrases that both mean the "right hand" (ἐκ δεξιῶν, 14:62; ἐν τοῖς δεξιοῖς, 16:5) from "right hand" in 14:62 to "right side" here in 16:5. The NRSV and NIV translators have seen in this phrase nothing more than a description of location in the tomb and, therefore, minimize the association with the Son of Man's place at the right hand of God.

6: He has been raised. ἠγέρθη.

The announcement of the resurrection is one word. But in the fourth UBS Greek edition, the editors have punctuated it as part of a longer period:

ἠγέρθη, οὐκ ἔστιν ὧδε· ἴδε ὁ τόπος ὅπου ἔθηκαν αὐτόν

The NRSV follows this punctuation partially but improves it by dividing it into two sentences with a full stop in place of the comma in the Greek edition: "He has been raised; he is not here. Look, there is the place they laid him." A study of Mark's use of short cola reveals that he uses short cola and periods for climactic effect. This indicates that the Markan storyteller stopped after this climactic announcement of the resurrection and invited

---

5. See Marcus, *Mark*, 2:1125.

the audience to reflect on the many dimensions of this fulfillment of Jesus' prophecy. The effect of this editorial decision about the punctuation of Mark's Greek is to make the announcement of the resurrection an introductory clause for which the climax is, "He is not here." This word "he has been raised" (ἠγέρθη) should be punctuated with a full stop.

The translation is difficult because inflections of the verb in Greek can specify the tense and person in a single word. This is not possible in English. However, English listeners can supply those implicit inflections if the word is translated as one word, "Raised!" rather than four words, "He has been raised." This translation makes the announcement of the resurrection climactically short. But it doesn't look as good in print as it sounds when the story is told. I have translated it with four words for the sake of those who are reading this exposition. But I would encourage you, when you tell the story, to make this astonishing announcement with only one word: "Raised!"

8: Because trembling and amazement had seized them / Because they were afraid" / εἶχεν γὰρ αὐτὰς τρόμος καὶ ἔκστασις / ἐφοβοῦντο γάρ

These two explanations to the audience are a thicket of sound mapping and translation issues.

The first recognition is that the four cola in 16:8 are distinct cola. The question is whether they are four simple periods with one colon in each period, two complex periods with two cola in each period, or one complex period with four cola. The fourth edition of the UBS Greek text punctuates 16:8 as one period with four cola separated by a comma and two half stops:

> καὶ ἐξελθοῦσαι ἔφυγον ἀπὸ τοῦ μνημείου, εἶχεν γὰρ αὐτὰς τρόμος καὶ ἔκστασις· καὶ οὐδενὶ οὐδὲν εἶπαν· ἐφοβοῦντο γάρ.

The NRSV adopts the UBS edit, effectively combining all four of these cola into one period. And it follows the UBS punctuation, with the exception that it substitutes a comma for the UBS semicolon after "they said nothing to anyone."

> So they went out and fled from the tomb, for terror and amazement had seized them; and they said nothing to anyone, for they were afraid.

In the UBS edition of the Greek text, the two comments to the audience with γάρ are each separated from the preceding colon but by different punctuation: a comma between 16:8a and 8b, and by a half stop between 16:8c

The Resurrection (16:1–8)

and 8d. The implication for the sound of the episode is that the explanation "for terror and amazement had seized them" comes after a minor pause, indicated by the comma, and the explanation "for they were afraid" comes after a short half breath, indicated by the English semicolon. However, both comments are identical in their storytelling function: they are asides to the audience that explain a puzzle in the preceding colon. And there is no grammatical or syntactical difference between the two. Whatever the punctuation decision, 16:8a–b and c–d should be punctuated the same.

The NRSV at least alters the UBS punctuation to make the pauses before the narrative comments consistent:

> So they went out and fled from the tomb, for terror and amazement had seized them; and they said nothing to anyone, for they were afraid. (NRSV)

As a sound map for the performance of the story, the NRSV indicates that 16:8 should be read as one sentence—the semicolon indicating a half breath between the two halves, and the commas indicating only slight pauses before the narrative comments. In order to read this as one sentence, it is necessary for the tempo to be relatively fast.

The New American Bible, the standard American Catholic translation, makes a significant change in the translation of the first narrative comment:

> Then they went out and fled from the tomb, seized with trembling and bewilderment. They said nothing to anyone, for they were afraid.

In this translation, the first narrative comment is translated as a participial phrase. This erases the direct address to the audience. A full breath with a longer pause is indicated by the full stop or period between the two halves and leads to a somewhat slower tempo.

The NIV completely eliminates the first narrative comment and moves the participial phrase to the beginning of the sentence:

> Trembling and bewildered, the women went out and fled from the tomb. They said nothing to anyone, because they were afraid.

This translation eliminates the first aside to the audience and the intimacy between the storyteller and the audience it establishes at the end of the gospel.

These variations in the translation of these cola and periods are signs of the uncertainty among scholars about their function and meaning. These cola do not look like a conclusion to the gospel. This ambiguity and apparent strangeness has been a factor in the conclusion of many that 16:8 was not the original ending of Mark.[6]

These asides have four distinctive characteristics as elements of the story. They are (1) audience asides with γάρ that explain a puzzle in the previous period, (2) unusually short cola/periods, (3) inside views of the feelings of a character, (4) enigmatic explanations that raise more questions than they answer. Each of these elements of Mark's storytelling occurs earlier in the story and is used here in a climactic manner. Greater specificity about each element will help to clarify these characteristics of Mark's ending.

Audience asides with γάρ

Mark's asides to the audience introduced by the conjunction γάρ usually explain confusing or puzzling elements in the previous sentence (e.g., 1:16, 22; 2:15; 3:21; 5:8, 28, 42; 6:17, 18, 20, 31, 48; 9:6, 34; 10:22; 11:13; 14:2, 40, 56; 15:10; 16:4, 8). They answer questions that the storyteller intentionally raises. These asides usually occur in the middle or at the end of units within the story. Mark's description of the women's response to the divine messenger's commission in 16:8 has a higher concentration of asides to the audience than any comparable episode in the gospel.

Short cola/periods

The units of Mark's story are often ambiguous, and the units in contemporary editions of the Greek text and English translations of the texts are always the creation of contemporary editors. Nevertheless, a survey of the units in the UBS Greek text of the four Gospels that are usually adopted in English translations provides a picture of the tendencies of the four evangelists. These are the instances of relatively unambiguous short cola/periods at the ends of units of the Gospels' stories in the UBS text: Mark 6:6; 11:14b; 12:12b, 17b, 34b, 37b; 14:11b, 31b, 72; 16:8; Matt 16:4b; 17:23b; 26:35b; Luke 1:66b; 9:9b; 14:6; John 10:42; 18:40b. While all four evangelists use short cola to give emphasis to endings, Mark has more than three times as many short endings as the other Gospels (Mark, 10; Matthew and Luke, 3 each; and John, 2). Furthermore, there is a concentration of short cola/

---

6. In a recent major monograph, Clayton Croy has argued that the first and last pages of Mark's original codex were lost. That is the reason for no birth narrative and no appearance stories in Mark's gospel. The need for the highly speculative hypothesis of mutilation arises from the fact that many readers find the ending at 16:8 improbable and unacceptable. See Croy, *Mutilation*.

The Resurrection (16:1–8)

periods in Mark 16:8 with the four progressively shorter cola/periods of the Greek text having 6, 6, 4, and 2 words.

Inside views

An inside view occurs when a storyteller shifts from telling the ongoing events of the story as an objective observer to telling what is happening inside the mind or heart of particular characters. In contrast to contemporary literary, oral, and film storytelling, ancient storytellers used inside views sparingly. Three stories in Mark prior to the resurrection story end with an inside view: Jesus' walking on the water (6:45–52), Jesus' second passion prophecy (9:30–32), and the conflict about paying taxes to Caesar (12:13–17).

The end of the walking-on-the-water story is a description of the internal responses of the disciples. Here is a rather literal translation of the ending that follows Jesus getting into the boat with them and the wind ceasing:

> And they were utterly totally amazed in themselves. Because they did not understand about the loaves but their hearts were hardened.
>
> λίαν ἐκ περισσοῦ ἐν ἑαυτοῖς ἐξίσταντο. Οὐ γὰρ συνῆκαν ἐπὶ τοῖς ἄρτοις, ἀλλ' ἦν αὐτῶν ἡ καρδία πεπωρωμένη. (6:51–52)

Thus, Mark explicitly names the disciples' response as extreme and as what was happening in their hearts.

The ending of the second passion prophecy also names the internal response of the disciples: "But they did not understand the saying and they were afraid to ask him" (9:32). It is notable that, like the response of the women at the tomb, the disciples' response to the prophecy was to be silent out of fear.

The conflict story about paying taxes to Caesar ends with an inside view of the response of the Pharisees and Herodians to their effort to trap Jesus in his talk: "And they were utterly amazed (ἐξεθαύμαζον) at him" (12:17b, NRSV). Their surprise is that Jesus so deftly escaped their trap.

Thus, Mark consistently uses inside views at the ends of stories to describe emotional reactions to Jesus' words or actions by other characters. And in 16:8 there is a higher concentration of inside views of highly emotional responses to Jesus' resurrection and to the messenger's commission than at any other point in the gospel.

Enigmatic explanations that raise more questions than they answer

Among Mark's audience asides with γάρ, there is only one earlier instance in which the aside occurs at the end of a story: the ending of the walking-on-the-water story (6:45–52). The comment to the audience at the end of the walking-on-the-water story explains the disciples' amazement at Jesus' walking on the water: "For they didn't understand about the loaves, but their hearts were hardened" (NRSV). The first explanation of their amazement refers back to two earlier stories—the feeding of the five thousand, which is in turn an allusion to the feeding of the people of Israel in the wilderness; the second explanation refers to the Exodus motif of the hardening of Pharoah's heart (e.g, see Exod 4:21; 7:13, 22; 8:19, 32; 9:35; 10:20). The allusion to the feeding of Israel in the wilderness makes some sense because of the comparison between the manna and the multiplication of the loaves and fish. But the reference to Pharaoh's hard heart is more puzzling than clarifying. Nevertheless, the story leaves a full understanding of the significance of the loaves in the realm of mystery—a mystery that remains, as we have seen above, until it is illumined by Jesus' interpretation of the bread at the Last Supper.[7]

But to explain that the disciples do not understand the meaning of the loaves by alluding to the hardening of Pharoah's heart is even more puzzling. Are the disciples like Pharoah? Is the amazement of the disciples as wrong as Pharoah's unwillingness to let Israel go? Are the disciples unwilling to see the hand of the Lord in this action of Jesus? Furthermore, the disciples are highly sympathetic characters. This inside view of their response to Jesus' walking on the water intensifies the audience's emotional intimacy with the disciples. Their response, therefore, also invites the listeners to examine their hearts: listeners might ask, Am I unwilling in some way to understand and accept the implication of this story? In what way might my mind be hardened and closed? Jesus' walking on the water and speaking the divine name, ἐγώ εἰμι ("I am") from the story of the burning bush (Exod 3:14, LXX) implies that Jesus is, in some profound way, God. That implication is called blasphemy both by the scribes at the healing of the paralytic (Mark 2:7) and later by the high priest at Jesus' trial before the Sanhedrin (14:64). Is this implication a reason to harden one's heart and mind against the story and against Jesus?

This is the logic of the story. In the end, these are questions that can only be answered by each listener after an examination of the heart. Thus,

---

7. See Quesnell, *Mind of Mark*, for a redaction-critical study of the puzzle of the ending of the story of Jesus' walking on the water.

The Resurrection (16:1–8)

this comment by the storyteller at the end of the walking-on-the-water story is profoundly enigmatic and raises more questions than it answers. Mark provokes his audiences to explore the implications of Jesus' feeding five thousand people with five loaves and two fish and then walking on the water to the disciples in the boat and saying, "I am." And when they encounter their internal resistance to the implication that Jesus is divine, Mark in this provocative explanation of the disciples' amazement invites his listeners to open their hearts and minds rather than to harden them.

The second instance of a concluding audience aside occurs at the end of the introduction to the PRN: "Because they were saying, 'Not during the feast, or there will be a riot of the people'" (14:2). As we have seen above, this aside is also an enigmatic explanation that raises more questions than it answers. The implication in this aside is that the authorities have resorted to a treacherous conspiracy because they have to arrest Jesus on this last day, Wednesday, before the feast begins on Thursday. This in turn raises questions about whether they will abandon their plot if they are unable to arrest him. And this leads to the questions about the fulfillment of Jesus' prophecy and the will of God.

Thus, Mark's two earlier explanations at the end of major episodes have the same storytelling function as do these explanations in 16:8. These asides are also a concentration of progressively shorter cola and inside views. This combination of climactic uses of storytelling techniques in a manner that is consistent with their earlier uses in Mark's story is conclusive evidence that this was an intentional and consciously structured ending.[8] This could not have happened accidentally.

The storytelling function of these enigmatic explanations is to provoke the audience into thinking about the issues raised by the initial puzzle and the ambiguity of the storyteller's explanation. That function requires time for the listeners to ponder for a moment. If these comments are delivered rapidly, there is no time for the storyteller to make the shifts from narration to explanation and for the audience to think.

This brings us back to the issue of the character of the breaths between the cola, the same issue we discussed above in relation to the explanation about the stone (16:4). The conclusion we have arrived at from the above examination of the four narrative characteristics of Mark's narrative comments is that the breaths between the narration of the women's responses and the explanations of those responses need to be long enough to allow the storyteller to turn or move closer to the audience in order to mark the shift

---

8. For a more detailed discussion of the narrative characteristics of this ending, see Boomershine and Bartholomew, "Narrative Technique."

from narration to explanation. These progressively shorter cola are structured for maximum climactic effect, and they require a significant pause between the narration and the explanation during which the audience can ponder the implications of the flight and silence of the women. In fact, the story is best told with the three pauses becoming progressively longer, the tempo becoming steadily slower, and the volume becoming quieter. *The sound map needs, therefore, to indicate a full breath between each of the four cola with full stops.* In English translation, this means that the story should be punctuated as four separate sentences, preferably beginning at the left margin so that the progressive shortening can be seen as well as heard.

Furthermore, in order to convey the impact and meaning of Mark's ending, the translation of Mark 16:8 must be faithful to Mark's order of the cola, which alternate between narration and explanation to the audience. A narrative comment with γάρ cannot be translated as a participial phrase (NAB, NIV) and still convey the combination of enigma and intimacy that is present in Mark's composition.

There is stylistic continuity between the young man's announcement to the women (16:6–7) and the ending. Mark loves to end the most important episodes of the story with short, simple periods with pauses that give the listeners time to respond before moving on. Here also the major translations give preference to the eye rather than the ear. The young man's announcement is best punctuated as a series of simple periods in Greek and as separate sentences in English. This punctuation indicates that the tempo is slow and that the announcement gives the audience time to ponder the significance of what the young man says. In this regard the NRSV follows the editors of the Greek text and combines the cola and periods into several complex sentences. The study of the sound of Mark's story does not support this editorial practice.

Comments on the Meaning and Impact of the Story

16:1: the day after the Sabbath / διαγενομένου τοῦ σαββάτου

Mark's empty-tomb/resurrection story begins with a description of the time, as is often the case at the beginning of new sections of the story. (See, e.g., 14:1, the beginning of the passion story and the plot; 14:12, the Passover meal; 15:1, the trial before Pilate; 15:25, the second period in the crucifixion; 15:33, the death; 15:42, the burial). "When the Sabbath was past" means Saturday evening when the stores opened after sundown. At the beginning of the burial story, the time was "the day before the Sabbath" (15:42). Thus, the sequence of the days is made clear: the day before the Sabbath, the Sabbath,

The Resurrection (16:1–8)

the day after the Sabbath. This is, therefore, the third day as was predicted in the three passion/resurrection prophecies (8:31; 9:31; 10:34). This notice enables the listeners to count the days. It is the first of the allusions to the possibility that Jesus' prophecy might be fulfilled.

1. the names of the three women / Μαρία ἡ Μαγδαληνὴ καὶ Μαρία ἡ [τοῦ] Ἰακώβου καὶ Σαλώμη.

The naming of the three women identifies them as the three who were present at Jesus' death (15:40), two of whom saw where the body was laid (15:47). This story is the conclusion of the characterization of Jesus' mother. She is identified here as Μαρία ἡ [τοῦ] Ἰακώβου, Mary the one of James, by verbal echo the mother of the first, younger brother, in the list of the witnesses of Jesus' death (15:40). She, along with Mary Magdalene, is present at Jesus' death and burial and now at the empty tomb. As I suggested above, her presence in Jerusalem implies that she had changed her mind about her conclusion that her son was crazy (3:21, 31), and that she had traveled with him in Galilee. Now she joins the two other women in buying spices to anoint and care for Jesus' body. The repetition of their names and the report that they bought spices for the anointing establish a mood of mourning. This story is thereby connected with the death and burial in mood and theme. But it also evokes connections with earlier elements of Mark's story: e.g., the leitmotif of Jesus' mother Mary, the passion/resurrection prophecies, and the anointing by the woman in Bethany.

The question raised by this indirect way of naming Jesus' mother is a particular instance of the overall puzzle of Mark's method of indirection and implication.[9] The answer that emerges from performing the story is that this is the composer's way of engaging audiences that are being invited to listen to a long story. It is a way of engaging their participation in a long and potentially boring story. That is the biggest challenge for anyone who tells Mark's gospel. This way of telling the story of Jesus' mother leaves her shrouded in mystery.

---

9 As Crossan has written, "I have given up trying to imagine why Mark names the women so differently in each case" (Crossan, *Who Killed Jesus?*, 182).

2. very early on the first day . . . when the sun had risen / καὶ λίαν πρωῒ τῇ μιᾷ τῶν σαββάτων . . . ἀνατείλαντος τοῦ ἡλίου

The time named at the beginning of the second period is, "very early on the first day of the week." The implication of the term "very early" (λίαν πρωῒ) is that it is still dark when the three women set out for the tomb. The precise time that Mark indicates by this phrase has provoked an extensive scholarly discussion.[10] The dominant conclusion is that the phrase describes a period of darkness just before dawn. In earth time it is then the last part of the night that began with the end of the Sabbath at sunset. In story time it is the end of the darkness that descended upon the story at the sixth hour, prior to Jesus' death (15:40–41). As we have seen above (see the note on "when the sun had risen"), the phrase "when the sun had risen" at the end of the period is a surprise that has a grammatical component: never before in the story has a period ended with a circumstantial participial phrase. In the context of the darkness that has been the context of the story since noon on Friday, this surprising dawning of a new day brings light streaming into the story. It is another intimation of what may come next.

3. the tone of the women's question about rolling away the stone

The trip out to the tomb focuses on the women's conversation about the problem of finding someone to roll away the stone. These are the first and only words of the three women who are the heroines of the story. Their question recalls the final act of the burial:

> 15:46c—and rolled a stone over the door of the tomb
> 16:3—Who will roll away the stone for us out of the door of the tomb?

The tone of their question to one another is sad, and the tempo is slow—the tempo of a funeral march.

4: the stone rolled back! / ἀποκεκύλισται ὁ λίθος!

The discovery of the stone rolled back is reported from the women's point of view. Once again there is a grammatical dimension to the impact of the opening phrase. The construction of καὶ or δε plus a circumstantial participle usually occurs in beginnings. When this construction occurs in endings, it is used consistently for moments of climax (e.g. earlier in the PRN for the young man's naked flight, 14:52; for Peter's realization of his

---

10 See Taylor, *Gospel according to St. Mark*, 604–5.

denial, 14:72; for the crowd's coming up to Pilate, 15:8; and for Jesus' death, 15:37). The emphasis here is on what the women saw: "and looking up," καὶ ἀναβλέψασαι. The audience is invited to see the open door to the tomb through the women's eyes. It is another intimation about the mystery inside the tomb. The composer uses two different verbs of seeing: "looking up" (ἀναβλέπω) and "they saw, perceived" (θεωρέω). This second verb has been used in the earlier descriptions of the women's witnessing Jesus' death and burial (15:41,47).

4b: Now it was really big! / ἦν γὰρ μέγας σφόδρα

The storyteller's explanation responds to the question raised by the tone of extreme surprise in the storyteller's description of the women's discovery. The implicit dialogue between the audience and the storyteller is, why were they so surprised? Because it was a really big stone! As we have discussed earlier (see note above in "Notes on Details and Translation"), this is a climactic and delightful moment in the relationship between the storyteller and the audience. The storyteller gives the audience inside information that heightens this moment of anticipation and suspense.

2–8: going out / going into / going out they fled / ἔρχονται ἐπὶ / εἰσελθοῦσαι εἰς / ἐξελθοῦσαι ἔφυγον

The stages of the women's trip to the tomb are introduced by the theme and variations on the verb "to go" (ἔρχομαι) and the noun "the tomb" (μνημεῖον): "they went out to the tomb" ἔρχονται ἐπὶ τὸ μνημεῖον (16:2), "and going into the tomb" εἰσελθοῦσαι εἰς τὸ μνημεῖον (16:5), "and going out, they fled from the tomb" ἐξελθοῦσαι ἔφυγον ἀπὸ τοῦ μνημείου (16:8a). This sonic theme frames the three parts of the resurrection section and is a mnemonic link to the three beginnings.

5: the young man / νεανίσκον

The young man in the tomb is described from the women's point of view. This is the most extensive and detailed description from a character's point of view since the description of what Jesus saw and heard at his baptism (1:10b–11). As I outlined above, an element of the surprise implicit in the description of the young man is the echoes of earlier motifs in the stories of the young man's fleeing naked and Jesus' confession before the Sanhedrin:

> And a certain **young man** was following him, **clothed** in a linen cloth over his nakedness
> Καὶ **νεανίσκος** τις συνηκολούθει αὐτῷ **περιβεβλημένος** σινδόνα ἐπὶ γυμνοῦ (14:51)

> And you will see the Son of Man **seated on the right hand** of power
> καὶ ὄψεσθε τὸν υἱὸν τοῦ ἀνθρώπου **ἐκ δεξιῶν καθήμενον** τῆς δυνάμεως (14:62)

> they saw **a young man seated on the right hand clothed** in a white robe
> εἶδον **νεανίσκον καθήμενον ἐν τοῖς δεξιοῖς περιβεβλημένον** στολὴν λευκήν (16:5)

This description of the young man resonates with the earlier sounds of the Son of Man seated on the right hand of Power and with the young man's naked flight that symbolized the shame of the disciples' running away. In contrast to the young man who flees naked, this young man is the presence of divine authority and splendor. The only prior use of the word "white" (λευκήν) in Mark is in the description of Jesus' glistening white garments in the transfiguration story (9:3). And the cultural associations of this clothing with divine messengers is evident in the use of this same phrase, "clothed in a white robe" περιβεβλημένος στολὴν λευκήν, in the Revelation to John to describe angelic beings (see, e.g., Rev 7:9, 13). The symbol of the shame of naked flight is transformed into a symbol of the glory of divine presence. The transformation of the verbal fabric of the story is the objective correlative of this big surprise for the women. This young man is a divine messenger!

they were astonished / ἐξεθαμβήθησαν

The storyteller's statement that they were astonished/amazed/alarmed is the first direct description of the women's feelings. The women's feelings of grief have been implicit since the first introduction of the women as the climax of the story of Jesus' death, but those emotions had to be inferred by the audience. This explicit inside view of their emotions creates a high degree of sympathetic identification with the women. In fact, this is the climax of a dynamic reduction of aesthetic distance in which the emotional identification with the women has steadily intensified. These are good women who have followed Jesus, loved him, and mourned his death and burial.

Mark alone among the composers of the Gospels uses the word ἐκθαμβέω to describe the women's response to the sight of this young divine messenger. It is an emotionally intensive word. The root of the word, θαμβέω, means "astounded." With the particle ἐκ as a modifier, literally "out of," it means something like "beyond astonishment," "totally astonished," or "overcome with astonishment." Mark also uses this word in the Gethsemane story to introduce Jesus' words to Peter, James, and John about his soul, something like "terribly distressed" (14:33): "he began to be terribly distressed and troubled . . ." Mark also uses this word to describe the crowd's response to seeing Jesus after the transfiguration (9:15). There it is associated with the surprise and wonder of a theophanic vision. This is one of those Greek words that means an ambiguous combination of astonishment, wonder, surprise, alarm, awe, and fear—for which English has no equivalent. The translators of the NRSV, NIV, and GNT have chosen "alarmed," and the RSV team chose "amazed." The closest that colloquial English could come is something like "shocked out of their minds." This is also one of those words in Greek that requires different English words in the varied contexts in which it occurs. Thus, none of the best English words for translating this Greek word here in 16:8, such as "alarmed," "amazed," or "astonished," would be appropriate as a description of Jesus' emotional distress in Gethsemane. If we conclude that Mark's gospel was the earliest of the four Gospels, then the other tellers of Jesus' stories apparently found Mark's word either too intense or too ambiguous since they used other words in all these contexts, including in the tomb. The original root meaning of "astounded, astonished" has been chosen here as the closest English equivalent.

6: But he says to them / ὁ δὲ λέγει αὐταῖς

The formula introducing the young man's speech is ὁ δὲ λέγει αὐταῖς, literally "But he says to them." This is an unusual formula. The only full parallel to this formula is in the feeding of the five thousand. There it introduces Jesus' order in response to the disciples' question about his command to give the people something to eat: "'Do you want us to go and buy two hundred denarii worth of bread and give it to these people to eat?' **But he says to them**, 'How many loaves do you have? Go and see'" (6:38). Here the young man's command is the exact antithesis of the women's "astonishment": "Don't be astonished."

6: the Nazarene who was crucified / τὸν Ναζαρηνὸν τὸν ἐσταυρωμένον

The messenger's identification of Jesus refers back to his hometown and to his crucifixion. The name Nazarene was last used by the servant girl of the high priest as an accusation of Peter (14:67): "that Nazarene, Jesus." The last word of the period is the participle, "who was crucified" (τὸν ἐσταυρωμένον), an echo of the most frequently repeated word in the stories of the trial before Pilate and the execution (15:13, 14, 15, 20, 24, 25, 27). The use of this term by the divine messenger transforms its associative meaning from shame to honor. The young man in white says these words with a tone of the highest respect.

raised. ἠγέρθη.

The announcement of the resurrection is a period with only one word, "Raised" (ἠγέρθη). The verb is in the passive voice and carries with it the implication of divine action: to paraphrase, "he has been raised by God." The announcement is a fulfillment of Jesus' prophecy at the end of the three passion prophecies and in his promise to the disciples on the way out to Gethsemane: "After I have been raised, I will go before you to Galilee" (14:28). The crucified/raised juxtaposition resonates back through the whole story.

the evidence of the empty tomb

The evidence of the resurrection offered by the young man is the empty tomb. Jesus is not here. And he points to the place where Jesus was laid. The words refer back to the climax of the burial episode:

> Mary Magdalene and Mary the mother of Joses **saw where he was laid**
> ἡ δὲ Μαρία ἡ Μαγδαληνὴ καὶ Μαρία ἡ Ἰωσῆτος **ἐθεώρουν ποῦ τέθειται** (15:47)
>
> **Look at** the place **where they laid him**
> **ἴδε** ὁ τόπος **ὅπου ἔθηκαν αὐτόν.** (16:6d)

The sounds of these words evoke the audience's memory of the place they saw in their imaginations through the women's eyes. And once again the words used earlier to describe the place of defeat are now used to describe the evidence of victory.

The Resurrection (16:1–8)

> 7: go, tell . . . he is going ahead of you to Galilee / ὑπάγετε εἴπατε
> . . . Προάγει ὑμᾶς εἰς τὴν Γαλιλαίαν

The young man's command to the women is the next step in this logic of transformation. He turns from describing the place where Jesus is no longer present to the place where he will be present in the future. The command to tell the disciples and Peter that he is going ahead of them to Galilee recalls the earlier stories of Jesus' prophecies and their fulfillment in the flight of the disciples and Peter's denial. The implication of the message to be delivered is that the failure of the disciples and Peter is not an unforgivable sin. Jesus' promise that he would go ahead of them to Galilee after his resurrection followed his prophecy of their scandalization and flight.

That prophecy is now being fulfilled. With only a minor modification of the verb in order to make it agree with a different subject, the message that the women are to give to the disciples and Peter is an exact remembrance of Jesus'promise after the prophecy of their desertion and denial:

> But after I have been raised, **I will go before you into Galilee**.
> ἀλλὰ μετὰ τὸ ἐγερθῆναί με **προάξω ὑμᾶς εἰς τὴν Γαλιλαίαν** (14:28).
>
> **He is going before you into Galilee**
> Προάγει ὑμᾶς εἰς τὴν Γαλιλαίαν (16:7)

> There you will see him / ἐκεῖ αὐτὸν ὄψεσθε

The message concludes that they will see him there. The contrast is thereby drawn to the young man's announcement of Jesus' absence from the tomb: to paraphrase, "He isn't here, he's out there ahead of you in Galilee." The previous uses of the verb "to see" (ὁράω) are all in the context of divine epiphanies:

> And there **appeared** to them Elijah with Moses
> Καὶ **ὤφθη** αὐτοῖς Ἡλίας σὺν Μωυσεῖ (9:4, NRSV)
>
> And then **they will see** 'the Son of Man coming on the clouds'
> Καὶ τότε **ὄψονται** τὸν υἱὸν τοῦ ἀνθρώπου ἐρχόμενον ἐν νεφέλαις (13:26, NRSV)
>
> And **you will see** the Son of Man seated at the right hand
> καὶ **ὄψεσθε** τὸν υἱὸν τοῦ ἀνθρώπου ἐκ δεξιῶν καθήμενον τῆς δυνάμεως (14:62)

The implication is that they will see Jesus in a divine epiphany, a postresurrection appearance. The implication is also that this will be a fulfillment of Jesus' implicit promise of postresurrection reconciliation.

just as he said to you / καθὼς εἶπεν ὑμῖν

The final phrase of the report the women are commanded to give the disciples points once again to the fulfillment of Jesus' prophecies and commands. The fulfillment of Jesus' prophecies is made explicit by the phrase, "just as he said to you":

> But they told them **just as** Jesus **had said to them**
> Οἱ δὲ αὐτοῖς **καξὼς εἶπεν αὐτοῖς** (11:6)

> ... and they found everything **just as he had said to them**.
> καὶ εὗρον **καθὼς εἶπεν αὐτοῖς** (14:16)

> There you will see him **just as he said** to you
> ἐκεῖ αὐτὸν ὄψεσθε, **καθὼς εἶπεν** ὑμῖν (16:7)

The exact repetition of this key phrase implies that this prophecy will be fulfilled just as happened with these earlier prophecies. Thus, the two primary points of emphasis in the young man's speech deal with the fulfillment of Jesus' prophecies of resurrection and his appearance to the disciples in Galilee.

Prophecy fulfillment in the PRN

The story of the resurrection is the culmination of the detailed fulfillment of Jesus' three passion/resurrection prophecies, in particular the third passion prophecy (10:33–34), which is fulfilled virtually word for word in the course of the story. The implication of the imminent fulfillment of the promise of a reunion in Galilee is that all of Jesus' earlier prophecies are beginning to be fulfilled. There are more which remain to be fulfilled: saving and losing one's life (8:35); the coming of the kingdom of God with power (9:1); houses, brothers and sisters, mothers and children, and fields for those who have left them in order to follow Jesus (10:29–30); the prophecies of the apocalyptic discourse, including the destruction of the Temple and the coming of the Son of Man (13:6–27); and the coming of the Son of Man (14:62). The probability is that some of these prophecies, such as the wars, the trials, the desolating sacrilege, the destruction of the Temple, and the handing over of family members to death have been fulfilled in the experience of persons in

Mark's audiences. But still unfulfilled are the prophecies of the final victory of the kingdom of God and the coming of the Son of Man.

The logic of eschatological transformation

The young man's words to the women are the reversal of a series of earlier defeats and disappointments in the PRN. The expectation of condemnation for the disciples and Peter is changed into a promise of reconciliation. The tomb as a place of grief has been transformed into a place of joy. The humiliation of a young man's naked flight is reversed into the glory of a young man in a white robe seated at the right hand. The disappointment of the hopes for Jesus' escape in the stories of the arrest, trial, condemnation, mocking, and crucifixion of Jesus is now experienced as the road to victory. Jesus has been confirmed as a true prophet and as the Christ, the Son of God and the Son of Man. Thus, the young man's speech changes the causes of grief into reasons for joy. It proclaims the beginning of the complete fulfillment of Jesus' prophecies concerning the coming Kingdom of God.

The logic of the resurrection story in Mark is the logic of symbolic reversal and transformation. Specifically, the elements of the story associated with defeat and death are transformed into symbols associated with life and victory.

darkness	light
stone rolled over the door of the tomb	stone rolled back
shame	pride
young man in a linen garment running away naked	young man in a white robe sitting at the right hand (of Power)
astounded	not astounded
the place for Jesus' dead body	the place empty
Nazareth as no place	Nazareth as honored hometown

Virtually every element of the story is a reversal of earlier associations. The story teaches its listeners to look and listen for the transformational power of God in the midst of the apparent dominance of the powers of evil. Jesus' messianic leadership is vindicated in each new dimension of the resurrection.

8: the women fled / ἔφυγον

The women's response is flight. The connotations of the word ἔφυγον are determined by its earlier use in the flight of the disciples and the young man, where flight is associated with cowardice and failure (14:50-52). These associations constitute the norm of judgment for the women's flight. This action by the women is surprising in light of the good news of the resurrection of Jesus.

8b: trembling and astonishment had them / εἶχεν γὰρ αὐτὰς τρόμος καὶ ἔκστασις

The storyteller responds to the audience's surprise by explaining the reason for their flight: literally translated, "they had trembling and astonishment." The verb "they had" (εἶχεν) is consistently used earlier to describe what someone possessed: e.g., the Syro-Phoenician woman had a daughter (7:25), they had a few small fish (8:7), the widow put in everything she had (12:44). In this case, they had something over which they had no control, something which had them! The word τρόμος denotes a physical response of shaking, and ἔκστασις is an extreme emotion often associated with fear and joy. Mark uses this word, ἔκστασις, in his description of the response of Jairus and his wife to the raising of their daughter to new life (5:42). And even though Jesus says that the girl was just sleeping, awaking from sleep is a frequent image for resurrection from death (e.g., John 11:11).

As is often the case in Mark's composition, the description of response to the unprecedented resurrection of a person from three days of death has a verbal objective correlative. This is the first time that Mark has explained an action of a character to the audience by reporting the character's inner feelings. Mark comes close to this in the explanation of the disciples' falling asleep in Gethsemane ("because their eyes were weighed down" ἦσαν γὰρ αὐτῶν οἱ ὀφθαλμοὶ καταβαρυνόμενοι—14:40b). But this is a more intimate and explicit naming of the women's emotions.

Thus, Mark combines two storytelling elements. He describes an action, fleeing, that is associated with a strongly negative norm of judgment, and explains this action by an aside addressed to the audience that names highly charged, positive emotions. A strongly negative norm of judgment creates a higher degree of emotional distance or alienation in relation to the character: e.g., Judas offering to hand Jesus over to the chief priests. Likewise, a highly charged inside view of a character's emotions creates a reduction of aesthetic distance and increases sympathy in relation to the character: e.g, the inside view of Jesus' being deeply disturbed and troubled in Gethsemane. When combined in this manner, the audience is invited to experience the women's wrong response of fleeing from the tomb with the knowledge that the reasons for their flight are completely understandable.

The Resurrection (16:1–8)

Furthermore, in the context of the communities of those telling the stories of Jesus, the memories of the persecution and execution of Jesus' followers by Nero may have also been a factor in the audience's sympathy for the women. Flight and fear were fully appropriate responses to the threat of torture and execution by the Roman authorities. In addition to the memories of Nero, there were also the more present threats of reprisals against Judeans in the aftermath of the war. That is, the political contexts of Mark's audiences may have also increased their ability to identify with the women's response to the commission by the young divine messenger.

8c: They said nothing to anyone / καὶ οὐδενὶ οὐδὲν εἶπαν

The women's second action is even more surprising. Their saying nothing to anyone is direct disobedience of the young man's command to go and tell. Furthermore, it is the exact reversal of Jesus' command to the leper to say nothing to any one and the leper's immediate response: "But he went out and began to proclaim it everywhere and to spread the word"(1:45). Likewise after the healing of the deaf and dumb man, Jesus "ordered them to tell no one; but the more he ordered them, the more zealously they proclaimed it" (7:36, NRSV). The command to the leper is the first instance of the distinctive Markan motif of the messianic secret (1:45; 3:12; 5:43; 8:26, 30). Therefore, the women's silence is ironically related to this element of the plot. It is also in ironic contrast to the foreign Gerasene demoniac whom Jesus commanded to go home and tell his friends, and who "went away and began to proclaim in the Decapolis how much Jesus had done for him" (5:20, NRSV). Their silence is also an echo of Jesus' silence at the trials before the Sanhedrin and Pilate. Literally translated, this leitmotif runs as follows:

> But he was silent and did not answer anything
> ὁ δὲ ἐσιώπα καὶ οὐκ ἀπεκρίνατο οὐδέν (14:61)

> **But Jesus answered nothing**, so that Pilate wondered.
> ὁ δὲ Ιησους οὐκέτι οὐδὲν ἀπεκρίθη, ὥστε θαυμάζειν τὸν Πιλᾶτον (15:5)

> And to no one they said nothing
> καὶ οὐδενὶ οὐδὲν εἶπαν (16:8c)

As can be seen, a double negative in Greek constitutes an emphatic negative rather than a positive, as in English. In Jesus' case, his silence was a right response and a hopeful surprise. But in the case of the women, it is a reversal of the expectation that they will tell the good news of the resurrection to the disciples and Peter. If anything, therefore, the women's silence is an even greater surprise than their flight.

8d. For they were afraid / ἐφοβοῦντο γάρ

The storyteller once again explains this surprise by describing their feelings to the audience: "because they were afraid" ἐφοβοῦντο γάρ. This two-word period is the shortest period in the gospel outside the speeches (see e.g. 5:24a; 9:34a; 10:22b; 11:14b; 12:12b; 12:16b; 14:50; 14:72b). It is the second audience aside after the explanation of their flight that is an inside view of a character's feelings. The word "fear" is used earlier several times to describe a response to an act of divine power by Jesus: the disciples' response to Jesus' calming of the sea (4:41); the crowd's response to Jesus' healing of the demoniac (5:15); the woman's response to Jesus' calling her after the healing of her flow of blood (5:33); the disciples' response to seeing Jesus walking on the water (6:50). In each of these instances, the response of fear is appropriate even if Jesus tells the disciples not to be afraid in both sea stories (4:40–41; 6:50). If anything, the audience is invited to identify with the disciples in their experience. This motif is in continuity with the theme in the Old Testament of fear/awe in the presence of the Divine (see Judg 6:22–23; 13:5; Isa 6:5). That is, the women's fear is once again understandable. However, in this story the women's silence and fear, while not wrong in itself, is not a response to the Divine presence but to the commission to go and tell the news of the resurrection and the promise of Jesus' appearance to the disciples and Peter.

Their fear is particularly resonant for audiences that would have heard this story in the period following the Judean–Roman War. Potential audiences of the gospel probably knew about the persecution of Christians by the Emperor Nero in 64 CE that is described by Tacitus in *The Annals* (see above). Being publicly associated with Christ was dangerous and could lead to extreme persecution. The fear of public persecution was probably, therefore, a dimension of the background of the women's fear that would have been inferred by Mark's audiences.

Regardless of the justifiable reasons for fear that may be implied or inferred, however, the women's silence is clearly wrong. It is the ultimate irony. Those who were earlier commanded to be silent, the leper (1:45) and the people of the Decapolis (7:35), aggressively proclaimed the news. Now those who are commissioned to announce even greater good news are silent. But while their fearful silence is wrong, it is understandable and even sympathetic. Thus, the description of the women's wrong response is combined with an unprecedented degree of insight into the reasons for this failure of a highly sympathetic character.

The provocative impact of the ending at 16:8

What then is the meaning and impact of this ending? This ending has the same basic characteristics as two earlier climactic moments in Mark's story: the astonishment (ἐξίστημι) of the disciples in response to Jesus' walking on the water (6:51–52), and Peter's denial of Jesus after Jesus' condemnation by the Sanhedrin (14:72). Each of these endings is a sympathetic, inside view of a wrong response by Jesus' disciples to a climactic event in the story. These endings in Mark have many of the same characteristics as some of Jesus' parables and some stories in the Old Testament. Among Jesus' parables, the parables of the Ten Virgins (Matt 25:1–13), the Talents (Matt 25:14–30), and a Father and Two Sons (Luke 15:11–32) have many of the same structural elements as Mark's stories. In the Old Testament, the ending of the book of Jonah (Jonah 4:1–11), Nathan's parable to David after David's adultery with Bathsheba and murder of Uriah (2 Sam 12:1–7), and the Genesis story of the man and the woman in the garden (Gen 2:4—3:24) are examples that also share many of these storytelling elements. In each of these stories, a highly sympathetic character does something unambiguously wrong. And in some form of suspended or surprising ending, the audience is invited to reflect on the reasons for the character's actions. Mark's ending is not, therefore, idiosyncratic or accidental but is in continuity with a broad and deep stream of provocative storytelling in the traditions of Israel. This combination of storytelling elements has produced some of the most memorable stories in the biblical tradition. And it is no surprise that some of these stories have provoked intensive debate about their meaning.

When seen and heard as a storytelling tradition, these stories also share a consistent impact. All these stories require the listeners to reflect on the reasons for the actions and responses of the characters. They create enigmatic puzzles that invite pondering and reflection. They are provocative.[11] The issues about which they provoke reflection vary widely. The endings of Jonah and the prodigal son invite reflection about anger as a response to the forgiveness and redemption of Assyrian enemies or a prodigal brother. The stories of the garden and Nathan's parable to David invite audiences to ponder engagement in the worship of fertility cult gods and goddesses or

---

11. Richard Swanson's title for his commentary series on the four Gospels, *Provoking the Gospel*, is in direct continuity with this generative impulse of the storytelling tradition of the Gospels.

adultery. Mark's enigmatic endings of Jesus' water walking, Peter's denial, and the commission of the women involve audiences in the issues related to Jesus' divine identity, the cost of discipleship, and the consequences of announcing Jesus' resurrection. All these stories share a common storytelling structure and purpose. Rather than reinforcing a particular moral or theological point or simply giving a happy or sad ending to a climactic story, these endings are open ended rather than closed, and move the story into the realm of audience response. Each listener is invited to enter into and to think about her or his own response to these paradigmatic situations in which the characters, often women, are involved.

The particular focus of the ending of Mark is the resurrection of Jesus and the commission to go and tell the disciples and Peter. The structure of the story suspends the happy ending and invites the listeners to reflect on the response of flight and silence to this apostolic commission. This theme of apostolic commissioning is shared by the endings of the other three Gospels. Matthew's gospel ends with the great commission to make disciples of all nations. The Gospel of John ends with the risen Jesus' threefold examination and provocation of Simon Peter to care for Jesus' flock regardless of the sure consequence of martyrdom. And Luke's story ends with the commission to proclaim repentance and forgiveness of sins to all the nations and the promise of empowerment by the Holy Spirit that takes place at Pentecost.

An integral dimension of the impact of the ending at 16:8 is the increasingly long silences between the climactic periods. The response to the issues raised by the story for the listeners takes place in those periods of silence. As can be seen from the commentary, those issues are complex and multidimensional.

Mark's ending provokes the listeners to think specifically about their response to the commission to go and tell. Full involvement in the story's dynamics creates an impact that could appropriately be called a purging of fear. In contrast to a Greek tragedy, whose impact is "the catharsis of pity and fear" (Aristotle's *Poetics*), Mark's story does not end with tragedy but with the transformation of tragedy into victory and the promise of a future full of hope. The purging of fear takes place in a place of detachment in the silence of the ending. The telling of the story is itself a sign that the women did eventually tell the disciples. The purging of fear is connected with the call to each listener to become a teller of the story of Jesus. Not coincidentally, that is also an underlying purpose of this commentary.

9

THE MESSIAH OF PEACE

JESUS' CANDIDACY AS THE ANOINTED MESSIAH OF ISRAEL AND of the world is based on the implicit appeal of the Gospel to follow a non-violent Messiah of peace. When heard against the background of the predominant stories of the ancient world, the epic poems of Homer and the stories of the anointed Messiahs of Israel, Jesus' story stands in striking contrast to those paradigmatic stories. Jesus acts in loving-kindness for the people of his own nation and for the people of the nations of his enemies. In his last days, he does not attack his enemies or attempt to mount a revolt but submits in non-violent resistance to execution by his Roman and Judean opponents.

Mark's implicit appeal was to believe in and follow Jesus' way rather than the way of alienation and warfare that led to the great tragedy of the Judean–Roman War. Mark's story of Jesus' passion and resurrection has five major climaxes: the last supper, the flight of the disciples, Peter's denial, the crucifixion, and the resurrection. Each of these major moments in the story is set in the context of a fulfillment of Jesus' prophecy of his suffering, death, and resurrection. Jesus' Passover meal with his disciples and the symbolic offering of his body and blood is set in the context of the story of the priests' plot and Judas' betrayal. The implication of the story is that Judas was present and that Jesus gave the bread and cup to the one who made himself Jesus' most treacherous enemy. Jesus' prayer and arrest in Gethsemane are framed by Jesus' prophecy that the disciples would all be offended and scattered. The prophecy is fulfilled in the flight of the disciples. Jesus' non-violent submission to arrest rather than violent resistance is the implied reason for their desertion. Jesus' confession of his identity as Messiah and his acceptance of condemnation to death is surrounded by the prophecy and fulfillment of Peter's denial. The issue for Peter is saving his life rather than dying with Jesus. The frame of Jesus' crucifixion and death is the crowd's choice of Barabbas and his connection with "the insurrection" and the mocking of Jesus first by the Roman soldiers and then by the Judean passersby, the chief priests and scribes, and the insurrectionists with whom he is crucified. This defection by "the crowd," Jesus' most consistent support group throughout the story, is a proximate cause for his condemnation, mockery, and crucifixion by the Romans. Finally, the announcement of Jesus' resurrection is preceded by the presence and implied mourning of the women at Jesus' death and burial and is followed by their post-resurrection flight and silence because of fear. In each instance, the story sets the events of Jesus' passion, death, and resurrection in the context of the issues related to the consequences of belief in Jesus as the Messiah of peace: giving oneself for one's friends and enemies, non-violent submitting to arrest, sharing Jesus' condemnation and death, being rejected and killed rather than killing others, and risking persecution by the announcement of Jesus' victory.

With the possible exception of Judas' betrayal, each of these framing stories involves the audience in a highly sympathetic relationship with a character who acts in a manner that is profoundly wrong according to the story's implicit norms of judgment. Thus, the disciples' desertion, Peter's denial, the crowd's choice of Barabbas and demand for Jesus' crucifixion, and the flight and silence of the women all share a similar set of storytelling elements: sympathetic characterization of those who respond wrongly, unambiguous norms of judgment of the right and wrong response, and a surprising reversal of expectations.

The allusions to recent events in the story, particularly in Jesus' apocalyptic discourse (Mark 13), point to the period after the Judean–Roman War as the historical context of the composition and original proclamation of Mark's Gospel. A further dimension of that context was the conflicts between the various factions of Israelite religion that were active at the time of Jesus and that survived the war. The implicit norms of judgment and the dynamics of audience address indicate that Mark composed his story to be told to audiences that were predominantly Judeans. However, he also explicitly included Gentiles in his audiences. If the story was told in these contexts, the performances of Mark's Gospel were occasions to which persons on both sides of the wall of separation between Judeans and Gentiles were invited.

Mark composed a story that could be told in a variety of contexts in the cities and towns of the Diaspora. These storytelling evenings were an integral part of the mission of this Israelite sect to convince Judeans and sympathetic Gentiles that Jesus is the Messiah God has sent to save the world from the powers of evil. The stories may also have been told at the various meals and worship celebrations of the sectarian communities. But in all of these occasions, the audiences were addressed as persons who were in various stages of belief in Jesus as Messiah. Mark's passion and resurrection story is structured to change rather than confirm the minds of the audience about Jesus.

A pervasive tragedy in the subsequent history of the interpretation of Mark's story as a whole, and of the PRN in particular, has been the reading of Mark as anti-Jewish. The study of Mark as performance literature does not support this reading of Mark's meaning and impact in its original historical context. When heard as a story told to audiences, Mark's story was addressed to audiences that were predominantly Judean but that included Gentiles. It was composed for performance in the context of the post-war community of Judeans and Gentiles who were seeking a way that would lead to peace and reconciliation. The tragedy is that the later hearing of the PRN by Christians, who identified themselves as not Jewish, has led to the experience of Mark's story as a rhetoric of condemnation rather than a rhetoric of involvement and implication. As a result, the story that was structured to appeal to its audience to recognize "our" involvement in the death of the Messiah became a story that was interpreted to mean that "they" were responsible for the death of the Messiah. This has led to the implication of Mark's story in the development of Christian anti-Judaism and anti-Semitism with its widespread tragic consequences in the history of western civilization. One of the ironies of contemporary biblical scholarship has been the reinforcement of this conclusion about the meaning and purpose of Mark's Gospel in its first-century context. A hope implicit in this commentary is that the study of Mark as performance literature will change this widespread conclusion about Mark's original meaning and purpose.

The structure of Mark's Gospel has a threaded theme and focus that had particular relevance in the post-war context of the late first century. But the issues raised by the story also have relevance in every subsequent age. The Gospel of Mark addresses the need to change the minds of the nations to belief in the power of love, healing, and compassion across the boundaries of ethnic, national, and religious identity that divide the human community. The nations then and now, such as the Roman empire and the American empire, presuppose that redemptive violence is the only way to overcome the power of evil and establish peace. This belief is reinforced every day in television news and dramas, in films, and in video games. The human race now lives in the context of the widespread development and acquisition of nuclear weapons and the growing capability of the nations to destroy the world. Ongoing warfare has become a way of life. As an American born in 1940, my country has been at war much of my life.

The celebration of American warfare and its warriors is a perpetual theme of daily life in the United States. We spend vast amounts of our national resources on weapons research and training for war but we spend little on research into non-violence, peacemaking, and training in conflict resolution and reconciliation.

We must find another way as a human community. The story of Jesus is a paradigmatic story that invites the peoples and nations of the world to change our minds about the ways that will lead to peace and reconciliation in the human community. This invitation includes the nations of the United States and Israel.

As it was in the first century, the telling and interpretation of the Gospel of Mark in the twenty-first century will be addressed to persons who are in various stages of non-belief in Jesus as the Messiah of peace. Mark's passion and resurrection narrative is a story of Jesus' suffering and death for the redemption of the world from the corporate powers of evil. It ends with the paradigmatic story of his victory over those powers and the commission to tell the story. The story of Jesus' passion and resurrection continues to be a story about the ways that will lead to peace.

Appendix 1

THE HISTORICAL CONTEXT OF MARK AND HIS AUDIENCES

THE JUDEAN-ROMAN WAR FROM 66 TO 70 CE WAS THE GREATest tragedy in the history of Israel. We can review a few of the salient facts to get an overall picture of the postwar context of the performances of Mark. Josephus estimates that some one million one hundred thousand Judeans were killed. His further estimate is that approximately an additional one hundred thousand were taken as prisoners. The tallest and most handsome were separated and reserved for the triumph in Rome. His description of the fate of the rest gives a sense of Roman policy for vanquished peoples:

> Those over seventeen years of age he [Titus] sent in chains to the works in Egypt, while multitudes were presented by Titus to the various provinces, to be destroyed in the theaters by the sword or by wild beasts; those under seventeen were sold. (*JW* 6.418)

About a month after the end of the siege of Jerusalem and the destruction of the Temple (on September 26, according to Josephus), Titus celebrated his brother's eighteenth birthday (October 24) by a festival in Caesarea and, as Josephus reports, "reserving [or 'postponing'] in his honour for this festival much of the punishment of his Jewish captives. For the number of those destroyed in contests with wild beasts or with one another or in the flames exceeded two thousand five hundred" (*JW* 7.37-38). Later in the Roman colony of Berytus in Phoenicia, on the occasion of his father's sixty-first birthday (November 17), Titus mounted an even greater spectacle in which "multitudes" of captives perished (*JW* 7.39-40).

Jerusalem was devastated as were a number of other cities that fought against the Roman legions. The Temple was destroyed and the walls were torn down. The institutions and the persons of the priesthood disappeared from history as did the Essenes. The only institutional system for self-governance remaining after the war was the Jamnia Academy under the leadership of Johanan ben Zakkai, a Pharisee from the school of Hillel, who had escaped through the walls in 69 CE in a coffin. The Judean community in Palestine was eviscerated, and the power of Jerusalem as the capital city of the Judean community ended.

Most Judeans lived in the diaspora cities of the Roman and Parthian Empires before the war. The editors of *Encyclopedia Britannica*, for example, estimate five million Judeans outside Palestine before the war, four-fifths within the Roman Empire.[1] Tacitus estimated a Jerusalem population of six million Judeans during the war. Josephus' estimate of 1,200,000 who were killed or taken as prisoners during the war may have been somewhat inflated but is not outside the realm of possibility, given the extensive casualties in the Galilean and Judean campaigns of 68–69 CE. Given the probable exodus from Palestine during and after the war, an even higher percentage of the four to five million Judeans who survived the war lived in the Diaspora cities outside Palestine in the aftermath of the war.

As one might expect, there were high levels of tension between Judeans and Gentiles in the postwar period. In his concluding book 7 of *The Jewish War*, Josephus reports a history of ongoing conflict between Judeans and Gentiles, and between the various Israelite factions after the war. Judeans were widely dispersed among the various native populations of the Roman and Parthian Empires. A particularly dense population of Judeans lived in Syria with a concentration in Antioch (*JW* 7.43). A sign of the tension was the request of the people of Antioch to Titus to expel "the Judeans" from the city. When he refused, they requested that he remove the "brazen tablets" on which the privileges of the Judeans were inscribed, which he also refused. The Judeans thereby escaped further retribution at the hands of Titus but continued to suffer Gentile hostility as a consequence of the war (*JW* 7.103–111).

In Alexandria, a major conflict was engendered by a large group of Sicarii, the revolutionary faction, many of whom had occupied the fortress at Masada but who had fled to Alexandria. They advocated a revolt and murdered many moderate Judeans of rank who opposed them. Finally the council of elders called a general assembly and "exposed the madness of the Sicarii" and advocated seizing them in order to prevent a major retaliation from the Romans (*JW* 7.103–11). According to Josephus, the moderate Judeans seized six hundred Sicarii while others escaped who were later caught and brought back to Alexandria. All these were apparently handed

---

1. See online: http://www.britannica.com/EBchecked/topic/161756/Diaspora/.

over to the Romans because the next report is that those captured, including children, endured torture and death rather than call Caesar lord (*JW* 7.417–419). As a precaution against further revolt, the Roman governor closed the temple at Onias (*JW* 7.420).

Another major revolt inspired by the remnants of the Sicarii occurred in the cities around Cyrene. When the Sicarii leader, Jonathan, was captured, he accused many rich Judeans of involvement in the conspiracy. Catullus, the Roman administrator, apparently believed Jonathan and thought to win his own Judean War. He executed some three thousand Judeans and encouraged Jonathan to implicate the leading Judeans in Alexandria and Rome of conspiracy. Catullus finally ended up in Rome with Jonathan before Vespasian, where they accused many prominent Judeans, including Josephus, of plotting revolt. Vespasian, however, saw through Jonathan's accusations and executed him, while Catullus later suffered a miserable death (*JW* 7.437–453).

Josephus' story, which has a high degree of historical credibility, is a window into the postwar tensions both within Israelite communities and between Israelites and Gentiles throughout the Roman world. The fact that Josephus concludes his history with these stories is a sign of a rhetorical purpose of his book, namely, advocacy among the Judeans dispersed throughout the Roman and Parthian empires of the acceptance of Roman government and an end to revolutionary activism. Josephus' primary audience was the Roman aristocracy, for whom Josephus' account was an inside story of the motives and outcomes of the war for the Israelite people. His account, along with Mark's gospel, is a primary source for the reconstruction of the language and culture of the postwar Israelite community. These major events in Syria, Palestine, and northern Africa were only the eruptions of an underlying pervasive and ongoing tension that undoubtedly manifested itself in a variety of ways in different places during this period.

In the immediate aftermath of the war, the Roman leaders, Vespasian and Titus, were merciless in their punishment of the Judeans. But, after the initial retributions and the surrender of the holdouts in the fortress at Machaerus and the deaths of the Sicarii and their families at the Masada fortress, the postwar policy of Vespasian and Titus was apparently relatively beneficent. Vespasian levied an annual two-drachma tax on all Judeans throughout the empire to be paid "into the Capitol," that is, Rome; this was the levy that had previously been paid by Judeans to the Temple in Jerusalem (*JW* 7.218). Other than this, the Roman government allowed the communities of Judeans to live without ongoing retribution.

Two Israelite religious sects survived the war. The one was promoted by the rabbinic Academy at Jamnia under the initial leadership of Johanan ben Zakkai. The focus of this sect was the Torah and the laws that marked Israel off from the Gentiles as a self-consciously separate people. The name "Judeans" and later "Jews" was increasingly applied to this sect exclusively. This was largely because the other sect of Judeans adaptable enough to survive the war was the followers of Jesus, variously called "the Way" and "the church," who later became known as "Christians." Because of their inclusion of Gentiles decades before the war, they did not continue many of the practices that marked off Judeans from Gentiles and made social intercourse with Gentiles difficult. As a result, they had no reason to describe their community to outsiders as "Judean" or "Jewish." That label was incongruous with the new identity into which they were calling Gentile converts to the religion of Israel. The long-term consequence of this is that the term "Jewish" became a label that marked the division between these two Israelite sects. This term and the name "Christian" disguised the fact that both were thoroughly rooted in the traditions of Israel, and that both interpreted Israel's traditions under the influence of various dimensions of Hellenistic culture.

Given this context, a major issue that faced Mark and the Judean and Gentile communities of the last three decades of the first century for whom he composed this gospel was the future of the relationship between Judeans and Gentiles in the postwar Roman Empire.[2] How could the community of Israel, known to outsiders as "Jews," and the allegiance of this community to the God of Israel be reconceived and reconstructed in the wake of this immense tragedy? What was the way forward in the relationship between Judeans and Gentiles? Would Israel continue the revolution and the quest for an independent state, as the Sicarii continued to violently pursue in postwar Alexandria? Would Judeans withdraw from interaction with Gentiles as much as possible, or would they seek active reconciliation and community with Gentiles?

The two sects had much in common. Both were nonviolent, although Rabbi Akiba championed the revolt led by Simon bar Kokhba some sixty years later (132–135 CE). Both maintained a policy of refusal to worship the emperor, for which the consequences were different, since the Romans recognized the rights of "Jews" to observe their religion but not the

---

2. See Marcus, "The Jewish War." As Marcus writes, "Instead of speaking vaguely of the Gospel's context as one of 'persecution,' we may specify the context of intra- and intercommunal tension produced by the upheaval of the Jewish War . . . Mark may thus be situated along a time line of developing opposition between Christian communities and the Jewish world from which they sprang. Many of the inhabitants of the latter world took a disastrous plunge into revolutionary activism, then responded to the wreckage of their dreams by closing ranks around a new leadership and a new definition of who was and was not a Jew" (462).

ethnically mixed followers of Jesus. The rabbis pursued a strategy of separatism while the church continued its policies of proselytism of Gentiles and the transformation of Roman society. The "church" of the followers of Jesus grew rapidly, and the community of the "Judeans" gradually recovered its former numbers. But the options available to the Judean survivors of the Judean-Roman War only emerged through a process that was long, messy, and complex. Mark composed his narrative about the Messiah of peace as a contribution to what at the time was an anguished and often violent struggle both within the community of Israelites and with their foreign neighbors. The search for an appropriate understanding of Mark's gospel requires us to learn as much about that struggle as we can and to listen to performances of Mark, not from the perspective of the options that emerged later in their ongoing history, but from the perspective of a struggle that lacked the clarity with which we have become accustomed to view it today.

Appendix 2

A SOUND MAP OF MARK'S PASSION-RESURRECTION NARRATIVE

THIS SOUND MAP IS DESIGNED TO INDICATE SOME OF THE dimensions of the sound of Mark's climactic story. This follows the conclusion of Margaret Lee and Bernard Brandon Scott based on the discussions of the Greek grammarians[1] that the sounds of ancient Greek compositions were structured in breath units of cola and periods. There are some modifications of their analysis of the sounds of Mark's crucifixion story[2] in this sound map. A comparison of the two maps may help to clarify the way the criteria shape the decisions about the sounds of the story. A listing of the criteria I have used is offered here in an effort to be as specific and objective as possible about my criteria for the analysis of the story's sounds.

This kind of analysis is a foundational step in a performance-criticism study of a biblical story. It alone provides a basis for many of the decisions about the performance of a text and the construction of its meaning. However, the decisions about the cola and periods are sometimes artistic decisions about emphasis and rhythm, for which the objective signs are ambiguous and the decisions, therefore, subjective. For example, the decisions about whether a particular colon is a new period or is a second colon in a period such as in the introduction to the Sanhedrin trial (14:53–54) or the crucifixion descriptions (15:24–25) are essentially artistic judgments based on what is most expressive.

---

1. Lee and Scott, *Sound Mapping*.
2. Ibid., 199–218.

The Criteria of Comma, Cola, and Period Construction

1. Breath test for cola. If the phrase is too long to be said with relative ease in one breath, divide into two cola. Periods with multiple cola are good Greek construction. An example is the list of the women witnesses in 15:40–41.[3] This is not a possible colon because it doesn't pass the breath test; also this is a description of the women mourners and should be slow rather than fast.

2. Cola for speech introductions and the speeches that follow are separated into new cola in order to change voice and breathe after introduction. Specifically, a new cola begins after ὅτι when it is used to introduce a quotation. These cola can be considered as commas and a long colon can have multiple commas.

3. A new speaker/character = a new period.

4. A longer pause or bigger breath is taken between periods than between cola within a period.

5. A speed test. Long cola = fast tempo; short cola = slow tempo.

6. A γάρ clause always begins a new colon in order to enable the change in the storyteller's relationship to the audience.

7. An unambiguous stop constitutes the end of a period.

8. An interrogative stop followed by an indicative is the end and beginning of successive cola or periods.

9. Successive participial phrases can constitute separate cola (as in the introduction to the Pilate trial—15:1a-b).

10. Successive verb clauses usually are separate cola (as in the mockery by the soldiers—15:16–20).

11. ἵνα clauses usually are separate cola.

12. Multiple nominative phrases can constitute separate colas (as in the women witnesses—15:40–41).

13. The introduction of a new character is an indication of a new period.[4]

The delineation of cola and periods is in part related to an estimate of the length of pauses between segments of the story. Cola and periods are

---

3. Ibid., 213.
4. See Lee and Scott's analysis of Luke 2 for a contrasting decision: ibid., 293.

also shaped by the relationship between the storyteller and the audience, variations in voice and tone related to characters, and variations in tempo.

There are areas of significant ambiguity in the identification of commas, cola, and periods. In long periods it is unclear whether a long introductory nominative clause with multiple phrases would have a second cola with the verb clause (instances: introduction to the anointing in Bethany—14:3, introduction to Judas' betrayal—14:10, introduction to the Passover preparations—14:12, introduction to the prophecy of denial—14:26, introduction to the arrest—14:43). I clearly disagree on the number of cola in the introductory periods because of the speed factor (the cola of John 20 for example).

Finally, a factor in the analysis of cola and periods is that the editors of modern Greek texts have made decisions about the cola, periods, paragraphs, and stories of the text that are indicated by punctuation, paragraphing, and titles. The criteria for the punctuation and units of the Greek texts are often inconsistent and have generally not considered the sounds of the text as a factor. This is even more characteristic of the various translations. For the purposes of objective sound mapping, it is a good idea to begin with a Greek text that has no punctuation. But it is virtually impossible to avoid being influenced by the textual editions we have studied. If sound mapping is valid, the arrangement of the Greek texts and the English translations will need to be reevaluated.

A new period always begins at the left margin and in the sound map below the periods and cola are numbered. If it is a complex period with more than one colon, the additional cola are indented. A comma within a colon is further indented but will have no number on the left. If a period or colon is too long for a line, the remaining words will be right justified. The asterisks mark instances of hiatus in which two sequential vowels are present rather than the more usual vowel/consonant. The hiatus marks the brief interruption that is required in order to pronounce two vowels in sequence. One way of conceiving these markings in sound is as a hierarchy of shorter to longer pauses between segments of the composition: the hiatus, the comma, the colon, the period, the episode, the story, and the section.

I have arranged the Greek and English texts in sections, stories, and episodes. The stories and sections are given titles and numbers. An empty line marks the pauses between the episodes. The purpose of these headings is to indicate the character of the pauses between the various segments of the stories. The ancient Greek grammarians do not discuss any of these units of composition. The delineation of the episodes is based on patterns of usage. The episode analysis is included because it facilitates memorization of the story. I make no claims about these units of the story in the ancient context. It is probable that the colon and period were units of composition that the composer of this story understood and used consciously. Because the characteristics of the episode are so consistently present, it is also likely that the composer was consciously aware of this unit of composition. The same is true for the units of the stories and the sections. But there is no way of knowing whether this was conscious and intentional. It is hard to imagine, however, that the degree of artistic shaping present was only instinctive.

The marks or sounds of an opening period in an episode include repetition of words either within the episode (14:26–29, 50–52) or in parallel with a contiguous episode beginning (14:60 and 61b; 15:9, 12, 15); appositives and genitive absolutes (14:3, 10, 66; 15:21, 42); settings of time and place (14:1, 3, 12, 32, 53; 15:1, 33, 42); a new character (14:3, 10, 12, 43, 53, 66; 15:1, 16, 21, 42–43; 16:5); "immediately" (εὐθὺς—14:43, 72; 15:1); verbs of motion (14:3, 10, 17, 25, 32, 43, 53, 66, 68b; 15:16, 43; 16:1, 5, 8); circumstantial participles (14:17, 22, 35, 50, 67, 15:1, 21, 42); and purpose clauses (ἵνα), usually translated as "in order to" (14:10, 12, 35; 16:1).

The characteristic marks or sounds of episode endings are rounding, that is, repetition of sounds from earlier openings or parallel endings in contiguous episodes (e.g., 14:10 and 11b; 14:50 and 52; 14:56 and 59; 14:68 and 70); extremes in colon/period length, often quite short (14:5b, 11, 31b, 72c; 15:20b; 16:4b, 8d) but sometimes unusually long (14:62; 15:40–41); ellipsis and asyndeton that shorten cola by requiring the listener to supply a missing particle or word (14:3; 21b; 38); "begin to" combined with an infinitive (ἤρξατο—14:19, 71; 15:8); and climactic circumstantial participial phrases (14:52, 72; 15:8, 37) and purpose (ἵνα) clauses (15:15, 20). Thus, the beginnings and endings of episodes are consistently marked by colon/period length, repetitions, and formal patterns of grammatical usage, as well as by subject matter.

The story is almost always composed of two or more episodes. The stories with one episode in Mark's PRN are: the plot of the chief priests and scribes (14:1–2)/Judas' offer to hand Jesus over to the chief priests (14:10–11) and the preparations (15:21–23)/the mocking (15:29–32). This may be a sign that Mark wove the story of the anointing into an already-formed story of the plot. Luke's version of the plot story with no Bethany anointing (Luke 22:1–6) may be evidence that a pre-Markan version was circulating in the community of those telling Jesus stories. *Story* is an ambiguous name for a formal category like this because it is the most natural term for everything. Lee and Scott use the term *part* for the larger unit of multiple cola in Mark's crucifixion narrative, and *unit* and *section* in the Sermon on the Mount. But for now *story* will do: thus, the stories of the prophecy of Peter's denial, the Pilate trial, the burial, and so forth.

Since the formal characteristics of episodes are melded into the form of the story, the specific formal marks of stories are often the same as episodes. However, there are discernible patterns to the story. A story usually begins with an indication of time and/or place and describes an event in that setting. The boundaries of a story are sometimes marked by a rounding repetition in the ending of a key word or phrase introduced at the beginning of the story. Thus, the Pilate-trial story begins with the authorities handing over (παρέδωκαν) Jesus to Pilate (15:1) and ends with Pilate handing Jesus over (παρέδωκεν) to the soldiers (15:15). Likewise, the boundaries of the stories of the plot (the chief priests and scribes "sought how to arrest and kill him," and Judas "sought how to hand him over"—14:1, 11), and the preparations for the Passover (the disciples asked "where do you want us to prepare the Passover?" and "they prepared the Passover"—14:12, 16) have a linked verbal motif at the beginning and end of the story.

Another pattern that marks the boundaries of stories is contiguous stories with parallel endings that indicate where the stories end. Three instances of this pattern are: (1) Pilate hands Jesus over "in order to crucify him," and the soldiers lead him away "in order to crucify him" (15:15 and 20); (2) they "crucified with him" two insurrectionists, and "those crucified with him" reviled him (15:27 and 32b); and (3) "there were women watching from a distance . . . Mary Magdalene and Mary the mother," and "Mary Magdalene and Mary watched where he was laid" (15:40 and 47). A consistent pattern is that episodes with appositives and genitive absolutes in their first periods always occur at the beginning of stories (e.g., 14:3, 10, 43, 66; 15:21, 42), and verbs of motion and circumstantial participles after καὶ and δὲ usually occur in the opening of a story (e.g., 14:3, 10, 17, 25, 32, 43, 53, 66, 15:16, 43; 16:1, 5. 8; some exceptions include 14:37, 39, 48, 60, 68b). Finally, the most extreme variations in long and short colon/period length tend to occur at the ends of stories (e.g., 14:9, 11, 16, 25, 31b, 72; 15:20b, 32b, 40–41; 16:4b, 8b). The identification of these marks of story beginnings and endings will be another set of memory hooks for those explorers who want to learn and tell Mark's PRN. The building of mnemonic structures was probably one of the motives for these sonic constructions.

The resurrection section is formally ambiguous. The most natural way to evaluate its form is that it is both a story and a section. However, it has the markings of story beginnings in the verbs of motion and descriptions of the three distinct places: "out to the tomb," "into the tomb," and "going out from the tomb." There are also climactic cola at the end of the three potential stories: the big stone, "there you will see him," and "for they were afraid." But on first take, these do not appear to be three different stories because they are so short.

However, in this section everything is short, and everything gets shorter and shorter. The periods are mainly simple periods with a single colon. The only complex periods are the introductory periods that describe the women buying the spices, going out to the tomb (16:1–2), and going into the tomb (16:5). There appears to be a correlation between length and tempo elsewhere, and, if so, the whole resurrection section gets slower and slower. This fits with the frequent use of short cola at moments of major climax in the overall story. In this case, it may be that there are three stories in the section, each of which gets shorter, as do the episodes and the cola. If so, this is the composer's way of giving maximum emphasis to the resurrection. Everything builds to the climax of the women saying nothing to anyone: ἐφοβοῦντο γάρ.

Finally, the largest unit is the section. A section has two or more thematically unified stories, begins with a change in place and usually time, and ends with a major climax. Statements of continuity or connection in time or place link otherwise disparate stories together. For example, in contrast to the other sections, the stories of the plot are not linked by being at the same place, but they are connected by being on the same day, Wednesday, the day before the feast. This linkage in time connects the conflict between some of the disciples and Jesus with Judas Iscariot's going from Bethany to the chief priests' place to hand Jesus over to them. And the stories of the crucifixion and death sections are located at the same place, Golgotha, but are marked by the hours rather than by distinctive places.

The analysis here is that there are eight sections in Mark's PRN: the plot on the day before the feast (14:1–11), the Passover meal at the upper room (14:12–24), the night on the Mount of Olives (14:25–52), the night at the house of the high priest (14:53–72), the morning at Pilate's place (15:1–20), the crucifixion (15:21–32), the death and burial (15:33–47), and the announcement of the resurrection at the tomb (16:1–8). The same patterns of repetition that mark the boundaries of the stories are also used to mark the beginnings and endings of the sections: the ring in which beginnings and endings are sonically linked and the parallel endings. With the exception of the Passover-meal section, all the sections in Mark 14 have a ring structure. In the ring sections, the stories that begin and end each section are thematically unified and surround a story with a related but fundamentally different subject. Thus, in section 1, the plot of the chief priests surrounds the anointing at Bethany. In Section 3, the prophecy and fulfillment of the disciples' flight frames the Gethsemane story; and in section 4, the stories of Peter's following and denying Jesus in the courtyard of the high priest introduce and conclude the trial before the Sanhedrin.

The endings of the sections in Mark 15 are marked by parallel endings in the stories of the section. The endings of the stories at Pilate's place (of the trial and of the soldiers' mocking) are "in order that he might be crucified" (ἵνα σταυρωθῇ), and "in order to crucify him" (ἵνα σταυρώσωσιν αὐτόν). The two concluding stories in the crucifixion section end with descriptions of the two insurrectionists crucified with Jesus: "And with him they crucified" (καὶ σὺν αὐτῷ σταυροῦσιν), echoed by "and those crucified with him" (καὶ οἱ συνεσταυρωμένοι σὺν αὐτῷ). And the stories of the death section end with the women who were watching and, by implication, grieving: "And there were women watching from a distance, among whom were Mary Magdalene, Mary, the mother of James, the younger brother, and Joses, and Salome" (ἦσαν δὲ **καὶ** γυναῖκες ἀπὸ μακρόθεν θεωροῦσαι, ἐν αἷς **καὶ** Μαρία ἡ Μαγδαληνὴ **καὶ** Μαρία ἡ Ἰακώβου τοῦ μικροῦ καὶ Ἰωσῆτος μήτηρ **καὶ** Σαλώμη); and at the burial, "And Mary Magdalene and Mary, the mother of Joses watched" (ἡ δὲ Μαρία ἡ Μαγδαληνὴ καὶ Μαρία ἡ Ἰωσῆτος ἐθεώρουν). Whatever we name these units of Mark's narrative, the attention to detail and the consistency of formal structures of sound composition is at some level amazing. A lot of care and compositional sophistication has been spent on this story. Detailed study of the sound maps will enable you to see and hear the high degree of artistic shaping present in Mark's narrative.

In summary, the most important technique for the structuring of the units of sound in Mark's narrative is repetition. The repetitions mark the boundaries of episodes, stories, and sections. The repetitions are constructed with consistency and attention to detail. Among the marks of beginnings and endings, the most important technique is the use of grammatical constructions that facilitate the initial orientation to the story that follows in longer and more elaborate complex periods, and the conclusion of the story in climactic, usually simpler but sometimes markedly more complex periods. All these are ways of constructing sound for maximum audience impact.

I would highly recommend the reading of the ancient theoreticians as well as the major works of recent "sound" scholarship, of which the most important for New Testament study is *Sound Mapping the New Testament*,[5] by everyone who is interested in the theoretical foundations for the analysis of the compositions of the New Testament as sound. This is the foundation for the reconception of the New Testament as performance literature.

---

5. For New Testament study, see Lee and Scott, *Sound Mapping*. Others include James Kleist, Lausberg, and Stanford (all cited in Lee and Scott, *Sound Mapping*).

In the sound map or score, the following marks are used to indicate the various features of the episodes, stories and sections of the passion-resurrection narrative:
- **bold** = repetitions
- (parentheses) = settings of time and place
- *italics* = genitive absolutes and appositives
- underline = γὰρ ("for") clauses (not in direct discourse)
- underline = ἤρξαντο ("to begin") with an infinitive
- underline = ἵνα ("in order to") clauses
- underline + *italics* = verbs or participles of motion
- ^ = asyndeton
- >< = short and long endings
- * = hiatus, the succession of vowels in the final and initial sounds of adjoining words

Section 1. The Day before the Feast

Story 1. The Plot of the Chief Priest and Scribes

1.1 (ην δὲ τὸ πάσχα καὶ τὰ ἄζυμα μετὰ δύο ἡμέρας.)
2.1 **καὶ ἐζήτουν** οἱ ἀρχιερεῖς καὶ οἱ γραμματεῖς **πῶς αὐτὸν** ἐν δόλῳ κρατήσαντες ἀποκτείνωσιν.
3.1 ἔλεγον <u>γάρ</u>,
3.2 Μὴ* ἐν τῇ* ἑορτῇ, μήποτε* ἔσται θόρυβος τοῦ λαοῦ.

Story 2. The Anointing at Bethany

1.1 (*Καὶ ὄντος αὐτ<u>οῦ</u> ἐν Βηθανίᾳ ἐν τῇ οἰκίᾳ Σίμωνος τ<u>οῦ</u> λεπροῦ*) *κατακειμέν<u>ου</u> αὐτοῦ*
1.2 <u>*ἦλθεν*</u> γυνὴ <u>*ἔχουσα*</u> ἀλάβαστρον μ<u>ύρου</u> νάρδου πιστικῆς πολ<u>υτελοῦς</u>.
2.1 ^συντρίψασα τὴν ἀλάβαστρον κατέχεεν αὐτοῦ τῆς κεφαλῆς.

3.1 ἦσαν δέ τινες ἀγανακτοῦντες πρὸς ἑαυτούς,
3.2 Εἰς τί* ἡ* ἀπώλεια* αὕτη τοῦ μύρου γέγονεν;
4.1 ἠδύνατο <u>γὰρ</u> τοῦτο τὸ μύρον πρα**θῆ**ναι* ἐπάνω δηναρίων τριακοσίων καὶ δο**θῆ**ναι τοῖς πτωχοῖς·
5.1 >καὶ* ἐνεβριμῶντο* αὐτῇ.<

6.1 ὁ δὲ Ἰησοῦς εἶπεν,
6.2   Ἄφετε* αὐτήν·
7.1 τί* αὐτῇ κόπους παρέχετε;
8.1 καλὸν ἔργον ἠργάσατο* ἐν ἐμοί.

9.1 **πάντοτε** γὰρ τοὺς πτωχοὺς **ἔχετε** μεθ᾽ ἑαυτῶν,
9.2   καὶ* ὅταν θέλητε δύνασθε αὐτοῖς εὖ ποιῆσαι,
9.3   ἐμὲ δὲ* οὐ **πάντοτε* ἔχετε**. (rounded period with **πάντοτε* ἔχετε**)
10.1 ὃ* ἔσχεν ἐποίησεν·
10.2   προέλαβεν μυρίσαι **τὸ σῶμά μου*** εἰς τὸν ἐνταφιασμόν.
11.1 >**ἀμὴν** δὲ **λέγω ὑμῖν**,
11.2   ὅπου* ἐὰν κηρυχθῇ τὸ* εὐαγγέλιον εἰς ὅλον τὸν κόσμον,
11.3   καὶ* ὃ* ἐποίησεν αὕτη λαληθήσεται* εἰς μνημόσυνον αὐτῆς.<

Story 3. The Betrayal by Judas Iscariot

1.1 Καὶ **Ἰούδας** Ἰσκαριὼθ ὁ* **εἷς τῶν δώδεκα**
1.2   <u>ἀπῆλθεν</u> (πρὸς **τοὺς ἀρχιερεῖς**) <u>ἵνα</u>* <u>αὐτὸν</u> <u>παραδοῖ</u>* αὐτοῖς.
2.1 οἱ δὲ* ἀκούσαντες ἐχάρησαν
2.2   καὶ* ἐπηγγείλαντο* αὐτῷ* ἀργύριον δοῦναι.
3.1 >**καὶ*** ἐζήτει πῶς αὐτὸν εὐκαίρως **παραδοῖ**.< (rounded with ἐζήτουν πῶς αὐτὸν in 14:2 and with αὐτὸν παραδοῖ in 14:10)

Section 2. The Last Passover

Story 1. The Preparations for Passover

1.1 (Καὶ τῇ πρώτῃ* ἡμέρᾳ τῶν ἀζύμων, ὅτε τὸ πάσχα* ἔθυον,)
        λέγουσιν αὐτῷ* οἱ μαθηταὶ* αὐτοῦ,
1.2   **Ποῦ** θέλεις ἀπελθόντες **ἑτοιμάσωμεν** ἵνα **φάγῃς τὸ πάσχα**;
2.1 καὶ ἀποστέλλει δύο τῶν μαθητῶν αὐτοῦ καὶ λέγει αὐτοῖς,
2.2   Ὑπάγετε* εἰς τὴν πόλιν,
2.3   καὶ* ἀπαντήσει* ὑμῖν ἄνθρωπος κεράμιον ὕδατος βαστάζων.

3.1 ἀκολουθήσατε* αὐτῷ, καὶ **ὅπου*** ἐὰν εἰσέλθῃ* εἴπατε τῷ* οἰκοδεσπότῃ* ὅτι
3.2   Ὁ διδάσκαλος λέγει,
3.3   **Ποῦ*** ἐστιν τὸ κατάλυμά μου
3.4   **ὅπου τὸ πάσχα** μετὰ τῶν μαθητῶν μου **φάγω**;
4.1 καὶ αὐτὸς ὑμῖν δείξει ἀνάγαιον μέγα ἐστρωμένον ἕτοιμον
4.2   καὶ ἐκεῖ **ἑτοιμάσατε** ἡμῖν.

A Sound Map of Mark's Passion-Resurrection Narrative

5.1 καὶ <u>ἐξῆλθον</u> οἱ μαθηταὶ
5.2 καὶ <u>ἦλθον</u> εἰς τὴν πόλιν
5.3 καὶ εὗρον καθὼς εἶπεν αὐτοῖς.
6.1 καὶ **ἡτοίμασαν τὸ πάσχα.** (rounded with **ἑτοιμάσωμεν . . . τὸ πάσχα**)

Story 2. The Prophecy of the Betrayal

1.1 (Καὶ* ὀψίας γενομένης) <u>ἔρχεται</u> μετὰ **τῶν δώδεκα**.
2.1 καὶ* ἀνακειμένων αὐτῶν καὶ* ἐσθιόντων ὁ Ἰησοῦς εἶπεν,
2.2 **Ἀμὴν λέγω* ὑμῖν** ὅτι*
2.3 **εἷς** ἐξ ὑμῶν **παραδώσει** με,
2.4 ὁ* ἐσθίων μετ' ἐμοῦ.
3.1 ^ἤρξαντο λυπεῖσθαι καὶ λέγειν αὐτῷ* **εἷς** κατὰ* **εἷς**,
3.2 Μήτι* ἐγώ;

4.1 ὁ δὲ* εἶπεν αὐτοῖς,
4.2 **Εἷς τῶν δώδεκα,**
4.3 ὁ* ἐμβαπτόμενος μετ' ἐμοῦ* εἰς τὸ τρύβλιον.
5.1 ὅτι* ὁ μὲν υἱὸς τοῦ* ἀνθρώπου* ὑπάγει καθὼς γέγραπται περὶ* αὐτοῦ,
5.2 οὐαὶ δὲ τῷ* **ἀνθρώπῳ* ἐκείνῳ** δι' οὗ* ὁ* υἱὸς τοῦ* ἀνθρώπου
παραδίδοται:
6.1 καλὸν αὐτῷ* εἰ* οὐκ ἐγεννήθη* ὁ* **ἄνθρωπος ἐκεῖνος**.

Story 3. The Last Passover

1.1 Καὶ *ἐσθιόντων* αὐτῶν *λαβὼν* ἄρτον εὐλογήσας ἔκλασεν καὶ* **ἔδωκεν αὐτοῖς**
καὶ εἶπεν
1.2 Λάβετε.
2.1 >τοῦτό ἐστιν τὸ σῶμά μου.<

2.1 καὶ ποτήριον εὐχαριστήσας **ἔδωκεν αὐτοῖς,**
2.2 καὶ ἔπιον ἐξ αὐτοῦ πάντες.
2.3 καὶ εἶπεν αὐτοῖς, **Τοῦτό* ἐστιν τὸ*** αἷμά μου τῆς διαθήκης τὸ* ἐκχυννόμενον
ὑπὲρ πολλῶν.
3.1> **ἀμὴν λέγω* ὑμῖν** ὅτι* οὐκέτι* οὐ μὴ **πίω*** ἐκ τοῦ γενήματος τῆς ἀμπέλου*
3.2 ἕως τῆς ἡμέρας ἐκείνης ὅταν αὐτὸ **πίνω** καινὸν ἐν τῇ βασιλείᾳ τοῦ
θεοῦ.<

Section 3. The Night in the Garden of Gethsemane.

Story 1. The Prophecy of Scandalization and Denial

1.1 (Καὶ ὑμνήσαντες ἐξῆλθον εἰς τὸ Ὄρος τῶν Ἐλαιῶν.)
2.1 **Καὶ λέγει αὐτοῖς ὁ Ἰησοῦς ὅτι**
2.2   **Πάντες σκανδαλισθήσεσθε,** ὅτι γέγραπται,
2.3   Πατάξω τὸν ποιμένα, καὶ τὰ πρόβατα διασκορπισθήσονται,
2.4   ἀλλὰ μετὰ τὸ ἐγερθῆναί με **προάξω ὑμᾶς εἰς τὴν Γαλιλαίαν.**
3.1 δὲ Πέτρος ἔφη* αὐτῷ,
3.2   Εἰ καὶ **πάντες σκανδαλισθήσονται,** ἀλλ' οὐκ ἐγώ.

4.1 **καὶ λέγει αὐτῷ ὁ Ἰησοῦς,**
4.2   Ἀμὴν λέγω σοι ὅτι σὺ σήμερον ταύτῃ τῇ νυκτὶ
        πρὶν ἢ **δὶς** ἀλέκτορα φωνῆσαι
        τρίς με* ἀπαρνήσῃ.
5.1 ὁ δὲ ἐκπερισσῶς ἐλάλει,
5.2   Ἐὰν **δέῃ** με συναποθανεῖν σοι,
        οὐ μή σε* ἀπαρνήσομαι.
6.1 >ὡσαύτως δὲ καὶ **πάντες** ἔλεγον.< (rounded with **πάντες**)

Story 2. Prayer in Gethsemane

1.1 (Καὶ <u>ἔρχονται</u> εἰς χωρίον οὗ τὸ ὄνομα Γεθσημανί,) καὶ λέγει τοῖς μαθηταῖς
                                                                    αὐτου,
1.2   Καθίσατε **ὧδε** ἕως προσεύξωμαι.
2.1 καὶ παραλαμβάνει τὸν Πέτρον καὶ [τὸν] Ἰάκωβον καὶ [τὸν] Ἰωάννην μετ'
                                                                    αὐτοῦ,
2.2   καὶ <u>ἤρξατο</u> ἐκθαμβεῖσθαι καὶ ἀδημονεῖν, καὶ λέγει αὐτοῖς,
2.3   Περίλυπός ἐστιν ἡ ψυχή μου ἕως θανάτου.
3.1 >μείνατε **ὧδε** καὶ **γρηγορεῖτε.**<

4.1 καὶ <u>προελθὼν</u> μικρὸν ἔπιπτεν ἐπὶ τῆς γῆς,
4.2   καὶ **προσηύχετο*** ἵνα εἰ **δυνατόν** ἐστιν παρέλθῃ ἀπ' αὐτοῦ* ἡ* ὥρα,
5.1 καὶ ἔλεγεν, Αββα ὁ πατήρ, πάντα **δυνατά** σοι,
5.2   παρένεγκε τὸ ποτήριον τοῦτο* ἀπ' ἐμοῦ.
6.1 **ἀλλ'** οὐ **τί*** ἐγὼ θέλω
6.2   **ἀλλὰ τί** σύ.

7.1 καὶ <u>ἔρχεται</u> καὶ **εὑρίσκει** αὐτοὺς καθεύδοντας, καὶ λέγει τῷ Πέτρῳ,

7.2   Σίμων, **καθεύδεις**;
7.3   οὐκ ἴσχυσας μίαν ὥραν **γρηγορῆσαι**;
8.1 **γρηγορεῖτε** καὶ **προσεύχεσθε**, ἵνα μὴ ἔλθητε εἰς πειρασμόν.
9.1 τὸ μὲν πνεῦμα πρόθυμον
9.2   ἡ δὲ σὰρξ ἀσθενής.

10.1 καὶ **πάλιν** *ἀπελθὼν* προσηύξατο τὸν αὐτὸν λόγον εἰπών.
11.1 καὶ **πάλιν** *ἐλθὼν* εὗρεν αὐτοὺς **καθεύδοντας**.
12.1 ἦσαν γὰρ αὐτῶν οἱ ὀφθαλμοὶ καταβαρυνόμενοι,
12.2   καὶ οὐκ ᾔδεισαν τί ἀποκριθῶσιν αὐτῷ.

13.1 καὶ *ἔρχεται* τὸ τρίτον καὶ λέγει αὐτοῖς,
13.2   **Καθεύδετε** τὸ λοιπὸν καὶ ἀναπαύεσθε;
14.1 ἀπέχει.

15.1 **ἦλθεν ἡ ὥρα**.
16.1 **ἰδοὺ παραδίδοται** ὁ υἱὸς τοῦ ἀνθρώπου εἰς τὰς χεῖρας τῶν ἁμαρτωλῶν.

17.1 ἐγείρεσθε ἄγωμεν.
18.2 **ἰδοὺ ὁ παραδιδούς** με ἤγγικεν.

Story 3: The Arrest

1.1 (Καὶ *εὐθὺς* ἔτι αὐτοῦ λαλοῦντος *παραγίνεται* Ἰούδας εἷς τῶν δώδεκα)
1.2   καὶ μετ' αὐτοῦ ὄχλος **μετὰ μαχαιρῶν καὶ ξύλων**
                παρὰ **τῶν ἀρχιερέων καὶ τῶν γραμματέων καὶ τῶν πρεσβυτέρων**.
2.1 δεδώκει δὲ **ὁ παραδιδοὺς** αὐτὸν σύσσημον αὐτοῖς λέγων,
2.2   Ὃν ἂν **φιλήσω αὐτός ἐστιν**.
2.3 >**κρατήσατε αὐτὸν** καὶ ἀπάγετε ἀσφαλῶς.<

3.1 καὶ *ἐλθὼν* *εὐθὺς* *προσελθὼν* αὐτῷ λέγει, Ῥαββί, καὶ **κατεφίλησεν αὐτόν**.
4.1 οἱ δὲ ἐπέβαλον τὰς χεῖρας αὐτῷ **καὶ** *ἐκράτησαν* *αὐτόν*.   (Fast)
5.1 >εἷς δέ [τις] τῶν παρεστηκότων σπασάμενος τὴν **μάχαιραν**
        ἔπαισεν τὸν δοῦλον τοῦ ἀρχιερέως καὶ ἀφεῖλεν αὐτοῦ τὸ ὠτάριον.<

6.1 καὶ ἀποκριθεὶς ὁ Ἰησοῦς εἶπεν αὐτοῖς,
6.2   Ὡς ἐπὶ λῃστὴν ἐξήλθατε **μετὰ μαχαιρῶν καὶ ξύλων** συλλαβεῖν με;
7.1 καθ' ἡμέραν ἤμην πρὸς ὑμᾶς ἐν τῷ ἱερῷ διδάσκων καὶ οὐκ **ἐκρατήσατέ** με.
8.1> ἀλλ' ἵνα πληρωθῶσιν αἱ γραφαί.<

9.1 καὶ ἀφέντες αὐτὸν <u>ἔφυγον</u> **πάντες**.
10.1 Καὶ νεανίσκος τις συνηκολούθει αὐτῷ περιβεβλημένος **σινδόνα ἐπὶ γυμνοῦ**,
καὶ κρατοῦσιν αὐτόν.
11.1 >ὁ δὲ καταλιπὼν τὴν **σινδόνα** γυμνὸς <u>ἔφυγεν</u>.< (rounded with <u>ἔφυγον</u> and σινδόνα ... γυμνοῦ)

Section 4. The Trial at the Home of the High Priest

Story 1. The Trial before the Sanhedrin

1.1 Καὶ <u>ἀπήγαγον</u> τὸν Ἰησοῦν πρὸς τὸν **ἀρχιερέα**.
2.1 καὶ <u>συνέρχονται</u> πάντες **οἱ ἀρχιερεῖς καὶ οἱ πρεσβύτεροι καὶ οἱ γραμματεῖς**.

1.1 **καὶ ὁ Πέτρος** ἀπὸ μακρόθεν <u>ἠκολούθησεν</u> αὐτῷ ἕως ἔσω **εἰς τὴν αὐλὴν**
τοῦ ἀρχιερέως.
2.1 **καὶ** ἦν **συγκαθήμενος** μετὰ τῶν ὑπηρετῶν **καὶ θερμαινόμενος** πρὸς τὸ φῶς.

3.1 οἱ δὲ **ἀρχιερεῖς** καὶ ὅλον τὸ συνέδριον ἐζήτουν κατὰ τοῦ Ἰησοῦ **μαρτυρίαν**
εἰς τὸ θανατῶσαι αὐτόν, καὶ οὐχ ηὕρισκον.
4.1 πολλοὶ <u>γὰρ</u> **ἐψευδομαρτύρουν κατ' αὐτοῦ**, καὶ ἴσαι αἱ **μαρτυρίαι** οὐκ ἦσαν.

5.1 καί τινες **ἀναστάντες ἐψευδομαρτύρουν κατ' αὐτοῦ** λέγοντες ὅτι
5.2 Ἡμεῖς ἠκούσαμεν αὐτοῦ **λέγοντος ὅτι**
5.3 Ἐγὼ καταλύσω τὸν ναὸν τοῦτον τὸν **χειροποίητον**
5.4 καὶ διὰ τριῶν ἡμερῶν ἄλλον **ἀχειροποίητον** οἰκοδομήσω.
6.1 καὶ οὐδὲ οὕτως **ἴση** ἦν ἡ **μαρτυρία** αὐτῶν.

7.1 καὶ **ἀναστὰς ὁ ἀρχιερεὺς** εἰς μέσον **ἐπηρώτησεν** τὸν Ἰησοῦν λέγων,
7.2   Οὐκ ἀποκρίνῃ* οὐδέν;
7.3   τί* οὗτοί σου **καταμαρτυροῦσιν**;
8.1 ὁ δὲ* ἐσιώπα καὶ* οὐκ ἀπεκρίνατο* οὐδέν.

9.1 πάλιν ὁ **ἀρχιερεὺς ἐπηρώτα*** αὐτὸν καὶ λέγει αὐτῷ,
9.2   Σὺ* εἶ* ὁ Χριστὸς ὁ* υἱὸς τοῦ* εὐλογητοῦ;
10.1 ὁ δὲ Ἰησοῦς εἶπεν,
10.2   Ἐγώ* εἰμι,
10.3   καὶ* ὄψεσθε τὸν υἱὸν τοῦ* ἀνθρώπου*
10.4   ἐκ δεξιῶν καθήμενον τῆς δυνάμεως
10.5   καὶ* ἐρχόμενον μετὰ τῶν νεφελῶν τοῦ* οὐρανοῦ.

11.1 ὁ δὲ **ἀρχιερεὺς** διαρρήξας τοὺς χιτῶνας αὐτοῦ λέγει,

A Sound Map of Mark's Passion-Resurrection Narrative

11.2 Τί* ἔτι χρείαν ἔχομεν μαρτύρων;
12.1 ἠκούσατε τῆς βλασφημίας.
13.1 τί* ὑμῖν φαίνεται;

14.1 οἱ δὲ πάντες κατέκριναν αὐτὸν ἔνοχον εἶναι θανάτου.
15.1 Καὶ <u>ἤρξαντό</u> **τινες ἐμπτύειν** <u>αὐτῷ</u>
15.2   καὶ περικαλύπτειν <u>αὐτοῦ</u> τὸ πρόσωπον
15.3   καὶ κολαφίζειν <u>αὐτὸν</u>
15.4   καὶ λέγειν <u>αὐτῷ</u>, Προφήτευσον.
16.1 >καὶ οἱ* ὑπηρέται ῥαπίσμασιν <u>αὐτὸν</u> ἔλαβον.<

Story 2. Peter's Denial

1.1 (Καὶ ὄντος τοῦ Πέτρου κάτω **ἐν τῇ αὐλῇ**) <u>ἔρχεται</u> μία τῶν **παιδισκῶν** τοῦ
                                                                      ἀρχιερέως,
1.2   καὶ **ἰδοῦσα τὸν Πέτρον** θερμαινόμενον ἐμβλέψασα* αὐτῷ λέγει,
1.3   Καὶ σὺ μετὰ τοῦ Ναζαρηνοῦ* ἦσθα τοῦ* Ἰησοῦ.
2.1 ὁ δὲ* **ἠρνήσατο** λέγων,
2.2   **Οὔτε* οἶδα*** οὔτε* ἐπίσταμαι σὺ τί λέγεις.

3.1 (καὶ <u>ἐξῆλθεν</u> ἔξω εἰς τὸ προαύλιον) καὶ ἀλέκτωρ ἐφώνησεν.
4.1 καὶ ἡ **παιδίσκη ἰδοῦσα αὐτὸν** <u>ἤρξατο</u> **πάλιν** λέγειν **τοῖς παρεστῶσιν** ὅτι
4.2   Οὗτος ἐξ αὐτῶν ἐστιν.
5.1 >ὁ δὲ πάλιν ἠρνεῖτο.<

6.1 (καὶ μετὰ μικρὸν) **πάλιν οἱ παρεστῶτες** ἔλεγον τῷ Πέτρῳ,
6.2   Ἀληθῶς **ἐξ αὐτῶν εἶ**,
6.3   καὶ γὰρ Γαλιλαῖος εἶ.
7.1 ὁ δὲ <u>ἤρξατο</u>* ἀναθεματίζειν καὶ ὀμνύναι ὅτι
7.2   **Οὐκ οἶδα** τὸν ἄνθρωπον τοῦτον ὃν λέγετε.

8.1 (**καὶ* εὐθὺς**) ἐκ δευτέρου* **ἀλέκτωρ ἐφώνησεν**.
9.1 καὶ* ἀνεμνήσθη* ὁ Πέτρος τὸ **ῥῆμα*** ὡς εἶπεν αὐτῷ* ὁ* Ἰησοῦς ὅτι
9.2   Πρὶν **ἀλέκτορα φωνῆσαι δὶς τρίς με* ἀπαρνήσῃ**.
10.1 >καὶ* ἐπιβαλὼν ἔκλαιεν.<

Section 5. The Handing Over to the Gentiles

Story 1. The Trial before Pilate

1.1 (Καὶ *εὐθὺς*/*πρωῖ*) συμβούλιον ποιήσαντες οἱ ἀρχιερεῖς μετὰ τῶν πρεσβυτέρων καὶ γραμματέων καὶ ὅλον τὸ συνέδριον
1.2   δήσαντες τὸν Ἰησοῦν *ἀπήνεγκαν* καὶ **παρέδωκαν** Πιλάτῳ.
2.1 καὶ ἐπηρώτησεν αὐτὸν ὁ Πιλᾶτος,
2.2   Σὺ* εἶ* ὁ βασιλεὺς τῶν Ἰουδαίων;
3.1 ὁ δὲ ἀποκριθεὶς αὐτῷ λέγει,
3.2   Σὺ λέγεις.

4.1 καὶ **κατηγόρουν** αὐτοῦ οἱ ἀρχιερεῖς πολλά.
5.1 ὁ δὲ **Πιλᾶτος** πάλιν ἐπηρώτα αὐτὸν λέγων,
5.2   Οὐκ ἀποκρίνῃ* οὐδέν;
5.3   ἴδε πόσα σου **κατηγοροῦσιν**.
6.1 ὁ δὲ Ἰησοῦς **οὐκέτι*** οὐδὲν ἀπεκρίθη, ὥστε θαυμάζειν τὸν Πιλᾶτον.

7.1 Κατὰ δὲ ἑορτὴν **ἀπέλυεν αὐτοῖς** ἕνα δέσμιον ὃν παρῃτοῦντο.
8.1 ἦν δὲ ὁ λεγόμενος **Βαραββᾶς** μετὰ τῶν **στασιαστῶν** δεδεμένος οἵτινες ἐν τῇ <u>στάσει</u> φόνον πεποιήκεισαν.
9.1 καὶ ἀναβὰς ὁ **ὄχλος** ἤρξατο αἰτεῖσθαι καθὼς ἐποίει **αὐτοῖς**.

10.1 ὁ δὲ **Πιλᾶτος ἀπεκρίθη** αὐτοῖς λέγων,
10.2   Θέλετε ἀπολύσω ὑμῖν τὸν βασιλέα τῶν Ἰουδαίων;
11.1 ἐγίνωσκεν γὰρ ὅτι διὰ φθόνον **παραδεδώκεισαν** αὐτὸν οἱ ἀρχιερεῖς.
12.1 οἱ δὲ ἀρχιερεῖς ἀνέσεισαν τὸν ὄχλον ἵνα μᾶλλον τὸν **Βαραββᾶν ἀπολύσῃ αὐτοῖς**.

13.1 ὁ δὲ **Πιλᾶτος** πάλιν ἀποκριθεὶς ἔλεγεν αὐτοῖς,
13.2   Τί οὖν θέλετε ποιήσω ὃν λέγετε **τὸν βασιλέα τῶν Ἰουδαίων;**
14.1 οἱ δὲ **πάλιν ἔκραξαν**,
14.2   Σταύρωσον αὐτόν.

15.1 ὁ δὲ **Πιλᾶτος** ἔλεγεν αὐτοῖς,
15.2   Τί γὰρ ἐποίησεν κακόν;
16.1 οἱ δὲ περισσῶς **ἔκραξαν**,
16.2   Σταύρωσον αὐτόν.
17.1 ὁ δὲ **Πιλᾶτος** βουλόμενος τῷ ὄχλῳ τὸ ἱκανὸν ποιῆσαι ἀπέλυσεν αὐτοῖς τὸν Βαραββᾶν,
17.2   καὶ **παρέδωκεν** τὸν Ἰησοῦν φραγελλώσας ἵνα σταυρωθῇ.

Story 2. *The Mocking by the Roman Soldiers*

1.1 (Οἱ δὲ στρατιῶται* *ἀπήγαγον* αὐτὸν ἔσω τῆς αὐλῆς, ὅ ἐστιν πραιτώριον,)
1.2   καὶ συγκαλοῦσιν ὅλην τὴν σπεῖραν.
2.1 καὶ **ἐνδιδύσκουσιν αὐτὸν πορφύραν**
2.2   καὶ περιτιθέασιν αὐτῷ πλέξαντες ἀκάνθινον στέφανον:

3.1 καὶ *ἤρξαντο** ἀσπάζεσθαι* αὐτόν, Χαῖρε, βασιλεῦ τῶν Ἰουδαίων:
3.2   καὶ ἔτυπτον αὐτοῦ τὴν κεφαλὴν καλάμῳ
3.3   **καὶ ἐνέπτυον αὐτῷ,**
3.4   καὶ τιθέντες τὰ γόνατα προσεκύνουν αὐτῷ.
4.1 καὶ ὅτε **ἐνέπαιξαν** αὐτῷ, **ἐξέδυσαν αὐτὸν τὴν πορφύραν**
4.2   καὶ **ἐνέδυσαν αὐτὸν τὰ* ἱμάτια* αὐτοῦ.**
5.1 >καὶ **ἐξάγουσιν αὐτὸν ἵνα σταυρώσωσιν αὐτόν.**< (rounded with **ἵνα σταυρωθῇ**)

Section 6. The Crucifixion of Jesus

Story 1. *The Preparations and Crucifixion*

1.1 Καὶ ἀγγαρεύουσιν παράγοντά τινα Σίμωνα Κυρηναῖον ἐρχόμενον ἀπ' ἀγροῦ,
1.2   τὸν πατέρα* Ἀλεξάνδρου καὶ Ῥούφου,
1.3   **ἵνα* ἄρῃ τὸν σταυρὸν αὐτοῦ.**
2.1 (καὶ *φέρουσιν* αὐτὸν ἐπὶ τὸν Γολγοθᾶν τόπον,)
2.2   ὅ ἐστιν μεθερμηνευόμενον Κρανίου Τόπος.
3.1 καὶ ἐδίδουν αὐτῷ ἐσμυρνισμένον οἶνον,
3.2   ὃς δὲ οὐκ ἔλαβεν.

Story 2. *The Crucifixion*

1.1 **καὶ σταυροῦσιν αὐτὸν**
1.2   καὶ διαμερίζονται **τὰ ἱμάτια αὐτοῦ,**
1.3   βάλλοντες κλῆρον ἐπ' αὐτὰ τίς τί ἄρῃ.
2.1 (<ἦν δὲ ὥρα τρίτη
2.2   καὶ **ἐσταύρωσαν αὐτόν.**<)

3.1 καὶ ἦν ἡ ἐπιγραφὴ τῆς αἰτίας αὐτοῦ ἐπιγεγραμμένη, Ὁ **βασιλεὺς τῶν Ἰουδαίων.**

4.1 Καὶ **σὺν αὐτῷ σταυροῦσιν** δύο λῃστάς,
4.2   ἕνα ἐκ δεξιῶν καὶ ἕνα ἐξ εὐωνύμων αὐτοῦ.

Story 3. The Mocking

5.1 Καὶ οἱ παραπορευόμενοι ἐβλασφήμουν αὐτὸν
κινοῦντες τὰς κεφαλὰς αὐτῶν καὶ λέγοντες,
5.2 Οὐὰ ὁ καταλύων τὸν ναὸν καὶ οἰκοδομῶν ἐν τρισὶν ἡμέραις,
5.3 σῶσον σεαυτὸν καταβὰς ἀπὸ τοῦ σταυροῦ.
6.1 ὁμοίως καὶ οἱ ἀρχιερεῖς ἐμπαίζοντες πρὸς ἀλλήλους μετὰ τῶν γραμματέων
ἔλεγον,
6.2 Ἄλλους ἔσωσεν, ἑαυτὸν οὐ δύναται σῶσαι,
6.3 ὁ Χριστὸς ὁ βασιλεὺς Ἰσραὴλ καταβάτω νῦν ἀπὸ τοῦ σταυροῦ,
ἵνα ἴδωμεν καὶ πιστεύσωμεν.
7.1 >καὶ οἱ συνεσταυρωμένοι σὺν αὐτῷ ὠνείδιζον αὐτόν.< (rounded with σὺν αὐτῷ σταυροῦσιν)

Section 7. The Death and Burial of Jesus

Story 1. The Death of Jesus

1.1 (Καὶ γενομένης ὥρας ἕκτης σκότος ἐγένετο* ἐφ᾽ ὅλην τὴν γῆν ἕως ὥρας ἐνάτης.)
2.1 (καὶ τῇ* ἐνάτῃ* ὥρᾳ*) ἐβόησεν ὁ* Ἰησοῦς φωνῇ μεγάλῃ,
2.2 Ελωι ελωι λεμα σαβαχθανι;
2.3 ὅ ἐστιν μεθερμηνευόμενον Ὁ θεός μου ὁ θεός μου, εἰς τί ἐγκατέλιπές
με;

3.1 καί τινες τῶν παρεστηκότων ἀκούσαντες ἔλεγον,
3.2 Ἴδε* Ἠλίαν φωνεῖ.
4.1 δραμὼν δέ τις [καὶ] γεμίσας σπόγγον ὄξους περιθεὶς καλάμῳ* ἐπότιζεν
αὐτόν, λέγων,
4.2 Ἄφετε* ἴδωμεν εἰ* ἔρχεται* Ἠλίας καθελεῖν αὐτόν.
5.1 >ὁ δὲ Ἰησοῦς ἀφεὶς φωνὴν μεγάλην ἐξέπνευσεν.< (rounded with φωνεῖ and φωνῇ μεγάλῃ)

6.1 Καὶ τὸ καταπέτασμα τοῦ ναοῦ ἐσχίσθη εἰς δύο ἀπ᾽ ἄνωθεν ἕως κάτω.
7.1 Ἰδὼν δὲ ὁ κεντυρίων ὁ παρεστηκὼς ἐξ ἐναντίας αὐτοῦ
7.2 ὅτι οὕτως ἐξέπνευσεν εἶπεν,
7.3 Ἀληθῶς οὗτος ὁ ἄνθρωπος υἱὸς θεοῦ* ἦν.
8.1 >ησαν δὲ καὶ γυναῖκες ἀπὸ μακρόθεν θεωροῦσαι,
8.2 ἐν αἷς καὶ Μαρία* ἡ Μαγδαληνὴ   (SLOW)
8.3 καὶ Μαρία ἡ Ἰακώβου τοῦ μικροῦ καὶ* Ἰωσῆτος μήτηρ
καὶ Σαλώμη,
8.4 αἳ* ὅτε* ἦν ἐν τῇ Γαλιλαίᾳ* ἠκολούθουν αὐτῷ

καὶ διηκόνουν αὐτῷ,
8.5   κα**ὶ*** ἄλλ_αι_ πολλ_αί_* _αἱ_ συναναβᾶσαι* αὐτῷ* εἰς Ἱεροσόλυμα.<

Story 2. The Burial of Jesus

1.1 (Καὶ ἤδη ὀψίας γενομένης, ἐπεὶ ἦν παρασκευή, ὅ ἐστιν προσάββατον,)
1.2   _ἐλθὼν_ Ἰωσὴφ [ὁ] ἀπὸ Ἀριμαθαίας εὐσχήμων βουλευτής,
1.3   ὃς καὶ αὐτὸς ἦν προσδεχόμενος τὴν βασιλείαν τοῦ θεοῦ,
1.4   τολμήσας _εἰσῆλθεν_ πρὸς τὸν Πιλᾶτον καὶ ᾐτήσατο τὸ σῶμα τοῦ Ἰησοῦ.
2.1 ὁ δὲ **Πιλᾶτος ἐθαύμασεν εἰ** ἤδη **τέθνηκεν**,
2.2   καὶ προσκαλεσάμενος **τὸν κεντυρίωνα** ἐπηρώτησεν αὐτὸν **εἰ** πάλαι
                                                                    ἀπέθανεν,
2.3   καὶ γνοὺς ἀπὸ τοῦ **κεντυρίωνος** ἐδωρήσατο τὸ πτῶμα τῷ Ἰωσήφ.

3.1 καὶ ἀγοράσας **σινδόνα** καθελὼν αὐτὸν ἐνείλησεν τῇ **σινδόνι**
3.2   καὶ **ἔθηκεν αὐτὸν** ἐν μνημείῳ ὃ ἦν λελατομημένον ἐκ πέτρας,
3.3   καὶ προσεκύλισεν **λίθον** ἐπὶ τὴν θύραν τοῦ **μνημείου**.
4.1 ἡ δὲ **Μαρία ἡ Μαγδαληνὴ καὶ Μαρία ἡ Ἰωσῆτος ἐθεώρουν ποῦ τέθειται**.
      (parallel ending with Μαρία* ἡ Μαγδαληνὴ καὶ Μαρία... Ἰωσῆτος)

Section 8. The Resurrection

1.1 (Καὶ διαγενομένου τοῦ σαββάτου) **Μαρία ἡ Μαγδαληνὴ**
                       καὶ Μαρία ἡ [τοῦ] Ἰακώβου
                       καὶ Σαλώμη
1.2   ἠγόρασαν ἀρώματα _ἵνα ἐλθοῦσαι_ ἀλείψωσιν αὐτόν.
2.1 (καὶ λίαν πρωῒ τῇ μιᾷ τῶν σαββάτων _ἔρχονται_ **ἐπὶ τὸ μνημεῖον**
2.2   ἀνατείλαντος τοῦ ἡλίου.)

3.1 καὶ ἔλεγον πρὸς ἑαυτάς,
3.2   Τίς **ἀποκυλίσει** ἡμῖν **τὸν λίθον** ἐκ τῆς θύρας τοῦ μνημείου;
4.1 καὶ ἀναβλέψασαι θεωροῦσιν ὅτι **ἀποκεκύλισται ὁ λίθος**.
5.1 >ἦν _γὰρ_ μέγας σφόδρα.<

6.1 (καὶ _εἰσελθοῦσαι_ **εἰς τὸ μνημεῖον**) εἶδον νεανίσκον
6.2   **καθήμενον** ἐν τοῖς δεξιοῖς
6.3   **περιβεβλημένον** στολὴν λευκήν,
6.4   καὶ ἐξεθαμβήθησαν.
7.1 >ὁ δὲ λέγει αὐταῖς, Μὴ **ἐκθαμβεῖσθε**.<

8.1 Ἰησοῦν ζητεῖτε τὸν Ναζαρηνὸν **τὸν ἐσταυρωμένον**.
9.1 >ἠγέρθη.<

10.1 οὐκ ἔστιν ὧδε.
11.1 >ἴδε ὁ τόπος **ὅπου ἔθηκαν αὐτόν**.<

12.1 ἀλλὰ ὑπάγετε εἴπατε τοῖς μαθηταῖς αὐτοῦ καὶ τῷ Πέτρῳ ὅτι
12.2   **Προάγει ὑμᾶς εἰς τὴν Γαλιλαίαν**.
13.1 >ἐκεῖ αὐτὸν ὄψεσθε, καθὼς εἶπεν ὑμῖν.<

14.1 (καὶ _**ἐξελθοῦσαι**_ _ἔφυγον_ ἀπὸ τοῦ μνημείου.)
15.1 >εἶχεν _γὰρ_ αὐτὰς τρόμος καὶ ἔκστασις.<

16.1 καὶ οὐδενὶ οὐδὲν εἶπαν.
17.1 >ἐφοβοῦντο _γάρ_.<

Appendix 3

THE PRONUNCIATION OF KOINE GREEK IN THE ROMAN PERIOD

With Adam Gilbert Bartholomew

HOW WAS GREEK PRONOUNCED IN MARK'S TIME? THE EVIdence is clear that Koine Greek was not pronounced in the way most Western students of Greek have been taught. The system of pronunciation taught in Western schools today can be traced to an essay by Desiderius Erasmus, a Dutch Renaissance humanist who lived in the latter part of the fifteenth century and the early part of the sixteenth century. It is a pronunciation that attributes to each vowel and consonant its own peculiar sound (with a few duplications in the vowels and diphthongs). It appears that this system is somewhat like the system employed in Greece prior to the spread of Greek that resulted in the Koine.[1] It is useful in studying classical Greek texts, especially poetry. But it is clearly not the system that prevailed in the time of Mark.

We don't know exactly how Greek was pronounced in Mark's world, and even when we gather evidence that gives us an approximate pronunciation, there were surely differences from one part of the Roman Empire to another. Browning writes that early in the period of the Koine, there was a structural change in pronunciation that spread rapidly.[2] Moulton describes the transition from old Attic dialects of ancient Greek to the more widely used vernacular of the Koine:

---

1. See Browning, *Medieval and Modern Greek*, 32–35, for a description of that system.
2. Ibid., 32.

The undeniable fact that phonetic spelling—which during the reign of the old dialects was a blessing to all—was entirely abandoned by educated people generations before the Christian era.... That αι and ε, ει (η) and ι, οι and υ were identities for the scribes of our MSS, is certain.[3]

Besides the evidence of scribal errors referred to by Moulton, other evidence for pronunciation of Koine includes old Greek inscriptions, bilingual Greek-Latin coins, and loanwords from Greek in Latin. The consequence of this is stated by Robertson: "We may be sure of one thing, the pronunciation of the vernacular κοινή was not exactly like the ancient literary Attic nor precisely like the modern Greek vernacular, but veering more towards the latter."[4]

Robertson recounts the "fiery controversy" over the "knotty problem" of pronouncing Greek since the revival of the study of Greek by Byzantine scholars in Italy, apparently in the thirteenth century.[5] Johann Reuchlin, who in the fifteenth century extended the study of Greek further west beyond Italy, had studied in Italy and adopted the Byzantine pronunciation. Reuchlin's contemporary, Erasmus, was responsible for introducing another pronunciation system. According to Faulkner, a man named Glareanus, "knowing that Erasmus was fond of novelty and credulous," reported to Erasmus that some very learned Greeks had come to Paris and had spoken Greek with a different pronunciation than that one in use in the West.[6] So Erasmus published a dialogue between a lion and a bear, *De Recta Latini Graecique sermonis pronuntiatione*, in which the bear claims that the "true sounds" of ancient pronunciation had been lost and were "those of the Dutch letters, with a few sounds borrowed from the French and German." Erasmus was writing to make it look as though he himself was the one who discovered the true pronunciation.

Was Erasmus serious about his proposal? A contemporary of Erasmus, Erasmus Schmidt, said that his namesake "as it were, had sucked it [the pronunciation] out of his fingers." A few centuries later John Stuart Blackie pronounced Erasmus' dialogue "more witty than wise." A nineteenth-century French critic, A. E. Egger, criticized Erasmus and wrote in response to Erasmus' written proposal:

> not only are the proofs which it brings forward against these objections insufficient, but he himself is not prepared to attach

3. MHT, 1:34.
4. Robertson, *Grammar*, 239.
5. Ibid., 236–37.
6. Faulkner, *Erasmus*, 233.

great value to his innovation . . . [T]he author, according to his ingenious and skeptical spirit, puts down many questions without resolving them and without considering them with serious attention.[7]

Faulkner reports that Erasmus himself

expressly acknowledged more than once the validity of the pronunciation of the native Greek scholars, follows them in his 'Colloquies,' and uniformly taught their method. And even if this was not the case, his own knowledge of Greek was not sufficient to entitle him to propound a revolutionary theory. He was a man of letters, of brilliant talents, but not a philologist.[8]

Blass, however, thought that Erasmus was serious about his system and comprehensive in presenting it. Thus, Caspar Rene Gregory wrote to Robertson, saying, "The philologians . . . gladly sided with Blass. It was much easier to go on with the totally impossible pronunciation that they used than to change it."[9]

For a time the Erasmian pronunciation was forbidden at Cambridge "under penalty of expulsion from the Senate, exclusion from the attainment of a degree, rustication for students, and domestic chastisement for boys."[10] The Byzantine pronunciation reigned at Cambridge and Oxford till the early twentieth century, while the pronunciation of Erasmus was employed on the continent. In the early twentieth century Oxford and Cambridge adopted the Erasmian pronunciation as well. Moulton and Howard declare that the "practical awkwardness" of the Byzantine pronunciation to be "too great a price to pay for the approximation gained."[11]

Despite all the evidence that in Mark's time Greek was pronounced more like modern Greek and not with the Erasmian pronunciation,[12] the system of Erasmus has been adopted for the recording of the performance of Mark's PRN in Greek that accompanies this commentary. The pragmatic reality is that those most likely to read this commentary and listen to the performance are those who have studied Greek in the West and have learned Erasmian pronunciation. While the pronunciation of Greek in the

---

7. Egger, *Hellenisme*, 1:452; cited in Faulkner, *Erasmus*, 234.

8. Faulkner, *Erasmus*, 233.

9. Robertson, *Grammar*, 237.

10. Ibid., 237, quoting Blass, *Pronunciation of Ancient Greek*, 3.

11. MHT, 2:42.

12 For a detailed description of the phonemic pronunciation system prevalent in the Roman period that is also more akin to contemporary Greek pronunciation, as well as a comprehensive program of language training designed to enable students to become fluent in speaking biblical languages, see http://www.biblicallanguagecenter.com/koine-greek-pronunciation.

recording is not the same as in Mark's time, there are many other ingredients of the original sound that remain the same: the rhythm set up by the cola and periods, the echoes among words with shared roots and grammatical endings, the word order that is often impossible to mimic in English. These other dimensions of the sound will be heard and felt by the listener despite the change in pronunciation. The difference in the sound of Greek between the Erasmian pronunciation and the pronunciation of Greek in Mark's time is similar to the difference in the sound in English between a story told in English by a Bostonian and the same story by someone from the American Deep South.

Appendix 4

THE RHETORICS OF BIBLICAL STORYTELLING

THIS APPENDIX IS AN EXPANSION OF THE DISCUSSION OF THE rhetorics of biblical storytelling in the introduction. The history of composition here is that even the limited discussion of the instances of these rhetorics in the biblical storytelling tradition was too long for an introduction. The full discussion, including the material in the introduction, is included here for the sake of readers who want to explore this subject more extensively.

In order to clarify the impact of Mark's rhetorical structures, the patterns of different storytelling rhetorics in the traditions of Israelite storytelling need to be distinguished. This discussion is also only an introduction to some of the rhetorics of biblical storytelling that are central to the understanding of Mark, and a fuller and more comprehensive exposition is needed.

For the purposes of this discussion, the contrasting rhetorics implicit in Mark's PRN can be called "the rhetoric of alienation or condemnation" and "the rhetoric of involvement or implication." We are all familiar with the rhetoric of alienation because of its perpetual presence in contemporary movies and politics. The rhetoric of involvement or implication is less familiar.

The Rhetoric of Alienation and Condemnation

The rhetoric of alienation and condemnation has a characteristic set of appeals and dynamics in respect to *aesthetic distance*, a technical term in literary criticism meaning how alienated from or close to a character a listener or reader feels.[1] *Aesthetic distance* refers to the dynamics of relationship established between a receiver (generally a reader) and a character in a novel. A highly sympathetic characterization will generate a dynamic of emotional intimacy and sympathy with a character (hence, a minimal degree of aesthetic distance). The characterization of a hostile, alienating character will result in a high degree of aesthetic distance.

The general plot structure associated with the rhetoric of alienation is the introduction of a conflict in which a character has a major role as an enemy. This "bad guy" character never does anything good, right, or in any way sympathetic. The dynamics of aesthetic distance in relation to the character are only negative, and those dynamics are intensified in the course of the story. Elements that escalate negative aesthetic distance are negative images, the implementation of negative norms of judgment, recurring themes/motifs of wrong doing, insight into hostile motives or attitudes, negative asides or comments to the audience by the storyteller, plots to do evil, and evil actions by the character. Storytellers, novelists, and dramatists have a broad repertoire of gestures, tones, and attitudes for the intensification of the rhetoric of alienation. As the conflict in the plot escalates, the actions of the enemy become progressively more evil until the climax of the conflict in which the enemy is killed or destroyed. The appeal to the audience is to celebrate and rejoice at the death or marginalization of the character. This is the rhetoric of countless action movies and of political rhetoric such as the characterization of Saddam Hussein in the build up to the Iraq War and his eventual capture and execution.

Goliath

There are many instances of this rhetorical structure in Israelite storytelling tradition. Examples of this rhetoric in Israel's storytelling traditions are Goliath, Pharaoh, Ahab and Jezebel, and Haman. Goliath is a classic example of this rhetoric of alienation. He is introduced as a giant warrior, and his challenge to send someone to fight with him fills the armies of Israel and the audience with fear. When David goes to meet him, Goliath curses him by his gods and mocks David: "Am I a dog, that you come to me with sticks?" (1 Sam 17:43, NRSV). David taunts him in return in the name of the Lord of hosts and then kills him with a sling, a stone, and Goliath's sword. For Israelites who originally heard this story, Goliath's cursing and mockery of David and Israel's God is highly alienating and creates high aesthetic distance.

---

1. See Booth, *Rhetoric of Fiction*, 156.

Every child who has heard this story over the centuries has cheered at Goliath's demise.

This set of negative rhetorical appeals is used in the storytelling traditions of Israel in the characterization of foreign enemies such as Haman and Jezebel, and in the characterization of Israelites: e.g., Korah and his allies, who rebelled against Moses (Numbers 16); the Benjaminites in Gibeah, who raped and killed the Levite's concubine (Judges 19-20); Ahab (1 Kgs 16:31—22:40); and Manasseh (2 Kgs 21:1-17). In each of these stories, the storyteller invites the audiences to join in the condemnation of these characters, a condemnation that the storyteller expresses by her tone of voice and body language. Silent reading of the story of the Levite's concubine, for instance, will create this visceral feeling of outrage at the behavior of the men of Gibeah and thus alienation from them even for modern readers. In the context of its original telling, the evil of the Benjaminites was poignantly experienced in the war between that tribe and the rest of Israel, the deaths of tens of thousands of warriors, and the destruction of the city of Gibeah. The dynamics of alienation and condemnation were made only more intense by means of the tone of voice and body language of the tellers of the story. In the Gospel of Mark, this rhetoric of alienation or condemnation is present in the characterization of the chief priests, scribes, and elders.

Pharaoh

A variation of this rhetorical pattern is what can be called the rhetoric of disappointment and alienation. This is the more complex rhetorical pattern of characters who are initially presented as enemies who become for a time sympathetic helpers but then revert to their status as enemies. At some point in the story these characters speak and behave in ways that raise the hope that the character will change and do what is right and good. But that hope is disappointed, and the character is confirmed as evil and as an enemy.

The classic instance of this characterization in the storytelling traditions of Israel is Pharaoh. The pharaoh of the Exodus is established as an enemy by his enslavement of the Israelites and his campaign to kill the male babies of the Israelites (Exodus 1). At several points in his interactions with Moses, Pharaoh relents and promises to let the people go; but then he changes his mind (the frogs—8:8-15; the flies—8:25-31; the hail—9:27-33; the firstborn—12:30-32). In each instance, especially when Pharaoh asks Moses to pray for him, the hope is raised that he may relent and let the people go. The climax of Pharaoh's reversions to his evil self is his pursuit of the Israelites with his army to the Red Sea. The audiences of the Exodus are invited to rejoice with Miriam at the Egyptians and by implication, Pharaoh, dead on the shore.

Ahab

Another instance of this rhetorical structure is the characterization of Ahab. He is initially presented as evil ("did evil in the sight of the Lord more than all who were before him"—1 Kgs 16:30, NRSV). In his dialogues with Elijah and in his hesitation to take Naboth's vineyard (1 Kgs 21:4), the hope is raised that he will do the right thing. Indeed, he repents of his evil plan to take the vineyard for a short time (21:27–29) but after talks with his wife, Jezebel, she engineers the stoning of Naboth and Ahab takes the vineyard. He later has a moderately sympathetic dialogue with the prophet Micaiah (22:13–28). But he rejects Micaiah's prophecy and returns to his way of not listening to the Lord and is killed at Ramoth-Gilead (22:29–40). Other instances of this rhetorical pattern are the characterizations of Nebuchadnezzar and Antiochus IV Epiphanes. This set of rhetorical appeals is used often in the characterizations of rulers, and some of these men are the worst characters in the stories of Israel. This is the rhetorical structure of Mark's characterization of Pilate.

The Rhetoric of Involvement and Implication

The most complex rhetorical pattern of characterization can be called the rhetoric of involvement and implication, the noun *implication* carrying the verbal sense of being or becoming involved in or implicated in what is taking place. In contrast to the rhetoric of disappointment and alienation, this rhetorical strategy involves good characters who do something that is wrong but with whom the storyteller appeals for sympathy in both their goodness and their failure.

The stories exhibiting this rhetorical strategy have a common structure in biblical literature. A covenant is made between God (or God's representative) and the central characters of the story, a covenant that often carries with it unambiguous norms in regard to what will constitute violation of the covenant. Various details create a high degree of sympathetic identification between the character and the audience. The characters are introduced in a positive manner. The actions and words of the character are in agreement with the ethical and cultural norms of the storyteller and the audience. There are intimate inside views of feelings and perceptions that are sympathetic in their emotional dynamics. This last narrative technique is one of the most readily identified marks of this rhetorical structure. There are often also recurring images, actions, and even phrases that are used to draw the characterization and to reinforce the positive dynamics in the relationship between the audience and the character.

In the rhetoric of involvement or implication, this character who has been presented in a highly sympathetic manner then does something that is unambiguously wrong, but at the same time perfectly understandable for the listener. The character's action is a violation of the basic structure of the covenant between the character and the Lord. The consequences of this violation of the covenant are named and carried out in words and acts of judgment. Sometimes the character's grief and repentance from this violation of covenant are explicitly described, often as weeping, shame, or confession. Because the character's violation is something the listener can fully understand, the impact of this story structure for the audience is an experience of being involved and implicated in this action and its consequences. A frequent response of a listener to this rhetorical dynamic is a sharing of the feeling of guilt and grief, reflecting on what led to this wrongdoing, and turning away from that action or thought. This audience response is particularly present when there is an immediate connection between the decisions of the character and existential issues facing the listeners. Thus, there is a direct correlation between the degree of sympathetic identification with the character and the degree to which the audience is itself involved in the character's action.

This narrative strategy is also characteristic of Israelite storytelling. The most graphic examples of this rhetorical structure occur in the central moments in the larger story of the covenant of the people with God: creation, the covenant with Yahweh and the golden calf at Sinai (Exodus 32), David's violation of the covenant in his adultery with Bathsheba and murder of Uriah (2 Samuel 11), the covenant renewal after the exile in Ezra's reading of the Torah at the Water Gate (Nehemiah 8). The distinguishing feature of this rhetorical structure is a highly sympathetic characterization of a figure with whom the audience is invited to identify, who then does something that is, according to the norms shared by the storyteller and the audience, wrong. And in each of the stories listed above, the story concludes with the recognition and confession of the violation of the covenant with God. A more detailed analysis of this rhetorical dynamic will help to clarify the impact of these stories.

The Man and the Woman in the Garden of Eden

The story of the man and the woman in the garden of Eden is a highly developed instance of this rhetorical structure. The earth-man is introduced by the story of the Lord mixing water and clay to form the man and then to give him life by breathing into him the breath of life. The Lord blesses the man by creating a garden into which the man is placed. The man's place in paradise is a strong invitation to the audience to identify with the man. The covenant between the Lord and the man is established by the pronouncement of the Lord in which the man is invited to eat from the fruit of all the trees in the garden except the fruit of the tree of the knowledge of good and evil, which is explicitly forbidden to him. The following episode, in which God brings all the creatures of the world to the man in his search for a companion, is delightful and establishes a highly positive audience relationship with the Lord, the man, and the woman. This sympathetic relationship with God has its climax in the image of the Lord bringing the woman to the man.

The formation of the woman is the culmination of the story of creation. The story implies that she is brought to the man naked. The man becomes an instant poet and proclaims her name in ecstasy. The sexual union of the man and the woman is explicitly implied in the description of their becoming one flesh. And the invitation to complete identification with the man and the woman culminates in the storyteller's aside to the listeners that they were naked and were not ashamed.

The serpent's temptation of the woman is an engagement of this superbly beautiful character with an enemy. An easily recognized hint to the audience of the woman's being vulnerable to violation of the covenant with God is her exaggerated quotation of God's prohibition against eating from the tree of the knowledge of good and evil: "You shall not eat of the fruit of the tree that is in the middle of the garden, nor shall you touch it" (Gen 3:3 [NRSV]; compare Gen 2:17 with 3:3). Every listener can remember and recognize that she has exaggerated God's command. The prelude to the eating of the fruit is an intensive threefold inside view of her seeing the fruit, anticipating its good taste, and recognizing that it is to be desired to make one wise—all qualities generally attractive to human beings. By taking the listener inside the woman's mind to see these attractive things and to desire them with her, the narrator invites the listener into the most intimate sympathetic identification with her. When she eats the fruit and gives it to "her man with her" and he eats, the audience can identify fully with this action by the woman and the man.

The discovery of their violation of the covenant is immediate, both in their recognition that they are naked and in their ensuing conversation with the Lord. The pronouncement of the Lord's judgment against the serpent, the woman, and the man follows this violation of the covenant with its prophecies of the consequences with which every listener can identify (Gen 3:14–19). The story ends with the Lord's clothing the man and the woman as an act of mercy and casting them out of the garden.

The distinctive characteristic of the storytelling dynamics of this story is the high degree of sympathetic identification that is established between the characters and the audience leading up to the violation of an unambiguous norm of judgment in their relationship with God. A virtual elimination of aesthetic distance is created by the utopian descriptions of the garden, the woman, and the man that are universally attractive to men and women everywhere. By means of this identification the listeners become involved and implicated in the actions of the woman and the man. Sympathetic identification is, then, the central mark of the rhetoric of involvement and implication.

Tragically, the man's effort to blame "the woman" for his sin, meant as an ironic joke in the original telling, has been read without irony in major streams of the theological tradition, making women responsible for the fall. This is similar to the way the theological interpretation of the ironies in the Passion Narrative has led to the momentous conclusion that "the Jews killed Jesus." As is evident in the theological tradition associated with blaming "the fall" on the woman, the possibility is present that members of the audience, and especially readers of the text, will not identify with the character and will experience the story as alienation and condemnation rather than as involvement and implication. But the story's rhetoric is structured to create audience involvement in the actions of the woman *and* the man.

Israel at Sinai and the Golden Calf

The exodus of the people of Israel from Egypt and the covenant at Mount Sinai (Exodus 1–40) includes another major instance of the rhetoric of implication. This story has a more fully developed structure. But the basic elements of the vicarious experience of sympathetic involvement in rebellion against God are present. The appeal for sympathetic identification with "the sons of Israel," usually translated as "the Israelites," is established at the very beginning of Exodus in the description of their enslavement in Egypt. The other name for this communal character is "the people" (in Hebrew, *ha'am*). That identification with "the people" is deepened in the stories of the flight from Egypt, the crossing of the Red Sea, and the journey through the wilderness to Mount Sinai. Throughout the story leading up to the covenant at Sinai, the Lord—the god of Abraham, Isaac, and Jacob—does a series of good things for the people: hearing their cry, calling and sending Moses, bringing the plagues on Pharaoh and Egypt culminating in the slaying of the first born of Egypt and passing over the Israelites, delivering the people from the Egyptians at the sea, and providing the manna and water during the journey through the wilderness. This unambiguously positive characterization of the God of Israel invites the listeners to enter into a highly sympathetic relationship with the Lord.

The story's norms of judgment are established with elaborate clarity in the long and detailed description of the covenant between the Lord and Israel in Exodus 19–31. The story of the preparations for the giving of the law (Exodus 19) intensifies the audience's sympathetic involvement with Moses and "the people" when "the people all answered as one: "Everything that the Lord has spoken we will do" (Exod 19:8, NRSV). This communal character, "the people," has a similar rhetorical function to "the crowd" in Mark.

The prelude to the violation of the covenant in the worship of the golden calf is an appeal for further intensification of the audience's sympathetic identification with "the people." It begins with an inside view of what they "saw," i.e., "when they saw that Moses delayed to come down from the mountain" (32:1, NRSV) and reaches its climax with their offering of burnt offerings to the golden calf and celebrating their new god: "the people sat down to eat and drink, and rose up to revel" (32:6, NRSV). The punishment for this violation of the covenant begins with the slaying of three thousand sons and brothers by the sons of Levi (32:25–29), a plague, and a promise by the Lord not to go up with them to the land of Canaan. The episode concludes with the storyteller's comment to the audience: "When the people heard these harsh words, they mourned, and no one put on ornaments" (33:4, NRSV).

The Davidic Covenant and David and Bathsheba

A further instance of this rhetorical structure occurs in the story of David. The covenant of the Lord with David is established in the story of Samuel finding and anointing David and "the spirit of the LORD came mightily upon David from that day forward." (1 Sam 16:1–13). The characterization of David is supremely sympathetic from his introduction as the "ruddy" youngest son of Jesse who is chosen by the Lord to his initial playing of the lyre and driving out the evil spirit from Saul to his courageous triumph over Goliath and his many victories in battle against the Philistines. The Lord maintains his covenant with David throughout the long ordeal of his succession to the throne and the conflicts with the supporters of Saul. The culmination of the appeals to the audiences to identify with David is the story of David's anointing as king at Hebron, his bringing the ark to Jerusalem (2 Samuel 5-6) and the Lord's pledge of an everlasting covenant with the house of David and David's prayer in response (2 Samuel 7).

The stories of David's adultery with Bathsheba and his murder of her faithful husband, Uriah, have all of the dynamics of the rhetoric of implication. The story begins with an inside view of what David saw, the naked Bathsheba: "he saw from the roof a woman bathing; the woman was very beautiful" (2 Sam 11:2, NRSV). He found out who she was, sent for her, and lay with her. The appeal of the story is for every man in the audience to identify with David. The attraction to the woman is as irresistible for a male listener as it was for David. The consequences of David's action, however, are equally unavoidable, and the norms of judgment in the story of his arranging the death of Uriah are crystal clear.

The parable of Nathan is an example of the rhetoric of implication as experienced by David. Nathan leads him into sympathetic identification with the poor man who loses his one beloved lamb who has been part of his family to the rich man. David is enraged and states: "As the LORD lives, the man who has done this deserves to die. He shall restore the lamb fourfold, because he did this thing, and because he had no pity" (2 Sam 12:6, NRSV). And Nathan says, "You are the man" and goes on to list all of the actions of covenant loyalty that the Lord has done for him and the consequences of his sin in his own house. David confesses his sin, fasts and weeps pleading for the life of his newborn son, who dies.

The effect of the story of Bathsheba for the audience is self-examination in regard to the attractiveness of adultery. The effect is also sympathetic involvement with David, even in the midst of the realization of the consequences of David's sin that will continue to play out. This is not the rhetoric of alienation and condemnation. The norm of judgment that David has done a great wrong and violated the covenant with the Lord is clear. But the impact is radically different because of the high degree of sympathetic identification with David that has been created by the story. The same effect is created by the audience identification with the man and the woman in the garden and with the people of Israel at Sinai.

There are many other instances of this rhetorical structure in the storytelling traditions of Israel: e.g., the story of the reading of the Torah to the people of Israel at the Water Gate after the return from the exile, which ends with the people weeping (Nehemiah 8-10), the story of Samson and Delilah (Judges 13-16), the story of Judah and Tamar (Genesis 38), and the book of Jonah. There is a sense in which the entire story of Israel is a recurring story of appeals for sympathetic identification with the Israelite people and their descendants as they/we continue to rebel against and reject the covenant with the Lord.

Some Parables of Jesus

The Judean storytellers who composed the stories of the New Testament continued this structure of storytelling rhetoric. The most concentrated use of the rhetoric of involvement and implication is in the parables of Jesus. Jesus frequently appeals for sympathetic identification with a character who does something that is wrong according to the norms of the parable. The major instances of the rhetoric of involvement and implication in Jesus' parables are the parable of the Rich Fool (Luke 12:16-21), the parable of the Ten Virgins (Matt 25:1-13), the parable of the Talents (Matt 25:14-30; Luke 19:12-27), the parable of the Unmerciful Servant (Matt 18:23-35), and the parable of the Great Feast (Matt 22:1-10; Luke 14:16-24), the guest without a wedding garment (Matt 22:11-14), the servant entrusted with supervision (Matt 24:45-51; Luke 12:42-46), and the parable of the Father and Two Sons (Luke 15:11-32). The dynamics of identification with these characters vary greatly. Sometimes they are just sympathetically stupid, like the one-talent servant, and the five virgins who didn't plan ahead. And just as in the story of the guest without a wedding garment, the exact nature of the character's wrongdoing may remain ambiguous. The identification with the goats to the left hand of the Son of the Human One (Matt 25:31-46) depends on the listeners' ambiguous connections with their failure to act with compassion for "the least of these." But Jesus casts a sufficiently wide net of the ones for whom the goats at his left had done nothing that no one can escape being implicated.

A more detailed analysis of two of the parables may be helpful. The appeals for sympathetic identification with the main character in the parable of the Unmerciful Servant are the description of his massive indebtedness, the king's decision to throw him and his family into prison, and his pleas on his knees for mercy—the poor guy! The norm of judgment that he should extend mercy just as he had received mercy is crystal clear. The king's judgment is thoroughly appropriate.

In the parable of the Rich Fool, the inside-view description of the rich man's dilemma with inadequate storage is the envy of every listener. His "new barns" solution is smart and his internal dialogue with his soul is what every investor hopes for. The appeals for sympathetic identification are brief and powerful. The fool's condemnation is both a surprise and an invitation to self-examination. Both these parables are remarkable in the universality of the issues they explore. The eschatological judgment with which each parable ends is so hyperbolic and surprising that every listener is required to at least think and is invited to change.

The Covenant Renewal after the Exile at the Watergate

Another form of the rhetoric of involvement and implication occurs in two structurally similar stories in Nehemiah and Acts. The story of the renewal of the covenant between the people of Israel and God at the Water Gate in Jerusalem and its aftermath is a graphic instance of this rhetorical structure (Nehemiah 8–13). A dimension of this story is the extensive description of the response that is generated by the people's experience of implication in the violation of the covenant with God. The occasion of the people's recognition of their violation of the covenant is described in the story of Ezra's ceremonial reading of the Torah at the Water Gate (Nehemiah 8). The sympathetic identification of the audience with the people as well as Ezra and Nehemiah has been established by the whole story of the return from the exile, the devastation of Jerusalem, and the rebuilding of the Temple and the walls of the city in the whole book of Ezra and the earlier sections of Nehemiah. But the audience's experience of full involvement in the recognition of their breaking of the covenant does not happen until Ezra's recital of the story of Israel and its covenant with God in Nehemiah 9, which ends with an official signing of a new written covenant. The central violations of the covenant that are identified in this story are the marriage of foreign wives, the nonobservance of the Sabbath, and the failure to provide for the Temple and its leaders. The story of Nehemiah ends with the description of the condemnation of those marriages and the cleansing "from everything foreign" (Neh 13:23–31, NRSV).

Pentecost

The story of Pentecost (Acts 2) has a similar rhetorical structure as well as a virtually identical setting. The story begins with the sound of the mighty wind, the tongues of fire, and the Galilean apostles speaking in the languages of the world. A great crowd of "Judeans, devout men from every nation under heaven" gathers together outside the house (2:5). In response to their puzzlement, Peter speaks to them and, therefore, to the audience as Israelites. Peter's speech is a retelling of the story of Jesus' death and resurrection in light of this outpouring of the Spirit. The themes of Peter's speech are the implication of the people in the death of Jesus "whom you crucified and killed by the hands of those outside the law" (2:23, NRSV) and the exaltation of Jesus to the right hand of God "as Lord and Messiah, this Jesus whom you crucified" (Acts 2:36). The response of the crowd is "to be cut to the heart" and to ask, "Brothers, what shall we do?" (2:37, NRSV). Many are baptized and become members of the community by selling their possessions and giving to all those who had need. The impact of this rhetorical structure is to appeal for the listeners to identify with the experience of the Israelites gathered at Pentecost in a manner that is virtually identical to the appeals of the story of the covenant renewal by Ezra and Nehemiah. The focus of the content is different, but the rhetorical structure is the same. In both instances, the response of repentance by the people is explicitly described as the climax of the story. This is indicative of the impact of the rhetoric of involvement and implication.

There are similarities between the stories we have covered in this appendix. Many of the central characters are communal characters: the man and the woman, who represent men and women; the people of Israel in the Exodus story; the inhabitants of Jerusalem and returned exiles in the story of covenant renewal at the Water Gate; Israelites from every nation living in Jerusalem at Pentecost; and the crowd in the trial of Jesus before Pilate. In the stories of individuals such as Samson, David, Jonah, Peter, and the women witnessing Jesus' death, the characters are highly sympathetic characters with whom audiences easily identify. The characters in the parables of Jesus are often highly sympathetic figures who are often poor and enslaved. In the parable of Nathan to David, the poor man with only one lamb is a highly sympathetic character for whom David has instant compassion (2 Sam 12:1–6). In the stories that involve the audience with communal characters such as the "people" the issues underlying the stories are often Israelite communal issues. These issues include the worship of other gods (Genesis, Exodus) and the marriage of foreign wives (Ezra and Nehemiah).

These stories make clear the difference between this distinctive rhetorical pattern in Israelite storytelling and the rhetoric of alienation and condemnation. In each instance the storyteller's purpose is an invitation to appeal for repentance from a particular act that symbolizes a broader way of behavior and life. The appeal is for recognition of *our* involvement in sinful ways that violate the covenant with God. It is not an appeal for condemnation or alienation from those characters. In fact, if that happens for particular listeners, the inherent purpose of the stories will be subverted and reversed. The extent and popularity of this mode of storytelling in Israel's tradition is the context within which Mark's story of Jesus' death and resurrection was conceived and told.

In each instance, a common structure is present: a high degree of sympathetic identification is established with characters who are involved or recognize their involvement in a violation of the covenant with God. The storytelling purpose of this type of story is involvement based on sympathetic identification rather than condemnation based on alienation. The purpose of this rhetorical structure is not condemnation or judgment of the characters but is an appeal for recognition of *our* involvement in this wrong and for repentance in relation to that wrong.

The Rhetorics of Alienation and Implication in Mark's PRN

Both the rhetoric of alienation and condemnation, and the rhetoric of involvement and implication, are present in Mark's PRN. The characterization of the chief priests is a flat characterization in which the dynamics of alienation or condemnation are established in the first episode of the PRN by their stealthy plotting and fear of Jesus' popularity (14:1–2) and are intensified until the climax of their mocking of Jesus on the cross (15:31–32). The climax of the rhetoric of alienation is the joining of the chief priests and scribes with the insurrectionists on Jesus' right and left in the taunting and mockery of Jesus.

The story of Pilate, in contrast, exhibits the variation of the rhetoric of alienation in which an enemy becomes a helper for a moment but then disappoints and reverts to his status as an enemy. This rhetorical structure has been interpreted as pro-Roman apologetic and a lessening of Roman responsibility for Jesus' death. This interpretation is a curious distortion of the impact of Pilate's characterization. The characterization has the same structure as that of Herod in the earlier story of the execution of John the Baptist. The fact that there are sympathetic dimensions to the characterization of Herod and the possibility is raised that he will continue to protect John from his wife's rage in no way diminishes his responsibility for John's death. If anything, it heightens the scale of injustice and of alienation from Herod. The same is true of the characterization of Pilate. He has the power to execute Jesus or to release him. Because of political calculations like those of Herod, Pilate orders the crucifixion of a man he knows is innocent of any crime. The magnitude of his cynicism in regard to the tradition of Roman justice is stunning. The characterization of Pilate is structured by the rhetoric of condemnation no less than is the characterization of the Judean authorities and, in particular, of the chief priests and Herod.

The characterizations of the disciples, Peter, the women, and the crowd are complex examples of the rhetoric of involvement and implication. The audience is invited to sympathize and identify with these characters, including the crowd, in a variety of ways prior to a climactic action or response that is unambiguously wrong. The accurate identification of this rhetorical structure is an essential element in the appropriate interpretation of the stories. A central argument here is that the perception of Mark's story as anti-Israelite is related to the misperception of the rhetorical dynamics involved in the characterization of the crowd. The analysis of the characterization of the crowd in the commentary on the Pilate trial, above, is of particular importance. While the rhetorical strategy in Mark's presentation of the disciples, Peter, and the women is usually perceived as one of involvement or implication, the strategy in the presentation of the crowd at the Pilate trial has been widely understood to be that of alienation or condemnation.

The problem with the rhetoric of involvement or implication is that the meaning and impact of the story is dependent on the audience's sympathetic identification with the characters. As is evident in the interpretation of the story of Adam and Eve as well as the Gospel Passion Narratives, in the absence of that vital connection with the characters, the same story that is structured to involve the listener in self-recognition and self-reflection can become a story that is experienced as alienating, causing the listener to criticize and condemn the character rather than to share the character's involvement in violation of the covenant with God.

One of the reasons why hearing the story rather than reading it in silence makes a difference is that the storyteller is in a position to narrate the events and the words of the characters in a tone other than factual information, and thereby to draw listeners into identification even with people who are outwardly different. This doesn't mean that sympathetic identification with characters doesn't happen in silent reading of stories. If a reader is attentive to and psychologically open to the clues inherent in the narrator's invitations, full engagement in sympathetic identification with the characters of the story is fully possible for a silent reader. But if the reader maintains a high degree of psychological distance in the reading of the story, its actual meaning can become virtually the opposite of the purpose inherent in the structure of the story. The source of that distance, therefore, may be a change either in the self-identity of the listener (from identifying oneself as Judean/Jewish to identifying oneself as Christian/non-Jewish), or in the psychological distance to the story (sympathetic hearing to critical silent reading), or both in combination. But, regardless of the cause of this shift, the story can undergo a radical transformation in its meaning. Thus, the story of the man and the woman in the garden can change, especially for male readers and theologians, from meaning "*we* violated God's covenant and our effort to blame it on the woman is a joke" to "*the woman* violated God's covenant." Likewise in Mark's story, the meaning of the story, especially for Christians who identify themselves as not being Jews in later periods, can shift from "*we* were involved in the death of the Messiah" to "th*e Jews* killed Jesus."

This is then a brief orientation to the dynamics that are implicit in the now silenced text of Mark's story and the possible ways in which the story can be restored to sound and reexperienced. The problem for our exploration of Mark's PRN is that while Mark's original audiences were familiar with this type of story and its characteristic dynamics in Israel's storytelling tradition, most contemporary readers of Mark's story are at best only vaguely familiar with these earlier stories, and virtually none of those readers have ever heard them told in the grand and forceful style of public performances in the biblical world.[2]

Furthermore, experiencing the appropriate dynamics of the passion-and-resurrection story is dependent on having heard the whole gospel prior to the ending. The impact of the flight of the disciples, Peter's denial, and the women's silence, and also of the crowd's choice of Barabbas rather than Jesus is in all cases, including that of the crowd, dependent on the audience's sympathetic relationship with the characters, which is established in the earlier parts of the story. Thus, the traditional practice in recent Christian worship of reading individual stories out of context and in an emotionally detached manner works against the possibility of experiencing the original meaning of a story, which is implicit in the rhetorical structure of the entire gospel. This tendency has only been increased by the practice of detached, critical reading of biblical compositions in silence. This practice is directly related to the misperception of the central stories of Mark's PRN as structured according to the rhetoric of alienation rather than the rhetoric of involvement and implication. The conclusion that follows from this misperception is that Mark's purpose was anti-Jewish polemic rather than the creation of an experience of involvement in the events that led to the death of the Messiah of peace.

2. See Shiner, *Proclaiming the Gospel,* 89: the rhetorical handbooks identify three styles of speech: 1. plain, suited to teaching that addresses the intellect; 2. grand or forcible, aimed at the emotions; and 3. intermediate. In Shiner's view, Mark is "full of forceful emotion," and emotion serves "as a primary determinate of the meaning of the Gospel in its original setting." The plain style is clearly the style that Western Christian readers have come to practice when reading aloud in liturgical settings. It is the style favored by "critical readers," as we shall note below. Some "critical readers" find an oral performance that is full of emotion to be a hindrance to their critical reflection.

Appendix 5

MARKAN TERMINOLOGY

AN ISSUE IN THE IDENTIFICATION OF MARK'S AUDIENCES IS the terminology that we will use. The interpretive community in recent centuries has become accustomed to naming the religious and cultural communities of the first century that were both the subject and the producers of the New Testament as Jews and Christians. Recent study of the use of these terms has made it clear that this usage only became customary in later periods and is anachronistic in the time of Mark.

The source for this reassessment is an article by John H. Elliott that can be introduced by a substantial quotation of the abstract of his article:

> Distinguishing between insider and outsider groups and their differing nomenclatures is essential for accurate interpretation and translation. Jesus and his earliest followers, were called 'Israelites,' 'Galileans' or 'Nazoreans' by their fellow Israelites. 'Israel,' 'Israelites' were the preferred terms of self-designation among members of the house of Israel when addressing other members—not Ἰουδαῖος, 'Jew' or 'Judaism.' Modern interpreters and translators of the Bible, it is argued, should respect and follow this insider preference. Ἰουδαῖος, an outsider coinage, is best rendered 'Judaean,' not 'Jew,' to reflect the explicit or implied connection with Judaea. The terms "Jew," "Jewish," and "Judaism" were predominantly employed by Israelites when addressing outsiders as an accommodation to outsider usage.[1]

Elliott thereby argues that in the first century the Greek terms, οἱ Ἰουδαῖοι, Ἰουδαῖος, and Ἰουδαίων were terms used by and in interaction with "outsiders" to the community of Israel. The translation of the term Ἰουδαῖος here will be "Judean."

---

1. Elliott, "Jesus the Israelite," 119–54.

As is understood today, these terms reflect the context of the fourth-century and communities shaped by the Mishnah and the Talmud and by the creeds and canon of the church. *Judaism* was not a term used by Israelites in the first century in discussions with other Israelites. They used terms that were more specific to various factions within the Israelite community and that reflected its geographical, political, and religious differences, such as *Nazarene, Judean, Pharisee, Sadducee, Galilean, scribe,* and *Herodian.* Elliott's argument is that the use of the terms *Jewish* and *Christian* is an anachronistic reading back into the first century of names that were only widely used with a very different meaning in a later context. In its original historical context, the Greek term Ἰουδαϊσμός refers to the practices of a religious community that took its definitive form as rabbinic Judaism only after the publication of the Mishnah and the emergence of Christianity as the official religion of the Roman empire in the fourth century. It was a relatively small segment of the wide range of groups and sects that were dimensions of the religion of Israel at the time of Jesus and Mark. Of course, the major difference was that the religion of Israel prior to the war had its center and major organization in the Temple, the priesthood, and the sacrificial rites that were conducted there.

A major reason for the adoption of this terminology for this commentary is that Elliott's analysis corresponds exactly with the terminology in Mark. Jesus is described as a Nazarene, never as a Judean. Thus, the maid of the high priest (14:67) and the young man in the tomb (16:6b) both describe Jesus as "the Nazarene." And the bystanders in the courtyard of the high priest identify Peter as "a Galilean" (14:70). The only characters who call Jesus a Judean are Pilate and the Roman soldiers in the stories of the Pilate trial (15:2, 9, 12), the mocking in the Praetorium (15:18), and the crucifixion (15:26), where they call him "King of the Judeans."

This usage may have been a factor in the way that Jesus' response to Pilate's initial question was understood by Mark's predominantly Judean audiences. Pilate's question is whether Jesus is "King of the Judeans." Jesus' response is certainly equivocal but it also may have been heard as, to paraphrase, "That's your term and your accusation." Pilate later asks the crowd a question that implies that they use this term for Jesus: "What then do you want me to do with the one you call 'King of the Judeans'?" The question implies that this is a term that was used by "the crowd" as a name of honor. But the people never use this term to describe Jesus. The closest that the people of Jerusalem ever came to this, according to Mark, is at the triumphal entry into Jerusalem when "those who went ahead and those who followed" said, "Blessed is the one who comes in the name of the Lord! Blessed is the coming kingdom of our ancestor David!" (11:9–10, NRSV). But no one before Pilate has used the term "King of the Judeans." Only Pilate and the Roman soldiers, who are clearly outsiders to the people of Israel, use this term and implicitly call Jesus a "Judean." In their mouths it becomes a term of mockery and derision, a term of ethnic and racial ridicule used by outsiders. Thus, the final two uses of this term occur during the mockery by the Roman soldiers and in the description of the sign on the cross.

In the context of the crucifixion story, in which the Romans repeatedly use this term, the term used by the chief priests and scribes is in marked contrast. The chief priests mock him as "the Messiah" and "the King of Israel" but not as "King of the Judeans." Thus, Mark primarily uses the term "the Judeans" (οἱ Ἰουδαῖοι) in the mouths of outsiders to the community of Israel.

The only use of "the Judeans" (οἱ Ἰουδαῖοι) other than by the Romans occurs in the explanation of the purity laws (7:3-4). This audience aside explaining Israelite purity laws also fits Elliott's terminological distinctions. In this aside, the Markan storyteller, an Israelite, addresses the non-Judeans in his projected audiences. In the one place in the gospel in which he explicitly addresses the outsiders to the community of Judeans in the audiences of the performances of the Gospel, he uses an outsider term: "the Pharisees and all the Judeans" (7:3, NRSV).

Mark's use of the term τὰ ἔθνη, "the nations, Gentiles," also corresponds with Elliott's description of terminology that is used for outsiders who are lumped together as one group. Among themselves, non-Judeans also used more specific geographical, political and religious terms such as *Greeks, Parthians,* and *Epicureans*; the Greek name for outsiders, non-Greeks, was "barbarians." In the third passion prophecy, Jesus says, "the Son of Man will be . . . condemned to death and handed over to 'the Gentiles'" (τοῖς ἔθνεσιν—10:33), and in the subsequent story he instructs the disciples "those who rule over the Gentiles lord it over them . . . but it shall not be so among you"(10:42-43, NRSV). Here the contrast between "them, the Gentiles" and "you Judeans" is explicit.

Elliott's proposal is adopted here, both in the commentary on the story itself and also in the commentary on Mark's audiences and the meanings of the story for them. An initial impression might be that the term "Christian" would apply to Mark since there was a higher degree of self-definition of the followers of Jesus in the later decades of the first century than in Jesus' time. The fact that the term is only used three times in the New Testament in Acts (11:26; 26:28) and 1 Peter (4:16), however, indicates that it was rarely used in the first century, and the instances of extensive usage were decades later than Mark.

The use of this terminology is also important in relation to the reading of Mark as "anti-Jewish." Jesus' highly agonistic engagement with other Israelite groups is "anti-Israelite" only if one assumes that the storyteller and the audience are outsiders, that is, non-Israelites. As Bruce Malina has written,

> Since the dialogue between personages represented in the documents [of the New Testament] and the authors of the documents themselves take place among members of the house of Israel, within Israelite society, or with positive reference to Israelite society, it would be simply silly to designate such interaction as 'anti-Semitic.'[2]

And it is equally silly to designate such interaction as "anti-Jewish." Unfortunately, the extent to which Mark is characterized as intentionally sowing the seeds of anti-Judaism and anti-Semitism is anything but silly. The terms *Christian* and *Jewish* are appropriately used now to describe the two sectarian groups of Israelite religion that survived the Judean-Roman War and gradually became distinct religious groups in the second to the fourth centuries.

---

2. Malina, 'Three Theses," 46.

Appendix 6

THE AUDIENCES OF MARK

THE BASIC DATA OF AUDIENCE ADDRESS IN THE PRN IS CHARTed and discussed in the introduction. The purpose of this appendix is to provide access to the broader data of audience address in the gospel as a whole. This appendix is a revision of a contribution to a recent collection of articles: *Mark as Story: Retrospect and Prospect.*[1]

The identification of audience identity in performance literature is based on the identification of the storyteller's assumptions about the characters with whom the projected audiences can readily identify. A storyteller who addresses the audience as someone the audience can't relate to will lose that audience. The audience will just walk away. In a story with a major character such as Jesus in the Gospels, the storyteller will spend a lot of the story addressing the audience as the character of Jesus as he teaches, interacts and argues with various persons and groups. In most of those instances, the storyteller as Jesus will address the audience as particular characters in the story. Thus, in first sections of the PRN, the storyteller as Jesus speaks to the audience as his disciples: in the conflict in Bethany over the woman's anointing, at the Last Supper, in the prophecy of flight and denial, and sleeping in Gethsemane. In the later parts of the PRN, the major addresses to the audience are by the high priest to the audience as the Sanhedrin jury at Jesus' first trial, by Pilate to the audience as the crowd at the second trial, and by the divine messenger to the audience as the women. With the exception of the address to the women, these addresses to the audience are the culmination of relationships with characters that have been established throughout the story. Of those the most important are the disciples and the crowd. That is, Mark the storyteller assumes that by the last part of the

---

1. Boomershine, "Audience Address," 115–44.

story, the projected audiences will readily identify with the crowd and the disciples.

Thus, we can identify the character of the audience for whom Mark may have performed by identifying the characters by whom the audience is addressed. The chart that follows lists the stories in which the audience is addressed for at least two sentences (periods in Greek) by a character in the story. I would suggest looking through the list in the right hand column as the indications of the characters with whom the audience is invited to identify:

Audience Address in Mark

Story and Address to the audience	Speaker Embodied by the Storyteller	Audience Addressed as
John's baptism (1:7–8)	John the Baptist	Judeans, etc.
Proclamation of the Kingdom (1:15)	Jesus	People of Galilee
Healing of paralytic (2:8–10)	Jesus	Scribes
Eating with tax collectors (2:17)	Jesus	Scribes of the Pharisees
Question about fasting (2:19–22)	Jesus	Disciples of John and the Pharisees
Shucking grain on Sabbath (2:25–28)	Jesus	Pharisees
Healing of man with withered hand (3:4–5)	Jesus	The people in the synagogue
Jesus and Beelzebul (3:23–29)	Jesus	Scribes from Jerusalem
Jesus and his mother and brothers (3:33–35)	Jesus	The group sitting around Jesus
Parable of the Sower (4:3–9)	Jesus	The crowd
Purpose of parables, the meaning of the sower parable, and parables of the Kingdom (4.11–32)	Jesus	Those around Jesus with the twelve
Rejection of Jesus at Nazareth (6.4)	Jesus	People in Nazareth synagogue

Mission of the twelve (6:10–11)	Jesus	The twelve
Tradition of the elders: cleanliness laws (7:3–4)	Mark	Audience as non-Judeans
Tradition of the elders (7:6–13)	Jesus	Pharisees and scribes
Tradition of the elders (7:14–15)	Jesus	The crowd
Tradition of the elders (7:18–22)	Jesus	Disciples
Demand for a sign (8:12)	Jesus	Pharisees
Leaven of the Pharisees and bread discourse (8:15–21)	Jesus	Disciples
Messianic confession, first passion prophecy, and discipleship (8:34—9:1)	Jesus	Crowd with the disciples
Transfiguration (9:12–13)	Jesus	Peter, James and John
Second passion prophecy (9:31)	Jesus	Disciples
Who is the greatest? (9:35–37)	Jesus	Disciples
The other exorcist (9:39–50)	Jesus	Disciples
Teaching about divorce (10:5–9)	Jesus	Pharisees
Teaching about divorce (10:11–12)	Jesus	Disciples
Blessing the children (10:14–15)	Jesus	Disciples
Rich man (10:18–21)	Jesus	The rich man
Rich man (10:23–27)	Jesus	Disciples
Rich man (10:29–31)	Jesus	Peter
Third passion prophecy (10:33–34)	Jesus	Disciples
James and John's request for position (10:42–45)	Jesus	Disciples

The cleansing of the Temple (11:17)	Jesus	The chief priests and crowd in the Temple
The fig tree (11:22–26)	Jesus	Disciples
Parable of the vineyard (12:1–11)	Jesus	The chief priests, scribes and elders
The resurrection controversy (12:24–27)	Jesus	Sadducees
Messiah David's son? (12:35–37)	Jesus	Large crowd in the Temple
Denouncing of the scribes (12:38–40)	Jesus	Crowd in the Temple
The widow's gift (12:43–44)	Jesus	Disciples
Apocalyptic discourse (13:4–37)	Jesus	Peter, James, John and Andrew
Anointing by woman (14:6–9)	Jesus	Those who rebuked the woman
Preparations for Passover (14:13–15)	Jesus	Two disciples
Betrayal prophecy (14:18–21)	Jesus	Twelve
The Last Supper (14:22–25)	Jesus	Twelve
Prophecy of desertion and denial (14:27–30)	Jesus	Twelve and Peter
Gethsemane (14:37–38, 41–42)	Jesus	Peter and Peter, James and John
The arrest (14:48–49)	Jesus	The crowd from the priests, scribes, and elders
The trial before the Council (14:63–64)	High priest	The Council
The trial before Pilate (15:9, 12–14)	Pilate	The crowd
The resurrection (16:6–7)	Young man	Mary Magdalene, Mary, and Salome

The category of "Speaker Embodied by the Storyteller" in the chart above reveals the basic structure of audience address. In speeches of two or more periods, the storyteller addresses the audience as Jesus most of the time (45 of 50 times). The other characters who address the audience are John the Baptist, Mark as the storyteller, the high priest, Pilate, and the young man at the tomb. The category of "Audience addressed as" reveals another fact that is surprising in the context of the audiences envisioned by many Markan scholars as Gentile Christian. The most striking fact about the addresses to the audience is that the audience is almost always addressed as various groups of Judeans and never as believers and only once as Gentiles. That is, the audience is never addressed as Gentiles who have joined communities who believe in and follow Jesus as the Messiah.

The only exception to this Israelite audience occurs in the story of Jesus' dispute with the Pharisees over the purity laws. The storyteller's explanation of the cleanliness laws (7:3–5) is addressed to the audience as persons who do not know these Israelite customs. This is a sign that the composer of the gospel recognizes and wants to include non-Israelites in the audiences of the story. That is, the audiences that are projected as the potential audiences for the performances of the gospel are primarily, but not exclusively, Judean.

This is a paradigmatic example of the difference made by the medium in which Mark is experienced. When the gospel is read in silence, this comment appears to be an inside address to the reader. Scholars have often inferred from this comment that the audience of Mark is Gentiles. When the gospel is heard as addressed to audiences, however, this comment is not directed to a reader but is directed to any in the audience who may not be familiar with Israelite legal and cultural customs. The comment indicates only that Mark as the composer of this story projects that there may be Gentiles in the potential audiences. This comment is a storytelling gesture of audience inclusion. The storyteller introduces it after a considerable amount of time during which he has been inviting his listeners to experience being a series of various Judean characters who are addressed by Jesus. The purpose of explaining the purity laws is to keep on board any Gentiles who might find it difficult to maintain involvement with the story without this essential information.[2]

Another revealing dimension of audience address in Mark is the way the audience is invited to move from being addressed as those who are Jesus' opponents to those who are Jesus' disciples. In this structure of audience address, the storyteller as Jesus moves from addressing the audience as (1) those who are in conflict with Jesus to addressing them as (2) those around Jesus, often the disciples or the twelve. This pattern is first established in the opening section of the gospel. After the initial brief addresses by the

---

2. For a more extensive discussion of the implications of the reassessment of Mark's narrative comments, see Boomershine, "Audiences Asides."

storyteller as John the Baptist to the audience as the people of Judea (1:7–8) and then by Jesus to the audience as the people of Galilee (1:15), the audience is addressed by the storyteller as Jesus for a long time as various groups with whom Jesus is in conflictual dialogue about the observance of the law: the scribes (2:8–10), the scribes of the Pharisees (2:17), the disciples of John and the Pharisees (2:19–22), the Pharisees (2:25–28), the people in the synagogue who are, by inference, Pharisees (3:4–5), and climactically the scribes from Jerusalem (3:23–29). That is, the audience is predominantly addressed in the early parts of the story as various groups of Israelites who are in conflict with Jesus.

Furthermore, there is a distinct escalation in the tone and content of the conflict. Jesus' address to the audience as the scribes in the paralytic story is moderate in tone. In each story that follows, the address is increasingly intense in tone and content. The longest and most conflictual address in this series is the address to the audience as the scribes who have come down from Jerusalem. They accuse Jesus of being possessed by Beelzebul and of casting out demons by the prince of demons. The climax of Jesus' speech is his description of their accusation as blasphemy against the Holy Spirit that will never be forgiven.

This series of stories ends with the most intimate address to the audience to this point in the gospel: the story of Jesus' mother and brothers (3:31–35). The storyteller as Jesus says to the audience as those seated around Jesus: "Who are my mother and my brothers?" And looking around at those who were seated around him, he says, "Here are my mother and my brothers. Whoever does the will of God is my brother and sister and mother" (NRSV). In the performance of the story, the storyteller addresses this saying to all those in the audience with a gesture of wide-open arms of inclusion. This is implicitly an invitation to the audience to move from identifying with those who are in conflict with Jesus to being one of those in Jesus' intimate circle of friends. This address to the audience as Jesus' followers is then continued throughout Jesus' parabolic address (4:1–32).

The next instance of this pattern in Mark's story is the dialogue about the purity laws. This story begins with the storyteller's description to the audience of the Pharisees' critique of Jesus for allowing his disciples to eat with unwashed hands and his explanation of Israelite purity customs (7:1–5). This introduction is followed by a highly confrontational address by Jesus to the audience as the Pharisees and scribes. This speech begins with Jesus' citation of Isaiah as prophesying their hypocrisy and ends with the accusation that in many ways they abrogate the law of God by the handing on of their tradition (7:6–13). Then the audience is briefly addressed as the crowd (7:14–15). The climax of the dialogue is an extensive address to the audience as his disciples. This speech is introduced by the relocation of the address from a public to a private place, "When he had left the crowd and entered the house..."(7:17, NRSV). In the telling of the story this introduction was probably accompanied by some gesture, perhaps a simple movement to the side and sitting down. It is also an indication of a lowering of the volume of the speech. The storyteller as Jesus moves from heated public argumentation through explanation to a sympathetic crowd to private explanation to the audience as the disciples. These storytelling moves in sound and gesture create intimacy between the character of Jesus and the audience.

There are two smaller instances of this pattern in audience address prior to the stories of Jesus in Jerusalem. The first is the story of the Pharisees' demanding a sign, followed by Jesus' speech in the boat to the disciples about the leaven of the Pharisees and the bread (8:11–13 and 8:14–21). The audience is addressed as the Pharisees who were testing Jesus in expressing their desire for a sign. The tone of the storyteller's voice as Jesus is best described as exasperation mixed with anger. The discussion is abruptly ended with the description of Jesus' getting back into the boat. The trip back to the other side of the lake is the context in which the storyteller as Jesus discusses the significance of the loaves with the audience as the disciples (8:14–21). While Jesus continues to express exasperation with the disciples, his tone is more the exasperation of a teacher whose students just don't get it. There is a real possibility that the storyteller smiled and even laughed in the delivery of this speech of Jesus. The dynamic of these two stories is an invitation to the audience to experience Jesus as moving from public prophet to private teacher, from being addressed as an ongoing adversary to being addressed as a disciple who is also confused about the meaning of the seven and twelve baskets, as is the audience.

The second instance of this pattern in audience address is the divorce controversy. Once again, the Pharisees engage Jesus in another test, this time about divorce law. The public discussion is addressed to the audience as the Pharisees (10:5–9). In contrast to the earlier stories of legal dispute, there is no sign here that the words of Jesus were delivered with a tone of anger or frustration. This rabbinic ruling about divorce law appears to have been delivered in a straightforward and authoritative manner in spite of the fact that the Pharisees' question is introduced as still another testing of Jesus. Once again the scene shifts to the more intimate setting of the house (10:10–12). The storyteller as Jesus addresses the audience as the disciples for a short explanation of his legal opinion. This move from public pronouncement to private discussion about the law has the same rabbinic dynamic as the earlier story about the purity laws.

The most extensive and highly developed instance of this pattern of audience address is the stories of Jesus in Jerusalem. The longest address to the audience as Jesus' opponents in the gospel is the parable of the Vineyard and the Wicked Tenants (12:1–11). It is addressed to the audience as the chief priests, scribes, and elders. This highly confrontational parable is followed by the controversy about paying taxes to Caesar. Next comes the controversy about resurrection, in which the audience is addressed as Sadducees. Jesus' pronouncement in this story ends with a dismissal of the Sadducees: "You are quite wrong" (12:27, NRSV). After the relatively cordial story of Jesus' discussion with the scribe (12:28–34), the audience is addressed as the crowd in the Temple (12:35–40). The storyteller presents Jesus addressing the audience as a large and sympathetic crowd. He first speaks with them about the scribes' teaching that the Messiah must be the Son of David and then levels a climactic denunciation against the scribes. The next move toward more intimate and confidential address to the audience is the story of the widow's gift where the audience is addressed as the disciples (12:41–44).

The climax of the stories of Jesus in Jerusalem prior to the Passion Narrative is the most extensive and intimate conversation in the entire gospel. The so-called apocalyptic discourse (13:4–37) is addressed to the audience as the four disciples who are sitting with Jesus on the Mount of Olives overlooking the Temple. In this long address, the storyteller invites the audience into a relationship of intimacy with and belief in Jesus. This intimacy and reinforcement of belief is directly related to Jesus' prophecies about the Judean-Roman War, which have probably been fulfilled in the audience's recent experience of the war and the destruction of the Temple.[3]

This invitation to an intimate relationship with the character of Jesus is the culmination of the storyteller's appeals to the audience throughout the story. Repeatedly in narrative sequence after narrative sequence, Mark as the teller of the tale invites the audience to move from a relationship of opposition and confrontation with Jesus to a relationship of belief and discipleship. In this structuring of audience address, Mark first engages his audience as adversaries of Jesus. The listeners are invited to enter into a series of testing confrontations with Jesus, revolving primarily around the interpretation of the law. The listeners are then invited to engage with Jesus as the members of a sympathetic crowd. This climactic setting in the narrative sequences described above resonated with the real-world setting of a storytelling performance, in which a crowd of people gathered around a

---

3. See Marcus, "The Jewish War." The social and political context of Mark that Marcus outlines in this article is congruent with the picture of Mark in performance.

storyteller. The culmination of this implicit appeal to the members of the audience is a storytelling invitation to enter into and identify themselves with Jesus' disciples listening to Jesus in small, private settings usually in a house. This setting of the story is consistent with the most frequent setting for the telling of Mark's story in private homes to relatively small groups of people who would gather for an evening of storytelling.

Further evidence that this pattern of audience address was intentional is the progressive structure of engagement with the dynamic of being addressed as a disciple. The first significant address to the audience as persons close to Jesus occurs, as we have seen above, in the story of Jesus and his mother and brothers (3:31–35). There the character with whom the audience is invited to identify is named "the crowd sitting around him" (καὶ ἐκάθητο περὶ αὐτὸν ὄχλος), literally "the sitting-around-him crowd." In the first teaching discourse that immediately follows this story, there is an elaborate description of the super-large crowd (ὄχλος πλεῖστος) that gathered along the shore of the sea. The storyteller Jesus then addresses the audience as that large crowd, with Jesus probably seated and speaking in a loud voice with a slow tempo, as one would find it imperative to use in speaking to such a crowd. After the parable, the storyteller shifts the setting to an unnamed place where Jesus is alone, and the character addressed in the long discourse that follows is "those who were around him with the twelve" (οἱ περὶ αὐτὸν σὺν τοῖς δώδεκα). This name is a step closer to the audience's being addressed as a disciple, but this character is "those who were around him *with* the twelve" rather than "the twelve" by themselves. The probable purpose of this rather strange name is the construction of a dynamic structure that invites the audience to draw closer to Jesus in small, incremental steps.

Furthermore, the content of Jesus' speech in this discourse (4:10ff.) is a series of implicit invitations to the audience to experience being insiders in the Jesus group and to reflect on the quality of their engagement with the story. The first episode of Jesus' speech about the mystery of the kingdom of God is an explicit address to the audience about the gift offered to them as followers of Jesus. Furthermore, the identification of "the mystery," like the motif of the Messianic secret, is a classic storytelling lure to an audience to stick around and hear the rest of the story. The contrast between those who are inside and those who are outside identifies a choice that the audience must make about whether to remain outsiders or to become insiders. Both the interpretation of the parable of the Sower (4:13–20) as a parable about different ways of "hearing" and the saying about "hearing" (the saying can mean both "Pay attention to *what* you hear" and "Pay attention to *how* you hear" [as in Matt 7:14 and Luke 12:49, see BDAG, 3b]) address the quality of the audience's present engagement with the story. This series of teaching stories (4:1–32) is the longest and most intensive interaction up to this point in the story between the main character, Jesus, and the audience, who are addressed first as "the great crowd" and then as "those around the twelve."

The first speech addressed to the audience as "the twelve" does not occur until the story of the mission of the twelve (6:10–11). Jesus' speech has an interesting structure. The storyteller reports the first half of Jesus' instructions to the twelve in indirect discourse (6:7–9). Only after this introduction does the storyteller as Jesus address the audience directly as "the twelve." This is the final incremental step in the storytelling process of inviting the audience to accept being addressed as disciples.

Prior to the Messianic confession and discipleship discourse, the audience is addressed once more as "the disciples" in the concluding speech about the purity laws (7:18–22). The major discipleship discourse that follows Peter's realization (8:27ff.), however, is addressed to the audience as "the crowd with the disciples" (8:34). Once again, the storyteller steps back from having Jesus address the audience as "the disciples" or "the twelve" and addresses them as "the crowd with the disciples." Like the earlier address to the audience as "those who were around him with the twelve," this name for Jesus' addressee is initially puzzling because it is difficult as a description of the actual scene. How did Jesus gather a crowd in between his confrontation with Peter and his pronouncements about discipleship? The function of this comment, however, is probably less to describe what happened at Caesarea Philippi than to describe the gestures and gathering of the audience by the storyteller.

This is the turning point in the addresses to the audience as Jesus' disciples. After the discipleship discourse, the audience is addressed as the disciples most of the time (chs. 9–10) in the story of the journey up to Jerusalem. Only the teaching about divorce and the conversation with the rich man are exceptions, and both of those introduce discussions with the audience as the disciples. These stories firmly establish the relationship between the storyteller as Jesus and the audience as disciples prior to the events in Jerusalem that end with the longest and most intimate conversation with the four disciples seated on the Mount of Olives.

Thus, the addresses to the audience as disciples are structured to move the audience *from* a distanced relationship with the character of Jesus *to* an identification of themselves as Jesus' disciples. This dynamic in the relationship between the storyteller and the audience is experienced far more clearly when the Gospel of Mark is orally performed for a listening audience than when it is read alone in silence. In oral performance the storyteller can generate waves of emotional interaction upon which she or he seeks to carry the audience towards an intimate relationship with Jesus, which readers reading in the context of a wholly different rhetorical tradition do not experience.

Another sign of the importance of audience address for the composition of the Gospels is the structure of the other three gospels. While similar patterns of audience address, namely interspersed addresses to the audience as opponents and disciples throughout the prepassion story, are present in Matthew and Luke, John has a highly distinctive structure of audience address that engages audiences in a clearly marked, progressive relationship with Jesus over the entire story prior to the Passion Narrative.[4]

In the first four chapters of the Gospel of John, the storyteller as Jesus addresses the audience as a series of Israelite groups that are either interested in him or even believe in him: the audience as themselves in the Prologue, then in subsequent narratives first as the disciples (particularly Nathanael), then as the Judeans in the Temple, then as Nicodemus, then as disciples of John, and as the Samaritan woman.

In John 5 there is a major shift in audience address. Beginning with Jesus' response to the Judeans who persecute and seek to kill him after the Sabbath healing of the man at the pool of Bethzatha (5:16, 18), the storyteller as Jesus consistently addresses the audience as various groups of Judeans, who for eight chapters (5–12) alternate between extreme opposition to Jesus (7:1, 19ff.; 8:48ff.; 10:31–39) and belief in him (7:31, 40–41; 8:30–31; 11:45; 12:42–43). This continues through the entry into Jerusalem with the only exception being the brief address to the audience as his disciples at the end of the bread discourse (6:60–70). These long addresses to the audience as Judeans torn between opposition and belief have their climax in a series of four addresses by the storyteller as Jesus to the audience, first as Philip and Andrew (12:23–28), then as the crowd (12:29–36), by John the storyteller to the audience as themselves (12:37–43), and finally as Jesus to the audience as themselves (12:44–50).

The third section of audience address in John is Jesus' last words to the eleven disciples in the aftermath of the washing of the disciples' feet and the departure of Judas (13–17). This is the longest and most intimate discourse of Jesus in the entire gospel tradition. Thus, in John the same pattern of audience address that is present in smaller sections of Mark provides the structure for the whole of John's story prior to the Passion Narrative.

The sign that the composer of John consciously constructs this pattern of audience address is that there are only two relatively short addresses to the audience as the disciples from the story of the man at the pool of

---

4. For a fuller discussion of the structure of audience address in John, see Boomershine, "Medium and Message of John," 92–120.

Bethzatha to the triumphal entry (6:60–70; 12:23–28). In fact, there are only two additional addresses to the audience as the disciples in the initial section of John's story (chapters 1–4): Jesus' response to Nathanael's over-the-top confession (1:50–53) and his response to the disciples' wanting him to eat something after his conversation with the Samaritan woman (4:34–38). This is in marked contrast to the three Synoptic Gospels, in which there are addresses to the audience as the disciples throughout the stories prior to the Passion Narrative.

This pattern of audience address in John is similar to the pattern in Mark and may have been a distinctive adaptation of Mark's story. Mark establishes initial engagement with Jesus in the addresses to the audience by John the Baptist and Jesus himself (1:7–8, 15), moves to an extended series of addresses to the audience as various Judean groups opposed to Jesus (2:8–10, 17, 19–22, 25–28, 3:4–5, 23–29), and ends this initial part of the story with an extended address to the audience as those close to Jesus (3:33–35; 4:11–32). But while Mark repeats this pattern several times, it is always within a shorter storytelling compass, the longest being four chapters (1–4, 11–13). In John this pattern is extended with minor variations over the entire story prior to the PRN (1–17). These patterns of audience address in the story world of the Gospels of Mark and John are evidence that this was a structural dimension of the gospel storytelling tradition.

The addresses to the audience in Mark's passion story are further confirmation of this compositional structuring in the Gospel of Mark. As can be seen from the chart, prior to the arrest, the storyteller as Jesus addresses the audience as various groups of the disciples. With the exception of the Passover-preparation instructions to the two disciples and the highly intimate speech interpreting the meaning of the bread and wine at the meal, Jesus' speeches address the responses of the disciples to the events of the passion. Jesus' counter rebuke of those who rebuked the woman who anointed him is implicitly linked with Judas' offer to betray him. Once again, this is more evident when the story is performed than when it is read in silence because of the level of Jesus' conflict and rebuke of those who denounce the woman. The prophecies of betrayal (14:18–21) and desertion/denial (14:27–30) engage the audience in identification with the disciples' disbelief and resistance to the prophecies that are more or less immediately fulfilled.

The climax of Jesus' addresses to the audience prior to the arrest is Gethsemane. This is the quietest, the most intimate and the most emotionally intense interaction of the storyteller as Jesus with the audience as Jesus' disciples in the entire story. The three-fold repetition of Jesus' plea that they stay awake may have had a direct connection with the audience's struggle to stay awake after an evening of some nearly two hours of storytelling. The audience is invited to identify fully with Peter, James, and John as they hear the disappointment in their teacher's voice. In each of these instances the audience is invited to recognize the disciples' responses of betrayal, flight, and denial as wrong responses but with which they can fully identify.

The storyteller's addresses to the audience as Jesus, the high priest, and Pilate are the climax of the plot of Jesus' opponents. In each of these addresses, the audience is directly addressed as *you*. Thus, after the arrest, the storyteller as Jesus asks the audience as the crowd from the authorities, "Have *you* come out as against an insurrectionist (λῃστὴς) . . ." (14:48-49) After Jesus' confession, the storyteller as the high priest asks the audience as the council, "*You* have heard his blasphemy. How does it appear to *you*?" (14:63-64) And the storyteller as Pilate addresses the audience as the crowd: "Do *you* want me to release for *you* the King of the Jews?" (15:9) and "What then shall I do with the one *you* call King of the Jews?" (15:12). These speeches all share the same performance dynamic of requiring the audience to answer these questions internally. It is also significant that the questions at the arrest and the Pilate trial address issues directly related to the audience's experience of the insurrection that led to the Judean-Roman War. Jesus' question to the crowd arresting him as an insurrectionist (λῃστὴς) and the crowd's choice at the Pilate trial between Barabbas, an insurrectionist(στασιαστής), and Jesus frame these direct questions to the audience in the same terms that Josephus uses frequently to describe the various groups that led the revolution.[5] These questions are formed to resonate with the experience of Judean audiences who lived in the aftermath of the destruction of Jerusalem and the Temple. The storyteller's implicit appeal to the audiences of the story is to identify the arrest and crucifixion of Jesus as mistakes that are associated with the disasters of the war.

The final address to the audience in Mark's story by the storyteller as a character in the story is the address of the storyteller as "the young man" dressed in white to the audience as Mary Magdalene, Mary, and Salome (16:6-7). This speech is the climax of the entire two-hour story. The speech is quiet, slow and intimate. The audience's identification with the women has been established in the stories of their presence at Jesus' crucifixion and burial (15:40-41, 47). As a result, the audience experiences the young man's words as addressed to them. The climactic imperative addressed to the audience is the command to "go, tell . . ." (16:7). The women's response of flight

---

5. The terms that Mark uses to describe Barabbas would have had the implications of revolutionary activity for Mark's audiences in the aftermath of the Judean-Roman war. This is evident from Josephus' usage of these same terms to refer to the insurgents. For documentation and an excellent discussion of this dimension of Mark's language in the arrest and trial stories, see Marcus, *Mark*, 2:1029.

and of saying nothing to anyone completes the cycle of wrong responses by the characters with whom the audience has been invited to identify. In each instance, the impact of this story experience is for the audience to be implicated in these wrong responses and implicitly invited to reflect on this response and to do its opposite: staying awake, staying with Jesus in times of persecution, openly confessing being a disciple, choosing Jesus as Messiah rather than the insurrectionists, and telling the story. This final address to the audience is consistent with the performance function of the addresses to the audience throughout the story. These addresses involve the audience in direct interaction with the characters and events of the story.

The Characteristics of Mark's Audiences

The instances and patterns of the Markan storyteller's addresses to the audiences of the story as various characters in the story are a source of direct information about the characteristics of Mark's audiences.

The audiences are almost always addressed as various groups of Judeans. The sequence of Israelite groups can be seen on the chart and can be summarized here: the people of Judea and Galilee; the scribes, and scribes of the Pharisees; the disciples of John the Baptist, and the Pharisees; the Pharisees at several points in the story; the scribes from Jerusalem; the crowd at several points in the story, including at the Pilate trial; the group sitting around Jesus; those around Jesus with the twelve; the people in the Nazareth synagogue; the twelve and the disciples many times; the crowd with the disciples; Peter/Andrew/James/John; the chief priests/scribes/elders; the Sadducees; the crowd in the Temple; the Sanhedrin; and Mary Magdalene/Mary/Salome. By far the most frequent character embodied by the storyteller in these addresses to the audience is Jesus. No other character has more than one major address to the audience. Thus, the primary dynamic of address by the storyteller to the audience as characters in the story is as a wide-ranging spectrum of Judean groups.

Non-Judeans are addressed as a minor but integral part of Mark's audiences. At one point in the story (7:3–5), Gentiles are addressed directly by the storyteller and are thereby included in the projected audiences of the gospel.

The translations of Hebrew and Aramaic terms by the storyteller are an indication that the audiences are addressed as Greek-speaking Judeans and Gentiles who may not know Hebrew or Aramaic.

Mark's audiences are addressed as Judean persons who are invited to move from identifying with groups who are opposed to Jesus to identifying with Jesus' disciples. This pattern is present in progressive sections of the gospel (2–4; 7:1–22; 8:11–21; 10:1–12; 12–13) and in the majority of stories before and after the Messianic confession. Before the Messianic confession, the audience is addressed most of the time as groups who are opposed to Jesus. After Peter's moment of recognition, the audience is predominantly addressed as disciples.

The audiences are addressed as persons who are implicitly asked to move gradually from being identified as part of crowds interested in listening to Jesus to being identified as Jesus' disciples. This movement in audience address from being addressed as those outside to those inside is carefully nuanced in incremental steps. These include addresses to the audience in relatively long discourses by Jesus as, for example, "those around Jesus with the twelve" and "the crowd with the disciples." The addresses to the audience as those inside are sometimes located in a story space where Jesus is alone or inside a house. This storytelling location is also a sign that these talks are quieter, smaller in gesture, and more intimate than the public discourses.

This data has implications for our reconstructions of the actual historical audiences of Mark's gospel. The data of audience address in Mark's gospel indicates that the story was structured for predominantly Judean audiences who did not believe that Jesus is the Messiah. Mark's purpose is evident in the structure of audience address in the story. The story is structured to move the audiences from identifying themselves as Jesus' opponents to identifying themselves as Jesus' disciples. Furthermore, those who are interested in Jesus, as are most of those who would have begun listening to Mark's story, are invited by the storyteller to move from a relationship of interest on the periphery of the story to a place inside the community of those who have an intimate relationship with Jesus.

There is nothing in this data that would indicate that Mark's story was directed to those outside the nascent Christian communities to the exclusion of those who were already members of believing communities. However, believers are *addressed as* Judeans who are either opposed to Jesus or are only interested in his teaching from a distance. That is, the structure of audience address does not support the assumption that Mark was composed for performances to audiences that were either an individual believing community, as Joel Marcus envisions, or the network of Christian communities in the Greco-Roman world, as Richard Bauckham has proposed. The story may have been told in believing communities, but those believers are addressed as persons who are either outside or on the periphery of discipleship communities. The audiences are addressed as disciples but only after a long period of storytelling invitations to move from a position of identification with opponents or with a supportive crowd on the outer perimeters of the communities of disciples. Thus, there are many allusions in Jesus' apocalyptic discourse to the experience of communities of Jesus' followers. But that only happens after a long process of audience inclusion in which the audience is invited by the dynamics of audience address to move from a position of opposition to the interested periphery to the inner circle of the twelve and then with the four and three disciples closest to Jesus.

The Gospel of Mark has a radically different structure of audience address than the letters of Paul, which are addressed to small communities of believers. Mark is addressed to the great community of Israelites throughout the Greco-Roman world, all of whom were seeking for a way forward in the aftermath of the Judean-Roman War. A major theme implicit in the structure of audience address is an appeal to the audience to reject the way of insurrection and to believe in a Messiah who taught and practiced healing and feeding of both Israelites and Gentiles. A dimension of Jesus' teaching was a critique of the purity laws that were a barrier to Israelites having virtually any relationship with Gentiles. However, while Gentiles are the object of Jesus' actions in several stories, the audience is addressed as Gentiles only once in the story. The Gospel of Mark is addressed to Israelites and Gentiles in a manner that assumes they are fully cognizant of the realities of hostility between Israelites and Gentiles. This relationship is, however, addressed from an Israelite perspective. The Gentiles are those on the other side of the sea (5:1ff); those who are appropriately called "dogs" (7:27); those who will mock, spit on, and kill the Messiah (10:34); and those who practice leadership by domination rather than service (10:42), Gentiles are, therefore, invited to be part of the audiences of the gospel but only as they are willing to enter into the Israelite world of Mark's story. As one might expect in the aftermath of the war, the Gospel of Mark addresses audiences in which the relationships between Israelites and Gentiles are even more highly polarized than they are in the letters of Paul.

The analysis of the dynamics of audience address requires that Markan scholarship reexamine the conclusion that the Gospel of Mark was "anti-Jewish." The central fact that requires this reexamination is that the audiences of the story were, with one exception, addressed as Judeans. Furthermore, for the first hour of the story the storyteller presents Jesus addressing the audiences as Judeans who are opponents and critics of Jesus. This is a structure of audience interactions characteristic of *intra-Israelite* conflict *rather than anti-Jewish* conflict. In its original context, the Gospel of Mark is no more "anti-Jewish" than the book of Jeremiah or the book of Exodus. It may be "anti-chief priests" just as opposition to the priests in Jerusalem is characteristic of the sectarian community in Qumran. Likewise, in both Jeremiah and Exodus, the audience is addressed as members of

Israelite communities by storytellers who embody characters such as Moses and Jeremiah who are in constant conflict with the people of Israel as well as with priests and other prophets. In both of those books, the audience is addressed as members of Israelite communities by storytellers who embody characters such as Moses and Jeremiah—figures in steady conflict with the people of Israel. The literature of Israel is full of violent intra-Israelite conflict in which various authors are appealing to Israelites to reject the policies and actions of other Israelite groups.

What is distinctive about Mark's story in the context of the literature of Israel is the inclusion of Gentiles in the projected audiences of the story. Gentile members of Mark's audiences were invited to join audiences of Israelites and to experience the story of Jesus as an integral part of the wider community of Israel. The storytellers of Mark's gospel did not address their audience as Gentiles, for whom Israelites are "the others," as would be required if the story's purpose was "anti-Jewish." The audiences of Mark are addressed as Judeans, for whom Gentiles are "the others." The structure of audience address in Mark requires that we imagine a social and political context in which non-Israelites were invited to join Israelites in listening to an Israelite story of which they were an integral part, both in the story itself, and in their participation in the audiences for whom the story was performed. This is congruent with the social and political context of the Israelite community in the immediate aftermath of the war outlined by Joel Marcus.[6] But the data of audience address indicates that the audiences of Mark were not addressed as communities in which either Gentiles or members of believing communities were the majority. The audiences of Mark were addressed as Israelites and Gentiles who were invited by the story to move from a position of opposition to Jesus to a position of identifying with Jesus' disciples. The audiences of Mark are, therefore, primarily addressed repeatedly as Judeans who do not believe that Jesus is the Messiah. The historical probability is that this was the dominant character of the audiences for which the gospel was performed. The primary purpose of the story implicit in the structure of audience address was to move its listeners from opposition to Jesus to belief in Jesus as the Messiah.

---

6. See Marcus, "Jewish War," 441–62.

Appendix 7

THE PRONUNCIATION OF JESUS' CRY OF ABANDONMENT AND THE BYSTANDERS' MISHEARING (MARK 15:34–35)

With Adam Gilbert Bartholomew

THE PERFORMANCE OF JESUS' CRY OF ABANDONMENT FOLlowed by the misunderstanding or deliberate mishearing on the part of the bystanders that leads them to mock him presents a challenge to the American English-speaking storyteller. To put it most simply, there is no sonic connection for American speakers of English between "Eloi," which is a widely employed transliteration of Ελωι (KJV, NRSV, NAB, NJB, NET), and the name Elijah. In fact, it is in no way certain how Americans might pronounce "Eloi" when they meet it in the translated text from which they may be working. There are options, but in order even to show in print what they are, we have to agree on which of a variety of phonetic keys we are going to use to represent the sounds we have in mind.

We begin with the phonetic key we shall employ in this appendix: Ā, ā—day; Ă, ă—father; Ē, e—beat; Ĕ, ĕ—bet; Ī, ī—site; Ĭ, ĭ—it. Using this phonetic key, here are the various ways Americans might pronounce "Eloi" when they meet it in a translation of Mark's text: Ĕlōē, Ĕlōī, Ēlōē, or Ēlōī. The fourth option gets closer to the sounds of the name Elijah than any of the others; but the presence of the long *o* sound (ō) in Ēlōī and of the *j* sound in Elijah requires of the listeners a great stretch of the imagination if they are to hear in Ēlōī something like the name Elijah.

Mark's audience would not have had our problem. First of all, Mark and the storytellers who told his story after him pronounced Ελωι for their listeners. The listeners did not have to figure out how to pronounce the word from a silent text. But even if it had been necessary to do that, the Greek letters of Ελωι had a rather standard pronunciation. Mark and his successors would have pronounced it Ĕlōē. The second reason those listening to the story in Greek would not have had our problem is that the name of the prophet in Greek is 'Ηλίαν, pronounced Ālēyăn (Erasmian) or Ēlēyăn (Koine).[1] The sound of the name of the prophet in Greek is much closer to the sound of Ελωι in Greek than the sound of "Elijah," the English translation of the name of the prophet.

If our American listeners are to hear what Mark's listeners heard in this episode in Mark's story, it seems there are two strategies open to us. One is to transliterate the Greek form of the name of the prophet as well as the Greek letters Ελωι. In this way the American storyteller would have the bystanders say, "Listen, he is calling Ālēyăn" (or "Ēlēyăn"). The difficulty with this option is that Ālēyăn (or Ēlēyăn) is quite unintelligible to English speaking audiences. We could add a narrative comment the way Mark does after Jesus' cry, such as "which means Elijah." That solution feels rather cumbersome, but it is an option.

The second strategy is to go the route Matthew did. According to most translations of Matthew, Jesus cried, "Eli!" This is the standard transliteration of Ηλι.[2] Seeing "Eli" most Americans would pronounce it Ēlī. That mimics exactly the beginning of the English translation of the prophet's name, allowing the storyteller to retain the familiar form of the name, and makes the bystanders' misunderstanding of Jesus' cry immediately intelligible.

The chart below gives most of the textual data involved in relation to the problem we have dealt with here. It is clearly rather complex. The one thing we have not tried to include in the chart is the Aramaic that Mark and Matthew are transliterating.

Mark 15:34, 35		
Greek New Testament	Ελωι	'Ηλίαν
Erasmian pronunciation of Greek in American Phonetics (see key below)	Ĕlōē	Ālēyăn
Possible Koine pronunciation of Greek in American Phonetics (see key below and Appendix III)	Ĕlōē	Ēlēyăn
NRSV transliteration of Ελωι, translation of 'Ηλίαν	Eloi	Elijah

1. See appendix 3 for the difference between Erasmian and Koine pronunciation.
2. It may be that Matthew is not drawing on the MT but using a different Aramaic dialect: cf. Davies and Allison, *Matthew 19–28*, 624.

The Pronunciation of Jesus' Cry of Abandonment

Possible American Phonetic Pronunciation of NRSV Transliteration	Ĕlōē Ĕlōī Ĕlōē Ĕlōī	
Matt 27:46, 47		
Greek New Testament	Ηλι	'Ηλίαν
Erasmian Pronunciation of Greek in American Phonetics (see key below)	Ālē	Ālēyăn
Possible Koine Pronunciation of Greek in American Phonetics (see key below and Appendix III)	Ēlē	Ēlēyăn
NRSV Transliteration of Ηλι, Translation of 'Ηλίαν	Eli	Elijah
American Phonetic Pronunciation of NRSV Transliteration	Ĕlī	Ĕlījuh
Key to American Phonetics Used Here		
Ā, ā—day Ă, ă—father Ē, ē—beat Ĕ, ĕ—bet Ī, ī—site Ĭ, ĭ—it		

Appendix 8

THE MOCKING OF JESUS AND SAMSON AND THE LXX A TEXT OF JUDGES

With Adam Gilbert Bartholomew

THIS STORY EVOKED MEMORIES OF EARLIER STORIES OF RITUAL humiliation of Israelites by their enemies. The oldest of these stories was the story of Samson and his ritual humiliation by the Philistine nobility that led to his action of mutual destruction. The central verb of this story tradition, ἐμπαίζω, "to ridicule, make fun of, mock," is used twice in Judg 16:25 and 27 in one of the two Greek LXX texts offered by Rahlfs. Rahlfs' A text, based on Codex Alexandrinus, has virtually the same exact phrase as Mark's summary: καὶ ἐνέπαιζον αὐτῷ (Judg 16:25), and καὶ ὅτε ἐνέπαιξαν αὐτῷ (Mark 15:20). Rahlfs' B text, based on Codex Vaticanus, translates 16:25 καὶ ἔπαιζεν ἐνώπιον αὐτῶν, "and he began to perform for them" (NETS parallel text translation). The NRSV translation of Judges is based on the Hebrew text and also renders this phrase "he performed for them." But the Greek in Codex Alexandrinus means "they mocked, made fun of him." This may well be an instance in which the LXX translators made an ambiguous Hebrew phrase clearer. Furthermore, this may be a sign that the Markan composer had heard the A text of the Septuagint and was sounding that note in his new composition.

The history of the LXX text of Judges is particularly complex. The note in the 2007 edition of *The New English Translation of the Septuagint (NETS)*, produced by the International Organization for Septuagint and Cognate Studies, states that there is as yet no full critical edition of the LXX of Judges. Rahlfs included two texts in his edition, one above the other. The *NETS* make translations of both of Rahlfs' texts available. The *NETS Notes* include an extensive discussion and clarifies why Rahlfs included two texts:

> In Judges Rahlfs based his edition on the readings of about twenty manuscripts. He identified two main textual traditions, which he believed were so diverse that they amounted to separate recensions (editions) of the book. He printed these as separate texts, designated A and B. NETS Judges, accordingly, offers a translation of both the A and the B texts.
>
> Rahlfs based his A text upon Codex Alexandrinus (A) and two groups of manuscripts representing the recensions of the LXX associated, respectively, with Origen (c. 185–253 CE) and Lucian (c. 250–312 CE). His B text was based upon Codex Vaticanus (B).[1]

In the story of the mocking by the Roman soldiers, Mark may well be alluding to the textual tradition of the Greek translation of Judges in codex Alexandrinus.

---

1. Pietersma and Wright, *NETS Notes*, 1.

BIBLIOGRAPHY

Alec McGowen in His Solo Performance of St. Mark's Gospel. Videorecording. New York: Arthur Cantor Films, 1990.
Pietersma, Albert, and Benjamin G. Wright, eds. *A New English Translation of the Septuagint.* New York: Oxford University Press, 2007.
Achtemeier, Paul J. "*Omne Verbum Sonat*: The New Testament and the Oral Environment of Late Western Antiquity." *JBL* 109 (1990) 3–27.
Auerbach, Erich. *Mimesis: The Representation of Reality in Western Literature.* Princeton: Princeton University Press, 1953.
Bauckham, Richard, ed. *The Gospels for All Christians: Rethinking the Gospel Audiences.* Grand Rapids: Eerdmans, 1998.
———. *Jesus and the Eyewitnesses: The Gospels as Eyewitness Testimony.* Grand Rapids: Eerdmans, 2006.
Bauer, Walter, et al. *A Greek-English Lexicon of the New Testament and Other Early Christian Literature.* 3rd ed. Chicago: University of Chicago Press, 2000.
Beilby, James K., and Paul Rhodes Eddy, eds. *The Historical Jesus: Five Views.* Downers Grove: IVP Academic, 2009.
Blass, F. A. *Pronunciation of Ancient Greek.* Translated by W. J. Purton. Cambridge: Cambridge University Press, 1890.
Bligh, P. H. "A Note on *Huios Theou* in Mark 15:39." *ExpTim* 80 (1968–69) 51–53.
Bonhoeffer, Dietrich. *Life Together.* John W. Doberstein. New York: HarperOne, 2009.
Boomershine, Thomas E. "Audience Address and Purpose in the Performance of Mark." In *Mark as Story: Retrospect and Prospect*, edited by Kelly R. Iverson and Christopher W. Skinner, 115–44. SBL Resources for Biblical Studies 65. Atlanta: Society of Biblical Literature, 2011.
———. "Audience Asides and the Audiences of Mark: The Difference Performance Makes." In *From Text to Performance: Narrative and Performance Criticisms in Dialogue and Debate*, edited by Kelly R. Iverson, 80–96. Biblical Performance Criticsm 10. Eugene, OR: Cascade Books, 2014.
———. "Biblical Megatrends: Towards a Paradigm for the Interpretation of the Bible in Electronic Media." In *American Bible Society Symposium Papers on the Bible in the Twenty-First Century*, edited by Howard Clark Kee, 209–30. Philadelphia: Trinity, 1993.
———. "Mark, the Storyteller: A Rhetorical-Critical Investigation of Mark's Passion and Resurrection Narrative." PhD diss., Union Theological Seminary, 1974.
———. "Mark 16:8 and the Apostolic Commission." *JBL* 100 (1981) 225–39.

———. "The Medium and Message of John: Audience Address and Audience Identity in the Fourth Gospel." In *The Fourth Gospel in First-Century Media Culture*, edited by Tom Thatcher and Anthony LeDonne, 92–120. London: T. & T. Clark, 2011.

———. "Peter's Denial as Polemic or Confession: The Implications of Media Criticism for Biblical Hermeneutics." *Semeia* 39 (1987) 47–68.

———. *Story Journey: An Invitation to the Gospel as Storytelling.* Nashville: Abingdon, 1988.

Boomershine, Thomas E., and Gilbert L. Bartholomew. "The Narrative Technique of Mark 16:8." *JBL* 100 (1981) 213–23.

Booth, Wayne C. *The Rhetoric of Fiction.* Chicago: University of Chicago Press, 1966.

Boys, Mary C. *Redeeming Our Sacred Story: The Death of Jesus and Relations between Jews and Christians.* Studies in Judaism and Christianity. New York: Paulist, 2013.

Brighton, Mark A. *The Sicarii in Josephus's Judean War: Rhetorical Analysis and Historical Observations.* Edited by Judith H. Newman. Early Judaism and Its Literature 27. Atlanta: Society of Biblical Literature, 2009.

Brown, Raymond E. *The Death of the Messiah: From Gethsemane to the Grave; A Commentary on the Passion Narratives in the Four Gospels.* 2 vols. ABRL. New York: Doubleday, 1994.

———. *The Gospel according to John.* 2 vols. AB 29–29A. Garden City, NY: Doubleday, 1966.

———. *The Gospel and Epistles of John: A Concise Commentary.* Collegeville, MN: Liturgical, 1988.

———. *An Introduction to the New Testament.* ABRL. New York: Doubleday, 1997.

Browning, Robert. *Medieval and Modern Greek.* 2nd ed. Cambrdige: Cambridge University Press, 1983.

Bultmann, Rudolf. *History of the Synoptic Tradition.* Translated by John Marsh. New York: Harper & Row, 1963.

Campbell, William S. "Engagement, Disengagement and Obstruction: Jesus' Defense Strategies in Mark's Trial and Execution Scenes (14:53–64; 15:1–39)." *JSNT* 26 (2004) 283–300.

Carson, D. A. *The Gospel according to John.* Leicester, UK: Inter-Varsity, 1991.

Chariton. *Callirhoe.* Edited and translated by G. P. Goold. LCL. Cambridge: Harvard University Press, 1995.

Charlesworth, James H., ed. *The Old Testament Pseudepigrapha.* 2 vols. Garden City, NY: Doubleday, 1983.

Collins, Adela Yarbro. *Mark: A Commentary.* Hermeneia. Minneapolis: Fortress, 2007.

Collins, John J. *The Scepter and the Star: The Messiahs of the Dead Sea Scrolls and Other Ancient Literature.* ABRL. New York: Doubleday, 1995.

Colwell, E. C. "A Definite Rule for the Use of the Article in the Greek New Testament." *JBL* 52 (1933) 12–21.

Crossan, John Dominic. *Who Killed Jesus? Exposing the Roots of Anti-Semitism in the Gospel Story of the Death of Jesus.* San Francisco: HarperSanFrancisco, 1996.

Croy, N. Clayton. *The Mutilation of Mark's Gospel.* Nashville: Abingdon, 2003.

Davies, W. D., and Dale C. Allison. *A Critical and Exegetical Commentary on the Gospel according to Saint Matthew.* Vol. 3, *Commentary on Matthew 19–28.* ICC. Edinburgh: T. & T. Clark, 2004.

Dibelius, Martin. *From Tradition to Gospel.* Library of Theological Translations. Cambridge: James Clarke, 1971 (German orig. 1933).

Dunn, James D. G. *The Oral Gospel Tradition*. Grand Rapids: Eerdmans, 2013.
Egger, Emile. *L'hellénisme en France: leçons sur influence*. 2 vols. Paris: Didier, 1869.
Elliott, John H. "Jesus the Israelite Was Neither a 'Jew' Nor a 'Christian': On Correcting Misleading Nomenclature." *JSHJ* 5 (2007) 119–54.
Faulkner, John Alfred. *Erasmus: The Scholar*. Men of the Kingdom. Cincinnati: Jennings & Graham, 1907.
Fowler, Robert M. *Let the Reader Understand: Reader-Response Criticism and the Gospel of Mark*. Minneapolis: Fortress, 1991.
Freedman, David N., ed. *The Anchor Bible Dictionary*. 6 vols. New York: Doubleday, 1992.
Frei, Hans W. *The Eclipse of Biblical Narrative: A Study in Eighteenth and Nineteenth Century Hermeneutics*. New Haven: Yale University Press, 1974.
Gamble, Harry Y. *Books and Readers in the Early Church: A History of Early Christian Texts*. New Haven: Yale University Press, 1995.
Gruen, Erich S. *Diaspora: Jews amidst Greek and Romans*. Cambridge: Harvard University Press, 2002.
Haas, Christina. *Writing Technology: Studies on the Materiality of Literacy*. Mahwah, NY: Earlbaum, 1996.
Hadas, Moses. *Ancilla to Classical Reading*. Columbia Bicentennial Editions and Studies. New York: Columbia University Press, 1954.
Hanson, K. C. "Jesus and the Social Bandits." In *The Social Setting of Jesus and the Gospels*, edited by Wolfgang Stegemann, Bruce J. Malina, and Gerd Theissen, 283–300. Minneapolis: Fortress, 2002.
Harner, P. B. "Qualitative Anarthrous Predicate Nouns: Mark 15:39 and John 1:1." *JBL* 92 (1973) 75–87.
Harris, William V. *Ancient Literacy*. Cambridge: Harvard University Press, 1989.
Harris-McCoy, Daniel E. *Artemidorus' Oneirocritica: Text, Translation and Commentary*. Oxford: Oxford University Press, 2012.
Hayes, Christine E. *Gentile Impurities and Jewish Identities: Intermarriage and Conversion from the Bible to the Talmud*. Oxford: Oxford University Press, 2002.
Hearon, Holly E., and Philip Ruge-Jones, eds. *The Bible in Ancient and Modern Media: Story and Performance*. Biblical Performance Criticism 1. Eugene, OR: Cascade Books, 2009.
Hengel, Martin. *Crucifixion in the Ancient World and the Folly of the Message of the Cross*. Translated by John Bowden. Philadelphia: Fortress, 1977.
Homer. *The Iliad of Homer*. Translated by Richmond Lattimore. A Phoenix Book. Chicago: University of Chicago Press, 1951.
Horsley, Richard A. *Jesus and Empire: The Kingdom of God and the New World Disorder*. Minneapolis: Fortress, 2003.
Horsley, Richard A., with John S. Hanson. *Bandits, Prophets, and Messiahs: Popular Movements in the Time of Jesus*. San Francisco: Harper & Row, 1988.
Ihde, Don. *Listening and Voice: A Phenomenology of Sound*. Athens: Ohio University Press, 1976.
Iverson, Kelly R., ed. *From Text to Performance: Narrative and Performance Criticisms in Dialogue and Debate*. Biblical Performance Criticism 10. Eugene, OR: Cascade Books, 2014.
Jeremias, Joachim. *The Eucharistic Words of Jesus*. Rev. ed. Translated by Norman Perrin. New York: Scribner, 1966.

Josephus, Flavius. *The Jewish War.* Vol. 2. Translated by H. St. J. Thackeray. LCL 210. Cambridge: Harvard University Press, 1997.

Juvenal. *Juvenal and Persius: The Satires.* Translated by G. G. Ramsay. LCL 91. Cambridge: Harvard University Press, 1969.

Kelber, Werner. *The Kingdom in Mark: A New Place and a New Time.* Philadelphia: Fortress, 1974.

———. *The Oral and the Written Gospel: The Hermeneutics of Speaking and Writing in the Synoptic Tradition, Mark, Paul, and Q.* Philadelphia: Fortress, 1983.

Klein, G. "Die Verleugnung des Petrus: Eine traditionsgeschichtliche Untersuchung." *ZTK* 58 (1961) 285–328.

Knibb, M. A. "Martyrdom and Ascension of Isaiah: A New Translation and Introduction." In *OTP*, 2:143–76.

Knox, B. W. "Silent Reading in Antiquity." *GRBS* 9 (1968) 421–35.

Lagrange, P. M.-J. *Evangile selon Saint Marc.* Etudes bibliques. Paris: Lecoffre, 1929.

Lee, Margaret Ellen, and Bernard Brandon Scott. *Sound Mapping the New Testament.* Salem, OR: Polebridge, 2009.

Lindars, Barnabas. *New Testament Apologetic: The Doctrinal Significance of the Old Testament Quotations.* Philadelphia: Westminster, 1961.

Linnemann, Eta. "Die Verleugnung des Petrus." *ZTK* 63 (1966) 1–32.

Lohmeyer, Ernst. *Das Evangelium des Markus.* KEK 1/2. Göttingen: Vandenhoeck & Ruprecht, 1954.

Mack, Burton L. *A Myth of Innocence: Mark and Christian Origins.* Philadelphia: Fortress, 1988.

Malina, Bruce J. "Three Theses for a More Adequate Reading of the New Testament." In *Practical Theology: Perspectives from the Plains,* edited by Michael G. Lawler and Gail S. Risch, 33–60. Omaha, NE: Creighton University Press, 2000.

———. *The New Testament World: Insights from Cultural Anthropology.* 3rd ed. Louisville: Westminster John Knox, 2001.

Marcus, Joel. "The Jewish War and the *Sitz Im Leben* of Mark." *JBL* 111 (1992) 441–62.

———. *Mark: A New Translation with Introduction and Commentary.* 2 vols. AYB 27, 27A. New York: Doubleday, 2000–2009.

———. *The Mystery of the Kingdom of God.* SBL Dissertation Series 90. Atlanta: Scholars, 1986.

———. *The Way of the Lord: Christological Exegesis of the Old Testament in the Gospel of Mark.* Studies in the New Testament and Its World. Edinburgh: T. & T. Clark, 1992.

Martyn, J. Louis. *History and Theology in the Fourth Gospel.* 3rd ed. Louisville: Westminster John Knox, 2003.

Mayo, C. H. "The *Gallicinium*." *JTS* 22 (1921) 367–69.

McDonald, Dennis R. *The Homeric Epics and the Gospel of Mark.* New Haven: Yale University Press, 2000.

Metzger, Bruce M. *Manuscripts of the Greek Bible: An Introduction to Greek Palaeography.* New York: Oxford University Press, 1981.

Moore, George Foot. *Judaism: In the First Centuries of the Christian Era.* 3 vols. Cambridge: Harvard University Press, 1966.

Moulton, James H., et al. *A Grammar of New Testament Greek.* 4 vols. Edinburgh: T. & T. Clark, 1908.

Moulton, James H., and George Milligan. *The Vocabulary of the Greek Testament*. Grand Rapids: Eerdmans, 1930.

Myers, Ched. *Binding the Strong Man: A Political Reading of Mark's Story of Jesus*. Maryknoll, NY: Orbis, 1988.

Ong, Walter. *Orality and Literacy: The Technologizing of the Word*. New Accents. London: Methuen, 1982.

———. *The Presence of the Word: Some Prolegomena for Cultural and Religious History*. The Terry Lectures. New Haven: Yale University Press, 1967.

Pesch, Rudolf. *Das Markusevangelium*. 2 vols. HTKNT 2. Freiburg: Herder, 1976.

Philostratus. *The Life of Apollonius of Tyana*. Translated by F. C. Conybeare. LCL. Cambridge: Harvard University Press, 1912.

Plummer, Alfred. *The Gospel according to St. Mark*. Cambridge Bible for Schools and Colleges. Cambridge: Cambridge University Press, 1915.

Quesnell, Quentin. *The Mind of Mark: Interpretation and Method through Exegesis of Mark 6, 52*. AnBib 38. Rome: Pontifical Biblical Institute, 1969.

Rhoads, David. "Performance Criticism: An Emerging Methodology in Second Testament Studies—Part I." *BTB* 36 (2006) 118–33.

———. "Performance Criticism: An Emerging Methodology in Second Testament Studies—Part II." *BTB* 36 (2006) 164–84.

Robertson, A. T. *A Grammar of the Greek New Testament in the Light of Historical Research*. Nashville: Broadman, 1934.

Sanders, E. P. *The Historical Figure of Jesus*. London: Penguin, 1993.

Suetonius, C. Tranquilus. *The Lives of the Twelve Caesars: To Which Are Added His Lives of the Grammarians, Rhetoricians, and Poets*. Translated by Alexander Thomson and revised by T. Forester. Bohn's Classical Library. London: Bell, 1914.

Shiner, Whitney. *Proclaiming the Gospel: First-Century Performance of Mark*. Harrisburg, PA: Trinity, 2003.

Smallwood, E. Mary. *The Jews under Roman Rule: From Pompey to Diocletian*. Corrected ed. SJLA 20. Leiden: Brill, 1981.

Stark, Rodney. *The Rise of Christianity: How the Obscure, Marginal Jesus Movement Became the Dominant Religious Force in the Western World in a Few Centuries*. San Francisco: HarperCollins, 1997.

Stendahl, Krister. *The School of St. Matthew, and Its Use of the Old Testament*. Acta Seminarii Neotestamentici Upsaliensis 20. Lund: Gleerup, 1954. 2nd ed., 1968.

Strack, Hermann L., and Paul Billerbeck. *Kommentar zum Neuen Testament aus Talmud und Midrasch*. 6 vols. Munich: Beck, 1922–1961.

Suhl, Alfred. *Die Funktion der alttestamentlichen Zitate und Anspielungen im Markusevangelium*. Gütersloh: Mohn, 1965.

Swanson, Richard. *Provoking the Gospel of Mark: A Storyteller's Commentary. Year B*. Cleveland: Pilgrim, 2005.

Tacitus, Publius Cornelius. *The Annals*. Translated by Alfred John Church and William Jackson Brodribb. Modern Library. New York: Random House, 1942. Online: classics.mit.edu/Tacitus/annals.html/.

Taylor, Vincent. *The Gospel according to St. Mark*. 2nd ed. London: Macmillan, 1966.

Tolbert, Mary Ann. *Sowing the Gospel: Mark's World in Literary-Historical Perspective*. Philadelphia: Fortress, 1989.

Weeden, Theodore J. *Mark—Traditions in Conflict*. Philadelphia: Fortress, 1971.

Welborn, L. L. *Paul, the Fool for Christ: A Study of 1 Corinthians 1–4 in the Comic-Philosophic Tradition*. Early Christianity in Context. London: T. & T. Clark, 2005.

Wellhausen, J. *Das Evangelium Marci*. 2nd ed. Berlin: Reimer, 1909.

West, Martin L. "Colometry." In *Brill's New Pauly*. Antiquity volumes: edited by Hubert Cancik and Helmuth Schneider. Brill Online, 2014, http://referenceworks.brillonline.com/entries/brill-s-new-pauly/colometry-e618300/.

Wink, Walter. *The Bible in Human Transformation: Toward a New Paradigm for Biblical Study*. Philadelphia: Fortress, 1973.

———. *The Bible in Human Transformation: Toward a New Paradigm for Biblical Study*. Facets. Minneapolis: Fortress, 2010.

———. *Engaging the Powers: Discernment and Resistance in a World of Domination*. The Powers 3. Minneapolis: Fortress, 1992.

Wrede, William. *The Messianic Secret*. Translated by J. C. G. Greig. Library of Theological Translations. Cambridge: James Clarke, 1971 (German orig. 1901).

Zeitlin, Solomon. *The Rise and Fall of the Judaean State: A Political, Social and Religious History of the Second Commonwealth*. Vol. 3, *66 CE–120 CE*. Philadelphia: Jewish Publication Society of America, 1978.

INDEX

aesthetic distance, 23–24, 28, 69, 231, 323, 348, 354, 391–92, 397
Alexander and Rufus, 261, 264, 266
Alexandria, 18, 364–66
allusion, 15, 41, 47, 74, 97–98, 122, 143–44, 151, 219, 248, 253, 264, 266, 276, 278, 280, 286–87, 290, 301, 303–6, 308, 316, 342, 345, 360, 425
ambiguity, 1, 33, 75, 89, 152, 211, 225, 267, 299–300, 310, 340, 343, 370
anti-Jewish polemic, x, 31, 34–35, 241, 405
anti-petrine polemic, 107–8
anti-Semitism, 20–21, 361, 409, 434
Antiochus IV Epiphanes, 25, 67, 160, 206–7, 219, 232, 241, 250, 257, 261, 281, 315, 324, 394
apologetic, x, 20, 29, 107, 308, 324, 403, 436
applause, 141, 165
assassination, 63, 68, 88, 150–53, 209, 277
asyndeton, 47, 371, 375
atmosphere, 47, 164–65, 182, 192, 255, 296, 305, 318
attitude, 23–24, 43, 131, 139–40, 146, 168, 244–45, 258–59, 292, 322, 324, 326, 392
audience, vii, ix–xi, 1–2, 4–5, 7–19, 22–32, 34–35, 39–41, 43–44, 46, 48, 55, 60, 63, 66, 68, 70, 75–76, 80–82, 85–89, 92–93, 97–98, 103, 106–11, 113, 118, 121, 125–27, 129, 131, 134–35, 138, 140–42, 146–47, 149–52, 155, 158–59, 161, 163, 165–67, 169, 171–72, 177–84, 186–88, 190, 193, 196–200, 202, 204, 206, 208, 210, 213–16, 219, 221–45, 247–48, 250, 252, 255–59, 264, 266–69, 271–77, 281, 285–86, 289–91, 293, 296–304, 306–7, 311–16, 320–21, 323, 325–27, 329–36, 338–40, 342–45, 347–48, 350, 353–58, 360–61, 363, 365, 367, 369–70, 374, 392–99, 401–2, 404–28, 433–34
audience address, 7, 14–16, 229, 237, 360, 410–11, 413–14, 416–18, 420–21, 424–26, 433–34
audience, horizon of, 15
audience, original, 31

Barabbas, 18–20, 22, 31–32, 34, 67, 202, 204, 209–11, 213–15, 225–26, 233–36, 238–39, 242–44, 246, 274, 300, 304, 360, 405, 422
Bartimaeus, 47, 222, 264, 285, 289
Bathsheba, 18, 27, 97, 188, 235, 357, 395, 398–99
Beelzebul, 15, 36, 105, 229, 284, 301–3, 315, 411, 415
Belkira, 160, 208, 218, 281–82, 291

Callirhoe and Chaereas, 185–86, 192, 287, 288, 307, 434
characterization, 7, 20, 23–27, 29–30, 68–69, 108–11, 113–14, 121–22, 128, 130, 137–38, 140, 180, 192, 199, 206–8, 227–28, 230–32, 237, 240–42, 250, 276, 302, 312, 319, 321–25, 345, 360, 392–95, 398, 403–4

439

climax, 6, 14, 24–25, 27, 29, 47, 50, 62, 81–82, 90, 96–97, 101, 127–30, 132, 136, 140–42, 149, 153, 155, 171, 175, 180, 183, 189, 195, 197–200, 208–11, 221, 237, 242, 245–46, 250, 255–58, 260, 263, 271–72, 274, 285, 293, 298–99, 305–6, 310, 312, 314, 324–25, 327, 333, 335–36, 338, 346, 348, 350, 359, 373, 392–93, 396, 398, 402–3, 415, 417, 420–22

codex, 3, 134, 189, 212, 247–48, 340, 430–31

cola, xi, 4, 6–8, 40, 47, 58–60, 65, 90, 117, 119, 122, 146, 183, 192–93, 200, 208, 210–11, 250–51, 262–63, 274–75, 297–98, 308, 314, 316, 318, 332–33, 335, 337–41, 343–44, 368–73, 390

colometry, 6, 438

comma, 8, 337–39, 369–70

communication, xiii, 1–5, 8–9, 13, 33, 169, 311, 333

composer, 6, 9, 65, 76, 81, 101, 136, 191, 193–94, 215, 219, 228, 236, 247–48, 253, 259, 266, 270, 280, 282, 290, 297, 306, 308, 320, 327, 335, 345, 347–48, 371, 373, 414, 420, 430

composition, ix–xi, xiii, 1–6, 8–9, 13–14, 18, 31, 35, 121, 131, 154, 175, 186, 211, 247, 250, 281, 313, 322, 335, 344, 354, 360, 368, 370–71, 374, 391, 405, 420, 430

conclusion, ix–xii, 1–2, 14, 16, 19, 21–22, 28, 31, 35, 52, 57, 60, 82, 105, 109, 112, 136, 145–47, 190, 210–11, 225, 237, 239–41, 252, 257–58, 260, 264, 272, 302, 309, 312, 314–15, 318–19, 324, 340, 343, 345–46, 361, 368, 374, 397, 405, 425

connotation, 74, 85–86, 93, 103, 105, 109, 193, 214–15, 219, 236–37, 254, 256, 274, 299, 307, 310–12, 315, 318, 321, 323, 353

crescendo, 82, 86, 89, 113, 127, 129, 139, 153, 173, 183, 190, 193, 195, 200, 210, 245, 255, 258, 278, 292–93, 308

darkness, 257, 295–96, 305, 316, 332–33, 346, 353

David, ii, xii, xv, 3, 13, 18, 24, 26, 43, 46–47, 54, 88–89, 97, 121, 158, 165, 174, 177, 187–88, 197, 222–23, 231, 234–36, 241, 278–79, 282–83, 357, 392, 395, 398–99, 402, 407, 413, 417, 435, 437

Delilah, 235, 399

detachment, 9, 13, 22, 154, 245, 358

dialogue, ii, x, 25, 92, 122, 211, 255, 318, 347, 388, 394, 400, 409, 415, 433, 435

direct discourse, 110, 121–22, 129, 176, 210, 326, 375

distance in characterization, 108–10, 206, 231; *see also* psychological distance, aesthetic distance, sympathetic distance, emotional distance, and dynamics of distance

Domitian, 313, 329

drama, 6, 130, 183, 189, 361

dramatizing, 150, 258–59, 296

dynamics of distance, 206, 228, 231, 237, 240, 312, 321, 323

Eleazar, 160, 206–7, 218–19, 250, 261–62, 265–68, 296

Elijah, 25, 54, 80, 87, 108–10, 126, 205, 295–97, 306–9, 316, 324, 351, 394, 427–29

Elisha, 47, 88, 108, 177

ellipsis, 122, 304, 332, 371

embody, 14, 61, 89, 129, 183–84, 292, 316, 326, 426

emotion, 12, 31–32, 55, 62, 85, 110, 113, 116, 119–20, 129–30, 141, 197, 215, 259, 292, 348, 354, 405

emotional distance, 182, 257, 323, 354

Emperor, 253, 313, 331, 356, 366

emphasis, 19, 50–51, 105, 130, 152, 171, 195, 198–99, 209, 211, 242–43, 263, 265, 285, 340, 347, 352, 368, 373

Index

empire, 19, 21–22, 38, 55, 92, 175, 314, 321, 361, 364–66, 387, 407, 435
enemies, 1, 24–25, 31–33, 41, 43, 64, 66, 70, 96–97, 140–41, 148, 152, 174, 176, 179, 184, 199, 235, 242, 247, 254, 276, 286, 289, 291, 293, 308, 357, 359–60, 393, 430
enemy, 23–25, 27, 29, 44, 64, 99, 137–38, 149–50, 158, 165, 219, 225, 235, 239, 241–42, 248, 254, 319, 323–24, 359, 392–93, 396, 403
engagement, 13, 22, 27, 30, 33–35, 168, 176, 235, 357, 396, 404, 409, 418, 421, 434
enigma, 35, 117, 344
episode, xi, 8, 27, 29, 41–44, 47, 51, 64, 73, 76, 78, 85, 93, 107, 114, 121, 123–30, 136, 140–42, 145, 162, 167, 169, 183, 186–87, 190–92, 194–95, 197–98, 200, 209–10, 214, 223, 227, 230, 232, 238, 250, 256, 260, 270–72, 275, 280, 287–88, 292, 294, 296, 300–301, 303, 306, 311, 316, 323, 327, 333, 335, 339–40, 343, 350, 370–75, 396, 398, 403, 418, 428
Erasmian pronunciation, 389–90, 428–29
Eve, 30, 404
expectation, 78, 86, 109, 125, 142, 144, 146, 148, 150–51, 172, 187, 208, 219, 221–22, 224, 227, 232, 234, 236, 238, 241, 244, 255, 301, 309, 312–13, 321, 323, 353, 356, 360
explanation, 8, 15, 40–41, 44, 48, 57–61, 63, 66, 81, 92, 106–7, 110–11, 126, 130, 166, 180, 182, 190, 210, 212, 221, 229, 233, 244, 289–90, 299, 320, 323, 325, 333–35, 338–40, 342–44, 347, 354, 356, 408, 414–16
eyewitness, 152, 170, 200, 269, 272, 329, 433

flashback, 42, 138–39
formula, 57–58, 60, 77, 93, 96, 111, 141, 146, 173, 194–95, 213, 215, 221, 272, 309, 349

garment, 36, 137, 163, 177, 183, 230, 253, 256, 269–70, 274–76, 278, 285–86, 289, 297, 301, 305, 310, 316, 324, 337, 348, 353, 400
genitive, 95, 324, 332, 371–72, 375
Gerasene, 43, 93, 95, 148, 230, 256, 289, 299, 355
Golgotha, 261, 263, 265, 267, 278, 298, 314, 321, 373
Goliath, 18, 24, 279, 282, 392–93, 398

Haman, 24, 392–93
hero, 12, 186, 199
Herod, 29, 66, 85, 195, 204–6, 232, 239, 241, 403–4
Herodians, 40, 124, 171, 209, 212, 228, 341
Herodias, 195, 200, 205–6, 239
hiatus, 370, 375
Hillel, 364
historical present, 114, 116, 127, 136, 139, 149, 163, 189, 263, 269, 272–73, 275
Homer, 270, 279, 282, 284, 359, 435

ideal reference, 9, 22
identification, x, 13, 15–17, 22, 26–30, 33, 109–10, 127, 141, 151–52, 173, 177, 189–90, 192, 194, 197, 199–200, 218, 227, 229–30, 232, 235, 240, 242, 285, 300, 304, 306, 312, 316, 326–27, 348, 350, 370, 372, 394–401, 403–4, 406, 410, 418–19, 421–22, 424
identity, 15–16, 19, 22, 30, 42–43, 54–55, 85, 89, 131, 137, 140, 155, 170–73, 176–78, 180–82, 186, 189, 192, 194, 200, 222–23, 256, 278, 286, 290, 313, 358–59, 361, 366, 388, 404, 410, 434–35
immediacy, 149, 190, 263, 269, 273, 275
implication, rhetoric of, 127, 152, 188, 197, 199, 235, 240, 397, 399
inclusion, 15, 22, 58, 98, 106, 129, 229–30, 314, 325, 366, 414–15, 425–26

indirect discourse, 110, 121, 129, 200, 210, 232, 293, 322–23, 326, 419
inference, 92, 117, 151, 190, 264, 274, 415
intention, xii, 20–21, 65, 114, 116, 136, 237, 239–40, 287
intonation, 170, 200
irony, 28, 69–70, 108, 113, 138, 144–48, 153–54, 179, 211, 239, 241, 245–46, 253, 255–56, 271, 278–79, 284–85, 287, 296, 305, 356, 361, 397
Israel, ii, xi, xiii, 1, 15, 17–19, 21, 23–25, 31–32, 34, 40, 42–44, 46–47, 49, 55, 66–69, 77–78, 80–81, 88, 91–92, 94, 96–98, 109, 144, 148–49, 151, 158, 160, 165, 174–75, 179–80, 187, 199, 206–8, 217–19, 223, 230, 234–35, 238, 241, 246, 254–55, 258, 268, 271, 276, 278–79, 283, 288–91, 306, 308–10, 312–13, 342, 357, 359, 362–63, 366, 392–94, 397–99, 401–2, 405–9, 426
Israelite, xi, xiii, 13–18, 21–22, 24–27, 38, 43–44, 46, 54, 60, 68–69, 75, 77, 93–94, 96–97, 99, 149, 160, 162, 165–66, 179–81, 187, 204, 206–8, 218–19, 224–25, 230, 241–42, 247–48, 250, 254–55, 261, 264, 270–71, 275, 281–82, 284–86, 288–93, 306–7, 315, 320, 323, 360, 364–67, 391–93, 395, 397–98, 400–402, 406–9, 414–15, 420, 423, 425–26, 430, 435

Jacob, 177, 398
Jairus, 36, 41, 137, 230, 285, 289, 301, 335, 354
James, ii, xii–xvi, 15–16, 47, 50–51, 55, 105, 109–10, 115, 118–20, 124–25, 129, 171, 176, 193, 219, 264, 278, 295, 301, 304, 314–15, 324–25, 328, 332–35, 345, 349, 374, 412–13, 422–23, 433–38
Jamnia, 68, 364–65
Jehu, 46–47, 88

Jeremiah, 69, 113, 134, 142–44, 148, 159, 165, 181, 219, 234, 288, 425–26
Jeroboam, 86, 88
Jerusalem, xvi, 17, 32, 42–43, 47–48, 53, 55, 65–66, 69, 76, 81, 105, 107, 111, 131, 137, 143, 160, 168, 179–81, 189, 212–13, 222–23, 227–31, 234, 240–41, 253, 266, 278, 281, 295, 297–98, 302–3, 310, 314–15, 320–21, 345, 363–65, 399, 401–2, 407, 411, 415–17, 419–20, 422–23, 425
Jezebel, 18, 24–25, 392–94
Joab, 150–51, 158
Joel, x, 19, 303, 424, 426, 436
Johanan ben Zakkai, 364
John, xi, 7, 13, 15–16, 20–21, 29, 36, 41, 47, 51–52, 55–56, 58–61, 67, 75–76, 78, 80, 85, 87, 96, 105, 109–10, 115, 118–20, 123–26, 129, 138, 148, 171, 173, 176–77, 190, 193, 195, 200, 204–7, 214, 219, 221, 226–27, 230–31, 239, 241, 255, 264, 277–78, 289, 304–5, 309, 318, 321, 323, 340, 348–49, 354, 358, 370, 388, 403, 406, 411–15, 420–23, 433–37
John of Gischala, 67, 214, 226
John the Baptist, 29, 36, 41, 60, 80, 87, 138, 200, 204–5, 230, 241, 318, 403, 411, 414–15, 421, 423
Jonah, 42, 120, 235, 357, 399, 402
Jonathan, 97, 365
Jordan, 93, 95
Joseph, 288, 294, 317–26
Josephus, xv, 14, 63, 67, 69, 75, 134, 168, 214, 226, 234, 236, 244, 274, 287, 303, 363–65, 422, 434, 436
Joses, 264, 295, 301, 304, 314–15, 317, 324–26, 332, 350, 374
Judas Iscariot, 51, 60, 62–65, 67, 70, 74, 76, 88, 91, 137, 164, 233, 307, 373, 376
Judean, ix, xi, xiii, 1, 13–20, 22, 30–35, 38, 42, 44, 54–55, 60, 63, 66–67, 69, 82, 84, 88, 91–93, 95–96, 102, 106, 134, 142, 144, 151, 165,

180–81, 202–4, 206–10, 213–14, 219–23, 225–26, 228, 231–34, 236, 240–41, 243–44, 247, 251, 254–60, 264, 266–67, 270, 272–77, 279–82, 286–87, 289–90, 303, 305, 313–14, 320–21, 325–26, 329–30, 355–56, 359–61, 363–67, 400–401, 404, 406–9, 411–12, 414, 417, 420–26, 434
Julius Caesar, 68, 313, 329

Koine, vii, xi, 6–7, 387–89, 428–29
Korah, 24, 393

laughter, 228–29, 289, 292–93, 309, 316
leitmotif, 91, 138, 170, 174–75, 275, 299, 345, 355
Levi, 264, 398
Levite, 24, 286, 288, 393
listener, xi, 9, 11–12, 15–16, 22–23, 26–28, 30, 36, 43–44, 51, 55, 60–61, 63, 68, 70, 72, 74, 85–86, 89–90, 92, 95–96, 100, 109–11, 119, 122–23, 125–28, 130, 138, 144, 146, 150–52, 163, 167, 171–72, 177, 188, 191, 194–95, 197, 199, 221–23, 229, 242, 246, 263–64, 270, 274–75, 280, 287, 296–97, 300, 303–5, 308, 312–13, 315, 317, 322, 324–25, 327, 330–33, 336–38, 342–45, 353, 357–58, 371, 390–91, 395–402, 404, 414, 417, 426–28
literacy, ii, 2, 10, 435, 437
Luke, 14, 20, 51–54, 60–61, 79, 139, 142, 173, 190–91, 193, 216, 226, 254–55, 265, 323, 340, 357–58, 369, 371, 400, 418, 420

Maccabean martyrs, 207, 218, 224, 248, 268, 270, 288, 290, 312
Maccabees, 160, 207, 248, 261, 267, 270, 290, 312
Manasseh, 24, 160, 218, 281–82, 291, 393

manuscript, ii, xi, xiv, 1–2, 4–5, 7, 52, 131, 134, 189–90, 211–12, 299, 319, 431, 436
Martyrdom and Ascension of Isaiah, 160, 173, 208, 279, 281–82, 288, 291, 436
Mary, 51–52, 61, 131, 264, 295, 301, 303–4, 314–15, 317, 324–26, 328, 332, 345, 350, 372, 374, 413, 422–23, 434, 437
Mary Magdalene, 295, 317, 324, 326, 328, 345, 350, 372, 374, 413, 422–23
Masada, ix, 364–65
Matthew, 20, 51–52, 58–59, 61, 87, 106, 139, 190–91, 218, 226, 255, 265, 323, 340, 358, 420, 428, 434, 437
meaning as reference, xiii, 8–9, 12; *also see* ostensive reference and ideal reference
media, ii, xii, 2, 5, 12–13, 33, 155, 433–35
memorization, 4–5, 370
memory, xi, 4–6, 46–47, 54, 57, 60, 90, 98, 110, 153, 158–59, 167, 188, 196, 204, 219, 226, 230, 247, 256, 265, 270, 274, 277, 279, 289–90, 308, 315, 325, 329–31, 336, 350, 355, 372, 430
Messiah of peace, i, iii–iv, vii, xiii, 1–2, 4, 6, 8, 10, 12, 14, 16–18, 20, 22, 24, 26, 28, 30–32, 34–35, 38, 40, 42, 44, 46, 48, 50, 52, 54, 56, 58, 60, 62, 64, 66, 68, 70, 74, 76, 78, 80, 82, 84, 86, 88, 90, 92, 94, 96, 98, 102, 104, 106, 108, 110, 112, 114, 116, 118, 120, 122, 124, 126, 128, 130, 132, 134, 136, 138, 140, 142, 144, 146, 148, 150, 152, 154, 156, 158, 160, 162, 164, 166, 168, 170, 172, 174, 176, 178, 180, 182, 184, 186, 188, 190, 192, 194, 196, 198, 200, 204, 206, 208, 210, 212, 214, 216, 218, 220, 222, 224, 226, 228, 230, 232, 234, 236, 238, 240, 242, 244, 246, 248, 250, 252, 254, 256, 258, 262, 264,

Messiah of peace (*continued*), 266, 268, 270, 272, 274, 276, 278, 280, 282, 284, 286, 288, 290, 292, 296, 298, 300, 302, 304, 306, 308, 310, 312, 314, 316, 318, 320, 322, 324, 326, 328, 330, 332, 334, 336, 338, 340, 342, 344, 346, 348, 350, 352, 354, 356, 358-62, 367, 405

messianic secret, 155, 168, 171, 222, 355, 418, 438

methodology, ii, x, 1, 5, 437

Miriam, 25, 394

Mithridates, 186, 288, 322

mnemonic, 100, 347, 372

mockery, 24, 29, 124, 180, 183, 249, 253-56, 258-59, 271, 282, 285, 288-90, 292-93, 306-8, 316, 327, 331, 360, 369, 392, 403, 408

Moses, 3, 24-25, 46, 76-80, 82, 92, 94, 98, 109, 126, 160-61, 166, 230, 249, 351, 393, 398, 426, 435

motif, 9, 19-21, 23, 36, 46, 52, 67, 70, 72, 78, 91, 93, 100-101, 119, 127, 129, 138, 155, 160, 168, 172-73, 186, 192, 208-9, 212, 222, 231, 253, 258, 260-61, 267, 272, 276-77, 281-82, 287, 290-91, 294, 296, 298-99, 307-8, 310, 312, 315, 342, 347, 355-56, 372, 392, 418

motive, 20-21, 23, 61-63, 65, 68, 88, 155, 179-80, 210-11, 233-34, 236, 239-41, 245, 323, 365, 372, 392

Mount of Olives, 102, 105, 113, 118, 120-21, 123, 132, 149-52, 155, 194, 198, 373, 417, 419

mystery, 51, 54, 72, 88, 93, 150, 155, 172, 180, 244, 277, 298, 314, 334-35, 342, 345, 347, 418, 436

Naboth, 25, 394

narrative, ii-iv, vii, ix-x, xiii, 1, 6, 9, 11, 15, 17, 19, 21, 23, 26, 29, 32-33, 35, 41, 68, 76, 79, 90, 96-97, 100-101, 109, 119, 131, 136, 138, 141, 150, 155, 172, 192, 197, 208, 264, 268, 271, 281, 300, 308, 319, 327, 339-40, 343-44, 362, 367-69, 371, 373-75, 377, 379, 381, 383, 385, 394-95, 397, 404, 414, 417, 420-21, 428, 433-35

narrator, 23, 28, 53, 58, 126, 137, 145, 276, 312, 396, 404

Nathan, 47, 187-88, 197, 357, 399, 402

Nazarene, 103, 185, 189, 193, 200, 350, 407

Nazareth, ix, 103, 120, 189, 301, 303-4, 315, 329, 332, 353, 411, 423

Nebuchadnezzar, 25, 206-7, 394

Nehemiah, 27, 238, 395, 399, 401-2

Nero, xv, 329-31, 355-56

Nicanor, 254, 288

norm of judgment, 28, 59, 219, 225, 228, 286, 354, 397, 399-400

norms, 23, 26-27, 44, 69, 86, 151, 179, 181, 197, 219, 225, 235, 237-38, 240, 255, 360, 392, 394-95, 398-400

novel, 23, 160, 185, 275, 287, 392

oath, 97, 185, 195, 201, 205, 239

onomatopoeia, 7, 47, 164, 197, 209, 251, 285, 297, 310

opponents, 42, 47, 53, 147-48, 154, 160, 198, 214, 228, 231, 244, 282, 284-85, 359, 414, 417, 420, 422, 424-25

opposition, 107, 181, 235, 312, 321, 366, 417, 420, 425-26

oral, ii, xiii, 2, 6, 9-11, 23, 30-31, 35, 52, 108, 134, 213, 233, 240, 334, 341, 405, 419, 433, 435-36

orator, xv, 169

original historical context, 1-2, 9, 13, 21, 35, 361, 407

ostensive reference, 8, 22

outsider, xi, 189, 207, 256, 289, 366, 406, 408-9, 418

Palestine, 55, 83, 267, 364-65

paradox, 42, 70

parallelism, 121-22, 144, 220, 224-25, 263, 265

paraphrase, 59–60, 87, 96, 106, 108, 243, 284, 286, 307, 322, 327, 350–51, 407
participation, 9, 345, 426
Passover, vii, 17, 36–39, 41, 43, 45, 47, 49, 51, 53, 55, 57, 59, 61–63, 65, 67, 69, 71–83, 85, 87, 89–91, 93, 95–100, 105–6, 118, 122, 125–26, 132, 141, 154, 164, 179, 225, 227, 239, 263, 266–67, 294, 320, 344, 359, 370, 372–73, 376–77, 421
Paul, xvi, 102, 425, 433, 436–38
performance, ii–iv, ix–xii, 1–5, 7–15, 18–19, 21, 31, 33, 35, 44, 52, 61, 70, 82, 89, 98, 106, 108, 113, 116, 128–29, 131, 134, 141, 152, 182, 190, 197, 199, 206, 213, 216, 228, 230, 240–42, 245–46, 258, 266, 268–69, 278, 281, 292, 298, 313–14, 316, 318, 322, 325, 339, 360–61, 363, 367–68, 374, 389, 405, 408, 410, 414–15, 417, 419, 422–24, 427, 433, 435, 437
performance criticism, ii, iv, x, xii, 1, 3, 13, 33, 435, 437
period, vii, x–xi, 1–4, 6–8, 13, 19, 39–40, 44, 47–48, 52, 55, 59–60, 63–64, 66–67, 73–74, 83, 118, 122, 131, 134, 140–41, 143, 153, 160, 165, 185–86, 189, 191–92, 197, 206, 208–11, 225–26, 232, 234, 245, 250–51, 262, 269, 271–72, 274–75, 281–82, 285, 290, 293–94, 296–98, 301, 306, 310, 313–14, 316, 318, 322, 325, 327, 332–35, 337–41, 344, 346, 350, 356, 358, 360, 364–65, 368–74, 376, 387, 389–90, 405–6, 411, 413, 424
perspective, 11–12, 19, 123, 128, 151–52, 167, 192, 194, 198, 235, 241, 258, 268, 272, 316, 325, 367, 425, 436–37
Pharaoh, 24–25, 49, 207, 288, 342, 392–94, 398
Pharisees, 15, 31, 40, 92, 105, 119, 124, 171, 209, 212, 228, 341, 408, 411–12, 414–16, 423

Philip, ii, 205, 420, 435
Philistines, 248, 286, 288, 398
Phoenicia, 17, 363
Pilate, 7, 15, 19–20, 25, 29–30, 34, 75, 111, 163, 202–4, 206, 208–13, 215–28, 232–34, 236–46, 250–52, 254–55, 257, 260, 271–72, 277, 300, 305, 311–12, 317–27, 331, 344, 347, 350, 355, 369, 371–74, 382, 394, 402–4, 407–8, 410, 413–14, 422–23
plosive, 48, 61, 251
plot, 17, 23–24, 32, 36–38, 40–42, 48, 53, 60–61, 65, 69–70, 72, 75, 89, 96, 100–101, 137–38, 140, 145, 155, 165, 179, 181, 185, 198–99, 206, 208, 212, 225, 228, 260, 276, 301, 343–44, 355, 359, 371–73, 375, 392, 422
plot, conspiracy, 17, 25, 37–42, 44, 47, 53, 62, 69–70, 88–89, 132, 138–40, 164–65, 208, 212, 233–34, 343, 365
plot, reversal of expectations, 109, 146, 232, 234, 236, 241, 244, 301, 313, 321, 323, 360
plot, prophecy fulfillment, 17, 76, 352
poem, 3, 330, 359
poet, 3, 27, 396, 437
point of view, 123, 128, 150, 167, 180, 192–94, 196, 198, 311, 325, 346–47
polemic, x, 19–20, 31, 34–35, 107–8, 241, 245, 405, 434
Polycharmus, 186, 192, 287–88
prelude, 28, 52, 128, 282, 336, 396, 398
priests, 17, 24, 29, 36–37, 39–40, 42–44, 46–48, 53, 61, 63, 65–66, 68–70, 74, 76, 85–86, 132–33, 137–39, 143, 148, 157, 159–61, 164–65, 169, 175, 179–82, 203–4, 209–13, 215–18, 220, 223, 225, 228, 231–36, 240–41, 243–44, 251, 255, 260, 271–72, 277–79, 284–86, 288–93, 309, 323, 354, 359–60, 371–73, 393, 403–4, 408, 413, 417, 423, 425–26
pro-Roman apologetic, x, 20, 29, 403

proclamation, 17–19, 33–34, 52, 60, 224, 360, 411
pronouncement, 27–28, 62, 86, 111–12, 177, 183, 277, 284, 316, 396–97, 416–17, 419
pronunciation, vii–viii, xi, 6–8, 259, 306, 387–90, 427–29, 433
psychological distance, 9–12, 30, 197, 404
punctuation, 4, 127, 335, 337–39, 344, 370
purity laws, 105, 320, 408, 414–16, 419, 425

Quintilian, 5, 7
quotation, iv, xi–xii, 15, 27, 39, 89, 102–3, 106–7, 121–22, 134, 143, 181, 185, 209, 213, 219, 248, 270, 276, 280, 286, 289–91, 296, 305–6, 369, 396, 406, 436

rabbi, 15, 68–69, 80, 82, 86, 126, 133–34, 139–40, 366–67
rabbinic, 14, 75, 92, 365, 407, 416
reader, ix–xii, 1–4, 7–15, 19, 21–24, 28, 30–31, 82–83, 108, 191, 213, 227, 240, 264, 312, 334, 340, 391–93, 397, 404–5, 414, 420, 435
rebuke, 47–48, 54–58, 61, 65, 69, 93, 105, 109–10, 112, 171, 197, 230, 303, 421
recital, 210, 262, 316, 401
reconciliation, 1, 12, 35, 87, 151, 184, 234, 237, 352–53, 361–62, 366
redaction, 9, 93, 342
redundancy, 103, 134
reflection, 9, 11, 26, 30–32, 34, 150, 314, 357, 404–5
repetition, 7, 21, 69, 76, 85, 125–29, 135, 137, 139, 164, 167, 169, 179, 196, 210–11, 213, 219, 251, 253–54, 275, 285, 287, 299, 310, 345, 352, 371–75, 421
resonance, 68, 119, 130, 173, 313
response, 9–12, 16–17, 26, 29, 34, 43, 48, 55–61, 70, 81–82, 84–89, 92, 94, 99, 101–13, 116–17, 119–20, 122, 125–27, 130, 135, 141–42, 146, 148, 150, 155, 159, 162–63, 165–68, 171–73, 176–77, 180, 183, 193, 197–99, 209–11, 213–14, 217, 221–26, 228, 230–34, 236, 238–39, 243–45, 256, 269, 277–78, 288, 290, 293–94, 296–301, 303–5, 309–14, 316, 321–22, 327, 329, 334–35, 340–43, 348–49, 353–58, 360, 388, 395, 399, 401–2, 404, 407, 420–23, 435
resurrection, iii–iv, vii, ix–x, 1, 6, 16–18, 29, 31–32, 34, 42, 52, 101, 104–5, 110, 172, 176, 202, 218, 252, 304, 324, 327, 329, 331, 333, 335–39, 341, 343–45, 347, 349–62, 369, 371–73, 375, 377, 379, 381, 383, 385, 401, 403, 405, 413, 417, 433
retelling, 35, 100, 304, 401
rhetoric, vii, x, xii, 3, 16, 18, 22–32, 127, 152, 180, 187–88, 197, 199, 235, 239–40, 244, 361, 391–95, 397, 399–405, 434
rhetoric of alienation and condemnation, 18, 23–24, 29–31, 180, 240, 361, 391–93, 399, 402–3, 405
rhetoric of disappointment and alienation, 25–26, 393–94
rhetoric of involvement and implication, 18, 25, 28–29, 31, 152, 187, 199, 239–40, 361, 394, 397, 400–405
ridicule, 247, 408, 430
righteous sufferer, 276, 286, 305, 308, 311
ritual, 37, 91, 93, 98, 177, 247–48, 253, 255, 268, 284, 297, 430
robe, 183, 253, 329, 336–37, 348, 353
Romans, xi, 12, 17, 19, 21–22, 38, 63, 68, 88, 181, 222, 226, 234–35, 238, 240–41, 271, 273–74, 326, 360, 364–66, 408, 435
Rome, 2, 18–19, 33, 66–67, 92, 150–51, 264, 313, 324, 329–31, 363, 365, 437
rounded, 376–78, 380, 383–84
rounding, 69, 209, 211, 246, 250–51, 257, 260, 271, 313, 327, 371–72

Index

Sadducees, 105, 147, 413, 417, 423
Salome, 295, 328, 374, 413, 422–23
salute, 247, 255–56, 316
Samson, viii, 235, 247–48, 255, 258, 268, 286, 288, 399, 402, 430–31
Samuel, 11, 46, 76, 78–82, 89, 143, 235, 395, 398–99
Sanhedrin, 17, 19, 48–49, 100–101, 111–13, 155–56, 164–67, 175, 177–83, 191–92, 198–99, 204, 208, 211–13, 216–17, 220, 222–25, 228, 237, 242–43, 267, 284–87, 289, 292, 310, 321, 323, 342, 347, 355, 357, 368, 373, 380, 410, 423
Satan, 15, 56, 61, 109, 124
satire, 48, 59, 61, 242, 320, 436
Saul, 43, 46, 54, 78–82, 88, 97, 158–59, 165, 234, 238, 278, 288, 398–99
scene, 61, 87–89, 119, 139, 178, 182–83, 230, 333, 416, 419, 434
scribes, 15, 17, 24, 29, 36–37, 39–40, 44, 48, 53, 61, 65, 69–70, 132–34, 137–39, 148, 157, 164–65, 169, 175, 177, 179–80, 182, 190, 203, 209, 211–12, 217–18, 222, 227–29, 231, 233, 240, 255, 260–61, 265, 271, 278–79, 284–86, 288–92, 302, 309, 315, 323, 342, 360, 371–72, 375, 388, 393, 403, 408, 411–13, 415, 417, 423
Scriptures, 15, 81–82, 91, 106, 133, 135, 145–47, 153, 199, 235, 270, 276
scroll, 3–5, 434
secrecy, 38, 41, 46, 153, 182
Septuagint, xv–xvi, 15, 54, 77, 81, 106, 134, 143, 161, 247–48, 254, 280, 288, 430, 433
Shakespeare, 327
Shiloh, 143, 159
Sicarii, 63, 66–67, 140, 151, 364–66, 434
Sidon, 93, 95, 282
silence, 2, 5, 11, 23, 30–32, 34–35, 38, 101, 150, 168, 171–73, 177–78, 183, 197, 201, 209, 213, 221–25, 240–41, 243, 271, 299, 312, 316, 322, 325–26, 329, 344, 355–56, 358, 360, 404–5, 414, 419, 421
Simon Peter, 109, 123–24, 170, 243, 358
sonic, sonic echoes, xi, 8, 40, 46, 90–91, 120, 135, 142, 162–63, 166, 168, 170, 173, 208–9, 211, 219–20, 252–54, 268, 270, 277, 279, 285, 287, 297–98, 303–4, 309, 319, 324, 332, 347, 372, 427
sound map, vii, xi, 6–8, 17, 37, 45, 62, 72, 83, 90, 101, 114, 132, 156, 184, 202, 204, 210, 246, 260, 269, 279, 294, 302, 317, 327, 339, 344, 368–71, 373, 375, 377, 379, 381, 383, 385
speaker, 7, 33, 95, 213, 369, 411, 413, 427
spectacle, 186, 331, 363
speech, ii, 4–5, 14, 31, 38, 56, 58, 62, 73, 80–81, 84, 92, 96, 102, 110, 114, 120–21, 127–28, 134, 136, 142–48, 153, 178, 181, 193, 195, 197, 245, 288, 293, 312, 349, 352–53, 356, 369, 401–2, 405, 413, 415–16, 418–19, 421–22
storyteller, ix, xii–xiii, 3, 6–7, 9–12, 14–16, 24, 26–27, 30, 35, 39–40, 42–44, 47–48, 53, 58, 60, 62, 64, 66, 69–70, 75, 77, 81, 85, 89, 91–92, 94, 98, 105–6, 108–10, 112–13, 119, 121–27, 129–31, 138, 140, 144–46, 150, 152, 163, 165–72, 177–81, 183, 187, 190–98, 200, 210, 213, 215, 220, 223–25, 227–35, 237, 239–41, 243–45, 256, 258–59, 264, 266, 268–69, 272, 276–79, 285, 289, 292–93, 296, 301–2, 306–7, 309, 312, 314–16, 323, 325–26, 333–35, 337, 339–41, 343, 347–48, 354, 356, 369–70, 392–96, 398, 400, 402, 404, 408–11, 413–28, 433, 437
Susanna, 160–62, 165–67
suspense, 7, 12, 104, 155, 172, 347
suspension of disbelief, 11

sympathetic distance, 123, 235, 240, 260
Syro-Phoenician woman, 43, 232, 289, 354

tablet, 3, 243, 364
Tacitus, xv, 329, 331, 356, 364, 437
Talmud, xvi, 267, 407, 435, 437
tempo, 7, 82, 128, 131, 137, 139, 141, 152, 262–63, 268, 271, 275, 296, 305, 325–26, 339, 344, 346, 369–70, 373, 418
threefold, 28, 111, 123, 126–27, 129, 137, 358, 396
Titus, 67, 287, 312–13, 363–65
tone, 7, 24, 30, 39–40, 42, 44, 48, 56, 59, 61, 70, 81–82, 84, 86–87, 89–90, 92, 98, 113, 118, 124, 126, 128–31, 137, 139–41, 145, 147, 152–53, 162, 165, 169–71, 182–83, 194, 197, 200–201, 210–11, 213, 215, 223–24, 227, 230, 241–45, 259, 268, 272, 277–79, 285, 292–93, 298–301, 309, 312, 316, 322, 325–26, 333, 335, 346–47, 350, 370, 392–93, 404, 415–16
tragedy, 33–34, 42, 238, 358–59, 361, 363, 366
transfiguration, 109–10, 119, 126, 140–41, 170–71, 175, 178, 194, 230, 256, 299, 313, 337, 348–49, 412
transformation, 9, 13, 30, 32, 43, 236, 348, 351, 353, 358, 367, 405, 438
translation, ii, x–xi, xv–xvi, 6, 15, 18, 37, 45, 48–51, 54, 56, 63–65, 68, 73–74, 77–78, 81, 83–84, 90, 94, 102–4, 106, 115–18, 130, 133–36, 141, 143, 152, 157, 160–63, 185, 189–93, 201, 203, 211–16, 221, 230, 233, 246–48, 253–54, 257, 261, 263–65, 267, 269–70, 272–74, 280–82, 286, 291–92, 295–99, 302, 304, 306, 314–19, 328, 332–41, 344, 347, 370, 406, 423, 427–31, 433–36, 438
treason, 88, 166, 210, 243

Uriah, 27, 97, 121, 188, 312, 357, 395, 399

verbal threads, xi, 7, 56, 73, 91, 94, 135, 140, 270, 272, 280, 285
Vespasian, 313, 365
volume, 1, 7, 113, 129, 166, 183, 195, 200, 210, 229, 245, 266, 271, 292–93, 296–97, 305, 310, 316, 344, 416, 438

woe, 83, 86–87, 168, 176

Zealot, 66–67, 69, 142, 226
Zechariah, 88, 103, 106–7, 146, 148

www.ingramcontent.com/pod-product-compliance
Lightning Source LLC
Chambersburg PA
CBHW021231300426
44111CB00007B/506